Creating Social Value Through Social Entrepreneurship

Mine Afacan Fındıklı
Beykent University, Turkey

Duygu Acar Erdur
Beykent University, Turkey

IGI Global
PUBLISHER of TIMELY KNOWLEDGE

A volume in the Advances in Business Strategy and Competitive Advantage (ABSCA) Book Series

Published in the United States of America by
IGI Global
Business Science Reference (an imprint of IGI Global)
701 E. Chocolate Avenue
Hershey PA, USA 17033
Tel: 717-533-8845
Fax: 717-533-8661
E-mail: cust@igi-global.com
Web site: http://www.igi-global.com

Library of Congress Cataloging-in-Publication Data

Names: Afacan Findikli, Mine, 1971- editor. | Acar Erdur, Duygu, 1985- editor.
Title: Creating social value through social entrepreneurship / Mine Afacan Findikli, and Duygu Acar Erdur, editors.
Description: Hershey PA : Business Science Reference, [2021] | Includes bibliographical references and index. | Summary: "The book helps readers understand the role of social entrepreneurship in creating social value and highlights the importance of social entrepreneurs in emerging economies through investigation of topics such as social value, social impact, social entrepreneurship ecosystem, triggers and challenges of social entrepreneurship, social entrepreneurship in emerging economies"-- Provided by publisher.
Identifiers: LCCN 2020033562 (print) | LCCN 2020033563 (ebook) | ISBN 9781799847274 (hardcover) | ISBN 9781799868668 (paperback) | ISBN 9781799847281 (ebook)
Subjects: LCSH: Social entrepreneurship. | Social values--Economic aspects. | Crowd funding--Social aspects.
Classification: LCC HD60 .C75 2021 (print) | LCC HD60 (ebook) | DDC 658.4/08--dc23
LC record available at https://lccn.loc.gov/2020033562
LC ebook record available at https://lccn.loc.gov/2020033563

This book is published in the IGI Global book series Advances in Business Strategy and Competitive Advantage (ABSCA) (ISSN: 2327-3429; eISSN: 2327-3437)

British Cataloguing in Publication Data
A Cataloguing in Publication record for this book is available from the British Library.

Advances in Business Strategy and Competitive Advantage (ABSCA) Book Series

Patricia Ordóñez de Pablos
Universidad de Oviedo, Spain

ISSN:2327-3429
EISSN:2327-3437

Mission

Business entities are constantly seeking new ways through which to gain advantage over their competitors and strengthen their position within the business environment. With competition at an all-time high due to technological advancements allowing for competition on a global scale, firms continue to seek new ways through which to improve and strengthen their business processes, procedures, and profitability.

The **Advances in Business Strategy and Competitive Advantage (ABSCA) Book Series** is a timely series responding to the high demand for state-of-the-art research on how business strategies are created, implemented and re-designed to meet the demands of globalized competitive markets. With a focus on local and global challenges, business opportunities and the needs of society, the **ABSCA** encourages scientific discourse on doing business and managing information technologies for the creation of sustainable competitive advantage.

Coverage

- Differentiation Strategy
- Economies of Scale
- Innovation Strategy
- Resource-Based Competition
- Value Chain
- Value Creation
- Strategy Performance Management
- Strategic Management
- Competitive Strategy
- Customer-Orientation Strategy

IGI Global is currently accepting manuscripts for publication within this series. To submit a proposal for a volume in this series, please contact our Acquisition Editors at Acquisitions@igi-global.com or visit: http://www.igi-global.com/publish/.

The Advances in Business Strategy and Competitive Advantage (ABSCA) Book Series (ISSN 2327-3429) is published by IGI Global, 701 E. Chocolate Avenue, Hershey, PA 17033-1240, USA, www.igi-global.com. This series is composed of titles available for purchase individually; each title is edited to be contextually exclusive from any other title within the series. For pricing and ordering information please visit http://www.igi-global.com/book-series/advances-business-strategy-competitive-advantage/73672. Postmaster: Send all address changes to above address.

Titles in this Series

For a list of additional titles in this series, please visit: http://www.igi-global.com/book-series/advances-business-strategy-competitive-advantage/73672

Revolutionizing Institutional Theory Through Stakeholder Capitalism
Neslihan Aydogan-Duda (UC Berkeley Extension, USA)
Business Science Reference • © 2021 • 300pp • H/C (ISBN: 9781799844921) • US $235.00

Handbook of Research on International Business and Models for Global Purpose-Driven Companies
Rafael Ignacio Perez-Uribe (EAN University, Colombia) Carlos Largacha-Martinez (Fundación Universitaria del Área Andina, Colombia) and David Ocampo-Guzman (EAN University, Colombia)
Business Science Reference • © 2021 • 589pp • H/C (ISBN: 9781799849094) • US $345.00

Cases on Internationalization Challenges for SMEs
António Carrizo Moreira (University of Aveiro, Portugal)
Business Science Reference • © 2021 • 333pp • H/C (ISBN: 9781799843870) • US $185.00

Impact of Disruptive Technologies on the Sharing Economy
Ford Lumban Gaol (Bina Nusantara University, Jakarta, Indonesia) Natalia Filimonova (Vladimir State University, Russia) and Chandan Acharya (City University of New York, USA)
Business Science Reference • © 2021 • 350pp • H/C (ISBN: 9781799803614) • US $245.00

Innovation Management and Growth in Emerging Economies
Heather C. Webb (Higher Colleges of Technology, Dubai, UAE) Wendy Wu (Edinburgh Napier University, UK) and Hussain Al Numairy (Higher Colleges of Technology, Dubai, UAE)
Business Science Reference • © 2021 • 288pp • H/C (ISBN: 9781799841951) • US $195.00

Handbook of Research on Nascent Entrepreneurship and Creating New Ventures
António Carrizo Moreira (University of Aveiro, Portugal) and José Guilherme Leitão Dantas (CARME, School of Technology and Management, Polytechnic of Leiria, Portugal)
Business Science Reference • © 2021 • 483pp • H/C (ISBN: 9781799848264) • US $295.00

Reshaping Entrepreneurship Education With Strategy and Innovation
Ayansola Olatunji Ayandibu (University of Zululand, South Africa)
Business Science Reference • © 2021 • 422pp • H/C (ISBN: 9781799831716) • US $205.00

IGI Global
PUBLISHER of TIMELY KNOWLEDGE

701 East Chocolate Avenue, Hershey, PA 17033, USA
Tel: 717-533-8845 x100 • Fax: 717-533-8661
E-Mail: cust@igi-global.com • www.igi-global.com

Table of Contents

Section 2
Financial Tools in Social Entrepreneurship

Section 3
Selected Cases on Social Value Creation

Detailed Table of Contents

Despite the discussion of social sustainability, which has been a crucial component of sustainable development for decades, unfortunately, the desired successful outcomes have not been realized in practice. This failure caused the need to examine the concept of social sustainability differently than ever before. Social entrepreneurship is a valuable tool to meet this need. Concordantly, this chapter purposes to evaluate the relations between social sustainability and social entrepreneurship by comprehensively analyzing them. Discussing this relationship and proposing a new perspective will support overcome theoretical dilemmas and practical struggles. Therefore, the concept of sustainability was explained in detail through a wide literature review, and then the concept of social entrepreneurship was examined, and links, similarities, and gaps were revealed between the two concepts. As a result, the effective implementation of social sustainability policies depends on the social impact and value created by social entrepreneurship.

Research on social entrepreneurship has increased especially in the last 10 years. The reason for this is the contribution of social entrepreneurship to both social and economic development. The purpose of this research is to perform a bibliometric analysis of a total of 926 social entrepreneurship articles in the WoS (Web of Science) database. These data reveal the most prestigious authors, countries, journals, and articles in the field of social entrepreneurship. In addition, other concepts related to social entrepreneurship were visualized with co-word analysis. As a result of the analysis, the chapter is presented with ideas to show how scientific research progresses in the field and for future studies. At the same time, it explains the recent form in Turkish studies using the TR-Index database.

Preface

In the last decades in order to generate a long-term and permanent social value, besides various actors such as governments, NGOs, corporations, social entrepreneurship has emerged through their constructive thoughts and motives focusing on social problems (Santos, 2012). Such that, they have been often characterized as heroes or ''an obsessive individual'' amid the public insight (Bornstein, 2004:3). Because social entrepreneurs have been often found to be well ahead of governments or established organizations which reflect a 'top down' understanding in discovering social needs and offering innovative solutions (Bornstein, 2004:9). For instance, Ashoka and its members with their mission to create an everyone a changemaker world explicitly act as visionaries and role models (Ashoka 2012).

Not only in broad-based public but also in previous literature, social entrepreneurs have been denoted such as a "great man" in finding innovative and sustainable solutions, especially to societal problems (Spear, 2006). Their main point of view has centered around social entrepreneurs' characteristics and their social mission (Dacin, 2010). However, today, it is seen that social entrepreneurship activities and the creation of social value cannot be sustainable with the efforts of a "heroic" single individual. Thus, social entrepreneurship has transformed to be a collective action where different actors - teams, governments, universities, NGOs, companies etc. - come together and cooperate. Successful and long-lasting social change needs always a collaborative endeavor. Although their potential to enhance social value, it is seen that social entrepreneurs struggle in balancing social mission and economic sustainability. In order to encounter this dual mission, numerous lack of resources, cultural barriers, and institutional voids while they fight for the well-being of society (Mair and Marti,2009). From this insight, the collaboration of the other actors with social entrepreneurs has the power to provide a 'bottom-up' understanding and significant benefits in the solution of social problems. (Dacin et.al.,2010; Hellström et al., 2015). Then, the social value flourishes. In this respect, social entrepreneurship creates an ecosystem and benefits from this ecosystem.

Creating Social Value Through Social Entrepreneurship sought to address the following questions: "How do social entrepreneurship/ enterprises create social value and sustain the initiatives in a challenging environment", and "What are the challenges they face and what kind of tools they can benefit to create and sustain the social value?". In this context our framework originates from social value creation which include the use of networks and social resourcing, financial funds, strategies of effectuation, and fit in societal culture. As is known, the social value is related to basic and long-standing needs and wellbeing of individuals and society. On the other hand, well-being encompasses economic, social, cultural, and political components (Wiseman & Brasher 2008). For this reason, built on a collaborative and collective awareness, to generate sustainable community-based solutions social entrepreneurship is needed (Hellström et al., 2015).

The first section titled "Evolution of Social Entrepreneurship" investigates the theoretical context of how social entrepreneurship has developed over time. Align with the context of the first section:

Chapter 1 starts with the context of social sustainability which is one of the primary goals of the 2030 Agenda for Sustainable Development launched in 2015 by The United Nations Development Program (UNDP). It continues by building the assumptions related to the inefficient and unsustainable practices which have been conducted by business organizations, governments as well as NGOs due to a lack of innovative ways of delivering superior social value. It highlights the role of social entrepreneurship as a phenomenon emerging to solve societal problems and extends the current literature by providing insight into social entrepreneurship in achieving social sustainability goals.

Chapter 2 goes deeper into the question of how social entrepreneurship has proceeded within the scope of social impact theory and the social value creation approach. In this chapter, the author has realized a bibliometric analysis including researches between 1978 to 2019 in order to provide a theoretical contribution to the relevant field by monitoring the evolution in the field of social entrepreneurship, via citation and co-word analysis.

Chapter 3 questions how social enterprises manage symbolic meanings while pursuing their dual missions based on an inductive qualitative study examining web pages and social media accounts of 38 social enterprises in Turkey. It reveals that social enterprises as hybrid organizations engage in symbolic management and convert their accumulated resources to symbolic meanings to acquire resources. Furthermore, the study identifies four symbolic management categories, which are domain expertise, the credibility of the product/ service, collaboration and cooperation, and commercialization potential, that support social enterprises to deal with dual mission conflicts.

Chapter 4 pointing out the tension between value creation and value capture strategies of social enterprises, suggests that rather than suffered from this tension, there is another way of creating value: hybrid organizations. Conducting a single case study, the main purpose of this chapter is to advance an argument about how hybrid social enterprises perform well for promoting social entrepreneurs' goals and investigate the effect of dual objectives on social enterprise's sustainability and social impact and highlight the opportunities and challenges of a hybrid 'social enterprise'.

Chapter 5 examines the concept of societal culture, social innovation, and social entrepreneurship in a conceptual manner in order to display the significance of macro-level contextual factors on the social innovation process. The study argues that social context and cultural values have an impact on social entrepreneurial initiatives and there is an interaction between cultural values in the process of social innovation. It also provides an insight to practitioners in realizing the importance of societal culture on social innovation via the effects on social entrepreneurs' activities.

Chapter 6 denotes an alternative view to social entrepreneurship emphasizing that digitalization generates new opportunities for the creation of social value to social entrepreneurship. The study puts forward the concept of social digital entrepreneurship and its facilitator role of digitalization in the creation of social value. The study presents a comparative analysis by revealing the European Index of Digital Entrepreneurship Systems (EIDES), the 2020 Digital Economy and Society Index (DESI), and the table of Estimated number and degree of acceptance of Social Enterprises in Europe. Then, it explores technology-enabled social innovation contributes towards extending the success of social initiatives coping with business and social requirements.

The second section titled "A Financial Lens for Social Entrepreneurship" tackles financial lens in social entrepreneurship. It is known that as social entrepreneurs have a social mission, they may financial challenges to sustain their initiatives. Concordantly, they need to struggle harder than commercial entrepreneurs in order to accrue and gather financial support. From this point of view, the second section of the book provides alterative financial solutions.

Chapter 7 discuss crowdfunding as bottom-up microfinance practices that seek to provide convenient ways to contribute to social initiatives. Crowdfunding platforms have become a new tool for social entrepreneurs. It points to various types of benefits. The first one indicates that crowdfunding provides useful information to funding seekers and shows new ways of investing in the future. The second benefit reveals that crowdfunding offers a chance to use previous experiences and knowledge in creating social value. Last but not least social entrepreneurs benefit human capital via accrued new knowledge and experience and provide moral support. Based on this perspective, this chapter explains the concept of the crowdfunding concept and its four types. Also, it provides current examples from the world and Turkey.

Chapter 8 argues previous research provides some insight into what motivates crowds to support projects, but it is little known about how social or environmental concerns affect the crowd crowdfunding. In this respect, the study address this gap by investigating the research question of "How does a platform's framing of campaigns as 'social' or 'environmental' affects project funding performance?" based on data from Kickstarter, one of the leading rewards-based crowdfunding platforms in the world.

Chapter 9 argues that due to the pressure caused by the temporary or permanent crises in societies, the governments need increasingly to optimize the effectiveness and efficiency of their social policies and the way they finance them. In this respect, the study claims social impact bonds (SIBs) may be an efficient tool to reduce the gap between speculative financial investments and the productive-real economy for solving social problems. It offers insight into social impact investment as a new financial asset and new techniques that aim to encourage social impact investments. Following that, it discusses social impact bonds' structure, benefits, and challenges for social entrepreneurs.

The third section titled "Selected Cases on Social Value Creation" seeks to highlight the crucial role of social entrepreneurs in fostering social impact in practice. In this way, the readers have the opportunity to understand one more time that a top-down "one size fits all" practices can't give essential support to answer efficiently and timely the needs of the societal environment. The selected cases confirm the necessity to focus on a bottom-up approach to bear a hand to the real needs of society's needs.

Chapter 10 questions a particular way of doing sustainable entrepreneurship in South America by realizing an exploratory study. Based on the shared value approach, it prevails against myths such as "social innovation is not profitable" and "social entrepreneurship is not scalable" by identifying and providing successful entrepreneurial projects in South America.

Chapter 11 begins with the necessity of equitable healthcare access to all individuals in communities by focusing on the sustainable development goal of the United Nations Millennium Development Goals. Then, it presents a new digital platform, named HERA, designed to increase access to healthcare for refugee and migrant populations. The chapter claims that innovative intervention models for the vulnerable population can align themselves with the sustainable social value aims in the UN's millennium development goals and explains how the HERA project evolved into a social enterprise from a grant-based field project.

Chapter 12, based on inclusive growth through creating shared value examines a Turkish social initiative; Future is Brighter Youth Platform(FBYP) which offers solutions to the fight against the inequality and social exclusion experienced by Turkish youth related to skill development and employment. Through FBYP, the chapter discusses the contributions of social enterprises to social inclusiveness.

Chapter 13 linking the creation of shared value and business development, tries to understand the capabilities of social entrepreneurship or social business models in developing countries for the generation of shared value by implementing the strategy of smart specialization. Then, it questions how an entrepreneurial ecosystem can be generated under the concept of the smart specialization strategy. In order to answer this question, the analysis was conducted starting with a preliminary research phase, a field phase for information gathering and analysis, and a bibliometric analysis of sources queried in the Scopus bibliographic database. From the results obtained, the chapter proposes practical implications for benefiting smart specialization methodologies.

Chapter 14 aims to reveal how social entrepreneurship generates a solution for a long-lasting problem of the country, women empowerment. As is known, in developing countries, like Turkey gender inequality is highly widespread and gender-based discrimination is apparent. In this context, a case study is conducted with the help of the semi-structured interview realized with the founder of Çöp(m)adam (Garbage Lady). Furthermore, as a secondary data source, the website of çöp(m)adam, the published media and the internet news were examined meticulously and the identified information which is relevant to the purpose of the study were included. The qualitative data suggests that Çöp(m)adam makes a direct positive contribution to the women's economic and psychological empowerment in Turkey.

The fourth section titled "Social Entrepreneurship in the Face of COVID-19" values on the raising importance of social entrepreneurship in this pandemic. Since December 2019, the world is under the threat of the Coronavirus disease (Covid-19), and right after its spread over, its socio-economic effects have begun to be discussed. During this period, it is seen that this crisis brought up some of the hidden problems in societies such as increasing number in mortality in elderly care homes, on the other hand it enables some new initiatives emerge and spread over rapidly.

Chapter 15 shows how social entrepreneurs play a triggering role in increasing society's welfare by offering constructive and permanent solutions in remedying the unprecedented effects of the crisis caused worldwide in the Covid-19 era. The chapter tries to find answers from secondary data such as reports from academic publications, reports declared by WHO, IMF, UNESCO, UNDP, ILO, WIEGO. The content of the section searches for the socioeconomic effects of the Covid-19 outbreak, the crucial role of social entrepreneurship in creating social value, how the groups experiencing social exclusion were affected during this pandemic. It reveals the increasing critical value of social entrepreneurs in terms of the services they provide to vulnerable groups during the pandemic.

Chapter 16 puts forward an alternative way of creating social value by giving an equal chance to access quality education and democratization of education. In this perspective, it explicit MOOCs (Massive open online courses) entrepreneurs who pursue both social and profit missions at varying degrees, and explains how they share educational material to a global audience without any time and any place restrictions via technology-based tools. Then, it provides different examples of Social Entrepreneurs Offering MOOC to Create Social Value and Social Impact. Especially focusing on Covid-19 pandemic, it reveals the need the transformation of traditional business models toward a renewed and more comprehensive lifelong learning view. In a nutshell, it summarizes how MOOCs can be valuable sources of social value creation and significant social impact through examples.

This book, including 16 chapters with the contributions of 26 authors from 4 different countries, aims to underline the role and development of social entrepreneurship in the creation and maintenance of social value through a valuable theoretical and practical insight. We hope this book can make a contribution to further understand the dynamics of social entrepreneurship and social value creation.

REFERENCES

Bornstein, D. (2004). *How to change the World, social entrepreneurs and power of the new ideas*. Oxford University Press. http://mason.gmu.edu/~progers2/howtochangetheworld.pdf

Dacin, P. A., Dacin, M. T., & Matear, M. (2010). Social entrepreneurship: Why we don't need a new theory and how we move forward. *Academy of Management Perspectives, Vol, 24*(3), 37–57.

Hellström, E., Hämäläinen, T., Lahti, V., Cook, J. W., & Jousilahti, J. (2015). Towards a Sustainable Well-being Society From Principles to Applications. In E. Hellström, J. Jousilahti & T. Heinilä (Eds.), *Sitra working paper*. https://media.sitra.fi/2017/06/19134752/Towards_a_Sustainable_Wellbeing_Society_2.pdf

Mair, J., & Marti, I. (2009). Entrepreneurship in and around institutional voids: A case study from Bangladesh. *Journal of Business Venturing, 24*(5), 419–435. doi:10.1016/j.jbusvent.2008.04.006

Santos, F. M. A. (2012). Positive Theory of Social Entrepreneurship Social Entrepreneurship in Theory and Practice. *Journal of Business Ethics, 111*(3), 335–351. doi:10.100710551-012-1413-4

Wiseman, J., & Brasher, K. (2008). Community wellbeing in an unwell world: Trends, challenges, and possibilities. *Public Health Policy, 9*(3), 353–366. doi:10.1057/jphp.2008.16 PMID:18701903

Acknowledgment

No matter how brilliant your mind or strategy, if you're playing a solo game, you'll always lose out to a team.

– Reid Hoffman

"Many ideas grow better when transplanted into another mind than the one where they sprang up."

– Oliver Wendell Homes

In January 2019, we set out with the idea to highlight the critical role of social entrepreneurship in creating social value. In the light of previous studies, our aim was to reveal the evolvement of social entrepreneurship in a new and broad perspective, the challenges they face in sustaining their initiatives, the social, economic, and ecological added values they create, and we made this dream come true thanks to our valuable researchers, friends and colleagues.

We would like to express our gratitude to 26 authors from 4 countries for their dedication and support, not only in the editing process of the book but also in the unprecedented Covid-19 period that affected us all physically and emotionally. Thanks to their contributions, 16 original episodes are presented to the readers.

In Columbia, we are grateful to colleagues at Politécnico Grancolombiano and at CESA Colegio de Estudios Superiores de Administración including Manuel Mendez Pinzon, Adela Margarita Vélez Rolón, Marcela Gómez Osorio, In Chile, we thank Katherina Kuschel from Universidad Tecnológica Metropolitana, In the USA, we are grateful to colleagues at HERA Project including Neeru Narla and Caitlyn Hoeflin, and Aral Sürmeli at the Medical Rescue Association of Turkey.

In Turkey, we extend our thanks to all Turkish colleagues and contributos at Bezmialem University, Beykent University, Istanbul Technical University, Uludag University, Marmara University, TED University, Medipol University, Gelişim University, Future is Brighter including Kerem Toker, Muhammet Fatih Şengüllendi, Kutay Güneştepe, Merve Güngördü Arıoğlu, Deniz Tunçalp, Mehlika Saraç, Gaye Karaçay Aydın, Hale Cide Demir, Erkut Altındağ, Işıl Yılmaz, Esen Kara, Tuba Bozaykut, Serra Titiz, Gözde Morgül, Çağla Arıker.

We also acknowledge the distinguished members of the Editorial Advisory Board members for their contributions during the peer review process.

Acknowledgment

We extend our special thanks to the valuable support given by the professional staff of the publisher, IGI Global. This book would not have been possible if it were not for our beloved family members.

Mine Afacan Fındıklı
Beykent University, Turkey

Duygu Acar Erdur
Beykent University, Turkey
December 2020

Section 1

Evolution of Social Entrepreneurship

Chapter 1
From Social Sustainability to Social Entrepreneurship:
A Path for Social Value Creation

Kerem Toker
https://orcid.org/0000-0002-1904-1406
Bezmiâlem Vakıf University, Turkey

ABSTRACT

Despite the discussion of social sustainability, which has been a crucial component of sustainable development for decades, unfortunately, the desired successful outcomes have not been realized in practice. This failure caused the need to examine the concept of social sustainability differently than ever before. Social entrepreneurship is a valuable tool to meet this need. Concordantly, this chapter purposes to evaluate the relations between social sustainability and social entrepreneurship by comprehensively analyzing them. Discussing this relationship and proposing a new perspective will support overcome theoretical dilemmas and practical struggles. Therefore, the concept of sustainability was explained in detail through a wide literature review, and then the concept of social entrepreneurship was examined, and links, similarities, and gaps were revealed between the two concepts. As a result, the effective implementation of social sustainability policies depends on the social impact and value created by social entrepreneurship.

INTRODUCTION

Despite the struggle for the sustainable solution of social problems, our world is still far from achievement. In particular, poverty continues to be a critical social problem for our planet. According to Alkire and et al. (2015), poverty is an actual and potential situation in which people are exposed to multiple disadvantages. Disadvantages include homelessness, landlessness, unemployment, health disasters, low income, violence, humiliation, and poor education, etc. Thus, researchers examine poverty in a multidimensional framework. Multidimensional poverty consists of three dimensions. These are health (nutrition and child mortality), education (participation and attendance time), living standards (cooking fuel, sanitation, drinking water, electricity, housing, assets). In the United Nations Global Multidimensional Poverty

DOI: 10.4018/978-1-7998-4727-4.ch001

Index (UN, 2020a), 1.3 billion people (23.1%) are multi-dimensionally poor in 101 countries. Two-thirds of the poor live in middle-income countries. There are big differences in poverty among countries. For example, Uganda's national poverty rate (55.1%) is similar to the Sub-Saharan Africa average (57.5%), but it ranges from 6% to 96.3% in the provinces of Uganda. The rates of poverty in Sub-Saharan Africa have similar differences. (6.3% - 91.9%). Also, half of the 1.3 billion MDP people are children under the age of 18. One third are children under the age of 10. There are significant variations in child poverty in South Asia. 10.7% of South Asian girls live in poor households outside of school, while in Afghanistan, this rate is 44%. In South Asia, 22.7% of children under the age of 5 live with inequality in the absence of nutrition (at least one child at home is malnourished, and there is more than one child in the home). In Pakistan, over a third of children experience similar domestic inequality under the age of 5. There is a wide variety of inequality, that is, the intensity of poverty among multidimensional poor people in different countries. For example, Egypt and Paraguay have similar MDP index values, but the disparity among poor people is very high in Paraguay. Even in poverty, inequality is experienced in our world.

Social issues are deeper and more comprehensive beyond Africa and Asia. According to Eurostat (2019), the total population rate at the risk of poverty or social exclusion in the European Union (EU) is 21.8% (113 million people). 22.8% of women, 20.8% of men, 24.2% of under 18, 18.7% of over 65, 11.6% of employees, and 64.5% of unemployed people face the same risk. Also, 11% of the EU population in higher education is at risk of poverty or social exclusion. This is 4% in the Czech Republic and Malta, while it is 17% in Greece. Poverty and social exclusion can reveal in various ways. While household income has a major impact on living standards, other aspects, such as access to labor markets and material deprivation, also prevent individuals from full participation in society. This is reflected in three sub-indicators that constitute the indicator of "poverty risk or social exclusion rate": monetary poverty, serious material deprivation, and very low labor intensity. These sub-indicators tend to overlap. Since people may be affected by two or three of this poverty at the same time, if a person falls into more than one category, it is counted only once in one indicator. More than 33 million people in the EU have been affected by more than one-third of poverty in the same period, at least one third (29.8%) of all people at risk of poverty or social exclusion. Of these, seven million were affected by all three forms (6.3%) of those at risk of poverty or social exclusion. Social problems are not yet resolved within the European Union, but the United States is struggling with similar social problems.

According to the "Poverty USA 2018" data, 10.6% of men and 12.9% of women are poor in the USA. In married couples, the poverty rate is 4.7%. Besides, the poverty rate is 12.7% for single-parent families without a wife and 24.9% for single-parent families without a husband. The poverty rate for the disabled is 25.7%. This means that approximately 4 million people with disabilities live in poverty in the USA. 16.2% (11.9 million children) of all children are poor. This rate corresponds to about 1 in 6 children. In 2015, the National Center on Family Homelessness analyzed state-level data and found that 2.5 million children across the country experienced homelessness within a year. Although official census data only gave the elderly a 9.7% poverty rate in 2018, the Supplemental Poverty Measure, which covers expenses such as increased costs of health care, announced the elderly poverty rate as 14.1%. According to the 2018 US Census Data, the highest poverty rate is among Native Americans (25.4%), while Blacks (20.8%) are the second-highest poverty rate and Hispanics (any race) is the third-highest poverty rate (17.6%). The poverty rate of whites is 10.1% and the poverty rate of Asians is 10.1%. Poverty thresholds are determined each year by the USA government and vary depending on the size of a family and the age of its members. In 2018, the poverty threshold, also known as the poverty line for an individual, is $ 12,784. The weighted average threshold for two people is $ 16,247 (Poverty USA, 2020). According to the US Census Bureau (2020), the overall poverty rate in the USA was 11.8% in 2018. These social problems experienced in almost every part of the world reveal that the concept of sustainable development should be discussed repeatedly with a different perspective.

The definition of sustainable development in the 1987 Brundtland Commission report *Our Common Future* is regarded as the milestone of sustainable development. Briefly, sustainability, defined as "development that meets the needs of the present without compromising the ability of future generations to meet their own need," has attracted considerable attention in society (WCED, 1987). Accordingly, the relations between society, the environment, and economic development are an integral part of sustainable development. To ensure sustainable development in both industrialized and developing countries, the links and interactions between the sustainability of these three components are examined. Among these interactions, social sustainability is one of the primary goals of sustainable development, but it is an endless discussion of how to achieve social goals. The reason for this is confusion about the indicators of social success, which are quite vague, costly, and complicated. However, governments and businesses are under big pressure from society to establish and sustain social policies. Despite this pressure, governments and businesses are reluctant to accept and share responsibilities. However, the social belief continues that a socially responsible public or private organization has to meet sustainability criteria at every stage of its operations.

The costs incurred by businesses for social policies have an impact on this reluctance. This cost concern makes the social sustainability practices of the enterprises a display object, rather than their legal obligations. Businesses that treat the issue only as a public relations activity cannot put forward integrated and meaningful social sustainability policies. Governments, on the other hand, are increasingly breaking away from society in the process of restructuring the global world. They also move away from the role and vision of joining the society. It is undisputed that this withdrawal creates more space for social organizations in society. One of the reasons for this is that society turns its attention to non-profit organizations (NPO). For example, social services such as aged care are often provided by NPOs. As NPOs expand and diversify their operations in the community, their responsibilities increase. Therefore, they are forced to adopt a competitive position and follow innovative ways of delivering superior value by capturing competitive advantage in their target markets. There has been an increase in the evaluation of social entrepreneurship as a new phenomenon emerging to solve social problems, as well as social, green, and sustainable business models to define new business logic that can have positive effects on business and society (Sinthupundaja, et al., 2020).

Increased public awareness reveals the need to address social problems with an entrepreneurial approach. In terms of sustainability, the concept of social sustainability should be developed within a new perspective, and it needs to be instrumentalized for community welfare. This new perspective could not be developed yet, many public institutions and non-governmental organizations (NGOs) have lagged far behind the expectations of society. The main social institutions are generally inefficient, ineffective, and unresponsive. There is also a great deal of confusion as to what benefits institutions can contribute to resolving social problems. The new perspective proposed here is quite obvious. Social entrepreneurs are needed to develop new social models in the new century.

Social entrepreneurship is a response to market imperfections characterized by simultaneous government and market failure (Betts et al., 2018). It leads to the establishment of new social organizations, or NPOs, and innovation in existing ones. NPOs represent a wide range of economic, educational, research, welfare, social, and spiritual activities carried out by various organizations. Entrepreneurship in the social field is of great scientific interest, particularly as it relates to the leadership of social organizations or social development. The wide research field of social models and social entrepreneurship activities stems from the significant role these concepts play in serving social sustainability and thus in the lives of future generations.

Surely, the principles, rules, and methods applied by the business community to develop new social models can also be applied to non-profit social projects. Social entrepreneurs are a kind of entrepreneur, and to examine social entrepreneurship, it is necessary to consider what constitutes this type. Therefore, the social entrepreneurship concept should be based on the accumulation of entrepreneurial theory. Also, to understand social entrepreneurship, it is necessary to grasp conventional entrepreneurship. It is important to treat and evaluate social entrepreneurs as a sub-system of the large entrepreneurial ecosystem. One of the common mistakes here is to believe that problems can be solved by placing the word social next to business concepts. The main concern of social entrepreneurship is to create social value by solving social problems. This differentiation in mission seen in social entrepreneurs is principal and obvious. This well-known mission directly affects how social entrepreneurs perceive and evaluate opportunities. This mission is the key and critical point that encompasses and guides social sustainability.

The basis of the discussion in this chapter is that the establishment and development of social entrepreneurship standards can play a key role in achieving social sustainability objectives. To achieve this, social needs and problems must be clearly defined. Also, the balance between economic benefit and social benefit should be used in favor of society. Here, social entrepreneurship turns the focus from meeting the needs of individuals to meeting the community's needs in a new and innovative solution to social problems. This perspective shift makes social sustainability goals concrete and possible. The purpose of this chapter is to begin a discussion about the scope and depth of the relationship between social entrepreneurship and social sustainability. For this, the connections between the two concepts have been explained and defined so that the foundations of a theoretical framework have been established. Thus, this chapter is expected to develop different theoretical expansions on the role and importance of social entrepreneurship in achieving social sustainability goals.

BACKGROUND

At the beginning of the third millennium, we are overwhelmed by unprecedented complexities in human history. Now, humanity can produce much more knowledge than anyone can absorb, increase interdependencies much more than anyone can manage, and accelerate change much faster than anyone can keep up with (Mebratu, 1998). These rapid changes bring with it many problems. With an increasing global population, accelerated global development, and consequently increasing resource use and environmental impacts, it seems more obvious that doing business, as usual, is not an option for a sustainable future. So much so that, in today's world, resources equivalent to 1.5 planets are spent to support human activities (Bocken et al., 2014). It is not possible to leave a habitable planet for coming generations under these conditions.

As stated by Costanza and Daly (1992), economic growth destroys natural capital and, after a stage, it costs more than the value it adds to humanity. In other words, natural capital reduced for economic growth will be more valuable over time than man-made capital. In this respect, economic growth has an anti-economic and impoverishing role rather than an enriching one for society (Sikdar, 2003). In this regard, NGOs, politicians, and businesses are increasingly understanding and accepting that the negative environmental, social, and economic conditions are unsustainable (Toker, 2017). Sikdar (2003) states that development, as a qualitative development, will occur without destroying natural capital. According to the author, growth has certain economic limits, but development is unlimited. Hence, the philosophy that underlies sustainable development is not to limit the living standards of natural resources.

Thus, concerns about the sustainability of human activity have increased, and questions have been raised as to whether the planet can reach its limited capacity to support human civilization in the last part of the 20th century. It is crucial to understand how quickly the planet can regenerate itself and how much it will absorb human influence before it is consumed (Horton & Horton, 2019). Because of these concerns, and particularly since the Brundtland report publishing, sustainable development has become a crucial factor in environmental discourse and widely accepted through many explanations (Mebratu, 1998). Sustainable development aims to build and maintain strong social, economic, and ecological systems. These systems are strictly interconnected. Human development depends on ecosystems serving humanity for social welfare and security. Moreover, people can adjust ecosystems to operate under desired conditions. Humanity receives many ecosystem services from the environment such as clean water, clean air, food, and energy. When ecosystems fail to provide these services, significant consequences can occur, such as low food security and famine. Such negative changes also represent a loss of flexibility in the economy (Folke et al., 2002). People better understood that natural resources should be evaluated as capital instead of income sources to meet the demands of future generations as the concept of sustainability developed. (Randhawa & Kumar, 2017). To this end, the 2030 Agenda for Sustainable Development was launched in 2015 by The United Nations Development Program (UNDP) to end poverty and put the world on the path to peace, prosperity, and opportunity for a healthy planet. The 17 Sustainable Development Goals (SDGs) demand nothing more than the transformation of the financial, economic, and political systems that govern our societies today to guarantee all human rights.

Notably, the first of these 17 goals is to end poverty. The global multidimensional poverty problem explained in the introduction part of the chapter has been listed as the priority problem of the United Nations' development goals (UNDP, 2020). UNDP demands the active participation of individuals and institutions in the policy-making process to prevent poverty. This goal promotes human rights, knowledge sharing between generations, and innovation and critical thinking at all ages. Therefore it supports transformational change in people's lives and communities. The program also expects governments to help create a conducive environment for creating productive employment and job opportunities for the poor and the excluded. The private sector also has an active role to play in this regard. Determine if the growth it generates is inclusive and contributes to poverty reduction. It can promote economic opportunities for the poor. The contribution of science to ending poverty has been significant. For example, access to safe drinking water has provided improved hygiene to reduce deaths from water-borne diseases and reduce health risks associated with unsafe drinking water and lack of sanitation (UN, 2020b). Is UNDP's role assigned to governments and the private sector sufficient for 2030 sustainable development goals? To better understand the issue, an examination of the components of sustainability is required. So much so that we have to comprehend the sustainability of ecosystems as a whole to safeguarding humanity's future.

THE COMPONENTS OF SUSTAINABLE DEVELOPMENT

The phrase *"triple bottom line"* (TBL) was developed in 1977 by environmentalist and economist John Elkington. TBL has become an internationally understood term used in corporate reporting processes involving environmental, social, and economic concerns. This term is widely used in sustainability discussions (McKenzie, 2004). Elkington's TBL statement captures the essence of sustainability by measuring the impact of an organization's operations on the world (Slaper & Hall, 2011). It is not possible to achieve environmental, social, or economic sustainability separately, without commonly achieving all three components of sustainability (McKenzie, 2004). It is clear that effectively communicating with stakeholders on prosperity, environmental quality, and social justice will become a decisive feature of corporate responsibility in the 21st century (Elkington, 1998). Therefore, the TBL approach requires determining the links between social, economic, and environmental factors for the needs of sustainability (Strulak-Wöjcikiewicz & Lemke, 2019). This approach meets all stakeholder demands that businesses need to contribute, as well as offers accountability and legitimacy to society (Norman & MacDonald, 2004). It is a comprehensive and efficient standpoint on this issue.

The environmental dimension is the first performance criterion of the TBL approach, which focuses on the impact of organizations on living and inanimate natural systems such as ecology, soil, air, and water (Jamali, 2006). According to Sikdar (2003), sustainability occurs only when ecological powers that support the social and physical conditions necessary for human and environmental health are maintained or developed. Therefore, achieving environmental sustainability aims to sustain global life support systems endlessly (this refers to natural systems that sustain human life) (Goodland, 1995). When the scope of environmental responsibility is examined, it is seen that it includes more than compliance with all government regulations and even initiatives such as recycling or energy efficiency (Jamali, 2006). So, the environment–human interaction requires a sensitivity that exceeds legal regulations.

Economic sustainability, the second component of sustainability, is an effort to manage the vital impacts of organizations and business networks on society, ecosystems, and the planet. It is generally well understood by economic actors. Enterprises balance its cost goals with its production to maintain its economic sustainability (Gimenez et al., 2012). Thus, it has two different aspects. One aspect is about traditional financial performance (cost reduction) and the other one is concerning the external stakeholders' interests (economic prosperity and improvement to living standards) (Saunila et al., 2018). In this way, major developments are achieved in facilitating sustainable development by identifying options and alternatives for more effective natural resource management. Therefore, reducing poverty in the world is the main concern of sustainable economic development. According to the Brundtland Report, the main goal of the economy in sustainable development is to create solutions when evaluating or predicting environmental and ecological destruction (Rasouli & Kumarasuriyar, 2016). It seems that the business world has come a long way in this regard.

Sustainability means staying within planetary boundaries. The Brundtland Commission Report stated that sustainability is meeting today's needs without sacrificing future generations and then expanded to include economic sustainability and social equality ideas (Horton & Horton, 2019). However, social problems along with economic growth are considered critical dimensions, as they represent growth in humans' well-being (Randhawa & Kumar, 2017). For example, stakeholders may be concerned about child labor recruitment, purchasing a workforce from sweatshops, supporting controversial political systems, or bad human rights records, and so forth, while the organization is doing business (Jennifer Ho & Taylor, 2007). For this reason, in addition to the planetary boundaries, social boundaries should not be exceeded (Horton & Horton, 2019). Thus it is mandatory to focus on the social aspect of sustainability. Figure 1 shows the main sustainable development components in the TBL approach.

Figure 1. Schematic illustration of the triple bottom line (inspired by Elkingnton, 1998)

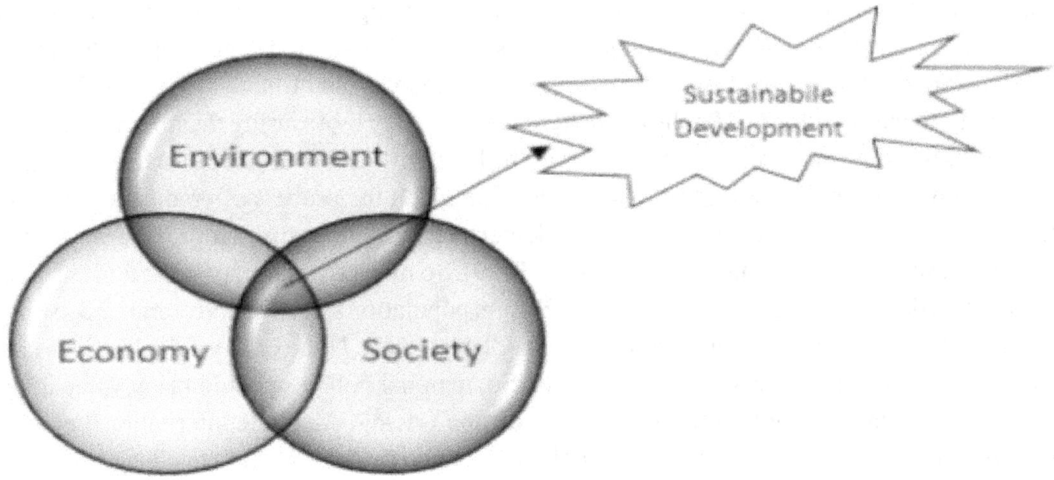

Addressing sustainable development and sustainability concepts with the TBL approach reflects a major change in thinking that forces organizations to re-evaluate their approaches to measuring their corporate performance (Hubbard, 2009). Regarding the corporate performance realization, the responsibility of businesses is at least as much as the states. Businesses play a dynamic role as essential elements in achieving the national development goals of countries, such as economic growth, poverty reduction, employment, and income, which will ensure a fairer income distribution and increased productivity (Toker, 2018). Also, NGOs were attended to the state and business actors after some time. In practice, it is seen that NGOs are more interested in the social sustainability aspect of the TBL approach. The reason for this is that the state and businesses have directed their interest in environmental and economic performance more than social sustainability. As mentioned in the introduction, the practical deficiencies occurring within the framework of social sustainability prevent the environmental and economic performance indicators from being achieved effectively. In addition to environmental and economic concerns, many social and ethical problems such as poverty, slavery, corruption, and overpopulation are now a major part of sustainability issues. In this regard, it would be appropriate to begin discussions on the implementation and success of social sustainability.

SOCIAL SUSTAINABILITY

While concerns of social sustainability, human capital development, the generation of employment, health, and safety development, it is also concerned with socio-economic processes such as organizations' ability to compete by ensuring their economic productivity and respect for the environment (Saunila et al., 2018). It can be stated that social sustainability is related to how social issues should be managed, which increases the probability of the organization's long-term survival (Ahmadi et al., 2017). To this end, social sustainability aims to positively influence all current and future relationships with stakeholders. It also focuses on meeting the needs of stakeholders and ensuring their loyalty to the organization (Baumgartner & Ebner, 2010). Thus, it is also seen as a positive contribution to environmental and economic components.

Notable economic development trends in many parts of the world include both a significant environmental stress factor and other environmentally related challenges. The negative trends discussed in this direction are environmental stress (rapid changes, shocks, disruptions), hunger and malnutrition, rapid and distorted urbanization, inequality, scarce energy sources, and financial systems. These trends reveal the need to build a reinforced policy and present it to society by ensuring that the current scientific knowledge supports the implementation policies in the best way (Gill et al., 2019). Many examples can be given within the framework of these trends. For example, in the process of eradicating poverty and reducing gender discrimination, governments implement various programs that provide ways and tools for women's development and empowerment (Rao, 1999). So much that poverty reduction should come from qualitative development, redistribution and sharing, population stability, and community solidarity, rather than a quantitative increase in production (Goodland, 1995). None of these applications can take place without changes in the economic playground. So, national policies should bring value to natural capital and cost to unsustainable activities, such as carbon pricing. Also, the international governance of global partners should be strengthened through binding agreements on climate change, stopping the loss of biodiversity and ecosystem services, and addressing other sustainability concerns (Griggs et al., 2013). At this point, policymakers have a crucial role to restructure the existing economic systems.

In recent years, there has been an improvement in principles for a paradigm shift and social sustainability implementations. For example, institutions are prioritized by reducing poverty and hunger, increasing health and well-being, and creating sustainable patterns of production and consumption. Also, the goal of improving lives and livelihoods will protect biodiversity and ecosystem services while promoting sustainable access to food, water, and energy (Griggs et al., 2013). In addition to these practices, fair wages in business life or expanding the scope of health services can be shown. As can be seen, these practices add value to the society and "return" those received from it. In addition to the moral aspect of being "good" to society, ignoring social responsibility can negatively affect the performance and sustainability of the business (Alhaddi, 2015). Although businesses have to be kneaded with this awareness, they deliver their social responsibilities to the government. According to Elkington (1998), sustainability partnerships can be initiated and managed by government agencies, companies, NGOs, or other stakeholders. A partnership approach that should be propagated by the government can be developed through contracts or voluntary environmental agreements between the entity and the government. However, in practice, both the reluctance and inability of the governments to initiate these processes and the reluctance of the enterprises to allocate resources to social processes have created an important gap in the implementation of the social aspect of sustainability. Such that government and philanthropic funds of non-profit organizations are becoming increasingly unsustainable (Betts, 2018). Social entrepreneurship, which has been on the agenda in recent years, and as a critical research topic can play a crucial role in filling this gap. Before discussing the establishment of links between social sustainability and social entrepreneurship, it would be appropriate to consider social enterprise and social entrepreneurship.

SOCIAL ENTERPRISE

Social enterprises are businesses run by nonprofits and/or small businesses that have a clear commitment to social impact (Saxena, 2019). It is necessary to mention the concept of social impact here. Social impact is the evaluation of the outcomes of work based on the social context. Social impact may occur in organizations that leave traditional commercial concerns behind and carry out operations that positively affect the community's well-being and quality of life. The concept of social impact should encompass and enrich all stakeholders and society. In this framework, social entrepreneurs have a role in shaping social value in society and creating social value in a complex social system. These various goals of creating social value are poverty reduction, health services improvement, and climate change prevention (Situmorang & Mirzanti, 2012). The similarity between social impact targets and social sustainability targets is remarkable.

Sustainability issues such as increased inequality and the deterioration of a natural livelihood make the transformation into a more sustainable economic system increasingly attractive. To realize this transition, private enterprises are critical stakeholders that manage the most resources and capabilities (Geissdoerfer et al., 2018). However, there is an important problem. Do these critical stakeholders take the initiative to solve the problems they produce? As mentioned earlier, the understanding of—and perhaps obsession with—the economic growth of enterprises lies at the root of the current problems. So long as economic growth is a key performance criterion for both business and government management, the destruction of the environment and society will continue. The interesting part of the issue is that businesses and governments that cause environmental and social disruption are also trying to develop various policies to prevent this disruption (Toker et al., 2020). For example, the official development aid of developed countries will be provided to low-income countries during 2015–2030. However, when today's low-income countries reach the middle-income level as a result of economic growth, the role and amount of these aids will decrease. Also, private philanthropy and volunteering are encouraged in practice, rather than the aid programs of official authorities. All countries except the poorest countries should share the financing they need to supply goods and services based on their economic capacity and the principle of common but differentiated responsibilities. Safe, predictable, and agreed-upon formulations are needed to end the failure to meet formal financing commitments for public goods to ensure sustainable development (Sachs, 2012). In this context, many developed countries with traditionally welfare programs have recently attempted to restructure the economic policies of the welfare state (Kibler et al., 2018). Thus, the roles of all these policy and strategy actors in the global economic system are changing. Sekliuckiene and Kisielius (2015) defined these new community-oriented roles and tasks as social entrepreneurship. Table 1 shows the social enterprise spectrum.

Social enterprises are social businesses and are defined as a generic term that generates income for society. It also creates or supports economic opportunities for poorly living and disadvantaged populations, referring to the lower social stratum. However, the importance of the personal characteristics of social entrepreneurs should not be underestimated (Rahdari et al., 2016). Saxena (2019) classified the strategies adopted by social entrepreneurs to ensure financial sustainability in a non-profit activity area as follows: 1) non-profit income strategies of earnings and 2) non-profit income strategies in the mission-oriented strategies of businesses. Thus, two forms in the literature are repeatedly differentiated: one for non-profit organizations and the other for social missions. Traditionally, non-profit organizations have worked in the social sector and have received funding from donors as well as some government resources. To get funding, non-profit organizations can commercialize some of their programs and thus act as if they are making a profit (Roy et al., 2014). However, the profit obtained here is spent on activities that will create social impact and value instead of creating capital accumulation. The lack of mission orientation and profit motivation increases the role and power of social enterprises in achieving social sustainability. According to Kibler et al. (2018), social enterprises can generate more social benefits than key national components (educators, policymakers, researchers, investors, and entrepreneurs) from the government and NGOs.

Table 1. The social enterprise spectrum Source: (Angelica, 2019)

		Purely Philanthropic	← Social Enterprise →	Purely Commercial
Motives		Appeal to goodwill	Mixed motives	Appeal to self-interest
Methods		Mission-driven	Mission and market-driven	Market-driven
Goals		Social value	The social and economic value	Economic value
Key stakeholders	Beneficiaries	Pay nothing	Subsidized rates, or a mix of full payers and those who pay nothing	Market-rate prices
	Capital	Donations and grants	Below-market capital, or a mix of donations and market-rate capital	Market-rate capital
	Workforces	Volunteers	Below-market wages, or a mix of volunteers and fully-paid staff	Market-rate compensation
	Suppliers	Make in-kind donations	Special discounts, or a mix of in-kind and full-price donations	Market-rate prices

Thus, social enterprises develop a society with the innovation and resourcefulness of individuals or groups. These individuals or groups create new and improved ways to address the problems of society, similar to traditional initiatives creating new and innovative products that enrich a developed society (Stephan et al., 2015). To sum up, social enterprises are organizations that aim to create a social impact through their activities, and they plan financial models for this purpose. A social entrepreneur is a person or group whose motivation is to make a social impact rather than a profit. Therefore, to understand the social entrepreneurs, it is necessary to explain their motivation first.

Social Entrepreneurship

The term "social entrepreneurship" emerged as a new label to describe the work of private firms working in the social field for society, volunteers and public institutions, and NPOs. Social entrepreneurship was the basis for Victorian-period private hospitals in England. Indeed, it has been a key feature of philanthropic work, and this feature is visible in the hospice movement. Social entrepreneurship has its roots in the 18th and 19th centuries, until charitable business owners and industrialists such as Robert Owen improved their working, educational, and cultural lives, and showed a concern for the well-being of employees. Since then, social entrepreneurship has been associated with community initiative and development, education, churches, charities, the non-profit sector, and voluntary organizations. Collectively, it expanded into a social economy or "third sector," and its growth was often linked to structural and managerial problems in social services run by the state (Shaw & Carter, 2007). Currently, the concept is at the focus of academic discussions.

Although there are many predictions about the social economy's scale, the descriptive differences in what constitutes social enterprise disappoint efforts to produce a comprehensive understanding of the sector size (Shaw & Carter, 2007). So the question is, what is social entrepreneurship? Any definition of the term "social entrepreneurship" should begin with the word "entrepreneurship." The word "social" changes entrepreneurship. If entrepreneurship has no clear meaning, characterize it with social would not be very successful. The word entrepreneurship is a mixed concept. On the positive side, it combines thinking out of the box with a unique brand of determination to create or bring something new to the world, expressing a special, innate ability to perceive and take action. The downside is that it takes time for the real effects of entrepreneurship activities to become visible (Martin & Osberg, 2007). Therefore, the entrepreneurial operations' results cannot be quickly evaluated. It stems from the nature of entrepreneurship.

The critical distinction between entrepreneurship and social entrepreneurship comes from the value proposition. The value proposition for the entrepreneur is foreseen and organized for markets that can easily buy new products or services and thus is about to make a financial profit. From the start, entrepreneurs and investors expect to earn financial profits. Profit is primary for the sustainability of any enterprise and the adoption of the large-scale market and achieving results with a new balance (Martin & Osberg, 2007). Within the narrow definition, social entrepreneurship is the phenomenon of practicing business expertise and market-based skills in the non-profit sector, typically as non-profit organizations develop innovative approaches to earning income (Austin et al., 2012). Discussing social entrepreneurship in the literature is a fairly new and complex phenomenon. Many authors define social entrepreneurship differently.

The components included in these definitions are social justice, social value, viable socio-economic structures, a new social-economic balance, innovation, entrepreneurship skills, market gaps, solving social problems, and social entrepreneurs as a change agent (Sekliuckiene & Kisielius, 2015). According to Béchervaise and Benjamin (2013), the social entrepreneurship paradigm requires a broader social commitment, visionary and self-sacrificing moral pursuit of entrepreneurship, to transition from a purely profit-oriented entrepreneurial operation to social entrepreneurship. For Roy et al. (2014), the social entrepreneur creates social value by combining resources with new methods, promotes social change, or explores and uses opportunities to create social value by meeting social needs. Another definition of the social entrepreneur is the alliance of individuals, groups, networks, and organizations seeking a sustainable, large-scale change through ideas that determine what or how governments, non-profit organizations, and businesses are doing to address major social problems (Light, 2006). Thus, social entrepreneurship works on different scales, ranging from individual to organizational alliances.

According to the Social Enterprise Coalition (2020), social enterprises should have a clear social and/or environmental mission in their management documents, generate most of their income through trade, re-evaluate most of their profits, be independent of the state (that is, autonomous), be under control in the interests of the social mission, and be accountable and transparent. Accordingly, the main driving force for the social entrepreneur is his/her social issue. The social problem addressed by a social enterprise becomes a decision based on which particular organizational form will most effectively mobilize the resources needed to solve this problem (Béchervaise & Benjamin, 2013). After these definitions, the motivation of the social entrepreneur will be examined in more detail.

Entrepreneurship directs the focus of entrepreneurial projects to the search for freedom and autonomy based on an existing location. Furthermore, the great narrative of emancipation is about the desire for autonomy against the status quo, breaking off from someone else's strength and the current social order (Haugh & Talwar, 2016). Social entrepreneurs are people who think of innovative, sustainable business models for social change and transform these models into reality as a social enterprise. This reality concept (social enterprise) brings together various organizational structures from commercial non-profit organizations to profit-making businesses that claim to have social goals on the same platform (Saxena, 2019). According to Zahra et al. (2009), social entrepreneurship provides a refined example of how it can inspire individuals in designing, building, and operating organizations for social problems that are deemed personally crucial. Following this logic, organizations whose only purpose is profit are outside of social entrepreneurship. Similarly, for-profit businesses engaged in charitable efforts or socially responsible activities generally fall outside the boundaries of social entrepreneurship. In this context, social entrepreneurs' lack of profit and focus on social value is a dominant view in the literature and practice.

Social entrepreneurs are motivated around personal satisfaction such as helping the community through their activities, focusing on non-monetary gains, the tendency to succeed, and proximity to social problems. Contributing to social sustainability by solving critical social problems is another factor that motivates social entrepreneurs. The importance of any social problem can be determined by whether entrepreneurs see an opportunity to solve this problem or whether others see it as a social problem. For example, an entrepreneur may be convinced of the importance of combating blindness, a serious and common problem in developing economies. At the same time, the benefits of providing vocational training to young people and empowering women in these economies can capture the entrepreneur's attention more strongly (Zahra et al., 2008). So, the problem must have social content rather than who has perceived it. Social entrepreneurs play the role of change in the social sector as follows (Dees, 1998):

- Adopting the mission of creating and maintaining social value (not just custom value),
- Recognizing new opportunities and continuously monitoring to serve this mission,
- To enter the continuous innovation, adaptation, and learning process,
- Acting bravely without being limited to the resources available,
- Increased sense of accountability for results

Also, social entrepreneurs, like conventional entrepreneurs, are the pioneers of society in pursuing freedom and autonomy. According to Haugh and Talwar (2016), the quest for autonomy involves breaking environmental constraints to create new possibilities. This includes exploring and repairing cracks in social and economic relationships that impose restrictions on specific activities that society cares about. Thus, positive social change is based on the removal of restrictions that hinder or slow progress. For example, the business integration of social initiatives aims to help individuals who are excluded from the labor markets to get rid of unemployment. According to Stephan et al. (2015), alike to traditional entrepreneurs, social entrepreneurs are innovative and motivated to continue their ventures. The characteristics of the two types of entrepreneurs are very similar. However, there are differences in purpose and motivation. While the traditional entrepreneur is interested in obtaining profit and growing his/her business, the social entrepreneur is interested in meeting a social need and benefiting society to be better than yesterday. Social entrepreneurs believe that life is more than just business and profit. Caring for people and providing them with opportunities are critical to the advancement of a better world.

Creating Social Value

The main mission of social entrepreneurship is to create social value. Social entrepreneurs are very social in conducting their activities, sharing their knowledge, and honoring their achievements (Dacin, et al., 2011). To create social value in social practice, community members must participate in the process broadly. Capturing social value in a social enterprise is the difference between the cost of the resources used by the social entrepreneur and the value created by the activity. This means that creating value is a concept measured at the social or system level, and capturing value is measured at the organizational or unit level. The traditional profit logic is nothing more than an estimate of the value obtained by a business (Santos, 2012). Unlike other businesses, the legitimacy of a social enterprise depends on its ability to successfully show its social impact to internal and external stakeholders (Molecke and Pinkse, 2020). This effect can only be achieved by creating social value. So what is social impact and social value? How are they realized? Explaining and discussing these questions will provide a clear understanding of social entrepreneurship. We will then support these definitions and explanations by giving a few tangible examples.

First, let's explain what is social impact?. Social impact is the individual's attitude towards a particular point being influenced by other people in the community. This situation is defined as the effect of others' explicit or implicit presence/actions on an individual's emotions, thoughts, or behaviors (Chang et al., 2020). In this context, "influence" refers to the ability of many actions to create "permanent changes" in the lives of people and their communities (Molecke and Pinkse, 2020; Rangan and Gregg, 2019). So much so that the success of a social enterprise depends on how well it shows social impact. The critical issue here is how to measure social impact. Such that the success of a social enterprise depends on how clearly it shows social influence (Molecke and Pinkse, 2020). There should be strong relationships between the outcomes of social enterprises and the social outcomes they influence. To this end, social enterprises must produce quantitative measures on the results of their activities.

So how can we overcome the difficulty and uncertainty in impact measurement? Molecke and Pinks (2020) discussed the social impact with 24 social entrepreneurs. According to social entrepreneurs, 2 questions need to be asked to examine the social impact in a social enterprise. The first of these; "Is there any effect?" it is the question. The answer is not to assess the amount of impact produced, but to create symbols of the status of the organization as a promising social enterprise. The second question is; to what extent the social enterprise has reached and succeeded. The authors found that social entrepreneurs often find answers to this question to prove the legitimacy of their social enterprises. There are implicit admissions that larger-scale social enterprises will have greater social impacts. However, how effective are social entrepreneurs? They cannot answer the question. According to the authors, the amount of the effect is unknown x. This situation is far from satisfactory for those who fund social enterprises.

Social impact measurement helps social enterprises set realistic goals, improve performance, prioritize decisions, and access capital markets more competitively (OECD, 2015). Therefore, despite the difficulties in measuring it, researchers have been working more and more in recent years to measure social impact. The Organization for Economic Co-operation and Development (OECD) developed several approaches to the measurement of social impact in the report "Policy Brief on Social Impact Measurement for Social Enterprises" published in 2015. The first of these approaches is the positivist approach that creates a picture of the real world by adopting accounting, rational, and objective value measurements. The second is the critical approach. This approach plays a role between (and within) organizations and society based on the principles of accounting, democracy, and accountability. The third and final approach is the interpretive approach. In this approach, accounting acts as a symbolic mediator between various social groups and acts as a tool for dialogue between initiatives and their stakeholders to encourage social change.

The literature also highlights many different methods adopted by public actors, social enterprises, and private funders to measure their social impact. The current debate on social impact measurement revolves around two main approaches. The 'one size fits all' approach depends on their size, industry, country, governance mechanisms, etc. It considers the indiscriminate application of a defined set of indicators (including economic and social indicators) to all social enterprises regardless. Social enterprises are considering adopting different criteria to capture their differences. It requires determining the most appropriate social impact measurement tools for each specific situation (OECD, 2015). Besides, the European Commission has developed an analytical guide on social impact measurement in the report "Proposed Approaches to Social Impact Measurement," published in 2014 by the GECES subgroup. GECES (2014) clearly states: "A single set of top-down indicators cannot be designed to measure social impact in all cases." The report provides several reasons why a unique set of indicators or metrics might not be suitable. For example, 'the diversity of social impacts sought by social enterprises is immense. Therefore, no single methodology can capture all impacts fairly or objectively. GECES also advocates adopting a measurement process rather than imposing specific criteria or indicators. It defines the following five-step process for all social impact measures: 1) plan (identify objectives); 2) engage (identify stakeholders); 3) set relevant measurements; 4) measure, validate, and value; 5) report, learn and improve. (see: Figure 2). It also proposes a framework based on developing a matrix of expected outcomes and sub-results, each of which includes potential indicators and explains their best practice. The report states that 'there is the freedom to use which indicator ensures that the measurement is intervened and aligned with stakeholders' needs.

Figure 2. Stages of impact measurement, and the benefits to stakeholders (GECES, 2015)

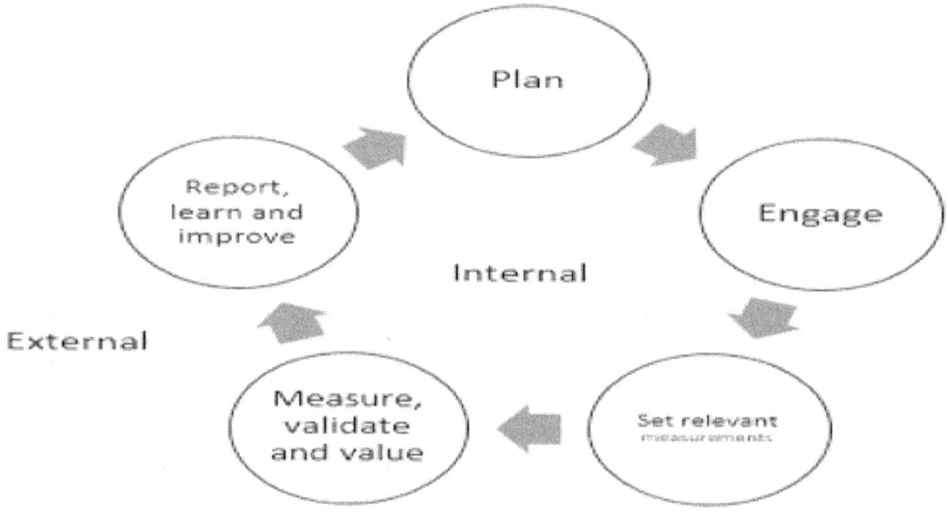

There are problems in measuring social impact, but we know that this effect is created through social value. Therefore, creating social value is the primary goal of the social entrepreneur. So now let's define what social value is.

How is social value created and delivered? According to Houston (2019), social value refers to the total impact on people's quality of life. This quality of life requires a comprehensive assessment of economic, environmental, social impact and value for all key stakeholder groups. One of the methods of creating social value is that businesses do not distribute dividends; therefore, all excess cash is invested to achieve the social goal pursued. Another method is to establish for-profit companies owned by low-income people. Thus, poor individuals can improve their social conditions through to the firm's profit production. Inclusive social business models mean for-profit businesses that contribute to poverty reduction by including disadvantaged people and low-income communities. Therefore, it supports the idea that such business models can help explain sustainable value creation (Canestrino et al., 2019).

The Cases of Creating Social Value in Social Entrepreneurship

Social sectors can be distinguished by three different sources of social value opportunities. The first source is activism. Activists are the main actors that give moral legitimacy to social enterprises. Activists monitor communication and information distribution through networks and encourage social value proposals or social concerns supported by activist groups. The second source of social value opportunities is self-help, where the beneficiaries themselves are social entrepreneurs. In this model (for example, a food bank), the economic value proposition is based on low-cost labor and marketing, affordable capital, and loyal and patient customers. The social needs or concerns of the main beneficiaries are at the core of the social value proposition. The third source of social value opportunities is philanthropy. Here, donors are the main actors, and economic value proposals are donations by philanthropists. The social value proposition is based on social issues defined by donors (Helmsing, 2015). Thus, the income obtained is used for the solutions of these defined social problems. Providing examples of creating social impact will help to understand the issue.

A self-managed collective and anarchist cuisine in Brussels can be a meaningful example of creating social value (Petteni, 2020): The initiative begins with given the loan of a greenhouse to politically active social entrepreneurs. In the beginning, several people belonging to the international anarchist network, which was present and active in places such as the Calais Migrant Camp, southern France, were interested in this greenhouse. This group saw that a structure that could provide regular food support to the refugees staying in Maximilien Park in Brussels was missing and decided to establish this well-known kitchen. The group of non-Belgian international members hoped to continue to move this project elsewhere, after finding enough local volunteers within a few months. However, since a lot of energy was required to set up the kitchen, they had a hard time finding a reliable and organized volunteer base that could operate the kitchen autonomously and locally without the help of one of the first group. The experience and energy of this group was not easily adopted by others. It was normally necessary to cook four times a week and six days during social isolation, which meant 700 cups of vegan and halal meals a day, 80 kg of rice or 150 liters of soup, about 80 to 100 kg of recycled net vegetables.

Generally, the project budget is quite low as 800 euros per week. The main factor enabling this kitchen to operate economically (which can continue the project independently of any institution) is the purchase of vegetables and bread from the markets and shops that accept the products because they cannot sell. These shops give their products, which are not sold, to volunteers, not because of the help, but because of the extra expense created by unloading excess products. Another job of the volunteers is to pick up these unsold products from Brussels in the early morning - between five and a half to six - by pickup trucks and to remove fresh vegetables and toss away rotten ones.

In this example, the social impact created by the entrepreneur group, which defines themselves as an "anarchist" in Brussels, is measured. The social impact feeds 800 refugees a day, with a weekly budget of 800 Euros. People and institutions who want to provide resources to these volunteers see what tangible social value their resources contribute. We will give two more examples for a better understanding of the social value. The second example is "The Shoe That Grows" project by social entrepreneur Kenton Lee.

More than 1.5 billion people worldwide suffer from soil-borne diseases. Children without shoes are particularly vulnerable to soil-borne diseases and diseases, and even parasites that can cause death. Sick children destitute of school, cannot help their families, and suffer unnecessarily. Since the feet of children overgrow, they often cannot use the donated shoes within a year and are once again exposed to illness and disease. The Shoe That Grows social enterprise can change this disadvantageous condition. The small size of the growing shoe is designed for a child of 5-10 years old to use for five years, while the large size for a child of 10-15 years old to use it for five years. The project is enlarged with donations from all over the world. So, 70 thousand pairs of shoes are delivered to children in 80 countries (Because International, 2020).

The third example of social impact is the Better World Books social initiative. Founded in 2002 by Notre Dame alumni Xavier Helgesen, Chris Kreece Fuchs, and Jeff Kurtzman, the mission of Better World is to maximize each book and promote literacy worldwide. The company works by reusing or recycling old books through sales on websites and donations to schools. So far, it has evaluated 84 million old books to raise $12.1 million for the literacy fund. The company attributes its success to using a "triple profit" model that attaches importance not only to financial profit but also to the social and environmental impact. In search of used book resources, Xavier soon made a discovery that drastically changed the business model and the environment. As new editions are created in thousands of libraries each year, millions of more books emerge. Some books are left in storage areas or thrown away. "I threw it away !." Social entrepreneurs, who believed that something could be done to save these thrown books and help the planet a bit in this process, started to partner with librarians worldwide. They could not only save the books from the dumps but also sell these books and raise money for the libraries themselves. The environmental and social impact created in this example of social entrepreneurship is measured in numbers. Since its foundation in 2002, Books Donated 26,502,000 funds raised for literacy & libraries 28,430,000 books reused or recycled 320,019,014 (Better World Books, 2020). These numbers represent the impact and strength of social enterprise on a world scale.

These examples show us that social entrepreneurship contributes permanently to the solution of complex problems in various parts of the world. After these social enterprise examples, the link between social entrepreneurship and social sustainability emerges. It will be useful to explain the relationship between the two concepts in detail.

LINKING SOCIAL ENTREPRENEURSHIP AND SOCIAL SUSTAINABILITY

There is a natural tension among those within the social entrepreneurship ecosystem, ensuring that everyone works towards the common goal, with the same goals and methods, using the same metrics in success criteria, and also promoting entrepreneurship (Waddock & Post, 1991). Therefore, the struggles faced by social entrepreneurs vary depending on their motivations, the resources required to pursue their ambitions, and the governance and control mechanisms used to regulate their behavior. Because the goals of social enterprises are deeply based on the values of their founders, it can also be difficult to balance motives with the need for profit and economic efficiency to create social wealth (Zahra et al., 2009). With all these obstacles, the critical role of social entrepreneurship in generating social sustainability cannot be denied. Therefore, it is useful to examine the relationship between the two concepts in more detail.

A strong entrepreneurial orientation based on efficient business models is required to sustain social enterprises (Zahra et al., 2009). Accordingly, social entrepreneurship pursues economic, social, and environmental rational goals similar to conventional enterprises. This approach provides a more idealized perspective by defining social entrepreneurs as *"change agents"* in the social sector (Santos, 2012). Social entrepreneurs are concerned with repairing the perceived market and government failures. The focus is on providing sustainable solutions rather than on sustainable advantage. Sustainable solutions are approaches that permanently eliminate the root causes of the problem, or, at a minimum, institutionalize a system to deal with the problem (Santos, 2012). Also, social entrepreneurship is a more ethical form of entrepreneurship, with a focus on the innovative use of resources to explore and use opportunities that meet a social need sustainably (Haugh & Talwar, 2016). Therefore, the effects of social entrepreneurship on the implementation processes of social sustainability are inevitable. Figure 3 shows the role and impact of social entrepreneurship in sustainable development.

Figure 3. The role of social entrepreneurship in sustainable development

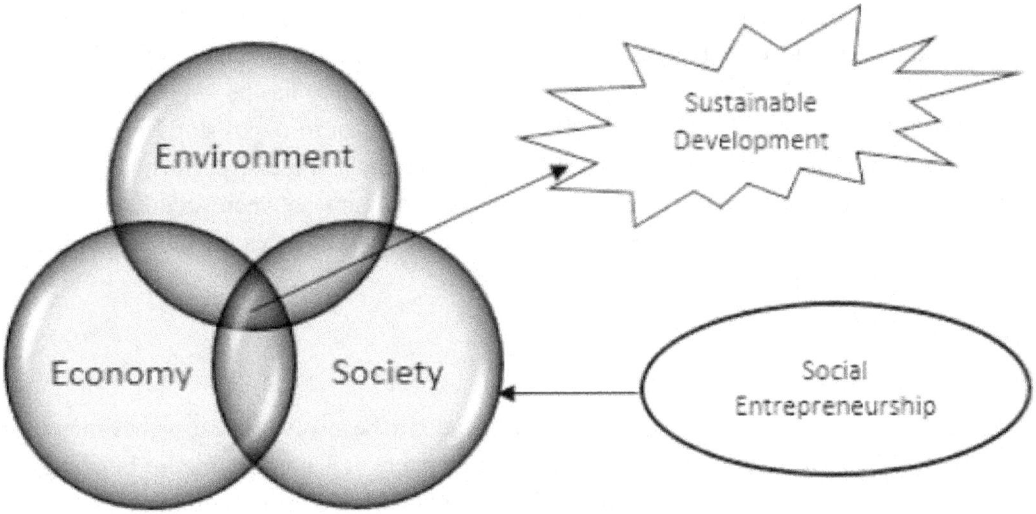

Social entrepreneurs establish unique organizations amidst a broad scale of philanthropy at one end and for-profit businesses at the other. They sometimes tend to be closer to commercial institutions due to the limitations imposed on philanthropic organizations. However, social entrepreneurs are focused on developing communities and helping disadvantaged social classes. Social enterprises of non-profit organizations are willing to give up profit and growth to create a higher social value (Stephan et al., 2015). This reveals the interconnection between social enterprise and social sustainability. So, sustainable development is a complex issue that requires systemic thought solutions to the social issues, and developing a social enterprise ecosystem may be just one of the viable solution options (Rahdari et al., 2016). For this reason, social enterprises put normative and implicit pressure on profit-making businesses to consider social issues through value-generating activities.

There is another critical issue regarding this relationship. Social enterprise movements in a society often initiate social changes with passion, and this change moves from the bottom (practice) to the top (policy-making) (Rahdari et al., 2016). This is a crucial point. The years of inadequacy in social sustainability processes result from the inability of the social practices initiated above to fall into the base of the community. However, as social change agents, social entrepreneurs operating at the community base provide critical support to policymakers by implementing the most basic social practices.

Similarly, Rahdari et al. (2016) stated that these change agents (social entrepreneurs) produce innovative solutions (usually technology-based) to social and environmental problems, often overlooked by traditional players in the government and social sectors. But social entrepreneurial ideas cannot be expected to create a big difference in society without further support from policymakers. For this reason, many governments establish policies that support the formation of social enterprises as legal entities to provide more support and encouragement to social entrepreneurs. For example, in the EU, the Microfinance and Social Entrepreneurship pillar supports actions in two thematic areas: (1) groups that need special attention and microcredit for micro-enterprises (2) development of social entrepreneurship. In this context, micro-financing opportunities and facilitation of access to financial institutions for those faced with the risk of being excluded from the labor market, who want to establish or develop their businesses or micro-enterprises, facilitate access to these institutions, especially for those who employ these segments. It aims to improve the development of the social investment market and enable access to finance through social equity, equity-like instruments, credit instruments, and grants up to 500,000 Euros, with an annual turnover or balance sheet not exceeding 30 million Euros (AB, 2020). Thus, the close relationship of social entrepreneurship with social sustainability has begun to be accepted.

Accordingly, Austin et al. (2012) proposed a framework for an in-depth study of social entrepreneurship. Within this framework, there are market, mission, stakeholders, performance, and context components. From this point, evaluating the relationships and gaps between social sustainability and social entrepreneurship can provide information on essential consequences for the increasing role and importance of social entrepreneurship.

Market

Businesses often cause many serious social problems that need to be resolved because they focus on results directly related to their profitability performance. Unfortunately, it is not feasible for businesses to find solutions to permanent social problems with traditional market logic, as it is often costly, complex, or unprofitable. This created a gap that worsened with institutional failures that policymakers did not have the will, power, or tools to lead to market-based solutions to sustain social reforms or reduce permanent social problems. Worse, in some parts of the world, market and institutional failures are not only common but also driven by government failures, and constant power struggles prevent reconciliation (Zahra et al., 2008). According to the 2020 report of the UK-based international aid organization Oxfam, the wealth owned by the richest 2,153 people in the world is more than the total wealth of 4.6 billion people (Oxfam, 2020). Another example of sustainable development failure, in Sub-Saharan Africa, more than 40 percent of the population still lives with less than $ 1.90 a day, and the number of extremely poor people today is significantly higher than it was twenty years ago. Worryingly, the pace of progress in poverty eradication has slowed significantly in recent years. According to UN DESA estimates, in May 2019, the number of people living in extreme poverty has increased in several Sub-Saharan African countries, where poverty levels are already very high. These countries are the Democratic Republic of the Congo, Madagascar, Mozambique, and Nigeria. Poverty rates have increased in some parts of Latin America and the Caribbean, including the region's largest economies, such as Argentina, Brazil, and the Bolivarian Republic of Venezuela (United Nations, 2020). For this reason, there is a need for organizations that have abstracted themselves from the state-business competition, and that can penetrate the market independently and are actively sensitive to social issues. Increasing the clustering of these organizations within the economic system constitutes the social sector.

Social entrepreneurs operate in markets. However, these markets generally do not provide the right discipline. Many social organizations charge fees for some of their services. They also compete for donations, volunteers, and other types of support. However, this market discipline is not often compatible with the social entrepreneur's mission. It depends on who pays or provides resources, what their motivation is, and how well they can evaluate the social value created by the enterprise. It is naturally difficult to measure creating social value. How much social value is created by reducing pollution in a specific stream, protecting the spotted owl, or accompanying the elderly? Calculations are not only difficult but also contentious. Even though improvements can be measured, it is often difficult to attribute them to a particular social enterprise (Dees, 1998).

It is assumed that social enterprises will replace existing business models that exclude the potential to develop new models. For example, social enterprises should be part of a solution to stimulate and strengthen local economies, but it should not be seen as a sideshow of the real economy (Parkinson & Howorth, 2008). For this reason, the effects of market forces on the formation of social entrepreneurship and the behavior of social enterprises towards these forces are a critical subject of study. In mixed markets where non-profit organizations operate, the determination of relative competitiveness, advantages, disadvantages, and interactive dynamics can determine the scope and form of potential collaborations. Thus, it can be determined to what extent social enterprises can correct market failures. However, social enterprises involve the process for individual entrepreneurs to create a market by reassembling resources to create creativity, vision, commitment, and new products (Surie, 2017). Therefore, social entrepreneurship eliminates the inadequacy of social sustainability caused by the effort to find solutions to social problems without building a market. Sustainable development policies could not see this gap for a long time and failed to create social impact. In other words, the social entrepreneurship paradigm has emerged to fill this gap.

Mission

While social sustainability policies just focus on creating value, social entrepreneurs aim to create and capture value. While this focus difference in objects makes social entrepreneurship more concrete and feasible, it also provides a solid basis for social sustainability.

Social entrepreneurs, however, identify social opportunities through a combination of external and internal drivers. Therefore, together with perceived social needs, their own life experiences also define the social value proposition (Helmsing, 2015). For this reason, social entrepreneurs can produce extraordinary ideas not only about what is done but also about how it happened. This situation, in a sense, defines entrepreneurship more broadly, including "using old things in new methods" as well as institutional and administrative reforms (Light, 2006). What is remarkable here is the development of socially based solutions initially linked to markets or government mechanics by social entrepreneurs (Santos, 2012). Thus, by building new initiatives or innovatively managing existing organizations, opportunities are discovered, identified, and used to increase social welfare (Zahra et al., 2009). Accordingly, Nandan et al. (2015) defined social entrepreneurship as the construction of transformative opportunities for social change through innovative activities within or between economic and social communities in a historical and cultural context.

Stakeholders

In the value exchanges between social enterprises and stakeholders, the stakeholders are disadvantaged people, consumers, donors, business partners, institutions, or internal stakeholders. The aims (beneficiaries and donors) to which the social value proposition is directed should be taken into account as it affects the way this value is created (Hlady-Rispal & Servantie, 2018). Also, social entrepreneurship does not necessarily begin with an individual initiative. Teams of small groups, organizations, networks, and even communities can also come together to create radical social change (Light, 2006). An interesting aspect is that individuals know themselves as social entrepreneurs and identify with other individuals belonging to the social entrepreneur community. This sense of belonging among stakeholders is not found among the social sustainability policymakers. While two parties are implementing and needing social sustainability policy practitioners, the people practicing and needing social entrepreneurship can be the same. Previously, it has been shown different roles of these stakeholders at different levels of the enterprises in Table 1.

Performance

Social entrepreneurs are activists with creative thoughts, visions, and a wide network of work. These activists can carry out their social enterprises through organizations such as foundations, associations, and NGOs, or they can be under government control. These organizations have aims and duties for social benefit. Performance evaluation systems are very critical, as social enterprises lack operational methods, especially business and management skills (Wongphuka et al., 2017) which adopt traditional approaches that evaluate social operations with both success and failure. Therefore performance assessment has become critical in social enterprises as they have to tell their success stories through reliable social and financial impact indicators against all stakeholders (Mamabolo & Myres, 2020).

Performance in social enterprises is related to the efficiency of achieving the intended social impact target rather than the income-generating capacity of the operations (Hlady-Rispal & Servantie, 2018). Social entrepreneurs may find it difficult to measure the social impact of their activities as they cannot use the usual profitability indicators (Sastre-Castillo et al., 2015). Although the social impact is considered, as a performance variable, related to social entrepreneurship, the increase in terminology related to social impact should be considered. For example, social impact is conceptualized as the social value in the literature (Rawhouser et al., 2019).

Performance measures for social entrepreneurship are less standardized and more specific for a particular organization. For example, take a new initiative created to provide educational services to children in cities. How do the leaders of this initiative evaluate performance? Using profitability as a performance measure will most likely not be beneficial as the organization's mission does not include financial earnings. Instead, a questionnaire designed to assess the program's impact on students may be more useful. Also, the increase in the number of students receiving education may represent another indicator that the program is well received by the local community. Although it is difficult to evaluate the performance of a social enterprise, developing mechanisms that support solving this problem is a significant task of academic research that contributes to the legitimacy of social entrepreneurship (Certo & Miller, 2008). However, the level of social entrepreneurship activity can vary greatly. Some individuals and organizations are very prolific entrepreneurs, while others may restrict entrepreneurship activities to a specific program or unit (Light, 2006). Therefore, performance criteria differ according to the scope of the social enterprise.

Also, organizations/individuals attempt to measure social impacts in areas that may be difficult to compare such as education, health care, environmental sustainability, and poverty (Rawhouser et al., 2019). Social entrepreneurs can sometimes fail. Although this is a reality, focusing on success stories makes it impossible to determine the failure rate. Social entrepreneurs trying to create a change that breaks the patterns can face serious obstacles to success. It may be difficult to break social habits (Light, 2006). Therefore, performance standards are crucial to define whether the social entrepreneur is achieving his/her objectives.

The hybrid nature of social enterprises means that their legitimacy is assessed by audiences expecting evidence-based performance demonstrations, both socially and financially. However, in traditional performance measurement forms, they produce social outputs that are not easily converted into required units (Molecke and Pinkse, 2020). Accordingly, while social sustainability sets general performance standards at the macro-level, social entrepreneurship determines project-based performance criteria at the micro-level.

Context

Contextual factors play a major role in the development of social entrepreneurship operations. Especially institutional, legal, and social environmental factors may be an obstacle or support in the development of social initiatives (Sekliuckienea & Kisielius, 2015). The context for the social entrepreneur changes with economic, political, social, and demographic conditions. The ability to combine seemingly unrelated factors or conditions and recognize opportunities is an entrepreneurial skill. Combining and merging conditions produces new products or services areas to solve social problems (Nandan et al., 2015). According to Light (2006), the social entrepreneurship intensity may increase and decrease over time. As the context is constantly changing, it can cause economic, political, social, and organizational pressures that can create pauses and restarts in social enterprises.

Social entrepreneurs follow goals related to the solution to certain problems in the social economy (Stephan et al., 2015). While social entrepreneurs often start with small enterprises, they target solutions to problems that have a local expression but have a global context such as access to water, encouraging the establishment of small businesses, and reintegration into individuals' workforce or waste management. Innovative solutions that social entrepreneurs endorse in their local context are often replicated to other geographies and can stimulate the global industry (Santos, 2012). Thus, there is a context from local to global. For example, social enterprises in the UK offer many essential services in some of the most deprived regions in the country. The concept of social entrepreneurship is still emerging in China. Some researchers argue that many small businesses in rural areas should be considered social entrepreneurs because they contribute not only to business development but also to the social well-being of local communities (Zhang & Swanson, 2014).

Now, opportunities for social entrepreneurs increase according to the increase in social needs. Many entrepreneurs are accepting these opportunity increases by building themselves into the social platform. Dreams of benefiting society can come true by establishing NPOs. As more and more entrepreneurs are interested in beginning social entrepreneurship projects, barriers to entry and competition increase in this area. NPOs operate in a tighter financing environment due to increased needs in target communities and increased competition for donations and grants. Society needs more social solutions than ever before.

Therefore, society prefers to cooperate with organizations that produce solutions that best satisfy its needs (Stephan et al., 2015). Attempts to realize social sustainability from the top of the socio-economic system are failing. Social entrepreneurs making breakthroughs at the micro-level penetrate the cells of the social-economic system and make the greatest contribution to the implementation and development of social sustainability. Accordingly, the close relationship between social sustainability and social entrepreneurship should be examined, and the ways of evaluating social issues should be changed in favor of social entrepreneurship. The basic indicators that the concepts are related are summarized in Table 2.

Table 2. Main indicators of social sustainability and social entrepreneurship

Main Indicators	Social Sustainability	Social Entrepreneurship
Market	The local and national economy	Local economy and specific disadvantaged groups
Mission	Creates social value	Creates and Captures social value
Stakeholders	Disadvantaged communities Companies Governments International organizations "Us and them" perspective	Disadvantaged individuals Donors Non-profit organizations Activists High identification with stakeholders
Performance	Social impact Social benefit More standardized	Social impact Social benefit Activity-specific standards
Context	Economy Society Regulations Political system Global but regionally and nationally focused Influencing context	Economy Society Regulations Political system Local but globally focused Affected by context

Social entrepreneurship is an innovation process that can occur in different institutional contexts in the economy, is based on creating value, and operates with its own rules and logic. It is a very appropriate approach to address some of the most pressing problems in modern society and to develop capitalism (Santos, 2012). The tools used so far to overcome the sustainable development crisis in the world have failed to achieve the goals. The need for overview change is more urgent than ever. For this reason, social entrepreneurship is the most remarkable tool that will contribute to the realization of social sustainability, which is one of the major components of sustainable development. It is a significant origin in building a livable world.

CONCLUSION

Sustainable development and its components (environmental, economic, and social) have been discussed for decades. Economic sustainability is mostly achieved because businesses have archaic profit goals. Also, environmental sustainability is achieved by legal regulations through strong social pressure on governments. Accordingly, it can be said that both of them are supported by legal regulations. However, the social sustainability component has not generated satisfactory results in practice. One of the reasons for this is the idea that the economic and environmental components of sustainable development contradict social goals. This approach confirms itself as the world witnesses inadequate practices of social sustainability. With increased unemployment and poverty; malnutrition and hunger; epidemic diseases; unhealthy living conditions; insecure, unhealthy working conditions; child labor employment; increased violence tendency; harmful substance use; violence against women; racism; struggles in reaching education opportunities; and others, the world has had to deal with social problems more than ever.

Businesses and governments that are expected to provide solutions to these problems are also the sources of these problems. Therefore, the economic and political actors that should be the founders and implementers of social sustainability policies could not go beyond what should be done. Now, social sustainability needs to be handled with a new approach. This new approach should consist of practical concrete bases rather than legal and normative bases. Over the past decade, with the discovery, existence, and discussion of this need, it has produced knowledge and practices that can create a knowledgeable perspective. Social entrepreneurship is a crucial tool produced by these discussions.

Social entrepreneurship suggests a very strong practical approach by focusing on the solutions for social problems facing individuals, who make up the smallest unit of society. The focus on the local perspective contributes significantly to improving public welfare. However, social entrepreneurs are consumers of their social activities at the same time. So they intensely identify with their work. Another major element is the close collaborations and social entrepreneurship networks brought by this identification. These collaborative networks, which gradually form the social entrepreneurship sector, begin to create upward pressure from the bottom of society. It should never be forgotten that social entrepreneurs are part of society itself. For this reason, the real success of social sustainability practices can be realized with a serious paradigm shift.

The use of social entrepreneurship's resources to create a positive social impact prepares us for a livable world. Thus, measuring the performance of the social entrepreneur is critical. If these performance measures are not carried out, it can be trapped in failure. For this reason, each social entrepreneur should measure the social value produced by limited resources and quickly identify the areas of failure and their causes. Uncertainties in the establishment of performance criteria are known. However, these measurements must be made despite the difficulties. Otherwise, the social entrepreneur may lose credibility and have difficulty reaching donor resources. Transparency and accountability are the most valuable weapons for social entrepreneurs to achieve their goals.

However, the level of being affected by the social, economic, and political context of social entrepreneurs is crucial. This fragility forces them to do work on a knife's edge. Therefore, they have to struggle with many contextual obstacles. When they overcome these obstacles, they can create broad and powerful social effects, from local to global arenas. The depth and permanence of these effects depend on the continuous development of social entrepreneurial networks. This impact and value movement, which is experienced from the bottom up, can earn the years lost by social sustainability.

It would also be helpful to review the up-to-date literature panorama about social entrepreneurship. One of the reasons that make social entrepreneurship an exciting and challenging topic is that practitioners move quicker than theorists. So, many examples of social entrepreneurship are emerging every day in the world. The literature on what social entrepreneurship is and what it serves has developed a lot. However, constitute the core of the subject, there is no consensus on the creation and measurement of social value. Studies examining the relationship between social innovation and social entrepreneurship has been increasing in recent years. (Douglas, & Prentice, 2019; Tracey & Stott, 2017; Phillips et al., 2015; Nandan et al., 2015). However, there is a lot of research about social entrepreneurship education as the subject is extremely critical (Kickul et al., 2018; Steiner et al., 2018; Zhu et al., 2016). It is crucial to provide entrepreneurship features by giving social entrepreneurship education to individuals at an early age and establishing a livable and sustainable future. Another area of research related to social entrepreneurship concerns the creation and management of social value (Cherrier et al., 2018; Beugré, 2016; Hitt et al., 2011). Sustainable business models and strategy options that social entrepreneurship can use to achieve its goals are also researched in the related literature (Sparviero, 2019; Dentchev et al., 2016). Studies on measuring social impact contribute to determining social enterprises' performance criteria (Mamabolo & Myres; Rawhouser et al., 2019; Lall, 2019). Performance researches have intensified in recent years due to the demand for measurable performance results from stakeholders. The publication of academic journals and books on social entrepreneurship contributes to limited scientific knowledge. Although there are few limited studies between social entrepreneurship and sustainability (Rahdari et al., 2016; Zhang & Swanson, 2014), no investigations are considering the links between social entrepreneurship and social sustainability.

FUTURE RESEARCH DIRECTIONS

This study aims to contribute to the acceleration of the social entrepreneurship process and to raise the perspective shift by influencing to policymakers. Redesigning the ecosystem with social entrepreneurial motivation from the bottom will make the world more livable now and in the future. Future research in this regard will provide an undoubtful contribution to the increase of social value spread by affecting cultures in all regions. Finally, conducting studies that are mobilizing economic, legal, and political dynamics that speed up social entrepreneurship practices is an imperative task that should be completed with urgency—right now.

REFERENCES

AB. (2020). *Microfinance and social entrepreneurship*. Retrieved from https://www.ab.gov.tr/files/SBYPB/birlik%20programlari/easi_brosur.pdf

Ahmadi, H. B., Kusi-Sarpong, S., & Rezaei, J. (2017). Assessing the social sustainability of supply chains using Best Worst Method. *Resources, Conservation and Recycling*, *126*, 99–106. doi:10.1016/j.resconrec.2017.07.020

Alhaddi, H. (2015). Triple bottom line and sustainability: A literature review. *Business and Management Studies*, *1*(2), 6–10. doi:10.11114/bms.v1i2.752

Alkire, S., Foster, J. E., Seth, S., Santos, M. E., Roche, J. M., & Ballon, P. (2015). *Multidimensional poverty measurement and analysis*. Oxford University Press. doi:10.1093/acprof:oso/9780199689491.001.0001

Angelica, M. H. (2019). Social entrepreneurship: Evolutions, characteristics, values and motivations. *The Annals of The University of Oradea. Economic Sciences*, *28*(1), 63–71.

Austin, J., Stevenson, H., & Wei-Skillern, J. (2012). Social and commercial entrepreneurship: Same, different, or both? *Revista ADM*, *47*(3), 370–384.

Baumgartner, R. J., & Ebner, D. (2010). Corporate sustainability strategies: Sustainability profiles and maturity levels. *Sustainable Development*, *18*(2), 76–89. doi:10.1002d.447

Because International. (2020). *A shoe that expands 5 sizes and lasts for years, created for kids living in poverty*. Retrieved June 9, 2020, from https://becauseinternational.org/the-shoe-that-grows

Béchervaise, N. E., & Benjamin, C. G. (2013). Visionary or criminal: From profit through morality to socially sustainable entrepreneurship. *Procedia: Social and Behavioral Sciences*, *99*, 339–350. doi:10.1016/j.sbspro.2013.10.502

Better World Books. (2020). *Better World Books: History*. Retrieved June 19, 2020, https://about.betterworldbooks.com/history/

Betts, S. C., Laud, R., & Kretinin, A. (2018). Social entrepreneurship: A contemporary approach to solving social problems. *Global Journal of Entrepreneurship*, *2*(1), 31–40.

Beugré, C. (2016). *Social entrepreneurship: Managing the creation of social value*. Taylor & Francis. doi:10.4324/9780203442609

Bocken, N. M., Short, S. W., Rana, P., & Evans, S. (2014). A literature and practice review to develop sustainable business model archetypes. *Journal of Cleaner Production*, *65*, 42–56. doi:10.1016/j.jclepro.2013.11.039

Canestrino, R., Ćwiklicki, M., Di Nauta, P., & Magliocca, P. (2019). Creating social value through entrepreneurship: The social business model of La Paranza. *Kybernetes*, *48*(10), 2190–2216. doi:10.1108/K-03-2018-0135

Certo, S. T., & Miller, T. (2008). Social entrepreneurship: Key issues and concepts. *Business Horizons*, *51*(4), 267–271. doi:10.1016/j.bushor.2008.02.009

Chang, S. H., Chang, C. W., & Chiu, H. J. (2020). A social impact theory perspective on consumers' intention to adopt recycling in China. *International Journal of Organizational Innovation (Online)*, *12*(4), 220–232.

Cherrier, H., Goswami, P., & Ray, S. (2018). Social entrepreneurship: Creating value in the context of institutional complexity. *Journal of Business Research*, *86*, 245–258. doi:10.1016/j.jbusres.2017.10.056

Costanza, R., & Daly, H. E. (1992). Natural capital and sustainable development. *Conservation Biology*, *6*(1), 37–46. doi:10.1046/j.1523-1739.1992.610037.x

Dacin, M. T., Dacin, P. A., & Tracey, P. (2011). Social entrepreneurship: A critique and future directions. *Organization Science*, *22*(5), 1203–1213. doi:10.1287/orsc.1100.0620

Dees, J. G. (1998). *The meaning of social entrepreneurship*. Retrieved June 16, 2020, from https://centers.fuqua.duke.edu/case/wp-content/uploads/sites/7/2015/03/Article_Dees_MeaningofSocialEntrepreneurship_2001.pdf

Dentchev, N., Baumgartner, R., Dieleman, H., Jóhannsdóttir, L., Jonker, J., Nyberg, T., Rauter, R., Rosano, M., Snihur, Y., Tang, X., & van Hoof, B. (2016). Embracing the variety of sustainable business models: Social entrepreneurship, corporate intrapreneurship, creativity, innovation, and other approaches to sustainability challenges. *Journal of Cleaner Production*, *113*, 1–4. doi:10.1016/j.jclepro.2015.10.130

Douglas, E., & Prentice, C. (2019). Innovation and profit motivations for social entrepreneurship: A fuzzy-set analysis. *Journal of Business Research*, *99*, 69–79. doi:10.1016/j.jbusres.2019.02.031

Elkington, J. (1998). Partnerships from cannibals with forks: The triple bottom line of 21st-century business. *Environmental Quality Management*, *8*(1), 37–51. doi:10.1002/tqem.3310080106

Eurostat. (2019). *At risk of poverty or social exclusion in the EU-28, 2018*. Retrieved July 17, 2020, from https://ec.europa.eu/eurostat/news/themes-in-the-spotlight/poverty-day-2019

Folke, C., Carpenter, S., Elmqvist, T., Gunderson, L., Holling, C. S., & Walker, B. (2002). Resilience and sustainable development: Building adaptive capacity in a world of transformations. *Ambio*, *31*(5), 437–440. doi:10.1579/0044-7447-31.5.437 PMID:12374053

Geissdoerfer, M., Vladimirova, D., & Evans, S. (2018). Sustainable business model innovation: A review. *Journal of Cleaner Production*, *198*, 401–416. doi:10.1016/j.jclepro.2018.06.240

Gill, J. C., Mankelow, J., & Mills, K. (2019). The role of Earth and environmental science in addressing sustainable development priorities in Eastern Africa. *Environmental Development*, *30*, 3–20. doi:10.1016/j.envdev.2019.03.003

Gimenez, C., Sierra, V., & Rodon, J. (2012). Sustainable operations: Their impact on the triple bottom line. *International Journal of Production Economics*, *140*(1), 149–159. doi:10.1016/j.ijpe.2012.01.035

Goodland, R. (1995). The concept of environmental sustainability. *Annual Review of Ecology and Systematics*, *26*(1), 1–24. doi:10.1146/annurev.es.26.110195.000245

Griggs, D., Stafford-Smith, M., Gaffney, O., Rockström, J., Öhman, M. C., Shyamsundar, P., Steffen, W., Glaser, G., Kanie, N., & Noble, I. (2013). Policy: Sustainable development goals for people and planet. *Nature*, *495*(7441), 305–307. doi:10.1038/495305a PMID:23518546

Haugh, H. M., & Talwar, A. (2016). Linking social entrepreneurship and social change: The mediating role of empowerment. *Journal of Business Ethics*, *133*(4), 643–658. doi:10.100710551-014-2449-4

Helmsing, A. B. (2015). Conditions for social entrepreneurship. *The International Journal of Social Quality*, *5*(1), 51–66. doi:10.3167/IJSQ.2015.050104

Hitt, M. A., Ireland, R. D., Sirmon, D. G., & Trahms, C. A. (2011). Strategic entrepreneurship: Creating value for individuals, organizations, and society. *The Academy of Management Perspectives*, *25*(2), 57–75.

Hlady-Rispal, M., & Servantie, V. (2018). Deconstructing the way in which value is created in the context of social entrepreneurship. *International Journal of Management Reviews*, *20*(1), 62–80. doi:10.1111/ijmr.12113

Horton, P., & Horton, B. P. (2019). Re-defining sustainability: Living in harmony with life on Earth. *One Earth*, *1*(1), 86–94. doi:10.1016/j.oneear.2019.08.019

Houston, R. (2019). *Social value and its relation to the SDGs*. Retrieved July 26, 2020, from https://www.ice.org.uk/ICEDevelopmentWebPortal/media/Documents/News/Blog/Social-Value-and-its-relation-to-SDGs-Simetrica-April-25-2019.pdf

Hubbard, G. (2009). Measuring organizational performance: Beyond the triple bottom line. *Business Strategy and the Environment, 18*(3), 177–191. doi:10.1002/bse.564

Jamali, D. (2006). Insights into triple bottom line integration from a learning organization perspective. *Business Process Management Journal, 12*(6), 809–821. doi:10.1108/14637150610710945

Jennifer Ho, L. C., & Taylor, M. E. (2007). An empirical analysis of triple bottom-line reporting and its determinants: Evidence from the United States and Japan. *Journal of International Financial Management & Accounting, 18*(2), 123–150. doi:10.1111/j.1467-646X.2007.01010.x

Kibler, E., Salmivaara, V., Stenholm, P., & Terjesen, S. (2018). The evaluative legitimacy of social entrepreneurship in capitalist welfare systems. *Journal of World Business, 53*(6), 944–957. doi:10.1016/j.jwb.2018.08.002

Kickul, J., Gundry, L., Mitra, P., & Berçot, L. (2018). Designing with purpose: Advocating innovation, impact, sustainability, and scale in social entrepreneurship education. *Entrepreneurship Education and Pedagogy, 1*(2), 205–221. doi:10.1177/2515127418772177

Lall, S. A. (2019). From Legitimacy to learning: How impact measurement perceptions and practices evolve in social enterprise–social finance organization relationships. *Voluntas, 30*(3), 562–577. doi:10.100711266-018-00081-5

Light, P. C. (2006). Reshaping social entrepreneurship. *Stanford Social Innovation Review, 4*(3), 47–51.

Mamabolo, A., & Myres, K. (2020). Performance Measurement in Emerging Market Social Enterprises using a Balanced Scorecard. *Journal of Social Entrepreneurship, 11*(1), 65–87. doi:10.1080/19420676.2018.1561499

Martin, R. L., & Osberg, S. (2007, Spring). Social entrepreneurship: The case for definition. *Stanford Social Innovation Review*, 29–39.

McKenzie, S. (2004). *Social sustainability: towards some definitions.* Hawke Research Institute Working Paper Series, 27. Hawke Research Institute, University of South Australia.

Mebratu, D. (1998). Sustainability and sustainable development: Historical and conceptual review. *Environmental Impact Assessment Review, 18*(6), 493–520. doi:10.1016/S0195-9255(98)00019-5

Molecke, G., & Pinkse, J. (2020). justifying social impact as a form of impression management: Legitimacy judgements of social enterprises' impact accounts. *British Journal of Management, 31*(2), 387–402. doi:10.1111/1467-8551.12397

Nandan, M., London, M., & Bent-Goodley, T. (2015). Social workers as social change agents: Social innovation, social intrapreneurship, and social entrepreneurship. *Human Service Organizations, Management, Leadership & Governance, 39*(1), 38–56. doi:10.1080/23303131.2014.955236

Norman, W., & MacDonald, C. (2004). Getting to the bottom of the "triple bottom line". *Business Ethics Quarterly*, *14*(2), 243–262. doi:10.5840/beq200414211

OECD. (2015). *Policy brief on social impact measurement for social enterprises*. Retrieved August 08, 2020, from https://www.oecd.org/social/PB-SIM-Web_FINAL.pdf

Oxfam. (2020). *World's billionaires have more wealth than 4.6 billion people*. Retrieved July 22, 2020, from https://www.oxfam.org/en/press-releases/worlds-billionaires-have-more-wealth-46-billion-people

Parkinson, C., & Howorth, C. (2008). The language of social entrepreneurs. *Entrepreneurship and Regional Development*, *20*(3), 285–309. doi:10.1080/08985620701800507

Petteni, O. (2020). *Capitalisme, progrès et entropie: Notes sur les chiffonniers du temps présent*. Retrieved May 19, 2020, from https://terrabayt.com/yasam/gunumuz-pacavracilarina-dair-notlar-brukselde-kolektif-mutfak-deneyimi/

Phillips, W., Lee, H., Ghobadian, A., O'Regan, N., & James, P. (2015). Social innovation and social entrepreneurship: A systematic review. *Group & Organization Management*, *40*(3), 428–461. doi:10.1177/1059601114560063

Poverty, U. S. A. (2020). *The Population of Poverty USA*. Retrieved June 21, 2020, from https://www.povertyusa.org/facts

Rahdari, A., Sepasi, S., & Moradi, M. (2016). Achieving sustainability through Schumpeterian social entrepreneurship: The role of social enterprises. *Journal of Cleaner Production*, *137*, 347–360. doi:10.1016/j.jclepro.2016.06.159

Randhawa, A., & Kumar, A. (2017). Exploring sustainability of smart development initiatives in India. *International Journal of Sustainable Built Environment*, *6*(2), 701–710. doi:10.1016/j.ijsbe.2017.08.002

Rangan, V. K., & Gregg, T. (2019). How social entrepreneurs zig-zag their way to impact at scale. *California Management Review*, *62*(1), 53–76. doi:10.1177/0008125619876903

Rao, P. K. (1999). *Sustainable Development* (Vol. 1). Blackwell Publishers.

Rasouli, A. H., & Kumarasuriyar, A. (2016). The social dimensions of sustainability: Towards some definitions and analysis. *Journal of Social Science for Policy Implications*, *4*(2), 23–34. doi:10.15640/jsspi.v4n2a3

Rawhouser, H., Cummings, M., & Newbert, S. L. (2019). Social impact measurement: Current approaches and future directions for social entrepreneurship research. *Entrepreneurship Theory and Practice*, *43*(1), 82–115. doi:10.1177/1042258717727718

Roy, A., Brumagim, A., & Goll, I. (2014). Predictors of social entrepreneurship success: A cross-national analysis of antecedent factors. *Journal of Social Entrepreneurship*, *5*(1), 42–59. doi:10.1080/19420676.2013.820783

Sachs, J. D. (2012). From millennium development goals to sustainable development goals. *Lancet*, *379*(9832), 2206–2211. doi:10.1016/S0140-6736(12)60685-0 PMID:22682467

Santos, F. M. (2012). A positive theory of social entrepreneurship. *Journal of Business Ethics, 111*(3), 335–351. doi:10.100710551-012-1413-4

Sastre-Castillo, M. A., Peris-Ortiz, M., & Danvila-Del Valle, I. (2015). What is different about the profile of the social entrepreneur? *Nonprofit Management & Leadership*, *25*(4), 349–369. doi:10.1002/nml.21138

Saunila, M., Ukko, J., & Rantala, T. (2018). Sustainability as a driver of green innovation investment and exploitation. *Journal of Cleaner Production*, *179*, 631–641. doi:10.1016/j.jclepro.2017.11.211

Saxena, G. (2019). Multidimensional competency construct for social entrepreneurs: A logistic regression approach. *Kasetsart Journal of Social Sciences*, *40*(3), 684–688.

Sekliuckiene, J., & Kisielius, E. (2015). Development of social entrepreneurship initiatives: A theoretical framework. *Procedia: Social and Behavioral Sciences*, *213*, 1015–1019. doi:10.1016/j.sbspro.2015.11.519

Shaw, E., & Carter, S. (2007). Social entrepreneurship. *Journal of Small Business and Enterprise Development*, *14*(3), 418–434. doi:10.1108/14626000710773529

Sikdar, S. K. (2003). Sustainable development and sustainability metrics. *AIChE Journal. American Institute of Chemical Engineers*, *49*(8), 1928–1932. doi:10.1002/aic.690490802

Sinthupundaja, J., Kohda, Y., & Chiadamrong, N. (2020). Examining capabilities of social entrepreneurship for shared value creation. *Journal of Social Entrepreneurship*, *11*(1), 1–22. doi:10.1080/19420676.2018.1543726

Situmorang, D. B. M., & Mirzanti, I. R. (2012). Social entrepreneurship to develop ecotourism. *Procedia Economics and Finance*, *4*, 398–405. doi:10.1016/S2212-5671(12)00354-1

Slaper, T. F., & Hall, T. J. (2011). The triple bottom line: What is it and how does it work. *Indiana Business Review*, *86*(1), 4–8.

Social Enterprise Coalition. (2020). *How do social enterprises work?* Retrieved April 5, 2020, from https://www.socialenterprise.org.uk/faq/

Sparviero, S. (2019). The case for a socially oriented business model canvas: The social enterprise model canvas. *Journal of Social Entrepreneurship*, *10*(2), 232–251. doi:10.1080/19420676.2018.1541011

Steiner, S. D., Brock, D. D., Pittz, T. G., & Liguori, E. (2018). Multi-disciplinary involvement in social entrepreneurship education: A uniquely threaded ecosystem. *Journal of Ethics & Entrepreneurship*, *8*(1), 73–91.

Stephan, U., Uhlaner, L. M., & Stride, C. (2015). Institutions and social entrepreneurship: The role of institutional voids, institutional support, and institutional configurations. *Journal of International Business Studies*, *46*(3), 308–331. doi:10.1057/jibs.2014.38

Strulak-Wójcikiewicz, R., & Lemke, J. (2019). Concept of a simulation model for assessing the sustainable development of urban transport. *Transportation Research Procedia*, *39*, 502–513. doi:10.1016/j.trpro.2019.06.052

Surie, G. (2017). Creating the innovation ecosystem for renewable energy via social entrepreneurship: Insights from India. *Technological Forecasting and Social Change*, *121*, 184–195. doi:10.1016/j.techfore.2017.03.006

Toker, K. (2017). Supply networks, value and sustainability. In I. M. Pekdemir (Ed.), *Sustainability Dynamics in Business* (pp. 271–323). Beta Publishing.

Toker, K. (2018). Industry 4.0 Declaration and its effects on sustainability. *Istanbul Management Journal*, *29*(84), 51–64.

Toker, K., Çinar, F., & Görener, A. (2020). Circular Economy Measurement and a Case of the Developing Country Context. In U. Akkucuk (Ed.), *Handbook of Research on Creating Sustainable Value in the Global Economy* (pp. 241–257). IGI Global. doi:10.4018/978-1-7998-1196-1.ch014

Tracey, P., & Stott, N. (2017). Social innovation: A window on alternative ways of organizing and innovating. *Innovation*, *19*(1), 51–60. doi:10.1080/14479338.2016.1268924

UN. (2020a). *World economic situation and prospects: October 2019 Briefing, No. 131*. Retrieved July 21, 2020, from https://www.un.org/development/desa/dpad/publication/world-economic-situation-and-prospects-october-2019-briefing-no-131/

UN. (2020b). *No poverty: why it matters*. Retrieved September 21, 2020, from https://www.un.org/sustainabledevelopment/wp-content/uploads/2016/08/1_Why-It-Matters-2020.pdf

UNDP. (2020). *Sustainable development goals*. Retrieved September 11, 2020, from https://www.un.org/sustainabledevelopment/sustainable-development-goals/

US Census Bureau. (2020). *United States | 2018 Poverty Statistics, All People Below Poverty Level Percent*. Retrieved July 21, 2020, from https://www.census.gov/search-results.html?searchType=web&cssp=SERP&q=Poverty

Waddock, S. A., & Post, J. E. (1991). Social entrepreneurs and catalytic change. *Public Administration Review*, *51*(5), 393–401. doi:10.2307/976408

WCED. (1987). *Out Common Future*. Oxford University Press.

Wongphuka, K., Chai-Aroon, T., Phainoi, S., & Boon-Long, P. (2017). Social entrepreneur competencies of social activists involved with children and youths: A case study of Nan province, Thailand. *Kasetsart Journal of Social Sciences*, *38*(2), 143–149. doi:10.1016/j.kjss.2016.02.002

Zahra, S. A., Gedajlovic, E., Neubaum, D. O., & Shulman, J. M. (2009). A typology of social entrepreneurs: Motives, search processes and ethical challenges. *Journal of Business Venturing*, *24*(5), 519–532. doi:10.1016/j.jbusvent.2008.04.007

Zahra, S. A., Rawhouser, H. N., Bhawe, N., Neubaum, D. O., & Hayton, J. C. (2008). Globalization of social entrepreneurship opportunities. *Strategic Entrepreneurship Journal*, *2*(2), 117–131. doi:10.1002ej.43

Zhang, D. D., & Swanson, L. A. (2014). Linking social entrepreneurship and sustainability. *Journal of Social Entrepreneurship*, *5*(2), 175–191. doi:10.1080/19420676.2014.880503

Zhu, Y., Rooney, D., & Phillips, N. (2016). Practice-based wisdom theory for integrating institutional logics: A new model for social entrepreneurship learning and education. *Academy of Management Learning & Education*, *15*(3), 607–625. doi:10.5465/amle.2013.0263

Chapter 2
Dynamic of the Evaluation of Social Entrepreneurship Concept:
A Bibliometric Analysis

Muhammet Fatih Şengüllendi
Beykent University, Turkey

ABSTRACT

Research on social entrepreneurship has increased especially in the last 10 years. The reason for this is the contribution of social entrepreneurship to both social and economic development. The purpose of this research is to perform a bibliometric analysis of a total of 926 social entrepreneurship articles in the WoS (Web of Science) database. These data reveal the most prestigious authors, countries, journals, and articles in the field of social entrepreneurship. In addition, other concepts related to social entrepreneurship were visualized with co-word analysis. As a result of the analysis, the chapter is presented with ideas to show how scientific research progresses in the field and for future studies. At the same time, it explains the recent form in Turkish studies using the TR-Index database.

INTRODUCTION

Bibliometric analysis was first introduced by Derek J. De Solla in 1965 (Boyack, et al., 2005). It consists of applying statistical methods to track changes in a particular scientific research subject, analyze the quantity of publications on the subject and objectively detect trends in a discipline (Calabretta et al., 2011). However, such analyzes provide useful information for specialists who want to evaluate scientific activity (Duque Oliva et al., 2006). In addition, it helps authors better recognize their field and thus create clearer publication policies (Zupic & Čater 2015). It is also used in the analysis of the structure or dynamics of a bibliometric research, an institute, a researcher, a field (Cobo et al.,2011).

There are different types of bibliometric analysis. These are Citation Analysis, Co-citation Analysis, Bibliographical Coupling, Co-author Analysis, Co-word Analysis. Among these types of analysis,

DOI: 10.4018/978-1-7998-4727-4.ch002

Citation Analysis, Co-citation Analysis, and Bibliographical Coupling use citation data for impact and similarity analysis. Co-author Analysis uses co-author data to find author relationships. Co-word Analysis analyzes links between concepts with the help of titles, keywords and summaries (Zupic & Čater,2015).

In this study, citation analysis and Co-word analysis, which are among the bibliometric analysis methods, were applied. Citation analysis is the application of "direct counts of references to or from other documents" to identify articles that are frequently cited within a specific area or journal and play a major role in the development of the research area (Charvet et al., 2008). Citation analysis enables to develop an objective perspective on the relationships between cited and quoted articles (Gundolf & Filser, 2013). In the Co- word analysis, the keywords used in scientific articles are taken as a basis to examine the conceptual structure of a field (Cobo et al., 2011). In the Co-word analysis, keywords accepted as data are considered to be conceptually related (Koseoglu et al., 2016). The network obtained at different times provides an understanding of the change of the conceptual structure (Coulter et al., 1998).

In this research, performing citation analysis and co-word analysis will enable to find the answers to the following questions about social entrepreneurship discipline (Zupic & Čater 2015):

- Citation Analysis;
  - Which journals were most influential on the flow of social entrepreneurship literature?
  - Who are the experts in the field of social entrepreneurship?
  - What is the recommended "reading list" in the field of social entrepreneurship?
- Co-word Analysis;
  - What are the issues related to the concept of social entrepreneurship?
  - How did the concept of social entrepreneurship develop?

In this research, the data obtained from the Web of Science (WOS) online database containing scientific studies in all disciplines and the VOSviewer program were used. The scanning in the WOS database was made under the title of "Social Entrepreneurship*" within the scope of academic articles. The study was carried out within the scope of citation analysis and co-word analysis on a total of 926 academic articles in SCI-EXPANDED, SSCI, A&HCI, CPCI-S, CPCI-SSH, BKCI-S, BKCI-SSH, ESCI indexes scanned in the WoS database.

SOCIAL ENTREPRENEURSHIP

In recent years, the interest in social entrepreneurship in the academia continues to increase. The reason for this interest is the contribution of social entrepreneurship to both social development and economic development (Paredo and McClean, 2006). Social entrepreneurship focuses on solving social problems and increasing individual welfare by adding value to the society. The process of adding value to the society and the individual starts with a sense of mission triggered by a social transformation or opportunity on the social entrepreneur candidate, and continues with the effective use of the resources held by the social entrepreneur. Finally, the initiative makes a deep contribution to society (Yunus, 2007).

Although the concept of social entrepreneurship is a new concept, they have been defined in different ways by researchers (Austin, Stevenson, & Wei-Skillern, 2006). While defining social entrepreneurship, the concept of researchers is "in the context of commercial entrepreneurship" (Macke et al., 2012), "in the institutional context" (Mair and Marti, 2009), "in the context of the public sector" (Dess, 2007), "in the context of education" (Miller and others, 2012) or "in the context of social entrepreneur typology" (Zahra et al., 2010). When the concept of social entrepreneurship is taken from a holistic perspective, it can be considered as a structure that includes many different perspectives (Macke et al., 2018). According to Mair (2010), when the concept of social entrepreneurship is considered as an umbrella, it is seen that it includes the concepts of social entrepreneurship, social change agency, corporate entrepreneurship, social entrepreneurship and social innovation.

Some researchers state that academic work on social entrepreneurship is still in its infancy (Short et al., 2009; Dacin et al., 2009; Bacq and Janssen, 2011). This results in a unifying paradigm deficiency (Dess, 2007). Research is based on a benefit-oriented attitude rather than a theory building (Macke et al., 2018). For this reason, the research revealed the issue of social entrepreneurship to increase social benefit with a bibliometric analysis method within the scope of social impact theory and creating social value.

In the literature, there are bibliometric studies made within the scope of social entrepreneurship. These studies are as follows: Desa (2007), Douglas (2008), Short et al. (2009), Hoogendoorn et al. (2010), Hill et al. (2010), Granados et al. (2011), Sassmannshausen and Volkmann (2013), Kraus et al. (2014), Rey-Martí et al. (2016), Ferreira et al. (2017), Dionisio, M. (2019). Some of the researches in the field of social entrepreneurship, which stand out in line with the momentum of its concept in the last 10 years, are as follows;

Table 1. Bibliometric Researches in the Field of Social Entrepreneurship

References	Used Database	Period of time	Search limitation	Analysis Type
Granados et al. (2011)	Business Source Complete (BSC); Science Direct (SD); Web of Knowledge (ISI); Social Enterprise Journal (SEJ); Journal of Social Entrepreneurship (JSE)	1991-2010	Articles	Citation
Sassmannshausen and Volkmann (2013)	Google Scholar and EBSCO Host	All period (most cited papers)	Journals and books	Citation
Kraus et al. (2014)	Emerald, EBSCO, ProQuest, ScienceDirect and Google Scholar	All period (most cited papers)	Articles, books and papers	Citation Analysis
Rey-Martí et al. (2016)	Web of Science	2003-2015	articles, proceedings, reviews, book review, editorial material, book chapters, meeting abstracts, notes, and letters	Descriptive
Ferreira et al. (2017)	Web of Science	1994-2014	journal articles	Co-citations
Dionisio, M. (2019).	EBSCO, Scopus and Google Scholar	2005-2017	A journal	Citations

The points that this research will contribute to the level of originality of bibliometric analysis in the other social entrepreneurship field in the literature are that it has the most recent time interval, contains both citation analysis and co-word analysis, and is focused on all journals in WOS. Another unique value is to try to explain the research through social impact theory and social value creation approach.

SOCIAL IMPACT AND CREATING SOCIAL VALUE

The effect of factors such as a social situation, activity, formation etc. on individuals arises from the "social forces" that are accepted depending on the size, proximity and strength of the stimulus (Latane, 1981). Social impact theory has three functions in terms of functionality. The first is that the effect of the social forces of the social being increases as a function of power so that it can be effective (the quantity of stimulus) (Latane and Wolf 1981). The second is that the impact of a social asset will have a greater impact as long as it is out of the hands of powerful institutions and individuals (universities and academics) in the community. The last principle is that the effect of social power will be divided among the targets (Argo et al., 2005). Our research focused on the first two principles of social impact theory.

In Figure 1, there is a model proposed within the scope of social impact theory and social value creation, in order to increase the social benefit of the effect of universities and academicians on social entrepreneurship activities. As seen in this model, the number of activities such as congresses, symposiums, panels, social entrepreneurship certificate programs organized by universities and the number of situations that universities encourage academics to publish on social entrepreneurship increase social benefit by creating social benefits by affecting social entrepreneurship and social entrepreneurs. According to Lan et al. (2014), the most important feature that social entrepreneurship should have in order for social entrepreneurship activities to achieve the goal of increasing the desired social benefit is formal education that they have taken apart from "learning by living". Therefore, in the following model, universities also increase their social benefit through social entrepreneurship activities by graduating social entrepreneur candidates.

Matthew (25:29) tells "For those who have will be given more, and they will have an abundance. As for those who do not have, even what they have will be taken from them." Merton (1988) calls it as "Matthew effect". According to"Matthew effect", "The accruing of greater increments of recognition for particular scientific propositions to scientists of considerable repute and the withholding of such recognition from scientists who have not yet made their mark". Therefore, it is understood that the amount of output of academicians within the scope of social entrepreneurship will also create social value.

Figure 1. The model of increasing the social benefit of the impact of universities and academicians on social entrepreneurship activities

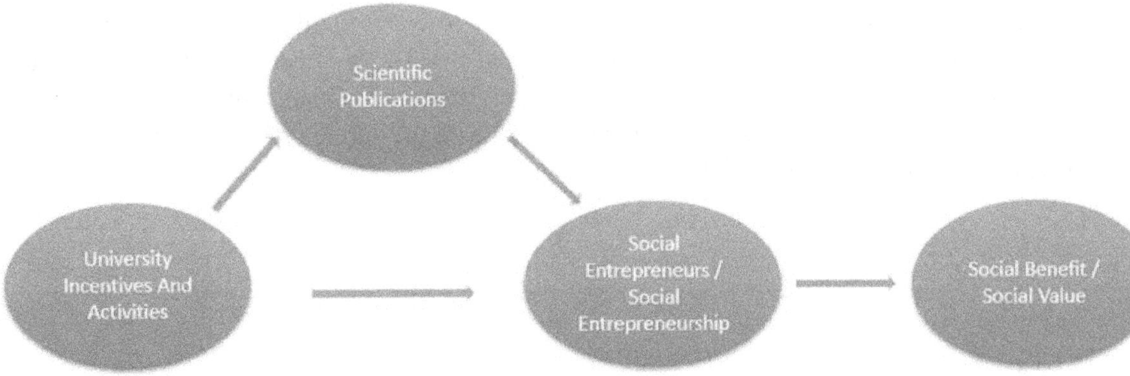

The values created by human beings, who are social creatures, in social life constitute social values. Social values that regulate social life bring order to the relations of the society with the individual and the individual with the society (Güngör,2008:102). Therefore, it is thought that universities' realization of various applications within the scope of social entrepreneurship and their desire to attract the attention of academics positively affect all issues related to social entrepreneurship. In addition, academic publications are also highly effective in the social value creation process of universities. This situation is as seen in Figure 1. In addition, the common output of all processes in the model is social value. Universities create social value; academic publications are social values; The aim of social entrepreneurship activities is to provide social benefit by creating social value.

Issues, Controversies, Problems

Aim of the research: This research aims to provide a theoretical contribution to the relevant field by monitoring the changes in scientific research in the field of social entrepreneurship, via citation and co-word analysis.

The Importance of Research: The number of social entrepreneurship research has been increasing in the literature for the past ten years. When the literature is examined, there are bibliometric analysis studies on the subject (Granados et al., 2011; Sassmannshausen and Volkmann, 2013; Kraus et al., 2014; Rey-Marti et al., 2016; Ferreira et al., 2017; Sassmannshausen and Volkmann, 2018; Macke et al., 2018). According to Corley and Gioia (2011), the contribution of a scientific research manifests itself on two levels. The first is the originality of the research in the level of development and discovery, and the second is its usefulness in the practical and theoretical level. While the research has contributed to the originality level of bibliometric analysis studies in the field of social entrepreneurship in the past by addressing the issue, it is the usefulness of the research in the practical and theoretical level in the future.

Number of Articles and Citations by Years

When the citations received by the 926 articles written within themselves are analyzed, it is seen that the citations to the articles have increased gradually over the years. Articles written in the field of social entrepreneurship received a total of 16,290 citations by 2020. When self-citations are removed, the number of citations is 13,487. The reference to the articles was mostly in 2019.

When the distribution of academic articles by social entrepreneurship is analyzed by years, it is seen that the first article was written in 1981. This article is titled "A New Paradigm for the Study of Entrepreneurship and Social Change" by Greenfield and Strickon (1981). The article describes the structure and transformation of the concept of entrepreneurship on the basis of Darwinism. Then, information was provided about the concept of "new entrepreneurship" with the aim of creating a new paradigm in order to achieve transformation in social life.

Figure 2. Citation Numbers by Years

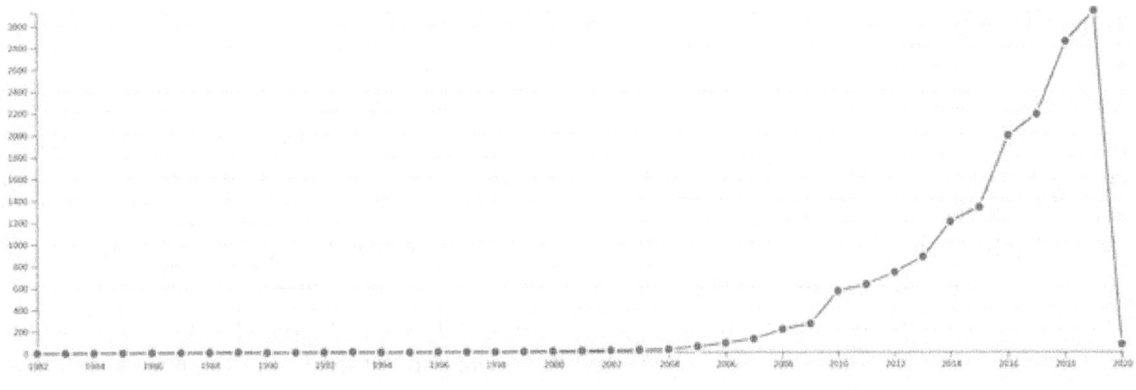

As can be seen in Table 2, most articles were written in 2018. This number has a ratio of 16.41% in total. As you can see, 834 articles have been written in total in the last 10 years and this number corresponds to approximately 90% of the total articles. The number of articles published in the last 5 years corresponds to approximately 64% of the total number of articles.

Table 2. Distribution of Social Entrepreneurship Research by Years

Year	Number	Percent (%)	Year	Number	Percent (%)
2020	-	-	2004	3	0.324
2019	114	12.311	2003	4	0.432
2018	152	16.415	2002	5	0.540
2017	121	13.067	2000	3	0.324
2016	126	13.607	1999	2	0.216
2015	78	8.423	1997	1	0.108
2014	56	6.048	1996	2	0.216
2013	45	4.860	1994	3	0.324
2012	47	5.076	1993	1	0.108
2011	37	3.996	1991	1	0.108
2010	54	5.832	1989	2	0.216
2009	19	2.052	1988	1	0.108
2008	9	0.972	1987	1	0.108
2007	11	1.188	1985	1	0.108
2006	15	1.620%	1982	1	0.108%
2005	6	0.648%	1981	1	0.108%

ANALYSIS

Citation Analysis

Citation analysis according to Moed (2005); It is one of the most important parts of bibliometric analysis in order to evaluate the scientific production performance based on criteria such as author, journal, publication, university, country. Citation analysis gives information about the real effect of a research based on the opinion that it is parallel to the number of citations received (Zan, 2013).

In this study, citation analyzes of articles written in the field of social entrepreneurship were made within the scope of author, journal, publication, university and country criteria. Citation analysis explains which articles on social entrepreneurship are the most dominant authors, journals, publications and universities among themselves. The most cited researchers in the field of social entrepreneurship are given to their research in the field of social entrepreneurship in Table 3.

Table 3. Citation Analysis (Authors)

Rank	Authors	Cited	Quantity
1	Holt, Diane	113	3
2	Littlewood, David	113	3
3	Rey-Marti, Andrea	86	3
4	Ribeiro-Soriano, Domingo	85	3
5	Bacq, Sophie	46	3
6	Dey, Pascal	42	4
7	Munoz, Pablo	41	3
8	Chandra, Yanto	34	4
9	Steayert, Chris	34	3
10	Kedmeneci Irena	34	3
11	Lewis, Kate V.	33	4
12	Shaw, Eleanor	27	3
13	Halberstadt, Jantje	37	3
14	Muradliharan, Eteyankara	25	5
15	Pathak, Saurav	25	5

As seen in Table 3, the authors who get the most citation from the publications in the field of social entrepreneurship are Holt, Diane and Littlewood, David. Rey-Marti and Andrea come after these two researchers.

In Figure 3 below, the citation map and cluster among the 15 most cited authors can be seen. As can be seen from Figure 3, it can be said that one of the pioneering researchers who feed the social entrepreneurship field are Chandra, Yanto and Dey, Pascal are 2 different schools in the field of social entrepreneurship. It can be said that Bacq, who is at the center of the writer's space, and Sophie is the author who feeds the most writers in the field.

Figure 3. Citation Analysis (Authors)

In Table 4, there is the ranking of the countries that are most cited by their authors from the field of social entrepreneurship. According to the table, USA ranks first with 152 studies and 1,202 citations, with 59 studies and 808 citations in second place, and French researchers with 28 studies and 274 citations in third place.

Table 4. Citation Analysis (Country)

Rank	Country	Cited	Quantity
1	USA	1202	152
2	England	818	59
3	France	274	28
4	Australia	218	22
5	Canada	178	27
6	Spain	170	35
7	Netherlands	160	18
8	Italy	151	30
9	China	144	19
10	Germany	116	23
11	India	113	29
12	Finland	106	11
13	Chile	75	6
14	Switzerland	67	11
15	Colombia	59	10

In Figure 4, there are citation networks and clusters of the 15 countries with the highest number of citations in social entrepreneurship. USA is at the center of the citation network among the countries it is seen. Therefore, it is the most nutritious country in the area. There are also 3 distinct clusters across countries. If an example is given over the blue cluster; Studies with references to authors from England, Canada, India and China are the most similar.

Figure 4. Citation Analysis (Country)

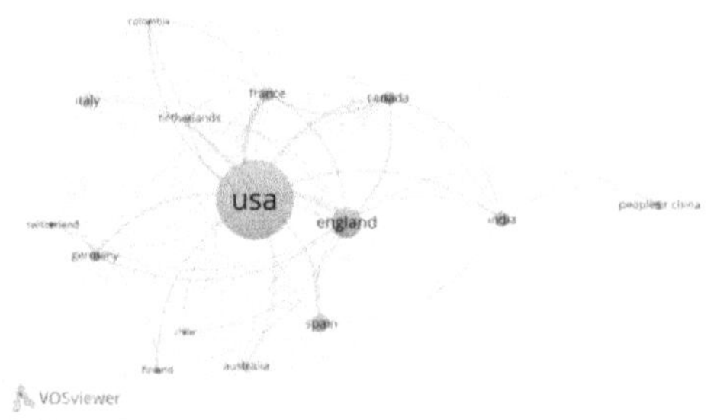

In Table 5, the ranking of universities that received more citations by academics in the field of social entrepreneurship is given. According to this ranking, University of Oxford comes first with 194 citations and 5 studies. The second place is the University of Sheffield with 187 citations and 5 studies, and the third place is the University of Essex with 119 citations and 6 studies. When the social entrepreneurship practices of the universities that rank high in the citation list are examined, the following results are obtained. There is "Skoll Center for Social Entrepreneurship" established within Oxford University. The mission of this center for social entrepreneurship research is as follows:

We also work to advance the field of social entrepreneurship through research insights and knowledge exchange. We are in a unique position to bridge the gap between theory and practice.

Table 5. Citation Analysis (University)

Rank	University	Cited	Quantity
1	University of Oxford	194	5
2	University of Sheffield	187	5
3	University of Essex	119	6
4	Universitat de València	95	9
5	Universitat Politècnica de València	77	6
6	Aalto University	70	4
7	University of North Carolina	68	6
8	Northeastern University	54	4
9	University of St.Gallen	52	6
10	Indiana University	47	5
11	University of Strathclyde	45	4
12	University of Zagreb	35	8
13	University of Tehran	35	6
14	Harvard University	35	4
15	City University of Hong Kong	34	4

Another university, University of Sheffield, has been working on social entrepreneurship education with South Korean Advanced Institute of Science and Technology (KAIST) since 2015. Therefore, it can be said that the universities with the highest number of citations value social entrepreneurship beyond being a course taught. The University of Essex, on the other hand, provides practical and theoretical services in the field of social entrepreneurship with the help of the "Interdisciplinary Studies Center (ISC)".

In Figure 5 below, the citation network and clusters of the universities with the most citation in the field of social entrepreneurship are shown. According to the network map, it is seen that the universities generally gather at the center. However, Kansas State University, which is not in the top 15 in citation ranking, is in a different place in this field. In other words, the references received by the works of Kansas State University academics in the field of social entrepreneurship differ from the universities located in the center of the country's space.

Figure 5. Citation Analysis (University)

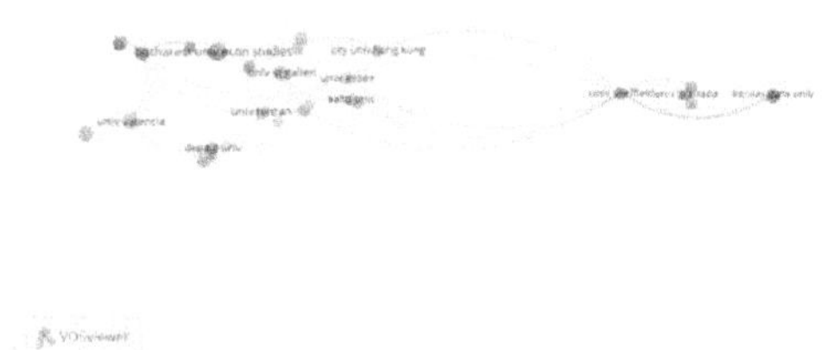

The number of articles published in the field of social entrepreneurship within the scope of journals is shown in Table 6. According to the table, the journal that gets the most citation from the articles published in the field of social entrepreneurship is "Journal of Business Ethics". The Journal of Business Ethics received a total of 207 citations from articles in social entrepreneurship. A total of 13 articles on social entrepreneurship have been published in the journal. The starting year of the journal is 1980 and the H-Index is 147. The Journal of Business Ethics is also available in Q1 quarter.

The highest number of articles was published by 22, "Journal of Social Entrepreneurship". The Journal of Social Entrepreneurship started its publication in 2010 and its H-Index is 20. The journal is also available in Q2 quarter. The journal that gets the most citation per article published is "Journal of Small Business Management". The journal has published a total of 6 articles in the field of social entrepreneurship and 103 citations (Average: 20.6). The starting year of the journal is 1996 and the H-Index is 94. "Journal of Small Business Management" is in Q1 quarter.

The journals listed in Table 6 are the most prestigious (most cited) journals in the field of social entrepreneurship. Therefore, researchers who want to publish in this field can focus on their own research by examining the current publications of the journals shown in this table.

Table 6. Citation Analysis (Journals)

Rank	Journal	Cited	Quantity
1	Journal of Business Ethics	207	13
2	Journal of Business Research	147	9
3	Journal of Cleaner Production	106	6
4	Journal of Small Business Management	103	5
5	Journal of Social Entrepreneurship	88	22
6	Entrepreneurship and Regional Development	45	9
7	Social Enterprice Journal	43	12
8	International Journal of Contemporary Hospitality Management	40	6
9	International Entrepreneurship and Management Journal	31	7
10	Voluntas	30	14
11	Sustainability	28	7
12	Social Entrepreneurship and Tourism	23	15
13	Canadian Journal of Administrative Sciences	18	5
14	Social Entrepreneurship and Social Business	10	6
15	Revija za Socijalnu Politiku	6	1

In Figure 6, there is a citation map of the journals that publish the most articles in the field of social entrepreneurship. In this map, it is seen that the journals are divided into 5 clusters. When the map is examined, the articles published in the "Journal of Social Entrepreneurship" are the articles that feed the area the most. Because when the citation network on the map is examined, it is seen that there is a connection with all the other clusters in terms of citation.

Figure 6. Citation Analysis (Journals)

Table 7 shows the total number of citations of articles written in the field of social entrepreneurship, both from within and outside of social entrepreneurship. According to the table, the article with the most citation is Short et al. (2009). In the article, it is based on the fact that the field of social entrepreneurship is at an infancy level and that the studies in the field are devoid of empirical efforts. In addition, for future research, they made a suggestion to mature the social entrepreneurship forehead:

Table 7. Citation Analysis (Articles)

Rank	Articles	Cited	Year
1	Short, J. C., Moss, T. W., & Lumpkin, G. T. (2009). Research in social entrepreneurship: Past contributions and future opportunities. Strategic entrepreneurship journal, 3(2), 161-194.	469	2009
2	Nicholls, A. (2009). 'We do good things, don't we?':'Blended Value Accounting'in social entrepreneurship. Accounting, organizations and society, 34(6-7), 755-769.	186	2009
3	Stephan, U., Uhlaner, L. M., & Stride, C. (2015). Institutions and social entrepreneurship: The role of institutional voids, institutional support, and institutional configurations. Journal of International Business Studies, 46(3), 308-331.	147	2015
4	Phillips, W., Lee, H., Ghobadian, A., O'Regan, N., & James, P. (2015). Social innovation and social entrepreneurship: A systematic review. Group & Organization Management, 40(3), 428-461.	110	2015
5	Calic, G., & Mosakowski, E. (2016). Kicking off social entrepreneurship: How a sustainability orientation influences crowdfunding success. Journal of Management Studies, 53(5), 738-767.	77	2016
6	Rivera-Santos, M., Holt, D., Littlewood, D., & Kolk, A. (2015). Social entrepreneurship in sub-Saharan Africa. Academy of Management Perspectives, 29(1), 72-91.	73	2015
7	Rey-Martí, A., Ribeiro-Soriano, D., & Palacios-Marqués, D. (2016). A bibliometric analysis of social entrepreneurship. Journal of Business Research, 69(5), 1651-1655.	66	2016
8	Littlewood, D., & Holt, D. (2018). Social entrepreneurship in South Africa: Exploring the influence of environment. Business & Society, 57(3), 525-561.	39	2018
9	VanSandt, C. V., Sud, M., & Marmé, C. (2009). Enabling the original intent: Catalysts for social entrepreneurship. Journal of Business Ethics, 90(3), 419-428.	38	2009
10	Haugh, H. M., & Talwar, A. (2016). Linking social entrepreneurship and social change: The mediating role of empowerment. Journal of Business Ethics, 133(4), 643-658.	37	2016
11	Dentchev, N., Baumgartner, R., Dieleman, H., Jóhannsdóttir, L., Jonker, J., Nyberg, T., ... & van Hoof, B. (2016). Embracing the variety of sustainable business models: social entrepreneurship, corporate intrapreneurship, creativity, innovation, and other approaches to sustainability challenges. Journal of Cleaner Production.	34	2016
12	Becker, S., Kunze, C., & Vancea, M. (2017). Community energy and social entrepreneurship: Addressing purpose, organisation and embeddedness of renewable energy projects. Journal of Cleaner Production, 147, 25-36.	31	2017
13	Muñoz, P., & Kibler, E. (2016). Institutional complexity and social entrepreneurship: A fuzzy-set approach. Journal of Business Research, 69(4), 1314-1318.	31	2016
14	Dey, P., & Steyaert, C. (2016). Rethinking the space of ethics in social entrepreneurship: Power, subjectivity, and practices of freedom. Journal of Business Ethics, 133(4), 627-641.	31	2016
15	Kedmenec, I., & Strašek, S. (2017). Are some cultures more favourable for social entrepreneurship than others?. Economic research-Ekonomska istraživanja, 30(1), 1461-1476.	30	2017

...Therefore, we recommend that scholars embrace key themes in strategic entrepreneurship and frame their research using established theories, such as contingency theory, creation theory, discovery theory, innovation diffusion theory, resource dependence theory, and other theoretical bases relevant to strategic entrepreneurship research.

Therefore, Short et al. (2009) (contingency theory, creation theory, discovery theory, innovation diffusion theory, resource dependence theory, and other theoretical) started to be used after 2009, the basis of the citation number of the article is causing. In the second row, Nicholls (2009), Short et al. As in (2009), it tried to explain the reporting and auditing functions in social entrepreneurship activities on the basis of a positivist, critical and interpretive approach in order to mature the concept of social entrepreneurship. Therefore, Macke et al. Efforts to overcome the common paradigm deficiency in the field of social entrepreneurship mentioned in (2018) actually started in 2009.

When Table 7 is interpreted in general, the following conclusion can be drawn: The articles in the table are the most cited articles among all articles written in the field of social entrepreneurship. The most cited article group in a field is the most prestigious and influential articles of the field. As a result, they are the most prominent works of the field.

In Figure 7, there is a citation map of articles in the field of social entrepreneurship. As can be seen from the map, Short et al. (2009) and Nicholls (2009) are the leading scientific studies in the field.

Figure 7. Citation Analysis (Articles)

Co-Word Analysis

In recent years, the interest in social entrepreneurship continues to increase. The reason for this interest is the contribution of social entrepreneurship to both social development and economic development (Paredo and McClean, 2006). As in Table 1, a total of 834 articles have been written in the last 10 years and this number corresponds to approximately 90% of the total articles. The number of articles published in the last 5 years corresponds to approximately 64% of the total number of articles. This visible change in recent years is a proof that the interest in the field has increased.

In co-word analysis, keywords often used in the same study in the field are considered to be related to each other. Therefore, in co-word analysis, the unit of analysis are concepts (Aria and Cuccurullo, 2017; Koseoğlu et al., 2016). With the development of computer technologies, visualization methods have become more used in co-word analysis studies and conceptual relationships have started to be explained more clearly (Yang & Cui, 2011).

The research questions in a co-word analysis in social entrepreneurship are as follows (Zupic & Carter, 2015);

- What is the conceptual structure of the social entrepreneurship field?
- What are the issues related to social entrepreneurship?
- How did the concept of social entrepreneurship develop?

The co-word analysis in this research was conducted from 2005 to 2019, when the concept of social entrepreneurship was frequently studied by scientists. This process has been analyzed by dividing it into 3 parts (2005-2009; 2010-2014; 2015-2019). In addition to these three groups, a total of 4 groups were examined by adding the map of articles in the field of social entrepreneurship in the 2005-2019 range.

When Part 1 (2005-2009) in Figure 9 is examined, it is seen that the benefit-oriented aspect of the concept of social entrepreneurship is mostly studied by the authors. In these years, concepts such as poverty, non-profit organizations, local economic development, public administration, and social enterprise have come to the forefront on the basis of social entrepreneurship to solve social problems. On the basis of these concepts, it can be said that social entrepreneurship is wanted to be brought to the fore in solving social problems.

When the group covering the second part of 2010-2014 is examined, it is seen that the concept of social entrepreneurship is working with educational areas such as interactive learning, learning by doing, pedagogy in order to increase the social value. The concept has also been studied locally, especially in China, for the social resolution of diseases such as HIV, MSM. In addition, the concept was continued to be studied with subjects such as creating social value, as in the 2005-2009 period.

Co-word analysis of the concept of social entrepreneurship between 2015-2019, which is the third part of Figure 9, is limited to the fact that the concept has been studied at least 5 times due to the increasing quantity in the studies. In this range, it is seen that the social aspects of concepts such as innovation, economy, enterprise, capital and business are studied with the concept of social entrepreneurship. Then, as seen in figure 8, the concept map created by the concepts studied at least 10 times with the concept of social entrepreneurship was created. This map shows that social entrepreneurship is now being handled together with the social aspects of the concepts worked with. In addition, it is seen that the concepts of corporate social responsibility and sustainability are the most studied concepts within the scope of social entrepreneurship.

Figure 8. Social Entrepreneurship Co-word Analysis (2015-2019)

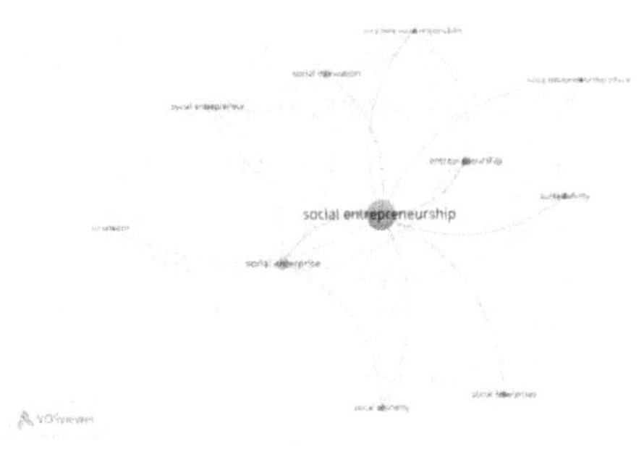

In the concept map, which is the 4th part of Figure 9 and covers the years 2005-2019, all the concepts in which the concept of social entrepreneurship is studied between these years are visualized within the relationship. At this point, the most important publication in the field, Short et al. As stated in (2009), there are developments related to placing the concept of social entrepreneurship on a solid theoretical ground. As seen in the concept map, there are theories in which the concept of social entrepreneurship is studied theoretically. Institutionalization theory and resource-based theory are among these theories.

The concept is also included in comparative entrepreneurship studies in terms of reaching sharper limits in entrepreneurship literature.

Figure 9. Social Entrepreneurship Co-word Analysis (2005-2019)

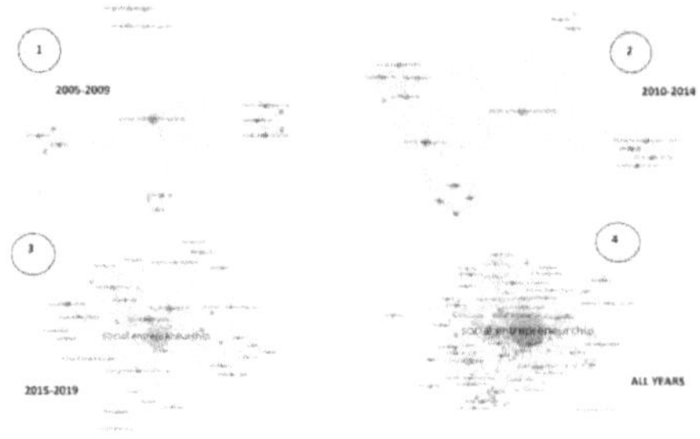

Tr-Index and Social Entrepreneurship

What's the name of that examination held in Turkey in social entrepreneurship TR-Index database is used. TR-Index; It consists of journals in the fields of Science and Social Sciences, Dentistry, Pharmacy, Engineering, Basic Sciences, Health Sciences, Veterinary Medicine, Social and Humanities sub-topics. National scientific journals that cover the scope of the TR- Index, ULAKBIM TR-Index experts It is selected by committees consisting of experts and academicians in their fields, depending on the Journal Evaluation Criteria. TR-Index can be scanned on the web page since August 2000. In addition to the bibliographic information (article name, author, essence, etc.) of the articles of the journals in the index, full texts of the article can also be accessed, depending on the authorization agreement signed between the ULAKBIM directorate and journal editors (https://trdizin.gov.tr/ about, 27.02.2020).

Considering the status of the article published in Turkey in the field of social entrepreneurship it is seen that a total of 20 articles published. The articles received a total of 24 citations. There are 1.2 citations per article. When the changes by year's total of 20 articles published in Turkey, it is observed that a total of 7 articles published in 2017. 16 of the articles have been written in business / economics, 3 in educational sciences and 1 in information / document management. The articles were written by a total of 33 different authors and there are no authors with at least 2 articles. Of 20 articles in total, 9 articles were written as single author, 9 articles were two authors, and 2 articles were 3 writers. When analyzed journals Articles published the third article in "Journal of Entrepreneurship and Innovation Management" was published in the journal, two articles of the "Journal of Erciyes University Faculty of Economics and Administrative Sciences," published in the journal shows that.

The first article is the titled "Social Entrepreneurship and Social Entrepreneurs: Theoretical Framework" published in Özdevecioğlu and Cingöz (2009). The article was published in the journal "Erciyes University Journal of Faculty of Economics and Administrative Sciences". In the article, social entrepreneurship is given as an example in this subject by mentioning that entrepreneurship is not only composed of efforts to bring together production factors and create a profit-oriented organization. It is emphasized that social entrepreneurship should increase the social benefits and non-profit factors. A type of entrepreneurship that explains social entrepreneurship activities to the development and development of societies in terms of both psychosocial and economic terms has been announced.

In 2010, two articles were published. The first one is the article titled "Urban Transformation and Enhancement of The Urban Life Quality In The Context of Social Entrepreneurship In Turkey" by See and Kara (2010). The article emphasized that the positive and negative opinions of non-governmental organizations and social entrepreneurs in the urban transformation process can affect the success of transformation projects in a positive and negative way. In addition, information and data on urban transformation, urban quality of life and social entrepreneurship were compiled by scanning the related literature. As a result, some suggestions were made that are expected to guide central and local decision makers on the success of urban transformation projects. The second article published in 2010 is the article titled "The Managerial and Conceptual Transformation in Third Sector: Social Profit Organizations" by Sarıkaya (2010). In the article, it is stated that the third sector is of great importance in terms of meeting social needs and filling the areas left by other sectors, the public and private sectors. Continuous increase in social needs and the need for deep-rooted solutions require a change and transformation in the third sector, both conceptually and in practice. In this transformation, especially the importance of social entrepreneurship and social profit concepts has been mentioned in recent years, the necessity of reconsidering third sector organizations and some concepts specific to these institutions and reshaping the management approach has been revealed.

The most cited article cited in Tr-Index is "Social Entrepreneurship in Combating With Poverty: Social Innovative Cases Of Ashoka Fellows" by Kümbül Güler (2011). In the article, it is emphasized that social entrepreneurship is defined as a whole of activities focused on the solution of social problems, and the concept can create social change in society rather than social entrepreneurs' own benefits, and benefit can be achieved in this way. The article focuses on the activities of social entrepreneurs, who have different strategies with an innovative approach to combating poverty, and examines the profiles of some selected members of Ashoka, an organization that provides significant funding to social entrepreneurs around the world, and how innovative social entrepreneurs perceive the problem of poverty and apply innovative strategies.

CONCLUSION

In this research, bibliometric citation analysis and co-word analysis were conducted in the world of social entrepreneurship within the scope of social impact theory and social value creation. Besides the WOS database, the analysis also benefited from the VOSviewer program. The scanning in the WOS database was made under the title of "Social Entrepreneurship*" within the scope of academic articles. Bibliometric analysis was carried out on 926 academic articles in SCI-EXPANDED, SSCI, A & HCI, CPCI-S, CPCI-SSH, BKCI-S, BKCI-SSH, ESCI indexes. As a result of the analysis, it is seen that the interest of both universities and academicians on social entrepreneurship has increased in the last 10 years. In terms of the subject, the social entrepreneurship phenomenon, which was first written in 1982, remained at low levels in the number of publications until 2004. However, it has shown a continuous trend after 2006. According to Short et al. (2009), social entrepreneurship researches, which were still in the infancy stage in 2009, are undoubtedly not at the end of their life after 10 years; It is still an area open to development and research.

Table 8. Social Entrepreneurship Articles in TR-Index

Article	Year	Author(s)	Journal	Key-words	Subject	Cited
Social Entrepreneurship and Social Entrepreneurs:Theoretical Framework	2009	Mahmut ÖZDEVECİOĞLU Ayşe CİNGÖZ	*Erciyes University Journal of Faculty of Economics and Administrative Sciences*	*Social Entrepreneurship, Social Entrepreneur, Social Enterprise.*	Business Man. Economy	3
Urban Transformation and Enhancement Of The Urban Life Quality in The Context Of Social Entrepreneurship In Turkey	2010	Mustafa GÖRÜN Mustafa KARA	*Journal of Administrative Sciences*	*Urban Transformation, Urban Quality of Life, Social Entrepreneurship, Participation.*	Business Man. Economy	3
The Managerial and Conceptual Transformation in Third Sector: Social Profit Organizations	2010	Muammer SARIKAYA	*Journal of Economics and Administrative Sciences*	*Third Sector, Social Profit, Social Profit Organizations*	Economy	2
Social Entrepreneurship in Combating With Poverty: Social İnnovative Cases Of Ashoka Fellows	2011	Burcu KÜMBÜL GÜLER	*Dokuz Eylul University The Journal of Graduate School of Social Sciences*	*Social Entrepreneurship, Social Entrepreneur, Social İnnovation, Poverty, Elimination of Poverty, Ashoka.*	Business Man.	5
Social, Entrepreneurship Dimensions of Libraries	2013	Ece HELVACIOĞLU	*Information World*	*Libraries, Social entrepreneurship, İnformation literacy, Access to information*	Information Management	1
Pre-serviceTeachers' Social Entrepreneurship Qualifications Scale: Validity and Reliability Study	2013	Tuğba KONAKLI Nur GÖĞÜŞ	*Gazi University Journal of Gazi Educational Faculty*	*Social entrepreneurship, Pre-service teacher, Scale development.*	Educational Research	3
The Role of Social Entrepreneurship on the Pre-service Teachers' Attitudes toward School Management	2015	Seval KOÇAK Murat ÖZDEMİR	*MersinUniversity Journal of the Faculty of Education*	*School management, social entrepreneurship, social skillsin management, attitudes toward school management*	Educational Research	3
A Field Study on Social İnnovation	2015	Fatih ÖZDEMİR İlker Murat AR	Journal of Entrepreneurship and İnnovation Management	Social innovation, social entrepreneurship, Turkey	Business Man. Economy	2
Social Entrepreneurship and Akhi Organization:Theoretical Framework	2016	İbrahim DURAK	Erciyes University Journal of Faculty of Economics and Administrative Sciences	Social Entrepreneurship, Akhism, Social Value	Business Man. Economy	0
Embeddedness in Social Entrepreneurship: The Role of Geographic Diffusion and Cultural Values	2017	Deniz KANTUR	Journal of Entrepreneurship and İnnovation Management	Social Entrepreneurship, Embeddedness, Geographic Diffusion, Cultural Values, Content Analysis	Business Man. Economy	0
The İmportance Of Social Entrepreneurship as a Part of Brand Positioning: A Study İn The Service Sector	2017	Bilal ASILSOY	İstanbul Commerce University Journal of Social Sciences	Brand, Brand Positioning, Business And Social Entrepreneurs, Social Entrepreneurs Marketing.	Business Man. Economy	0
Shaping The Future in The Management And Solution Of Social Problems: Social Entrepreneur Cooperatives and The Example Of Enterprise Europe Network	2017	Mehmet GÜNEŞ	Third Sector Social Economic Review	Entrepreneurship, Social Entrepreneurship, Cooperatives, Social Entrepreneur Cooperatives, Social Economic Network, The European Entrepreneurship Network	Business Man. Economy	0
The Effects Of Personal Values On Social Entrepreneurship Tendency: A Research on Tourism Students	2017	Cem IŞIK Ekrem AYDIN	Journal of Entrepreneurship and İnnovation Management	Social Entrepreneurship, Personal Values, İnnovation, Tourism	Business Man. Economy	1
The Effect of Perceived Social Support on Social Entrepreneurship: A Research on University Studensts	2017	Mustafa Fedai ÇAVUŞ Nazmiye Ülkü PEKKAN	Business and Economics Research Journal	Perceived Social Support, Social Entrepreneurship, University Students	Business Man. Economy	1
Mediation Role of Self-Efficacy Perceptions in the Relationship Between Emotional Intelligence Levels and Social Entrepreneurship Traits of Pre-Service Teachers	2017	Mehmet ÜSTÜNER Hüseyin AKAR	Journal of Education and Future	Self-efficacy, Emotional İntelligence, Social Entrepreneurship, Pre-service Teacher	Business Man. Economy	0
Social Entrepreneurship in Universities: Opportunities And Suggestions	2018	Mahmut KARĞIN Hüseyin AKTAŞ Ramazan GÖKBUNAR	Journal of Celal Bayar University Faculty of Economics and Administrative Sciences	Social Entrepreneurship, Social Entrepreneur, Entrepreneurship, Entrepreneur Universities, İnnovation-Driven Economies.	Business Man. Economy	0
KOSGEB Entrepreneurship Program: A Critical Assesment	2018	Mete Kaan NAMAL Mustafa KOÇANCI Beyhan AKSOY	The Academic Elegance	KOSGEB, Entrepreneurship Support, Social Entrepreneurship.	Economy	0
An Evaluation Of The Future of Entrepreneurship Education in Turkey in The Framework of Meb 2023 Education Vision	2019	Murat TARHAN	Journal of BoluAbant İzzet Baysal University Faculty of Education	2023 Education Vision, Entrepreneurship, Entrepreneurship Skills, MEB	Business Man.	0
Social Business Models and Social Entrepreneurship: Boğaziçi University Consumption Cooperative Case	2019	Çiğdem KAYA	Journal of Business Research-Turk	Social Entrepreneurship, Social Business Model, Consumption Cooperative	Information Management	0
The Role of Social Innovation and Social Entrepreneurship in The Future Of Social Work Profession	2019	Buğra YILDIRIM Tarık TUNCAY	Hacettepe University Journal of Economics and Administrative Sciences	Social Innovation, Social Entrepreneurship, Social Work Profession, Social Workers	Educational Research	0

The main factors in increasing this interest are the proof that both the social problems increase, the desire for the solution of social problems increases, and the universities and academicians are interested in the subject. Unless there is a decrease in the number of people suffering from epidemics, environmental problems and ongoing wars, there will be no decrease in the number of social entrepreneurs. This situation will keep the researchers' interest in the subject.

Citation analysis in the research gives information about who are the most influential experts in a field, which are the most effective journals, countries, universities, and the leading publications of the field. According to the results of citation analysis, the most effective journals in the field of social entrepreneurship are "Journal of Business Ethics", "Journal of Business Research" and "Journal of Cleaner Production". The reason why these journals are known as the most prestigious journals in the field of social entrepreneurship is that they received the most citations. When social entrepreneurs and researchers who want to do research on social entrepreneurship follow these journals, they can access the most up-to-date and most qualified social entrepreneurship research. These journals can be their source of inspiration for future researches.

The field's most influential authors on citation are Holt Diane, Littlewood David and Rey-Marti, Andrea. USA, England and France are the countries that get the most citation in the publications of their authors. The main reason why these authors are known as the most influential authors is that they received the most citations in their research in the field of social entrepreneurship. Therefore, they can be referred to as the theoretical gurus of the social entrepreneurship field.

The three most effective universities in the world are University of Oxford, University of Sheffield and University of Essex. The reason why these universities receive the most citations is that they have established various centers and international platforms in order to attract the attention of the academicians within their organization to the field of social entrepreneurship. This situation may have motivated academics and directed them to academic research. University of Oxford's international association with the "Skoll Center for Social Entrepreneurship" center and the University of Sheffield's South Korean Advanced Institute of Science and Technology (KAIST) can be given as an example. The University of Essex, on the other hand, provides practical and theoretical services in the field of social entrepreneurship with the help of the "Interdisciplinary Studies Center (ISC)".

The articles that get the most citation in terms of the citations made by social entrepreneurship studies are Short et al. (2009), Nicholls (2009) and Stephan et al. (2015). The most cited articles in the field of social entrepreneurship can be considered as the main works of the field. Researchers who want to do research in the field of social entrepreneurship are especially recommended to read the leading and most prestigious works of the field.

In the research, a co-word analysis was also made within the scope of social entrepreneurship. This analysis provides information on the conceptual structure of the social entrepreneurship field, issues related to social entrepreneurship and how the social entrepreneurship writing has developed. In 2005-2009, it is seen that the benefit-oriented aspect of the concept of social entrepreneurship is mostly studied by the authors. In these years, concepts such as poverty, non-profit organizations, local economic development, public administration, and social enterprise have come to the forefront on the basis of social entrepreneurship to solve social problems. 2010-2014 is examined, it is seen that the concept of social entrepreneurship is working with educational areas such as interactive learning, learning by doing, pedagogy in order to increase the social value. The concept has also been studied locally, especially in China, for the social resolution of diseases such as HIV, MSM. In addition, the concept was continued to be studied with subjects such as creating social value, as in the 2005-2009 period. 2015-2019, it is seen that the social aspects of concepts such as innovation, economy, enterprise, capital and business are studied with the concept of social entrepreneurship.

The bibliometric methods used in the research have been examined within the scope of social impact theory by creating social value for the purpose of increasing the social benefit inherent in social entrepreneurship. In this respect, it contributes to the theoretical level of social entrepreneurship studies. Studies conducted in Turkey in finally been examined in the study of social entrepreneurship in general. In the following years, he appeared in the literature within the concepts of social entrepreneurship, education area and health. In recent years, it is seen that social entrepreneurship has been working with basic topics such as social innovation, sustainability and social economy.

TR-Index database belonging to Turkey in the result of the examination shows that a total of 20 article was written. The first article was written in 2009 and the number of citations received by the most cited article is 5. Most articles were published in 2017. Based on these results, it may be wrong to conclude that the issue of social entrepreneurship is underestimated by Turkish academics. The conclusion may be that academics did not prefer TR-Index in their research on social entrepreneurship. But it is clear that the result is that social entrepreneurship at an early stage in Turkey.

One of the aims of bibliometric studies is to take a kind of photograph and interpret the studies made within the scope of a certain concept. Academic research on social entrepreneurship are not yet mature. This situation is due to the fact that humanity has been dealing with different problems in each passing time due to the situation of finding solutions to the social problems inherent in social entrepreneurship. Therefore, as long as social problems continue, scientific research on social entrepreneurship and social entrepreneurship will continue. Author collaboration analysis can be conducted within the scope of journals such as Journal of Social Entrepreneurship, Social Entrepreneurship and Tourism, Social Entrepreneurship and Social Business, which are directly linked to the field of social entrepreneurship in the future.

REFERENCES

Akar, H., & Üstüner, M. (2017). Mediation role of self-efficacy perceptions in the relationship between emotional intelligence levels and social entrepreneurship traits of pre-service teachers. *Journal of Education and Future*, (12), 95–115.

Aksoy, B., Koçanci, M., & Namal, M. K. (2019). *Girişimcilik motivasyonu: Uygulamalı girişimcilik eğitimi katılımcıları örneği.* Yönetim Ve Ekonomi. *Celal Bayar Üniversitesi İktisadi Ve İdari Bilimler Fakültesi Dergisi, 26*(1), 109–129. doi:10.18657/yonveek.526604

Aria, M., & Cuccurullo, C. (2017). Bibliometrix: An R-tool for comprehensive science mapping analysis. *Journal of Informetrics, 11*(4), 959–975. doi:10.1016/j.joi.2017.08.007

Austin, J., Stevenson, H., & Wei-Skillern, J. (2006). Social and commercial entrepreneurship: Same, different, or both? *Entrepreneurship Theory and Practice, 30*(1), 1–22. doi:10.1111/j.1540-6520.2006.00107.x

Bağdaş, Ç. K. (2019). Sosyal İş Modelleri ve Sosyal Girişimcilik: Boğaziçi Üniversitesi Tüketim Kooperatifi Örneği. *İşletme Araştırmaları Dergisi, 11*(3), 1433-1449.

Becker, S., Kunze, C., & Vancea, M. (2017). Community energy and social entrepreneurship: Addressing purpose, organisation and embeddedness of renewable energy projects. *Journal of Cleaner Production, 147*, 25–36. doi:10.1016/j.jclepro.2017.01.048

Boyack, K., Klavans, R., & Börner, K. (2005). Mapping the backbone of science. *Scientometrics, 64*(3), 351–374. doi:10.100711192-005-0255-6

Calabretta, G., Durisin, B., & Ogliengo, M. (2011). Uncovering the intellectual structure of research in business ethics: A journey through the history, the classics, and the pillars of Journal of Business Ethics. *Journal of Business Ethics, 104*(4), 499–524. doi:10.100710551-011-0924-8

Calic, G., & Mosakowski, E. (2016). Kicking off social entrepreneurship: How a sustainability orientation influences crowdfunding success. *Journal of Management Studies, 53*(5), 738–767. doi:10.1111/joms.12201

Charvet, F., Cooper, M. C., & Gardner, J. T. (2008). The intellectual structure of supply chain management: A bibliometric approach. *Journal of Business Logistics, 29*(1), 47–73. doi:10.1002/j.2158-1592.2008.tb00068.x

Cobo, M. J., López-Herrera, A. G., Herrera-Viedma, E., & Herrera, F. (2011). Science mapping software tools: Review, analysis, and cooperative study among tools. *Journal of the American Society for Information Science and Technology, 62*(7), 1382–1402. doi:10.1002/asi.21525

Coulter, N., Monarch, I., & Konda, S. (1998). Software engineering as seen through its research literature: A study in co-word analysis. *Journal of the American Society for Information Science, 49*(13), 1206–1223. doi:10.1002/(SICI)1097-4571(1998)49:13<1206::AID-ASI7>3.0.CO;2-F

Corley, K. G., & Gioia, D. A. (2011). Building theory about theory building: What constitutes a theoretical contribution? *Academy of Management Review, 36*(1), 12–32. doi:10.5465/amr.2009.0486

Çavuş, M. F., & Pekkan, N. Ü. (2017). Algılanan sosyal desteğin sosyal girişimciliğe etkisi: Üniversite öğrencileri üzerinde bir araştırma 1. *Business and Economics Research Journal, 8*(3), 519–532. doi:10.20409/berj.2017.64

Dentchev, N., Baumgartner, R., Dieleman, H., Jóhannsdóttir, L., Jonker, J., Nyberg, T., Rauter, R., Rosano, M., Snihur, Y., Tang, X., & van Hoof, B. (2016). Embracing the variety of sustainable business models: Social entrepreneurship, corporate intrapreneurship, creativity, innovation, and other approaches to sustainability challenges. *Journal of Cleaner Production, 113*, 1–4. doi:10.1016/j.jclepro.2015.10.130

Desa, G. (2007). *Social entrepreneurship: snapshots of a research field in emergence*. Paper presented at the 3rd International Social Entrepreneurship Research Conference, Centre for Corporate Values and Responsibility (CVR), Frederiksberg.

Dey, P., & Steyaert, C. (2016). Rethinking the space of ethics in social entrepreneurship: Power, subjectivity, and practices of freedom. *Journal of Business Ethics, 133*(4), 627–641. doi:10.100710551-014-2450-y

Dionisio, M. (2019). The evolution of social entrepreneurship research: A bibliometric analysis. *Social Enterprise Journal, 15*(1), 22–45. doi:10.1108/SEJ-05-2018-0042

Douglas, H. (2008). Creating knowledge: A review of research methods in three societal change approaches. *Journal of Nonprofit & Public Sector Marketing*, *20*(2), 141–163. doi:10.1080/10495140802224787

Duque Oliva, E. J., Cervera Taulet, A., & Rodríguez Romero, C. (2006). A bibliometric analysis of models measuring the concept of perceived quality inproviding internet service. *Innovar (Universidad Nacional de Colombia)*, *16*(28), 223–243.

Durak, İ. (2016). Sosyal Gırısımcılık Ve Ahılık Teskılatı: Teorık Çerçeve/Socıal Entrepreneurshıp And Akhı Organızatıon: Theoretical Framework. *Erciyes Üniversitesi Iktisadi ve Idari Bilimler Faküeltesi Dergisi*, (47), 101.

Ferreira, J. J., Fernandes, C. I., Peres-Ortiz, M., & Alves, H. (2017). Conceptualizing social entrepreneurship: Perspectives from the literature. *International Review on Public and Nonprofit Marketing*, *14*(1), 73–93. doi:10.100712208-016-0165-8

Görün, M., & Kara, M. (2010). Kentsel dönüşüm ve sosyal girişimcilik bağlamında Türkiye'de kentsel yaşam kalitesinin artırılması. *Yönetim Bilimleri Dergisi*, *8*(2), 137–164.

Granados, M. L., Hlupic, V., Coakes, E., & Mohamed, S. (2011). Social enterprise and social entrepreneurship research and theory. *Social Enterprise Journal*, *7*(3), 198–218. doi:10.1108/17508611111182368

Greenfield, S. M., & Strickon, A. (1981). A new paradigm for the study of entrepreneurship and social change. *Economic Development and Cultural Change*, *29*(3), 467–499. doi:10.1086/451267

Gundolf, K., & Filser, M. (2013). Management research and religion: A citation analysis. *Journal of Business Ethics*, *112*(1), 177–185. doi:10.100710551-012-1240-7

Günes, M. (2017). *Sosyal Sorunların Yönetim ve Çözümünde Geleceği Şekillendirmek: Sosyal Girişimci Kooperatifçilik Ve Avrupa Girişimcilik Ağı Örneği*. Third Sector Social Economic Review.

Güngör, E. (2008). *Ahlak Psikolojisi ve Sosyal Ahlak*. Ötüken Yayınları.

Haugh, H. M., & Talwar, A. (2016). Linking social entrepreneurship and social change: The mediating role of empowerment. *Journal of Business Ethics*, *133*(4), 643–658. doi:10.100710551-014-2449-4

Helvacıoğlu, E. (2013). Sosyal Girişimcilik Boyutunda Kütüphaneler. *Bilgi Dünyası*, *14*(1), 199–203.

Hill, T. L., Kothari, T. H., & Shea, M. (2010). Patterns of meaning in the social entrepreneurship literature: A research platform. *Journal of Social Entrepreneurship*, *1*(1), 5–31. doi:10.1080/19420670903442079

Hoogendoorn, B., Pennings, E., & Thurik, A. (2010). What do we know about social entrepreneurship: An analysis of empirical research. *International Review of Entrepreneurship*, *8*(2), 1–42.

Işık, C., & Aydın, E. (2017). Kişisel değerlerin sosyal girişimcilik eğilimine etkisi: Turizm öğrencileri üzerine bir araştırma. *Girişimcilik ve İnovasyon Yönetimi Dergisi*, *6*(2), 131–154.

Kantur, D. (2017). Sosyal Girişimcilikte Yerleşiklik: Coğrafi Yayılım ve Kültürel Değerlerin Rolü. *Journal of Entrepreneurship and Innovation Management*, *6*(1), 173–196.

Kargin, M., Aktaş, H., & Gökbunar, R. (2018). Üniversitelerde Sosyal Girişimcilik: Fırsatlar ve Öneriler. *Yonetim ve Ekonomi*, *25*(1), 155–170.

Kedmenec, I., & Strašek, S. (2017). *Are some cultures more favourable for social entrepreneurship than others?* Economic research-. *Ekonomska Istrazivanja, 30*(1), 1461–1476. doi:10.1080/1331677X.2017.1355251

Koçak, S., & Özdemir, M. (2015). Öğretmen Adaylarının Okul Yöneticiliğine Yönelik Tutumları Üzerinde Sosyal Girişimciliğin Rolü. *Mersin University Journal of the Faculty of Education, 11*(3).

Konaklı, T., & Göğüş, N. (2013). Aday Öğretmenlerin Sosyal Girişimcilik Özellikleri Ölçeği: Geçerlik ve Güvenirlik Çalışması. *Gazi University Journal of Gazi Educational Faculty (GUJGEF), 33*(2).

Koseoglu, M. A., Rahimi, R., Okumus, F., & Liu, J. (2016). Bibliometric studies in tourism. *Annals of Tourism Research, 61*, 180–198. doi:10.1016/j.annals.2016.10.006

Kraus, S., Filser, M., O'Dwyer, M., & Shaw, E. (2014). Social entrepreneurship: An exploratory citation analysis. *Review of Managerial Science, 8*(2), 275–292. doi:10.100711846-013-0104-6

Kümbül Güler, B. (2011). Yoksullukla mücadelede sosyal girişimcilik: Ashoka üyelerinden sosyal yenilikçi örnek uygulamalar. *Dokuz Eylül Üniversitesi Sosyal Bilimler Enstitüsü Dergisi, 13*(3), 79–111.

Lan, H., Zhu, Y., Ness, D., Xing, K., & Schneider, K. (2014). The role and characteristics of social entrepreneurs in contemporary rural cooperative development in China: Case studies of rural social entrepreneurship. *Asia Pacific Business Review, 20*(3), 379–400. doi:10.1080/13602381.2014.929300

Latane´, B. (1981). The Psychology of Social İmpact. *The American Psychologist, 36*(4), 343–356. doi:10.1037/0003-066X.36.4.343

Latane´, B., & Wolf, S. (1981). The Social İmpact of Majorities and Minorities. *Psychological Review, 88*(5), 438–453. doi:10.1037/0033-295X.88.5.438

Littlewood, D., & Holt, D. (2018). Social entrepreneurship in South Africa: Exploring the influence of environment. *Business & Society, 57*(3), 525–561. doi:10.1177/0007650315613293

Macke, J., Sarate, J. A. R., Domeneghini, J., & da Silva, K. A. (2018). Where do we go from now? Research framework for social entrepreneurship. *Journal of Cleaner Production, 183*, 677–685. doi:10.1016/j.jclepro.2018.02.017

Macke, J., Vallejos, R. V., Faccin, K., & Genari, D. (2012). Social Capital in Collaborative Networks Competitiveness: The case of the Brazilian Wine İndustry Clust*er. İnt. J. Comput. İntegr. Manuf., 25*, 1–8.

Mair, J., & Martí, İ. (2009). Entrepreneurship in and around İnstitutional voids: A case study from Bangladesh. *Journal of Business Venturing, 24*(5), 419–435. doi:10.1016/j.jbusvent.2008.04.006

Merton, R. (1988). The Matthew Effect in science, II: Cumulative advantage and the symbolism of intellectual property. *Isis, 79*(4), 606–623. doi:10.1086/354848

Moed, H. F. (2005). *Citation analysis in research evaluation* (Vol. 9). Springer Science & Business Media.

Muñoz, P., & Kibler, E. (2016). Institutional complexity and social entrepreneurship: A fuzzy-set approach. *Journal of Business Research, 69*(4), 1314–1318. doi:10.1016/j.jbusres.2015.10.098

Nicholls, A. (2009). 'We do good things, don't we?': 'Blended Value Accounting' in social entrepreneurship. *Accounting, Organizations and Society*, *34*(6-7), 755–769. doi:10.1016/j.aos.2009.04.008

Özdemir, F., & Ar, İ. M. (2015). Sosyal yenilik üzerine bir alan araştırması. *Girişimcilik ve İnovasyon Yönetimi Dergisi*, *4*(1), 17–43.

Özdevecioğlu, M., & Cingöz, A. (2009). Sosyal girişimcilik ve sosyal girişimciler: Teorik çerçeve. *Erciyes Üniversitesi İktisadi ve İdari Bilimler Fakültesi Dergisi*, (32), 81–95.

Paredo, A. M., & McLean, M. (2006). Social Entrepreneurship: A Critical Review of the Concept. *Journal of World Business*, *41*(1), 56–65. doi:10.1016/j.jwb.2005.10.007

Phillips, W., Lee, H., Ghobadian, A., O'Regan, N., & James, P. (2015). Social innovation and social entrepreneurship: A systematic review. *Group & Organization Management*, *40*(3), 428–461. doi:10.1177/1059601114560063

Rey-Martí, A., Ribeiro-Soriano, D., & Palacios-Marqués, D. (2016). A bibliometric analysis of social entrepreneurship. *Journal of Business Research*, *69*(5), 1651–1655. doi:10.1016/j.jbusres.2015.10.033

Rivera-Santos, M., Holt, D., Littlewood, D., & Kolk, A. (2015). Social entrepreneurship in sub-Saharan Africa. *The Academy of Management Perspectives*, *29*(1), 72–91. doi:10.5465/amp.2013.0128

Sarıkaya, M. (2010). Üçüncü Sektörde Yönetsel ve Kavramsal Dönüşüm: Sosyal Kâr Amaçlı Örgütler. *CÜ İktisadi ve İdari Bilimler Dergisi*, *11*(1), 87–100.

Sassmannshausen, S. P., & Volkmann, C. (2013). *A bibliometric based review on social entrepreneurship and its establishment as a field of research (No. 2013-003)*. Schumpeter Discussion Papers.

Short, J. C., Moss, T. W., & Lumpkin, G. T. (2009). Research in social entrepreneurship: Past contributions and future opportunities. *Strategic Entrepreneurship Journal*, *3*(2), 161–194. doi:10.1002ej.69

Stephan, U., Uhlaner, L. M., & Stride, C. (2015). Institutions and social entrepreneurship: The role of institutional voids, institutional support, and institutional configurations. *Journal of International Business Studies*, *46*(3), 308–331. doi:10.1057/jibs.2014.38

Tarhan, M. (2019). MEB 2023 Eğitim Vizyonu Çerçevesince Türkiye'de Girişimcilik Eğitiminin Geleceğine Yönelik Bir Değerlendirme. *Abant İzzet Baysal Üniversitesi Eğitim Fakültesi Dergisi*, *19*(2), 667–682. doi:10.17240/aibuefd.2019.19.46660-528071

VanSandt, C. V., Sud, M., & Marmé, C. (2009). Enabling the original intent: Catalysts for social entrepreneurship. *Journal of Business Ethics*, *90*(3), 419–428. doi:10.100710551-010-0419-z

Yang, Y., Wu, M., & Cui, L. (2011). Integration of three visualization methods based on co-word analysis. *Scientometrics*, *90*(2), 659–673. doi:10.100711192-011-0541-4

Yıldırım, B., & Tuncay, T. (2019). Sosyal İnovasyonun Ve Sosyal Girişimciliğin Sosyal Hizmet Mesleğinin Geleceğindeki Rolü. *Hacettepe Üniversitesi İktisadi ve İdari Bilimler Fakültesi Dergisi*, *37*(1), 169–188. doi:10.17065/huniibf.350375

Yunus, M. (2007). *Creating a world without poverty: Social business and the future of capitalism* (1st ed.). PublicAffairs.

Zahra, S. A., Rawhouzer, H. N., Bhawe, N., Neubaum, D. O., & Hayton, J. C. (2010). Globalization of Social Entrepreneurship Opportunities. *Strategic Entrepreneurship Journal*, *2*(2), 117–131. doi:10.1002ej.43

Zan, B. U. (2012). *Türkiye'de Bilim Dallarında Karşılaştırmalı Bibliyometrik Analiz Çalışması.* Yayımlanmamış Doktora Tezi, Ankara Üniversitesi, Sosyal Bilimler Enstitüsü.

Zupic, I., & Čater, T. (2015). Bibliometric methods in management and organization. *Organizational Research Methods*, *18*(3), 429–472. doi:10.1177/1094428114562629

KEY TERMS AND DEFINITIONS

Bibliometric Analysis: It is a numerical analysis of the publications produced by individuals or institutions in a certain period and in a certain region and the relations between these publications.

Cite: It is a scientific study citing another scientific study.

Keyword: Ideas and topics that describe exactly what the content is.

Scholar: Scholar is the person who tries to obtain information systematically using the methods of obtaining scientific data for facts and variables related to the universe.

Scientific Mapping: It is a method that shows how scientific studies, disciplines and subjects are connected to each other with the help of maps.

Social Entrepreneurship: Social entrepreneurship is a type of entrepreneurship where the social entrepreneur determines a social problem or need in the environment in which he lives, and creates permanent solutions by using entrepreneurship principles in order to eliminate or eliminate this problem.

Social Impact Theory: It is a theory that accepts that the effects of factors such as social status, activity, formation etc. on individuals/groups depend on the size, closeness, and strength of the stimulus.

Tr-Index: It is the Turkish database of journals in the sub-subject areas of Dentistry, Pharmacy, Engineering, Basic Sciences, Health Sciences, Veterinary Medicine, Social Sciences and Humanities in the main subjects of Social Sciences.

Web of Science (WoS): It is a subscription-based website that provides comprehensive citation data for many different academic disciplines.

Chapter 3
Conforming With Diverse Expectations:
How Do Social Enterprises Acquire Symbolic Capital?

Kutay Güneştepe
Istanbul Technical University, Turkey

Merve Güngördü Arıoğlu
Istanbul Technical University, Turkey

Deniz Tunçalp
Istanbul Technical University, Turkey

ABSTRACT

Social enterprises need to manage their dual missions. On the one hand, they have to develop a sustainable revenue model and maintain their businesses. On the other hand, they should communicate that they do not prioritize commercial objectives, as their primary focus is social impact. The authors explore how social enterprises manage symbolic meanings while pursuing their dual missions. They have examined symbolic actions with netnography and derived a resource acquisition model. This chapter has three contributions to the literature. Firstly, while symbolic capital is a crucial resource for entrepreneurial success, activities to capture this resource are understudied in the literature. The authors have developed a novel perspective to fill this gap. Secondly, there are various studies examining resource acquisition in the US context. This study enriches our understanding of the focal phenomenon as it is conducted in the Turkish context. Thirdly, this is one of the few studies collecting empirical data with netnography and may foster further studies based on online data sources.

DOI: 10.4018/978-1-7998-4727-4.ch003

INTRODUCTION

Social entrepreneurship is a promising research area in entrepreneurial studies with its novel dynamics, combining both for-profit and non-profit activities in one organization (Dacin et al., 2011). Unlike its commercial counterparts, social enterprises' primary objective is to offer social value rather than bringing prosperity to its shareholders. Accordingly, various studies have examined similarities and differences between social and commercial enterprises (e.g., Austin et al., 2006; Lumpkin et al., 2013; Yitshaki & Kropp, 2016). Although social enterprises, as hybrid organizations, do not prioritize maximizing profit, they still need to pursue economic value creation to maintain the business and increase the social impact (Costanzo et al., 2014; Siebold et al., 2018). This diverging logic of operation requires skillful management of activities to gain legitimacy and to acquire other resources.

Hybrid organizations pursuing dual missions employ varying strategies such as decoupling, compromising, and selective coupling (Pache & Santos, 2013) to sustain their business. While pursuing their dual missions, conflicts may arise from internal and external foundations (Bacq et al., 2016). Capabilities of the human resources and elasticity in the managerial approaches can solve or mitigate internal conflicts (e.g., Battilana & Dorado, 2010; Costanzo et al., 2014; Siebold et al., 2018; Gumusay et al., 2020). On the other hand, adopting and communicating symbolic meanings in line with the field's expectations can alleviate tensions with the external stakeholders (De Clecq & Voronov, 2009; Barbosa, 2020).

This chapter focuses on the symbolic sources and asks *how social enterprises manage symbolic meanings while pursuing their dual missions*. To answer this question, the authors conducted an inductive qualitative study and examined web pages and social media accounts of 38 social enterprises in Turkey. New enterprises carry out symbolic management to gain legitimacy to acquire various resources (Zott & Huy, 2007; De Clecq & Voronov, 2009). In the digital age, online channels are essential sources of symbolic communications (Tunçalp & Le, 2014; Kozinets, 2018) that provide rich information to scholars examining symbolic meanings (e.g., Seemen & Islam, 2020). Because of that, the authors explore the online sources about selected social enterprises with netnography (Kozinets, 2018).

Findings show that social enterprises engage in symbolic management and convert their accumulated resources to symbolic meanings to acquire resources. The authors have identified four symbolic management categories that support social enterprises to deal with dual mission conflicts. The authors also develop a framework relying on these categories and describe the constructs in detail.

This study has several contributions. First of all, balancing the dual mission of social entrepreneurs is a widely discussed topic in the literature, and scholars underline that social enterprises need to communicate the appropriateness of their activities to social value creation to maintain their legitimacy (Pache & Santos, 2013; Costanzo et al., 2014; Pret & Carter, 2017). While social enterprises are oriented more externally than their commercial counterparts (Gras & Lumpkin, 2012; Costanzo et al., 2014), there are a few studies about their symbolic management in the literature (Barbosa, 2020). Moreover, various calls for research on this topic exist (Austin et al., 2006; Chell et al., 2010; Dacin et al., 2011, Siebold). So, the research fills this gap and has practical implications for social enterprises.

Second, acquiring external resources is crucial for social enterprises to sustain their business without requiring governmental supports or public donations (Di Domenico et al., 2010). Symbolic management enables social enterprises to reach other resources. However, most empirical studies regarding resource acquisition of enterprises have considered tangible resources such as financial capital and carried out in the US context (Rawhaouse et al., 2017). This book chapter contributes to the entrepreneurship literature by examining one of the most critical intangible resource types, symbolic resources. It also extends our knowledge of how resource acquisition takes place out of the US context.

The third contribution of this study is regarding the source of data. Online environments such as websites and social media appear as a fruitful data source for scholars (Kozinets, 2019), particularly after social distancing because of the pandemic (Lobe et al., 2020). Moreover, management scholars widely use online sources of data to understand and explain "symbolic repertoires of different groups of interest" (Kozinets, 2018:385). Therefore, this chapter exemplifies using online data to study symbolic management and possibly inspires other entrepreneurship researchers to use this data source in their studies.

In this chapter following the introduction section, the authors review the literature regarding hybrid organizations and their dual mission conflicts. The authors introduce Bourdieu's notions of capital in the next section as an approach that supports developing the framework. Next, the authors give information regarding the case selection, data collection, and analytic approach in the methodology section before presenting the developed framework and the results in the findings and discussion section. Finally, the authors write their concluding remarks, limitations, and future research in the last part.

DIVERSE EXPECTATIONS IN HYBRID ORGANIZATIONS

Scholars have long been examining how hybrid organizations deal with their dual mission conflicts that arise through developing a self-sustaining business without undermining their social value creation. These organizations satisfy these diverging expectations by deploying different practices that may cause internal tensions, inconsistency with the external expectations, which may lead to the organization's failure (e.g., Tracey et al., 2011). On the other hand, studies have shown that hybrid organizations utilize various internal and external strategies and tools to manage this double-edged sword.

For example, the research shows that hybrid organizations resolve conflicts of dual missions internally with their human resources' capabilities and implement a flexible managerial approach. Siebold, Günzel-Jensen, and Müller (2018) have examined social enterprises in their early stages regarding human resource formation. The study has shown that the founders' emotional attachment to their missions helps them balance social and economic objectives, empowering one another. In another study, Battilana and Dorado (2010) have studied two microfinance organizations and explored how these organizations balance two conflicting logics. They expressed that such hybrid organizations can develop an organizational identity through hiring and socializing practices that facilitate to diminish tensions arising from dual missions to maintain their business. Costanzo et al. (2014) show that social enterprises, on the one hand, build up a disadvantaged workforce, indicating they care about societal problems and, on the other hand, empower them to deploy economic value creation activities. Also, social enterprises combine executers from various skills and knowledge sensitive to diverging objectives. Embracing a flexible managerial approach can help hybrid organizations lessen internal tensions when deploying contradictory activities. For example, social enterprises blend social and economic missions in their business plans and make managerial decisions accordingly (Costanzo et al., 2014). Gümüsay et al. (2020) show that hybrid organizations comprehend diverse practices, offer different choices, and foster openness to new ideas as their managerial philosophy.

Furthermore, hybrid organizations employ various strategies to convince external stakeholders to prioritize social problems while carrying out economic activities. These balancing strategies require managing symbolic meanings to some extent. Di Domenico, Haugh, and Tracey (2010) have found a new type of bricolage called persuasion. Social enterprises use this tactic to influence other stakeholders regarding the legitimacy of acquired resources and leveraging new ones. Accordingly, social enterprises communicate the message that these economic resources are useful for social value creation. Pache and Santos (2013) investigate four social enterprises running under competing logics. They show that social enterprises embrace the *trojan horse* tactic to gain legitimacy if they perform under a contested logic. These illegitimate organizations adopt symbolic behaviors to meet the expectations in the field and gain resources. A study investigating conflicting logics in an Islamic bank Gümüsay, Smets, and Morris (2020), reveals that hybrid organizations use presentational sources including artifacts, pictures, and statements carrying different symbolic meanings to resolve conflicts arising from multiple logics. Ramus et al. (2020) show that social enterprises' symbolic actions focusing on social and economic values vary as the time unfolds within a sequence determined according to stakeholders' demands.

Therefore, studies considering external sources of dual mission balancing have exerted that symbolic meanings are central in convincing others about the organization's ability to carry out conflicting missions. To be deemed legitimate in this context, symbolic meanings are used and manipulated (Zott & Huy, 2007) by hybrid organizations. According to the dominant order's expectations in the field, symbolic management relies on skillfully adopting and communicating meanings of the resources at hand. This process requires analyzing how existing resources are converted to meanings and expressed in the transmission channels as texts, statements, reports, and images to manifest a legitimate position of the enterprise in the field.

BOURDIEU'S NOTIONS OF CAPITAL

Bourdieu's notions of the capital provide a rich theoretical basis while examining relations of varying resources and their conversion to symbolic power expressing legitimacy (Tatli et al., 2014). According to Bourdieu (1986), actors accumulate objectified and embodied forms of available resources as different capital types. There are four types of capital: economic, social, cultural, and symbolic, and these are convertible into one another.

Economic capital is regarding material forms of resources accrued over time, such as commodities, physical and financial resources (Everett, 2002). Economic capital is the basis of all other forms of capital and can be converted to others easily (Bourdieu, 1986). Social capital is regarding the social network comprised of stable relationships and reciprocal recognition that provide resources to the owner (Bourdieu, 1986). The third form of capital is the cultural capital that covers three sub-categories, such as embodied, objectified, and institutionalized. Embodied cultural capital is slowly accumulated over time from an external source through learning and experiencing and mostly gained unconsciously. Objectified cultural capital is the material expression of culture valued in a particular field and conditioned to possess embodied capital. Institutionalized cultural capital manifests itself through certificates and recognition, implying trustworthiness in a specific field (Borudieu, 1986). The last type is symbolic capital representing the legitimacy of all other forms of capital and accumulated as celebrity, reputation, and prestige (Bourdieu & Wacquant, 1992; Bourdieu, 1993). Therefore, symbolic capital is the most valuable capital form as the owner has the power to "impose [...] the legitimate vision of the world" (Everett, 2002:63).

The entrepreneurship literature exerts that new enterprises can convert different forms of capital to symbolic capital (e.g., Pret et al., 2016) and impose their vision to shape the field and meet with external stakeholders (e.g., De Clercq & Voronov, 2009). As there is a substantial overlap between their findings, potential research can reconcile the studies regarding hybrid organizations' strategies to convince external stakeholders by symbolic management and entrepreneurship studies relying on Bourdieu's notions of capital. Accordingly, social enterprises can convert their economic, social, and cultural capital to develop symbolic capital through symbolic management and convince external stakeholders to generate economic and social value according to their expectations. Relying on this framework, the authors examine social enterprises' symbolic management activities in their web pages and social media accounts.

METHODOLOGY

The authors have conducted a qualitative study (Dyer & Wilkins, 1991) by examining online channels of social enterprises. Qualitative research is useful for performing exploratory studies (Denzin & Lincoln, 2018; Gehman et al., 2018) and identifying emerging patterns (Flick, 2008). Collecting data from multiple sources helps researchers to reveal similarities and differences between online channels of social enterprises. In this way, scholars can capture novelties in the data.

Case Selection

The authors selected 38 social enterprises as cases from the report (The Impact Investing Ecosystem in Turkey, 2019) on stakeholder mapping and preliminary analysis for impact investing in Turkey. The UNDP (United Nations Development Programme) Istanbul International Center for Private Sector in Development team prepared this report in partnership with the Republic of Turkey Investment Office. The Turkish startup ecosystem is growing year after year, and, more recently, new social enterprises have started to emerge in this ecosystem. Among 45 biggest economies, Turkey is listed as 11th in the ranking of 2019 Youth Poll by Thomson Reuters under "The Best Countries to Be a Social Entrepreneur" (Thomson Reuters Foundation, 2019).

The Impact Investing Ecosystem in Turkey (2019) report lists more than 9.000 social enterprises, where 38 of them are startups. Moreover, these social enterprises pursue different Sustainable Development Goals (SDGs). This diversity is essential to capture as much variety as possible from the data and make a broader exploration of the focal phenomena (Eisenhardt & Graebner, 2007). Names of these social enterprises and their SDGs are in Table 1.

Table 1. List of Social Enterprises

Enterprise Name	SDGs
Airqoon	Sustainable Cities & Communities
Atık Nakit	Responsible Consumption & Production
Baby Academy	Quality Education
BacPolyZym	Responsible Consumption & Production
B-fit	Good Health & Well Being
BillionToOne	Good Health & Well Being
Biolive	Responsible Consumption & Production
Devecitech	Affordable & Clean Energy, Sustainable Cities & Communities
E-Bursum	Quality Education
Enevo	Responsible Consumption & Production
Engelsiz Çeviri	Reduced Inequalities
Evreka	Sustainable Cities & Communities, Responsible Consumption & Production
Fazla Gıda	No Poverty
Gane On Biotech	Good Health & Well Being
Givin	Quality Education, Responsible Consumption & Production
Haus Free Dry	Responsible Consumption & Production
Joon	Zero Hunger, Reduced Inequalities
Kodluyoruz	Quality Education, Decent Work & Economic Growth, Reduced Inequalities
MentalUP	Quality Education
Minorpreneurs	Quality Education
Mobilmed	Good Health & Well Being
Naturansa	Responsible Consumption & Production
Nymbly	Good Health & Well Being
Otsimo	Quality Education
Positive Energy	Affordable & Clean Energy
Reengen	Affordable & Clean Energy
Reflect	Responsible Consumption & Production
Sensgreen	Affordable & Clean Energy, Responsible Consumption & Production
Tarfin	No Poverty, Decent Work & Economic Growth
Tarlamvar	Zero Hunger, Decent Work & Economic Growth
Tolkido	Quality Education, Reduced Inequalities
Toma Biosciences	Good Health & Well Being
Toyi	Quality Education
Tutumlu Anne	Responsible Consumption & Production
Ubitricity	Responsible Consumption & Production
Uplifters	Good Health & Well Being
Vansan	Responsible Consumption & Production
Vivoo	Good Health & Well Being

Data Collection

The authors have preferred taking netnography as the method, as it provides data relevant to the research question, which relies on social enterprises' symbolic management. Social enterprises' online channels complement their business by revealing particular instantiations of managerial decisions and strategies. Accordingly, the authors performed a "symbolic netnography" (Kozinets, 2018:394), supporting theory-building scholars.

The authors collected qualitative data from web sites and social media accounts (Kozinets, 2018) of selected social enterprises. Social media accounts include Facebook, Instagram, Twitter, and LinkedIn pages of these social enterprises. The authors collected information from the whole web site and some particular parts of the social media accounts such as: about sections and cover photos for Facebook, bio section for Instagram, profile picture and pinned tweets for Twitter, about section and background photo for LinkedIn accounts. These social media accounts are relatively stable and communicate information regarding how the account owner wants to be perceived by the followers and visitors.

The number of entries extracted from websites, Facebook, Instagram, Twitter, and LinkedIn accounts is 215, 97, 68, 87, and 54, respectively, reaching a total of 521. One entry can be a sentence, a paragraph, or a visual. The data generated from these entries amounting to nearly 120 A4 pages with double line space.

Data Analysis

The authors find out constructs regarding the symbolic management of social enterprises through conducting an inductive data analysis. They followed the Gioia methodology while coding the empirical data (Gioia et al., 2012). By coding the content of web sites and social media accounts, the authors developed first-order concepts, second-order themes, and aggregate dimensions. The data's systematic analysis provides qualitative rigor and helps to represent the links between data and insights gathered from the data.

The first two authors of the study have performed open coding for fifteen social enterprises. While generating first-order concepts, the authors distilled the data as few as possible. Following that, the first two authors coded the rest of the data separately and then discussed their results together until agreement. Similarly, second-order themes and aggregate dimensions are developed, questioned, and discussed between the authors.

The data structure is in Table-2. By carrying out a systematic inductive approach, the authors identified four symbolic action categories that converted cultural, social, and economic capital to symbolic capital. These four categories have 11 sub-categories. As the aim is to cover all alternative ways of symbolic management via online channels, analyzed social enterprises' online content represents at least one of these categories and sub-categories.

Table 2. Data structure

First-order Concepts	Second-order Themes	Aggregate Dimensions
Showing solutions for the social problem	Knowledge and experience	Domain expertise
Applying global best practices to solve a social problem		
Relating solution with reports of global organizations and governmental strategic plans		
Information about the social problem by focusing on its direct effects	Raising awareness	
Information about the social problem by linking it with a more topical social problem		
Information about the social problem by showing quotations from people affected by the problem		
Personal social media accounts of the team members	Qualifications of the team	
Team members background showing academic career		
Sustainability related benefits of using a solution for a social problem	Material benefits of the product/service	The credibility of the product/service
Health-related benefits of using a solution for a social problem		
Economic benefits of using a solution for a social problem		
Social benefits of using a solution for a social problem	Non-material benefits of the product/service	
Cultural benefits of using a solution for a social problem		
Capabilities of the product/service used for the social problem	Product/service technical information	
Use-case presentation of the product/service with pictures and videos		
Trophies & Awards owned by the enterprise	Evidence of success	
News regarding the enterprise on the media and social media		
Case studies of customers/partners and customer feedbacks		
Access to expertise regarding a social problem	Contribution of partners	Collaboration and cooperation
Joint activities with other organizations and governmental bodies		
Partners of the enterprise providing perks		
Logo's showing affiliation with non-profit and for-profit organizations	Ties with other organizations	
Information of affiliation with non-profit and for-profit organizations		
Information about investments	Managerial competence	Commercialization potential
Information about affiliated acceleration programs and incubators		
Information regarding the potential market size		
Information regarding customer segments		
Call to action to buy the product/service	Revenue generation	
The difference from the competitors regarding price and qualities		
Showing customers of the product/service		
Price information regarding the product/service		

FINDINGS AND DISCUSSION

The framework that the authors developed, relying on the data analysis, is shown in Figure 1. Non-symbolic forms of capital take the form of symbolic capital when they are "grasped through categories of perception" (Bourdieu & Wacquant, 1992: 119), and entrepreneur is an "active shaper" (Zott & Huy, 2007:100) of perceptions. Therefore, social enterprises convert cultural, social, and economic capital to symbolic capital through symbolic management. Social enterprises make use of various communication channels for symbolic management, and in this study, the authors analyzed enterprises' online channels.

The social capital accumulated through symbolic management supports the enterprises to convince others about their adequacy to manage dual missions. Dual missions are the social value proposition and economic value proposition (Austin et al., 2006). The authors also argue that acquired resources are accumulated and expand the enterprise's cultural, social, and economic capital as time unfolds, like the studies mentioning the recursive nature of resource acquisition (e.g., De Clercq & Voronov, 2009).

Figure 1. Symbolic management for social enterprises

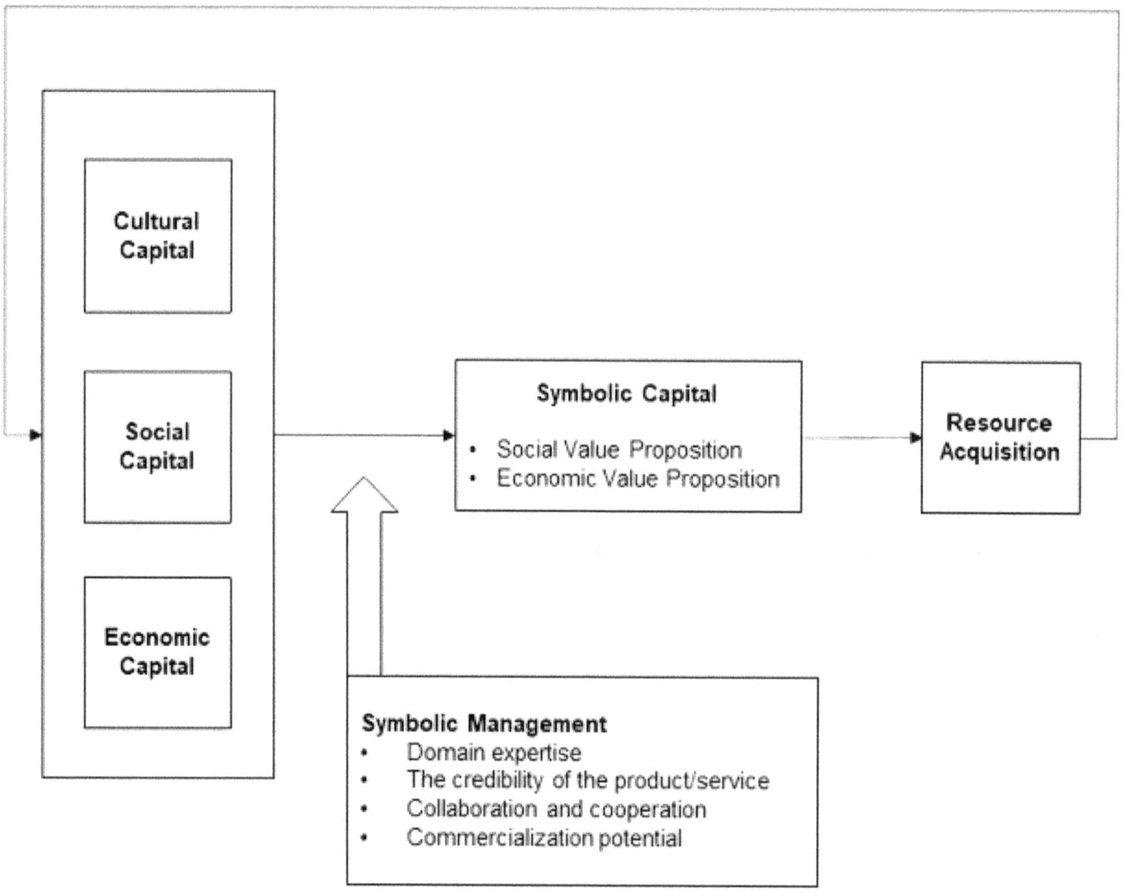

Domain Expertise

Domain expertise represents the extensive know-how in the social enterprise about the reasons and consequences of a particular social problem and its ability to carry out activities relying on this repertoire.

Symbolic management by displaying domain expertise is essential to convert the social enterprise's embodied cultural capital to symbolic capital. Accordingly, social enterprises communicate their adequacy in providing the social value proposition, which affords a source of legitimacy (Ramus et al., 2020). Moreover, expertise in the focal social problem meets the field's social welfare logic (Pache & Santos, 2013). Therefore, social enterprises convince their stakeholders, depending on their legitimacy, to provide resources that support them to grow their business and social impact further.

First of all, social ventures convey their knowledge and experience by symbolic management and represent their domain expertise in analyzing and solving social problems. They share their solution relating it with scientific information and the most up-to-date approaches to the social situation. Accordingly, they highlight they are performing best practices technical wise. Social entrepreneurs also link their solutions with the broader context by mentioning global organizations' reports and governments' long-term strategic plans. In this way, they imply their vision and activities are parallel with other bodies in the field that have a broader impact.

Furthermore, most social enterprises have placed a blog section on their web pages to share various external bodies' information regarding the social problem. These blog posts inform the website visitors and raise awareness about the social situation in detail, mostly through referring scientific knowledge and statistics. The content of the blog posts varies among the direct and indirect effects of the social problem. The authors identified that several social enterprises draw the links between Covid 19 and their focal social problem. In this way, they create more awareness, as people are already experiencing Covid 19 Pandemic's consequences. In addition to this, social enterprises share quotations from people who suffer from the focal social problem. Overall, they raise awareness by introducing information gathered from outside their organization that counts on scientific knowledge and ordinary people's lives with various audiences.

As of last, social enterprises convey their domain expertise indirectly by sharing the qualifications of the team. Social enterprises may prefer showing all the team members or founders and co-founders on the home page or a sub-page. If these team members have an academic background, they also mention their academic titles. Moreover, social enterprises can disclose their team members' social media accounts as these people use their personal social media pages to share information regarding the focal social problem.

The Credibility of the Product/Service

Social enterprises' embodied cultural capital represents itself in a materialized form as objectified cultural capital (Lee & Shaw, 2016). Accordingly, the product or service's credibility facilitates converting objectified cultural capital to symbolic capital. Social enterprises manage this by showing various texts and visuals regarding their online channels' products or services. The findings show that this symbolic management category has four foundations.

Material benefits cover the sustainability, health-related, and economic benefits of the offered product or service. Sustainability and health-related benefits support social enterprises in converting their objectified cultural capital to symbolic capital and developing social value propositions as these benefits mostly touch on society's wellbeing. On the other hand, texts and visuals about the product's economic benefits support social enterprise's economic value propositions. By introducing economic benefits, social enterprises attempt to express how they provide financial support to disadvantaged groups, reduce costs, and increase efficiency. Similar to sustainability and health-related benefits, non-material benefits of the product or service, including social and cultural advantages, support the enterprise's social impact. However, in addition to converting objectified cultural capital to symbolic capital, the product's economic benefits may include direct financial support from the social enterprise to disadvantaged groups. Therefore, this kind of symbolic management also covers converting economic capital to symbolic capital.

Moreover, social enterprises convey their product or services' credibility by presenting their capabilities through technical information, including numbers and statistics. They also share screenshots and pictures of their products and services and, if available, outcomes generated by them. Entrepreneurs engage in such symbolic actions to imply their solutions are working and can deal with problems on the focus (Zott & Huy, 2007). As social entrepreneurs need to manage both social and economic missions, representing how good they are in solving problems supports them in emphasizing social and economic value propositions. In this way, social enterprises convert their objectified cultural capital and accumulate symbolic capital.

Social enterprises also present the achievements relying on their products and services in their online channels as evidence of their success and convert institutionalized cultural capital to symbolic capital. Trophies and awards have an essential role in assigning legitimacy to organizations' innovative activities (Monteiro & Nicolini, 2015). Accordingly, attending contests is a widely preferred activity in the entrepreneurship ecosystem to gain legitimacy (Zott & Huy, 2007). Social enterprises inform their followers and customers regarding the prizes they have won to improve their credibility. Moreover, they share the news referring to their organization in the mainstream media or show social media posts of publicly recognized people mentioning their organization. Therefore, they reinforce their trustworthiness in the field. Another way of doing this is by displaying case studies from customers and partners using the social enterprise's products or services and posting feedback of customers. All of these symbolic activities support both the social and economic value proposition of social entrepreneurs.

Collaboration and Cooperation

Social enterprises collaborate and cooperate with other organizations and individuals that enhance their social impact and resolve the problems arising from scarce resources (Pearce, 2003). Di Domenico et al. (2010) show that successful social ventures use social bricolage and their networks to perform resource-poor environments. So, this symbolic management activity helps to convey they are not walking alone while dealing with social problems and convert the social enterprises' social capital to symbolic capital. In online channels of social enterprises, others collaborate and cooperate in two ways.

As first, social enterprises inform their followers and users about the contribution of their partners while delivering their products and services. They give detailed information about their network's expertise, share pictures, videos, and news regarding joint activities with partners or governmental bodies, and show perks provided to them by partner organizations to persuade others. The authors find out that most of their partner organizations are municipalities and non-profits that are the most prominent social enterprises (e.g., Korosec & Berman 2006; Lumpkin et al., 2013). As these organizations' primary goal is to generate positive social impact, this kind of symbolic management strengthens social enterprises' social value proposition.

Secondly, social enterprises show logos of affiliated for-profit and non-profit organizations on their web sites and give information about the relationship with these associated bodies in their social channels. In addition to the non-profit partner organizations contributing to the delivery of products and services mentioned above, social enterprises also show their ties with for-profit organizations such as venture capitals. Accordingly, these symbolic management activities can support both the social and economic value proposition of social enterprises.

Commercialization Potential

Although social enterprises' primary focus is on social impact, field incumbents also expect financial self-sufficiency (Austin et al., 2006) and should emphasize their knowledge about managing a business. Therefore, social enterprises need to convey their commercialization potential in their online channels and boost their economic value proposition. According to the findings, social enterprises communicate their commercialization potential in two ways. As first, managerial competence supports the commercialization potential of social enterprises. De Clecq and Voronov (2009) argue that entrepreneurs should show their management skills and knowledge to convince investors and take the risk of investment in an enterprise. In the case of getting investment from investors, social enterprises mention this in their online channels. Moreover, social enterprises represent their affiliation with acceleration programs and incubation centers, which train entrepreneurs to develop their managerial skills.

The knowledge regarding the spread of social impact, including market size and customer segmentation, is another managerial competence. In their online channels, social enterprises show how many people suffering from a particular social problem can be supported by the offered product or service. This number indicates the potential market size. Furthermore, social enterprises can provide detailed information about their customer segments and sometimes offer different solutions and products to these groups.

Signaling revenue generation activities is another way of communicating commercialization potential. In most web pages, the authors find out a call to action to purchase the product or service. Moreover, some social enterprises integrate payment services to their websites to ease the purchasing and do not miss any opportunity if someone is willing to pay for the product or services and share price information. Furthermore, some enterprises prefer to compare and contrast their products and services with their rivals. Moreover, social enterprises may demonstrate their customers on their websites. Such activities are in line with commercial logic (Ramus et al., 2020) and imply that social enterprise has the knowledge to generate revenue.

So, all of these symbolic actions in the online channels support social enterprises to convert their embodied cultural capital regarding their managerial competence to symbolic capital. Moreover, as integrating payment systems needs investment, it is possible to argue that social ventures convert their economic capital to symbolic capital that supports their economic value proposition.

Overall Evaluation of the Framework

The developed framework shows that symbolic management activities help social enterprises convert their cultural, social, and economic capital to symbolic capital. Symbolic capital helps social enterprises to gain legitimacy and exercise power to convince their stakeholders. In this way, social enterprises manage their dual mission relying on social and economic impact.

The relationships between symbolic management categories, different forms of capital, and value proposition affected by the conversion are in Table 3. According to the findings of the study, the conversion rates of cultural, social, and economic capital differ among symbolic management categories in parallel to the study of Pret et al. (2016). As an overall evaluation, it is possible to argue that social enterprises most commonly transform their cultural capital into symbolic capital by using their online channels.

Table 3. Relationships between symbolic management, forms of capital, and value proposition

Symbolic Management Category	Conversions between forms of capital	Contribution to the value proposition
Domain expertise	· Embodied Cultural Capital to Symbolic Capital	· Social Value Proposition
The credibility of the product/ service	· Objectified Cultural Capital to Symbolic Capital · Institutionalized Cultural Capital to Symbolic Capital · Economic Capital to Symbolic Capital	· Social Value Proposition · Economic Value Proposition
Collaboration and cooperation	· Social Capital to Symbolic Capital	· Social Value Proposition · Economic Value Proposition
Commercialization potential	· Embodied Cultural Capital to Symbolic capital · Economic Capital to Symbolic Capital	· Economic Value Proposition

The research shows that examined enterprises convert their embodied cultural capital to symbolic capital by implying their domain expertise and commercialization potential. Moreover, commercialization potential also indicates the conversion of economic capital to symbolic capital. On the other hand, symbolic management relying on the credibility of the product or service converts objectified cultural capital, institutionalized cultural capital, and economic capital to symbolic capital. Collaboration and cooperation activities mentioning in the online channels transform social capital to symbolic capital.

When the relationships between the symbolic management category and contribution to the value proposition are evaluated, it is possible to conclude that while symbolic actions relying on domain expertise promote social value proposition, commercialization potential strengthens the economic value proposition. Moreover, representing the credibility of the product or service and collaboration and cooperation in the online channels boost both social and economic value propositions.

The recursive relationship drawn in the framework has an essential role in managing dual missions and supporting resource accumulation as time unfolds. By performing symbolic management, social enterprises gain various tangible and intangible resources. For example, successfully managing their symbolic environment helps social ventures to represent their expertise and collect economic resources as the customers believe in the social impact of the organization, or by communicating the message that the management works professionally in the organization, new partners can join to the social network of the enterprise. In the end, the successful accumulation of resources boosts the symbolic capital of the social enterprise and help them to manipulate the opinions of others (Lounsbury & Glynn 2001; De Clercq & Voronov, 2009).

CONCLUSION

In this study, the authors explore how social enterprises manage symbolic meanings while pursuing their dual missions. Social ventures as hybrid organizations need to manage their dual-mission conflicts. They can perform this by focusing on the internal and external roots of this problem. The authors take an external perspective in this study and examine the symbolic management activities of social enterprises. Relying on the findings, the authors draw a framework and show how different sources of capital, symbolic management, and resource acquisition relate to each other.

This study contributes to the literature by providing a different perspective in terms of the developed framework explaining the relationship between symbolic management and resource acquisition in the Turkish context. Moreover, the data source of the study has the potential to inspire other researchers as it relies on netnography, which is relatively new in entrepreneurship and management studies. Furthermore, entrepreneurs can realize the importance and role of symbolic management while acquiring resources. Practitioners in the field can benefit from the relationships drawn in the framework and determine their symbolic management strategies by considering this study's insights. Moreover, this chapter is more meaningful in Covid 19 Pandemic times as organizations focus on their online channels because social distancing does not allow any physical activities.

LIMITATIONS AND FUTURE RESEARCH

As symbolic management is in question, online channels provide an excellent source of information regarding such activities. Accordingly, the research question and methodological approach has a good fit and complement each other. However, the study is not free from limitations. Further studies relying on offline sources of data can enrich the understanding of symbolic management in social enterprises.

Moreover, the authors of this study focus on the external environment of hybrid organizations. However, the extant literature highlights that hybrid organizations also deal with the tensions arising from their dual missions by managing conflicts internally. So, the symbolic management of social enterprises to solve internal disagreements will contribute to the literature.

Furthermore, temporality appears as an underexamined and important construct for managing dual missions. Researchers can carry out longitudinal studies to show how symbolic management activities change as time unfolds.

REFERENCES

Austin, J., Stevenson, H., & Wei-Skillern, J. (2006). Social and commercial entrepreneurship: Same, different, or both? *Entrepreneurship Theory and Practice*, *30*(1), 1–22. doi:10.1111/j.1540-6520.2006.00107.x

Bacq, S., & Eddleston, K. A. (2016). A Resource-Based View of Social Entrepreneurship: How Stewardship Culture Benefits Scale of Social Impact. *Journal of Business Ethics*, 1–23.

Barbosa, A. M. (2020). What's in a Hybrid? Framing, Meaning, and Symbols in Hybrid Organizing. *The Academy of Management Annals*, *2020*(1), 20690. Advance online publication. doi:10.5465/AMBPP.2020.20690abstract

Battilana, J., & Dorado, S. (2010). Building Sustainable Hybrid Organizations: The Case of Commercial Microfinance Organizations. *Academy of Management Journal*, *53*(6), 1419–1440. doi:10.5465/amj.2010.57318391

Bourdieu, P. (1986). The Forms of Capital. In J. G. Richardson (Ed.), *Handbook of Theory and Research for the Sociology of Education* (pp. 241–258). Greenwood Press.

Bourdieu, P. (1993). *The Field of Cultural Production*. Polity Press.

Bourdieu, P., & Wacquant, L. J. D. (Eds.). (1992). *An Invitation to Reflexive Sociology*. University of Chicago Press.

Costanzo, L. A., Vurro, C., Foster, D., Servato, F., & Perrini, F. (2014). Dual-Mission Management in Social Entrepreneurship: Qualitative Evidence from Social Firms in the United Kingdom. *Journal of Small Business Management*, *52*(4), 655–677. doi:10.1111/jsbm.12128

Dacin, M. T., Dacin, A. P., & Tracey, P. (2011). Social Entrepreneurship: A Critique and Future Directions. *Organization Science*, *22*(5), 1–11. doi:10.1287/orsc.1100.0620

De Clercq, D., & Voronov, M. (2009). Role of cultural and symbolic capital in entrepreneurs' ability to meet expectations about conformity and innovation. *Journal of Small Business Management*, *47*(3), 398–420. doi:10.1111/j.1540-627X.2009.00276.x

Denzin, N., & Lincoln, Y. S. (2018). Introduction: the discipline and practice of qualitative research. In N. Denzin & Y. S. Lincoln (Eds.), *The Sage Handbook of Qualitative Research*. Sage.

Di Domenico, M., Haugh, H., & Tracey, P. (2010). Social bricolage: Theorizing social value creation in social enterprises. *Entrepreneurship Theory and Practice*, *34*(4), 681–703. doi:10.1111/j.1540-6520.2010.00370.x

Dyer, W. G. Jr, & Wilkins, A. L. (1991). Better stories, not better constructs to generate better theory: A rejoinder to Eisenhardt. *Academy of Management Review*, *16*(3), 613–619. doi:10.5465/amr.1991.4279492

Eisenhardt, K. M., & Graebner, M. E. (2007). Theory building from cases: Opportunities and challenges. *Academy of Management Journal*, *50*(1), 25–32. doi:10.5465/amj.2007.24160888

Everett, J. (2002). Organizational Research and the Praxeology of Pierre Bourdieu. *Organizational Research Methods*, *5*(1), 56–80. doi:10.1177/1094428102051005

Gehman, J., Glaser, V. L., Eisenhardt, K. M., Gioia, D., Langley, A., & Corley, K. G. (2018). Finding Theory–Method Fit: A Comparison of Three Qualitative Approaches to Theory Building. *Journal of Management Inquiry*, *27*(3), 1–18. doi:10.1177/1056492617706029

Gioia, D. A., Corley, K. G., & Hamilton, A. L. (2012). Seeking Qualitative Rigor in Inductive Research: Notes on the Gioia Methodology. *Organizational Research Methods*, *16*(1), 15–31. doi:10.1177/1094428112452151

Gras, D., & Lumpkin, G. T. (2012). Strategic Foci in Social and Commercial Entrepreneurship: A Comparative Analysis. *Journal of Social Entrepreneurship*, *3*(1), 6–23. doi:10.1080/19420676.2012.660888

Gümüsay, A. A., Smets, M., & Morris, T. (2020). "God at Work": Engaging Central and Incompatible Institutional Logics through Elastic Hybridity. *Academy of Management Journal*, *63*(1), 124–154. doi:10.5465/amj.2016.0481

Korosec, R. L., & Berman, E. M. (2006). Municipal support for social entrepreneurship. *Public Administration Review*, *66*(3), 448–462. doi:10.1111/j.1540-6210.2006.00601.x

Kozinets, R. V. (2018). Netnography for Management and Business Research. In C. Cassell, A. L. Cunliffe, & G. Grandy (Eds.), *The SAGE Handbook of Qualitative Business and Management Research Methods* (pp. 384–397). Sage.

Kozinets, R. V. (2019). *Netnography: The essential guide to qualitative social media research* (3rd ed.). Sage.

Lee, R., & Shaw, E. (2016). Bourdieu's non-material forms of capital: Implications for startup policy. *Environment and Planning C. Politics and Space*, *34*(8), 1734–1758.

Lobe, B., Morgan, D., & Hoffman, K. A. (2020). Qualitative Data Collection in an Era of Social Distancing. *International Journal of Qualitative Methods*, *19*, 1–8. doi:10.1177/1609406920937875

Lounsbury, M., & Glynn, M. A. (2001). Cultural Entrepreneurship: Stories, Legitimacy and the Acquisition of Resources. *Strategic Management Journal*, *22*(6-7), 545–564. doi:10.1002mj.188

Lumpkin, G. T., Moss, T. W., Gras, D. M., Kato, S., & Amezcua, A. S. (2013). Entrepreneurial processes in social contexts: How are they different, if at all? *Small Business Economics*, *40*(3), 761–783. doi:10.100711187-011-9399-3

Monteiro, P., & Nicolini, D. (2015). Recovering Materiality in Institutional Work: Prizes as an Assemblage of Human and Material Entities. *Journal of Management Inquiry*, *24*(1), 61–81. doi:10.1177/1056492614546221

Pache, A. C., & Santos, F. (2013). Inside the Hybrid Organization: Selective Coupling as a Response to Competing Institutional Logics. *Academy of Management Journal*, *56*(4), 972–1001. doi:10.5465/amj.2011.0405

Pearce, J. (2003). *Social Enterprise in Anytown*. Calouste Gulbenkian Foundation.

Pret, T., & Carter, S. (2017). The importance of 'fitting in': Collaboration and social value creation in response to community norms and expectations. *Entrepreneurship and Regional Development*, *29*(7), 639–667. doi:10.1080/08985626.2017.1328903

Pret, T., Shaw, E., & Drakopoulou-Dodd, S. (2016). Painting the Full Picture: The Conversions of Economic, Cultural, Social and Symbolic Capital. *International Small Business Journal*, *34*(8), 1004–1027. doi:10.1177/0266242615595450

Ramus, T., Vaccaro, A., & Berrone, P. (2020). Time Matters! How hybrid organizations use time to respond to divergent stakeholder demands. *Organization Studies*. Advance online publication. doi:10.1177/0170840619900341

Rawhouser, H., Villanueva, J., & Newbert, S. (2017). Strategies and Tools for Entrepreneurial Resource Access: A Cross-Disciplinary Review and Typology. *International Journal of Management Reviews*, *19*(4), 473–491. doi:10.1111/ijmr.12105

Semeen, H., & Islam, M. (2020). Social impact disclosure and symbolic power: Evidence from UK Fair Trade Organizations. *Critical Perspectives on Accounting*, (102182), 102182. Advance online publication. doi:10.1016/j.cpa.2020.102182

Siebold, N., Günzel-Jensen, F., & Müller, S. (2018). Balancing dual missions for social venture growth: A comparative case study. *Entrepreneurship and Regional Development*, *31*(9-10), 710–734. doi:10.1080/08985626.2018.1554710

Tatli, A., Vassilopoulou, J., Özbilgin, M., Forson, C., & Slutskaya, N. (2014). A Bourdieuan Relational Perspective for Entrepreneurship Research. *Journal of Small Business Management*, *52*(4), 615–632. doi:10.1111/jsbm.12122

Istanbul International Center for Private Sector in Development. (2019). The Impact Investing Ecosystem in Turkey. United Nations Development Programme.

UNDP's Istanbul International Center for Private Sector in Development. (2019). *The Impact Investing Ecosystem in Turkey.* Retrieved from https://www.iicpsd.undp.org/content/dam/istanbul/docs/The%20Impact%20Investing%20Ecosystem%20in%20Turkey_final.pdf

Thomson Reuters Foundation & Deutsche Bank. (2019). *The best countries to be a social entrepreneur*. Retrieved from https://poll2019.trust.org/

Tracey, P., Phillips, N., & Jarvis, O. (2011). Bridging institutional entrepreneurship and the creation of new organizational forms: A multilevel model. *Organization Science*, *22*(1), 60–80.

Tunçalp, D., & Le, P. L. (2014). (Re)Locating boundaries: A systematic review of online ethnography. *Journal of Organizational Ethnography*, *3*(1), 59–79.

Yitshaki, R., & Kropp, F. (2016). Entrepreneurial passions and identities in different contexts: A comparison between high-tech and social entrepreneurs. *Entrepreneurship and Regional Development*, *28*(3), 206–233.

Zott, C., & Huy, N. (2007). How Entrepreneurs Use Symbolic Management to Acquire Resources. *Administrative Science Quarterly*, *52*(70), 70–105.

Chapter 4
Social Enterprises as Hybrid Organisations:
Balancing of Value Creating and Value Capturing

Mehlika Saraç
Bursa Uludağ University, Turkey

ABSTRACT

Social enterprises are organizations that seek to achieve social goals through innovative and social value-creating activities. However, besides their social objectives, they are confronting financial and resource-based challenges in the markets to provide their sustainability. The tension between these dual objectives leads organizations to focus on one of the strategies value-creating or value capture. However, in recent years, hybrid organizing is seen as an alternative way of balancing dual objectives. Thus this study aims to understand how hybrid social enterprises perform well and create social impact. A qualitative descriptive single case study approach will be used to analyze a hybrid organization and its consequences.

INTRODUCTION

There is now a growing belief that social enterprises play an important role in creating economic and social value. Social entrepreneurs who are motivated by social problems rather than solely making profits increase the quality of life in social and cultural aspects. Social enterprises can develop innovative solutions to social needs unfulfilled by either private enterprise or the public sector (Leadbetter, 1997). However, in addition to their social objectives, like any entrepreneur, social entrepreneurs have to present in the market and create sustainable and productive organizations by reaching valuable resources and developing capabilities that will maximize their outputs and outcomes (Bacq&Eddleston,2018).

According to the British Council's "Status of Social Initiatives in Turkey" research report (2019) there are more than 9000 social enterprises. % 83.6 percent of social enterprises are established by

DOI: 10.4018/978-1-7998-4727-4.ch004

entrepreneurs highly educated and they are expecting to grow. Unfortunately, the report also indicated that 38.3 percent of the social enterprises survived less than one year, 45.2 percent lasted 1-3 years, 8.7 percent lasted 4-6 years, 2.6 percent lasted 7-10 years and 5.2 percent lasted more than 10 years as a company. These numbers point out the sustainability problem of social enterprises. The failure of a social enterprise is much more sensitive than that of a traditional company. Because, when a social enterprise fails, it not only fails its employees and investors and the population it intended to benefit also affected negatively (Gasca, 2017). Thus most of the government policies intended to support and encourage social enterprises to grow, to become more sustainable organizations (Phillips, 2006).

Many researchers distinguish social enterprises from corporate enterprises by emphasizing the realization of social goals rather than economic gains (Austin et al., 2006, Santos, 2012) However, the paradox is, one of the main reasons for the failure of social enterprises is the lack of sustainable funding and they are seeking non-grant revenue to survive (Phillips, 2006; Dees, Emerson and Economy, 2001). Social entrepreneurs aim to create social value while also confronting financial challenges by exploiting market-based solutions and by utilizing a wide range of resources (Bacq & Janssen, 2011).

Besides on this rational explanation about the need of economic interest of social enterprises, drawing on institutional theory, Dart, (2004) believes that logic of the capitalist system', market political and ideological values highly affect the social economy through a process of isomorphism and the social enterprises are getting similar to profit-oriented enterprises close to market logic. However, it can be argued that the capitalist system is also affected by a social movement. For example, even most renowned capitalists, Bill Gates, the founder of Microsoft, argued a new form of capitalism: ''Such a system would have a twin mission: making profits and also improving lives for those who don't fully benefit from market forces.''(Certo & Miller, 2008). The interaction of both logic can be seen as the basis of hybrid social organizations, which will be discussed further.

Santos (2012) explain the sustainability of social enterprises by using *value capture* and *value creation* concepts. He recognizes that there is a tension between value creation and value capture. The emphasis on one of them allows for the differentiation of entrepreneurial activities. Considerable studies indicated that these two different missions create significant tension and occur on a two side continuum where at one end, social entrepreneurs are solving social problems as reflected in the social mission. However, at the other end of the continuum, social entrepreneurs prioritize profit-making that lead to neglect the social component of their organizations (Munoz and Kimmitt, 2019) When social entrepreneurs overemphasize the economic business component, this is often described as "mission drift" (Cornforth, 2014). Thus, evidence suggests that entrepreneurs adopt particular strategies such as stakeholder engagement, to mitigate the effects of this drift (Ramus & Vaccaro, 2014).

However, it is also suggested that social entrepreneurs can have dual objectives as social and economic missions and they try to achieve these two missions alongside. The social mission represents its main normative purpose and making the business economically functional is a more utilitarian objective (Moss, Short, Payne, & Lumpkin, 2011). Munoz and Kimmitt (2019) also argued that mission drift seems not to be the only possible outcome for those social entrepreneurs prioritizing economic goals. Social entrepreneurs can indeed remain competitive without drifting away from their social orientation. They indicated that there is a symbiotic link between the dual objectives (social and economic) where social mission works as a competitive advantage that allows social entrepreneurs to remain competitive through their social mission; social missions actually improve financial performance, and one does not necessarily compromise the other. A new idea growing that *"values are divided between the financial and the societal, but this is a fundamentally wrong way to view how we create value. Value is whole. The world is not divided into corporate bad guys and social heroes." (NYU Stern School of Business)*

Briefly, the problem "whether a social enterprise should aim for value capture or value appropriation to increase its chances of impact investment or prevent mission drift by avoiding value capture" was discussed well in the literature. It seems a new alternative, hybrid organizations rising rapidly and takes the attention of both academics and practitioners. There is a growing number of studies focusing on hybrid organizations and posit a new question about their performance and social impact (Munoz & Kimmett, 2019; Díaz-Correa & López-Navarro, 2018; Mitra et al., 2019; Doherty et al., 2014). Some studies have mentioned that hybrid organizing leads to economic-sustainability, efficiency and aids the redistribution of economic resources (Santos et al., 2015; Mitra et al., 2017; Wilson and Post, 2013). However, more studies from different contexts will make valuable contributions to literature.

Thus, the main purpose of this chapter is to advance an argument about how hybrid social enterprises perform well for promoting social entrepreneurs' goals and investigate the effect of dual objectives on social enterprise's sustainability and social impact and highlight the opportunities and challenges of a hybrid 'social enterprise'. Thus a qualitative descriptive single case study approach will be used to analyze a hybrid organization and its consequences.

The chapter is structured as follows. The key concepts of social enterprise, value creation, value capture are defined. Next controversial academic literature related to dual objectives of social entrepreneurship is presented to explore the potential role of balancing dual objectives on social enterprise's sustainability and their social impact. The methods section outlines the case study approach and introduces the case study organization used to explore the positive effect of balancing economic and social objectives. In the discussion and conclusion part, results gained from the case are fused with the background information.

BACKGROUND

In recent years social entrepreneurship, a subdiscipline within the field of entrepreneurship, has gained increasing attention from entrepreneurship scholars. The 2006 Nobel Prize given to Muhammad Yunus and the Grameen Bank of Bangladesh for their extraordinary efforts to promote economic and social development in the poorest sections of society, drew attention to the concept of 'social entrepreneurship' throughout the world. With the support of foundations such as Ashoka, Schwab and Skolls, many traditional civil society organizational forms such as non-profits, non-governmental organizations (NGOs), charities as well as for-profit enterprises have begun to identify themselves as 'social enterprises', because of the ambiguity surrounding its definition (Trivedi, 2010)

Although ''there are fundamentally different conceptions and interpretations of the concept of social entrepreneur and the entrepreneurial role (Venkataraman, 1997), focus on social value is consistent across various definitions of social entrepreneurship (Dees, 1998; Austin et al., 2006; Nicholls, 2008). Social value is defined as 'basic and long-standing needs of society' (Certo & Miller, 2008). Austin et al.(2006, p. 2) define social entrepreneurship as ''innovative, a social value-creating activity that can occur within or across the nonprofit, business, or government sectors.''. Social entrepreneurship involves the recognition, evaluation, and exploitation of opportunities that result in social value rather than profit generation and personal wealth (Austin et al., 2006). It is suggested there is two main point difference between social and commercial entrepreneurship (Bacq & Janssen, 2011, p.379). Social entrepreneurship has a strong social mission, whereas commercial entrepreneurship has a mission of profit. Second, the major part of the economic profit generated by the commercial activities of the social venture will need to be reinvested in the social mission, whereas in a traditional commercial venture, profit will be distributed to shareholders or reinvested in the commercial activities of the company. According to Boschee (1995), social entrepreneurship is the action of balancing moral imperatives and the profit motives – and that balancing act is the heart and soul of the movement.

To highlight the importance of balancing social mission and profit interest on social enterprise sustainability, it is also essential to understand the positioning of social enterprises in the contemporary economy (Phillips, 2006). According to Polanyi's (1977) notion of the economic principles of the market, the economy can be roughly divided into three co-existing systems such as (1) Private profit-oriented (2) Public service planned provision, (3) Self-help mutual social purpose. The private sector (or market economy) based on competition, focused on individual gain and with the goal of profit maximization. Public, operating through compulsory deductions such as taxation and organized around notions of the welfare state. As seen in figure 1, Pearce (2003) positions social enterprise within the third system which is based on reciprocity. It is is a particular type of circulation of goods and services among groups or individuals that signifies social connections, based on gifts or donations. It is different from the market exchange as it is regulated by human relationships rather than price mechanisms, and different from the redistributive exchange because it is not imposed (Phillips, 2006).

Thus social enterprises are different from private enterprises because they generate profit without profit maximization goal and they are also different from the public sector because they are independent of public authorities. However, they need to use market relations in their operations such as selling services and goods and have benefited from redistributive relations by utilizing government funding to finance their services. It is suggested that social enterprise's long-term sustainability is highly related to their ability to 'continuously hybridize these three poles of the economy. Also, isomorphism is seen as inevitable if social enterprises fail to balance these three poles (Laville & Nyssens, 2001).

Characteristics of a social entrepreneur are highly related to their outcomes and value creation nature of social entrepreneurship. However, it is argued that organizations don't have dichotomous outcomes, social entrepreneurs were considered on a continuum, that is, from purely social to purely socio-economical (Mair & Martí, 200). Wei-Skillern et al. (2007) defined social entrepreneurship as 'an innovative, social value-creating activity that can occur within or across the nonprofit, business, or government sector. This definition extends the boundaries of social enterprises and emphasizes the innovative aspect of social enterprises that creates social value, regardless of output and company structure. According to this approach, social entrepreneurship is commonly seen as a hybrid organization that combines elements of commercial and social sector organizations and maximization of the dual objective of ventures lead to hybrid organizing (Munoz and Kimmet (2019). In hybrid organizing, different institutional logics are combined in new ways (Battilana & Dorado, 2010). Hybrids are an organizational form combined of business and social purpose and defined as "enterprises that design their business models based on the alleviation of a particular social or environmental issue. They generate income and attract capital in ways that may be consistent with for-profit models, nonprofit models, or both" (Haigh et al., 2015, p. 5).

An important part of the scholars on social entrepreneurship maintains the effectiveness of dual objectives and hybrid organizations. For example; Martin and Osberg (2007, p. 35) submit that as long as social entrepreneurs' value propositions target a disadvantaged population there is no problem with aiming at turning a profit. Mair and Martı´ (2006) advocate the advantages of mixing social ventures and profit aims, while Kramer & Porter (2011) maintain that profit coupled with societal benefit is a higher form of profit. Munoz and Kimmet (2019) analyze social and economic goals in hybrid organizations and they indicated that the social mission of a hybrid venture may produce a competitive advantage in both the presence and the absence of economic priorities depends on different strategic conditions.

Figure 1.

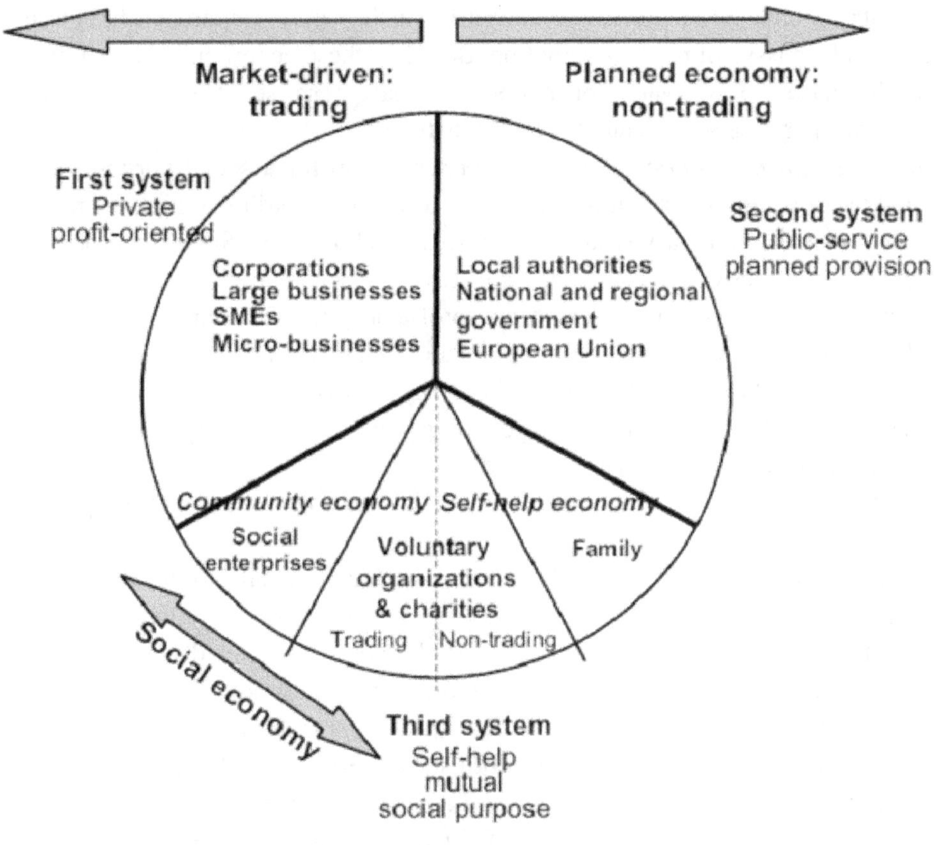

However, it is a controversial issue and there is a different point of views in the literature. Santos (2012) criticized this approach and he put social entrepreneurship in an analytical framework that has two ends of continuum consisting of value capture and value creation. He recognizes that there is a tension between value creation and value capture. Value creation happens when the utility of society's member's increases when resources used in this activity and value capture happens when the focal actor capture portion of the value created by the activity. Value creation is related to social outcomes while value capture is related to economic outcomes. He posits that social entrepreneurs maximize not on value capture, but on value creation, only satisficing on value capture to fuel operations and reinvest in growth. According to his theory, these two different dimensions do not complement each other well. The emphasis on either one or the other draws from the specific identity of an organization that allows for the differentiation of entrepreneurial activities. Since maximizing both value creation and value capturing in the same organizational unit is difficult, organizations need to choose one or the other and be clear in communication their choice. Rather than many hybrid alternatives, there is only one form of organization that fulfills Santos's criteria of maximizing value creation, while satisficing value capture and that is the social enterprise. Agafonow (2014) criticized his theory because shifting the focus away from the organization. Contrary to Santos, Agafonow maintains that by refocusing the theory on the organizational level and away from the system it is possible to understand that not all organizational solutions available to social entrepreneurs can create value, and not all value capture strategies can serve a social goal.

Bacq & Janssen, (2011) suggested that these different conceptions of social enterprises are due to differences between American and European conceptions of the social entrepreneurship. They observe that the different geographical perspectives mainly differ in the way they approach the enterprise concept, the legal form, and the issue of profit distribution. Based on these geographical perspectives, they have defined three different schools towards conceptions of social enterprises. These are (1) Social innovation school, (2) Social enterprise school, and (3) EMES network.

According to *social innovation school,* Enterprises set up for a social purpose but operating as businesses and in the voluntary or non-profit sector. However, according to him, the main world of the social entrepreneur is the voluntary sector (Thompson, 2002, pg.413). Social enterprises enact hybrid non-profit and for-profit activities (Dart, 2004, pg.415) and Social entrepreneurship can be seen to take many different organizational forms: for-profit, non-profit, or hybrid (Mair and Marti, 2004, pg.7). Social enterprises have a social purpose; assets and wealth are used to create community benefit; they pursue this with trade in a market place; profits and surpluses are not distributed to shareholders; 'members' or employees have some role in decision making and/or governance; the enterprise is seen as accountable to both its members and a wider community; there is a double- or triple-bottom-line paradigm: the most effective social enterprises demonstrate healthy financial and social returns (Thompson and Doherty, 2006, pg.362).

According to Social Enterprise School, the ventures started by social entrepreneurs typically fall into one of two categories: on the one hand, an 'affirmative business' is created to provide real jobs, competitive wages and career opportunities and ownership for people who are disadvantaged, whether it be physically, mentally, economically or educationally (the portion of disadvantaged employees is typically 60% or higher); on the other hand, a 'direct-service business' is kids, battered women, etc. [. . .] almost all of them emerge in some way from the non-profit sector (Boschee, 1995, pg.2)

Finally, according to the EMES network, social enterprises are organizations with an explicit aim to benefit the community, initiated by a group of citizens and in which the material interest of capital investors is subject to limits.

Based on this literature review above, it is seen that it is a kind of strategic choice for social enterprises to being pure value-oriented, profit-oriented, or some level of hybrid. It is very little known how these choices affect the sustainability and social impact of social enterprises. There is also a call for researches investigating these issues on an organizational level (Trivedi & Stokols,2011). Austin *et al.* (2006) called for further research to examine how the characteristics of SEs affect their management, particularly concerning mission and resource mobilization. It is also suggested that learning from successful and impactful social entrepreneurship in different countries and contexts would inform understanding of the influence of institutional conditions on the emergence of hybrid organizations? (Doherty et al., 2014). This chapter full fills this gap by focusing on dual objectives and hybrid organizations and tries to understand their structure and outcome linkages. For this purpose, a descriptive case study on hybrid organizing and balancing the dual objectives of social entrepreneurship will be presented and discussed in the next sections.

MATERIAL AND METHODS

A descriptive case study approach is followed to examine how a social hybrid organization has implemented a sustainable business model aiming to find a solution for food waste, carbon emission, and climate change. Using a single case is a common method in qualitative research to addressing why and how questions where little prior knowledge is available (Yin, 1994). Also, the literature review indicated that similar researches in the hybrid organization field preferred the same descriptive single-case study method (Alberti&Baron, 2017; Díaz-Correa & López-Navarro, 2018)

The data were collected from mixed sources which become the complementary data for each other (Yin 2014). The use of several sources of information (primary and secondary) improves the validity of the study. The primary method is semi-structured interviews. Two personal in-depth interviews were conducted with one of the company's founders and the product manager. The information was given via email and online call. The secondary sources were collected from the company's official web site, published articles, other websites, videos, news, and social media- Facebook, Instagram, Linked, and Twitter.

WHOLE SURPLUS CASE: SOCIAL ENTERPRISE AS HYBRID ORGANIZATIONAL MOTIVATION OF THE WHOLE SURPLUS AS A SOCIAL ENTERPRISE

Globally it is known that 1/3 of the produced foods end up as waste. In Turkey, 2 billion € worth foods are being wasted as well with an estimated 60% still being edible. Although this surplus food waste itself is a big cost to businesses in the food sector, there are also hidden costs come along such as warehousing, logistics, and demolishing these waste foods. Moreover, there is a 100% tax deduction incentive in Turkey for the foods to be donated instead of throwing away. To bring a creative solution to this global problem, which has an economic, ethical and environmental aspect "Whole Surplus", was founded by Olcay Silahli and Arda Eren as

A Privately Held company with nearly 50 employees. Following the United Nations global goals for sustainable development (2015), they focus on the problem of food waste which threat the world by starvation and 8% of the carbon emission that leads to climate change.

It is officially established in 2016 with the challenging vision of *"reducing food waste in the food supply chain by 50% until 2030, by using technology-based solutions"*. From the first day, they have started to create food waste awareness in the private sector, and try to be a good example of this responsible action and encourage its partners and new startups in this mission.

Business Model of Whole Surplus

The business model of Whole surplus (fig.2) is based on four modules. These are; **(1)** Food Donation **(2)** Commissioned Resale **(3)** Recycling and **(4)** Animal feed. Whole Surplus also provides data analysis applications to its customers.

Figure 2.

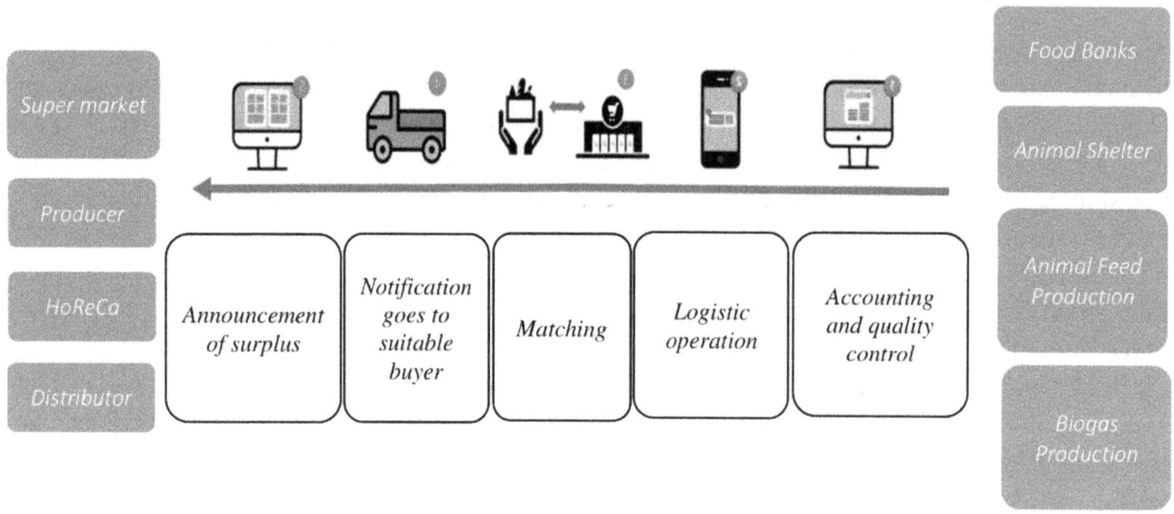

Donation platform is providing professionals in the food industry the opportunity to offer their unsold but safe-to-eat products online to food banks. Food industry professionals can donate safe-to-eat products that are discarded at an earlier stage due to several reasons such as not conforming to the norm in shape, being close to selling best by date, which although perfectly healthy. (Foodbank is a non-profit, charitable organization that distributes food to those who have difficulty purchasing enough food to avoid hunger.) With this donation, Food industry professionals provide a 30% income tax reduction and give a commission to the whole surplus. Also, food industry professionals pay a membership fee to the platform. There is no charge to Foodbanks.

As a second, with the commissioned resale module, the whole surplus expands its product to e-commerce for surplus foods between businesses to utilize foods considering sell best by date and other constraints through right redistribution and matching. This system will also make an advantage to the buyer side such as a Hotel or a catering firm to buy food close to sell best by date at discount and prevent food waste by consuming in a short period which is a new era of smart buying for HoReCa channel operators.

Finally, food industry professionals may choose recycling and animal feed modules by paying a membership fee to the platform.

The Focus of Organizational Objective

The whole surplus believes that profit-making companies and the private sector are as responsible as other institutions to solve social problems and they should change their business model. By reducing food waste, they have fulfilled three important sustainable development goals; responsible consumption and production, zero hunger, and climate action, on the other side they have supported the circular economy.

The whole surplus defined itself as

The whole Surplus is an effective waste management platform for businesses. It creates economic and social value from surplus food by managing the unsold products (food) of the businesses in the most effective way.

This definition highlights its hybrid structure and focuses on social values as well as economic values. The product manager of whole surplus mentioned that;

We all have the same goal, no hungry people remain in the world. It does not matter which connections and ways we use to reach those who need it. Respond to the partner's goal, move forward .. the main goal is not to leave hungry people.

Balancing and Managing Dual Objectives

The whole surplus product manager explained their dual objectives as below;

The whole surplus doesn't see social and economic goals as competing goals. Company goals are not a two end of the continuum. Whole surplus's success factor is achieving and balancing both goals at the same time.

Also surplus take the advantage of dual goals, they mentioned that sometimes economic and social goals conflict.

When economic and social goals coincide, The whole surplus always acts for social purposes. For example, in the food recovery pyramid, although global competitors prefer landfilling and burning, this method does not include in the business model of the whole surplus in line to reduce carbon emissions by 50 percent. Even, the whole surplus has the goal of reducing the use of this method. No action is taken that contradicts our social goal.

Structuring of The whole surplus helps to balance dual goals.

The whole surplus works as an Inc. It provides its workforce from salaried employees rather than volunteers, but it is ensured that everyone working with us has similar social values.

The whole surplus set up its food rescue association. Such a structuring helps in managing different corporate logic. We have a colleague in the head of the food rescue association... Being a catalyzer in the Food Bank ecosystem is one of the goals of the Whole surplus. Currently, we work with 47 active food banks and plans to add 80 more food banks to its network.

Performance / Social Impact

The whole surplus was one of the 9 startups and the only Turkish startup that was supported by the united nations development program (undp) the accelerate 2030 program. And it was invited to geneva social good summit in 2017. It is considered as one of the most valuable local ventures. After one year from its foundation, in May, 60 thousand dollars investment was received from 500 Istanbul. After this investment, the venture has received an investment of 120 thousand euros from the Metro Retail Accelerator powered by Techstars Berlin program, and finally received its third investment of 2.2 million TL. Finally, in 2019, Galata Business Angels invested

450 thousand dollars in the Whole surplus which was the highest investment in one round in Galata Business Angels history. In 2018, while ensuring food recovery in 19 cities of Turkey, the amount of food saved reached 1600 tons. In 2019, with the collaboration with Nestle Turkey in less than a year, the whole surplus turned 1550 tons of food into benefit with a donation, animal feed production, and biogas and protected the world and environment by preventing 735 tons of carbon emissions. The Product manager mentioned the Whole surplus social impact as below,

Since the platform is technology-based, social impact can be measured easily. For 2020, 1.1 million people received donations on the platform.

Mutually Beneficial Relationships with Stakeholders

The whole surplus serving a B2B Food Surplus Management System, which aims to maximize the donation of surplus foods to food banks with "food for people" priority and to maximize the tax break for retailers through donations. Their ambition is to minimize waste at the source by additionally providing data analytics. This provides a sustainable financial model that helps its stakeholders to profit from social work. It has business partnerships with 40 companies (70% of them are global and 30% are local.) in 36 cities such as Migros, Metro, Kipa, Uludağ İçecek, Pinar, Golf, Juico, Feast, Maritim, CarrefourSA and supported by several private companies and foundations such as UNDP, Accelerate2030, Impact Hub Istanbul, Mercedes-Benz, Sabancı Vakfı, Kelly Deli, P.O.Y.D. In addition to private companies, the whole surplus cooperates with 15 municipalities and 25 non-governmental organizations, foundations, and associations.

DISCUSSION AND CONCLUSION

The tension between value creation and value capture strategies of social enterprises is highly emphasized in literature (Santos, 2012). However, this study suggested that rather than suffered from this tension, there is another way of creating value: hybrid organizations. The whole Surplus is a revealing case of an innovative hybrid company that creates important social value in three main areas (1) responsible consumption and production (2) zero hunger (3) climate action and enhances sustainable development.

What makes the Whole Surplus so successful as a hybrid social enterprise is considered the shared value it offers to stakeholders through their Business to Business (B2B) food surplus management system. By working with retailers, food banks, producers, distributors, and recyclers, the Whole Surplus maximizes donations of surplus foods to food banks and minimizes waste at the source through smart data analytics technologies. This case is important to understand that business model that offers shared value to many stakeholders in a creative way is very crucial as the social value itself. Literature provides evidence that hybrid organizations can develop more creative and innovative management processes that help to bridge with stakeholders effectively (Doherty et al., 2014).

It is also obvious that the Whole Surplus set enough balance between social/welfare logic (value creation) and market/commercial logic (value capture). Lack of balance and overemphasize the economic business component lead to mission drift and negative consequences (Ramus & Vaccaro, 2014). The position of the enterprise as a connector rather than selling the product directly, reduce the emphasis on its economic aspect, and helps to sustain a balance between social/welfare logic.

It is suggested that hybrid organizations have been successful in engaging angel investors and attract different types of investor whose values align with those of the organization (Mitra et al., 2019). The Whole Surplus social business model had been very successful in attracting angel investors in each year. These investments played a major role in accelerating the enterprise by providing necessary financial flow.

Although the results of this research give insight, it has some limitations. This study focused on a hybrid organization in the specific case of a social enterprise. A single-case study reduces the generability of findings as compared to the multiple-case studies.

When evaluating the effectiveness of hybrid organizations, this study didn't consider the environmental variables such as the entrepreneurial ecosystem . However, these environmental factors take an important role in the social impact created by social enterprise. Therefore, ignoring these variables is another weakness of the study.

REFERENCES

Agafonow, A. (2014). Toward a positive theory of social entrepreneurship. On maximizing versus satisficing value capture. *Journal of Business Ethics, 125*(4), 709–713. doi:10.100710551-013-1948-z

Alberti, F. G., & Varon, M. A. (2017). Can profit and sustainability goals co-exist? New business models for hybrid firms. *The Journal of Business Strategy, 38*(1), 3–13. doi:10.1108/JBS-12-2015-0124

Austin, J., Stevenson, H., & Wei-Skillern, J. (2006). Social and commercial entrepreneurship: Same, different, or both? *Entrepreneurship Theory and Practice, 30*(1), 1–22. doi:10.1111/j.1540-6520.2006.00107.x

Bacq, S., & Eddleston, K. A. (2018). A Resource-Based View of Social Entrepreneurship: How Stewardship Culture Benefits Scale of Social Impact. *Journal of Business Ethics, 152*(3), 589–611. doi:10.100710551-016-3317-1

Bacq, S., & Janssen, F. (2011). The multiple faces of social entrepreneurship: A review of definitional issues based on geographical and thematic criteria. *Entrepreneurship and Regional Development, 23*(5-6), 373–403. doi:10.1080/08985626.2011.577242

Bansal, S., Garg, I., & Sharma, G. D. (2019). Social entrepreneurship as a path for social change and driver of sustainable development: A systematic review and research agenda. *Sustainability, 11*(4), 1091. doi:10.3390u11041091

Battilana, J., & Dorado, S. (2010). Building sustainable hybrid organizations: The case of commercial microfinance organizations. *Academy of Management Journal, 53*(6), 1419–1440. doi:10.5465/amj.2010.57318391

Boschee, J. (1995). Social entrepreneurship. *Across the Board, 32*(3), 20–25.

Certo, S. T., & Miller, T. (2008). Social entrepreneurship: Key issues and concepts. *Business Horizons, 51*(4), 267–271. doi:10.1016/j.bushor.2008.02.009

Cornforth, C. (2014). Understanding and combating mission drift in social enterprises. *Social Enterprise Journal, 10*(1), 3–20. doi:10.1108/SEJ-09-2013-0036

Dart, R. (2004). The legitimacy of social enterprise. *Nonprofit Management & Leadership, 14*(4), 411–424. doi:10.1002/nml.43

Dees, J. G. (1998). Enterprising nonprofits: What do you do when traditional sources of funding fall short. *Harvard Business Review, 76*(1), 55–67. PMID:10176919

Dees, J. G., & Anderson, B. B. (2003). For-profit social ventures. In M. L. Kourilsky & W. B. Walstad (Eds.), *Social Entrepreneurship* (pp. 1–26). Senate Hall.

Dees, J. G., Emerson, J., & Economy, P. (2001). *Enterprising Nonprofits: A Toolkit for Social Entrepreneurs*. Wiley.

Díaz-Correa, J. E., & López-Navarro, M. A. (2018). Managing sustainable hybrid organisations: A case study in the agricultural sector. *Sustainability, 10*(9), 3010. doi:10.3390u10093010

Doherty, B., Haugh, H., & Lyon, F. (2014). Social enterprises as hybrid organizations: A review and research agenda. *International Journal of Management Reviews, 16*(4), 417–436. doi:10.1111/ijmr.12028

Gasca, L. (2017). *Why Do Social Enterprises Fail? New Research Reveals Three Reasons (And Some Surprises)*. https://nextbillion.net/why-do-social-enterprises-fail-new-research-reveals-three-reasons-and-some-surprises/

Haigh, N., & Hoffman, A. J. (2014). The new heretics: Hybrid organizations and the challenges they present to corporate sustainability. *Organization & Environment, 27*(3), 223–241. doi:10.1177/1086026614545345

Haigh, N., Walker, J., Bacq, S., & Kickul, J. (2015). Hybrid Organisations: Origins, Strategies, Impacts and Implications. *California Management Review, 57*(3), 5–12. doi:10.1525/cmr.2015.57.3.5

Kramer, M. R., & Porter, M. (2011). *Creating shared value*. FSG.

Laville, J.-L., & Nyssens, M. (2001). The social enterprise: towards a theoretical socio-economic approach. In C. Borzaga & J. Defourny (Eds.), *The Emergence of Social Enterprise* (pp. 312–332). Routledge.

Leadbetter, C. (1997). *The Rise of the Social Entrepreneur*. Demos.

Mair, J., & Marti, I. (2004). Social entrepreneurship: What are we talking about? A framework for future research (No. D/546). IESE Business School.

Mair, J., & Martı´, I. (2006). Social entrepreneurship research: A source of explanation, prediction, and delight. *Journal of World Business, 41*(1), 36–44. doi:10.1016/j.jwb.2005.09.002

Martin, R. L., & Osberg, S. (2007). *Social entrepreneurship: The case for definition*. Academic Press.

Mitra, P., Kickul, J., Gundry, L., & Orr, J. (2019). The Rise of Hybrids: A Note for Social Entrepreneurship Educators. *International Review of Entrepreneurship, 17*(2).

Moss, T. W., Short, J. C., Payne, G. T., & Lumpkin, G. T. (2011). Dual identities in social ventures: An exploratory study. *Entrepreneurship Theory and Practice, 35*(4), 805–830. doi:10.1111/j.1540-6520.2010.00372.x

Muñoz, P., & Kimmitt, J. (2019). Social mission as competitive advantage: A configurational analysis of the strategic conditions of social entrepreneurship. *Journal of Business Research, 101*, 854–861. doi:10.1016/j.jbusres.2018.11.044

Nicholls, A. (Ed.). (2008). *Social entrepreneurship: New models of sustainable social change*. OUP Oxford.

Pearce, J. (2003). *Social Enterprise in Anytown*. Calouste Gulbenkian Foundation.

Phillips, M. (2006). Growing pains: The sustainability of social enterprises. *International Journal of Entrepreneurship and Innovation*, *7*(4), 221–230. doi:10.5367/000000006779111648

Polanyi, K. (1977). *The Livelihood of Man*. Academic Press.

Ramus, T., & Vaccaro, A. (2017). Stakeholders matter: How social enterprises address mission drift. *Journal of Business Ethics*, *143*(2), 307–322. doi:10.100710551-014-2353-y

Santos, F. M. (2012). A positive theory of social entrepreneurship. *Journal of Business Ethics*, *111*(3), 335–351. doi:10.100710551-012-1413-4

Thompson, J., & Doherty, B. (2006). The diverse world of social enterprise: A collection of social enterprise stories. *International Journal of Social Economics*, *33*(5-6), 361–375. doi:10.1108/03068290610660643

Trivedi, C. (2010). Towards a social ecological framework for social entrepreneurship. *The Journal of Entrepreneurship*, *19*(1), 63–80. doi:10.1177/097135570901900104

Trivedi, C., & Stokols, D. (2011). Social enterprises and corporate enterprises: Fundamental differences and defining features. *The Journal of Entrepreneurship*, *20*(1), 1–32. doi:10.1177/097135571002000101

Venkataraman, S. (1997). The distinctive domain of entrepreneurship research: An editor's perspective. In J. Katz & R. Brockhaus (Eds.), Advances in entrepreneurship, firm emergence, and growth vol. 3: Firm emergence and growth (pp. 119—138). Greenwich, CT: JAI Press.

Wei-Skillern, J., Austin, J. E., Leonard, H., & Stevenson, H. (2007). *Entrepreneurship in the social sector* (Vol. 13). Sage.

Wilson, F., & Post, J. E. (2013). Business models for people, planet (& profits): Exploring the phenomena of social business, a market-based approach to social value creation. *Small Business Economics*, *40*(3), 715–737. doi:10.100711187-011-9401-0

Yin, R. K. (1994). *Case Study Research: Design and Methods*. Sage Publications.

Chapter 5
The Role of Societal Culture in Social Innovation:
Creating Social Value via Social Entrepreneur Standpoint

Gaye Karacay
https://orcid.org/0000-0003-2465-0297
Istanbul Technical University, Turkey

ABSTRACT

Being at a development stage, the social innovation literature needs further contributions that would help to comprehensively find out the enablers of social innovation especially within macro level. Since the nature of social innovation is cumulative as well as interactive, the micro level practices of individual social innovation initiatives add up to the general patterns at the macro-level. On account of the fact that shared values among members of a society bring about similar expectations, perceptions, and behavioral patterns, it is essential to explore how various societal cultural attributes contribute to social innovation capacities of countries. This study aims to explore an evidence of the influence of societal culture on social innovation, specifically by shaping the perceptions of social entrepreneurs for social value creation. By discussing the relationship between societal culture and social innovation in a conceptual manner along with developing research propositions, this study offers a new direction for future research.

INTRODUCTION

In today's world, there has been revolutionary transformations in technology, business world and thus in the daily lives of individuals. The pace and the depth of these ongoing changes necessitate a rapid adaptation on the side of individuals, societies, and economic and social systems. Driven by these adaptation requirements, much more pervasive economic and societal problems have come in to the picture; and what is worse, these novel problems cannot be solved merely by governmental interventions and

DOI: 10.4018/978-1-7998-4727-4.ch005

public assets like done before. Therefore, a perspective change is required for developing effective and sustainable solutions for these problems.

Social innovations mostly keen on offering sustainable solutions for meeting societal needs that are not covered by the commercial market forces (Austin, Stevenson, Wei-Skillern, 2006). By providing novel solutions to societal problems, social innovations contribute to the welfare in a given community (Peredo & McLean, 2006), and so create social value (Moulaert, et. al, 2005). There is no standard definition of social innovation upon which all counterparts have totally agreed on; but the projects aligned with social innovation are characterized by social value creation which is the outcome of social need fulfillment through the development of innovative solutions that is transformational in social aspect (Mulgan, et al., 2007).

Any innovation process starts firstly with an exploration of an unmet need and then a solution proposal for meeting that need. Social entrepreneurs mainly aim to offer an unconventional way of developing innovative solutions for today's pervasive social, economic and environmental problems. Driven by the goal of developing sustainable novel solutions for societal problems, social entrepreneurs collaborate with various stakeholders in society and perform target-oriented activities with this purpose in their mind. Adopting an innovative perspective for fulfilling unmet societal needs, these collaborative efforts ensue social innovations to happen (Mulgan, Tucker, Ali, & Sanders, 2007).

Although theorized mostly through an economic perspective, the value concept necessitates also a sociological perspective since the perception of value depends on the receiver whose perceptions shaped by value systems (Pitelis 2009). In view of that, understanding the motives of social entrepreneurs necessitates also an understanding of individual values. Individual values are contingent upon a bigger value system imposed by societal environment. Members of a society perceive and understand the world by means of the values and norms in their culture, and behave accordingly (Singelis & Brown, 1995). Therefore, societal cultural norms and values are likely to be an important factor in shaping the perspectives of social entrepreneurs.

In the extant literature, the studies on social innovation mostly explored micro level elements of social innovation, while there is only a few study that focused macro-level contextual factors. Being one of a few, the study by Krley and colleagues point to the importance of the contextual conditions which are societal climate, resources, political, regulative and normative environment as part of a three layered social innovation system (Krlev, Bund & Mildenberg, 2014).

The current study aims to explore the relationship between societal culture and social entrepreneurship in a conceptual manner in order to display the significance of macro level contextual factors on social innovation process. In view of that, the literature on social innovation, social entrepreneurship, societal culture was investigated in order to comprehend how attributes of societal culture influence social innovation along the process stages of social innovation. While exploring the association among social innovation and societal culture, the main focus was on exploring the effect of societal culture on the social value perspectives of social entrepreneurs. Based on the literature review, the research propositions were developed to be tested by future empirical studies.

By discussing the relationship between societal culture and social innovation in a conceptual manner along with offering research propositions, this study presents a new direction for future research; and so it contributes to the social innovation and social entrepreneur aspects of the theory. Besides, this study provides an insight to practitioners in realising the importance of societal culture on social innovation via the effects on social entrepreneurs' activities.

LITERATURE REVIEW

Social Innovation

Unlike past, the amount and the variety of resources needed for developing sustainable solutions for economic, social and environmental problems have increased enormously. That's why; in today's world the solutions could no longer be offered by a single social system actor, i.e., private companies, public institutions or non-governmental organizations (Murray et al., 2010). In parallel to this requirement, at United Nation's Sustainable Development Summit in 2015, 193 countries accepted to adopt *'The 2030 Agenda for Sustainable Development'* which urges them to take action for 17 Sustainable Development Goals (SDGs). These SDGs, which address the global challenges of poverty, inequality, climate change, environmental degradation, peace and justice, require the joint efforts by public, private, non-governmental and international organizations both at the developing and developed countries (United Nations, 2015).

By adopting a similar point of view, various stakeholders in economic and social systems are making collaborations for developing systemic solutions to multi-dimensional societal problems. In such a background, social innovations whose reason of existence is social value creation by developing sustainable solutions for societal needs via new products, services, models and collaborations, have become much more important than ever (Mulgan, 2006, p. 146).

Basically, social innovations are *"innovations that are social both in their ends and in their means"* (Murray, Caulier-Grice, Mulgan, 2010, p.4). However, in the related literature, there are various social innovation definitions which are derived through different conceptualization perspectives. For instance, according to Mulgan and colleagues, *"social innovation includes innovative activities and services that aim to meet a social need; and the development and dissemination of these innovative activities and services are provided mostly by social-purpose organizations"* (Mulgan, Tucker, Ali, Sanders, 2007, p.8). Phills and colleagues defined social innovation as, *"developing more effective, efficient, sustainable novel solutions for a social problem, and by that creating social value for a social group or society"* (Phills, Deiglmeier, Miller, 2008, p.36). The research project supported by the 7th Framework Program of the European Commission adopted a different perspective for conceptualization of social innovation, and made the following definition, *"social innovations are new solutions (products, services, models, markets, processes etc.) that simultaneously meet a social need (more effectively than existing solutions) and lead to new or improved capabilities and relationships and/or better use of assets and resources. In other words, social innovations are both good for society and enhance society's capacity to act"* (Caulier-Grice, Davies, Patrick & Norman, 2012, p. 18). From another point of view quite different from the others, The European Union Policy Advisors Bureau defined social innovation as *"a factor enhancing the ability of society to mobilize in the axis of equal access to opportunities"* (BEPA, 2011). Alvord and colleagues conceptualized social innovation as *"a context mobilizing ideas, talents, social arrangements and resources that initiate social change required for sustainable development and social welfare to facilitate emergence of novel solutions to societal problems"* (Alvord, Brown, Letts, 2004).

Although there are some differences among the various definitions of social innovation stated in the literature, these several social innovation definitions share a common emphasis regarding the main goal of social innovation to be meeting the unfulfilled social needs and creating social value (Cahill, 2010,p.262).

Social Innovation as a System

Innovations, defined as *"the process to undertake a change in one or more of many aspects of production, distribution, and consumption of economic goods"* (Beije 2000), are critical for the different layers of economic system; that is, for countries' welfare at macro level; and for commercial businesses' competitiveness at micro level (Nelson 1993). Like technological and economical innovations, social innovations also contribute to the economic and social welfare at different layers of the system (Boelman et al., 2014, p. 9). Social innovations contribute to the economic and social system through the cumulative impact they create on fulfilling the unmet social needs by their effective and sustainable solution models (Neumeier, 2012, p. 49).

According to Krlev and colleagues (2014) social innovation is composed of three layered integrated system factors; which are, entrepreneurial activities at micro level, organizational outputs at meso level, and framework conditions at macro level. Each of these layers is operationalized by different system agents. At micro level, entrepreneurial activities include the necessary operations include identification of a social problem, knowledge/idea creation, idea selection, taking risks, realization of ideas, mobilizing resources, initiation of the innovation process, and then maintenance of the solution model. These initial steps are realized through the activities of social entrepreneurs.

In line with Krlev and colleagues' (2014) conceptualization of social innovation system, at the micro layer, the agents are social entrepreneurs who aim to create social value for the public wellbeing and so who recognize the social innovation opportunities and then who initiate social innovations at micro level (Austin, Stevenson, & Wei-Skillern, 2006, p.3). In parallel to this view, some of the social entrepreneurship definitions specifically highlight the agency role of social entrepreneurs. For instance, according to one of the definitions "social entrepreneurship is the construction, evaluation and pursuit of opportunities for transformative social change carried out by visionary, passionately dedicated individuals" (Roberts & Woods, 2005, p.49).

At meso level, social enterprises as organizational entities operate with an aim to develop and sustain innovative solutions for social problems. Social enterprises operate within the framework of a business model (Phillips, Lee, Ghobadian, O'Regan & James, 2015, p.430). These entities need to act in line with the requirements of commercial businesses in order to survive; as well as they need to develop innovative solutions for social problems in line with their reason for existence (Zahra et al, 2008, p.124). Social enterprises, which have the capacity to access and use the most up-to-date technology, knowledge, products and services in an effort to develop new and effective solutions to social problems, are the most important factors in initiating and disseminating social innovation processes (Westley & Antadze, 2010). The research findings confirm that the social innovation capacity in a country drives from the outputs of social enterprise projects by the activities of social entrepreneurs (Krlev, Bund & Mildenberg, 2014, p.202). Therefore, social enterprises as organizational structures and social entrepreneurs as the people who set up these structures are the initiators and operators of social innovation process.

In order to have a successful innovation, not only the physical and financial infrastructure, but also the efficient interactions among stakeholders are among the most critical factors (Wieczorek & Hekkert, 2012, p. 86). In this respect, the functionality of social innovations is contingent upon the cooperation among various actors (Doherty et. al, 2014, p.418). Additionally, such a cooperation among various actors for developing novel and sustainable solutions to social problems also initiate formation of new institutional structures (Karaçay and Alpkan, 2019). However, the emergence of new institutional structures, which would facilitate social innovation process, depends highly on the framework conditions at macro level (Krlev, Bund & Mildenberg, 2014).

According to the institutional approach, the national innovation frame conditions are the most critical factors in promoting innovations (Lundvall, 1988). Lundvall (2007) argues that in order to boost supply of innovations, rather than solely depending on a monetary based supply-push model, a demand-pull model based on nurturing the enabling conditions for innovations are more effective. In line with this reasoning, Krley and colleagues claimed that macro level framework conditions need to be considered as part of social innovation system. They argued that various individual framework conditions can be grouped into societal climate, resources, political, regulative and normative environment (Krlev, Bund & Mildenberg, 2014).

United Nations' 17 Sustainable Development Goals aim to be universal by being applicable both to developing and developed countries (Le Blanc, 2015, p.180). However, the research findings revealed that there is a noticeable difference in the focus, type and scope of social innovations between developing and developed countries (Eichler & Schwarz, 2019, p.9). For instance, in developed countries there are higher occurrence of social innovations related with the SDGs of 'partnerships for the goals' and 'sustainable cities, communities, and good health and well-being'; while in developing countries there are higher occurrence of social innovations related with the SDGs of 'poverty' and 'clean water and sanitation' (Eichler & Schwarz, 2019, p.10). By taking account this observed difference among developed and developing countries in terms of the type and scope of social innovations, it becomes much more clear that, there is a need for investigating the effects of framework conditions on social innovation (Matten & Moon, 2008). However, as being at an early stage of development the social innovation literature lacks the necessary research outputs that clearly demonstrate context-specific enablers of social innovation.

Social Innovation and Social Value

The concept of value and its creation is the focal issue for almost all types of establishments (Lepak, Smith & Taylor, 2007). Both private, public and third sector companies operate with an aim of creating and capturing some kind of a value. The value as a concept is usually theorized through an economic perspective particularly in strategy and management literature (Bowman & Ambrosini, 2000). Within social innovation context, the desired value indicates social value. Social value is mainly defined as enhancing well-being for the earth and its living organisms by fulfilling unmet societal needs (Brickson, 2007, p. 866). Therefore, social value are the wider financial and non-financial impacts on the wellbeing of individuals, groups and society (Erdur & Fındıklı, 2020, p.3). In view of that, the main reason for existence of a social innovation initiative is to create social value via meeting societal needs (Moulaert, et. al, 2005).

Some of the economic and technological innovations may also provide social value through their impact on macro level conditions like unemployment. However, these economic and technological innovations cannot be labelled as social innovation. The main reason for this depends on the requirement that the efforts that initiate and accelerate a social innovation process need to be driven by a desire for providing social value to the society by offering solutions to societal problems, rather than a desire for commercial value creation which is the case in economic and technological innovations (Mulgan et al., 2007, p.8).

Lepak and colleagues (2007) claimed that the value creation sources are multi-layered; and so, society, organizations and individuals need to be integrated into the evaluations of value creation since each represent a source as well as unit of analysis at different layers in social innovation system. Moreover, the interaction based value creation via the associated activities of actors needs also consideration for social innovation (Ramirez, 1999, p.56). Therefore, with regard to social innovation, social entrepreneurs function as the main initiators at micro level via their activities for recognizing the social innovation opportunities and taking the necessary entrepreneurial steps (Tortia, Degavre & Poledrini, 2020).

Social entrepreneurs have a guiding principle of actively doing good for serving collective interests (Fisscher, Frenkel, & Nijhof, 2005). Social entrepreneurs and social enterprises are expected to generate profit and then to reinvest it to the social venture (Harding, 2006, p.5). While the main purpose of commercial entrepreneur is creating profit for private gain, the main purpose of social entrepreneur is creating social value for public gain (Austin, Stevenson, & Wei-Skillern, 2006, p.3). In view of that, the main ambition for a social entrepreneur is increasing social value by contributing to the welfare in a given community, rather than increasing personal wealth (Austin et al., 2006, p.2;).

However, there are also some contradicting views about social entrepreneurs. For instance, although there is a common emphasis on the not-for profit nature of social entrepreneurship, some researchers claim that social entrepreneurship can be for-profit basis (Mair & Marti, 2006, p.39). Since the definition and legal structure of social entities have not been finalized all around the world, the discussions on these issues still continue.

Moreover, on the subject of social entrepreneurs, there are questions which require further research studies in order to be answered comprehensively. One of these questions is, what are the main reasons for social entrepreneurs to prefer social value more than private gain? Individual characteristics can be one of the driving forces, but they are out of the scope of this study. Regarding social innovation process, among macro level framework conditions societal culture requires additional attention, because the existence of a particular social need in a given context develops mostly from the perception of what social needs are; and this perception roots back in societal values and norms (Krlev, Bund & Mildenberg, 2014, p.207). For that reason, in this study, we aim to discuss the effects of societal culture as a driving force for social value creation.

Societal Culture

Societal culture is *"the collective programming of the human mind that distinguishes the members of one human group from those of another"* (Hofstede, 1980, p. 260). One of the most popular definition of societal culture is "shared motives, values, beliefs, identities; and interpretations or meanings of significant events that result from common experiences of members of communities, and are transmitted across age generations (House et al., 2004: 15).

Cultural values indicate the degree to which a society considers a certain type of behavior or action, for instance competition and risk taking versus collaboration to be desirable or not. Cross-cultural research reveals that individual behavior is contingent upon individual values, which have roots in societal cultural backgrounds. Societal culture is a formation that determines how to perceive and behave by means of rules on which members have compromised (Triandis, 1990). Additionally, by having an impact on how an individual bring up, socialize and learn, societal culture shapes the developmental psychology of individuals which would outline individual behavior (Singelis & Brown, 1995). Briefly, societal culture constitutes a general guideline for categorizing and understanding individual viewpoints by referring to norms of larger groups (House et al., 2004).

Cross-cultural researchers tend to describe national culture in terms of value dimensions. Cultural dimensions provide a perspective for explaining how cultural values affect personal values and attitudes of the members of a society; and so offer some answer for why individuals in a specific society behave in a particular way (De mooij, 2017). The most popular frameworks for identifying cultural dimensions are the ones developed by Hofstede (1980), Schwartz (1994), and the GLOBE Project (House, Hanges, Javidan, Dorfman, & Gupta, 2004); and Inglehart and Baker (2000).

Hofstede (1980) asserted that behavioral differences can be traced back to cultural differences. Based on empirical examinations, Hofstede's model of cultural values framework provides five dimensions of cultural variation worldwide; that is, "individualism-collectivism, masculinity-femininity, power distance, uncertainty avoidance and long-/short-term orientation". Later, a sixth dimension "indulgence/restraint" was found by Minkov (2007) and added to Hofstede's model.

Subsequently, some alternative frameworks for the cultural dimensions based on values were developed. Schwartz (1992) defined values as trans-situational life goals that guide human perception and behavior; and claimed that values are closely related to behaviors, social roles and processes. The Schwartz theory of basic values (1994) identifies ten basic personal values that are recognized across cultures.

On the other hand, The GLOBE project (House et al., 2004) examined the cultural dimensions at the social and organizational level. The Globe study focused particularly on the relationship between culture leadership via nine societal culture dimensions; that is, assertiveness, future orientation, gender differentiation, uncertainty avoidance, power distance, individualism-collectivism, in-group collectivism, performance orientation and humane orientation.

Moreover, based on the World Values Survey data, Inglehart and Baker (2000) identified two main dimensions of culture: one reflecting the polarization between traditional versus secular-rational orientations toward authority; and the other indicating the polarization between survival versus self-expression values.

Societal Culture and Social Entrepreneurship

There are many research studies which showed societal culture having a significant effect on entrepreneurship and social entrepreneurship (e.g., Byungku & Louise, 2019; Canestrino, Cwiklicki, Magliocca, & Pawełek, 2020; Puumalainen, Sjögren, Syrja, & Barraket, 2015). By investigating plenty of published papers on societal culture and entrepreneurship, Hayton and colleagues (2002, p. 41) concluded that societal culture affects the rates of entrepreneurship by influencing the supply of potential entrepreneurs. This logic applies also well to social entrepreneurship.

According to Mair and Marti (2006, p.37) social entrepreneurship is a process involving the innovative use and combination of resources to pursue opportunities to catalyze social change as well as address societal needs. Accordingly, social entrepreneurs aim for identifying social welfare solution opportunities which is shaped in a given context including societal culture.

The studies investigating the effect of societal culture on social entrepreneurship displayed various findings. For instance, according to the findings of Kedmenec and Strašek's (2017) research examining the role of societal culture on social entrepreneurship, it is found that in specific framework conditions low masculinity, high short-term orientation and high indulgence cultural attributes are effective on social entrepreneurship efforts.

Puumalainen, Sjögrén, Syrjä, and Barraket (2015) found by their research that there is a negative relationship between power distance cultural attributes and social entrepreneurship, while there is a positive relationship between social entrepreneurship and Inglehart and Baker's (2000) secular-rational values and self-expressive values.

In a similar research focus, Pathak and Muralidharan (2016) found that the high in-group collectivist cultural context is positively associated with social entrepreneurship. Moreover, the findings of a recent research by Canestrino, Ćwiklicki, Magliocca and Pawełek (2020) points to a positive association between social entrepreneurship and gender egalitarianism cultural attributes, and a negative association among social entrepreneurship and uncertainty avoidance cultural attributes.

THEORETICAL FRAMEWORK AND RESEARCH PROPOSITIONS

In reference to commercial entrepreneurship, individual perceptions and preferences are found to be the key determinants of entrepreneurial behavior (Busenitz & Barney 1997). It is also logical to assume a similar condition for social entrepreneurship, that is, individual perceptions and preferences to be main determinants of social entrepreneurship behavior. Established social psychology research clearly demonstrates that perception does not only depend on sensory input, but also subject to various factors that modify perceiver's appraisals (Rauthmann, 2012). That's why; the existence of a particular social need in a given context develops from a normative perception of what social needs are in general, while this perception roots back in societal values and norms (Bodenhausen & Hugenberg, 2009). Moreover, even though the perception of value depends on the sender and the receiver; the rank of value priorities is contingent upon social norms shaped by societal context (Pitelis 2009).

Structuration theory (Giddens, 1984) argues that human agency and social structure are not completely separated from each other, but they are interactively produced together. While behavioral approaches focus on agent's cognitive capacity for interpreting social systems, structuration perspective looks into agent's reflexivity capacity as well as institutional structures enabling and constraining actions ((Sarason, Dean, & Dillard, 2006).). According to structuration theory, since agent is enabled and constrained by the structure, social entrepreneurs are also expected to be subject for such an effect of the context. Therefore, social innovation happens through interaction among agents, institutional structures, and social systems (Cajaiba-Santana, 2014)

The agency role of social entrepreneurs for social innovation is a phenomenon that is commonly accepted in the literature (Roberts & Woods, 2005). Social entrepreneurs' activities that initiate and mobilize social innovation include identification of a social problem, knowledge/idea creation, idea selection, risk taking risks, realization of ideas, mobilizing resources, and initiation and maintenance of the innovation process (Krlev et al., 2014). The main driver for social entrepreneurs is fulfilling unmet social needs and so increase public welfare and wellbeing (Austin et. al, 2006). Social entrepreneurs mainly aim to serve collective interest, make improvements in the lives of individuals and as a whole society, and so create social value for the public wellbeing (Austin et. al, 2006, p.3). However, there are also opinions that advocate social entrepreneurs to aim for private gain together with creating and sustaining social value (Dees,1998; Peredo & McLean, 2006). Social entrepreneur's aspiration for private gain along a spectrum of non-private gain to private gain would in turn shape the social enterprises business level strategy. In line with structuration theory, social innovation happens through interaction among social entrepreneurs, and social systems. In case the social system prioritizes the social value creation more than private gain, then social entrepreneurs are likely to be affected from this contextual condition. On the other hand, when the social system prioritizes the private gain, then social entrepreneurs may have more freedom to choose their value aspirations. In case, this freedom results in higher private gain preference over social value creation on the side of social entrepreneurs, then social innovation is shaped via such a preference.

The point reached as a result of the above discussions brings us to the main research question of the current study, which is, *"How does national culture enable or constrain social innovation via its effect on social entrepreneurs' value creation preferences?"*.

Research Propositions

Members of a culture perceive and understand the world by means of their common cultural perspective (Triandis, 1990). Various social perception variables have been found to differ between countries because of the differences in cultural attributes, for instance. individualistic versus collectivistic value orientations (Triandis, 1990). Subjective well-being, which denotes one's emotional and cognitive evaluations of personal life with a specific reference to happiness, fulfillment and life satisfaction, is found to be contingent not only upon individual personality dispositions but also on societal cultural attributes (Diener, Oishi, & Lucas, 2003). Although economic conditions may explain some of the differences in subjective well-being between countries, the research findings indicate that most of the differences are attributable to the common norms and values in the cultural context dictating appropriateness and relative importance of feelings (Diener, Oishi, & Lucas, 2003; Hamamura, Heine & Paulhus, 2008). Moreover, there are more research findings displaying the moderation effect of societal culture on the relationship between individual personality characteristics and one's life satisfaction (Schimmack, Radhakrishnan, Oishi, & Dzokoto, 2002). In line with these research findings, the potential impact of social culture on the motivation and decisions of social entrepreneurs becomes much clearer (Byungku & Louise, 2019).

Entrepreneurial desires are shaped by the context (Schmutzler, Andonova & Diaz-Serrano, 2019). The research findings of Mitchell and colleagues (2002) showed that the environment, more specifically national culture, frames entrepreneurs' cognitive approach, that is entrepreneurs' knowledge structures and mental models used to make judgements and decisions for opportunity evaluation, venture creation and growth (Mitchell, Smith, Morse, Seawright, Peredo, & McKenzie, 2002). Social entrepreneurs, mainly aim to serve collective interest and create social value for the public wellbeing (Austin et al, 2006). The identification of opportunities for social value generation is also found to be context-specific (Baker, Gedajlovic, & Lubatkin, 2005). The notion of value and its creation necessitate a sociological perspective due to the fact that it is the value priorities of the focal source which would conceptualize values and their relative rankings (Pitelis 2009, p. 1118). In other words, the perception of value differs by the target or user of value, and also by how the value is conceptualized and prioritized. Accordingly, the perception of social value may vary in line with the cultural context, so it is likely that the efforts of social entrepreneurs that aim to generate social value may differ by societal cultural values (Puumalainen, Sjögren, Syrja, & Barraket, 2015).

Societal culture brings about constraints and availabilities for social innovation process by setting the value priorities (Krlev, Bund & Mildenberg, 2014, p.207). In order to understand social innovation capacity of a country via the outputs of social entrepreneur efforts, it is important to understand how societal culture affects the relative balance between the self-oriented entrepreneur orientation and other-oriented social orientation (Canestrino, Ćwiklicki, Magliocca, & Pawełek, 2020, p.134). Depending on the priority of values and needs in a social context, the perceptions, and so the efforts of social entrepreneurs may vary. Despite all these possibilities, the research studies conducted for investigating the effects of societal culture attributes on social innovation processes with a particular focus on social entrepreneurs' value creation preferences are almost not exist to our knowledge.

This study focuses on exploring whether the importance given to social value generation rather than economic value generation varies in line with the shared societal values. Based on the literature review results and the arguments given above, the propositions of the current study are developed and given in the below section.

According to Hofstede's model of cultural values framework, collectivism represents a preference for a tightly-knit social structure in which members of a group care and be loyal to each other (Hofstede, 1980). In a collectivist culture, the problems of one of the members become the problem of all because they identify themselves as "we" rather than as" I". Social innovation mainly initiates from caring the wellbeing of all. In this respect, in a collectivist cultural setting caring the problems of others and supporting these solutions are highly welcomed. Therefore, in such a cultural context socail value generation would be highly appreciated. Besides, Pathak and Muralidharan (2016) found that the high in-group collectivist cultural context is positively associated with social entrepreneurship. Therefore, the first research proposition is developed as follows:

Proposition 1. Higher collectivism may positively influence social innovation by increasing social entrepreneurs' desire for social value creation over economic value generation.

According to Hofstede's model of cultural values framework, masculinity indicates a preference for competition and achievement, and in such a cultural context material success is valued. Therefore, in a high masculine cultural context, economic value generation would be more appreciated compared to social value generation. Moreover, the research by Kedmenec and Strašek (2017) displayed that in specific framework conditions low masculinity is found to be effective on social entrepreneurship efforts. Accordingly, the second proposition of the study is developed as follows:

Proposition 2. Lower masculinity may positively influence social innovation by increasing social entrepreneurs' desire for social value creation over economic value generation.

According to Hofstede's model of cultural values framework, long-term versus short-term orientation indicates how societies balance their past with the future. Those high in long-term orientation prefer a pragmatic approach in balancing the past traditions with the requirements of the present and the future. On the other hand, societies with short-term orientation prefer a normative approach and focus on maintaining old-style traditions, and have suspicion about social change. However, social innovation requires change in products, services, relationships etc. in order to solve unfulfilled social needs. More importantly this desire for change should be for social value generation, because economic value generation is a much shorter target, while social value creation necessities a future focus. Accordingly, the third research proposition of the study is developed as follows:

Proposition 3. Higher long term orientation may positively influence social innovation by increasing social entrepreneurs' desire for social value creation over economic value generation.

According to Hofstede's model of cultural values framework, uncertainty avoidance refers to the extent to which members of a society feel uncomfortable with uncertain situations (Hofstede, 1980). High uncertainty leads to general avoidance of risk, and that's why members of the society prefer to preserve the rigid codes of behavior. On the other hand, low uncertainty leads to willingness to take risks, and members of the society in that context are much more relax about future and they let practice precede principles. Therefore, in a high uncertainty avoidance cultural context, it is expected to see established structures that are planned and operationalized for serving the needs of all. However, a society with low uncertainty avoidance most likely would not have all the required structures and established rules which had been planned and operationalized in advance. In such a societal context, there would be higher need for social innovations, and so social value generation would likely to be more appreciated. The finding of a recent study by Canestrino and colleagues (2020) points to a negative association among social entrepreneurship and high uncertainty avoidance cultural attributes. Accordingly, the forth proposition of this study is developed as follows:

Proposition 4. Lower uncertainty avoidance may positively influence social innovation by increasing social entrepreneurs' desire for social value creation over economic value generation.

According to Hofstede's model of cultural values framework, power distance indicates willingness of members of a society to accept unequal distribution of power at social level. The lower the power distance in a cultural context, the higher the access to resources and the higher the fairness (Vitell, Nwachukwu, & Barnes,1993). In such a cultural context, working to ensure fair access to resources and to develop solutions for meeting unfulfilled needs would likely be appreciated. Therefore, social value generation would likely to be more appreciated in low power distance culture. Besides, the research by Puumalainen and colleagues (2015) found that there is a negative relationship between high power distance cultural attributes and social entrepreneurship. Consequently, the fifth proposition of the study is developed as follows:

Proposition 5. Lower power distance may positively influence social innovation by increasing social entrepreneurs' desire for social value creation over economic value generation.

CONCLUDING REMARKS

Like in technological innovations, the initiation of a social innovation process depends on the first impulse to meet a particular social need, followed by taking the necessary entrepreneurship steps. That's why social entrepreneurs act as the main actors in a social innovation. The cumulative effect of micro-level social entrepreneurship outputs builds up to the macro level social innovation capacity of a country.

Since the existence of a social need in a given context develops from a normative perception of what social needs are, the societal cultural context which shapes such normative perceptions either enable or constrain social entrepreneurship via shaping social entrepreneurs' perspectives. The current study focused on exploring how societal cultural attributes influence social innovation along the process stages of identifying the social problem, clarifying the value generation aspects, formulating a strategy for the responsible social enterprise; and for that the main focus of the current study was on understanding how societal culture influences the perspectives of social entrepreneurs in social value generation aspects.

In order to explore the possible roles of societal culture in social innovation capacity of countries by shaping social entrepreneurs' perceptions and actions, the current study investigated the extant research findings on the subject by conducting a literature review study on on social innovation, social entrepreneurship, societal culture. The evidence gathered from previous research findings supports the current study's propositions that societal culture does effect social innovation capacities through its effect on social entrepreneurship efforts. Based on the literature review, the research propositions were developed to be tested by future empirical studies.

By discussing the relationship between societal culture and social innovation in a conceptual manner in addition to developing research propositions, this study presents a new direction for future research. In this respect, this study contributes to the social innovation and social entrepreneur aspects of the theory. Besides, this study provides a practical insight to the practitioners in social innovation arena to help them to realise the importance of societal culture on social innovation via the effects on social entrepreneurs' activities. The further studies may help to understand the effects of specific cultural attributes on social entrepreneurship; and this understanding may be helpful to develop country specific policies for supporting social entrepreneurs in their efforts for increasing social well-being.

Although the propositions of the current study represent a general view for future research, a limitation of the study is that there might be some other significant macro level factors that may affect social innovation processes by interacting with societal culture attributes. In future studies, by extending the scope of the propositions, a more comprehensive coverage of the macro level factors may be possible. More importantly, as a further study, there is need for empirical research to validate the assertions of these propositions.

REFERENCES

Alvord, S. H., Brown, L. D., & Letts, C. W. (2004). Social entrepreneurship and societal transformation: An exploratory study. *The Journal of Applied Behavioral Science*, *40*(3), 260–282. doi:10.1177/0021886304266847

Austin, J., Stevenson, H., & Wei-Skillern, J. (2006). Social and commercial entrepreneurship: Same, different, or both? *Entrepreneurship Theory and Practice*, *30*(1), 1–22. doi:10.1111/j.1540-6520.2006.00107.x

Beije, P. (2000). *Technological Change in the Modern Economy*. Edward Elgar.

Bodenhausen, G. V., & Hugenberg, K. (2009). Attention, perception, and social cognition. In F. Strack & J. Förster (Eds.), *Social cognition: the basis of human interaction* (pp. 1–22). Psychology Press.

Boelman V., Kwan A., Lauritzen J.R.K., Millard J., & Schon, R. (2014). *Growing social innovation: A guide for policy makers, A deliverable of the TEPSIE project*. EU 7th Framework Programme, Brussels: EU, DG Research.

Bowman, C., & Ambrosini, V. (2000). Value creation versus value capture: Towards a coherent definition of value in strategy. *British Journal of Management*, *11*(1), 1–15. doi:10.1111/1467-8551.00147

Bureau of European Policy Advisors. (2011). *Empowering people, driving change, social innovation in European Union*. Retrieved from https://ec.europa.eu/archives/bepa/pdf/publications_pdf

Busenitz, L. W., & Barney, J. B. (1997). Biases and heuristics in strategic decision-making: Differences between entrepreneurs and managers in large organizations. *Journal of Business Venturing*, *12*(1), 9–30. doi:10.1016/S0883-9026(96)00003-1

Byungku, L., & Louise, K. (2019). Cultural leadership ideals and social entrepreneurship: An international study. *Journal of Social Entrepreneurship*, *10*(1), 108–128. doi:10.1080/19420676.2018.1541005

Cahill, G. (2010). Primer on social innovation: A compendium of definitions developed by organizations around the world. *The Philantropist*, *23*, 259–271.

Cajaiba-Santana, G. (2014). Social innovation: Moving the field forward: a conceptual framework. *Technological Forecasting and Social Change*, *82*, 42–51. doi:10.1016/j.techfore.2013.05.008

Canestrino, R., Ćwiklicki, M., Magliocca, P., & Pawełek, B. (2020). Understanding social entrepreneurship: A cultural perspective in business research. *Journal of Business Research*, *110*, 132–143. doi:10.1016/j.jbusres.2020.01.006

Caulier-Grice, J., Davies, A., Patrick, R., & Norman, W. (2012). Defining social innovation: A deliverable of TEPSIE project. EU 7th Framework Programme, EU, DG Research, Brussels.

De Mooij, M. (2017). Comparing dimensions of national culture for secondary analysis of consumer behavior data of different countries. *International Marketing Review*, *34*(3), 444–456. doi:10.1108/IMR-02-2016-0047

Dees, J. G. (1998). *The meaning of social entrepreneurship*. Revised May 2001, original draft, available at http://www.fuqua.duke.edu/centers/case/documents/ Dees_SEdef. pdf

Diener, E., Oishi, S., & Lucas, R. E. (2003). Personality, culture, and subjective well-being: Emotional and cognitive evaluations of life. *Annual Review of Psychology*, *54*(1), 403–425. doi:10.1146/annurev.psych.54.101601.145056 PMID:12172000

Doherty, B., Haugh, H., & Lyon, F. (2014). Social enterprises as hybrid organizations: A review and research agenda. *International Journal of Management Reviews*, *16*(4), 417–436. doi:10.1111/ijmr.12028

Eichler, G., & Schwarz, E. (2019). What sustainable development goals do social innovations address? A systematic review and content analysis of social innovation literature. *Sustainability*, *11*(522), 1–18. doi:10.3390u11020522

Erdur, D., & Fındıklı, M. (2020). A conceptual model proposal for co-creation of social value: Insights from social entrepreneurs. *Istanbul Gelisim University Journal of Social Sciences*, *7*(1), 1–20.

Fisscher, O., Frenkel, D., Lurie, Y., & Nijhof, A. (2005). Stretching the frontiers: Exploring the relationships between entrepreneurship and ethics. *Journal of Business Ethics*, *60*(3), 207–209. doi:10.100710551-005-0128-1

Giddens, A. (1984). *The Constitution of Society*. Polity Press.

Hamamura, T., Heine, S. J., & Paulhus, D. L. (2008). Cultural differences in response styles: The role of dialectical thinking. *Personality and Individual Differences*, *44*(4), 932–942. doi:10.1016/j.paid.2007.10.034

Harding, R. (2006). *Social entrepreneurship monitor*. London Business School.

Hayton, J. C., George, G., & Zahra, S. A. (2002). National culture and entrepreneurship: A review of behavioral research. *Entrepreneurship Theory and Practice*, *26*(4), 33–52. doi:10.1177/104225870202600403

Hofstede, G. (1980). *Culture's consequences: International differences in work-related values*. Sage.

House, R. J., Hanges, P. J., Javidan, M., Dorfman, P. W., Gupta, V., & Globe Associates. (2004). *Leadership, culture and organizations: The Globe study of 62 societies*. Thousand Oaks, CA: Sage.

Inglehart, R., & Baker, W. (2000). Modernization, cultural change and the persistence of traditional values. *American Sociological Review*, *65*(1), 19–51. doi:10.2307/2657288

Karaçay, G., & Alpkan, L. (2019). The effects of digital transformation on labor markets: Social policy recommendations for labor market of Turkey [Dijital dönüşümün işgücü piyasalarına etkileri: Türkiye işgücü piyasası için sosyal politika önerileri]. *Türk İdare Dergisi*, *91*(488), 345–373.

Kedmenec, I., & Strašek, S. (2017). Are some cultures more favourable for social entrepreneurship than others? *Economic research- Ekonomska Istrazivanja*, *30*(1), 1461–1476. doi:10.1080/1331677X.2017.1355251

Krlev, G., Bund, E., & Mildenberger, G. (2014). Measuring what matters? Indicators of social innovativeness on the national level. *Information Systems Management*, *31*(3), 200–224. doi:10.1080/10580530.2014.923265

Le Blanc, D. (2015). Towards integration at last? The sustainable development goals as a network of targets. *Sustainable Development*, *23*(3), 176–187. doi:10.1002d.1582

Lepak, D. P., Smith, K. G., & Taylor, M. S. (2007). Value creation and value capture: A multilevel perspective. *Academy of Management Review*, *32*(1), 180–194. doi:10.5465/amr.2007.23464011

Lundvall, B. (1988). Innovation as an Interactive: From User-Producer Interaction to the National System of Innovation. In *Technical Change and Economic Theory* (pp. 349–369). Pinter.

Lundvall, B. (2007). National Innovation Systems-Analytical Concept and Development Tool. *Industry and Innovation*, *14*(1), 95–119. doi:10.1080/13662710601130863

Mair, J., & Marti, I. (2006). Social entrepreneurship research: A source of explanation, prediction and delight. *Journal of World Business*, *41*(1), 36–44. doi:10.1016/j.jwb.2005.09.002

Matten, D., & Moon, J. (2008). Implicit and explicit CSR: A conceptual framework for a comparative understanding of corporate social responsibility. *Academy of Management Review*, *33*(2), 404–424. doi:10.5465/amr.2008.31193458

Mitchell, R. K., Smith, J. B., Morse, E. A., Seawright, K. W., Peredo, A. M., & McKenzie, B. (2002). Are entrepreneurial cognitions universal? Assessing entrepreneurial cognitions across cultures. *Entrepreneurship Theory and Practice*, *27*(2), 9–29. doi:10.1177/104225870202600402

Moulaert, F., Martinelli, F., Swyngedouw, E., & Gonzalez, S. (2005). Towards alternative model(s) of local innovation. *Urban Studies (Edinburgh, Scotland)*, *42*(11), 1969–1990. doi:10.1080/00420980500279893

Mulgan, G. (2006). The process of social innovation. *Innovations: Technology, Governance, Globalization, 1*(2), 145–162. doi:10.1162/itgg.2006.1.2.145

Mulgan, G., Tucker, S., Ali, R., & Sanders, B. (2007). *Social innovation: what it is, why it matters and how it can be accelerated.* Working Paper, Skoll Centre for Social Innovation.

Murray, R., Caulier-Grice, J., & Mulgan, G. (2010). *The open book of social innovation.* NESTA.

Nelson, R. R. (1993). *National innovation systems: A comparative analysis.* Oxford University Press.

Neumeier, S. (2012). Why do social innovations in rural development matter and should they be considered more seriously in rural development research? Proposal for a stronger focus on social innovations in rural development research. *Sociologia Ruralis, 52*(1), 48–69. doi:10.1111/j.1467-9523.2011.00553.x

Pathak, S., & Muralidharan, E. (2016). Informal institutions and their comparative influences on social and commercial entrepreneurship: The role of in-group collectivism and interpersonal trust. *Journal of Small Business Management, 54*(S1), 168–188. doi:10.1111/jsbm.12289

Peredo, A. M., & McLean, M. (2006). Social entrepreneurship: A critical review of the concept. *Journal of World Business, 41*(1), 56–65. doi:10.1016/j.jwb.2005.10.007

Phillips, W., Lee, H., Ghobadian, A., O'Regan, N., & James, P. (2015). Social innovation and social entrepreneurship: A systematic review. *Group & Organization Management, 40*(3), 428–461. doi:10.1177/1059601114560063

Phills, J. A., Deiglmeier, K., & Miller, D. T. (2008). Rediscovering Social Innovation. *Stanford Social Innovation Review, 6*(4), 34–43.

Pitelis, C. N. (2009). The co-evolution of organizational value capture, value creation and sustainable advantage. *Organization Studies, 30*(10), 1115–1139. doi:10.1177/0170840609346977

Puumalainen, K., Sjögrén, H., Syrjä, P., & Barraket, J. (2015). Comparing social entrepreneurship across nations: An exploratory study of institutional effects. *Canadian Journal of Administrative Sciences, 32*(4), 276–287. doi:10.1002/cjas.1356

Ramirez, R. (1999). Value co-production: Intellectual origins and implications for practice and research. *Strategic Management Journal, 20*(1), 49–65. doi:10.1002/(SICI)1097-0266(199901)20:1<49::AID-SMJ20>3.0.CO;2-2

Rauthmann, J. F. (2012). You say the party is dull, I say it is lively: A componential approach to how situations are perceived to disentangle perceiver, situation, and perceiver situation variance. *Social Psychological & Personality Science, 3*(5), 519–528. doi:10.1177/1948550611427609

Sarason, Y., Dean, T., & Dillard, J. F. (2006). Entrepreneurship as the nexus of individual and opportunity: A structuration view. *Journal of Business Venturing, 21*(3), 286–305. doi:10.1016/j.jbusvent.2005.02.007

Schimmack, U., Radhakrishnan, P., Oishi, S., Dzokoto, V., & Ahadi, S. (2002). Culture, personality, and subjective well-being: Integrating process models of life satisfaction. *Journal of Personality and Social Psychology, 82*(4), 582–593. doi:10.1037/0022-3514.82.4.582 PMID:11999925

Schmutzler, J., Andonova, V., & Diaz-Serrano, L. (2019). How context shapes entrepreneurial self-efficacy as a driver of entrepreneurial intentions: A multilevel approach. *Entrepreneurship Theory and Practice*, *43*(5), 880–920. doi:10.1177/1042258717753142

Schwartz, S. H. (1994). Beyond individualism/collectivism: New cultural dimensions of values. In U. Kim, H. C. Triandis, C. Kagitcibasi, S.-C. Choi, & G. Yoon (Eds.), *Individualism and collectivism: theory, method, and applications*. Sage.

Singelis, T. M., & Brown, W. J. (1995). Culture, self, and collectivist communication: Linking culture to individual behavior. *Human Communication Research*, *21*(3), 354–389. doi:10.1111/j.1468-2958.1995.tb00351.x PMID:12349710

Smith, P. B. (2015). To lend helping hands: In-group favoritism, uncertainty avoidance, and the national frequency of pro-social behaviors. *Journal of Cross-Cultural Psychology*, *46*(6), 759–771. doi:10.1177/0022022115585141

Tortia, E., Degavre, F., & Poledrini, S. (2020). Why are social enterprises good candidates for social innovation? Looking for personal and institutional drivers of innovation. *Annals of Public and Cooperative Economics*, *91*(3), 1–19. doi:10.1111/apce.12265

Triandis, H. C. (1990). Cross-cultural studies of individualism and collectivism. In J. Berman (Ed.), *Nebraska Symposium on Motivation* (pp. 41-133). Lincoln: University of Nebraska Press.

United Nations (2015). *Transforming our world: The 2030 agenda for sustainable development*. General Assembly a/res/70/1.

Vitell, S. J., Nwachukwu, S., & Barnes, J. (1993). The effects of culture on ethical decision-making: An application of Hofstede's typology. *Journal of Business Ethics*, *12*(10), 753–760. doi:10.1007/BF00881307

Westley, F., & Antadze, N. (2010). Making a difference: Strategies for scaling social innovation for greater impact. *The Innovation Journal*, *15*(2), 1–20.

Wieczorek, A. J., & Hekkert, M. P. (2012). Systemic instruments for systemic innovation problems: A framework for policy makers and innovation scholars. *Science & Public Policy*, *39*(6), 74–87. doi:10.1093cipolcr008

Zahra, S. A., Rawhouser, H. N., Bhawe, N., Neubaum, D. O., & Hayton, J. C. (2008). Globalization of social entrepreneurship opportunities. *Strategic Entrepreneurship Journal*, *2*(2), 1–15. doi:10.1002ej.43

Chapter 6
The Effects of Digitalization on Social Entrepreneurship and Social Value

Hale Cide Demir
https://orcid.org/0000-0002-1876-504X
Kadir Has University, Turkey

ABSTRACT

The intense competition and change by globalization and digitalization in the 21st century have made organizations and people face opportunities, threats, and uncertainty. Digitalization allows new and original business models and thus, presenting changes as a service or benefit to the consumer has become more important. A network is the most powerful instrument of social entrepreneurs or other employees to adapt to the new order. A very important tool of the new order is the blockchain technology which allows more secure, efficient, and trustworthy social enterprises. Social entrepreneurship is the process of establishing social enterprises to create social benefits and the relevant social value is general non-financial effects of programs, organizations, and interferences that include the wellbeing of people and communities, social capital, and the environment. This study tries to define and theorize that the results of digitalization, can be managed by increasing social entrepreneurship and the resulting social impact and networking have an easing effect on this method.

INTRODUCTION

The World becomes increasingly digitalized and this indicates the switch from an information society to a digital society. As industries become digitalized, efficiency and speed in production increase while costs and defective manufacturing decrease. Digitalization is generally claimed to be the reason for the occurrence of new and productive business models. The digital age is usually associated with productivity and efficiency but it is obvious that the digital age has also influence on labor, resource and power allocation, equality in opportunity, and income. This fact remarkably increases the necessity of the potential effects of social entrepreneurs. This is the only way to balance equality in opportunity and the existing income.

DOI: 10.4018/978-1-7998-4727-4.ch006

As an unprecedented platform in history, digitalization has generated new occupations and jobs and has democratized the ways of reaching the masses, therefore, it is possible to consider these events and the effect of their scale as dynamic changes that can foster the development of social entrepreneurship.

This chapter describing social digital entrepreneurship reveals the facilitator role of digitalization in the creation of social value. The study presents a comparative analysis by revealing the European Index of Digital Entrepreneurship Systems (EIDES), the 2020 Digital Economy and Society Index (DESI), and the table of Estimated number and degree of acceptance of Social Enterprises in Europe. The European Index of Digital Entrepreneurship Systems (EIDES)(ec.europa.eu) contains the digital entrepreneurship scores of the European countries. To date, there is no social digital entrepreneurship index yet.

Understanding digital entrepreneurship offers new opportunities for social entrepreneurs for creating social value (Santana, 2017) that leads to well-being (Galindo-Martin, et al., 2019). However, there are limited studies investigating the effects of digitalization on social entrepreneurship. This study examines the social digital entrepreneurship concept within the scope of Network Theory. The main purpose of the study is to reveal the connections between digitalization and social entrepreneurship, how digitalization can pave the way for efficient and successful social enterprises, and comment on the future of both concepts in the context of a new – more digitalized – order after the COVID-19 crisis. Since there is a limited number of studies regarding social digital entrepreneurship, this study is a compilation study which aims to discuss these connections and forecast the future of them while comparing indices and aims to contribute to the related literature.

The chapter is organized as follows. In the first section, the rise of digitalization is explained through definitions and features of digitalization. Based this framework, digital entrepreneurship concept is described. In the second section, the impact of digitalization on social entrepreneurship is discussed and digital social entrepreneurship concept is presented. Lastly, future directions, limitations and contributions of the study are explained.

THE RISE OF DIGITALIZATION

Definitions and Features of Digitalization

Digitalization is not as simple as it sounds. It has many dimensions and fields of application. This is obvious in the variety of studies about digitalization and digitization. As a related concept, digitization is the complement of digitalization. This part consists of the definitions, structure, and features of digitalization and digitization.

According to Gardner Glossary (2018), digitalization is the utilization of digital technologies to change a business model and supply new income and value-producing opportunities and it is the process of moving to a digital business. The website I-scoop.eu (2018) defines digitalization as the conversion of interactions, communications, and business functions into more digital ones that often sums up as a mix of digital or physical as in multi-channel customer service, integrated marketing or smart production with a mix of autonomous, semi-autonomous and manual operations. The changing business models, business functions, and the resulting value chains are mentioned in the following part of the study.

To understand the structure of digitalization, it is necessary to examine the architecture and features of it. As digitalization spreads in the systems of firms, it forms its architecture. Sahut et.al. (2019) argue that digitalization creates its modular architecture which contains devices, networks, services, and contents and these are enabled by digital technology. This is called pervasive digitalization. On the way from an information society to digital society, people have started to gather, produce, distribute and consume information at an unprecedented speed. Also, an original characteristic of business digitalization is that the value is mostly created in the production process of digital information. Hence, the digital value can be strongly or weakly bonded to physical products. The authors also claim that value creation should be digitally implemented because value creation in non-digital ways seriously degenerates if not accompanied by digital value creation (Sahut, et.al., 2019). Digitalization and digital information should be pervasive consisting of a comprehensive system that is for the benefit of consumers, businesses, economy, and society. It is clear that underdeveloped or developing countries that cannot use digital information much suffer from poverty and lack of productivity.

Digitalization did not occur in one day. It had certain phases which Legner et.al. (2017) calls "waves". These waves are closely associated with technological advances. The authors mention three waves of digitalization seen since computers became widespread. The first wave was the replacement of paper with computers and automation in workplaces. The second wave was the emergence of the Internet as a global means of communication that changed the value chain perspective of firms and created new business types such as e-commerce and intermediaries. At present, we are in the third wave which denotes the transforming of SMAC technologies (social, mobile, analytics, and cloud computing) and the constant increase of processing power, storage capacity, and communication bandwidth. These developments have brought the prevalent computing very close to reality (Legner et.al., 2017). These waves and technology are parallel processes whereas all the factors of SMAC develop independently.

Digitization and digitalization are related but separate concepts. Legner et.al. (2017) indicate this difference. Digitization is a technical issue and it is about transforming analog data and signals into digital ones. Digitalization, on the other hand, expresses a wide range of sociotechnical facts and mechanisms of adopting and utilizing these technologies in broader individual, organizational, and social contexts. According to Rachinger et.al. (2018), digitization is the process of converting analog data into digital data sets and it is the framework for digitalization. Digitization can be considered to be a tool and the purely technical part of digitalization in various contexts.

Some researchers have studied the negative or destructive parts of digitalization. This is also necessary to avoid some consequences especially the effects on humans. Fossen and Sorgner (2019) define 'destructive digitalization' as the risk of employees being replaced by digital devices or machines. Legner et.al. (2017) emphasize the negative parts of digitalization as technostress, addictive behaviors, loss of privacy, and laws that have been in effect for an analog world. In many countries, technology and digitalization develop and expand more rapidly than laws and regulations. This may disturb some people as well as some business processes.

The internet and digitalization have many benefits as mentioned above. However, these benefits bring about many problems such as security gaps, data theft, etc. Since blockchain technology is a distributed database that is protected against security gaps, encrypted on a network, and ensures the management of the data, it is the ideal system for the creation and management of large networks such as a social enterprise. Blockchain technology ensures the security and digital accessibility of data with the applications working via blockchain. Blockchain technology presents solutions for many problems in today's economies (Yavuz, 2019).

Social entrepreneurship is a socioeconomic existence so, blockchain technology can be used extensively for the creation, protection, and management of social enterprises. If a social enterprise lacks data security then the "trust" factor, which is one of the pillars of social enterprises, will disappear and their social value will decrease dramatically. Today, many platforms supported by states and private companies work on creating blockchain-based ecosystems. As the “trust” factor is a prerequisite for economic transactions, blockchain has the potential to ensure trust in every social enterprise with a very powerful security system. Also, blockchain technology has the potential to enable the underdeveloped or developing countries to catch up with developed countries or at least shorten the gap. The development of blockchain technology provides the necessary trust and controllability for digital entrepreneurship to develop. That is why, technological advances are critical for the increase in the number, effectiveness, and impact area of digital entrepreneurship. There are very few studies in the literature regarding the connection of digital entrepreneurship and blockchain technology. For example, the study of Chalmers et.al. (2019) examines the digital entrepreneurs in the music industry who offer innovative services to make transactions cheaper, automated, and more secure.

Barbosa (2020) mentions the “Building Blocks – Blockchain for Zero Hunger” implemented in Pakistan and Jordan. The project benefits 100,000 refugees and aims to provide financial aid to these people. The project is an initiative within the World Food Program (WFP) and Houman Haddad, one of the managers of the WFP, had the idea of using blockchain technology to improve the program’s financial transfer system. The managers of the initiative have had the chance to observe the efficiency of the blockchain in a project within the social and humanitarian scope. Using the blockchain not only offers greater efficiency but also cost reduction. Efficiency in such a project is especially important because most of the funds come from donations.

Mukkamala et.al. (2018) give another example of the utilization of blockchain technology in a social enterprise. They mention the example of a micro-credit-based community development program in India. The program aims to support the economic empowerment of poor people through self-help employment and income generation by creating women entrepreneurs in Indian villages. The authors state that the blockchain technology has certain advantages in this social entrepreneurship project and similar projects. Blockchain technology can ensure trust in the operations of social enterprises. Transparency, anonymity, privacy, and decentralization are other advantages of blockchain technology.

There are some interesting facts and statistics about digitalization. They are the indicators of how prevalent digitalization is and also how much it contributes to efficiency. Today, 70% of organizations have a digital transformation strategy or are working on one (ptc.com). Digital business strategy is widely adopted in most of the sectors. The top three sectors in this field are services (95%), financial services (93%), and healthcare (92%) (idg.com). Personal computers increased from 700,000 in 1980 to 1.33 billion in 2019 (statistica.com). Smartphones mounted from 23,000 in 1980 to 3.5 billion in 2019 which means almost half of the people on earth had a smartphone on average (bankmycell.com). Microsoft Office had more than 1.2 billion users in 2019 (windowscentral.com). As of 2019, half of the private households in the world have a computer. In developed countries, this rate is 80 percent (statista.com). This year’s (2020) Covid-19 crisis has increased the demand and motivation of people for digitalization and seems to accelerate the evolution of it in the coming years.

Applications such as Uber is a good example of digitalizing a simple service in life: taxi service. Taxi service is not something innovative but Uber is not only about offering people a car and taking them to places but it is about presenting a more accessible, more practical, and easier service meeting both sides on a digital platform (Nogueira, 2018).

Governments have started to regard digitalization as a strategic priority as well (ex. Germany’s digital agenda) and have introduced research funds and cooperation schemes (Legner et.al., 2017). They have also developed electronic state systems. In recent years, these systems have become smart and personalized containing a ubiquitous infrastructure and offering a personalized and real-time public service. E-government services started around the year 2000 (e-government 1.0) with internet technology becoming prevalent and has reached the stage e-government 4.0 (Barcevicius, et.al., 2019). Fostering efficiency and avoiding paperwork, the electronic state platforms "accelerate" life.

Digitalization encourages innovation in business and society. Legner et.al. (2017) determined ten key areas that companies need to implement while digitalizing as follows: digital leadership and digital empowerment, data-driven nimbleness, customer and partner involvement, digital platform management, business model innovation, IT architecture transformation, process digitization and automation, and digital security and compliance (Legner et.al., 2017). These factors pave the way for more efficiency and innovation for companies.

Business models are turning into digital business models and digitalization is the main facilitator. Thanks to the power of computing and IT, managing information has been easier, calculations have accelerated, sharing has speeded up, marginal costs have been decreased, and scalability of operations have enhanced. As a result, technologies such as mobile computing, cloud computing, big data, the Internet of things, digital marketplaces, social media, smartphone apps, file-sharing, and software-as-a-service have led to digital business models and ways of working. The new business models enabled by digitalization include crowd financing, online supply chain management, internet marketplaces, "sharing" models, decentralized and remote work, online talent platforms, dynamic pricing, e-commerce, social entrepreneurship, and many more. Even sectors such as retail and health care in which digitalization is less prevalent have accelerated the process of becoming digitalized. Regarding the importance of digitalization, the authors claim that digitalization has facilitated and improved the collection, storage, exchange, and use of information. Digitalization also adds to the skills of workers and firms to add value to the value chain by enhancing the organizational, managerial, and analytic aspects of production while decreasing the value and need for other types of work. From the perspective of firms, digitalization adds to their performance. Specifically, both manufacturing and service firms have revealed cost savings, more output, and more productivity with digitalization (Muro et.al., 2017).

Some researchers define the utilization of digital opportunities. By bonding different technologies (ex. Cloud technologies, sensors, big data, 3D printing), digitalization opens unforeseen opportunities and provides the potential to create radically new products, services, and business models (Rachinger et.al., 2018). As technology advances and new tools are being used in digitalization, these products, services, and business models have the potential to diversify more. According to futurist thought, the singularity is one of the last stops of the digitalization process. After that, the weaknesses of human nature will be compensated like inequalities, etc.

In today's world of unforeseen economic, health, and natural crises and disasters, digitalization has proved to be vital in overcoming them. In some cases, like the latest Covid-19 virus pandemic of 2020, digitalization is observed to be the hope of people by enabling things like online shopping, working from home or following the news. It has been a very important factor for the hope of the world's people, perhaps the very thing that keeps some people going. Thanks to the opportunities that digitalization has provided, compared with past pandemics, many more people are informed and many more regions can receive aids.

Gobble (2018) indicates that before utilizing digitalization, firms should first understand it. For the author, digitized data is the basic knowledge and that knowledge can be used to start to move and produce change. That process is to let flourished and take root and later on lead to digital transformation. Digital transformation is about a whole remaking of the business around new opportunities and new demands presented by digital technology. When the transmitted data is used to estimate and obstruct failures, optimize planned maintenance schedules, and improve the product, that is digitalization. Digitalization may start as an innovation attempt and may be energized by a new business opportunity but in the end, it should go far beyond innovation to remake the company (Gobble, 2018). Gobble reveals the integrative approach of digitalization; thus, no element of digitalization should be ignored for businesses seeking productivity.

As digital technologies are inserted into the operations of firms, new business management practices and activities occur and this is called digital business. In the digital business platform, there are widely seen technologies such as mobile devices and applications, analytical tools, capacity-sharing platforms, and the Internet of things. E-business has evolved into a digital business today. With digital ecosystems, firms can have a great network impact (Martin-Pena et.al., 2018). As the authors indicate, digital business models have to be researched further. On the other hand, the firms that fail to adopt digitalization will probably fall behind the competition in their industries.

Like in other fields, sustainability is also a must in digitalization and digital models. According to Parida et.al. (2019), digitalization revolutionizes the way business is done and it does this by utilizing the Internet of Things (IoT), dense data exchange, and predictive analytics within industrial value chains. However, the researchers claim that technological implementation on its own is not enough. To be able to gain profit from digitalization, companies need to be innovative about their business models and should have the necessary skills to upgrade their business to developed and sustainable business models. The authors also indicate that digitalization creates value through three functions: operational data collection through sensors, efficient sharing of these data through connectivity among wireless communication networks, and transforming of the data into important insights and applicable instructions (Parida, et.al., 2019). After the Covid-19 crisis, many countries will probably make more investment in R&D activities and implement smart manufacturing and the Internet of things in more facilities.

The ultimate effect of digitalization on economies and organizations is digital transformation and the resulting "the whole remaking of the business". Ross, an MIT Sloan Management Review author, clearly indicates (2018) this and states that digital transformation and the whole remaking of the business constitute 'digitalization'. For her, while digitization is an operational necessity, digitalization is 'a visionary digital value proposition' and it redefines a business, even an industry. Digitization is a tool of digitalization and digitalization is an innovative "vision project" for every economy and firm that paves the way for efficiency, cost reduction, and competitive power.

Digital Entrepreneurship

Elia et.al. (2020) introduce the concept of the digital entrepreneurship ecosystem. According to the authors, the digital entrepreneurship ecosystem has two dimensions: the digital-output entrepreneurship ecosystem and the digital-environment entrepreneurship ecosystem. The digital-output ecosystem contains a network of entrepreneurial actors to establish digital enterprises which are organizations which are specialized in using digital technologies to design, produce and deliver innovative digital artifacts and services (ex. The Silicon Valley) (Elia et.al., 2020). The digital environment ecosystem is a broad network of heterogeneous and geographically distributed stakeholders who have the purpose to support the design and establishment process of a startup including digital platforms. This study is unique in that it mentions the infrastructure, formation, and different aspects of a "social digital entrepreneurship ecosystem". For example, Sarma and Sunny (2017) regard smart cities as an outcome of connecting social entrepreneurship with digital entrepreneurship. This is an example of a factor in the "social digital entrepreneurship ecosystem".

Digital entrepreneurship is about creating new ventures, converting existing businesses by developing original digital technologies or their original usage. Many countries consider these features of digital entrepreneurship crucial for economic growth, employment, and innovation. As a helping factor to digital entrepreneurship, digital technologies have brought about the possibility of linking owners and users and preventing the previous dualism of businesses and customers (Baierl et.al., 2019). As the world digitalizes, the need for digital entrepreneurship increases proportionally. Digital entrepreneurship not only means economic growth, employment, and innovation but also safer trade, efficiency, and productivity. The end of the 1990s and the beginning of the 2000s denote the new era of digital giants such as Google, Facebook, and YouTube and these companies have guided and inspired many digital entrepreneurs all over the world.

Consequently, digital entrepreneurship is an upward global trend for many years and has not reached its peak yet. Digital entrepreneurial activities "range from the origination of ideas and creative opportunities, the identification and sourcing of capital and other resources, and the institutional policy frameworks to risks and uncertainties related with the creation and development of 'digital start-ups', and more recently with their growth to scaling-up phases" (Murschetz, 2019). The recent global crises seem to continue to encourage digital entrepreneurial activities for a long time as well as to increase in volume.

Kraus et.al. (2018) identified six streams of research regarding digital entrepreneurship: digital business models, digital entrepreneurship process, platform strategies, digital ecosystem, entrepreneurship education, and social digital entrepreneurship. Social digital entrepreneurship represents the "social" side of digital entrepreneurship implying a more humane use of the digital world and entrepreneurship.

A NEW ERA IN SOCIAL ENTREPRENEURSHIP: DIGITAL SOCIAL ENTREPRENEURSHIP

An important aspect of digitalization is that it creates social value for communities, societies, and most importantly for people. It was a known fact that digitalization creates social value (Afonasova et.al., 2019). The Covid-19 crisis has shown that digitalization is a very important tool for the survival of people, fulfilling their needs, remote working, and more. Thus, during and after the crisis, digitalization has the potential to create even more social value depending on the incentives of governments and the motivation of social entrepreneurs. As digitalization develops, digital entrepreneurship and social entrepreneurship also develops. It is natural to expect social entrepreneurs to go digital. Their mindset is innovative and most of the innovation in the world progresses on digital platforms and via digital tools.

Many researchers have examined the "social part" and the social value creation process of digitalization. Among them are Fossen and Sorgner (2019) and they indicate that digitalization is an important factor in decreasing entry barriers for various sectors. According to the authors, this may lead to more entrepreneurship. Also, digitalization reduces the costs of communication and information. Another advantage of digital technologies is that they decrease labor costs through artificial intelligence and distant contracts. Another type of digitalization is the 'transformative digitalization' which means the powerful interaction and communication of digital machines and humans (Fossen and Sorgner, 2019). This classification of digitalization is due to its effect on the person, not on the economy or the firm implying the social value it creates.

Another aspect of digitalization is its relationship with young people. Young people are mostly digital natives and they can be trained in such a way that they can be supported and encouraged to become digital transformation leaders (Legner et.al., 2017). That is why the other generations should close the gap of digital nativeness. This area is important for creating social utility.

Biggiero (2007) studies the small and medium enterprises in territorial systems. He states that industrial districts and industrial clusters contain many firm relationships and thus they are large cognitive systems with their socio-cognitive integration. This structure enables firms to disseminate information among the member firms of the cluster. This information sharing of digitalizing industrial districts creates social values that benefit society and business life. These social values also appear in the effective collaboration of firms for innovation (Biggiero, 2007). As we see in the Covid-19 crisis, global information sharing is as important as the innovation process itself. Digitalization facilitates and accelerates information sharing, especially the global one.

Today's world is very much interested in sustainability. In their study, Jovanovic et.al. (2018) associate digitalization with society's sustainable development emphasizing the social benefits of digitalization. According to the Good Country Index, the culture, well-being, prosperity, and equality of a country have a strong positive relationship with digitalization. These results underline the fact that social components of countries are affected positively with the process of digitalization. The authors indicate that digitalized societies have more satisfied basic needs and better education. The researchers also conclude that digitalization significantly affects sustainable development. This development not only includes economic development but also the social aspect (Jovanovic et.al., 2018). After the Covid-19 crisis, the world will try to be more digitalized, more sustainable, and more valuable socially. With its results, this research reveals this hope for the post-crisis period.

In their study examining digitalization in retailing, Hanninen et.al. (2018) emphasized the social value of digitalization. The researchers indicate that retailing has evolved thanks to digitalization and large digital ecosystems connect suppliers with retailers. Digital platforms create consumer value through value-adding services. For them, multi-sided digital platforms can create different values and sets of values for users. The values created are social values as well. First of all, the user experience is a social value due to convenience and consumer satisfaction. Also, some digital platforms enable social interaction among users. Thus, consumers become information creators rather than simply being buyers of goods. Social value is also created in other social processes such as discussion boards and feedback systems. These social processes in digital systems allow communication, interaction, and trust among digital platform participants (Hanninen et.al., 2018). The social value creation of digital retail platforms has gained even more importance in the Covid-19 crisis because of people's increasing needs of interaction, communication, and trust as a result of the lack of physical interaction and communication. This is a very important factor that boosts the morale of people all around the world.

While associating digitalization with environmental sustainability in their study, Klymenko et.al. (2019) also emphasize the social value it creates in society. The researchers mention the Triple-Layered Business Model Canvas (TLBMC) which contains economic, environmental, and social layers. The authors indicate that social value is mostly about stakeholder views. In other words, the social layer of the model remarks on the social impact of an organization on its stakeholders. The authors studied digitalized and sustainable organizations in their study and thus, implemented the model on these organizations (Klymenko et.al., 2019). By providing more efficiency, especially at crisis times like the Covid-19, more income, and more democracy, digitalization influences stakeholder values positively and creates social value.

For individual workers and remote workers, whose number has increased dramatically after the Covid-19 crisis, digitalization in the workplace has changed the nature and rewards of work. This means that digitalization has created remarkable social value since the beginning of the crisis. After the crisis, if supported properly, digitalization can create even more social value. An example of a social digital entrepreneurship study in a cultural context is that of Huang and Cox (2014). They concluded that their model constitutes an efficient social digital entrepreneurship model that utilizes universal service funds to spread IT technologies, leads to greater social entrepreneurship, and reduces poverty for people with low income in Taiwan. Similarly, in their study examining the social and innovative activities of small and medium-sized enterprises, Maiolini et.al. (2016) express the drivers for social digital entrepreneurship. These are: (a) mobile as a device, (b) web and social as channels/platforms, (c) marketing, education, and e-commerce as relevant businesses. The researchers indicate that digitalization is important in shaping the boundaries of the social innovation sector, constantly feeding its cross-industry nature, and continually changing the social innovation phenomenon. Social innovation is about increasing attention on the role of communities that create and spread innovation and the way new technologies can support these. The results of the research give information to people who want to understand the appropriate technologies that can be used in social innovation projects. These people can be innovation strategists, innovation managers, entrepreneurs, social policymakers, etc. (Maiolini et.al., 2016). If digitalization improves and its boundaries span then social innovation and social digital entrepreneurship can also improve and span its boundaries. After the Covid-19 crisis, the conjuncture necessitates a "social" way of innovative thinking.

It is important to understand how entrepreneurs accrue social capital in the digital age. In their study, Smith et.al. (2017) examined the issue. The authors suggest that social capital is crucial for entrepreneurship as it can help entrepreneurs in realizing the opportunity, acquiring resources, gaining legitimacy, and attaining the other desired results. Entrepreneurs are increasingly using social media to create networks. They use social network sites differently than offline networks to accumulate the social capital that is necessary to build and grow their enterprises (Smith et.al., 2017). Social capital is, in a way, a step towards social digital entrepreneurship, and the authors point at this issue.

From a different perspective, Sarma and Sunny (2017) regard smart cities as an outcome of connecting social entrepreneurship with digital entrepreneurship. The main purpose of smart cities is fostering economic growth and social environment, facilitated by collaborative dialogue and technological innovations. The authors claim that smart cities can both boost economic growth and solve societal problems. Smart cities introduce an innovation process starting from local entrepreneurs. A smart city includes technology, government, and society and it is a city that digital technology is diffused across all city functions. The researchers emphasize that smart cities resemble a social movement that contains "the government, citizens, businesses and entrepreneurs". Therefore, the entrepreneurs in smart cities reveal their entrepreneurship in a social-digital movement in a social-digital system.

As more social entrepreneurs go digital or more digital entrepreneurs go social, societies, economies, and the world will benefit from this. Covid-19 crisis has urged the world to be more digital and more social. The education systems of all countries should train new entrepreneurs as social and digital ones.

Table 1. The European Index of Digital Entrepreneurship Systems (EIDES)

Country	Stand-up sub-index		Start-up sub-index		Scale-up sub-index		EIDES	
	Score	Rank	Score	Rank	Score	Rank	Score	Rank
Denmark	84.6	1	77.0	2	80.9	1	80.7	1
Sweden	73.4	4	76.4	1	78.9	2	77.6	2
Luxembourg	75.9	2	72.1	3	74.8	3	74.3	3
Finland	73.3	3	71.3	4	72.0	4	72.4	4
Leaders	76.8		74.2		76.6		75.7	
Germany	64.6	6	61.7	6	65.1	6	63.8	5
United Kingdom	65.0	5	60.6	7	65.6	5	60.7	6
Netherlands	64.1	7	57.9	8	64.7	7	62.2	7
Ireland	61.5	8	62.7	5	59.1	8	61.1	8
Belgium	57.5	9	57.0	9	58.1	9	57.6	9
Austria	52.8	11	54.2	11	57.9	10	54.7	10
Malta	54.6	10	58.2	10	52.0	11	54.3	11
Estonia	52.7	12	53.5	12	48.7	13	51.0	12
France	49.7	13	47.2	13	51.4	12	48.6	13
Followers	52.5		52.6		52.0		52.1	
Spain	45.2	14	44.6	14	42.9	15	44.2	14
Czech Republic	41.9	15	41.9	15	45.1	14	42.5	15
Lithuania	39.8	16	41.8	17	40.1	16	40.6	16
Slovenia	35.3	19	41.6	16	38.2	17	38.4	17
Portugal	38.9	17	39.7	18	36.8	18	38.1	18
Cyprus	36.7	18	38.5	19	34.0	20	36.5	19
Catchers-up	37.7		40.1		37.3		38.4	
Poland	31.6	22	33.6	20	33.4	21	32.9	20
Latvia	32.5	20	32.8	21	33.2	22	32.9	21
Italy	32.0	21	31.8	24	34.0	19	32.6	22
Croatia	29.7	23	32.2	22	29.9	25	30.6	23
Hungary	27.6	25	32.0	23	30.9	23	30.1	24
Slovakia	28.1	24	30.3	25	30.6	24	29.9	25
Greece	22.9	26	24.4	26	25.5	26	24.3	26
Bulgaria	22.8	27	25.6	27	25.2	27	25.9	27
Romania	21.6	28	22.4	28	20.1	28	21.9	28
Laggards	25.9		26.1		24.5		24.9	
EU/28 average	47.0		47.2		47.2		47.1	

Table 1 above shows the European Index of Digital Entrepreneurship Systems (EIDES)(ec.europa.eu) scores of the 28 countries of the EU. Denmark, Sweden, Luxembourg, Finland, and Germany occupy the first five ranks. The countries are classified into four groups as the "leaders, followers, catchers-up, and laggards". This table is the digital entrepreneurship report card for the European countries.

Table 2. The 2020 Digital Economy and Society Index (DESI)

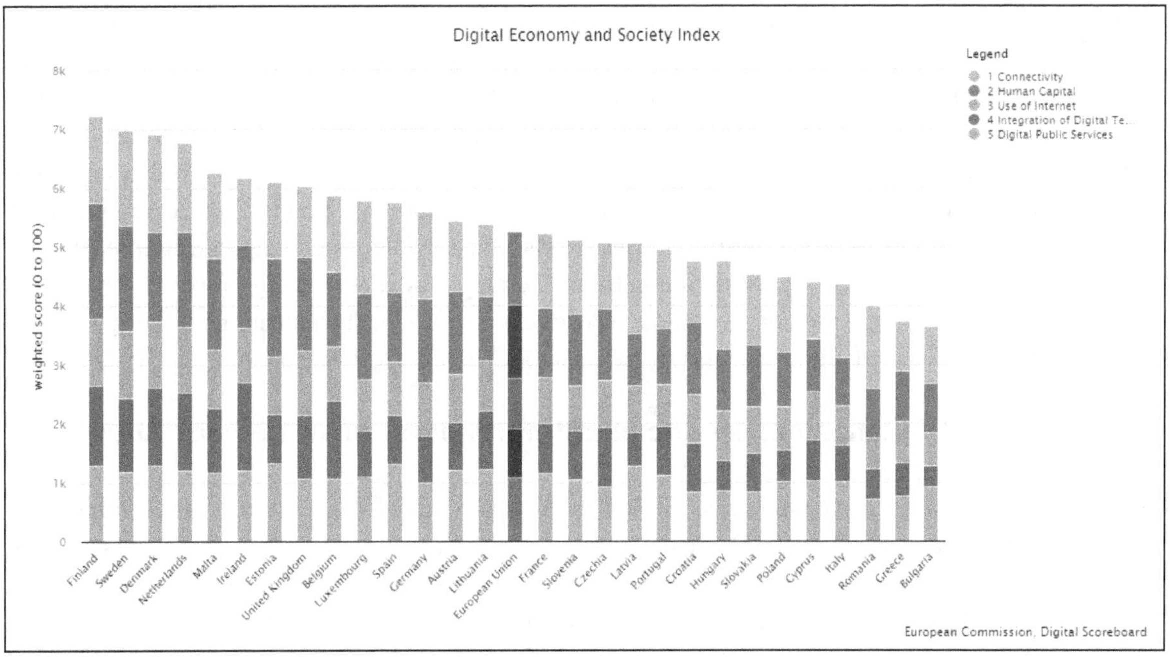

Table 2 is the 2020 Digital Economy and Society Index (DESI)(ec.europa.eu). The index reveals the digital performance of European countries based on certain indicators. A comparison of the two tables (Table 1 and 2) reveals that the top countries in digital entrepreneurship are also successful in the digital economy and society. These countries are Finland, Sweden, Denmark, Estonia, France, Belgium, Luxembourg, Spain, Austria, and Lithuania. This comparison implies that digitalization and digital entrepreneurship are closely interconnected.

Table 3. Estimated Number and Degree of Acceptance of Socail Enterprises in Europe

Country	Year	Estimated Number of SEs	Number of SEs per million inhabitants	Estimated number of employees	Degree of data reliability	SE concept use & acceptance
Albania	2015	379	132	2,000-2,500	Low	Low
Austria	2015	Approx. 1,535	Approx. 174	N.A.	Low	Low
Belgium	2017	18,004	1,580	572,910	Average	Average-High
Bulgaria	2015-2017	Approx. 3,700	Approx. 125	26,500	Average	Average
Croatia	2018	526	126	N.A.	Average	Average
Cyprus	2017	190	22	N.A.	Very low	Low
Czech Republic	2018	3,773	356	N.A.	Average	Average
Denmark	2018	411	71	N.A.	Low	Average
Estonia	2016	121	92	1,900	Average	Low
Finland	2016	1,181	214	Approx. 52,500	High	Average
France	2015-2017	Approx. 96,603	1,464	>1,187,249	Average	Average
Germany	2017	77,459	934	N.A.	Average	Low
Greece	2019	1,148	107	N.A.	High	Average
Hungary	2016	15,855	1,621	91,642	Average	Average
Iceland	2017	258	740	1,438	Low	Low
Ireland	2009	3,376	699	>25,000	Low	High
Italy	2017	102,461	1,694	894,800	Very High	Very High
Latvia	2019	Approx. 200	Approx. 103	N.A.	Average	Average
Lithuania	2016-2017	3,475	1,251	N.A.	Average	Average
Luxembourg	2017-2018	928	1,548	24,075	High	High
Malta	2019	31-62	65-130	N.A.	Low	Low
Montenegro	2018	150	241	<500	Low	Low
Netherlands	2015-2016	5,000-6,000	290-350	65,000-80,000	Low	Low
North Macedonia	2015-2015	551	266	N.A.	Low	Low
Norway	2018	250	47	N.A.	Average	Low
Poland	2016-2019	29,535	768	428,700	High	Average
Portugal	2013	7,938	773	185,716	Average	Average
Romania	2015-2017	6,317	321	17,117	Average	Average
Serbia	2012	411	58	4,379	Average	Low
Slovakia	2014	3,737	687	N.A.	Low	Average
Slovenia	2017	1,363	474	15,000	Average	Average
Spain	2017	9,680	208	>91,200	High	High
Sweden	2006-2016	Approx. 3,000	Approx. 298	N.A.	Low	Low
Turkey	2016-2018	1,776	22	N.A.	Average	Low
United Kingdom	2005-2017	30,753	464	153,517	Very high	Very high

Table 3 exhibits the fact that the number of Social Enterprises per million inhabitants is at a satisfactory level (1000+) in Belgium, France, Hungary, Italy, Lithuania, and Luxembourg. Certainly, the number of Social Enterprises is not the only factor to give an idea about the Social Enterprise ecosystem. The number of employees, data reliability, and the use and acceptance of the Social Enterprise concept are the other important factors shown in the table. Combining Tables 1 and 2 with Table 3, it is possible to observe that the countries which are successful in digital entrepreneurship and digitalization are also successful in social entrepreneurship. For example, Belgium, France, Luxembourg, and Lithuania are in this category. It is logical to conclude that these countries are also successful in social digital entrepreneurship.

At the moment, there is no social digital entrepreneurship index. It is being prepared for the year 2020. Therefore, the combination of these three indexes can reveal which countries have the appropriate ecosystem for social digital entrepreneurship.

The Effects of Digitalization on Social Entrepreneurship and Social Value

Social entrepreneurship is an ecosystem and digitalization is important for this ecosystem becoming widespread. The study describes in detail the structure and different aspects of social entrepreneurship. This ecosystem consists of helping disadvantaged and vulnerable groups for economic growth, providing equal opportunities for them, creating a platform that is accessible for everybody, especially the disadvantaged groups, contributing to the society, protecting sustainability and the environment, fostering employment, enhancing education, raising awareness, recovering the income injustice, encouraging social investors, and so on. For example, in the UK this ecosystem is quite wide and contains many actors, categories, and fields of social enterprises. However, other countries, especially the underdeveloped and developing ones, are not at that level. For example, in the UK, the British Council – a non-departmental public body – has been running the Global Social Enterprise Program which aims to "provide capacity building for social entrepreneurs, promotes social enterprise education in schools and universities, and forges international networks linking social entrepreneurs, intermediary organizations and social investors". The British Council also supports policy leaders to create ecosystems in which social entrepreneurship and social investment can succeed (The State of Social Enterprise in Turkey Report, 2019).

There are certain reasons for the inadequate number and quality of social enterprises in underdeveloped and some developing countries. The main reason for this seems the lack of government support and institutions like the British Council. Also, the awareness for and visibility of the concept of social entrepreneurship in societies is low in many countries. A common understanding should be created about the issue in those countries and this should be seen as a path to solidarity and prosperity in societies (The State of Social Enterprise in Turkey Report, 2019). The governments and local administrations should support social enterprises and relevant awareness.

About the policy aspect of the solution for the lack of social entrepreneurship, according to the British Council (The State of Social Enterprise in Turkey Report, 2019), serious policies should be adopted that include a holistic approach with ownership, coordination, and cooperation of different government departments. In some countries, bureaucracy creates many obstacles for social entrepreneurs. These should be removed and social entrepreneurship should be encouraged. Some social entrepreneurs may refrain from establishing a social enterprise due to tax policies in a country. Tax and employment policies should foster the foundation of social enterprises. Most social enterprises are innovative and policies should encourage innovations of social enterprises.

Prodanov (2018) states that one of the main reasons for the increase in social inequalities, crises, and unemployment is the spreading of digital technologies. However, digital technologies can also be a major tool for the solution of these problems. Building on the tenets of Actor-Network Theory, we argue that digitalization can actually avoid inequalities in the process of social value creation to society. As is known, the theory states that interrelated people tend to think and behave similarly. The theory examines the bonds between the actors in a certain group (individuals, groups, organizations) and explains the social behavior of the actor by addressing the system of networks as a whole. The network connections can both bond and separate the actors. Considering that social entrepreneurship is mostly about creating social networks aiming to generate social value, social network theory can explain the relationships between the actors of the network. The network impact is crucial for social enterprises. With digital ecosystems enabled by digitalization, enterprises can have a great network impact and this scale effect can foster the development of social enterprises. Actor-Network Theory and Social Network Theory contribute to the understanding of social entrepreneurship by focusing on the concept of network. These studies have the potential to provide a better understanding of social entrepreneurship. The better society understands the concept of social entrepreneurship, the more social entrepreneurship is supported by societies and governments. This will enable more developed social enterprises and therefore equality and more wealth in societies.

Social entrepreneurship emerged to attain social goals with the instruments of the market, not with those of the state and this was possible with digital technologies. Therefore, the researcher claims that there is a close connection between social entrepreneurship and the digital economy. This leads to the opinion that social entrepreneurship is a way of solving social problems in the context of Industry 4.0. In a rapidly changing digital environment, the entrepreneur has become an important person with innovative ideas. The rising inequalities in the world, especially under capitalism require new solutions like social entrepreneurship. Social entrepreneurship depends not on capitalistic expansion for profit but on the emotions of social responsibility, morality, and solidarity. A good example of a foundation of social entrepreneurship is the Ashoka Foundation which connects social entrepreneurs from all over the world. According to the author, an enterprise can be social only when the social goals are the main mission of its activity (Prodanov, 2018). Social entrepreneurs like Ashoka Foundation use mainly digital platforms to expand and operate. This fact implies that digitalization helps social enterprises not only in the founding stage but also in the operation stage.

In their study regarding women social entrepreneurs, Razak and Pisal (2016) mention the role of the digital economy in social entrepreneurship. They give examples of social entrepreneur women in Malaysia and state that these women sell their products online. They use a digital platform both in Malay language and English, they ship products abroad and their literacy rate has raised significantly by more than 80%. Their income has increased between 30 to 50%. This case is a typical example of the relationship between social entrepreneurship and digitalization. Some developing countries are encouraging women participation in the digital economy because governments are aware of the fact that if women use digital technologies more especially in rural areas and small towns, the society will benefit remarkably either through commercial or social enterprises. (Razak and Pisal, 2016). Although there are successful examples, the study emphasizes that there is a long way to go for the marginalized women in Malaysia. This study reveals a big hope for the poor and illiterate women in developing or underdeveloped countries who can be saved with the right social entrepreneurship policies with digital support.

Another study about women social entrepreneurs is that of Altinay and Altinay (2018). The researchers studied the women of the northern part of Cyprus. These women are social entrepreneurs who make projects for enhancing social responsibility to share knowledge, researching, and learning new things. According to the authors, technology has become a bridge to evaluate how social entrepreneurship can be enriched. Every society, especially women, should learn their experiences, beliefs, and values. Thus, technology becomes a bridge for women to adopt transformative learning for receiving education and gaining the capacity to understand their experiences, beliefs, and values. Digitalization and technology have made especially women more visible outside their local environment, enabled them to become pioneers of their employment, and increased their capacity to improve their skills. Digitalization has also made women adopt new changes and create new lifestyles (Altinay and Altinay, 2018). The results of the study confirm all these assumptions. In a closed community like the northern part of Cyprus, digitalization seems to have made a huge difference for women social entrepreneurs and all other women.

Bychkovska (2017) indicates that social entrepreneurship is influenced by digitalization and plays the role of the tool of technological change. The author mentions the two-way relationship between the two concepts. Being quite innovative, social entrepreneurs develop progressive business models. These works are interwoven with technological innovations to transform national innovation systems. Social entrepreneurs learn from international innovation systems, develop local capacities, and adopt international knowledge and social innovation to local needs (Bychkovska, 2017). Constant personal development and learning combined with open-mindedness and research can bring distinctive knowledge and innovation to locals which pave the way for social entrepreneurship.

There are numerous studies about the effect of digitalization on entrepreneurship (ex. Fossen and Sorgner, 2019) but the studies about the effect of digitalization on social entrepreneurship are very few. The literature on this subject is open to enrichment.

CONCLUSION

We live in an ecosystem age, based on technology-based developments, all of the shareholders of the communities can produce economic value and foster social-cultural development. In these ecosystems, social entrepreneurship thanks to the technology-based tools receives growing attention because of its potential for addressing societal problems. As technology develops, new digital devices and platforms are introduced, thus, as social entrepreneurs invent new types of social enterprises, new solutions, and new business models integrated with digitalization. This study relates digitalization to social entrepreneurship. The Covid-19 pandemic has shown that digitalization is an inseparable part of our lives. With digital ecosystems enabled by digitalization, social enterprises can have a great network impact and this scale effect can foster the development of social enterprises.

In this chapter, digitalization's facilitating role in the creation of social value is discussed through the block chain example. Also, the impact of the digitalization competence of countries on digital social entrepreneurship, which is a new concept, is shown by comparing EIDES, SEs Europe, and DESI indices. Then the subject is linked to social digital entrepreneurship and the countries having social digital entrepreneurship ecosystems are indicated. In addition, the subject is connected with the Actor-Network Theory which may also contribute to a clearer understanding. Moreover, the system of education suggested for the social entrepreneurs of the developing countries, which are not digitally mature, the road to this system, and its convenience discussed.

The relationship of digitalization with social entrepreneurship and social value is a relatively new concept and needs to be studied in different contexts such as countries, genders, and people with disabilities. Future research on digitalization can focus on types of digital social entrepreneurship and the effects of actor network theory and social network theory on social digital enterprises. Moreover, the legal basis for social digital entrepreneurship is a fruitful area. In addition, blockchain technology and its reliability effect on social digital entrepreneurship can be researched. The effect of the new funding options coming with the crowdfunding originating from the blockchain technology on social digital entrepreneurship should also be studied. Another research area can be social network usage on social digital entrepreneurship. The positive and negative network effects of digitalization can be studied as well. Also, the benefits of digitalization on social enterprises can be studied. The question of "How can digitalization be cost-effective?" can be taken into account in the research. Moreover, the concepts of crowdfunding and the effect of scale can also be considered. In terms of practical implications, research may be conducted on specific topics such as financial impacts of social digital entrepreneurship, and social entrepreneurship, especially in developing countries outside the EU or whether gender inequality in STEM is also valid for social digital entrepreneurs or not. Also, the impact of the proposed education system can be studied.

REFERENCES

Afonasova, M., Panfilova, E., Galichkina, M., & Slusarczyk. (n.d.). Digitalization in Economy and Innovation: The Effect on Social and Economic Processes. *Polish Journal of Management Studies, 19*(2), 22-32.

Baierl. (2019). *Digital Entrepreneurship – Interfaces between Digital Technologies and Entrepreneurship Reihe: FGF Studies in Small Business and Entrepreneurship*. Springer. doi:10.1007/978-3-030-20138-8

Barbosa, L. (2020). Social Entrepreneurship and Digital Technology – Case Study of the Blockchain for Zero Hunger Initiative. *52nd International Scientific Conference on Economic and Social Development*.

Barcevicius. (2019). *Exploring Digital Government Transformation in the EU*. European Commission JRC Science for Policy Report, 12.

Biggiero, L. (2007). Industrial and Knowledge Relocation Strategies Under the Challenges of Globalization and Digitalization: The Move of Small and Medium Enterprises Among Territorial Systems. *Entrepreneurship and Regional Development, 18*(6), 443–471. doi:10.1080/08985620600884701

British Council. (2019). *The State of Social Enterprise in Turkey Report*. Retrieved September 3, 2020 from https://www.britishcouncil.org.tr/en/programmes/education/social-enterprise-research

Chalmers, D., Matthews, R., & Hyslop, A. (2019). Blockchain as an External Enabler of New Venture Ideas: Digital Entrepreneurs and the Disintermediation of the Global Music Industry. *Journal of Business Research*. Advance online publication. doi:10.1016/j.jbusres.2019.09.002

Cresswell, K., Worth, A., & Sheikh, A. (2010). Actor-Network Theory and Its Role in Understanding the Implementation of Information Technology Developments in Healthcare. *BMC Medical Informatics and Decision Making, 10*(1), 67. doi:10.1186/1472-6947-10-67 PMID:21040575

Drencheva, A. (2019). Social Entrepreneurship: Blending Prosocial Motivation and Self-Interests in Business. In D. Ochnik (Ed.), *Selflessness in Business* (pp. 15–32). Vernon Press.

Dy, A. M. (2016). A Web of Opportunity or the Same Old Story? Women Digital Entrepreneurs and Intersectionality Theory. *Human Relations*, 286–311.

Elia, G., Margherita, A., & Passiante, G. (2020). Digital Entrepreneurship Ecosystem: How Digital Technologies and Collective Intelligence are Reshaping the Entrepreneurial Process. *Technological Forecasting and Social Change, 150*, 1–12. doi:10.1016/j.techfore.2019.119791

Eneza Education. (2017). Retrieved October 1, 2020 from http:// enezaeducation.com/

Eurodiaconia Briefing for Members, Measuring Social Value, What Do We Mean by Measuring Social Value? (n.d.). Retrieved September, 10 from www.eurodiaconia.org

European Commission. (2016). *Social Enterprises and Their Eco-systems: Developments in Europe, Directorate-General for Employment Social Affairs and Inclusion, 8. European Union Digital Transformation*. Retrieved August 21, 2020 from https://www.i-scoop.eu/digital-transformation/digitization-digitalization-digital-transformation-disruption/

Fossen, F. M., & Sorgner, A. (2019). Digitalization of Work and Entry into Entrepreneurship. *Journal of Business Research, 148*(2963), 1–16. doi:10.1016/j.jbusres.2019.09.019

Galindo-Martin, M. A., Castano-Martinez, M. S., & Mendez-Picaso, M. T. (2019). Digital Transformation, Digital Dividends, and Entrepreneurship: A Quantitative Analysis. *Journal of Business Research, 101*, 522–527. doi:10.1016/j.jbusres.2018.12.014

Gardner. (2018). *Gardner Glossary*. Digital Library Federation.

Gobble, M. (2018). Digitalization, Digitization, and Innovation. *Research Technology Management, 61*(4), 56–59. doi:10.1080/08956308.2018.1471280

Hanninen, M., Smedlund, A., & Mitronen, L. (2018). Digitalization in Retailing: Multi-Sided Platforms as Drivers of Industry Transformation. *Baltic Journal of Management, 13*(2), 152–168. doi:10.1108/BJM-04-2017-0109

Huang, S., & Cox, J. L. (2014). Establishing a Social Entrepreneurial System to Bridge the Digital Divide for the Poor: A Case Study for Taiwan. *Universal Access in the Information Society*, 219–236.

Human Development Report. (2015). *Work for Human Development*. New York: United Nations Development Program.

Hure, E., Picot-Koupey, K., & Ackermann, C. (2017). Understanding Omni-Channel Shopping Value: A Mixed Method Study. *Journal of Retailing and Consumer Services, 39*, 314–330. doi:10.1016/j.jretconser.2017.08.011

Jovanovic, M., Okanovic, M., & Dlacic, J. (2018). Digitalization and Society's Sustainable Development – Measures and Implications. *Proceedings of Rijeka School of Economics, 36*(2), 905–928.

Klymenko, O., Halse, L., Jeger, B., Nerger, A.J., (2019). Digitalization and Environmental Sustainability: Where are the Opportunities? *7th EurOMA Book of Proceedings,* 3880-3889.

Kraus, S., Palmer, C., Kailer, N., Kallinger, F. L., & Spitzer, J. (2018). Digital Entrepreneurship: A Research Agenda on New Business Models for the Twenty-First Century. *International Journal of Entrepreneurial Behaviour & Research, 25*(2), 353–375. doi:10.1108/IJEBR-06-2018-0425

Legner, C. (2017). Digitalization: Opportunity and Challenge for the Business and Information Systems Engineering Community, *Business. Information Systems, 59*(4), 301–308.

Maiolini, Marra, A., Baldassarri, C., & Carlei, V. (2016). Digital Technologies for Social Innovation: An Empirical Recognition on the New Enablers. *Journal of Technology Management & Innovation, 11*(4), 22–28. doi:10.4067/S0718-27242016000400004

Martin, R. L., & Osberg, S. (2007). Social Entrepreneurship: The Case for Definition. *Stanford Social Innovation Review*.

Martin-Pena, M.L. (2018). *The Digitalization and Servitization of Manufacturing: A Review on Digital Business Models.* Wiley.

Mukkamala, Vatrapu, R., Ray, P. K., Sengupta, G., & Halder, S. (2018). Blockchain for Social Business: Principles and Applications. *IEEE Engineering Management Review*, *46*(4), 94–99. doi:10.1109/EMR.2018.2881149

Muro, M. (2017). *Digitalization and the American Workforce*. Metropolitan Policy Program.

Murschetz, P. (2019). Editorial to Special Issue on "Digital Entrepreneurship". In P. Faustino & T. Flew (Eds.), *Journal of Creative Industries and Cultural Studies* (pp. 9–13). Routledge.

Nogueira, A. (2018). *Digital Entrepreneurship: What is it and How to Get Started*. Retrieved October, 7, 2020 from https://blog.hotmart.com/en/digital-entrepreneurship/

Nominet Trust Reveals 100 Leading Ventures Using Tech to Solve World's Biggest Social Problems. (n.d.). Retrieved September 27, 2020 from http://www.nominettrust. org.uk/news-events/news/nominet-trust-reveals-100-leading-ventures-using-tech-to-solve-world%E2%80%99s-biggest-soci

Parida, Sjödin, D., & Reim, W. (2019). Reviewing Literature on Digitalization, Business Model Innovation, and Sustainable Industry: Past Achievements and Future Promises. *Sustainability*, *11*(2), 391. doi:10.3390u11020391

Popov, E.V., Veretennikova, A.Y., & Kozinskaya, K.M. (2020). *The Impact of Digitalization on the Social Entrepreneurship Development, Institute of Economics*. The Ural Branch of the Russian Academy of Sciences.

Rachinger, Rauter, R., Müller, C., Vorraber, W., & Schirgi, E. (2018). Digitalization and Its Influence on Business Model Innovation. *Journal of Manufacturing Technology Management*, *30*(8), 1143–1160. doi:10.1108/JMTM-01-2018-0020

Sahut, J. M., Iandoli, L., & Teulon, F. (2019, September). The Age of Digital Entrepreneurship. *Small Business Economics*, 1–19.

Santana, M. (2017). Digital Entrepreneurship: Expanding the Economic Frontier in the Mediterranean. European Institute of the Mediterranean, 1-51.

Sarma & Sunny. (2017). Civic Entrepreneurial Ecosystems: Smart City Emergence in Kansas City. *Business Horizons*, 843–853.

Schwab Foundation for Social Entrepreneurship. (2017). Retrieved October 7, 2020 from http://www.schwabfound.org/

Small, A. (2014, Feb. 5). The New Social Entrepreneurs: Young, Tech-Savvy – and Improving the World. *The Guardian.*

Social Enterprises and Their Ecosystems in Europe. (2020). Comparative Synthesis Report, European Commission.

Social innovation mapping: Social entrepreneurs changing lives through ICT. (2014). *Ashoka*. Retrieved September 15, 2020 from https://sipa.columbia.edu/ system/files/ICT-Based-Social-Impact_09- 2014-report.pdf

Worldreader. (2017). Retrieved September 2, 2020 from https://www. worldreader.org/

Yavuz, M. S. (2019). Digital Transformation in Economy: A Review of Blockchain Technology and Application Areas. *Research of Financial, Economic, and Social Studies*, *4*(1), 15–29.

KEY TERMS AND DEFINITIONS

Blockchain: It is a distributed database that is protected against security gaps, encrypted on a network, and ensures the management of the data.

COVID-19: It is a disease caused by a new strain of coronavirus.

Digital Entrepreneurship: It is about creating new ventures, converting existing businesses by developing original digital technologies or their original usage.

Digitalization: It is the utilization of digital technologies to change a business model and supply new income and value-producing opportunities and it is the process of moving to a digital business.

Social Digital Entrepreneurship: Social digital entrepreneurship represents the "social" side of digital entrepreneurship implying a more humane use of the digital world and entrepreneurship.

Social Entrepreneurship: Social entrepreneurship is the process of establishing social enterprises to create social benefits.

Social Value: It is the quantification of the relative importance that people experience about the changes in their lives.

Section 2
Financial Tools in Social Entrepreneurship

Chapter 7
A Magical Tool for Social Entrepreneurship:
Crowdfunding

Erkut Altındağ
Beykent University, Turkey

ABSTRACT

In recent years, sharing behaviors, collective actions, and individual participation have gained momentum in terms of shared value creation understanding. Crowdfunding is one of the results of this new emphasis on collective participation. Where social entrepreneurship is a shining trend, financing of investments becomes increasingly essential. As social entrepreneurs struggle with the disadvantages of acquiring financial resources, crowdfunding appears to be an innovative tool to overcome financial shortcomings. In this chapter, the crowdfunding concept and its types are explained. Also, evidence of the organic bond between crowdfunding and social entrepreneurship with current examples from the world and Turkey is presented.

INTRODUCTION

In recent years, crowdfunding has become a new way for entrepreneurs to request financing in order to put their ideas and business plans into effect. Crowdfunding platforms such as Kickstarter, GoFundMe, and Indiegogo were introduced in order to host and mediate fundraising campaigns. Numerous reports about financing achievements of those who have had success using them have made such platforms very popular, and the growing interest from all kinds of entrepreneurs and investors has attracted participants to these platforms. Although it is relatively easy to create a project on these platforms, it is quite difficult to achieve the funding goals. There are many factors that may affect the results. For example, those things that may help increase the success rate of content creators is having previous experience, being able to promote the product on social media, using the right language describe the project, and the design of the reward package. For crowdfunding, all projects are shown to the backers on the online platform (Apostolos and Ioannis, 2012; Lin et al., 2018 ; Allon and Babich, 2020).

DOI: 10.4018/978-1-7998-4727-4.ch007

Crowdfunding can be used for supporting projects in the sciences and in many other fields. By using social media channels, a large number of micro-investors can be quickly reached. Social media such as Facebook, Twitter, YouTube, Flickr, and Tumblr make it possible to reach and link to thousands of media site for the project in way that is faster and more efficient than using traditional media. It thus is really important to take advantage of common interests in order to include investors in the platform environment. In the social sciences, crowdfunding has attracted significantly more interest recently. The advantages of crowdfunding for cultural organizations are quite clear, and the organizations does not constitute an exception. Crowdfunding also allows entrepreneurs to raise funds through an open call on the Internet. Perhaps the most important feature is the extra unique benefits that funders (i.e., "crowdfunding") enjoy by participating in the crowdfunding mechanism. These additional unique benefits vary with an equity-based model, profit-sharing scheme, and crowdfunding forms ranging from lending to direct donations. While crowdfunding can take different forms, there is little academic understanding of the economic factors that determine an entrepreneur's choice of a particular form of crowdfunding (Belleflamme et al., 2014). From social entrepreneurship, all the concepts discussed in this section will also give clues about the new economic period in the world undergoing a change in the shadow of the pandemic as an extension of popular culture and technological developments.

Crowdfunding is a suitable alternative method for other institutions and individuals who are not actively involved in a country's capital market. In traditional financing models, there is a structure where labor and expenses are extremely high, and entrepreneurs need to hold dozens or hundreds of meetings in order to access finance. In a sense, it centralizes available investment opportunities by enabling data access. Thus, mass investment portals allow the information of early-stage businesses to be quickly transferred to potential investors. Crowdfunding system is also an effective system for investors. In the crowdfunding literature, backers observe and are aware of decisions from other backers and are influenced by their behavior (Bretschneider et. al., 2014). The concept was recently promoted as a way to help small businesses and entrepreneurs looking for investment capital to take their business ventures from scratch. Traditionally, investment advice is given by professionals such as brokers and investment consultants, based on clients' investment objectives and their level of sophistication. This system allows investors to search for many potential investment opportunities at once and access detailed information about them online. The new trend in the developing world is donation-based crowdfunding platforms that investors use to monitor innovative products and companies. It is known that social entrepreneurs have difficulties in maintaining the continuity of their initiatives that they started to create social value. For this reason, crowdfunding emerges as an essential tool for the sustainability of initiatives. Especially, the difficulties of new entrepreneurs in accessing resources and financial problems make crowdfunding an important alternative.

The Concept of Crowdfunding

Crowdfunding was derived from the concept of crowdsourcing, which involves the use of a large number of people to gather ideas and solutions for a wide range of problems. This new concept was first introduced into the international literature by Jeff Howe in 2006. The crowdfunding method aims to fund new initiatives by collecting small and medium sized investments from a wide variety of people (Apostolos & Ioannis 2012). Crowdfunding was derived from microfinance, and it has grown and diversified significantly since its origins. New developments in internet-based financing have been coming on board since 2006. Since crowdfunding is internet-based, it has proliferated and has also already had a significant economic impact as it reaches all the countries globally. It can be defined as the collective effort of many individuals to network and pool their resources to support efforts initiated by specific organizations. The idea of crowdfunding dates back to the late 1990s. The first websites created primarily for charitable fundraising used the internet to extend traditional fundraising campaigns. The significant effects of crowdfunding for fundraising have been remarkable. This funding method accelerates cooperation among different people and organizations to speed up the financing of business projects while requiring new sets of behaviors by different actors. (Wallmeroth 2019). This concept goes back centuries or even thousands of years. People pooling their resources in order to finance a typical project is an idea that dates back to a long time when people who lived in communities together shared duties and responsibilities.

The basic idea behind crowdfunding, which is considered an innovative method of securing funding, is not a new phenomenon. A frequently cited early example in crowdfunding literature is the Statue of Liberty on Ellis Island in New York, which was constructed after seeking funds from the public in newspapers, unlike today's crowdfunding projects (Brüntje & Gajda 2016). In 1885, Joseph Pulitzer, the publisher of the New York newspaper *World*, asked New York citizens to make a financial contribution to make the pedestal of the statue. In return for doing this, he would print the individuals who provided their support in his newspaper. Five months after this notice, the *World* announced that the donation campaign had amassed $102,000. The most crucial point about this support was that up to 80% of the funds came from citizens in New York who had donated less than $1 US dollar each (Gierczak et al. 2016).

Crowdfunding is a bottom-up microfinance practice that seeks to mobilize people and resources. Therefore, it necessarily comes from a group cooperating together. It is a collective movement that results the efforts of individuals and organizations using websites dedicated to seeking these types of funds. The term "crowdfunding" comes from the word "crowdsourcing," which refers to the collective development of a product. Collective financing is generally used to promote innovative products. Therefore, it is different from other models in terms of the "reward" that is expected by the project's contributors. According to the Framework for European Crowdfunding, "the rise of crowdfunding in the last decade results from the increase in web applications and mobile services, and the conditions allowing entrepreneurs, businesses, and all kinds of creatives to communicate with the dialogue" (Biancone et al., 2019).

There are three essential features involved in crowdfunding (Hoque et al., 2018); there is a business project that requires financing, there are several investors, and a significant amount of the support is provided during the implementation period for the project and it brings investors and entrepreneurs together by means of an internet platform. The platform is called an interface where both the fundraiser and backers come together. Crowdfunding platforms are a place that online brokers can mediate between the entrepreneurs who have ideas and the backers who can support them. Therefore, the platform is a place that can be defined as an interface between founders and funders (Sharma & Lertnuwat, 2016). Furthermore, brokers need to provide a valuable service to be able to compete in the crowdfunding industry. Trust, reputation, legitimacy, sustainability, and success are key factors for these firms. Brokers generate income from different sources, such as commissions on the amount of funds raised, payment processing fees, and consulting services fees. Therefore, their performance and economic sustainability may depend on the number of projects they can draw to their platform as well as the amount of funding involved in these projects and the success of these campaigns. The cybersecurity used by the platforms and the potential failure of projects initiated there are among the risks backers face. In any event, crowdfunding platforms face two main problems. The first is the risk of the crash of a major platform due to neglect or the use of a bad application. The second is the risk of one of the projects on these platforms turning out fraudulent. If either of these occur with any frequency, this may damage the platform's reputation for potential content creators and funders (Rey-Martí, et al. 2019). Therefore, crowdfunding may lead to major changes in the relationship between investors and the people who need the crowdsourced funds. The use of social networks has only heightened the number of potential uses for crowdfunding, and information about a crowdfunding campaign can spread everywhere the need for the funding of original ideas that are deserving of such support.

An important difference between crowdfunding from traditional entrepreneur financing is that there is no intermediation. While transparency and reputation costs help to reduce the moral hazards involved, the information asymmetry in these markets is mitigated by the collective knowledge generated by the crowd. Furthermore, investors can achieve significant diversity by means of low search and online investment costs, which greatly improves the amount of risk-sharing. Essentially, these mechanisms are provided by the use of internet technologies to maintain the functioning of the markets engaged in crowdfunding(Hsu, 2015). By ensuring effective networking and interactions (usually online) providers are considered as the most important components of a crowdfunding project, allowing creators to connect with a potentially large audience ("crowd"). Furthermore, project creators are encouraged by the platforms to inform potential funding providers about their projects through the updates they provide on the crowdfunding platform (Borst et al., 2018).

Models of Crowdfunding

Crowdfunding can include various means of colleting funds, from online fundraising to the sale of stock. Each project typically has a financing goal that needs to be completed by a certain time. Therefore, depending on the fundraising approach, if a project's funding goal is not reached exactly by the desired time, the money that has already been contributed to the project is transferred back to the contributors. Thus, the funder (the project's owner or a place of business) cannot initiate the project. Therefore, all or nothing is valid on the platform. On the other hand, a fundraising fund can collect funds even if the predefined funding goal has not been fully met at the time of the deadline. There are different crowdfunding models, which depend on the type of returns (financial or non-financial) that contributors receive. The main crowdfunding models can be categorized under the following four broad categories (Spanos, 2016, p. 2-3):

The Donation-Based Crowdfunding Model

The donation-based crowdfunding model generally involves raising funds for social causes, artistic projects, or aid organizations that are seeking donations. Donors provide financing for these projects or companies without the expectation of monetary or financial returns. Therefore, the people who contribute form a sense of belonging, and nothing is expected in return (Arnold et al., 2019). The donation-based type of crowdfunding involves funding for an incredibly wide range of issues, from overcoming medical crises to rescuing homeless animals, eliminating social problems, or the reallocation of educational resources. As a distinct problem-solving strategy and as a widespread social practice, donation-based crowdfunding has become an alternative source of capital for various personal and public purposes (Xu, 2018).

Through donation-based crowdfunding, donors receive nothing for their contributions. This type of crowdfunding is essentially used to get financing for NGOs. Razoo, Crowdrise, and GoFundMe are among the donation crowdfunding platforms. The cooperation formed in this relationship that results donations exceeds the level of just being simple financial relations due to the high level of emotional participation by the backers for such projects. Individuals who contribute to the project can act as partners through the online platforms, and they not only contribute financially to the project but also can become an important member of the team for the film project. Therefore, viewers can play a significant role in a production when they move from a passive to active mode of engagement with a project. It may take a long time for a project's owners to bring together the number of backers they need on the platform to provide the necessary support for a project. Significant mistakes in crowdfunding include failing to pay attention to backers or to fully transfer the project to them. The funds (community) usually contain more than just monetary contributions. The backers of a project may be in contact with the producer and/or director during the production of the film. Therefore, they can also make additional contributions to the project. For example, backers can play a significant role by providing a free opportunity to use someplace as a location to shoot all or part of the film, or they could assist at different stages in terms of their technical skills or by promoting the film on social media and other platforms. Furthermore, backers can also inform the producer about upcoming film festivals or competitions (Fanea-Ivanovici, 2018).

The Reward-Based Crowdfunding Model

A type of crowdfunding in which the crowd is particularly useful for creating an added value beyond financing is the reward-based crowdfunding. Reward-based crowdfunding has certain features that make it particularly easy to interact with potential customers. One of the main features of reward-based crowdfunding is that it usually revolves around consumer goods and services. Therefore, it is perfectly suited to take advantage of potential customers in a creative manner during the value creation process of an initiative. Another important feature of reward-based crowdfunding is that it is based on a pre-sale agreement, which means that the firms that use reward-based crowdfunding can allow their backers to obtain the rights for a particular product or the rights related to a particular product (namely, the product itself or the previously discussed rewards) in return for their financial contribution. While such a pre-sale agreement brings with it a particular risk (namely, the business may run out of money before the product is produced), it also offers certain opportunities for both firms and customers. Since the product is generally not produced until it is financed by investors, new venture customers can use this arrangement to develop and commercialize their products and services, which allows them to use their potential customers as a valuable resource for creative activities (Lipusch et al., 2018).

In terms of reward-based crowdfunding, the definition of a "product" can be quite varied. For example, it can be a physical commodity, such as an electronic device. It can also be a service, such as a piece of software, movies, music, live shows, or even restaurants. An important feature of performing reward-based crowdfunding is that the backers who invest in a campaign usually buy the finished product and, therefore, serve as both the investors in the venture and the consumer of the product. If the campaign reaches its goal, it will succeed, and the content creator may provide rewards to backers who have donated to the campaign. Otherwise, the campaign fails, and consequently, the backers are refunded their money and no reward is given to them (Chakraborty & Swinney, 2020). For reward-based crowdfunding, backers typically make a small contribution in return for benefits from a proposed product or service. Kickstarter, PledgeMusic, and Indiegogo are examples of reward-based crowdfunding platforms.

The Lending-Based Crowdfunding Model

A lending-based crowdfunding platform allows individuals, organizations, and businesses to raise money to finance their activities. In other words, this type of crowdfunding mobilizes financial resources that are provided by a large number of investors and are directed through private platforms. It connects individual debtors to potential lenders through its online platform (Landström et al., 2019). For example, in the lending-based model, investors will receive their original investments plus interest (the rate of which depends on the level of risk involved). For lending-based crowdfunding, lenders provide money to entrepreneurs or organizations through a platform and expect repayment at an agreed upon time. Depending on the platform used, some lenders charge interest while others do not. Kiva is an example of this type of platform. The succession of lending-based crowdfunding platforms hinges on their own ability to solve moral hazard issues and overcome significant entry barriers related to scale and scope economies, adverse selection, and funding cost advantage of large incumbent banks. There are also risks related to excessive reliance on leveraged funding and 'too big to fail' institutional investors prone to runs and moral hazard problems (Havrylchyk, 2018).

The Equity-Based Crowdfunding Model

Finally, equity-based crowdfunding is one in which funders usually get an appropriate share of the project, including participation in the launch of a venture (Kuti et al., 2017). The project owner defines the duration and the targeted funding amount for the crowdfunding campaign. Bids continue until the target is achieved, and the investment stage starts at that moment. Product or service can be traded as a stock on any stock market, and its value may increase or decrease. Investors who generate cash through equity-based crowdfunding platforms become the shareholders of institutions (Fenwick et al., 2018). In sum, the crowd is an important force for change. Crowdfunding refers to fundraising by ordinary people who come together on online platforms. Backers wait until the financing is completed after they provide their support to a project they like. However, if backers do not like and support a project, then the funding will not be provided. The system operates by means of the participation of everyone on the social platform, and it is a way to bring people together with businesses in order to develop different ventures.Equity-based crowdfunding is generally used to finance the launch or growth of a company. CrowdCube, Seedrs, and CircleUp are some of the most popular platforms for this type of funding (Nevin et al., 2017). In view of the potential benefits, newly established companies and entrepreneurs generally use lending-based crowdfunding and equity-based crowdfunding to attract investments. Lending-based and equity-based crowdfunding are jointly called "investment crowdfunding." If the companies funded grow and develop, then their investors will usually receive financial returns.

The Potential Benefits of Crowdfunding for Social Enrepreneurs

In our business world, financing is the most basic need in all kinds of initiatives because the shortage of finance puts new firms at a clear disadvantage compared to established firms. This funding scarcity is a significant problem, especially in social entrepreneurship, as social motivation often takes precedence over financial concerns and is not compatible with the interests of traditional forms of finance (banks, angel investors, venture capital, etc.) (Rey-Marti, 2019). Although crowdfunding may seem similar to venture capital and angel investment, there are some differences in it. The purpose of all three financing methods is to create a source of funds for young entrepreneurs who cannot provide collateral to obtain loans from credit institutions, especially banks, and who do not have sufficient resources to implement their business ideas and projects. While the angel investor supports the business ideas that it deems appropriate individually, it provides the fund source institutionally through venture capital and ventures capital investment trusts. On the other hand, crowdfunding can collect resources for the project and business idea from the public, investors, through a crowdfunding platform from all over the world, without any time and place shortages (Fettahoğlu 2017, 517).

Social projects are not attractive to traditional lenders or investors because social goals sometimes conflict with maximization goals. This challenge is compounded by fierce competition between socially-oriented organizations for attracting donations and state aid. This aid's availability has declined dramatically in recent years, as the recent economic crisis has forced many national governments to reduce social spending. Concordantly, crowdfunding offers a convenient way to fund social entrepreneurship startups. Therefore, crowdfunding is accepted as a method for establishing an internet-based link between entrepreneurs who want to increase their amount of available capital and the investors who want to provide a new source of funds for a project and are willing to invest.

The crowdfunding can be defined as a virtual electronic platform where all of the communication and fundraising takes place between the entrepreneurs and the investors. This platform has a mission that brings these parties together for this common purpose. The entrepreneurs and groups involved are seeking a means for financing these initiatives through the provision of relatively small contributions by many individuals who use the internet, without the help of financial intermediaries. This absence of financial institutions that act as intermediaries in crowdfunding distinguishes crowdfunding from capital or credit market activities. Individuals, SMEs, and non-governmental organizations (NGOs) are usually in the role of being the entrepreneur. The financial return of crowdfunding plays a crucial role in backing firms and projects that would not be funded or only partially financed in old fashioned ways, that is, through the banking channel or financial markets, particularly in the case of SMEs (Bottiglia and Pichler, 2016).

Through crowdfunding, social entrepreneurs can not only receive support for their long term projects but also can take the opportunity to test their business ideas on these platforms. Thus, these social entrepreneurs have the opportunity to receive feedback about the critical features of their new products before they launch them, and this gives them the opportunity to make changes to products based on this feedback (Lam & Law 2016). Moreover, social entrepreneurs can benefit from crowdfunding mainly to reduce costs. Users make significant contributions to the creation of a project by being involved in the product's development and design. Companies can collect funds easily and quickly by means of a crowdfunding platform because crowdfunding creates a pool of funds provided in small amounts by individuals. Backers may sometimes be more effective and productive than using small teams or individuals. One idea behind using a crowd as a funding source is based on the principle that the more different individuals there are that are involved, the more effective and efficient the project can be. The fact that the members of the crowd have different backgrounds and act collectively can play an important role in the progress of a project (Hoque et al., 2018).

It should also be noted that crowdfunding, which is a unique aspect of creating social value, allows price discrimination. For example, in the case of pre-ordering, the capacity to best practice price discrimination between crowdfunders and other consumers can be limited by the amount of capital the entrepreneur must collect to meet the pre-order fixed costs (Belleflamme et al., 2014). Crowdfunding offers unique features in terms of new methods that have become a part of social entrepreneurship today.

The goal of crowdfunding is to raise many small donations through the online platform of a financial institution instead of making large amounts of demands from it. A crowdfunding opportunity is published during a limited period of time on the specified platform, and there is financial target that the creators seek before the campaign ends (Schäfer et al., 2018, p. 497). New donors are likely to repeat the behaviors of previous donors, who engage in peer influence on social media, and this can be an important driving force behind the success of a crowdfunding campaign. In addition, the use of social media can also augment the so-called "bystander" effect. In summary, it can be said that crowdfunding benefits all new business plan owners, especially small entrepreneurs, at different scales. At the last, with the opportunity to advertise the platforms used and announce the projects to the whole world itself, many more financial and advertorial benefits can be obtained.

Prominent Examples of Crowdfunding

The two biggest crowdfunding platforms are Kickstarter and Indiegogo. The Kickstarter crowdfunding platform follows the so-called "all-or-nothing" model, and it has hosted 473,941 campaigns since it began in 2008. Of these campaigns, 176,497 have successfully financed a total amount of over $4.5 billion. The Indiegogo crowdfunding platform is the second biggest crowdfunding platform, and it has hosted over 800,000 campaigns. Approximately 9% of them have been successfully financed with a total amount of more than $1.6 billions. Using Indiegogo, entrepreneurs can make a choice between the "keep-it-all" model and the "all-or-nothing" model. Platforms charge fees ranging from 3% to 9% of the funding volume collected. The Indiegogo platform is a more open platform when compared to Kickstarter that can be used by any company for any product. In 2017-2018, it launched several strategic projects that helped crowdfunding firms to develop their businesses after a campaign.

The program offers a number of services for entrepreneurs, including special product pages and comprehensive marketing packages. It also provides a significant amount of support for firms so that they can overcome many problems that are related to starting a new business. Both Marketplace and Amazon Launchpad have created an environment in which firms that use crowdfunding can compete with firms that do not use crowdfunding (Miglo, 2020, p. 1-2). The AngelList crowdfunding platform can form all kinds of funding unions, involving individuals, angel investors, and risk capital. Individual angel investors create an online union profile that provides their basic information for potential backers, such as how many unions they expect to syndicate each year and their typical investment sizes. Other accredited investors who apply to join one or more specific unions are referred to as "backers." These investments are made through the AngelList platform (Agrawal et al., 2016, p. 114). AngelList operates through a U.S.-based website for firms that facilitate syndication investments of accredited investors. Unions meet on the portal, and management is conducted by experienced investors who examine the target investment and invest personally in the agreement that they offer. Thus, they provide their confidence in the potential of the investment. The AngelList portal actively offers opportunities for more than 200 union candidates (Hornuf & Cumming, 2018). In particular, CircleUp helped 106 companies to exceed $125 million dollars in funding by focusing on consumer products and the retail market. In 2012, the passage of the JOBS Act made crowdfunding legal by loosening various restrictions on the sale of securities. Prior to that, companies that issued private securities could not advertise their offers or did not demand investors in general. Therefore, as a way to mobilize resources, this crowdfunding has become an increasingly important force in terms of global finance (Zhao et al. 2019). Equity-based crowdfunding platforms, such as SeedInvest, conduct a meticulous business process to prevent the prohibition of general demand and to take advantage of the JOBS Act. Since this process is complex, these platforms usually offer very few investment opportunities at the same time (Wessel et al., 2017). The platform shared by SeedInvest users serves like an umbrella, and their membership is more homogeneous and private (Talonen et al., 2020). Fundable is one of the few crowdfunding sites in India that focuses completely on small businesses. The Fundable crowdfunding portal links to campaigns for different business sectors in India. Entrepreneurs and businesses in these different sectors use this platform for collecting funds collection for such things low-cost clinical diagnoses and intellectual travel experiences in India. Banking, travel, food and beverage, and fitness are among other sectors involved on this platform (Vira, 2020). Wefunder is one of the most successful equity-based crowdfunding platforms in the U.S. today. One of the most successful campaigns on Wefunder was the launch of Beta Bionics (Cumming & Johan, 2019).

Crowdfunding Companies in Turkey

Crowdfunding platforms that operate in Turkey include the FonGoGo, CrowdFon, FonlaBeni, ArıKovanı, Buluşum, and FonBulucu platforms. Among these platforms, Buluşum is a donation-based funding platform, and the others are reward-based platforms. In addition, Buluşum only places on its platform projects that will benefit society. No commission is requested from its successful projects. The Buluşum platform, which is affiliated with the Boyner Foundation, is a non-profit platform, and it aims to bring together inventors and backers. The ArıKovanı platform, which is another non-profit crowdfunding platform, attaches a great amount of importance to innovation. The Arıkovanı platform publicizes only technology and innovation-based projects, the prototype of which has already been completed. However, no commission is charged for projects that have been successful on the platform because ArıKovanı is a Turkcell initiative. Therefore, the purpose of this platform is to support innovation and to make a contribution. Other crowdfunding platforms are profit-oriented platforms, and they charge a commission that can be between 7% and 15% of the funding total from successful ventures (Çubukçu, 2017). The CrowdFon crowdfunding platform, the first crowdfunding platform in Turkey, was launched in 2013 by Şavaş Ünsal, who took over Projemefon. This platform is a reward-based crowdfunding platform that provides financial resources for ideas. The projects placed on this platform are uploaded only when the site's administrators review them and consider them appropriate. It appears that the CrowdFon platform has adopted the "all-or-nothing" system. While the platform transfers its funds to successful projects that can collect the targeted amount, it charges 12% of the total amount collected. However, it does not demand this charge for unsuccessful projects that have not collected the entire targeted amount and has had to return the collected amount to funders. The platform allows projects to collect more funds than they originally targeted. The platform is not responsible for the transaction fees of the service providers that are used for payments (Vural, 2019).

The FonlaBeni platform was established in 2013 and has published 68 projects as of December 2017. This platform allows for the funding of projects in such categories as the environment, film, art, food, and technology, and it receives a commission fee of 9% from its successful projects. The funds collected for unsuccessful projects are paid back to the investors. For this reason, it can be stated that this platform has adopted the "all-or-nothing" model. The FonGoGo platform was established in 2013. This platform, which mediated the funding of 511 projects as of July 2019, helps support many projects in many areas such as the environment, film, education, design, and technology. The platform, which receives a commission fee of 7% from its successful projects that have met their targeted amount of funding, has given back funds to the investors for the 80 unsuccessful projects that did not reach their target amount of funding within the specified amount of time. This platform has adopted the "all-or-nothing" model. In addition to this information, these platforms in Turkey help support projects in a wide range of fields such as technology, art, film, music, and the environment (Akbaş, 2019). SPK (Turkish Capital Markets Board) communiqué has issued Share-based crowdfunding in 2019 in Turkey. Thus, all legal gaps regarding crowdfunding were filled. The number is expected to increase significantly in Turkey, the massive funding platform in near future.

CONCLUSION

Crowdfunding is considered to be a revolutionary innovation for providing financing to the entrepreneurial initiatives and has now turned into a worldwide known and applied tool. This chapter aimed to provide a general insight for crowdfunding and its potential benefits for social entrepreneurship. In line with this purpose, a comprehensive literature review has been presented and the current examples of global and local crowdfunding have been given.

Social entrepreneurship opens new doors in many fields with the innovative solutions it brings and the social value it creates. However, starting and maintaining a social initiative is often difficult, especially financially. As it is known, many project owners cannot realize their works that will provide significant benefits to society and the economy, as they cannot collect the funding they need to realize their ideas. While economic problems and the impulse not to take risks to cause good ideas to fade away, crowdfunding opens a unique door for social entrepreneurs. In this perspective, as an innovative financial tool crowdfunding appears to be an alternative for social entrepreneurs. With financial support from society, progress and efforts to turn commercial ideas into reality will become more widespread in the coming years, but it is also possible that people's brilliant ideas and initiatives will melt away in these systems. Having such a financial support opportunity attracts attention as an significant opportunity for social entrepreneurs and small businesses to create their own ecosystems.

The concept of crowdfunding has emerged as the main force of entrepreneurial finance. It has a structure that encourages financial strength and the revolutionary transformation of the financial sector. These platforms allow funders to evaluate and picking projects that they would like to finance. On the other hand, crowdfunding still has some risks. First, pre-investment work is required before using crowdfunding to raise funds. It is essential to understand whether the business can afford it by setting realistic budgets and timelines. The intellectual property acquired by small entrepreneurs under difficult conditions should also be protected with great precision. Unlike traditional funding methods, where a business has several potential investors presenting its ideas, crowdfunding involves many people who know a lot about the business and its idea. It has an unwanted side effect as it allows other businesses to copy ideas until they pay off without real inventors. Therefore, businesses must have the right intellectual property protection for their ideas before posting their campaigns online. This can be in the form of trademarks, patents, or copyrights. Businesses with good ideas should read the legal statement on their chosen crowdfunding platform and seek legal advice just before officially launching their invention. Finally, entrepreneurs should be careful about fraud. The increasing number of fake sites on the Internet copy projects and direct them to fraudsters. Entrepreneurs need to check the credibility of the crowdfunding platform they plan to use before committing. After these risks are eliminated and a suitable platform is found, crowdfunding is one of the best alternatives, especially for entrepreneurs in the incubation period. Moreover, in order to ensure the spread of this new technique, incentives can be provided by direct government or public support in developing countries as well as the success of the recently established platforms.

Crowdfunding can be preferred as a very effective tool for social entrepreneurs. In the new world order, it should be at the top of the list of preferences as a method that can be used by any entrepreneur or company who does not have high financial power but wants to enter the market with a great idea or product. Having the support of millions or having the ability to use a powerful financial instrument can male the created social value sustainable. Of course, if there is a good idea...

REFERENCES

Agrawal, A., Catalini, C., & Goldfarb, A. (2016). Are Syndicates the Killer App of Equity Crowdfunding? *California Management Review*, *58*(2), 111–124. doi:10.1525/cmr.2016.58.2.111

Akbaş, S. (2019). *Girişimciler ve Yatırımcıları Buluşturan Alternatif Finansman Yöntemi: Kitlesel Fonlama (Yüksek Lisans Tezi)*. Pamukkale Üniversitesi Sosyal Bilimler Enstitüsü.

Alexiou, K., Wiggins, J., & Preece, S. B. (2020). Crowdfunding Acts as a Funding Substitute and a Legitimating Signal for Nonprofit Performing Arts Organizations. *Nonprofit and Voluntary Sector Quarterly*, *49*(4), 1–22. doi:10.1177/0899764020908338

Allon, G., & Babich, V. (2020). Crowdsourcing and Crowdfunding in the Manufacturing and Services Sectors. *Manufacturing & Service Operations Management*, *22*(1), 102–112. doi:10.1287/msom.2019.0825

Apostolos, G., & Ioannis, M. (2012). Crowd-funding: Developing a Strategy for Crowd Participation. In *12th International Conference*. Economic Society of Therssaloniki.

Arnold, L., Brennecke, M., Camus, P., Fridgen, G., Guggenberger, T., Radszuwill, S., & Urbach, N. (2019). *Blockchain and Initial Coin Offerings: Blockchain's Implications for Crowdfunding*. Business Transformation through Blockchain.

Belleflamme, P., Lambert, T., & Schwienbacher, A. (2014). Crowdfunding: Tapping the right crowd. *Journal of Business Venturing*, *29*(5), 585–609. doi:10.1016/j.jbusvent.2013.07.003

Biancone, P. P., Secinaro, S., & Kamal, M. (2019). Crowdfunding and Fintech: Business Model Sharia Compliant. *European Journal of Islamic Finance*, (12), 1–10.

Borst, I., Moser, C., & Ferguson, J. (2018). From Friendfunding to Crowdfunding: Relevance of Relationships, Social Media, and Platform Activities to Crowdfunding Performance. *New Media & Society*, *20*(4), 1396–1414. doi:10.1177/1461444817694599 PMID:30581357

Bottiglia, R., & Pichler, F. (Eds.). (2016). *Crowdfunding for SMEs: A European Perspective*. Springer. doi:10.1057/978-1-137-56021-6

Bretschneider, U., Knaub, K., & Wieck, E. (2014). *Motivations for crowdfunding: What drives the crowd to invest in start ups?* Paper presented at the 22nd European Conference on Information Systems (ECIS 2014), Tel Aviv, Israel.

Brüntje, D., & Gajda, O. (2016). *Crowdfunding in Europe State of the Art in Theorey and Practice*. Springer.

Chakraborty, S., & Swinney, R. (2020). Signaling to the Crowd: Private Quality Information and Rewards-Based Crowdfunding. *Manufacturing & Service Operations Management*, •••, 1–15. doi:10.1287/msom.2019.0833

Çubukçu, C. (2017). Kitlesel fonlama: Türkiye'deki Kitlesel Fonlama Platformları Üzerinden Bir Değerlendirme. *Girişimcilik ve İnovasyon Yönetimi Dergisi*, *6*(2), 155–172.

Cumming, D. J., & Johan, S. A. (2019). *Crowdfunding: Fundamental Cases, Facts, and Insights*. Academic Press.

Fanea-Ivanovici, M. (2018). Crowdfunding – A Viable Alternative Source of Finance for the Film Industry? *Revista Economica*, *70*(3), 79–88.

Fenwick, M., McCahery, J. A. and Vermeulen, E. P. M. (2018). Fintech and the Financing of Smes and Entrepreneurs: From Crowdfunding to Marketplace Lending. *The Economics of Crowdfunding*, 103–129.

Fettahoğlu, S., & Khusayan, S. (2017). Yeni finansman olanağı: Kitle fonlama. *Uşak Üniversitesi Sosyal Bilimler Dergisi*, *10*(4), 497–521.

Gierczak, M. M., Bretschneider, U., Haas, P., Blohm, I., & Leimeister, J. M. (2016). Crowdfunding: Outlining the New Era of Fundraising. In *Crowdfunding in Europe*. Springer. doi:10.1007/978-3-319-18017-5_2

Hagedorn, A., & Pinkwart, A. (2016). The financing process of equity-based crowdfunding: An empirical analysis. In *Crowdfunding in Europe* (pp. 71–85). Springer. doi:10.1007/978-3-319-18017-5_5

Havrylchyk, O. (2018). Regulatory framework for the loan-based crowdfunding platforms. Organisation for Economic Co-operation and Development Unclassified Document.

Hoque, A. S. M. M., Awang, Z., Muda, H., & Salleh, F. (2018). Ramification of Crowdfunding on Bangladeshi Entrepreneur's Self-efficacy. *Accounting*, *4*(4), 129–138. doi:10.5267/j.ac.2018.4.001

Hoque, N., Hasmat Ali, M., Arefeen, S., Masrurul Mowla, M., & Mamun, A. (2018). Use of Crowdfunding for Developing Social Enterprises: An Islamic Approach. *International Journal of Business and Management*, *13*(6), 156–164. doi:10.5539/ijbm.v13n6p156

Hornuf, L., & Cumming, D. (2018). *The Economics of Crowdfunding: Startups, Portals and Investor Behavior. Taylor &amp.* Francis Limited.

Hsu, C. (2015). The Informational Role of Volume. University of British Columbia.

İedaNest Blog. (n.d.). *Türkiye'de Kitlesel Fonlamanın Faydaları ve Destekçi Motivasyonu*. https://blog.ideanest.org

Kuti, M., Bedő, Z., & Geiszl, D. (2017). Equity-based Crowdfunding. *Financial and Economic Review*, *16*(4), 187–200.

Lam, P. T. I., & Law, A. O. K. (2016). Crowdfunding for renewable and sustainable energy projects: An exploratory case study approach. *Renewable & Sustainable Energy Reviews*, *60*, 1–18. doi:10.1016/j.rser.2016.01.046

Landström, H., Parhankangas, A., & Mason, C. (Eds.). (2019). *Handbook of Research on Crowdfunding*. Edward Elgar Publishing. doi:10.4337/9781788117210

Lin, Y., Yin, P., & Lee, W. C. (2018). Modeling Dynamic Competition on Crowdfunding Markets. *World Wide Web Conference*, 1815–1824.

Lipusch, N., Dellermann, D., Oeste-Reiß, S., & Ebel, P. (2018). Innovating Beyond the Fuzzy Front End: How to Use Reward-Based Crowdfunding to Co-create with Customers. *Proceedings of the 51st Hawaii International Conference on System Sciences*, 4202–4211. 10.24251/HICSS.2018.528

Macht, S., & Chapman, G. (2019). Getting more than money through online crowdfunding. *Asia-Pacific Journal of Business Administration*, *11*(2), 171–186. doi:10.1108/APJBA-05-2019-0101

Marchegiani, L. (2017). From Mecenatism to Crowdfunding: Engagement and Identification in Cultural-Creative Projects. *Journal of Heritage Tourism, 13*(2), 1–9.

Miglo, A. (2020). Crowdfunding in a Competitive Environment. *Journal of Risk and Financial Management*, *13*(3), 1–38. doi:10.3390/jrfm13030039

Moysidou, K., & Hausberg, J. P. (2020). In crowdfunding we trust: A trust-building model in lending crowdfunding. *Journal of Small Business Management*, *58*(3), 511–543. doi:10.1080/00472778.2019.1661682

Nevin, S., Gleasure, R., O'Reilly, P., Feller, J., Li, S., & Cristoforo, J. (2017). Social identity and social media activities in equity crowdfunding. *Proceedings of the 13th International Symposium on Open Collaboration*, 1–8. 10.1145/3125433.3125461

Premier Line. (n.d.). *Crowdfunding Definition Page*. https://www.premierline.co.uk/

Price Water House Coopers (PWC). (n.d.). *Crowdfunding Page*. www.pwc.com.tr

Rey-Martí, A., Mohedano-Suanes, A., & Simón-Moya, V. (2019). Crowdfunding and social entrepreneurship: Spotlight on intermediaries. *Sustainability*, *11*(4), 1–23. doi:10.3390u11041175

Sakarya, Ş., & Bezirgan, E. (2018). Kitlesel Fonlama Platformları: Türkiye Ve Yurtdışı Karşılaştırması. *Düzce Üniversitesi Sosyal Bilimler Enstitüsü Dergisi*, *8*(2), 18–33.

Schäfer, M. S., Metag, J., Feustle, J., & Herzog, L. (2018). Selling science 2.0: What Scientific Projects Receive Crowdfunding Online? *Public Understanding of Science (Bristol, England)*, *27*(5), 496–514. doi:10.1177/0963662516668771 PMID:27647666

Sharma, S. ve Lertnuwat, N. (2016). The Financial Crowdfunding with Diverse Business Models. *Journal of Asian and African Social Science and Humanities*, *2*(2), 74–89.

Shen, W., Crandall, J. W., Yan, K., & Lopes, C. V. (2018). Information design in crowdfunding under thresholding policies. In *Proceedings of the 17th International Conference on Autonomous Agents and MultiAgent Systems* (pp. 632-640). International Foundation for Autonomous Agents and Multiagent Systems.

Spanos, L. (2016). Complementarity and Interconnection Between CSR and Crowdfunding: A Case Study in Greece. *5th International Conference on Social Responsibility, Ethics and Sustainable Business*, 1–15. 10.2139srn.2883191

Talonen, A., Pasanen, J., & Ruuskanen, O. P. (2020). Exploring the Co-operative Form ' s Potential in Crowdfunding : A Non-monetary Perspective. *FIIB Business Review*, 1–13.

Vira, K. S. (2020). Promoting Entrepreneurship Through Crowd Funding In India. *Studies in Indian Place Names*, *40*(35), 418–424.

Vural, A. (2019). Girişimciler İçin Yeni Nesil Bir Finansman Modeli "Kitle Fonlaması - Crowdfunding": Dünya Ve Türkiye Uygulamaları Üzerine Bir İnceleme Ve Model Önerisi (Doktora Tezi). Başkent Üniversitesi: Sosyal Bilimler Enstitüsü, Ankara.

Wallmeroth, J. (2019). Investor Behavior in Equity Crowdfunding. *Venture Capital*, *21*(2–3), 273–300. doi:10.1080/13691066.2018.1457475

Wessel, M., Thies, F., & Benlian, A. (2017). Opening the floodgates: The implications of Increasing Platform Openness in Crowdfunding. *Journal of Information Technology*, *32*(4), 344–360. doi:10.105741265-017-0040-z

Xu, L. Z. (2018). Will a Digital Camera Cure Your Sick Puppy? Modality and Category Effects in Donation-Based Crowdfunding. *Telematics and Informatics*, *35*(7), 1914–1924. doi:10.1016/j.tele.2018.06.004

Zhao, Y., Harris, P., & Lam, W. (2019). Crowdfunding Industry-History, Development,Policies, and Potential Issues. *Journal of Public Affairs*, *19*(1), 1–9. doi:10.1002/pa.1921

KEY TERMS AND DEFINITIONS

Backers: A person, institution, or country that supports someone or something, especially financially.

Crowdfunding: The practice of funding a project or venture by raising small amounts of money from a large number of people, typically via the internet.

Entrepreneurship: The creation or extraction of value. With this definition, entrepreneurship is viewed as change, which may include other values than simply economic ones.

Equity: Collective effort of individuals to support efforts initiated by other people or organizations through the provision of finance in the form of equity.

Reward-Based: Crowdfunding has been used for a wide range of purposes, including motion picture promotion, free software development, inventions development, scientific research, and civic projects.

Chapter 8
Crowdfunding as a Financial Tool for Social Enterprises:
The Funding Performance of Social and Environmental Projects in Crowdfunding

Işıl Sevilay Yılmaz
https://orcid.org/0000-0001-9499-5245
TED University, Turkey

Burze Yaşar
TED University, Turkey

ABSTRACT

Nevertheless, scholarly knowledge on crowdfunding has been accumulating, and the number of studies on the role of crowdfunding in financing social entrepreneurs is limited and results are mixed. This calls for a need to uncover the underlying dynamics of funding success for socially and environmentally oriented projects. To analyze these dynamics, the authors analyze the funding performance of campaigns tagged by the Kickstarter platform as 'public benefit', 'environmental', or 'LGBTQIA'. Results show that projects with these tags are more likely to be successful compared to projects without tags after controlling for other factors that are shown to affect project success in the literature. These findings provide guidelines to social entrepreneurs looking to fund their projects on crowdfunding platforms and open up the path for future research on the relationship between framing for social and environmental orientation and funding success.

INTRODUCTION

Social entrepreneurs, disruptive innovators who are our champions, are trying to solve the world's most pressing challenges and entering into markets where others have failed before. In the ongoing COVID-19 pandemic, we need social innovators more than ever before since the pandemic hit the vulnerable, ex-

DOI: 10.4018/978-1-7998-4727-4.ch008

cluded and employers in the informal economy the most in terms of health and economic effects (World Economic Forum, 2020). Humanity has surpassed the critical levels of environmental pollution (Steffen et al., 2015) and such environmental destruction may be increasing risks of current and future epidemics of pandemics (Brennan & Micklas, 2020). Incremental improvements are not sufficient to lighten the effects of threats facing our planet and more systematic change is necessary. Hence, supporting social entrepreneurs or sustainability oriented entrepreneurs who run for profit companies that pursue positive environmental or social objectives is of utmost importance. The main research question in this chapter is whether crowds favor them and crowdfunding platforms serve as an efficient funding mechanism for social entrepreneurs.

Access to finance has been a significant challenge for entrepreneurs and became even more difficult after the 2007 credit crisis (North et al., 2013). Raising capital through traditional financial sources can be difficult especially for social enterprises (Castellas et al., 2018; Emerson et al., 2007; Nicholls, 2010). Social enterprises seek out business solutions to solve social problems (Thompson & Doherty, 2006). They have dual missions of social purpose and financial stability (Doherty et al., 2014) and compared to for profit enterprises they face difficulties in mobilization of resources (Austin et al., 2006). Taking into account the unconventional business models and restrictions on profit sharing, raising capital from traditional capital providers is harder for social enterprises (Chertok et al., 2008; Choi & Gray, 2008).

Crowdfunding has emerged as a critical financing mechanism to fill especially the early stage funding gaps (Sorenson et al., 2016; World Bank, 2013). After the 2007 credit crisis, internet based crowdfunding has become a valuable method for entrepreneurs to solicit financial support online (Belleflamme et al., 2014; Bonini & Capizzi, 2019; Harrison, 2013; World Bank, 2013). It is an unconventional method of financing in which financial intermediaries are surpassed and crowds transfer funds to projects and enterprises (Lehner, 2014; Mollick, 2014; Schwienbacher & Larralde, 2010). The process of crowdfunding is described as the "successful interaction between a facilitating organization (or platform), a variety of campaign founders who seek financial support for their ideas and ventures, and a large dispersed "crowd" of individuals ("crowdfunders") who are enticed to invest, pledge, lend, or donate money toward these ideas and ventures" (Nielsen, 2018, p.1). Crowdfunding platforms provide financing opportunity for social entrepreneurs who do not have a track record or collateral and cannot access bank loans, democratizing the financial services (Ordanini et al., 2011; Rey-Martí et al., 2019).

Crowdfunding not only serves for financing but for a number of business purposes. Entrepreneurs can run early market tests for product ideas and estimate demand for their products and services (Belleflamme et al., 2014). Moreover crowdfunding supports marketing of entrepreneurs and raises product/service awareness (Mollick, 2014). Crowdfunding has become a powerful fundraising tool in the world and according to Statistica Crowdfunding -Statistics and Facts (2020), crowdfunding transaction value totals 8,537.3 million dollars with an expected annual growth rate of 12% and average funding per campaign is 780 dollars in 2020. Crowdfunding comes in four types based on what the funder expects to receive in return. The four main types of crowdfunding are: 1) donation based 2) debt based 3) equity based and 4) reward based. What funders receive in return for their contributions at these platforms vary from a simple thank you letter/mention to interest return, equity stake or a reward, respectively.

Debt based online crowdfunding platforms facilitate loans to consumers or businesses from institutional creditors or individual lenders. Debts can take the form of bonds as well as secured or unsecured loans. The digital nature of lending allows for lower overhead costs and interest rates and thus has become a viable financing option for borrowers that have difficulty accessing credit. The largest crowdfunding volume is generated by peer to peer or marketplace consumer lending (CCAF, 2020). Compared to debt based models, equity based crowdfunding market volume constitutes a much smaller share of the global alternative finance market. In equity based crowdfunding investors receive shares of a business, most often a small and medium size enterprise, in return for their investment. One subset of equity crowdfunding is real estate crowdfunding in which investors purchase shares in a property. Donation based and reward based models account for the smallest percentage of the overall alternative finance volume (CCAF, 2020). Unlike debt or equity based crowdfunding, individuals do not receive any financial return for the funds they provide in donation or reward based models.

Crowdfunding has grown rapidly as an alternative source of funding for entrepreneurs but scholarly knowledge has been building up slower. Academic literature has set out to explore why some projects meet their funding goals and others do not and what the underlying dynamics of crowdfunding are. Researchers have identified a number of factors leading to project funding success: Project creator's social network (Colombo et al., 2015; Giudici et al., 2018; Kromidha & Robson, 2016; Mollick, 2014; Vismara, 2016; Zheng et al., 2014; Zvilichovsky, David, Yael Inbar, 2015), project narratives (Bi et al., 2017b; Gafni et al., 2019a; Manning & Bejarano, 2017; Mollick, 2014), social media usage (Bi et al., 2017a; Datta et al., 2018; Hong, Yili & Burtch, 2015) and geography (Agrawal et al., 2011; Giudici et al., 2018; Ordanini et al., 2011).

While research provides some insight into what motivates crowds to support projects, we know little about how social or environmental concerns affect the crowd. The extant literature on the relation between social and environmental sustainability and crowdfunding is fragmented and provides contradictory results. A number of empirical papers suggest that socially or environmentally oriented projects are more likely to be funded (Calic & Mosakowski, 2016; Lehner, 2013). On the other hand, Hörisch (2015) finds no positive impact of environmental orientation on funding performance and this finding suggests that crowd funders, like traditional funders, may first look into potential financial returns. In this respect, there is a clear need for more research on the relation between environmental and social framing and funding success. The authors address this gap by investigating the research question of "How does a platform's framing of campaigns as 'social' or 'environmental' affects project funding performance?" based on data from Kickstarter, one of the leading rewards based crowdfunding platforms in the world. The results shed light onto crowdfunders' decision making criteria and have implications for platforms looking to attract qualified projects to the platform and improve the funding process.

The next section discusses the literature on crowdfunding and social or environmental orientation followed by hypothesis development. Then the sample is presented and empirical findings are discussed in relation to the literature. The chapter concludes by implications for social entrepreneurs, limitations and future research directions.

BACKGROUND

Crowdfunding takes place on online platforms that bring together funders and fund raisers. Investment crowdfunding platforms that offer debt and equity based crowdfunding, are regulated more heavily than platforms that facilitate non-investment crowdfunding models such as donation and reward based models. In the investment models, funders take on higher risks and expect monetary returns for the funds they provide. In this respect, trust of investors is critically important to develop crowdfunding and regulations on platform activities and processes are put in place in many countries. Unlike traditional fund raising methods, in crowdfunding, all information exchange is online and lack of face-to-face interaction results in a high level of information asymmetry. In order to reduce information asymmetry, fundraisers provide information to signal their quality and crowdfunders react to these signals (Stiglitz, 2002; Yasar et al., 2020). However there is no verification of the information disclosed by fund raisers (Dorfleitner et al., 2018).

In rewards based crowdfunding models there is no monetary return but the risk pertains to whether the fundraiser will be able to deliver the promised reward in due time or fail. Project creators share their projects or business ideas at the platforms and set fundraising goals at the beginning. For each level of pledged money, they define a reward which can range from a simple thank you note to early access to a product. Crowdfunding campaigns can be either fixed or flexible. In fixed campaigns, 'all or nothing' principle applies and if the fundraiser does not raise the target amount of money, he or she does not collect the raised funds. On the other hand, the fundraiser keeps the collected funds irrespective of reaching the initial goal amount in flexible campaigns. In rewards based crowdfunding pledge levels are usually low and it is critical for the project creator to reach and persuade as many crowdfunders as possible to participate.

Crowdfunders play a critical role in crowdfunding campaigns and they may have various motivations ranging from expectations of financial returns, being part of a community to recognition. Motivations of funders participating in campaigns at different platforms may show heterogeneity with respect to normative, gain and hedonic goal frames (Lindenberg & Steg, 2007). Normative or altruistic goals are related to meeting ethical or moral norms of a community. Hedonic goals refer to individuals' aims to improve the way they feel at a specific moment. Gain goals are related to individuals' objectives of increasing or preserving their resources. Vasileiadou et al. (2016) find that crowdfunders' motivations to participate in campaigns are actually a combination of these goals. Extant literature calls for more research on motivations of crowdfunders.

Empirical evidence suggests that crowdfunders look into worthy ideas and core values of the enterprise and are motivated by the opportunity to help others and support causes that they believe in rather than by material rewards (Allison et al., 2015; Gerber & Hui, 2013; Hui et al., 2014; Lehner, 2013; Lehner & Nicholls, 2014; Ordanini et al., 2011). Because crowdfunders' motivations differ from those of traditional investors who mainly seek financial returns and look into business plans and collaterals (Lehner, 2013), crowdfunding may especially fit financing needs of social entrepreneurs. This chapter explores whether this is the case and analyzes the funding performance of projects with social or environmental tags at Kickstarter.

Based on 'warm-glow giving' theory (Andreoni, 1990), literature suggests that social entrepreneurs may be more successful in raising funding but the empirical results are contradictory. Using 1507 Italian campaigns listed on Indiegogo, which is a reward-based crowdfunding platform, Lagazio & Querci (2018) find that social impact projects do not perform significantly better than other projects. They classify every project in the field of animals, community, environment, and politics as social impact projects and all the other fields such as technology, health and others as non-social impact. On the other hand, Allison et al.(2015) find that project funding success increases in debt securities crowdfunding when entrepreneurs frame the project as an opportunity to help others rather than a business opportunity. Pitschner and Pitschner-Finn (2014) compare the crowdfunding performance of non-profit and for profit campaigns and find that non-profit projects' likelihood of funding success and the average amount of funding committed are statistically significantly higher. On the other hand they find the total amount collected to be lower and suggest that the results are more likely driven by a few very successful for profit campaigns.

One strand of the literature focuses on renewable energy projects and investigates the effect of sustainability or environmental orientation on project funding success. Vasileiadou et al. (2016) show that sustainability or environmental orientations positively affect crowdfunding success and confirm crowdfunding's potential to finance renewable energy. Bonzanini et al. (2016) also investigate renewable energy projects' crowdfunding success and its determinants. They find that expectation of financial returns, entrepreneur's social capital and commitment and reputation of the platform (measured by the number of projects listed and platform's financial contributions to the campaign) significantly affect the probability of project funding success. Because investment amounts are low, investors do not seem to take into consideration risk factors such as size of the target capital or the leverage. Lam and Law (2016) also look into the potential of crowdfunding for financing sustainable and renewable projects. Unlike, Bonzanini et al. (2016), they use case methodology and analyze eight different international cases that use different crowdfunding models. They conclude that even though crowdfunding cannot substitute conventional venture capital such as venture capital, angel investment or bank loans, it can play a critical role at the early stages of project's life as seed capital. Rewards and donation based crowdfunding may be used initially and after initial tests loan or equity based crowdfunding are suggested.

MAIN FOCUS OF THE CHAPTER

The prior section shows that in spite of the knowledge accumulation on crowdfunding, the number of studies looking into the crowdfunding performance of social entrepreneurs is still very limited. Furthermore, findings on the relation between social or environmental orientation and crowdfunding success are contradictory. By examining whether social or environmental framing affects a project's funding success based on data from the Kickstarter platform, this chapter contributes to the literature on financing of social entrepreneurs.

Recent literature uses the theory of framing (Benford & Snow, 2000; Goffman, 1974) to analyze the relation between pro-social orientation and crowdfunding success (Defazio et al., 2020). A project is described as pro-socially oriented if it engages in initiatives for the well-being of the society or the environment (Brickson, 2007) and exhibits values of inclusiveness, caring for others and fairness. Framing is the assortment and organization of information so that the intended audience more easily comprehends it. Framing a project can help bring forth significant information about the project and attract more funders to the campaign. Giorgi and Weber (2015) analyze how analysts' framings of securities influence institutional investors' appraisals of analysts. They find that investors do appreciate analysts' framing of content such as fast moving security information which they need to process and act on to perform their jobs. Similarly in a crowdfunding context, a platform's framing of projects by adding tags such as 'public benefit', 'environmental' or 'LGBTQIA' to them may help bring forth such significant information about campaigns. Moreover, framing eases the search process for funders looking for projects that have social or environmental impacts among so many projects listed. Unlike prior studies that analyze pro-social framing of projects based on linguistic cues fundraisers use in titles, project descriptions and blurbs (Allison et al., 2015; Defazio et al., 2020; Moss et al., 2015), this chapter uses the intermediary's or platform's framing of projects in relation to funding success in line with Hörisch (2015).

Besides easing the search process for funders, framing may ease starting a community by decreasing the time to bring together like minded pro-socially oriented individuals at social impact campaigns. In crowdfunding platforms, communities are built online and a strand of literature investigates the role of community building for the success of a crowdfunding project. An online community is "a group of people with a common purpose whose interaction is mediated and supported by computer systems, and governed by formal and informal policies" (Preece, 2000; 2004). In online communities people mainly come together to exchange information and other resources, engage in conversations, play, learn or just to come together (Resnick & Kraut, 2012). Online community building is critical for a project's funding success and yet creating and maintaining online communities are not without challenges. The main challenges of online community building are 1) starting a new community 2) attracting and socializing new members 3) encouraging commitment 4) encouraging contribution and 5) regulating behavior (Resnick & Kraut, 2012).

As discussed above, platforms' framings of social and environmental projects help distinguish social impact projects from numerous others and ease the search process for pro-socially oriented funders. Moreover framing can help project creators overcome the challenge of starting an online community of pro-socially oriented funders more easily. For these reasons, framing of projects with social/environmental tags may enhance project funding success. The authors do not suggest that social tags will be preferred over environmental tags or vice versa and hypothesize that:

H1: Projects with a public benefit tag are more likely to succeed than projects with no tags
H2: Projects with an environmental tag are more likely to succeed than projects with no tags
H3: Projects with an LGBTQIA tag are more likely to succeed than projects with no tags
H4: Projects with a public benefit, environmental or LGBTQIA tag are more likely to succeed than projects with no tags.

A dummy variable which takes the value of one if the project has a public benefit, environmental or LGBTQIA tag and zero otherwise is generated to test the fourth hypothesis.

The following model is used to test the above described hypotheses:

Funding Performance = $\beta 0 + \beta 1$ Social/Environmental/LGBTQIA Tag +
+ k1 Project level control variables t + Year Dummies
+ *Category Dummies* + ε (1)

The authors first run this model as a probit analysis where funding performance is a dummy variable taking the value of one if the project achieves or surpasses its initial funding target and zero otherwise. They also run an OLS regression where the dependent variable is this time the logarithm of the pledge/goal ratio. The identification of social and environmental projects is based on the tags "public-benefit", "environmental" and "LGBTQIA" provided by Kickstarter. The analysis controls for a number of factors that are shown to affect project funding performance as well as time and sectoral differences.

In crowdfunding, besides community building, entrepreneurs depend on distributed and crowd work which involve collaboration of many people to reach a common goal (Hui et al., 2014). In distributed work, collaboration is with a group of individuals who are known but physically distributed while in crowd work individuals are not known. Entrepreneurs' distributed work in crowdfunding involves working with teams, subcontracted labor and supporters within their social network. In parallel, entrepreneurs make crowds work by motivating people who they do not know personally to support the campaign and spread the word about it (Hui et al., 2014). In this respect, the authors control for the number of stated collaborators in the project. Besides existence of collaborators, description length and image count are shown to signal project quality in the literature. The authors control for project quality proxied by entrepreneurs' preparedness for the campaign (Bi et al., 2017b; Gafni et al., 2019b; Mollick, 2014). This variable, is a composite metric of project quality and is obtained by summing up description length, image count and collaborator count. In constructing the measure the authors use the included variables as categorical variables of 4 groups. Therefore, Project Preparedness (PREP) is a categorical variable of 12 groups.

The authors also control for other project level variables such as creator bio-length, creator comment count, update count, number of backers, number of new backers, campaign duration, number of projects creator backed, whether the project is KickStarter staff pick, time and main category. Table 1 lists the variables used in the analysis.

FINDINGS

Data and descriptive statistics

Crowdfunding platforms may have different 'loose ideologies' (Überbacher, 2014) depending on the values and beliefs of users spending time at the platform and the mission of the platform (Calic & Mosakowski, 2016). Kickstarter is one of the leading reward based crowdfunding platforms in the world. Given its mission of 'help bring creative projects to life' and the demographics of its crowdfunders, Kickstarter can be classified as supportive of a sustainability orientation which includes social orientation and environmental orientation (Calic & Mosakowski, 2016). The authors test the above stated research hypotheses in a sample of campaigns on the Kickstarter platform.

Kickstarter is founded in 2009 and since then it is supporting project creators all over the world. Most common rewards offered in the platform are early access or cheaper access to products, creative experiences, mementos or collaborations. As of March 16, 2020, Kickstarter reports that a total of $4.84 billion has been pledged and 179,244 projects have been successfully funded. The number of total backers is 17,579,128 of which 5,815,608 are repeat backers. Kickstarter uses 'all or nothing' principle and funders can receive the pledged money only if they reach or exceed their initial goals. Average success rate is 37.61% and most of the funded projects raise less than $10,000 but the platform notes that the number of projects that have reached six to seven figures, has been increasing. Success rate differs across categories and technology has the lowest success rate, 20.65%.

The authors collect data for a total of 10,520 randomly selected projects posted between 2014 and 2018 on the Kickstarter platform, using a web crawling program. Projects with a goal amount equal to or higher than $5,000 are included because the success factors may also change with respect to the magnitude of target goals (Mollick, 2014). This funding threshold is comparable to amount of capital traditional entrepreneurs seek via conventional methods. Outliers constituting top 1% of project goal amount which is above 250,000 dollars are also excluded and the final sample includes 8,411 projects.

Table 2 and Table 3 summarize the distribution of projects in the sample over time and across categories, respectively. Majority of projects are listed in years 2017 and 2018. Overall success rate for the full sample is 43.06%. 824 of the projects have at least one of the public benefit, environmental or LGBTQIA tags. The social /environmental tags are scattered among various categories however design, film/video and publishing has the highest numbers.

Table 1. Description of Variables

Variable Type/Name	Definition
DEPENDENT VARIABLE	
Log. Pledge/Goal Ratio	Logarithm of Pledge/Goal Ratio
Successful (1,0)	Indicator variable which takes the value of one if the project is funded, and zero otherwise
SOCIAL IMPACT VARIABLE	
Social Impact Tag (1,0) (SEL)	Indicator variable which takes the value of one if the project has any environmental, LGBTQIA or public benefit tag, and zero otherwise
Environmental	Indicator variable which takes the value of one if the project has an environmental tag, and zero otherwise
Public Benefit	Indicator variable which takes the value of one if the project has a public benefit tag, and zero otherwise
LGBTQIA	Indicator variable which takes the value of one if the project has a LGBTQIA tag, and zero otherwise
PROJECT LEVEL VARIABLES	
Project Preparedness (PREP)	**Variable created by summing up description length, image count and collaborator count.**
Description Length(1-4)	Categorical variable of 4 Groups: takes the value of 1 to 4 for each quartile
Image Count (0-4)	Categorical variable of 5 Groups: 0 if there are no images and 1 to 4 for each quartile.
Collaborator Count (0-4)	Categorical variable of 5 Groups: 0 if there are no collaborators and 1 to 4 for each quartile.
Creator Bio Length (1-4)	Categorical variable of 4 Groups: takes the value of 1 to 4 for each quartile
Creator-Comment Count(0-4)	Categorical variable of 5 Groups: 0 if there are no comments and 1 to 4 for each quartile.
Update Count (0-4)	Categorical variable of 5 Groups: 0 if there are no updates and 1 to 4 for each quartile.
Creator-Social Media Link Count (0-4)	Categorical variable of 5 Groups: 0 if there are no social media links and 1 to 4 for each quartile.
Staff pick (1,0)	Indicator variable which takes the value of one if the project is picked by Kickstarter, and zero otherwise
Creator-Backed Project Dummy	Indicator variable which takes the value of one if the project creator has backed a project on Kickstarter before, and zero otherwise
Duration (days)	The time (days) difference between the project launch and deadline.
New backer ratio	New backers divided by total backers
Category Dummies	Indicator variables which takes the value of one if the main category of the project is from a category, and zero otherwise
Year Dummies	Indicator variables which takes the value of one if the project is from a given year, and zero otherwise

Note: Table describes variables used in the analysis

Table 2. Distribution of Projects over Time

Year	Full Sample (N)	Success Rate	Projects with at least one social impact tag (public benefit or environmental or LGBTQIA)	Projects with environmental tag	Projects with LGBTQIA tag	Projects with public benefit tag
2014	516	59.69%	140	7	65	69
2015	662	59.06%	163	46	43	85
2016	542	61.07%	177	54	43	90
2017	1,523	24.10%	183	63	78	56
2018	5,168	43.05%	161	71	72	25
Total	**8,411**	**43.06%**	**824**	**241**	**301**	**325**

Note: Table presents the distribution of projects over time and across tags. The annual success rate is reported by year in the third column

Table 3. Distribution of Social /Environmental Projects by Main Category

Main Category	Full Sample	Projects with public benefit or environmental or LGBTQIA tags	tagged environmental	tagged lgbtqia	tagged publicbenefit
Art	320	87	12	11	72
Comics	308	81	1	79	1
Crafts	86	3	0	0	3
Dance	29	4	0	3	1
Design	1,392	127	84	2	56
Fashion	476	62	32	5	28
Film & Video	722	122	9	94	21
Food	822	87	36	3	52
Games	1,175	8	0	8	0
Journalism	42	13	1	2	10
Music	485	27	2	20	5
Photography	138	25	5	11	10
Publishing	763	92	15	52	25
Technology	1,568	77	43	7	37
Theater	85	9	1	4	4
Total	**8,411**	**824**	**241**	**301**	**325**

Note: Table presents the distribution of social/environmental projects by main category.

Table 4 presents the descriptive statistics for the full sample and subsamples of projects with and without social/environmental tags. There are statistically significant differences in the mean values of our variables between these two groups. In particular, projects with social/environmental tags are more successful both in terms of success rate and pledge/goal ratio. The difference is much more emphasized in the success rate as the success rate of the social/environmental projects is twice that of the remaining projects. The average goal for social/environmental projects is also higher. The social/environmental projects seem to provide more detailed information about the project. The creators of the projects may be effective in attracting backers as the average number of backers for social/environmental projects is 580 individuals while this number is around 324 for the rest of the sample. The creators of social/environmental projects are more likely to use social media in promoting their projects as social media link count for these projects is significantly higher.

Table 7 in appendix presents a pairwise correlation matrix. We performed a variance inflation factor (VIF) analysis for all variables included in our model and the mean VIF is below the threshold of five, suggesting that multicollinearity does not pose a threat for our analysis

Table 4. Descriptive Statistics for Projects with and without Social/environmental Tags

	FULL SAMPLE (N:8,411)	PROJECTS WITHOUT PUBLIC BENEFIT -ENVIRONMENTAL or LGBTQIA TAG (N:7,587)	PROJECTS WITH PUBLIC BENEFIT --ENVIRONMENTAL or LGBTQIA TAG (N:824)	Mean Difference	Significance (TTEST)
Variable	(1)	(2)	(3)	(3-2)	
Pledge/Goal Ratio	1.41	1.3	2.09	0.75	*
Successful (1,0)	0.43	0.4	0.80	0.41	***
Goal (USD)	27,141.46	26,776.2	30,504.47	3,728.25	***
Average pledge level(USD)	481.34	462.2	657.30	195.07	***
Creator Bio Length	658.67	652.6	714.78	62.20	**
Image Count	16.16	16.2	15.90	-0.29	
Collaborator Count	0.55	0.5	0.58	0.04	
Description Length	6,086.27	5,984.2	7,026.38	1,042.21	***
Creator-Comment Count	57.02	60.1	28.20	-31.95	***
Update Count	7.71	7.2	12.43	5.24	***
Creator-Social Media Link Count	1.93	1.9	2.27	0.38	***
Staff pick (1,0)	0.26	0.2	0.81	0.61	***
Creator-Backed Project Count	8.66	8.5	9.78	1.24	
Duration (days)	33.21	33.2	33.10	-0.12	
Number of rewards	9.35	9.1	11.64	2.54	***
Backers Count	349.41	324.3	580.61	256.32	**
New backer ratio	0.42	0.4	0.39	-0.04	***

Notes: This table presents means of variables for the full sample as well as projects with and without social/environmental tags. All dollar values for projects that use non-dollar currencies are calculated using the static USD rates provided by Kickstarter. The fifth column shows the mean differences for the two groups, projects with and without social/environmental tags. The final column shows if there are any statistically significant differences in listed variables between projects with and without social/environmental tags subsamples based on two sample t-tests. ***, **, and * indicate statistical significance at the 1%, 5%, and 10% levels, respectively.

The hypotheses stated in the previous section all posit that social/environmental tags have a positive effect on the project funding performance. Table 5 and Table 8 (in appendix) report the coefficients of the five binary probit regression models in which success dummy is the dependent variable as well as average marginal effects of each variable on the probability of crowdfunding campaign success. Model 1 includes only one indicator variable "Social Impact Tag (1,0) (SEL)" which takes the value of one if the project has any of environmental, LGBTQIA or public benefit tags, and zero otherwise. The positive and significant coefficient and average marginal effect in Model 2 show that projects with a social/environmental tag are 12.3 percentage points more likely to succeed after accounting for project level control variables. In Models 3 through 6, we compare projects with public-benefit, environmental and LGBTQIA tags with projects with no tags, respectively. The coefficients for all type of tags turn out to be positive and significant.

Table 5 also presents information about other success factors in crowdfunding platforms. Better prepared projects (represented by a composite metric of project quality constructed by summing up description length, image count and collaborator count) are more successful. If the creator of the project has backed a project before it increases the likelihood of success. Staff pick variable has a positive and significant effect as in Mollick (2014). Results show that as the duration of the campaign is longer, the project is less likely to succeed. There are two opposing views related to the duration of the campaign. A number of papers argue that longer duration is not a good signal (as it is a signal for lack of confidence in the project) in goal setting theory and negatively affect project performance (Marelli & Ordanini, 2016; Mollick, 2014). (Lagazio & Querci, 2018), on the other hand, suggest that funders appreciate more time to effectively screen and analyze projects and show that campaigns that are longer than 30 days are more likely to succeed. Our findings support the first view with a negative and significant coefficient for the duration variable. Table 5 and Table 8 also suggests that as the proportion of new backers (backers who are new to the platform) in our backers increase, the probability of success increases in all models.

The second measure we use for project funding success is the logarithm of pledge/goal ratio and Table 6 and Table 9 (in appendix) present the regression analysis in which this ratio is used as the dependent variable. The findings are similar to the results reported for the probit analysis. The projects with a public benefit or environmental tag have a higher pledge/goal ratio even after controlling for the variables known to affect funding performance including year and category effects. The main difference between Table 5 and Table 6 is for the LGBTQIA tag as the coefficient for this tag is still positive but insignificant in Table 6.

Our empirical results indicate that, projects with either a social or an environmental tag are more likely to reach their funding goals compared to projects without tags. Moreover, they are also more likely to exceed their funding goals. The results are in line with Vasileiadou et al. (2016) and Bonzanini et al. (2016) who show that sustainability or environmental orientations positively affect crowdfunding success.

Table 5. Probit Regression with marginal effects-Dependent Variable Success Dummy (1,0)

DEPENDENT VARIABLE: SUCCESS_DUMMY (1,0)	**Model 1**		**Model 2**		**Model 3**		**Model 4**		**Model 5**	
	Coef.	**Marginal Effects**	**Coef.**	**Marginal Effects**	**Coef.**	**Marginal Effects**	**Coef.**	**Marginal Effects**	**Coef.**	**Marginal Effects**
Social Impact Tag (1,0) (SEL)	1.114***	0.416***	0.581***	0.123***						
	[0.052]	0.018	[0.076]	0.016						
Tagged Public-Benefit(1,0)					0.558***	0.12***				
					[0.120]	0.026				
Tagged Environmental (1,0)							0.440***	0.094***		
							[0.129]	0.028		
Tagged LGBTQIA (1,0)									0.597***	0.127***
									[0.112]	0.024
Project Preparedness (PREP)			0.027***	0.006***	0.031***	0.007***	0.023***	0.005***	0.024***	0.005***
			[0.008]	0.002	[0.008]	0.002	[0.008]	0.002	[0.008]	0.002
Creator Bio Length (1-4)			-0.039**	-0.008**	-0.045***	-0.01***	-0.039**	-0.008**	-0.038**	-0.008**
			[0.017]	0.004	[0.017]	0.004	[0.017]	0.004	[0.017]	0.004
Creator-Comment Count(0-4)			0.290***	0.062***	0.288***	0.062***	0.288***	0.062***	0.294***	0.063***
			[0.018]	0.004	[0.018]	0.004	[0.018]	0.004	[0.018]	0.004
Update Count(0-4)			0.595***	0.126***	0.591***	0.127***	0.604***	0.129***	0.599***	0.128***
			[0.018]	0.003	[0.019]	0.003	[0.019]	0.003	[0.019]	0.003
Creator-Social Media Link Count(0-4)			-0.111***	-0.024***	-0.114***	-0.024***	-0.112***	-0.024***	-0.112***	-0.024***
			[0.014]	0.003	[0.015]	0.003	[0.014]	0.003	[0.014]	0.003
Staff pick (1,0)			0.576***	0.122***	0.572***	0.123***	0.611***	0.131***	0.617***	0.132***
			[0.048]	0.010	[0.050]	0.011	[0.049]	0.010	[0.049]	0.010
Creator-Backed Project (1,0)			0.099**	0.021**	0.102**	0.022	0.088**	0.019**	0.094**	0.02**
			[0.039]	0.008	[0.040]	0.009	[0.040]	0.008	[0.040]	0.008
Duration (days)			-0.019***	-0.004***	-0.019***	-0.004***	-0.020***	-0.004***	-0.019***	-0.004***
			[0.002]	0.000	[0.002]	0.000	[0.002]	0.000	[0.002]	0.000
New backer ratio			1.164***	0.247***	1.145***	0.246***	1.141***	0.244***	1.180***	0.252***
			[0.088]	0.018	[0.090]	0.019	[0.089]	0.019	[0.090]	0.019
Constant	-0.278***		-1.383***		-1.322***		-1.208***		-1.358***	
	[0.015]		[0.160]		[0.167]		[0.168]		[0.171]	
Observations	8,411		8,399		7,903		8,118		8,075	
Year & Category Controls	No		Yes		Yes		Yes		Yes	

Notes: The table reports coefficient estimates and robust standard errors for the probit regression of Success Dummy (1,0) on the independent variables explained in Table 1.We also report the marginal effects for each probit regression. The numbers in parentheses are robust standard errors. ***, **, and * denote statistical significance at the 1%, 5% and 10% levels, respectively. We use the robust option of Stata regressions for estimating the standard errors using the Huber-White sandwich estimators. These standard errors take into account issues concerning heterogeneity and lack of normality while leaving the point estimates of the coefficients unchanged. Another version of this table which includes the variables of Description Length(1-4), Image Count (0-4) and Collaborator Count(0-4)separately instead of the constructed Project Preparedness (PREP)variable is available in Appendix (Table8).

Table 6. Regression - Dependent Variable Log. Of Pledge Goal Ratio

Dependent variable Log.Pledge/Goal Ratio	(1)	(2)	(3)	(4)	(5)
Social Impact Tag (1,0) (SEL)	0.838***	0.117**			
	[0.053]	[0.046]			
Tagged Public-Benefit(1,0)			0.132*		
			[0.068]		
Tagged Environmental (1,0)				0.160**	
				[0.075]	
Tagged LGBTQIA (1,0)					0.014
					[0.067]
Project Preparedness (PREP)		0.035***	0.034***	0.033***	0.033***
		[0.005]	[0.006]	[0.005]	[0.005]
Creator Bio Length (1-4)		-0.049***	-0.051***	-0.050***	-0.050***
		[0.011]	[0.011]	[0.011]	[0.011]
Creator-Comment Count(0-4)		0.314***	0.318***	0.319***	0.318***
		[0.011]	[0.012]	[0.011]	[0.012]
Update Count(0-4)		0.439***	0.432***	0.438***	0.437***
		[0.011]	[0.011]	[0.011]	[0.011]
Creator-Social Media Link Count(0-4)		-0.036***	-0.040***	-0.038***	-0.039***
		[0.009]	[0.009]	[0.009]	[0.009]
Staff pick (1,0)		0.405***	0.391***	0.391***	0.408***
		[0.032]	[0.033]	[0.032]	[0.032]
Creator-Backed Project (1,0)		0.118***	0.111***	0.112***	0.112***
		[0.026]	[0.026]	[0.026]	[0.026]
Duration (days)		-0.011***	-0.012***	-0.012***	-0.012***
		[0.001]	[0.001]	[0.001]	[0.001]
New backer ratio		0.896***	0.840***	0.871***	0.868***
		[0.057]	[0.057]	[0.057]	[0.057]
Constant	-0.902***	-2.295***	-2.215***	-2.232***	-2.233***
	[0.017]	[0.112]	[0.118]	[0.120]	[0.120]
Observations	8399	8399	7903	8118	8075
Adjusted R-squared	0.0278	0.5198	0.5119	0.5187	0.5171
Year & Category Controls	No	Yes	Yes	Yes	Yes
F	251.1	337.8	308.5	322.5	319

Notes: The table reports coefficient estimates and robust standard errors for the OLS regression of logarithm of pledged/goal ratio on the independent variables explained in Table 1. The numbers in parentheses are robust standard errors. ***, **, and * denote statistical significance at the 1%, 5% and 10% levels, respectively. We use the robust option of Stata regressions for estimating the standard errors using the Huber-White sandwich estimators. These standard errors take into account issues concerning heterogeneity and lack of normality while leaving the point estimates of the coefficients unchanged. Another version of this table which includes the variables of Description Length(1-4), Image Count (0-4) and Collaborator Count(0-4)separately instead of the constructed Project Preparedness (PREP)variable is available in Appendix (Table9).

FUTURE RESEARCH DIRECTIONS

One limitation of this chapter is that the analysis uses only the crowdfunding platform's framing and does not differentiate projects that frame themselves as having a social or environmental orientation in their narratives. A nice extension of this work would be to classify those projects based on linguistic cues and make comparisons and run the analysis. Another limitation of this study is that the number of projects with tags is a small percentage of the dataset. Further research can work with bigger datasets and look into other crowdfunding platforms including lending and equity crowdfunding platforms. Most of the campaigns in Kickstarter are US based, limiting the generalization of results in other cultures.

In reward based crowdfunding platforms, due diligence conducted by funders is limited because little information is available and data is typically self-reported, creating a significant uncertainty on a project's likelihood of success (Calic & Mosakowski, 2016). Thus, a good understanding of success factors is utmost importance for project creators. Further research can analyze the dynamics and success factors of crowdfunding for social entrepreneurs. What motivates the crowd in terms of social and environmental impact? How can social entrepreneurs use crowdfunding platforms more effectively? How can policy makers better address funding the needs of social entrepreneurs? How can platforms differentiate social entrepreneurs from traditional entrepreneurs and increase their visibility among huge number of projects listed on the platforms? Or do we need to increase platforms specialized on social entrepreneurs only? For example Ecocrowd in Germany is a crowdfunding platform which is committed to sustainability and lists only sustainable projects. Green Crowding and Oneplanetcrowd are lending platforms for sustainable projects. Brazilian Kickante, is a crowdfunding platform for projects committed to create social impact. Research on these platforms will answer the question of whether social entrepreneurs shall prefer these platforms.

CONCLUSION

With pressing social and environmental problems and risks of current and future pandemics, we need social entrepreneurs more than ever. Funding these critical actors is of utmost importance. Social entrepreneurs experience difficulty in getting funding from traditional capital markets and conventional financial instruments may underserve their needs. Crowdfunding has emerged as an important avenue for social entrepreneurs to obtain funding but little is known on its effectiveness as a funding tool. This chapter contributes to the entrepreneurial finance literature by examining whether platforms' framing of projects by adding social or environmental tags increase the likelihood of project funding success.

The empirical analysis based on 8,411 projects from Kickstarter platform presents evidence that framing for pro-social orientation pays off in reward based crowdfunding. The authors also document that higher project preparedness (represented by a combination of longer project descriptions, increased number of images and collaborating with other parties) increases the likelihood of success. Increasing the frequency and openness of communication by the project creators also help them increase their success rate. In particular, if the project creator is more engaged in the platform as represented by higher number of project creator comments, larger number of project updates and more experience in the platform as a backer, it pays off in the form of higher probability of success.

This chapter makes a number of contributions to the literature. First it contributes to filling the knowledge gap on the funding performance of social impact projects. By identifying potential success factors it also contributes to the literature on determinants of crowdfunding success. Last but not the least, it also provides empirical evidence for the theory of framing in a digital setting. The presented findings have practical implications for platforms that want to attract more qualified projects and increase the funding success rate, prosocial investors who are looking for promising ideas, project creators who want to increase their chances of being funded and policy makers who seek for regulations to govern crowdfunding.

ACKNOWLEDGMENT

The authors would like to thank Nurullah Hatipoğlu for his valuable contribution in data collection.

REFERENCES

Agrawal, A., Catalini, C., & Goldfarb, A. (2011). The Geography of Crowdfunding. SSRN Electronic Journal. doi:10.3386/w16820

Allison, T. H., Davis, B. C., Short, J. C., & Webb, J. W. (2015). Crowdfunding in a prosocial microlending environment: Examining the role of intrinsic versus extrinsic cues. *Entrepreneurship Theory and Practice*, *39*(1), 53–73. doi:10.1111/etap.12108

Andreoni, J. (1990). Impure altruism and donations to public goods: A theory of warm-glow giving. *Economic Journal (London)*, *100*(401), 464–477. doi:10.2307/2234133

Austin, J., Stevenson, H., & Wei-Skillern, J. (2006). Social and Commercial Entrepreneurship: Same, Different, or Both? *Entrepreneurship Theory and Practice*, *30*(1), 1–22. doi:10.1111/j.1540-6520.2006.00107.x

Belleflamme, P., Lambert, T., & Schwienbacher, A. (2014). Crowdfunding: Tapping the right crowd. *Journal of Business Venturing*, *29*(5), 585–609. doi:10.1016/j.jbusvent.2013.07.003

Benford, R. D., & Snow, D. A. (2000). Framing Processes and Social Movements: An Overview and Assessment. *Annual Review of Sociology*, *26*(1), 611–639. doi:10.1146/annurev.soc.26.1.611

Bi, S., Liu, Z., & Usman, K. (2017a). The influence of online information on investing decisions of reward-based crowdfunding. *Journal of Business Research*, *71*, 10–18. doi:10.1016/j.jbusres.2016.10.001

Bi, S., Liu, Z., & Usman, K. (2017b). The influence of online information on investing decisions of reward-based crowdfunding. *Journal of Business Research*, *71*, 10–18. doi:10.1016/j.jbusres.2016.10.001

Bonini, S., & Capizzi, V. (2019). The role of venture capital in the emerging entrepreneurial finance ecosystem: Future threats and opportunities. *Venture Capital*, *21*(2–3), 137–175. doi:10.1080/13691066.2019.1608697

Bonzanini, D., Giudici, G., & Patrucco, A. (2016). The Crowdfunding of Renewable Energy Projects. In *Handbook of Environmental and Sustainable Finance* (pp. 429–444). doi:10.1016/B978-0-12-803615-0.00021-2

Brennan, M., & Micklas, K. (2020). 5 things to know about climate change and coronavirus with WHO Climate Lead Dr . Campbell- Lendrum. *CBS News*, 1–4.

Brickson, S. L. (2007). Organizational identity orientation: The genesis of the role of the firm and distinct forms of social value. *Academy of Management Review*, *32*(3), 864–888. doi:10.5465/amr.2007.25275679

Calic, G., & Mosakowski, E. (2016). Kicking Off Social Entrepreneurship: How A Sustainability Orientation Influences Crowdfunding Success. *Journal of Management Studies*, *53*(5), 738–767. doi:10.1111/joms.12201

Castellas, E. I., Ormiston, J., & Findlay, S. (2018). Financing social entrepreneurship The role of impact investment in shaping social enterprise in Australia. *Social Enterprise Journal*, *14*(2), 130–155. doi:10.1108/SEJ-02-2017-0006

CCAF. (2020). *The Global Alternative Finance Market Benchmarking Report*. https://www.jbs.cam.ac.uk/faculty-research/centres/alternative-finance/publications/the-global-alternative-finance-market-benchmarking-report/

Chertok, M., Hamaoui, J., & Jamison, E. (2008). The Funding Gap. *Stanford Social Innovation Review*, *6*(2), 44–52.

Choi, D. Y., & Gray, E. R. (2008). The venture development processes of "sustainable" entrepreneurs. *Management Research News*, *31*(8), 558–569. doi:10.1108/01409170810892127

Colombo, M. G., Franzoni, C., & Rossi-Lamastra, C. (2015). Internal Social Capital and the Attraction of Early Contributions in Crowdfunding. *Entrepreneurship Theory and Practice*, *39*(1), 75–100. doi:10.1111/etap.12118

Crowdfunding - Statistics & Facts. (2020). *Statistica*. https://www.statista.com/topics/1283/crowdfunding/

Datta, A., Sahaym, A., & Brooks, S. (2018). Unpacking the Antecedents of Crowdfunding Campaign's Success: The Effects of Social Media and Innovation Orientation. *Journal of Small Business Management*. Advance online publication. doi:10.1111/jsbm.12498

Defazio, D., Franzoni, C., & Rossi-Lamastra, C. (2020). How Pro-social Framing Affects the Success of Crowdfunding Projects: The Role of Emphasis and Information Crowdedness. *Journal of Business Ethics*. Advance online publication. doi:10.100710551-020-04428-1

Doherty, B., Haugh, H., & Lyon, F. (2014). Social Enterprises as Hybrid Organizations : A Review and Research Agenda. *International Journal of Management Reviews*, *16*(4), 417–436. doi:10.1111/ijmr.12028

Dorfleitner, G., Hornuf, L., & Weber, M. (2018). Dynamics of investor communication in equity crowdfunding. *Electronic Markets*, *28*(4), 523–540. doi:10.100712525-018-0294-5

Emerson, J., Freundlich, T., Fructerman, J., Berlin, L., & Stevenson, K. (2007). Nothing ventured, nothing gained. In Nothing ventured, nothing gained: Addressing the critical gaps in risk-taking capital for social enterprise. doi:10.1108/09657960110696708

Gafni, H., Marom, D., & Sade, O. (2019a). Are the life and death of an early-stage venture indeed in the power of the tongue? Lessons from online crowdfunding pitches. *Strategic Entrepreneurship Journal*, *13*(1), 3–23. Advance online publication. doi:10.1002ej.1293

Gafni, H., Marom, D., & Sade, O. (2019b). Are the life and death of an early-stage venture indeed in the power of the tongue? Lessons from online crowdfunding pitches. *Strategic Entrepreneurship Journal*, *13*(1), 3–23. doi:10.1002ej.1293

Gerber, E. M., & Hui, J. (2013). Crowdfunding: Motivations and deterrents for participation. *ACM Transactions on Computer-Human Interaction*, *20*(6), 1–32. Advance online publication. doi:10.1145/2530540

Giorgi, S., & Weber, K. (2015). Marks of Distinction: Framing and Audience Appreciation in the Context of Investment Advice. *Administrative Science Quarterly*, *60*(2), 333–367. doi:10.1177/0001839215571125

Giudici, G., Guerini, M., & Rossi-Lamastra, C. (2018). Reward-based crowdfunding of entrepreneurial projects: The effect of local altruism and localized social capital on proponents' success. *Small Business Economics*, *50*(2), 307–324. doi:10.100711187-016-9830-x

Goffman, E. (1974). *Frame analysis: An essay on the organization of experience*. Harvard University Press.

Harrison, R. (2013). Venture Capital An International Journal of Entrepreneurial Finance Crowdfunding and the revitalisation of the early stage risk capital market: Catalyst or chimera? *Venture Capital*, *15*(4), 283–287. Advance online publication. doi:10.1080/13691066.2013.852331

Hemer, J. (2011). A snapshot on crowdfunding. In *Arbeitspapiere Unternehmen und Region, No. R2/2011*. Fraunhofer ISI. doi:10.1227/01.NEU.0000349921.14519.2A

Hong, Y., Y. H., & Burtch, G. (2015). How does Social Media Affect Contribution to Public versus Private Goods in Crowdfunding Campaigns? *Thirty Sixth International Conference on Information Systems*, 1–15.

Hörisch, J. (2015a). Crowdfunding for environmental ventures: An empirical analysis of the influence of environmental orientation on the success of crowdfunding initiatives. *Journal of Cleaner Production*, *107*, 636–645. doi:10.1016/j.jclepro.2015.05.046

Hui, J. S., Greenberg, M. D., & Gerber, E. M. (2014). Understanding the role of community in crowdfunding work. *Proceedings of the ACM Conference on Computer Supported Cooperative Work, CSCW*, 62–74. 10.1145/2531602.2531715

Kromidha, E., & Robson, P. (2016). Social identity and signalling success factors in online crowdfunding. *Entrepreneurship and Regional Development*, *28*(9–10), 605–629. doi:10.1080/08985626.2016.1198425

Lagazio, C., & Querci, F. (2018). Exploring the multi-sided nature of crowdfunding campaign success. *Journal of Business Research*, *90*(May), 318–324. doi:10.1016/j.jbusres.2018.05.031

Lam, P. T. I., & Law, A. O. K. (2016). Crowdfunding for renewable and sustainable energy projects: An exploratory case study approach. *Renewable & Sustainable Energy Reviews*, *60*, 11–20. doi:10.1016/j.rser.2016.01.046

Lehner, O. M. (2013). Crowdfunding social ventures: A model and research agenda. *Venture Capital*, *15*(4), 289–311. doi:10.1080/13691066.2013.782624

Lehner, O. M. (2014). The formation and interplay of social capital in crowdfunded social ventures. *Entrepreneurship and Regional Development*, *26*(5–6), 478–499. doi:10.1080/08985626.2014.922623

Lehner, O. M., & Nicholls, A. (2014). Social finance and crowdfunding for social enterprises: a public-private case study providing legitimacy and leverage. In Venture Capital (Vol. 16, Issue 3, pp. 271–286). Taylor & Francis. doi:10.1080/13691066.2014.925305

Lindenberg, S., & Steg, L. (2007). Normative, gain and hedonic goal frames guiding environmental behavior. *The Journal of Social Issues*, *63*(1), 117–137. doi:10.1111/j.1540-4560.2007.00499.x

Manning, S., & Bejarano, T. A. (2017). Convincing the crowd: Entrepreneurial storytelling in crowdfunding campaigns. *Strategic Organization*, *15*(2), 194–219. doi:10.1177/1476127016648500

Mollick, E. (2014). The dynamics of crowdfunding: An exploratory study. *Journal of Business Venturing*, *29*(1), 1–16. doi:10.1016/j.jbusvent.2013.06.005

Moss, T. W., Neubaum, D. O., & Meyskens, M. (2015). The Effect of Virtuous and Entrepreneurial Orientations on Microfinance Lending and Repayment: A Signaling Theory Perspective. *Entrepreneurship Theory and Practice*, *39*(1), 27–52. doi:10.1111/etap.12110

Nicholls, A. (2010). The institutionalization of social investment: The interplay of investment logics and investor rationalities. *Journal of Social Entrepreneurship*, *1*(1), 70–100. doi:10.1080/19420671003701257

Nielsen, K. R. (2018). Crowdfunding through a partial organization lens – The co-dependent organization. *European Management Journal*, *36*(6), 695–707. doi:10.1016/j.emj.2018.01.006

North, D., Baldock, R., & Ullah, F. (2013). Funding the growth of UK technology-based small firms since the financial crash : Are there breakages in the finance escalator? *Venture Capital*, *15*(3), 237–260. doi:10.1080/13691066.2013.804755

Ordanini, A., Miceli, L., Pizzetti, M., & Parasuraman, A. (2011). Crowd-funding: Transforming customers into investors through innovative service platforms. *Journal of Service Management*, *22*(4), 443–470. doi:10.1108/09564231111155079

Pitschner, S., & Pitschner-Finn, S. (2014). Non-profit differentials in crowd-based financing: Evidence from 50,000 campaigns. *Economics Letters*, *123*(3), 391–394. doi:10.1016/j.econlet.2014.03.022

Preece, J. (2004). Online Communities: Researching sociability and usability in hard to reach populations. *AJIS. Australasian Journal of Information Systems*, *11*(2), 146–152. doi:10.3127/ajis.v11i2.132

Resnick, P., & Kraut, R. (2012). *Building successful online communities: Evidence-based social design.* MIT Press.

Rey-Martí, A., Mohedano-Suanes, A., & Simón-Moya, V. (2019). Crowdfunding and social entrepreneurship: Spotlight on intermediaries. *Sustainability (Switzerland)*, *11*(4), 8–10. doi:10.3390u11041175

Schwienbacher, A., & Larralde, B. (2010). Crowdfunding of small entrepreneurial ventures. In *Handbook of Entrepreneurial Finance* (Vol. 11, p. 3,10). Oxford University Press. http://ssrn.com/abstract=1699183

Sorenson, O., Assenova, V., Li, G. C., Boada, J., & Fleming, L. (2016). Expand innovation finance via crowdfunding. *Science*, *354*(6319), 1526–1528. doi:10.1126cience.aaf6989 PMID:28008025

Steffen, W., Richardson, K., Rockström, J., Cornell, S. E., Fetzer, I., Bennett, E. M., Biggs, R., Carpenter, S. R., De Vries, W., De Wit, C. A., Folke, C., Gerten, D., Heinke, J., Mace, G. M., Persson, L. M., Ramanathan, V., Reyers, B., & Sörlin, S. (2015). Planetary boundaries: Guiding human development on a changing planet. *Science, 347*(6223), 1259855. Advance online publication. doi:10.1126cience.1259855 PMID:25592418

Stiglitz, J. E. (2002). Information and the Change in the Paradigm in Economics. *The American Economic Review, 92*(3), 460–501. doi:10.1257/00028280260136363

Testa, S., Nielsen, K. R., Bogers, M., & Cincotti, S. (2019). The role of crowdfunding in moving towards a sustainable society. *Technological Forecasting and Social Change, 141*(December), 66–73. doi:10.1016/j.techfore.2018.12.011

Thompson, J., & Doherty, B. (2006). The diverse world of social enterprise: A collection of social enterprise stories. *International Journal of Social Economics, 33*(5–6), 361–375. doi:10.1108/03068290610660643

Überbacher, F. (2014). Legitimation of New Ventures: A Review and Research Programme. *Journal of Management Studies, 51*(4), 667–698. doi:10.1111/joms.12077

Vasileiadou, E., Huijben, J. C. C. M., & Raven, R. P. J. M. (2016). Three is a crowd? Exploring the potential of crowdfunding for renewable energy in the Netherlands. *Journal of Cleaner Production, 128*, 142–155. doi:10.1016/j.jclepro.2015.06.028

Vismara, S. (2016). Equity retention and social network theory in equity crowdfunding. *Small Business Economics, 46*(4), 579–590. doi:10.100711187-016-9710-4

World Bank. (2013). Crowdfunding's Potential for the Developing World. In infoDev, Finance and Private Sector Development Department. Author.

World Economic Forum. (2020). *6 ways social innovators are responding to the COVID-19 pandemic*. Author.

Yasar, B., Kiesssling, T., & Martin, T. (2020). An Empirical Test of Signaling Theory. *Management Research Review*. doi:10.1108/MRR-08-2019-0338

Zheng, H., Li, D., Wu, J., & Xu, Y. (2014). The role of multidimensional social capital in crowdfunding: A comparative study in China and US. *Information & Management, 51*(4), 488–496. doi:10.1016/j.im.2014.03.003

Zvilichovsky & Inbar. (2015). *Playing both sides of the market: Success and reciprocity on crowdfunding platforms*. Available at SSRN 2304101

KEY TERMS AND DEFINITIONS

Crowdfunding: Financing a project or business by raising money from a large number of backers using online crowdfunding platforms.

Crowdfunding Platform: A website that acts as a fund transfer mechanism where project owners describe their projects and seek for money from the crowds and individuals back the projects if they are convinced.

Debt-Based Crowdfunding: The method of crowdfunding in which the project owners finance their projects in the form of a loan from several lenders. The debt amount is subject to a prespecified fixed interest rate.

Donation-Based Crowdfunding: The method of crowdfunding in which the project owners finance their projects in the form of donation from several backers. Mostly applicable to non-profit projects charities.

Equity-Based Crowdfunding: The method of crowdfunding in which the backers of the project receive ownership in the company/final product in return for their contribution.

Kickstarter: A reward based crowdfunding platform for creative projects.

Reward-Based Crowdfunding: The method of crowdfunding in which the backers of the projects generally contribute small amounts of money to projects and receive previously announced rewards (in the form of a final product/tangible asset or service) in return.

APPENDIX

Table 7. Correlation Matrix

Variables	(1)	(2)	(3)	(4)	-5	(6)	(7)	(8)	(9)	(10)	(11)	(12)	(13)	(14)	(15)	(16)	(17)	(18)	(19)	(20)	(21)	(22)
(1) Pledge/Goal Ratio	1																					
(2) Successful (1,0)	0.13	1																				
(3) Goal (USD)	-0	-0.1	1																			
(4) Average pledge level(USD)	-0	0	0.3	1																		
(5) Social Impact Tag (1,0) (SEL)	0.02	0.25	0.03	0.1	1																	
(6) Tagged Environmental (1,0)	0.04	0.13	0.03	0.04	0.52	1																
(7) Tagged LGBTQIA (1,0)	0	0.14	-0	0.02	0.58	-0	1															
(8) Tagged Public-Benefit(1,0)	0.01	0.15	0.05	0.12	0.61	0.12	-0	1														
(9) Description Length	0.03	0.17	0.14	0.09	0.07	0.07	0.01	0.06	1													
(10) Creator Bio Length	-0	-0	0.05	0.11	0.02	0	-0	0.05	0.1	1												
(11) Image Count	0.08	0.17	0.08	-0.1	0	0.07	-0	-0	0.44	-0.1	1											
(12) Collaborator Count	0.11	0.16	0.09	0.03	0.01	0.06	-0	0.02	0.15	-0	0.28	1										
(13) Creator-Comment Count	0.12	0.19	0.05	-0.1	-0	0	-0	-0	0.16	-0	0.23	0.22	1									
(14) Update Count	0.14	0.5	0.1	-0	0.14	0.07	0.11	0.07	0.31	-0	0.3	0.19	0.3	1								
(15) Creator-Social Media Link Count	0.02	0.06	0.04	0.05	0.07	0.05	0.04	0.04	0.15	0.14	0.11	0.12	0.08	0.15	1							
(16) Staff pick (1,0)	0.07	0.38	0.07	0.09	0.42	0.23	0.21	0.28	0.2	-0	0.12	0.08	0.04	0.34	0.11	1						
(17) Creator-Backed Project Count	0.23	0.18	-0	-0.1	0.01	-0	0.04	-0	0.13	-0.1	0.15	0.09	0.42	0.27	0.1	0.12	1					
(18) Project Comment Count	0.86	0.07	0.06	-0	-0	0	-0	-0	0.06	-0	0.09	0.11	0.17	0.21	0.01	0.05	0.21	1				
(19) Duration (days)	-0	-0.1	0.12	0.07	0	0.01	-0	0.02	-0	0.06	-0	-0	-0.1	-0.1	-0	-0.1	-0.1	-0	1			
(20) Number of rewards	0	0.22	0.08	0.21	0.17	0.06	0.11	0.11	0.27	0.06	0.16	0.04	-0	0.24	0.15	0.25	0.04	-0	-0	1		
(21) Backers Count	0.95	0.12	0.07	-0	0.03	0.03	0.01	0.01	0.07	-0	0.09	0.12	0.16	0.2	0.03	0.11	0.25	0.88	-0	0.02	1	
(22) New backer ratio	-0.1	-0.1	-0	0.11	-0	-0	-0.1	0	-0.1	0.13	-0.2	-0.1	-0.2	-0.2	-0	-0.1	-0.2	-0.1	0.04	0.02	-0.1	1

Table 8. Probit Regression with marginal effects-Dependent Variable Success Dummy (1,0)

DEPENDENT VARIABLE: SUCCESS_DUMMY (1,0)	Model 1		Model 2		Model 3		Model 4		Model 5	
	Coef.	Marginal Effects	Coef.	Marginal Effects	Coef.	Marginal Effects	Coef.	Marginal Effects	Coef.	Marginal Effects
Social Impact Tag (1,0) (SEL)	1.114***	0.416***	0.570***	0.12***						
	[0.052]	0.018	[0.076]	0.016						
Tagged Public-Benefit(1,0)					0.548***	0.117***				
					[0.120]	0.025				
Tagged Environmental (1,0)							0.447***	0.095***		
							[0.129]	0.027		
Tagged LGBTQIA (1,0)									0.574***	0.122***
									[0.112]	0.024
Description Length(1-4)			-0.006	-0.001	-0.009	-0.002	-0.01	-0.002	-0.009	-0.002
			[0.019]	0.004	[0.019]	0.004	[0.019]	0.004	[0.019]	0.004
Image Count (0-4)			-0.009	-0.002	0.003	0.001	-0.014	-0.003	-0.01	-0.002
			[0.019]	0.004	[0.019]	0.004	[0.019]	0.004	[0.019]	0.004
Collaborator Count(0-4)			0.102***	0.022***	0.104***	0.022***	0.101***	0.021***	0.099***	0.021***
			[0.015]	0.003	[0.016]	0.003	[0.016]	0.003	[0.016]	0.003
Creator Bio Length (1-4)			-0.039**	-0.008**	-0.044**	-0.009	-0.039**	-0.008**	-0.038**	-0.008**
			[0.017]	0.004	[0.017]	0.004	[0.017]	0.004	[0.017]	0.004
Creator-Comment Count(0-4)			0.293***	0.062***	0.290***	0.062***	0.291***	0.062***	0.296***	0.063***
			[0.018]	0.004	[0.018]	0.004	[0.018]	0.004	[0.018]	0.004
Update Count(0-4)			0.597***	0.126***	0.592***	0.126***	0.605***	0.129***	0.600***	0.128***
			[0.018]	0.003	[0.019]	0.003	[0.019]	0.003	[0.019]	0.003
Creator-Social Media Link Count(0-4)			-0.114***	-0.024***	-0.116***	-0.025***	-0.114***	-0.024***	-0.115***	-0.024***
			[0.014]	0.003	[0.015]	0.003	[0.014]	0.003	[0.014]	0.003
Staff pick (1,0)			0.591***	0.125***	0.588***	0.125***	0.624***	0.133***	0.632***	0.134***
			[0.048]	0.010	[0.051]	0.011	[0.049]	0.010	[0.049]	0.010
Creator-Backed Project (1,0)			0.108***	0.023***	0.111***	0.024***	0.098**	0.021**	0.104***	0.022**
			[0.039]	0.008	[0.040]	0.009	[0.040]	0.008	[0.040]	0.008
Duration (days)			-0.019***	-0.004***	-0.018***	-0.004***	-0.019***	-0.004***	-0.019***	-0.004***
			[0.002]	0.000	[0.002]	0.000	[0.002]	0.000	[0.002]	0.000
New backer ratio			1.161***	0.245***	1.140***	0.243***	1.139***	0.242***	1.176***	0.25***
			[0.088]	0.000	[0.090]	0.000	[0.089]	0.000	[0.090]	0.000
Constant	-0.278***		-1.239***		-1.176***		-1.058***		-1.211***	
	[0.015]		[0.163]		[0.170]		[0.170]		[0.173]	
Observations	8,411		8,399		7,903		8,118		8,075	
Year & Category Controls	No		Yes		Yes		Yes		Yes	

Notes: The table reports coefficient estimates and robust standard errors for the probit regression of Success Dummy (1,0) on the independent variables explained in Table 1.We also report the marginal effects for each probit regression. The numbers in parentheses are robust standard errors. ***, **, and * denote statistical significance at the 1%, 5% and 10% levels, respectively. We use the robust option of Stata regressions for estimating the standard errors using the Huber-White sandwich estimators. These standard errors take into account issues concerning heterogeneity and lack of normality while leaving the point estimates of the coefficients unchanged.

Table 9. Regression - Dependent Variable Log. Of Pledge Goal Ratio

Dependent variable Log.Pledge/Goal Ratio	(1)	(2)	(3)	(4)	(5)
Social Impact Tag (1,0) (SEL)	0.838***	0.111**			
	[0.053]	[0.046]			
Tagged Public-Benefit(1,0)			0.129*		
			[0.067]		
Tagged Environmental (1,0)				0.158**	
				[0.075]	
Tagged LGBTQIA (1,0)					0.002
					[0.068]
Description Length(1-4)		-0.038***	-0.043***	-0.038***	-0.037***
		[0.012]	[0.012]	[0.012]	[0.012]
Image Count (0-4)		0.047***	0.046***	0.042***	0.043***
		[0.012]	[0.012]	[0.012]	[0.012]
Collaborator Count(0-4)		0.103***	0.107***	0.103***	0.102***
		[0.011]	[0.011]	[0.011]	[0.011]
Creator Bio Length (1-4)		-0.044***	-0.045***	-0.045***	-0.045***
		[0.011]	[0.011]	[0.011]	[0.011]
Creator-Comment Count(0-4)		0.309***	0.312***	0.314***	0.314***
		[0.011]	[0.012]	[0.012]	[0.012]
Update Count(0-4)		0.438***	0.431***	0.437***	0.437***
		[0.011]	[0.011]	[0.011]	[0.011]
Creator-Social Media Link Count(0-4)		-0.037***	-0.041***	-0.040***	-0.040***
		[0.009]	[0.009]	[0.009]	[0.009]
Staff pick (1,0)		0.416***	0.403***	0.401***	0.418***
		[0.032]	[0.033]	[0.032]	[0.031]
Creator-Backed Project (1,0)		0.126***	0.121***	0.121***	0.121***
		[0.026]	[0.026]	[0.026]	[0.026]
Duration (days)		-0.011***	-0.011***	-0.012***	-0.012***
		[0.001]	[0.001]	[0.001]	[0.001]
New backer ratio		0.889***	0.831***	0.863***	0.861***
		[0.057]	[0.057]	[0.058]	[0.057]
Constant	-0.902***	-2.118***	-2.029***	-2.053***	-2.057***
	[0.017]	[0.116]	[0.121]	[0.124]	[0.124]
Observations	8,399	8,399	7,903	8,118	8,075
Adjusted R-squared	0.0278	0.5242	0.517	0.5232	0.5214
Year & Category Controls	No	Yes	Yes	Yes	Yes
F	251.1	322.2	295.4	307.4	304.3

Notes: The table reports coefficient estimates and robust standard errors for the OLS regression of logarithm of pledged/goal ratio on the independent variables explained in Table 1. The numbers in parentheses are robust standard errors. ***, **, and * denote statistical significance at the 1%, 5% and 10% levels, respectively. We use the robust option of Stata regressions for estimating the standard errors using the Huber-White sandwich estimators. These standard errors take into account issues concerning heterogeneity and lack of normality while leaving the point estimates of the coefficients unchanged.

Chapter 9
Social Impact Bonds as a Tool for Social Impact Investment

Esen Kara
Bursa Uludağ University, Turkey

ABSTRACT

Despite the rapid economic and technological transformations experienced today, all countries are faced with many social and environmental problems. With financial globalization, temporary or permanent crises in an economy affect other economies through cross-contamination and push governments to make serious budget cuts in the field of social spending. In this context, it is inevitable for governments to reconsider the way of financing social policies. The important role the finance industry plays in sustainable development and creating shared value for society has developed innovative and alternative funding approaches. In this context, social impact investments are a new concept that aims to integrate the positive social or environmental impact into the financial return of capital. One of the new techniques used in financing social impact investment is social impact bond programs. This chapter aims to provide information about social impact bonds and discuss the potential application of SIBs in Turkey.

INTRODUCTION

According to World Bank data, the population of G-7 countries which is 65 and over is 150.1 million, while in G-20 countries this population is around 568 million (data.worldbank.org). In line with the projections made by the United Nations for future population growth every two years, it is estimated that the world population will increase to 9.7 billion in 2050 and the fertility rate per woman will decrease worldwide. As an inevitable side effect of declining fertility, the global population will continue to age. Accordingly, governments will have to prepare for economic and social difficulties (https://www.cbo.gov/publication/55331). Because this means increasing retirement costs and decreasing tax base. Therefore, the increasing financing need for social services provided by states will become a growing problem for economies in the upcoming period (Wood, 2010).

On the other hand, the temporary or permanent crises that occur in economies cause pressure on governments to reduce deficits by making serious budget cuts in many social spending areas. In this

DOI: 10.4018/978-1-7998-4727-4.ch009

context, the need for governments to optimize the effectiveness and efficiency of their social policies and the way they finance them is increasing day by day (Carè & De Lisa, 2019). Especially in the aftermath of the Global Crisis, which emerged in the US mortgage market in mid-2007 but affected the entire world economy in a short time, the need for social support increased in societies, and the austerity policies implemented caused major cuts in social expenditures (Joy & Shields, 2019). In this respect, the idea of developing new assets that can reduce the gap between speculative financial investments and the productive real economy has emerged in the process of solving social problems (Schinckus, 2017). One of these is social impact bonds, that is thought to be a financial tool that can help solving social problems that are difficult to solve due to conflicting and changing needs by turning them into a form of profit for private sector investors (Joy & Shields, 2019).

Social impact bonds (SIBs) are new financial assets that aim to encourage private investors to fund pre-defined social programs (Schinckus, 2017). Looking at the last two decades, it is observed that the concept of business model, which seeks innovative formulas including business models for sustainability, has come to the fore. Innovative forms of business and finance based on cooperation and shared value are emerging in the world economy and financial system, which is characterized by great difficulties during the global crisis we are still experiencing. In this context, business models based on intersectoral partnerships for sustainability can be considered as an important new paradigm that can address complex social issues. From the perspective of the finance industry, it can be said that SIBs are innovative and alternative financing approaches that aim to increase social impact based on various factors such as sustainability, solidarity, cooperation and social impact beyond the risk and return relationship (La Torre et al., 2019).

From this point of view, the purpose of this chapter is to provide information about social impact bonds, one of the new techniques used in financing social impact investments. After the introduction, the chapter continues with a brief explanation on collaborative business model and social impact investment concept. Following that, the structure, benefits and challanges of SIBs are explained. Finally, the study focused on the potential application of SIBs in Turkey.

Collaborative Business Model and Social Impact Investment for Sustainability

Despite various gains in economy and technology in today's world, societies still face many social and environmental challenges. It is clear that in order to solve these difficulties, it is necessary to put forward sustainable contributions with the cooperation of public, individual and institutional actors. Today, government initiatives, customer expectations and pressures from the environment push companies to rethink the way they do business in a way that contributes to the solution of environmental and social problems. For this reason, an increasing number of companies are acting with a strategy that will bring economic, environmental and social value contributions, rather than focusing solely on profit maximization. At the same time, more and more entrepreneurs are implementing social business projects that are not only economically viable but will contribute to the environment and society. The way to achieve economic success through a specific environmental or social activity is possible only if the companies can systematically integrate sustainability into their business models (Yan et al., 2018; Schneider & Clauß, 2019). In this context, sustainability can be defined as the implementation of new business models as well as the renewal or improvement of products, services and processes in a way that creates social and environmental value in addition to economic returns in the short and long term (Stubbs, 2019).

Massachusetts Institute of Technology MIT Sloan Management Review and the Boston Consulting Group meets with a large number of managers, think tank leaders and investors at a global level in the context of corporate sustainability in order to shed light on the sustainable business world, and tries to reveal common perceptions and practices on this issue. Accordingly, the results have revealed that the majority of managers today believe in the necessity of having a sustainability strategy in order to remain competitive, be innovative and create permanent business value. In addition, it is stated in the report that increasing investor interest is the main driver of sustainability and that the overwhelming majority of investors find sustainability performance important. Another issue that draws attention in the report is that investors are looking for new investment products focused on sustainability and related bond markets are expanding rapidly. In line with this importance attributed to sustainability, it was observed that nearly half of the companies included in the study changed their business models due to sustainability opportunities, and leading large companies reassessed their entire business model with a lens of sustainability (https://sloanreview.mit.edu/projects/corporate-sustainability-at-a-crossroads/).

The concept of business model for sustainability was first discussed by Stubbs and Cocklin, and the researchers put forward a framework of six factors to describe the model. These factors can be listed as follows: an environmental and social organizational goal that shifts focus from short-term financial returns to long-term value creation through sustainability initiatives, rather than short-term financial goals that include profitability and stock returns; environmental and social performance measurement in addition to the financial reporting process; the need for a stakeholder perspective where all stakeholders, including shareholders and financial market participants, recognize that the vision of sustainability creates long-term value; leadership perspective striving to integrate sustainability values into organizational culture and institutionalize in the minds of key stakeholders; a collaborative approach that develops sustainability solutions for the entire system instead of individual components (organizations) in the system; organizations working in collaboration with stakeholders to achieve economic, social and environmental results (Stubbs & Cocklin, 2008).

Later studies on business model theory for sustainability, which is still in its early development stage, have revealed different insights. For example, Boons and Lüdeke-Freund (2013) defined a model that distributes economic costs and benefits equally among stakeholders in the business model through a value proposition that creates social and environmental value as well as economic value. Schneider and Clauß (2019) have introduced an integrative model definition that focuses on the creation of sustainable value by combining social, ecological and economic institutional logic and creates value with external stakeholders. Freudenreich et al. (2016) emphasized on a business model in which the actors causing social and ecological problems will contribute to the development and implementation of solutions, and in this context, each stakeholder will play an active role in the value-building process.

When studies emphasizing collaborative business models for sustainability are examined, it is seen that these collaborative forms are explained with concepts such as cross-sectoral partnerships, social alliances, and social partnerships. Collaborative business models for sustainability, expressed as an inter-agency solution-generating mechanism for social problems, are collaborative arrangements established between the business world, non-profit organizations and/or the government. Accordingly, inter-sectoral social partnerships for sustainability are expected to create a transformational impact in the envisaged areas by bringing together various stakeholders, expertise, resources and skills to achieve a collaborative advantage (Hille et al., 2018; La Torre et al., 2019). In this context, intersectoral partnerships are promising tools that address approaches to solving sustainability problems that fall within the competencies and responsibilities of business, government and/or civil society (Hille et al., 2018).

Feilhauer and Hahn have defined an intersectoral partnership for sustainability as any initiative in which a firm collaborates with a non-profit partner to pursue a sustainability goal (Feilhauer & Hahn, 2019). In another study, Cantele et al. discussed this model as a social alliance that includes the integration of economic and social dimensions and that protects the public good, with a positive impact, between organizations that are affiliated to each other from different sectors with mutual cooperation based on sustainability (Cantele et al., 2020). When these definitions are examined, a common concept of cooperation based on sharing the responsibility of all actors in the process stands out.

Today, cross-sectoral social partnerships are becoming increasingly common as a means of addressing complex, social and ecological issues that go beyond any organization's management ability in implementing sustainable development goals. There is a tendency among governments, non-profit organizations and profit-making businesses to cooperate in solving social problems, albeit with different motivations. The focus of these partnerships is the creation and implementation of collaborative strategic plans in solving societal challenges that cannot be solved by a single sector (Clarke & Fuller, 2010; Hesse et al., 2019).

In the economy literature, the main purpose of company managers is to maximize the wealth of shareholders. However, companies are increasingly being questioned about the role they have to take in generating innovative solutions to social problems that pose an obstacle to development. In this respect, considering that social participation is not the basic mission of a company, companies' participation in cross-sectoral social partnerships may arise from different motivations. Some of these may be the need to respond to external pressures, the desire to maintain a privileged position within the market and society, the desire to maintain positive relationships with stakeholders, especially the government, the ability to alleviate a social problem and gain access to a previously unreachable market or group of customers. In addition, participation in cross-sectoral partnerships can contribute to strengthening corporate brand and reputation. It can also be a way of showing commitment to the company's own values, principles, policies and traditions. These motivations will also serve the economic interests of the companies. On the other hand, governments may choose social alliances for reasons such as current budget deficits, lack of capability in the relevant field, and non-profit organizations not having the necessary operational efficiency. Because of such constraints, solving complex problems in a sustainable way often requires innovative intersectoral cooperation, combining expertise and resources from various sectors (Stadtler, 2011; La Torre et al., 2019).

Business models created for sustainability attract increasing attention in the field of finance. The important role the finance industry plays in sustainable development and creating shared value for businesses and society has developed innovative and alternative funding approaches. Social impact investments, one of them, is a new concept that aims to integrate the positive social or environmental impact created in developed and developing markets into the financial return of capital. This goal is pursued by the efforts of microfinance organizations or private sector organizations that apply the necessary business approaches to achieve social goals (Andreu, 2018).

Social impact investing aims to attract certain types of investors who consider the concept of investment not only in terms of financial gain, but also as a way of creating social value through the organizations they invest in. In this respect, social impact investment can be considered as an approach that requires investors to think about investment opportunities from an ethical point of view, and that influences financing policies with ethical discourses such as solving social and environmental problems and increasing solidarity. In other words, social impact investments are an asset allocation strategy that finances projects that combine a measurable social and environmental impact with economic sustainability and financial returns. In this context, it can be stated that the concept of social impact can be handled as a third dimension in addition to risk and return for investors. Therefore, it can be said that social impact investments differ from the concept of philanthropy in terms of the expectation of a certain financial return or at least the recovery of basic capital (http://gsgii.org/wp-content/uploads/2017/05/Impact-Investment-Report.pdf Report; Schrotgens & Boenigk, 2017; Chiodo & Michelucci, 2018; Andreu, 2018).

In the post-global financial crisis period, it is observed that social impact investments are supported by policy makers and investors as a tool that focuses on the creation of social change in order to promote sustainable development (Munoz & Kimmitt, 2019). In 2013, the Social Impact Investment Taskforce was established at the G8 summit chaired by the UK to develop social impact investments. In a series of recommendation reports published in 2014, the Taskforce emphasized that social impact investments, which benefit from entrepreneurship, innovation and capital in order to strengthen social development, are a force that can create radical change in solving difficult social problems. It has also been stated that impact investments are a response to the growing awareness in the public and private sectors that the challenges that society is facing in the 21st century are too large and complex to be solved by the government and the social sector alone. However, social impact-oriented organizations need to gain access to a market where they can generate revenue from the products and services they offer. The larger of these markets can only be provided by governments that pay for impact (http://gsgii.org/wp-content/uploads/2017/05/Impact-Investment-Report.pdf). In this context, one of the new techniques used in financing social impact investments is social impact bond programs based on success-oriented payments that contribute to positive social change (El Ebrashi, 2013; Biasin et al., 2019). One of the discussion areas of the financial sector after the 2008 Global Crisis, which was criticized by personal interests and ambitions regarding the sector, was the issue of directing finance towards a social purpose. Social impact bonds are new financial assets that serve this purpose by combining philanthropic capital with market-oriented solutions based on the idea that private sector business practices will always deliver greater efficiency and effectiveness (Ryan & Young, 2018).

Social Impact Bonds

SIBs first appeared in the United Kingdom in 2010, enabling third parties to outsource the financing, planning and evaluation of social programs while providing profit for private investors (Ryan & Young, 2018). Today, SIB programs are found in many developed and developing countries. SIB projects are especially applied in the solution of social problems such as unemployment, homelessness, health, child care, family welfare, education, juvenile delinquency, reduction of re-delinquency and environment (Jackson, 2013; Ryan & Young, 2018). However, the determinant of the potential scope for SIBs can be the welfare level of a country and the level of development of civil society and private sector in the country (OECD, 2016).

According to the Social Finance database, a total of 138 SIBs have been supported by various governments since 2010. Most of these bonds were issued in the UK (47), America (26) and Netherlands (11). Figure 1 shows the SIBs financed since 2010 on different social issues.

Figure 1.

Issue Area	Number of SIBs
Workforce Development	44
Housing/Homelessness	23
Health	22
Child and Family Welfare	20
Education and Early Years	14
Criminal Justice	12
Poverty and Environment	3

Designed with a 'performance-based payment' or 'success-oriented payment' approach, SIBs are a financial product that creates benefits such as saving on public spending and increasing the quality of social service provision with the support of private institutions and financial markets. In this context, the innovation of SIB programs is the inclusion of third-party investors in the system, who provide funds to finance a social service program with inter-sectoral cooperation. Therefore, it is possible to express SIBs as a multi-stakeholder partnership that creates synergy between public institutions, governments, social organizations and financial institutions. Thanks to this multi-stakeholder participation, SIBs can be interpreted as an innovative approach to sustainability (Berndt & Wirth, 2018; La Torre et al., 2019).

SIBs are essentially certain contracts based on performance results where private investors get upfront financing to improve some of the targeted social outcomes. With the contract made, the government undertakes to pay the investor at a certain rate of return when the determined social goal is reached. When the targeted social results are not achieved, the investors bear the costs, in other words, they lose all or part of their capital and cannot make a profit. Thus, the financial risks of innovative services are removed from public institutions and service providers and transferred to investors. Here, it will also serve to achieve better social results with a more intensive performance management, since payment is only made when the desired social outcomes are achieved, and investors will take care of this financial risk (Andreu, 2018; FitzGerald et al, 2019).

The Structure of SIBs

In fact, SIBs are structures that, unlike traditional bonds, provide private investors with the opportunity to earn a positive return, while also providing outsourcing opportunities to other parties in the financing, planning and evaluation of social programs (Ryan & Young, 2018). While traditional bonds promise their holders to pay fixed coupon payments at a predetermined rate for a specified maturity, SIB holders can only earn financial returns when they reach pre-determined social goals. In this regard, it can be argued that SIBs act as stocks in terms of earning income. In addition, SIBs are multi-stakeholder agreements that aim to develop social services through the cooperation of the government, service provider, investor and a special purpose (intermediary) organization (McHugh et al., 2013). Here, unlike the issuance process of traditional bonds, a special purpose institution is involved in the process.

Funds from private investors other than the public sector are used in SIBs to improve social outcomes. If the programs in question succeed in achieving predetermined social outcomes, a solution where all stakeholders won will emerge. For example, a SIB program eliminates government upfront costs for service delivery, while providing investors with the opportunity of return if set targets are met. People who benefit from public services can also access better quality service and increase their quality of life. In addition, SIBs can provide financing to solve the social problems experienced by some groups, such as criminals who receive less attention in terms of government spending and donors. On the other hand, SIB programs remove certain costs on the government by bearing financial risk on private investors in case the targets are not achieved. However, in this case, the government will not provide efficient service, and the investors will lose some or all of their investments (Disley et al., 2011).

SIB programs are a multilateral partnership that brings together the public sector, private sector and social sector and includes five main stakeholders. First of all, all SIB programs have target outputs defined by state institutions. All SIB programs include an external organization, referred to as a service provider, that uses funds from investors as working capital and provides services to the target population to achieve the projected social outcomes. A second stakeholder is social finance intermediaries who act as an intermediary in the relations between the stakeholders, find the necessary capital, lead agreement negotiations, identify service providers, design and issue financial instruments and manage financial flows. But the key role played by intermediaries is that they transform and reallocate project risk. Private investors are the stakeholders that provide the necessary financing for the project by purchasing the financial instruments issued by the intermediary. Another stakeholder is independent validators that assess the feasibility of the social mission and translate the various goals of the government into quantitative and objective indicators on which repayments to investors depend. Depending on the achievement of the goal or the different levels of results achieved, the government or government representative makes a refund. However, SIBs can take other forms. Their flexible nature makes SIBs potentially useful in a variety of situations (Baliga, 2013; Azman & Ali, 2016; Del Giudice & Migliavacca, 2019)

In the light of this information, the working mechanism of SIBs can be summarized as follows (Azman & Ali, 2016; La Torre et al., 2019; Del Giudice & Migliavacca, 2019):

1. A contract is concluded as a result of negotiations between the government and other stakeholders on program outputs and payment mechanisms.
2. Based on the contract, a social finance intermediary that coordinates all stakeholders issues "bonds" to raise funds from investors. These funds are used to provide a capital in advance for the social program to be implemented.
3. The social service provider receives the funds and provides the necessary services to the target population in order to find solutions to the relevant social problem.
4. An independent validator then evaluates the program outcomes and prepares the necessary reports and submits them to the government or its representative.

5. If the results agreed in the contract are achieved, the government or its representative pays the investors. These payments include the capital and financial returns depending on the degree of success. Therefore, the repayments to be made to investors in SIB programs are based on the logic of transferable savings obtained through preventive social programs. In addition, focusing on pre-defined outputs with such a mechanism transfers the risk of project failure to the private sector. In this context, SIBs are innovative financial tools in terms of cooperation between stakeholders in creating collective social impact as well as including market forces and investor control in social policy. Besides, while government interventions in most cases aim to solve social problems, SIB programs are designed to potentially prevent them. The success of preventive interventions funded by a SIB reduces future public spending and provide savings.

Figure 2.

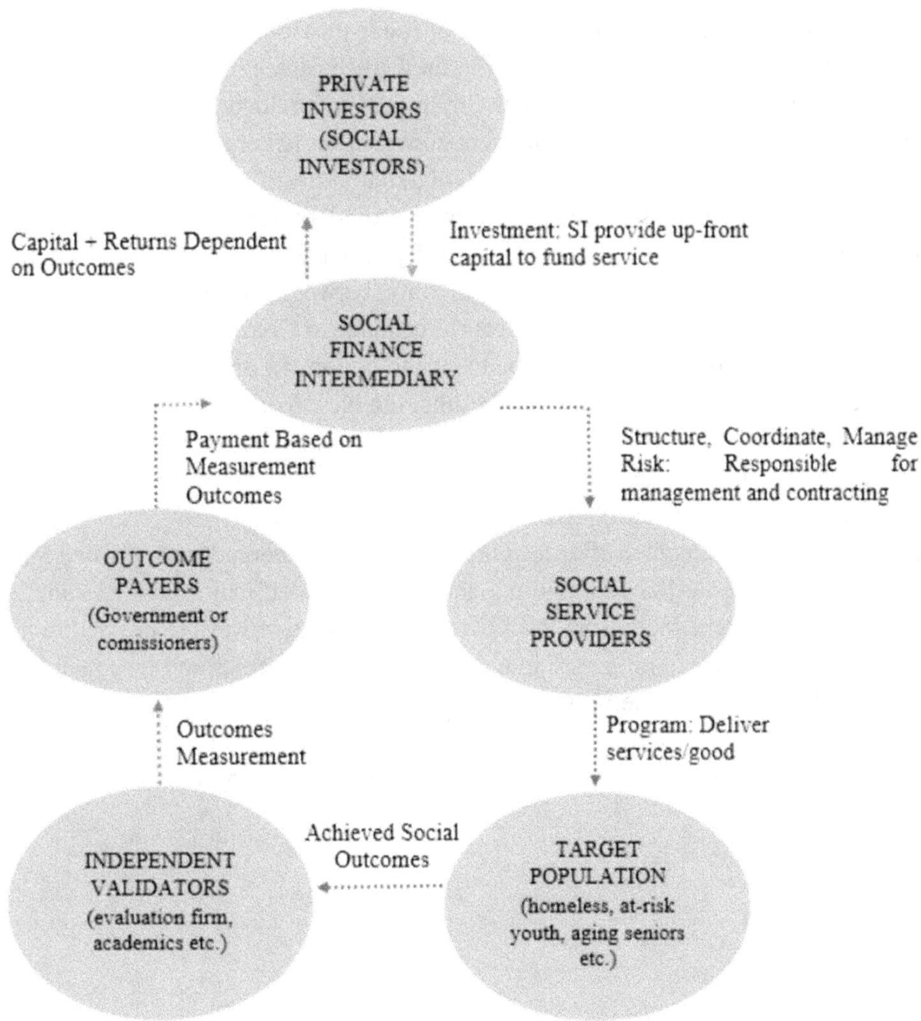

SIB Applications Around the World

The first SIB program in the world was launched in Peterborough, UK in September 2010. The program envisaged a reduction in the rate of recidivism within 12 months of 3,000 male short-term prisoners detained in Peterborough prison. The program was conducted on the basis of a contract between Social Finance, the Department of Justice, the Big Lottery Fund and the service provider One Service which acts as an intermediary and brings together the government, social service providers and other stakeholders. Funding for the program (£5M) has been obtained from a large pool of investors. In the event that the re-conviction rate for 3000 prisoners falls below 7.5 percent with regard to the comparison group within six years, which is the criteria for success of the project, a financial return ranging from 7.5 percent to 13 percent has been committed to investors. According to the contract, the rate of return of investors varies in proportion to the success of the program (Baliga, 2013; Berndt & Wirth, 2018).

The Peterborough example was quickly copied across the country and the UK was recognized as the epicenter of SIB activity. In addition, the UK and USA are the two leading countries in the world in terms of the number of applications and the amount of funds provided. Following the pilot implementation in the UK, the first social bond application in the United States took place in New York City in August 2012. Goldman Sachs Urban Investment Group (UIG) provided $ 9.6 million fund to support the rehabilitation of prisoners aged 16-18 who were convicted in Rikers Island Prison. Another of the stakeholders of the implemented SIB program is MDRC, a non-profit research institution. The MDRC used the loan to fund the Osborne Association, a service provider with extensive experience in providing services to inmate adolescents. Another responsibility of MDRC in its contract with the New York City Administration is determined as ensuring coordination between all stakeholders during the project implementation period and realizing the repayments to be made to Goldman Sachs. The validator of the program is the Vera Institute of Justice, an independent and non-profit organization. Accordingly, based on the twelve and twenty-four month evaluation results, the New York City Administration will make payments to the MDRC based on its success in reduction in re-conviction and projected cost savings. The MDRC will then pay the loan debt to Goldman Sachs along with the rate of return stipulated in the contract (Baliga, 2013; Berndt & Wirth, 2018; Ryan & Young, 2018).

The austerity policies implemented after the Global Crisis that emerged in the United States in 2007-2008 and affected the entire world economy in a short time, created major cuts in social services. In this context, states have become increasingly supportive of alternative ways to be used in the financing of protective and preventive social programs in a way to reduce their costs and responsibilities. Interest in SIB programs, which is one of them, is growing worldwide day by day. Figure 3 and Figure 4 list the SIB projects compiled from the database of Social Finance, a non-profit organization being funded since 2007 and working in collaboration with governments, social sectors and the financial community.

Figure 3.

Country	Service Provider	Issue Area	Year	Duration(years)	Amount
GBR	One Service	Criminal Justice	2010	7	£5M
GBR	Best Network	Workforce Development	2012	3.5	£3M
GBR	Nottinghamshire Futures	Workforce Development	2012	3.5	£1.7M
GBR	Career Connect	Workforce Development	2012	3.5	£1.5M
GBR	Perth YMCA	Workforce Development	2012	3.5	£0.9M
GBR	Action for Children	Child and Family Welfare	2012	8	£3.1M
GBR	St. Mungo's Broadway	Housing / Homelessness	2012	3	£1.2M
GBR	Thames Reach	Housing / Homelessness	2012	3	£1.2M
USA	The Osborne Association & Friends of Island Academy	Criminal Justice	2013	3	$9.6M
GBR	Consortium of Voluntary Adoption Agencies	Child and Family Welfare	2013	10	£2.4M
USA	Center for Employment Opportunities	Criminal Justice	2013	5.5	$13.5M
USA	Roca	Criminal Justice	2014	5.5	$22M
GBR	Core Assets	Child and Family Welfare	2014	4	£1M
USA	Chicago Public Schools	Education and Early Years	2014	4	$16.9M
USA	MHSA	Housing / Homelessness	2014	6	$3.5M
USA	FrontLine Service	Child and Family Welfare	2015	6	$4M
GBR	St. Basil's	Housing / Homelessness	2015	3.5	£1M
GBR	Ways to Wellness	Health	2015	3	£1.7M
GBR	Career Connect	Workforce Development	2015	4	£1.4M
GBR	Age UK	Health	2015	6	£0.85M
USA	Adobe Services	Housing / Homelessness	2015	3	$6.9M
USA	Nurse-Family Partnership	Health	2016	5	$30M
USA	Colorado Coalition for the Homeless	Housing / Homelessness	2016	3	$8.7M
USA	DC Water, Sewer Authority	Poverty and Environment	2016	4	$25M
USA	First Step House	Criminal Justice	2016	6	$4.6M
USA	The Road Home	Housing / Homelessness	2016	5	$4.4M
USA	Women in Recovery	Criminal Justice	2017	7	$10M
GBR	Crisis, Thames Reach	Housing / Homelessness	2017	5	£1.4M
USA	Interface Children and Family Services	Criminal Justice	2017	3	$2.64M
USA	Tuscaloosa VA Medical Center	Workforce Development	2018	3	$5.1M

Figure 4.

Country	Service Provider	Issue Area	Year	Duration(years)	Amount
Australia	The Benevolent Society	Child and Family Welfare	2013	7	AUD10M
Australia	UnitingCare Burnside	Child and Family Welfare	2013	7	AUD7M
Germany	Multiple service providers	Workforce Development	2013	2	€0.3M
Netherlands	Buzinezzclub	Workforce Development	2013	2	€0.7M
Belgium	Duo for a Job	Workforce Development	2014	3	€0.23M
Canada	EGADZ	Child and Family Welfare	2014	5	C$1M
Portugal	Lisbon primary schools	Education and Early Years	2015	1	€0.12M
Peru	The Rainforest Foundation UK	Workforce Development	2015	7	$0.11M
India	Educate Girls	Education and Early Years	2015	5	$0.27M
Switzerland	Caritas Bern	Workforce Development	2015	4.5	F0.27M
Austria	Gewaltschutzzentrum Upper Austria, Frauenhaus Linz	Child and Family Welfare	2015	8	€0.8M
Israel	Aluma	Workforce Development	2015	6	$2.1M
Netherlands	Buzinezzclub	Workforce Development	2015	4	€2.1M
Israel	Movement	Health	2016	8	$5.5M
Australia	Common Ground Adelaide, Hutt St Centre	Housing / Homelessness	2016	3	AUD9M
Netherlands	Work-Wise Direct Consortium	Criminal Justice	2016	3	€1.2M
South Korea	Daekyo Consortium	Education and Early Years	2016	30	₩1110M
Canada	Mother Teresa Middle School	Education and Early Years	2016	3.5	C$1M
Canada	Heart and Stroke Foundation	Health	2016	5	C$2M
N. Zealand	APM Workcare	Health	2017	6	N$1.5M
Finland	Epiqus Ltd.	Workforce Development	2017	8	€10M
Australia	Flourish Australia	Health	2017	7	AUD7M
India	Hindustan Latex Family Planning Promotion Trust (HLFPP)	Health	2017	4	$3.5M
Netherlands	ArboNed, Re-turn	Health	2017	1	€0.64M
Uganda, Kenya	Village Enterprise	Poverty and Environment	2018	3	$2.4M
South Africa	Foundation for Community Work	Child and Family Welfare	2018	4	$0.54M
France	Jeffco Public Schools, Jefferson County Human Services	Education and Early Years	2018	3	€0.78M
Australia	SYC Ltd	Workforce Development	2019	5.5	A$5M
Israel	Beit Yatziv	Education and Early Years	2019	5.5	₪14.8M

The Benefits and Challenges of SIBs

The benefits of SIB projects can be listed as follows (Mulgan et al, 2011; Griffiths & Christian Meinicke, 2014; Barajas et al., 2014):

- The most important benefit of SIB projects is that it eliminates the need to use the taxes collected by the state in financing the social programs and transfers the risk to the investors who provide the initial capital for the project. Paying investors when predefined targets are achieved provides savings in the public budget and links profits with socially valuable results.
- When the government or its representative is implementing a program or service, it bears the risks of spending on a public intervention that does not guarantee the desired results. A SIB program transfers this risk borne by the government or its representative to private investors. This allows for more efficient expenditures. It also paves the way for the public to come up with more innovative projects where financial risk is limited.
- SIBs offer potential opportunities in funding and testing innovative approaches to enable early intervention in societal problems. In this context, it can be stated that social investments can help to shift public funds to other support areas by creating new resources in funding the newly emerging social work interventions. In this context, SIB projects contribute to the spending of public funds on successful programs, as payments depend on the results achieved.
- SIB projects improve weak incentives and create new financing resources in that they focus on outputs rather than inputs, encourage results-oriented actions, direct scarce resources to areas where the most positive impact can be achieved, and transfer the risks over the public. In this context, it can provide the opportunity to save from the state treasury even when there is an intense pressure on public resources. Because it transfers costs from the public sector to the private sector.
- Philanthropic and other nonprofits spend a significant amount of resources on research on alternative programs and innovative solutions. However, they may then be deprived of the resources to run these programs. On the other hand, governments may avoid financing a program whose results are uncertain due to the risks involved. SIBs, unlike governments, lead the private sector, which grows with such high-risk and high-return investments.
- SIB programs divide resources and knowledge and enable collaboration between different actors in the public and private sectors, unlike the traditional structure that prevents social programs and related institutions from working together. In this respect, it can be said that SIB programs are unique in the context of social impact investment due to their structure that allows the actors involved in the project to operate in the field in which they are best.
- SIB programs divide resources and knowledge and enable collaboration between different actors in the public and private sectors, unlike the traditional structure that prevents social programs and related institutions from working together. In this respect, it can be said that SIB programs are unique in the context of social impact investment due to their structure that allows the actors involved in the project to operate in the field in which they are best. The government or its representative in the aforementioned structure has the legitimacy to set the goals of the SIB program due to the liability of public accountability. Here, the private sector provides start-up capital, the nonprofit service provider demonstrates its expertise in a particular area, and is actually running the program. Working together of these actors to address large-scale social problems makes SIB programs more effective than other models of government funding.

- SIB projects place the result oriented view at the heart of the process and encourage investors and social service providers to make a planning in a way that generates return on investment. In this context, it is possible to mention that well-grounded applications will be put forward. In addition, in the context of social impact investments, SIBs encourage more investment, especially in areas where social service providers often find it difficult to find sufficient resources, and to turn people-oriented investment rhetoric into action.
- Focusing on the success of the services offered may lead investors to make a special effort to realize the expected benefits during the implementation of SIB projects, to use new resources to solve the problems addressed, and to be flexible in developing new responses to emerging challenges.
- The SIB contract allows the government or its representative to enter into long-term contracts with social service providers and enables related services to be implemented for extended periods. The government or its representative ensures - provided that the SIB project is successful - that the funds required to finance the program are available throughout the project and investors cannot claim repayments until the specified period.
- The necessity to measure the impact of the SIB program very carefully, prompts the government or its representative to analyse the effectiveness of the program in depth. This leads to the provision of more efficient services by developing a culture of implementing proven programs.
- Social investors will demand more careful measurement of the social impact and financial performance of the program. In this context, continuous observations of external investors concerned with the success of the services provided will enable a more careful performance management in SIB programs compared to many standard service contracts.
- SIB projects increase the effectiveness of the social programs it finances by setting reliable criteria for performance measurement, creativity and financial flexibility, and by including quantitative metrics in non-profit performance standards. In this context, certain parameters of SIBs encourage more efficient use of financial and physical capital by optimizing the allocation of resources. In addition, it can maximize the impact on the target population.
- SIBs allow social service providers to gain advance access to large amounts of capital, allowing applications that have proven successful to rapidly scale. SIB programs transfer the fundraising function to private investors, rather than re-allocating them between non-profit organizations. Thus, SIB contracts help non-profit organizations to expand their service areas and operations by funding them.

As an innovative financial tool, SIBs offer great potential in increasing the quantity and quality of investments aimed at improving the welfare of society. However, SIB programs pose some inherent difficulties (Mulgan et al, 2011; Costa et al, 2012; Joy & Shields, 2013; Rizzello & Carè, 2016):

- Social impact investment variables differ due to variables considered in widely recognized financial models. Investing in SIBs involves a high level of uncertainty and risk of failure, given the high variability that can be observed in the performance of projects financed in this way and in the results achieved. For this reason, defining and evaluating the social risk variables involved in the investment process of a SIB project is an important focal point.
- There is a widespread opinion in the literature that SIB programs will not reduce existing bureaucracy and reduce public costs. In addition, the implementation of a comprehensive program will require new skills of civil servants who will carry out technical tasks in the context of defining the

market, evaluating the program and building the partnership. This will create a considerable cost of administrative changes.

- The fact that SIB payments are based on program outputs will pose a number of problems, especially in service approaches that lack a proven track record of financial success. Although pilot SIB programs have been proposed to solve this problem, the cost and time-consuming nature of such studies may cause the private sector to be reluctant to undertake the necessary additional investments.
- Failure to achieve the predefined goal may not mean that the program has failed if the results obtained as a result of the implemented program prevent the problem in focus from worsening or contribute to the provision of social justice and improvement of problems in the long term. In this context, the interruption of financing for preventive programs due to the failure to achieve the defined target may cause greater welfare problems and higher costs in the future.
- Some non-profits worry that progress on SIBs will reduce public, private and charitable funds provided as grants or donations. Linking financing especially to the results to be achieved creates problems for non-profit organizations as they do not have direct control over the outputs to be achieved. In this context, non-profit organizations are at a disadvantage compared to the public and private sectors. The transition to SIB programs, which requires new management and evaluation mechanisms, is an investment that non-profits cannot afford.
- Essentially, the private sector, which tends to avoid risk, will hesitate to make that investment unless it is confident that the investment will result in significant financial return. However, the prominent SIB framework conveys the opposite of this situation. SIBs are a unique - bond-like - financial instrument that can be expressed as risky in the sense that the rate of return is limited, cannot be converted into a liquid asset, and all financial investments can be lost. This risk of SIBs requires a proven financial viability and a large scale in terms of achieving an acceptable profit. However, it is difficult to state that these two situations exist in the majority of SIB projects.
- In the event that a SIB-funded program fails, private investors can use their power to get the payment stipulated in the contract, and firms cän profit from the complexity caused by delays in government regulations and auditing failures. In this context, it has been suggested that the SIBs are not completely different from the risky financial instruments that led to the deepening of the Global Crisis of 2008.
- It is unclear what kind of application will be continued if a major investor is in financial trouble during the project. In such a situation, the most likely outcome is that the social impact investment is abandoned and the government assumes full responsibility. Such scenarios are more likely to emerge, especially in times of economic slowdown when social needs reach high levels.
- The funders of the project may refrain from making a SIB contract if they feel that they will not be able to achieve the result and therefore cannot receive payment from the government. It can be said that the existence of such a risk limits the use of SIBs in providing basic government services such as education or public security. As a solution to this situation, mechanisms for terminating the contract within the framework of certain rules can be included in the process. However, this will also pose a risk of termination.
- SIB contracts may be relatively more expensive than a direct contract between a government agency and a social service provider, due to the additional costs incurred by the existence of the social finance intermediary institution and the evaluation institution in the system. In addition, all

stakeholders, including investors, should understand the importance of these additional costs in realizing the project and achieving the projected goal.

- The most technically complex issue with SIBs is exactly how to measure the expected impact. Funders and government should ensure that the measurement criterion used in a SIB project is not systematically biased and is a fair measure of performance on average. In this context, it can be said that a sound measurement should establish a clear link with the desired results and with prudent estimates and take second-degree effects into account.

Social Spending and Social Impact Bonds Potential in Turkey

When the data of the years 2008-2018 in Turkey are analyzed, it is observed that there has been a 74% increase in social spending during the mentioned period. The share of social protection expenditures in gross domestic product (GDP) decreased from 12.3% in 2017 to 11.9% in 2018. It can be said that the contraction in the country's economy in 2018 had an effect on this. When the structure of social spending in Turkey is observed based on the risk and needing groups, it is seen that the expenditures made to the retired / elderly people have the biggest share in GDP with 5.7%. This was followed by sickness / health care expenditures with 3.3% and widow / orphan expenditures with 1.4%. Here, 9% of social protection funds have been given conditionally. In 2018, family / child funds had the largest share in conditional funds with 37.7%. This was followed by disability funds with 28.1% and sickness / health care funds with 15.5%. Besides 67.3% of the social protection funds were given in cash. The largest share in cash funds in 2018 was the funds provided to retired / elderly people with 72.8%. This was followed by widow / orphan funds with 17.7% and unemployment funds with 3.4%. Indeed, 35.4% of the social protection income was made up by state contributions, 30.3% by employers' social contributions and 26.9% by individuals under protection. In this context, it can be stated that the main financial source of social protection expenditures is the state (https://www.tuik.gov.tr/).

Figure 5.

(Million TL)

	2008	2009	2010	2011	2012	2013	2014	2015	2016	2017	2018
Total social protection expenditure	113 512	134 522	148 450	171 668	195 663	220 429	247 244	280 074	336 520	382 665	442 607
Administartion costs and other expenditure	1 922	2 032	2 205	2 586	2 976	3 982	4 332	5 163	5 744	7 108	6 697
Total social protection benefits	111 591	132 490	146 245	169 082	192 687	216 446	242 912	274 912	330 776	375 557	435 910
Sickness/health care	39 571	47 384	49 429	56 046	60 518	65 839	73 322	80 463	91 330	103 077	121 444
Disability	2 506	3 538	4 280	5 654	7 035	8 088	9 251	10 124	11 982	13 317	14 840
Old age	52 891	63 236	71 725	80 243	92 137	104 554	117 390	133 515	162 139	184 984	214 133
Survivors	11 735	11 649	14 148	19 200	22 424	25 568	28 931	32 719	39 615	44 687	52 262
Family/children	2 946	3 418	3 681	4 603	5 597	6 899	7 580	8 901	12 319	14 966	16 986
Unemployment	721	1 856	1 624	1 739	2 431	2 572	3 167	5 263	8 172	8 672	10 358
Social exclusion and n.e.c.	1 220	1 408	1 359	1 596	2 545	2 927	3 271	3 927	5 218	5 853	5 887

In summary, considering the increase in all expenditure items in the 2008-2018 period, social impact bonds are considered to be an important tool of investment for Turkey. For this, first of all, it should be determined that SIB can be used in financing the expenditures for which public services. In addition, as our legal legislation is not suitable for SIB implementation, necessary arrangements should be made in the legislation. SIB programs are carried out with a contract signed between public institutions and private organizations. In this context, regulations that will guide the scope of the contract to be made, measuring the success of the service to be provided and preparing the repayment plan should be determined.

SIBs are a type of financial asset that offers investors the opportunity to generate financial returns and also have social returns. However, since they are a new class of assets, it can be said that they have a limited asset pool where they can have funds. Investors, on the other hand, do not yet have enough historical risk and return data that they can use in decision making. Therefore, government support is indispensable for the development of the SIB market. For this purpose, practices such as investment incentives, tax exemptions, undertaking some part of the underwriting by the state during the issuance process can be implemented (Social Finance, 2010).

CONCLUSİON

The projections regarding the world population and the temporary or permanent crises in the economies indicate that the need for financing for social services provided by the states will increase day by day. In this context, it can be said that there is a need to develop new financial assets in the process of solving social problems. In the post-crisis period, it is seen that social impact investments come to the fore as a tool that focuses on the creation of social change to promote sustainable development. Social impact investments is an asset allocation strategy used in financing public services and financing projects that combine a measurable social and environmental impact with economic sustainability and financial returns. One of the new techniques used in financing social impact investments is social impact bonds, a financial tool that focuses on inter-sectoral partnership and mutual cooperation in achieving sustainable development goals.

Designed with a success-oriented payment approach, SIBs, on the one hand, provide profit to private investors, on the other hand, provide third parties with the opportunity to access fund resources in financing, planning and evaluating social programs. In this way, public expenditures can be saved and the quality of social service delivery can be increased with the support of private institutions and financial markets.

It is observed that SIB programs, which were first implemented in the United Kingdom in 2010, are rapidly developing worldwide. SIB, which is mostly used in developed countries, especially in the UK and USA, will contribute to the solution of social problems in the world if also implemented in other countries that adopt the social state principle.

In Turkey, where the amount and structure of social policy spending are very inadequate, it can be stated that SIBs have the potential to provide innovation in the financing of social programs. However, it is necessary to establish the necessary legal basis and regulate the financial infrastructure for this. In addition, making SIBs attractive for investors is another issue that needs to be addressed, as they carry a higher risk than other bonds. In this framework, options such as tax advantages in interest incomes to be obtained from SIBs and in gains obtained from secondary markets can be taken into consideration. From this point of view, further studies can concentrate on the legal regulations to be made by examining the developed countries' practices.

REFERENCES

Baliga, S. (2013). Shaping the Success of Social Impact Bonds in The United States: Lessons Learned from the Privatization of U.S. Prisons. *Duke Law Journal*, *63*, 437–479.

Berndt, C., & Wirth, M. (2018). Market, Metrics, Morals: The Social Impact Bond as an Emerging Social Policy Instrument. *Geoforum, 90*, 27–35. doi:10.1016/j.geoforum.2018.01.019

Bolton, E. (2010). Social Impact Bonds Unlocking investment in rehabilitation. *Social Finance*. https://www.socialfinance.org.uk/resources/publications/social-impact-bonds-unlocking-new-investment-rehabilitation

Boons, F., & Lüdeke-Freund, F. (2013). Business Models For Sustainable Innovation: State of the Art and Steps Towards a Research Agenda. *Journal of Cleaner Production, 45*, 9–19. doi:10.1016/j.jclepro.2012.07.007

Calderini, M., Chiodo, V., & Michelucci, F. V. (2018). The Social Impact Investment Race: Toward an Interpretative Framework. *European Business Review, 30*(1), 66–81. doi:10.1108/EBR-10-2016-0134

Cantele, S., Moggi, S., & Campedelli, B. (2020). Spreading Sustainability Innovation through the Co-Evolution of Sustainable Business Models and Partnerships. *Sustainability, 12*(3), 1–19. doi:10.3390u12031190

Carè, R., & De Lisa, R. (2019). Social Impact Bonds for a SustainableWelfare State: The Role of Enabling Factors. *Sustainability, 11*(2884), 2–23.

Clarke, A., & Fuller, M. (2010). Collaborative Strategic Management: Strategy Formulation and Implementation by Multi-Organizational Cross-Sector Social Partnerships. *Journal of Business Ethics, 94*(S1), 85–101. doi:10.100710551-011-0781-5

Congress of the United States Congressional Budget Office. (2019). *The 2019 Long-Term Budget Outlook*. https://www.cbo.gov/system/files/2019-06/55331-LTBO-2.pdf

Del Giudice, A., & Migliavacca, M. (2019). Social Impact Bonds and Institutional Investors: An Empirical Analysis of a Complicated Relationship. *Nonprofit and Voluntary Sector Quarterly, 48*(1), 50–70. doi:10.1177/0899764018797480

Disley, E., Rubin, J., Scraggs, E., Burrowes, N., & May Culley, D. (2011). *Lessons Learned from the Planning and Early Implementation of the Social Impact Bond at HMP Peterborough*. Rand Europe.

El Ebrashi, R. (2013). Social Entrepreneurship Theory and Sustainable Social Impact. *Social Responsibility Journal, 9*(2), 188-209.

Feilhauer, S., & Hahn, R. (2019). Firm-Nonprofit Collaboration: Explaining the Rationale Behind Firms' Cross-Sector Partner Choices. *Long Range Planning, 3*, 1–19. doi:10.1016/j.lrp.2019.101952

FitzGerald, C., Carter, E., Dixon, R., & Airoldi, M. (2019). Walking the Contractual Tightrope: A Transaction Cost Economics Perspective on Social Impact Bonds. *Public Money & Management, 39*(7), 458–467. doi:10.1080/09540962.2019.1583889

Freudenreich, B., Ludeke-Freund, F., & Schaltegger, S. (2019). A Stakeholder Theory Perspective on Business Models: Value Creation for Sustainability. *Journal of Business Ethics, 166*(1), 3–18. doi:10.100710551-019-04112-z

Griffiths, A. & Meinicke, C. (2014). *Introduction To Social Impact Bonds And Early Intervention*. Early Intervention Foundation: Initial Report.

Hesse, A., Kreutzer, K., & Diehl, M.-R. (2019). Dynamics of Institutional Logics in a Cross-Sector Social Partnership: The Case of Refugee Integration in Germany. *Journal of Business Ethics, 159*(3), 679–704. doi:10.100710551-017-3775-0

Hille, I. G. A., de Bakker, H. E., Ferguson, J., & Groenewegen, P. (2018). Navigating Tensions in a Cross-Sector Social Partnership: How a Convener Drives Change for Sustainability. *Corporate Social Responsibility and Environmental Management, 26*(2), 317–329. doi:10.1002/csr.1684

Hille, I. G. A., de Bakker, H. E., Ferguson, J., & Groenewegen, P. (2020). Cross-Sector Partnerships for Sustainability: How Mission-Driven Conveners Drive Change in National Coffee Platforms. *Sustainability, 2020*(12), 1–23.

Investment, I. (n.d.). *The Invisible Heart of Markets.* http://gsgii.org/wp-content/uploads/2017/05/Impact-Investment-Report.pdf

Joy, M., & Shields, J. (2013). Social Impact Bonds. *The Next Phase of Third Sector Marketization Canadian Journal of Nonprofit and Social Economy Research, 4*(2), 39–55.

Joy, M., & Shields, J. (2018). Austerity in the Making: Reconfiguring Social Policy through Social Impact Bonds. *Policy and Politics, 46*(4), 681–695. doi:10.1332/030557318X15200933925397

La Torre, M., Trotta, A., Chiappini, H. & Rizzello, A. (2019). Business Models for Sustainable Finance: The Case Study of Social Impact Bonds. *Sustainability, 11*(1887), 2-23.

McHugh, N., Sinclair, S., Roy, M., Huckfield, L., & Donaldson, C. (2013). Social Impact Bonds: A Wolf in Sheep's Clothing? *The Journal of Poverty and Social Justice: Research, Policy, Practice, 21*(3), 247–257. doi:10.1332/204674313X13812372137921

Mulgan, G., Reeder, N., Aylott, M., & Bo'sher, L. (2011). *Social Impact Investment: The Challenge and Opportunity of Social Impact Bonds.* The Young Foundation.

Munoz, P., & Kimmitt, J. (2019). A Diagnostic Framework for Social Impact Bonds in Emerging Economies. *Journal of Business Venturing Insights, 12*, 1–9. doi:10.1016/j.jbvi.2019.e00141

OECD. (2016). *Understanding Social Impact Bonds.* http://www.oecd.org/cfe/leed/UnderstandingSIBsLux-WorkingPaper.pdf

Public Policy and International Affairs Fellowship Domestic Policy Workshop. (2014). *Social Impact Bonds A New Tool for Social Financing.* Academic Press.

Rizzello, A., & Carè, R. (2016). Insight into the Social Impact Bond Market: An Analysis of Investors. *ACRN Oxford Journal of Finance and Risk Perspectives, 5*(3), 145–171.

Ryan, S., & Young, M. (2018). Social Impact Bonds: The Next Horizon of Privatization. *Studies in Political Economy, 99*(1), 42–58. doi:10.1080/07078552.2018.1440985

Schinckus, C. (2017). Financial Innovation as a Potential Force for a Positive Socialchange: The Challenging Future of Social Impact Bonds. *Research in International Business and Finance, 39*, 727–736. doi:10.1016/j.ribaf.2015.11.004

Schneider, S., & Clauß, T. (2019). Business Models for Sustainability: Choices and Consequences. *Organization & Environment*, *00*(0), 1–24.

Schrötgens, J., & Boenigk, S. (2017). Social Impact Investment Behavior in the Nonprofit Sector: First Insights from an Online Survey Experiment. *Voluntas*, *28*(6), 2658–2682. doi:10.100711266-017-9886-5

Stadtler, L. (2011). Aligning a Company's Economic and Social Interests in Cross-Sector Partnerships. *Journal of Corporate Citizenship*, *44*(44), 85–106. doi:10.9774/GLEAF.4700.2011.wi.00007

Stubbs, W., & Cocklin, C. (2008). Conceptualizing a "Sustainability Business Model. *Organization & Environment*, *21*(2), 103–127. doi:10.1177/1086026608318042

Stubbs, W. (2019). Strategies, Practices, and Tensions in Managing Business Model Innovation for Sustainability: The Case of an Australian BCorp. *Corporate Social Responsibility and Environmental Management*, 1063–1072. doi:10.1002/csr.1786

Syed Azman, S. M. & Engku Ali, E. R. (2016). Potential Role of Social Impact Bond and Socially Responsible Investment Sukuk as Financial Tools that Can Help Address Issues of Poverty and Socio-Economic Insecurity. *Intellectual Discourse*, 343-364.

Jackson, T. (2013). Evaluating Social Impact Bonds: Questions, Challenges, Innovations, and Possibilities in Measuring Outcomes in Impact Investing. *Community Development (Columbus, Ohio)*, *44*(5), 608–616. doi:10.1080/15575330.2013.854258

TÜİK. (n.d.). https://www.tuik.gov.tr/

Wood, A. (2010). New Legal Structures to Address the Social Capital Famine. *Vermont Law Review*, *35*(045), 45–52.

Yan, X., Lin, H., & Clarke, A. (2018). Cross-Sector Social Partnerships for Social Change: The Roles of Non-Governmental Organizations. *Sustainability*, *10*(558), 1–17. doi:10.3390u10020558

Section 3
Selected Cases on Social Value Creation

Chapter 10
Creating Shared Value and Social Innovation:
Cases of Success From South American Entrepreneurial Ventures

Katherina Kuschel
CENTRUM PUCP, Peru & Pontificia Universidad Católica del Perú, Peru

Manuel Méndez Pinzón
Politécnico Grancolombiano, Colombia

ABSTRACT

This multiple case study of nine entrepreneurial ventures with social emphasis operating in Colombia, Peru, and Chile identifies vital elements that make these firms impactful in three dimensions: economic, environmental, and social. The results found that the founder's proximity to the social/ecological problem is a trigger to start up a business. The "purpose" is a motivational factor to both start up a business and keep the business during hard times, such as the COVID-19 pandemic. The purpose is the fuel, but it does not guarantee the success of the company. The value proposition is the critical factor for success. These companies are continually re-inventing and changing their value proposition while keeping the purpose of the organization as a keystone. The authors shed light on a model for social entrepreneurship in South America.

INTRODUCTION

"A healthy economy should be designed to thrive, not grow"

Kate Raworth

Nowadays, the world is facing extinction-level grand challenges (Pörtner et al., 2019; United Nations, 2015). The COVID-19 pandemic has shifted our economy dramatically in a matter of weeks. Moreover,

DOI: 10.4018/978-1-7998-4727-4.ch010

there is an ever-growing awareness of significant societal challenges, and government and NGOs lack sufficient resources and capabilities to meet these challenges (Porter, 2012). Therefore, the imperative for entrepreneurship for sustainable development and innovative solutions is profound.

Social innovation is on the rise in Latin America (Domanski, Howaldt, & Schröder, 2017), while the phenomenon of social entrepreneurship remains a poorly-understood (Santos, 2012; Sinthupundaja, Kohda, & Chiadamrong, 2020). As crises create new needs and therefore new business opportunities, natural disasters in South American countries boost social innovation. One example is shown by data from the GEM project in Chile. According to the data, during the economic downturn (2007-2010, including the earthquake of February 2010) the entrepreneurial attitude of the Chilean population changed: Entrepreneurial intention increases while fear of failure decreases. This means, that the community became more resilient.

South American countries have historically addressed social impact, mostly with philanthropy and corporate social responsibility. Paternalism, as an action that limits a person's or group's liberty or autonomy and is intended to promote their own good (Dworkin, 2010) has been the colonial root behind these practices. However, high collectivism (as described by the framework based on Geert Hofstede's work) and cooperativism are also valid values nowadays, shared in most Iberoamerican countries. This context makes South America a fertile land for social entrepreneurship and innovation.

"B Corporation" (*Sistema B*) is a certification for firms with triple impact (social, environment, financial). According to their website, the B movement works "for an economy where success is measured by the well-being of individuals, societies and nature"[1]. By 2020, B movement has certified 572 B corporations in Latin America (out of 3275 in the world), and joined 5 "+B cities" in South America (out of 7 in the world).

The interest in social innovation is continuously growing in South American countries. The academic community has also shown interest in studying sustainable business models.

For instance, Brillo de Luna, a school that creates shared value creation by recycling glass, and partnering with a glass company nearby (Villalobos Arayá, 2020). Another example is Algramo[2], a company that goes beyond traditional business models.

"We are continuously challenging our business model... We are not a delivery service, nor a detergent dispenser. We want to become a sustainability solution, we want to take waste out of the equation. We need to change consumer behavior. What a huge challenge". José Manuel Möller, Algramo CEO, April 2020.

Research Questions and Aim

Is there a particular way of doing sustainable entrepreneurship in South America? Do the perspectives of "shared value creation" and "entrepreneurial context" contribute to the understanding of the sustainable entrepreneurship phenomenon? What is the trigger for starting up a sustainable business? What is the driver? Does the social and/or environmental serve as a survival or as a success factor during hard times?

This exploratory study challenges the prevailing myths such as "social innovation is not profitable" and "social entrepreneurship is not scalable" by identifying and providing with successful entrepreneurial projects with social emphasis that serve as a model for social entrepreneurship in South America.

THEORETICAL FOUNDATION

This chapter combines two perspectives: shared value and a contextualized perspective of entrepreneurship.

First, shared value creation theory (Porter et al., 2011) challenges organizations to meet the social and environmental problems and State voids (Porter, 2006). According to Porter and Kramer (2011), *shared value* can be defined as policies and practices that increase the organizational competitiveness by improving the economic and social conditions of the communities where the company is located.

The role of a company in its communities has been evolved from *Philanthropy* (volunteering, donations to worthy social causes), to *Corporate Social Responsibility* (CSR - compliance with community standards, good corporate citizenship, "sustainability", and now to *Creating Social Value* (CSV - integrating societal improvement into economic value creation itself) (Porter, 2012). This new approach is also applicable to small businesses and new ventures.

It is suggested that once the organization strategy adopts shared value creation, the company becomes more profitable and it creates in turn value in society (Pongwiritthon, 2015) in the form of taxes, job/salaries, etc. Porter and Kramer (2011) suggest three ways to create shared value: by 1) reconceiving products and markets, 2) redefining productivity in the value chain, and 3) improving the local and regional business environment.

According to Welter (2011) a contextualized view of entrepreneurship contributes to our better understanding of its dynamics and impact. These historical, temporal, institutional, spatial, and social contexts for business creation provide individuals with opportunities while it also sets limitations. "Effectuation" (Sarasvathy, 2009), "bricolage" (Baker et al., 2003; Baker & Nelson, 2005; Ciborra, 1996), and "ecosystem" (Isenberg, 2010; 2011; 2014) O'Connor, Stam, Sussan, & Audretsch, 2018) approaches are also part of the contextual perspective. This analysis uses a contextual perspective of entrepreneurship (Welter, 2011; Zahra, Wright, & Abdelgawad, 2014) in emerging markets (Smallbone, Welter, & Ateljevic, 2013) such as Chile, Colombia, and Peru.

LITERATURE REVIEW

The shared value approach demystifies the concept of competency, as the clusters play a key role in increasing productivity, innovation, and competitiveness of the whole sector (Porter, 2011). Porter (2011) and Aspelund et al. (2017) state that collaboration between actors in the same industry has positive effects for the firm. Moreover, social emphasis has a positive impact on firm performance (Alberti & Garrido, 2017) when redefining the business strategy, business models, products or services to face social or environmental challenges. This is particularly important in times of societal and economic crisis.

Entrepreneurship and innovation go hand-in-hand. Idea generation processes are critical for identifying social or environmental necessities, and therefore, business opportunities (Arias, Franco, Sánchez, & Rojas, 2019). Entrepreneurship should be based on innovation development, in the level of venture strategy or the level of solutions offered to the market needs.

Shared Value and SMEs

A framework developed by Matinheikki et al. (2017) suggests that institutional change towards shared value creation requires a reformation of existing practices to meet new community-based logic within the field, since achieving a shared value paradigm is complicated by actors' relationships with their institutional, organizational, and socio-material environments. Another barrier for the full application of the CSV approach is that women entrepreneurs, compared to men, lack access to finance, training, and rights, besides differing in terms of economic opportunities (Véras, 2015). The unlocking of these cultural and structural difficulties will propel the implementation of a CSV approach among SMEs.

However, we are starting to see case studies that illustrate the practices inside companies that evidence successful implementations of a shared value creation approach into the value chain (Elamrani & Lemtaoui, 2016). For Lüth and Stierl (2015), the secret sauce for creating shared value that fosters regional development is what they call "Partners in Responsibility Method for SMEs". By networking activities with other businesses and pooling resources to address pressing social issues, companies can greatly increase the impact of their efforts. In several regions of Germany this method is successfully applied.

As suggested by Pavlovich and Corner (2014), the presence of spiritual practices increases conscious awareness which, in turn, shapes entrepreneurial intentions towards shared value creation. In other words, conscious awareness serves as a mechanism for creating shared value. Is then awareness enough for the founder? According to Blanchard and Gray (2019), shared value works as a mechanism for profit generating in rural locations, "but this is tempered with the ability to bring together visions of a shared nature within both customer base and business".

A Different Way of Doing Business

According to Sinthupundaja et al. (2020), social entrepreneurship can be represented as a transitional vehicle that serves for creating shared value among an entrepreneur, society and the environment.

Social entrepreneurship, sustainable entrepreneurship, and entrepreneurship with social impact are often used interchangeably and as overlapping concepts. We have also found the terms sustainopreneurship, green entrepreneurship, ecopreneurship, and environmental entrepreneurship, for those ventures oriented to tackle environmental problems. Nikolaou, Tasopoulou, and Tsagarakis (2018) created a typology of green entrepreneurship according to the seeking mission (social or profit) and the business stage (startup or an established firm). In our study, we selected for-profit and not-for-profit "social ecopreneurs" in an early stage of the business, as defined by Nikolaou et al (2018).

The motivation of social, environmental, and sustainable entrepreneurs deviates from the one-sided pursuit of profit that tends to characterize the regular entrepreneur (Van de Ven et al. 2007; Dacin et al. 2010). The social and environmental values become a source of competitive advantage for social entrepreneurial ventures (Muñoz & Kimmitt, 2019; Sinthupundaja et al., 2020). Now, due to the emergence of the Sustainable Development Goals (SDG) as a pressure to the global society, it has been pointed out that entrepreneurship should not be based solely on generating wealth (Dean & McMullen, 2007; Shepherd & Patzelt, 2011).

The SDGs were adopted by all United Nations Member States in 2015. They agreed to aim at ending poverty, taking care of the planet, and a peaceful living by 2030. Seventeen integrated SDGs may overlap or conflict with each other, however, the "development must balance social, economic, and environmental sustainability." (UNDP, 2020).

Social Impact in the Education Sector

As 4 out of 9 selected ventures come from the education sector, we decided to review the literature on sustainability and education in South American countries.

Latin America is now the fourth largest edtech market in the world (Lustig, 2019). The increasing levels of mobile and Internet access is the main driver of edtech opportunities. These opportunities are being scaled in Latin American countries as most of these countries shared similar educational problems, culture, and language. HolonIQ (2020) launched LATAM EdTech 100 — a list of the 100 most innovative education technology companies across Latin America. According to this list, Brazil, Mexico and Chile are leading innovations in the edtech sector.

Vélez and Gairin (2019) explored students within dual models of education in a university in Bogota. They analyze knowledge transfer from the classroom to the company, and back to the classroom. They confirmed that this educational model contributes to the sophistication of the business sector through knowledge transfer processes.

From an entrepreneurial education perspective, Vélez (2015) indicated that the inclusion of education for sustainable development in higher education should be seen as the route to develop future entrepreneurs' competencies. These skills will allow them to understand the 21st century complex problems, develop and start up new business models with a sustainability strategy. Similarly, Pico et al. (2018) define different learning models that help internalize concepts of sustainable development. Entrepreneurial training programs at the university level were analyzed by Garmendia, Barrientos, and Castro (2019) in Venezuela. They found that the introduction of social and environmental awareness to the program would improve the student entrepreneurship skills, particularly for social and environmental problem recognition.

METHODOLOGY

This chapter combines the analysis of multiple case studies with the approach of shared value creation. The authors selected nine specific contemporary case studies from Chile, Colombia, and Peru and identified the common differences and similarities.

As selection criteria, we decided to include only for-profit enterprises whose founders were reachable for the authors, from two different sectors: productive and educational sectors.

Table 1. Characteristics of the nine companies included in this study

Company	Country & year of foundation	Value proposition
Laboratoria	Peru, 2014	A startup in edtech aiming at training women developers for a digital world.
Greenglass	Chile, 2009	A trading company that extends the life of bottles made of glass, and recycles them into glasses (for drinking water).
Lab4U	Chile, 2014	A startup in the edtech sector with an app that simulates a science laboratory in smartphones.
School Brillo de Luna	Chile, 2015	A shared value creation project that generates a new income to the school by collecting glass and partnering with the community and a glass factory.
Mejor en Bici	Colombia, 2010	A sustainable solution to mobility.
Algramo	Chile, 2012	A sustainable way of buying that aims at removing waste from the equation. It is not just a system for detergent refill, nor a distribution channel.
La Cucha	Chile, 2019	A short food supply chain, with a focus on local and organic products, and fair trade.
ENI Foundation	Colombia, 2010	An institution of technical education.
LULU	Peru, 2019	A digital platform that improves the quality of life of mothers and their children with disabilities.

Source: Authors' own.

During the COVID-19 pandemic, we have interviewed some founders (via phone or videoconference), and attended webinars with founder's discussion on their strategies to overcome the crisis. We included these companies with secondary data (i.e., business cases from Emerald Emerging Markets Case Studies, private webinars, conferences and company's information uploaded into YouTube) prior and during the global crisis.

Table 2. Data sources

Primary data	Secondary data
Interviews to - Andreas Aron, founder and CEO of La Cucha - Jimmy Leonardo Castro, founder and CEO of ENI Foundation - Mónica Villanueva, co-founder of LULU	Emerald Emerging Markets Case Studies - School Brillo de Luna - Mejor en Bici Private webinars - Algramo Youtube videos - Laboratoria - Greenglass - Lab4U

Source: Authors' own.

In all cases we have reviewed company websites and social networks such as the Facebook fanpage or their Instagram accounts.

We have gathered and analyzed the data, particularly regarding:

- Contextual data from the industry (e.g., competitors, city, sector)
- Data from the (co)founder(s) (e.g., motivation to start up a business, background)

- Data from business (age, stage, structure, team building, size measured by employees and sales)
- Strategy
    - Business Model
    - Shared Value Creation: Innovation, value chain, impact (Porter and Kramer, 2011)
- Purpose, sustainable development goals, and measures of success
- Strategies during and after the COVID-19 pandemic and other crises.

RESULTS

In this exploratory study, we have found that there is a higher social and/or environmental "mission", a "cause", a "purpose" that operates as a motivational factor to both start up a business and keep the business during hard times, such as the COVID-19 pandemic.

A. The Proximity to the Social/Environmental Problem as a Trigger to Start Up a Business

The founder must be immersed in the situation to understand the problem better and offer a viable solution.

"During a trip I took around South America, I realized that some countries don't have clean drinking water, and most of the water available was commercialized in bottles. The bigger the bottle, the cheaper. However, poor people only have money for small bottles. Then, with other backpackers, we bought a 20 liters jerrycan, and refilled our own 5-liters-bottles. We definitely accessed a better price just by simply association, by aggregating the demand. This became my motto, and I committed myself to contribute with a solution." Andreas Aron, La Cucha Puerto Varas (Chile). April 2020.

Mónica, the co-founder of LULU (Peru), was participating in a network of women. She noticed a common interest of some women: getting information and taking care of disabled people. She decided to create LULU, a support online platform that shares best practices and advice for taking care of people with disabilities and their caregivers.

Jimmy, the founder of ENI Foundation (Colombia) —an academy that offers technical education— was already in the education sector. He was asked by some students to change the class schedule, to better fit their work schedule. Little by little, students that were enrolled in a course in the morning shift were attending the course in the evening shift or vice versa. ENI Foundation was born to assist a market of adults that work on shifts, and who cannot enroll in a virtual course, as they have no online skills. Jimmy knew the reality of the technicians.

As we can evidence in this section, the founder has to be "very close to" or "in" the situation to better understand the problem.

B. Is the Pursuit of Social Impact a Success Factor?

Making a social impact becomes a purpose. The purpose becomes the driver, the North star, that helps align the team during difficult times.

"The purpose is contagious. People can relate with it... collaborators, suppliers, customers... everyone". José Manuel Möller, Algramo (Chile). April 2020.

The purpose is the glue that keeps the team together and aligned towards the goal. However, this purpose will not create money for its own. The value proposition is key. The business model (i.e., the creation, delivery, and capture of value) of a social enterprise has to both serve and fit the market.

"In our case, people come back with their reusable container for detergent because they save money. That's the final value of our company. And by doing so, they are saving the planet. Ultimately, money saving is the driver for the consumers". José Manuel Möller, Algramo (Chile). April 2020.

All the participants of this study, as founders of social enterprises, often have a conflict. This is an ethical conflict. They perceive themselves as agents of change, and this self-perception often conflicts -in early stages of the company- with the stereotypes around leading a for-profit organization.

"We have to change the current paradigm of either making money or saving the planet (...) We can do both". José Manuel Möller, Algramo (Chile). April 2020.

The conflict starts to dissolve once the founder understands the importance of alliances with big corporations, and the social role of employment creation.

C. Similarities Among Social Firms in South America

We have found several similarities among these companies with social impact. However, we have selected those similarities that were most relevant to both the concept of shared value creation, and to the current context of economic downturn.

These relevant similarities are:

C.1. Identification of Social and Environmental Business Opportunities

These firms identified in a more agile and flexible ways the social and environmental needs. As they are often underlying and latent needs that may not necessarily be very attractive to traditional business models, they may be overlooked by traditional companies.

The best way of identifying market needs is to ask the community. These companies do exactly that. They work hand by hand with the society, which ensures a business strategy success.

"The model of education under flexible shifts wouldn't have been thought of if our own students hadn't suggested it".

Jimmy Leonardo Castro, founder and CEO of ENI Foundation (April 2020)

C.2. They are Constantly Re-Inventing and Changing their Value Proposition

These companies evolve and pivot around their purpose, testing and adapting their value proposition for a better product-market fit.

"We are a startup in education that changes and evolves to maximize our impact". Landing page from Laboratoria.la (retrieved on April 24, 2020)

C.3. Keep the Purpose of the Organization

As mentioned before, during times of crisis, the purpose becomes more relevant, as it is contagious. That purpose serves as the business strategy. An SVC organizational strategy includes the idea of developing solutions for social and environmental issues while being profitable.

"[The COVID-19 pandemic is an opportunity] is a change in the form, but not the substance. We are going to keep our purpose."

Mónica Villanueva, co-founder of LULU (April 2020)

We analyzed how these firms align with Porter and Kramer (2011) ways of creating shared value. According to them, there are three ways of SVC.

1. Reconceiving products and markets (i.e., innovation)
2. Redefining productivity in the value chain (i.e., value chain)
3. Improving the local and regional business environment (i.e., cluster)

Results are shown in table 3.

Table 3. How firms create shared value, according to Porter and Kramer (2011) definition

Company	Way to create Shared Value	Sustainable Development Goal (SDG)
Laboratoria	Innovation, Value Chain	4, 5
Greenglass	Innovation	12
Lab4U	Innovation, Value Chain	4
School Brillo de Luna	Value chain	4
Mejor en Bici	Innovation	11
Algramo	Innovation, value chain	12
La Cucha	Cluster, Value chain	12
ENI Foundation	Innovation	1, 4, 10
LULU	Innovation	3, 4, 5

Source: Authors' own.

As seen, most companies innovate in their products and markets, regardless of the business stage.

In addition to the similarities, we have also identified some differences among the analyzed firms. They are in different business stages, they have focused on diverse markets with different social and environmental needs, and they contribute differently to the SDG (see table 3 above).

DISCUSSION

The findings in our exploratory study confirms some statements found in the literature.

Unlike big and established companies, social entrepreneurship is more agile and flexible. It can offer market solutions with positive impact to society and environment and does not need to have a philanthropic view of its role, as more prominent companies do (Gundry et al., 2011; OECD, 2014; Méndez & Gómez 2017). These entrepreneurial projects and young SMEs are continually looking for ways to positively impact society and their stakeholders, confirming what was found in previous studies (Méndez & Gómez, 2017). We also confirm that founders put the emphasis on value creation instead of value capture (Agafonow, 2014).

The founders become agents of change. Owners' purpose or motivation is key to create social value with their firms. Entrepreneurial values seem to match the creation of shared value (Blanchard & Gray, 2019).

As previously suggested, the companies studied co-create social innovation with their stakeholders. This means that they co-create innovative solutions to social or environmental problems or needs. This co-creation is a warranty of the success of the business strategy (Bacq & Janssen, 2011; Gundry et al., 2011). However, these companies go a step beyond. They are not aiming at maximizing profit, but a broader understanding of benefits for the stakeholders, as stated by Andreas from La Cucha.

In the same line, Mónica, the co-founder of LULU, agree that there are many differences for men and women in entrepreneurship, however, she acknowledges the variety of funds and training programs intended for women, nowadays in Latin American countries.

Although not fully captured in our results, we can see that these firms have a long-term vision. Shared Value Creation makes companies competitive in the long run (Porter & Kramer, 2011).

CONCLUSIONS

Summarizing, our results show that the founder's proximity to the social/environmental problem is a trigger to start up a business. The "purpose" is a motivational factor to both start up a business and keep the business running during hard times. The purpose —similarly to the SDGs— is the fuel but it does not guarantee the success of the company. The value proposition is the key factor for success. This is why these companies are constantly re-inventing and changing their value proposition, while keeping the purpose of the organization.

A World After the Crisis

The "low-touch economy"[3] is emerging. The pandemic has set a new normal of social distancing and its effects on human behavior and organizational habits; such as changes in personal health habits, limited travelling and social gatherings, different patterns in consumption, tele-working, online meetings, and online teaching, just to name a few.

We expect organizational transformation and decentralization caused by the new social norms for avoiding further COVID-19 infection (or other future pandemics). This is an opportunity for business models such as short supply chains companies (such as La Cucha and Algramo), and online businesses (such as Laboratoria and LULU).

Flexible small businesses are reinventing themselves in a short period of time to adjust their business models to these "new normal" scenarios. New social and environmental needs will emerge post crisis. Those founders and leaders who quickly adapt with resilience and agility will get competitive advantages (Lepeley, forthcoming).

There are plenty of new opportunities for business to re-calibrate their value proposition. Otherwise, they could disappear. Co-creating solutions with the community more easily achieve fast adjustment to the VUCA (i.e., Volatile, Uncertain, Complexity, Ambiguity) environment. This is a "lean startup" approach to innovation. This approach is ideal for entrepreneurial ventures and SMEs, as it is cheap and does not need R&D or any initial investment. Therefore, a key step is to build the community first (Martez & Dieste, 2019).

Future Research Opportunities

The selection process of companies in this study, does not allow us to generalize our results. We have intentionally selected businesses founded by young men and women in South America. For the moment, we cannot state that a specific variable such as gender, city of origin, particular background or experience as a variable that can be strongly associated to start up a social venture. However, a study with 601 male and female undergraduate students in Germany showed that women are more likely to translate positive desirability into social entrepreneurial intentions (Dickel & Eckardt, 2020). More research is needed in our South American context.

What are the business models that can navigate the crisis better? How do we ensure they fulfill the SDG mandate? How can entrepreneurs pivot their business model to hit Creation of Shared Value? As found by Méndez, Henao, and Vélez (2017) in a Peruvian sample, is sustainable entrepreneurship first driven by necessity? How does it look like to pivot after a health/social crisis and again for an economic crisis? What is the role of the team? What aspects of the CSV strategy can be easily applied? What are specific local variables that can contribute to the creation of a model for communicative entrepreneurship in South America? We believe that factors that are specific to the South American context can help us build an integrative model for social innovation enablers.

This model of shared value creation and social innovation in entrepreneurial ventures has the potential of becoming a phenomenon that facilitates innovation and competitiveness while contributing to regional development once social-economic and environmental problems are mitigated (Porter & Kramer, 2011).

REFERENCES

Agafonow, A. (2014). Toward a positive theory of social entrepreneurship. On maximizing versus satisficing value capture. *Journal of Business Ethics*, *125*(4), 709–713. doi:10.100710551-013-1948-z

Alberti, F. G., & Varon Garrido, M. A. (2017). Can profit and sustainability goals co-exist? new business models for hybrid firms. *The Journal of Business Strategy*, *38*(1), 3–13. doi:10.1108/JBS-12-2015-0124

Aspelund, A., Fjell, L., & Rødland, S. E. (2017). Doing good and doing well? international entrepreneurship and social responsibility. *International Journal of Entrepreneurship*, *21*(2).

Arias, J. A., Franco, L. C., Sánchez, M., & Rojas, M. J. (2019). Prácticas innovadoras en el contexto de la de educación superior: Una experiencia de la Institución Universitaria Politécnico Grancolombiano y la Corporación Universitaria Rafael Núñez. In *Investigación e innovación en la enseñanza superior. Nuevos contextos, nuevas ideas, primera edición* (pp. 470-480). Recuperado de https://octaedro.com/wp-content/uploads/2019/11/16152-Investigacion-e-innovacion-en-la-ES.pdf

Bacq, S., & Janssen, F. (2011). The multiple faces of social entrepreneurship: A review of definitional issues based on geographical and thematic criteria. *Entrepreneurship and Regional Development*, *23*(5-6), 373–403. doi:10.1080/08985626.2011.577242

Baker, T., Miner, A. S., & Eesley, D. T. (2003). Improvising firms: Bricolage, account giving and improvisational competencies in the founding process. *Research Policy*, *32*(2), 255–276. doi:10.1016/S0048-7333(02)00099-9

Baker, T., & Nelson, R. E. (2005). Creating something from Nothing: Resource Construction through Entrepreneurial Bricolage. *Administrative Science Quarterly*, *50*(3), 329–366. doi:10.2189/asqu.2005.50.3.329

Blanchard, K., & Gray, D. (2019). Can shared value and entrepreneurship contribute to SME development within rural locations? *Strategic Change*, *28*(2), 147–155. doi:10.1002/jsc.2256

Ciborra, C. U. (1996). The platform organization: Recombining strategies, structures and surprises. *Organization Science*, *7*(2), 103–118. doi:10.1287/orsc.7.2.103

Dacin, P. A., Dacin, M. T., & Matear, M. (2010). Social entrepreneurship: Why we don't need a new theory and how we move forward from here. *The Academy of Management Perspectives*, *24*(2), 36–56.

Dean, T. J., & McMullen, J. S. (2007). Toward a theory of sustainable entrepreneurship: Reducing environmental degradation through entrepreneurial action. *Journal of Business Venturing*, *22*(1), 50–76. doi:10.1016/j.jbusvent.2005.09.003

Diaz, J. T., Bolivar, H., Gomez, J., & Prada, J. (2018). Business diagnostic technology for sharing value and social innovation in one-person companies. *2017 Congreso Internacional De Innovacion y Tendencias En Ingenieria, CONIITI 2017 - Conference Proceedings,* 1-6. doi:10.1109/CONIITI.2017.8273342

Dickel, P., & Eckardt, G. (2020). Who wants to be a social entrepreneur? The role of gender and sustainability orientation. *Journal of Small Business Management*, 1–23. doi:10.1080/00472778.2019.1704489

Domanski, D., Howaldt, J., & Schröder, A. (2017). Social Innovation in Latin America. *Journal of Human Development and Capabilities*, *18*(2), 307–312. doi:10.1080/19452829.2017.1299698

Dworkin, G. (2010). Paternalism. The Stanford Encyclopedia of Philosophy.

Elamrani, J., & Lemtaoui, M. (2016). Creating shared value in Moroccan companies: A case study of OCP SA. *Transnational Corporations Review*, *8*(4), 280–288. doi:10.1080/19186444.2016.1266131

Inkpen, A. C., & Tsang, E. W. (2005). Social capital, networks, and knowledge transfer. *Academy of Management Review*, *30*(1), 146–165. doi:10.5465/amr.2005.15281445

Isenberg, D. J. (2014). What an entrepreneurship ecosystem actually is. *Harvard Business Review*, *5*, 1–7.

Isenberg, D. J. (2010). How to start an entrepreneurial revolution. *Harvard Business Review*, *88*(6), 40–50.

Isenberg, D. J. (2011). *The entrepreneurship ecosystem strategy as a new paradigm for economic policy: principles for cultivating entrepreneurship*. Babson Entrepreneurship Ecosystem Project, Babson College. Available at: http://www.innovationamerica.us/images/stories/2011/The-entrepreneurship-ecosystem-strategy-for-economic-growth-policy-20110620183915.pdf

Lepeley, M. T. (forthcoming). Soft Skills: The lingua franca of Human Centered Management. In *Soft Skills in Human Centered Management. Global Dimensions*. Routledge.

Garmendia, J., Barrientos, E., & Castro, J. (2019). Management context of entrepreneurship in engineers and architects in Tachira, Venezuela. *Journal of Physics: Conference Series*, *1418*, 012015. doi:10.1088/1742-6596/1418/1/012015

Gundry, L., Kickul, J., Griffiths, M., & Bacq, S. (2011). Creating Social Change Out of Nothing: The Role of Entrepreneurial Bricolage in Social Entrepreneurs' Catalytic Innovations. In Social and Sustainable Entrepreneurship (Advances in Entrepreneurship, Firm Emergence and Growth, Vol. 13). Emerald Group Publishing Limited. doi:10.1108/S1074-7540(2011)0000013005

Holon, I. Q. (2020). *LATAM EdTech 100*. Available from: https://www.holoniq.com/notes/latam-edtech-100/

Lustig, N. (2019). *An Overview of Edtech in Latin America*. Available from: https://www.nathanlustig.com/an-overview-of-edtech-in-latin-america/

Lüth, A., & Stierl, M. (2015). Creating Shared Value by Fostering Regional Development: The 'Partners in Responsibility 'Method for SME. *Global Policy*, *6*(4), 507–509. doi:10.1111/1758-5899.12238

Martez, N., & Dieste, E. (2019). Measurement system for the analysis of social innovation in projects. *Proceedings - 2019 7th International Engineering, Sciences and Technology Conference, IESTEC 2019*, 311-316. 10.1109/IESTEC46403.2019.00064

Matinheikki, J., Rajala, R., & Peltokorpi, A. (2017). From the profit of one toward benefitting many–Crafting a vision of shared value creation. *Journal of Cleaner Production*, *162*, S83–S93. doi:10.1016/j.jclepro.2016.09.081

Méndez, M., & Gómez, M. (2017). Factores incidentes para crear valor compartido en las mipymes de Bogotá. *Suma de Negocios*, *8*(18), 96–105. doi:10.1016/j.sumneg.2017.10.003

Méndez, M., Henao, A., & Vélez, A. (2017). Factores críticos de éxito para el desarrollo de una empresa en sus primeras fases de desarrollo. Espacios, 38(18).

Muñoz, P., & Kimmitt, J. (2019). Social mission as competitive advantage: A configurational analysis of the strategic conditions of social entrepreneurship. *Journal of Business Research, 101*, 854–861.

Nikolaou, I. E., Tasopoulou, K., & Tsagarakis, K. (2018). A typology of green entrepreneurs based on institutional and resource-based views. *The Journal of Entrepreneurship, 27*(1), 111–132. doi:10.1177/0971355717738601

O'Connor, A., Stam, E., Sussan, F., & Audretsch, D. B. (Eds.). (2018). *Entrepreneurial Ecosystems. Place-Based Transformations and Transitions*. Springer.

OECD. (2014). *Cultivating successful entrepreneurs*. Available at: http://www.oecd.org/cfe/leed/entrepreneurship.htm

Pavlovich, K., & Corner, P. D. (2014). Conscious enterprise emergence: Shared value creation through expanded conscious awareness. *Journal of Business Ethics, 121*(3), 341–351. doi:10.100710551-013-1726-y

Pico Bonilla, C. M., Pico Bonilla, A., Méndez Pinzón, M., Ramírez Triana, C. A., Chicas Sierra, S. M., Mateus Tovar, R. F., & Tunjano Pinzón, I. F. (2018). *Experiencias de aprendizaje significativo para la apropiación de conocimientos en ciencias económicas, administrativas y contables*. Institución Universitaria Politécnico Grancolombiano.

Pongwiritthon, R. (2015). Creating shared value of Thai SMEs for competitive advantage. *International Journal of Applied Business and Economic Research, 13*(5), 3109–3120.

Porter, M., & Kramer, M. R. (2011). Creating shared value. *Harvard Business Review, 89*(1/2), 62–77.

Porter, M. (2012). *New Opportunities for Company Performance and Purpose: Creating Shared Value*. Hitachi Innovation Forum 2012, *Video Conference*, Boston, MA.

Porter, M. E., & Kramer, M. R. (2006). Strategy & Society. *Harvard Business Review*, 84. PMID:17183795

Porter, M. E., Hills, G., Pfitzer, M., Patscheke, S., & Hawkins, E. (2011). *Measuring shared value: How to unlock value by linking social and business results*. Available at: https://www.hbs.edu/faculty/publication%20files/measuring_shared_value_57032487-9e5c-46a1-9bd8-90bd7f1f9cef.pdf

Pörtner, H. O., Roberts, D., Masson-Delmotte, V., Zhai, P., Tignor, M., Poloczanska, E., Mintenbeck, K., Nicolai, M., Okem, A., & Petzold, J. (2019). *IPCC Special Report on the Ocean and Cryosphere in a Changing Climate*. IPCC Intergovernmental Panel on Climate Change.

Rawhouser, H., Cummings, M., & Newbert, S. L. (2019). Social impact measurement: Current approaches and future directions for social entrepreneurship research. *Entrepreneurship Theory and Practice, 43*(1), 82–115. doi:10.1177/1042258717727718

Santos, F. M. (2012). A positive theory of social entrepreneurship. *Journal of Business Ethics, 111*(3), 335–351. doi:10.100710551-012-1413-4

Sarasvathy, S. (2008). *Effectuation: Elements of entrepreneurial expertise*. Edward Elgar., doi:10.4337/9781848440197

Shepherd, D. A., & Patzelt, H. (2011). The new field of sustainable entrepreneurship: Studying entrepreneurial action linking "what is to be sustained" with "what is to be developed". *Entrepreneurship Theory and Practice*, *35*(1), 137–163. doi:10.1111/j.1540-6520.2010.00426.x

Sinthupundaja, J., Kohda, Y., & Chiadamrong, N. (2020). Examining capabilities of social entrepreneurship for shared value creation. *Journal of Social Entrepreneurship*, *11*(1), 1–22. doi:10.1080/19420676.2018.1543726

Smallbone, D., Welter, F., & Ateljevic, J. (2014). Entrepreneurship in Emerging Market Economies: Contemporary Issues and Perspectives. *International Small Business Journal*, *32*(2), 113–116. doi:10.1177/0266242613511479

UNDP. (2020). *What are the Sustainable Development Goals?* Available at: https://www.undp.org/content/undp/en/home/sustainable-development-goals.html

United Nations. (2015). *Transforming our world: The 2030 agenda for sustainable development.* General Assembley 70 Session.

Van de Ven, A. H., Sapienza, H. J., & Villanueva, J. (2007). Entrepreneurial pursuits of self-and collective interests. *Strategic Entrepreneurship Journal*, *1*(3–4), 353–370. doi:10.1002ej.34

Véras, E. Z. (2015). Female entrepreneurship: from women's empowerment to shared value creation. Journal on Innovation and Sustainability. *RISUS, 6*(2), 109-123.

Villalobos Araya, R. (2020). School "brillo DE luna": Sustainable business model. *Emerald Emerging Markets Case Studies*, *10*(1), 1–22. Advance online publication. doi:10.1108/EEMCS-11-2019-0314

Welter, F. (2011). Contextualizing entrepreneurship—Conceptual challenges and ways forward. *Entrepreneurship Theory and Practice*, *35*(1), 165–184. doi:10.1111/j.1540-6520.2010.00427.x

Zahra, S. A., Wright, M., & Abdelgawad, S. G. (2014). Contextualization and the advancement of entrepreneurship research. *International Small Business Journal*, *32*(5), 479–500. doi:10.1177/0266242613519807

ENDNOTES

1 https://sistemab.org/en/

2 Algramo started by trading OMO and Quix brand products from Unilever. However, Algramo pivoted and they are offering in 2020 a mobile dispensing system, which allows neighbours to request the product that arrives on an electric tricycle at home, in order to reuse the container without having to move. This project began in the commune of Las Condes (Santiago de Chile). Algramo won in December 2019 the *Ocean Plastic Innovation Challenge* organized by *National Geographic*. It is the equivalent to a prize for the best company in the Circular Economy.

3 "Low-Touch Economy" is a report prepared by the Board of Innovation in April 2020. https://www.boardofinnovation.com/blog/what-is-the-low-touch-economy/

Chapter 11
Social Enterprises and Sustainable Development Goals:
How a Global Health Project Transformed Into a Social Venture – The Case of HERA App for Refugees

Aral Surmeli
HERA Inc., USA

Nirmala Priya Narla
Boston Children's Hospital, USA & Harvard Medical School, USA

Caitlyn Hoeflin
HERA Inc., USA

ABSTRACT

In line with Sustainable Development Goals (SDGs) put forth by the United Nations (UN), social entrepreneurship models in global health are on the rise. While SDG Goal 3: Good Health and Wellbeing is the direct focus of global health sector, the majority of other SDG goals affect and are affected by 'good health and wellbeing'. While global health interventions create social value by increasing healthcare access in vulnerable populations, the effect is often limited by the timeline and availability of funds. In a social venture model, where value creation is paired with a sustainable financial income, this issue can be alleviated. In addition, innovative intervention models for vulnerable populations can align themselves with the sustainable social value aims in the UN's new Global Goals. This chapter describes a project (HERA) designed to decrease mortality and morbidity due to preventable diseases in refugees. The authors examine how it transformed to a sustainable and collaborative social initiative working to create lasting social value and discuss this process contextualized by the SDGs.

DOI: 10.4018/978-1-7998-4727-4.ch011

INTRODUCTION

Global health is a relatively new term in medicine (Beaglehole et al., 2010). Koplan et al. initially defined global health as 'an area for study, research, and practice that places a priority on improving health and achieving health equity for all people worldwide.' However the history goes back centuries to when imperial countries had to figure out 'foreign diseases' among occupying soldiers that were transmitted from local and indigenous people (Farmer, 2013). With this as its history –in which the goal was not necessarily to 'heal the world', Global Health is now understood as 'collaborative transnational research and action for promoting health for all' (Beaglehole et al., 2010). Historically, Global Health is an area of medicine and public health that has been primarily funded by donations and not equity grants, as it was presumed to have no financial returns. Until several decades ago, the notion that investment in people's health was actually a great investment was not mainstream. Prioritizing the value in economic participation and productivity of a society was an important step in not just the health of nations, but also the wealth of nations. This realization, in addition to progress on human rights and the belief that every human deserves healthcare, has made Global Health attractive to a larger community. Meanwhile, the United Nation's ongoing efforts through the Millennium Development Goals, and more recently with the Sustainable Development Goals, has further pushed forward emphasis on the health of people and equitable healthcare access.

However, the resources needed to 'save the world' are still scarce in the non-profit sector. Relying heavily on donations and grants puts many global health efforts on financially volatile grounds, as was recently made clear with COVID-19 pandemic (Finnegan, 2020). Furthermore, organizations are obliged to align their activities and goals in accordance with the available funds. In 2020, the global community has witnessed that even the most established organizations such as the World Health Organization (WHO), are vulnerable to the political agenda of donor countries (Mcneil et al, 2020). In light of this uncertainty, social entrepreneurship – *which at its core is designed to bridge the intention of both worlds: the sustainable revenue streams and business strategy of private corporate work with the desire to create social impact from non-profit work* – was born. Given a larger space of work, and considerable amount of financial freedom, social entrepreneurship slowly started to make its way into more mainstream efforts and intentions of creating a better world. As new initiatives, existing ventures, non-profits and other organizations move towards social entrepreneurship.

Although social entrepreneurship has existed since the 1970's, formal research into the growth and phenomenon are fairly new (Nicholls, 2010). The term underlines the creation of 'social value' while focusing on the 'entrepreneurial' method as a way of creating this social value (Mair et al., 2006). In this two dimension definition is where for profit and non-profit work intersects. While creating social value has been a fundamental goal of non-profit work, primarily through donations and grants, entrepreneurship, which arose from business world, has taken over the modality of sustaining ongoing social value creating activities by up-taking market methods in revenue creation (Schmitt et al., 2017). This shift in financial model stems from the need for sustainable funding that donations or grants lack. The phenomenon presented itself as a new way of looking at non-profit work, keeping the primary goal of social value creation the same, while finding more cost-effective ways to sustain the work.

Here, we present the case of HERA, a digital platform designed to increase access to healthcare for refugee and migrant populations and discuss how the HERA project evolved into a social enterprise from a grant-based non-profit project.

USING MOBILE TECHNOLOGIES FOR REFUGEES: THE HERA APP EXPERIENCE IN TURKEY AND CHALLENGES IN PRACTICE

HERA App is a mobile health (mhealth) intervention designed for Syrian refugees under temporary protection in Turkey, a population of almost 4 million people (UNHCR, 2020). The application was envisioned as a guide and a bridge for refugees, especially women and children, to access healthcare services in Turkey. Increasing demand for preventive services, such as childhood immunizations and antenatal visits, will eventually lead to saving lives, reducing the hospitalization times, and lowering healthcare costs in this population. HERA is an acronym for 'Health Recording App' and is the name of a powerful Greek Goddess.

HERA was envisioned when one of the founders saw first-hand the possibilities of smartphone applications in improving public health outcomes at Harvard's Center for Global Development in Dubai. Here, he researched the usage of text message reminders in increasing vaccination rates. The results were significant enough that he saw the need to integrate this technology throughout vulnerable refugee populations globally. Initial funding of CAD $100,000 for the development and piloting of the app was provided by Grand Challenges Canada. Grand Challenges Canada is a non-profit that funds innovative healthcare solutions in the developing world.

HERA was designed to decrease maternal and infant mortality and morbidity by increasing the uptake of vaccinations and prenatal care. The crucial distinguishing feature of HERA is that it focuses on the demand-side of the care equation: while the majority of healthcare solutions focus on increasing the supply of healthcare, HERA works by increasing the demand for existing health services. To achieve this goal, HERA sends push notifications to users about upcoming important medical appointments. The app also provides information in English, Turkish, and Arabic about the Turkish health and legal system, which is unfamiliar to many refugees. Additionally, users are able to locate nearby medical clinics and store their personal health records in a secure encrypted location.

Implementing these interventions, however, is always a struggle. 2019 started with many unforeseen issues for HERA. The team had to divert their efforts to operational hurdles, including solving logistical and managerial problems, rather than performing impact evaluation, networking or funding activities. But the bigger struggle was the team had to simultaneously increase their efforts in finding sustainable funding, creating the 'perfect app', and evaluating the app's impact in the field.

A crucial decision was on how to create sustainable impact on the lives of the Turkish Syrian refugee population. For most global health projects, sustainability relies on a constant influx of money. Thus, obtaining global health grants is often the first priority of non-profit work. However, most grants offer a limited funding stream over a specified and discrete project period.

In August 2020, still in the midst of COVID-19 pandemic, the HERA team began pushing forward on a sustainable social enterprise model, while simultaneously focusing on scale-up and creating more robust evidence on health gains attributable to their solution.

This case study describes HERA's progress from a global health project to a social enterprise and how the organization altered its business model in order to become a sustainable solution for increasing the healthcare access of refugee populations. As of now, HERA's work is more agile and social business oriented.

BACKGROUND

War and the Syrian Refugee Crisis

In 2011, as the Arab Spring spread to Syria, demonstrations protesting the government began (Rogers, 2020). Protests spread nationwide, and more and more armed groups in the region started to take part in the conflict. The resultant civil war caused almost half of the population, 12 million people, to forcibly migrate (UNHCR, 2019).

Turkey's open-door policy, which saved many lives, led millions to migrate through its eastern borders. As of 2019, the official number of Syrian refugees is 3.65 million, and accounts for more than 60% of all Syrian refugees (Ferris et al., 2016; WHO, 2020). This rapid influx of millions of people required an adaptive and flexible response in Turkish infrastructure to ensure the population's housing, health, and other living needs.

Syrian Refugees in Turkey

Health outcomes in pre-war Syria were of a middle-income country: immunization rates for the majority of vaccines were at or over 80%, and life expectancy was 74 years, ranking 72nd globally in 2010 – better than Turkey. Social insurance including all medical benefits are free of charge for Syrian nationals in the country (WHO, 2020; ILO, 2020). Syria has a young population in early stages of demographic transition (World Population Review, 2020).

War crippled the public health system and massive migration made health services impossible for the neediest communities. Additionally, moving populations are always prone to preventable diseases and usually suffer more mortality and morbidity. Trauma and war-related injuries are the most common reason for mortality in Syrians for the last eight years (IHME, 2017). The Syrian population that took refuge in Turkey is very young; 50% are under the age of 18 (WHO, 2020). The majority of the population resides in urban areas and is minimally integrated into the local society.

Healthcare in Turkey and Turkey's Refugee Response

Turkey is an upper middle-income country, ranked 64th in Human Development Index, with a population of almost 80 million people. Life expectancy is 75.1 years, and the country is moving towards a more non-communicable disease-characterized mortality pattern, consistent with its demographic and epidemiological transition, as fertility rates decrease and the population ages.

Turkish nationals are all under the national insurance scheme, which entitles them to free healthcare and has led to positive public health outcomes. As the refugee influx started, public health authorities grew concerned about backsliding. Many refugees did not receive necessary vaccinations and lacked antenatal care, leading to increased susceptibility for disease outbreaks in both the refugee and host-country populations.

Free access to healthcare services is the largest determinant of a good health system (Yates et. al, 2013). All registered Syrian refugees qualify for 'Temporary Protective Status' and are part of the Turkish national insurance scheme. Despite entitled access to free healthcare, it is challenging to improve health outcomes due to the many barriers for healthcare access in practice. The Syrian population often live primarily outside of the formal camps, and in slums of big cities in the hopes of earning a livelihood (Todd, 2019). Because of this, it is hard to track this population, maintain their health records, and ensure their awareness of the available services. The demand side of the problem is further aggravated by increasing xenophobia from the Turkish population, rumors about deportation, and competing priorities for survival as a recent refugee. Ultimately, these barriers result in refugees mostly utilizing healthcare services only in emergency situations, or in very serious conditions that prevent them from working. Service delivery is lacking in preventive care and primary care services, and lack of demand is the biggest challenge.

BRIDGING THE PEOPLE'S NEEDS WITH AVAILABLE HEALTHCARE SERVICES

Issues on the Ground: Experience of the Team

HERA's founding team in Turkey had been working in refugee response efforts for some time. Most of their work was part of the Medical Rescue Association of Turkey (MEDAK)'s response in Istanbul and Syria bordering cities.

Their NGO, MEDAK, successfully developed and led health screening projects and health literacy training for Syrian refugees around Turkey. Even though the small-scale projects were helping the communities they were working with, the team leads recognized that the problem was endemic on a much larger scale. Everywhere they worked, Syrian mothers were saying that they only received some vaccines (which they were unable to name) and had received several vaccine series multiple times. One of the co-founders met with a few families who had received the polio vaccine six times during the same campaign period because neither the providers nor refugee families had access to any immunization records.

Fortunately, access to hospital birth was not an issue. Turkey, in accordance to its transformative health agenda, made sure access to health services, including vaginal and C-section deliveries, was accessible. However, the rates of prenatal check-ups, iron or folic acid supplementation, and prenatal tetanus checks were still extremely low. An OBGYN who worked in one of the largest local public OBGYN and Children's Hospital said, 'They do not come for prenatal care if they do not have big problems. Even the ones who come are further along in the pregnancy, mostly in 3rd trimester.' Why were there these many problems in a country where healthcare is free? How were these basic needs are not being met? These were the questions that led the founders of HERA to think about a more comprehensive solution beyond planning new health campaigns.

The founders recognized the importance of mobilizing resources and had witnessed firsthand the scope of transnational collaboration. They put together a diverse team in Boston, where the primary lead of HERA had done postgraduate studies in Public Health, to offer a complementary skillset of experiences in global health capacity building, social business, publicity, and networking activities. The team understood that sustainable impact could only be achieved by being an international social venture.

The Idea

The very first idea was rooted in one of the co-founder's internship in Harvard Medical School's Global Health Delivery Center in Dubai working with Dr. Subhash Chandir and Dr. Salmaan Keshavjee. In 2016, the Center was focused on working with research teams in the area and providing funding for global health projects. Dr. Chandir's work also included SMS reminder projects in Pakistan for immunizations. It was shown that a behavioral nudge-sending reminders for vaccination dates to the families increase the number of people getting vaccinated. These type of demand interventions were extremely cheap and effective in increasing uptake of health services in low resource settings (Hall et al., 2015). There is a growing evidence base on SMS reminders' use with medication adherence, timely immunization uptake doctor's appointments and smoking cessation (Ghorai et al., 2014; Wakadha et al., 2013; Raifman et al., 2014).

After coming back from the internship, co-founders (just classmates then) met for dinner to catch up, which ended as an all-night brainstorming on how they could utilize demand-side interventions for the populations they were working with. Increasing immunization rates, antenatal care uptake, medication adherence, and a myriad of other health-related applications could be very beneficial for Syrian refugees in Turkey. The initial draft of the innovation they designed included many small interventions compacted into one overarching intervention. Their main goal was to increase the uptake of healthcare services and to provide refugees information about resources available to them. It was also an empowerment tool, giving the women control over their healthcare needs.

HERA was envisioned as a 'guide' for refugee populations in Turkey: Someone who did not know their rights, where to go to receive care, how to get registered, and who spoke a different language would be able to use HERA to navigate through the system. The founders thought of every possible barrier in the pathway to health access and tried to come up with a solution. This plan came from trying to 'solve all the problems' angle. The rationale was that having isolated interventions might miss the perspective of all stakeholders in the journey or the macro-level barriers they might face. In the end, the first draft had 16 different features in one platform, which would then to become a mobile app.

The first iteration of the mobile app (Exhibit 1) tracked the immunization dates using the Turkish vaccination calendar and sent reminders to mothers for the dates of upcoming appointments. The app would also do the same for prenatal care dates for pregnant women. Even though this was the main intervention, HERA would also allow the storage of medical records on a cloud server, direct users to nearby health facilities, call 911 emergency services, and provide health information and various other features.

A Tech Solution for a Demand Gap: Context and Enablers

An important aspect of designing interventions is the mode, or the platform, of delivery. When the targeted gap is on the demand side, considerations on human behavior, financial effectiveness, innovation, and implementation have to be balanced. Traditionally, there have been many successful demand interventions that increase the uptake of desired health services, such as conditional cash transfers or massive ad campaigns (Rawlings et al., 2005; Snyder et al., 2004). However, modern interventions, and in the context of humanitarian crisis, have to be designed more agile, mobile, and adaptable to different contexts.

There were also unique opportunities about this specific humanitarian crisis that allowed for technology to have greater potential: First, the Turkish government provides healthcare services free of charge, in contrast to other humanitarian contexts. Normally local or international NGO's (INGO) provide care. Although good-willed, it is challenging to provide high standard, evidence-based care to an entire population in accordance with recommended guidelines during humanitarian crises and in times of resource scarcity. Turkey's coordinated response, taking the lead off of INGOs, helped with regulated and standard care provision. This would also become an important factor in designing the scalability of HERA in Turkey.

Another opportunity was that the Turkish Health System was starting to include more electronic health solutions as part of their comprehensive services, in alignment with its health system goals. The country had digitalized all of its health records starting 2015 and was already starting to implement tele-health interventions in remote areas and creating a digital platform for end-users to view their health records. Although mobile health interventions were relatively new and not tested robustly in Turkey, let alone in vulnerable populations, the country's health infrastructure was becoming more suitable for health programs.

Just like in the supply of health services, it is also important to consider whether the target population will have access to the platform of delivery. In this context, a phone – particularly a smartphone – was needed. This is where the experience of the team played an important role. MEDAK, the NGO, had been working with Syrian health networks in İstanbul. One important observation they had was that all of the information transaction (i.e. about new laws, regulations), communication, and organization was done through social media and messaging apps such as WhatsApp. This was not because the refugees were 'rich' – but phones, and smartphones were a way to connect with their dispersed families and receive updates about their country and changing regulations. Smartphones were also described as 'lifeline' for refugees during their flight (Alencar et al., 2019). The team believed that using a smartphone platform was not only good opportunity but also an issue of equity; they always believed in making new technologies available to vulnerable communities.

While deciding on the model of delivery for these set of features (interventions), the team had to weigh the risks of using a high-tech solution (mobile app) rather than a low tech (SMS-based reminder). There was a tradeoff: The tech infrastructure need was more complicated and might seem 'out of touch with reality.' However, the benefits outweighed the costs. Technology meant easier modifications, real time data sharing, and more agility. The HERA team finally choose a mobile app because it was a digital platform that could be further improved. Furthermore, the main idea behind HERA was not just a mobile app: It was a set of interventions, which could be adapted to the context, modified according to the needs of the population. In addition, the HERA founders knew that going from a higher to lower tech as needed would be easier than the reverse.

TRANSLATING AN IDEA TO INNOVATION

Development Process

Even though the idea of HERA was designed with a rigorous evidence base and with people who had field experience with the target population, developing an idea into an innovation is an iterative process. Going back to the drawing board happens a lot more often than desired. This concept is a very important phase of the development process, as the journey is not in fact a straight line, but a cyclical and often chaotic one. Innovating is finding new way of thinking about a relatively old problem. Yet, an innovative idea does not necessarily translate into actionable designs or programs unless the design of implementation is also innovative.

The core team had no experience in mobile health applications before. This meant numerous discussions with people with a mhealth background in order to understand everything from the feasibility of incorporation of various features in a mobile application to pricing strategies and the costs of the app itself. This process was a whole new learning process for the team because it involved communicating with people who had a very different perspective on the project, and the concept of a 'business model'.

Early on in the innovation phase the team approached several people to involve them as their advisors. From their medical school, Dr. Figen Demir, an epidemiologist, and Dr. Ata Akın, the dean of medical engineering faculty, agreed to advise them on the project. In addition, the team approached Dr. Nitika Pai of McGill University, who had already implemented large-scale mobile health projects in Africa. Advisors played an important role in helping the team develop actionable next steps from the idea. Many things had to be mapped out for each step of the innovation: stakeholders in the refugee response, the predicted evolution of health issues and in country regulations, the feasible range of services HERA could provide, financial strategy, and monitoring and evaluation (M&E) plans.

As HERA was growing from an idea to an innovation, the team started to focus on its implementation as a field project. How would HERA work if they had the perfect product? Who would use it? How would they know about it? How would it help with the uptake of health services? Unfortunately, these questions took several years to answer — and even be asked — as the development process was ongoing.

ACTION LEARNING

Preliminary Needs Assessment and Organizational Scale up

In 2017, the search for funding started after the innovation became more solid when HERA was invited to apply for Grand Challenges Canada's Stars in Reproductive, Maternal, Newborn and Child Health Seed funding program.

During the months leading up to application deadline, a small acceptability and feedback study was performed. The main idea was to understand the needs of the target refugee population and get their ideas on what sort of features would be useful for their lives in Turkey. At the same time, the team believed that comprehensive inclusion of the target population, especially if it is a vulnerable community, is an important part of all phases of the innovation from design to implementation to evaluation. This was an important aspect of field ethics and equity as part of guiding global health principles.

Since there was limited time, the interviews had to be done strategically. The most important discussions for the design of the intervention were with the target group, refugee women, and their first contact in healthcare services, healthcare providers. Specifically, these practitioners included OBGYNs and pediatricians who received Syrian population in their clinics. Initial interviews, though small in number (n=8), provided significant insights on the needs and value of such a mobile application from the perspective of the target population. When refugee women were asked about what they would expect from a mobile app to help them, the issue of language barriers repeatedly came up. Eventually, this user experience study became a guiding tool for revising HERA more directly to the needs of the population. This process of being in close contact and receiving constant stakeholder feedback became a routine part of field activities and has proven to be very beneficial.

Grand Challenges Canada funding would also mean that that HERA' features had to be distilled. Even though all of the features are believed to be useful for the target community, the more complex the mobile app is, the more difficult it is to use. The argument on including all features, squarely planned for each potential barrier, is comprehensive and focused on the journey of healthcare access, not only directed at a single healthcare barrier, such as language barrier. This rationale suggests that chances of improved access to care would increase if all barriers were tackled simultaneously. However, the reality of implementation in the field seldom allows for complete integration. In addition, being focused, on a range of services provided and also a specific target population (women with young children and pregnant women) allowed for more detailed evaluation of the impact.

The capacity of the implementing organization is essential for success of the project. HERA was envisioned by the same team that co-founded MEDAK in 2013 with the goal of providing medical aid in disasters and humanitarian crises. However, MEDAK was a grassroots NGO with a yearly budget of less than 20.000 USD and run by volunteers. To put this into more perspective, HERA's proof of concept funding was bigger than MEDAK's budget over a 5-year period.

Prior to HERA's implementation MEDAK had to scale up its administrative and organizational structure. They always relied on volunteers, as motivation was a desired characteristic in field workers. However, now they needed a multidisciplinary professional team, including lawyers to make sure all documents signed were safe, and accountants who knew how to process international funding for Turkish organizations.

Organizational scale up was a grueling process, during which the team had to learn from their mistakes on the way. Among other issues that became valuable lessons for the NGO, the biggest one involved a lawsuit filed by the project team against the app developer due to poor quality of HERA app version 1. In addition to a 6-month delay to the delivery date, without a complete product, this issue cost MEDAK 'profit lost' due to being unable to procure remaining funding from Grand Challenges Canada during that time. This problem forced MEDAK to minimize its other activities to continue financing HERA amongst other issues.

Accelerating the Development

In 2019, HERA was gaining much momentum both in the field and also in Boston, as the newly formed Harvard (Boston / MA) team from the same Master of Public Health cohort was looking for opportunities to develop the project and also plan for sustainability. Two design thinking shifts were especially important in the transformation of the initial project into a professional innovation venture with the potential for significant impact.

The first shift began as a scale-up plan for HERA that was completed as part of their course's final assignment. Scaling up can be done in different ways: a) providing the intervention to a larger population or a larger geography, b) the scope of services provided can be increased but the number of users can stay the same, and c) both geography and scope can increase in tandem, marginally scale up in both dimensions[1].

Figure 1.

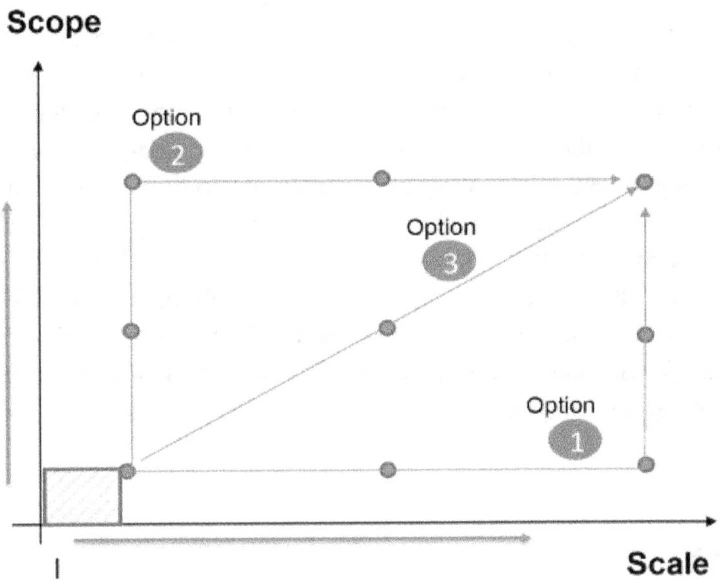

For HERA, both dimensions of scale up meant more sustainable funding. But scale up plans were also what attracted many humanitarian donors. Increasing the scope to include other interventions could potentially the project's increase impact. HERA could provide medication reminders, or even serve as an information tool for dissemination of non-health issues. Population scale up would mean including more children and pregnant women in the program, because under-5 and maternal mortality are still significantly high in refugee populations.

The third option, scaling up in both dimensions at the same time, seemed overambitious at the beginning. In the end, the team decided to include conditional credit transfers as a way of increasing the uptake of preventive services together with scaling to include a larger population of women and children refugees in Turkey.

The other shift in thinking was that before, the co-founders did not really consider HERA as a 'venture' or themselves as 'entrepreneurs.' For them, they were doctors who worked in the field, where they found a gap in services that they then tried to solve. They believed that scientific evidence was the sole proof of possible success. However, HERA's successful implementation as an innovation did not only depend on scientific evidence from the proof of concept study, but rather, a contextualized, but bold, implementation strategy.

Successful implementation and impact on a large scale is possible with the right partners in the right places for the right people. In order for HERA to reach this goal, the team had to progress in all dimensions of the innovation: product, health system integration, financial sustainability, scientific validity, and technology infrastructure.

Formal Scale Up: HERA Inc. (Boston /MA)

Towards the end of 2019, the team decided to further expand in the United States, specifically in Boston where the founders were located at that moment. The main rationale behind it was the realization that the United States offered vast resources-- financial, networking, and technology. In addition, Boston was the hub of innovation, healthcare and academia. Establishing a non-profit was a regulatory process that required bureaucracy as well as setting up an international co-founder team that could engage and connect with the resources in the U.S., all while the field work was ongoing in Turkey.

HERA Inc. was officially established in October 2019 to serve as a business and resource strategy hub for all of HERA's activities. The new board of directors, co-founders of HERA Inc., were people with background in operations, networking, and business administration. This expansion allowed for pushing forward strategic planning on a dimension other than field work or scientific research. This collaboration set up the groundwork and infrastructure to evolve from a grant-based model into a sustainable social business.

LESSONS LEARNED

Evaluating the Innovation

As with any other global health intervention, HERA was designed with a feasibility and effectiveness study. The first study protocol was approved by the Acıbadem University School of Medicine, İstanbul Institutional Review Board. The study had two intervention and two control arms. One intervention group was pregnant women, who would be given the app, receive reminders about their prenatal checkup dates, and be followed for an increase in timely appointment dates. The second intervention arm was refugee women who had children under the age of two. They were also to be given the app and receive reminder notifications for vaccination dates of their child (if they had multiple children, they could track all, but only one was to be used for analysis) and followed for timely uptake of vaccines and completeness of immunization calendar. In addition to this quantitative analysis, selected persons from the target group were to be invited for in depth and focus group interviews to better understand acceptability and technical issues that might occur. Howeverb technical planning is rarely implemented perfectly in the field. They would soon realize this.

When the proof of concept study was planned, the assumption was the app would work with minimal issues, or at least have similar issues as other attempted health interventions in the field. The team did not fully appreciate that it was an innovative way of looking, in contrast to using existing strategies. The team never anticipated that the places they were meeting with groups of people had no internet with which to download the app . They also had no idea what to do when the app crashed after participant put in all their information. There were also unforeseen important cultural aspects to consider with the target population; for instance, during Ramadan Month, people were a lot less interested in meetings or talking about importance of immunizations. Furthermore, the addition of new team members or new activities caused diversion of focus from the innovation's evaluation in the field.

Finally, the team decided to discontinue all other activities until the minimum viable product was ready and field tests for feasibility were started. Although this feels intuitive in hindsight, for a long time the team did not realize they needed to spend much of their time on a minimum viable product. In parallel to this shift, evaluation plans were also altered. In addition to understanding the impact of HERA, creating the 'perfect app', through a rigorous scientific process – with both qualitative and quantitative analysis – was included in the revised future study protocols.

Designing Agile Interventions in Humanitarian Contexts

Humanitarian crises present unique opportunities for agile interventions. By nature, they are very distinct from each other, but the affected are usually poorer populations with low quality of healthcare services. The 'limited resources' rhetoric tends to be far more severe in humanitarian contexts. These attributes can be addressed more effectively with agile interventions rather than with rigid standard operation procedures.

Solution design agility is very suitable for conditions that are rapidly changing. As the problem evolves, an intervention that is flexible and responsive can more readily be transformed. In addition, humanitarian contexts often lack reliable quantitative data, which is an essential tool for choosing between alternatives. Agile designs are more focused on lean development rather than on planned processes (Eisenmann et al., 2012). This allows real-time accommodation of feedback in every step, because the development is more impact focused, rather than plan, or output, focused.

HERA, which was designed in response to Syrian refugee crisis, the biggest humanitarian crisis since World War 2, has evolved into an agile innovation. The way that the HERA team went about it is through strategic M&E. Rather than treating evaluation as a tool to understand the outcomes, it was used as means of discussing improvement as the project proceeded. Instead of project milestones, the team chose to react with a smaller feedback loop with quick reactivity time. Feedbacks were evaluated and communicated to higher levels - team leads, advisory board – with possible reactions to the issues. This allowed the team to work coherently and faster in plan- do- study- act cycles.

Having an Agile Organization

MEDAK was founded by a young group of volunteers, with mean age of 26 at that time, who mostly came from disaster response experience. Working in disaster contexts, members were used to adapting to rapid changes in the field. In 2017, when the HERA team applied to Grand Challenges Canada for funding, MEDAK had only one externally funded project. SOSyria Project, funded by International Medical Corps, was a health literacy and first aid training program designed for Syrian families.

There was some traction on increasing accountability and professionalism in the NGO with SOSyria Project. However, with HERA's proposal, MEDAK had to step up to a new level. Implementing a long-term intervention would only be possible with a capable group of people and a flexible organizational structure that could allow for quick decision making. Fortunately, MEDAK's tradition of rapid analysis and agile response to changing conditions was preserved. The team was able to use the same methods, sometimes involuntarily, in HERA's decision-making process.

Establishing an Agile Team

Growth from two people to a big team across two different continents was not planned in the beginning. The way HERA chose to go about it was via marginal growth strategy: After the core team was founded, the inclusion of new people happened incrementally. Even though there were predictions of human resource needs, there was not a defined list of personnel. After each stage of progress – being accepted to a venture program, preparing a new strategic plan, updating from the field — the team would consider their capacity and discuss the needs.

HERA team members were mostly around the same age, late twenties/early thirties and at the beginning of their careers. The resultant drive, passion, and flexibility has been an important determinant of HERA's agility and resilience to issues with team members.

Adapting to Rapidly Changing Conditions

The ability to adjust to the dynamic needs of the target population proved important. A good example of immediate responsiveness is the creation of a website and short message service (SMS) versions of HERA App. Being able to utilize the high penetration of smartphones in the refugee community was the original reason for opting for a mobile app. However, HERA was first envisioned as a responsive platform, rather than a mobile app, the final product. This flexibility allowed the team to quickly design other versions of HERA for deployment. Having a variety of delivery modes would also help them in deploying HERA in different contexts in the future.

Applying agile design process to health innovations in humanitarian contexts is difficult. Most of the available funding for humanitarian response is usually either saved for new emergencies or devoted to capacity building with already existing response strategies. For those who are more reliant on a robust evidence base of success, it is always a point of hesitation to invest in new strategies and innovations, particularly a humanitarian context. Despite this, innovative interventions created and processed through agile process design present many opportunities. Rapidly changing situations, low quality data for decision-making, and high stress scenarios can benefit hugely from flexible intervention designs that focus on practicality rather than documentation and which can respond quickly to feedback from different directions.

Moving from Innovation to Practice: Agility and Resilience to Shocks

The realities of the field, socio-political instability, different life paths of team members, and other variables are hard to plan for in the beginning. Being agile means HERA's team had to respond to changes but also consider unanticipated issues.

As a grassroots NGO, MEDAK never had to file a lawsuit or go to court for any legal reason. Therefore, there was no protocol for when a contractor did not fulfill their part of the agreement and caused the project significant harm. That is what happened when the first app developer company did not deliver the mobile app on deadline. Since the continuation of funding from Grand Challenges Canada relied on deliverables, this became a major problem for the team. After six months, it was obvious that the company would not be able to reliably deliver the product and was unwilling to refund: the only option was to file a lawsuit.

The team knew that a lawsuit might take several years and also that the verdict, which they believed would be in their favor, would not help with the project progress, and could possibly hurt their external relationship. Instead of waiting for results, a new agreement with an international company was made. This time, three people from HERA's team would be in constant contact during the development process and visit the company at least once a week to work together on the app design. To make up for lost time and traction due to the delay in application launch, the rest of the team would focus on scale up plans, financial sustainability, and networking. This rapid and simultaneous movement instead of sequential or milestone approach helped them to minimize the damages in unfamiliar, uncharted, and unpredicted territory.

COVID-19 and HERA

In March 2020, in response to the rapid spread of the 2019 novel coronavirus disease (COVID-19), and ongoing contextualized risks for the Syrian refugee population in Turkey, the decision was made to incorporate a COVID-19 response into the HERA platform. The aim of this decision was to access the current and growing user base of women and children to provide health education outreach and reduce exposure risks within the health system. Educational content was adapted to include general information about COVID-19 (including basic protective measures), a virus tracking map, government restrictions, and testing site referrals. Users were notified of these updates on their mobile devices; the user base was then contacted for symptomatic assessment at two-week intervals. A description of this intervention was published in October of 2020 as an example of the ability of mhealth platforms to be rapidly distributed at a low cost to improve the health of vulnerable populations. HERA served as proof of concept that similar mhealth applications can be rapidly adapted to emerging challenges, including both humanitarian crises and evolving infectious outbreaks, such as the COVID-19 pandemic.

TOWARDS SCALE AND SUSTAINABILITY: A SOCIAL BUSINESS MODEL (EXHIBIT 2)

Suitable Conditions for Scale Up

HERA was envisioned in an environment that is suitable for technological innovations and for a well-defined, and appreciated, need. The Syrian refugee crisis is known worldwide because the migration route for displaced persons included the Western world and made it 'their problem' too. It was also obvious to many stakeholders in the humanitarian sector that traditional approaches to disaster response were not enough because the specific needs of each refugee group in different countries were different. Turkey had excellent conditions and institutional settings for growth of such an innovation.

Transformation in the Health Program of Turkey's Ministry of Health (MoH) had led to significant health outcome improvements, but this process was far from over. Starting from 2015, the MoH increased its focus on building technological infrastructure, creating telehealth capacity, and opening a new branch that would regulate electronic health interventions. HERA was aligned with these efforts, which made it more acceptable for scaling up and eventual integration to MoH services.

Another important opportunity in Turkey was that Turkish Government was the major provider of health services which are all free of charge. A demand side innovation such as HERA would rely on the presence of a fairly guaranteed supply stream. Being the major provider also meant that the adoption system would be relatively easy as there would be one integration process. Adoption of the innovation itself by end users was also favorable due to high usage of smartphones in the target community.

While the field team in İstanbul working on the proof-of-concept project got back on track with many useful, practical solutions, the Boston team grew to four people who decided to work on HERA. The team was now advised by professionals in the global health systems and innovation arena such as

Dr. Rıfat Atun. Although this rapid growth and transnational collaborator coordination was intimidating, the team believed that a variety of expertise and knowledge would be the key to HERA's success.

After the proof-of concept study data collection and analysis concluded, the team was confident about the wide-reaching potential of HERA. With favorable conditions, the team now had to decide on how to continue with scaling up plans. Deciding on scale up strategy early on is important for sustainable growth and prioritizing the organizational activities.

Scale up discussions always included integration of HERA into the Ministry of Health's refugee health services. The core team believed that sustainability would be best ensured with this plan, as MoH was the major health provider for refugees in Turkey. Also, successful medical care uptake would help the MoH make data collection easier and digital as users of HERA could put their health records in the app, should they choose to do so. A major risk was the funding of refugee responses. Since the early 2010s, the government of Turkey has been receiving large grants for European Union and United Nations for its response to the Syrian refugee crisis but is unclear for how long this funding will continue. Integration with the MOH also meant handing the operation to MoH, or at least parts of it. In practice, it introduced many issues as the priorities of HERA team and Ministry of Health might not always be the same.

Another option for scale up was to stay completely independent as an entity. This ideally would be through external funding from humanitarian and global health donors with sustainable grants. A major advantage is that HERA team would be in complete control of the program and could keep the priorities it was designed for. Also, having international donors would pave the way for international scale up or different versions of HERA App for other refugee communities around the world. However, as the team knew, having a grant generally meant a rigid timeline, stable milestones and finite funding duration. They would still have to spend a lot of energy on actively seeking new sources of funding.

Alternatively, working with a large company, particularly a telecom company in Turkey could be beneficial. As a corporate social responsibility agreement, the company could reach the end users easily. In addition, integration of conditional credit transfers – that is currently not done and is planned as a part of agile scale up design – would be seamless: Instead of sending cash transfer, the telecom company could give discount on the bill or provide free internet or data to the user as a reward for getting the vaccine or going to the prenatal checkup appointment. The major risk identified in this plan was the buy-in of the telecom company with possible unwillingness to cooperate due to fear of pushback or negative advertisement from xenophobic parts of the host community.

The last scale up strategy that the team thought of is working directly with United Nation charters. In humanitarian crises, United Nation charters and a few international organizations are coordinated by United Nations Office for Coordination of Humanitarian Affairs (UNOCHA) through a cluster approach. Each cluster is responsible for an aspect of the crisis or the needs of the population (health cluster, water and sanitation cluster, shelter cluster etc.). Approaching the UN with the HERA project could be beneficial in integrating HERA to UN humanitarian response programs and scale up in different contexts with a fairly stable funding stream. However big and rigid organizations are usually hard to mobilize due to long and arduous bureaucratic processes. In addition, the team was afraid that HERA might be swallowed by a bigger organization with a misaligned vision for equity and end up out of control of the original HERA team.

Sustainable Development Goals and HERA

As health sector reform becomes an increasing priority amongst the international community, access, quality, efficiency, and equity are key intermediate objectives in the approach to successful reform (Roberts et al., 2003). Key aspects of reform that require ongoing and rigorous assessment include problem definition, causal diagnosis and policy development. Yet, a 'deep sensitivity to local circumstances' is an important part of understanding and affecting global change (Roberts et al., 2003). Our global health efforts have to be adjusted and contextualized for highly mobile populations, including displaced persons.

The sustainable development goals (SDGs) adopted by 193 countries in 2015, materialized from some of the most comprehensive and cross-sector collaborative negotiations in the United Nations history. Developed as a replacement for the continued vision put forth by the Millennium Development Goals (MDGs), the SDGs are the world's shared plan to end extreme poverty, reduce inequality, and protect the planet by 2030 (United Nations, 2020). Incorporating health efforts for refugee care is an important part of the SDGs, including good health and well-being (Goal 3) and inequality reduction (Goal 10) within and among communities, through creating inclusive and resilient human settlements (Griggs et al. 2013).

The SDGs are in fact interconnected, often related to the cyclical relationships created by social determinants of health. Social determinants of health are conditions in the environment in which people are born, live, work, and play, that affect a wide range of health risks and outcomes (WHO, 2020). They are often linked to the complex, interrelated social structures and economic systems that shape these conditions (Centers for Disease Control, 2019). For example, poverty, poor living conditions, and downstream effects of climate change and humanitarian crises, have a major impact on the health of individuals and communities. However, economic productivity can similarly be cyclically linked to health. Disability caused by chronic disease affects days of work lost, and health costs (including catastrophic health expenditures) associated with various disease states, may push people towards unemployment, or employment in unsafe and usually underpaid jobs; thus, powering the poverty cycle.

HERA works to leverage information and communication technologies in an era of rapid communication, to improve the wellbeing of difficult to reach patients. When considering access for highly mobile or other vulnerable populations, creative approaches to ensure equitable achievement of the SDGs is important. In the intersection of health and human flourishment, the use of innovative interventions is an important tool for providing target populations more control over their own health and well-being (Vernon et al., 2016). Unfortunately, it is estimated that at least 200 million people, up from current estimates of 80 million, will be forcibly displaced from their homes by 2050, driven by humanitarian crises often fueled by conflict and climate change (Myers, 2005). Contextualized approaches to healthcare access for this population are, such as HERA's platform, required for equitable achievement of the SDGs by 2030.

Financial Sustainability and Becoming a Social Enterprise

From an idea to full blown enterprise, initiatives take a lot of unexpected turns, sometimes in a good direction and sometimes bad. The majority of these turns cannot be forecasted perfectly, though resilience can be built. Ever-changing political, economic and social environment affects social impact work swiftly because it is seen as an elastic expenditure, meaning that it is sensitive to small changes in economic power or willingness to pay.

Becoming a social enterprise is about the sustainable funding of all activities of the organization before anything else. As discussed before, grant based funding strategies can be vulnerable to changing priorities and economic and political contexts.

HERA's metamorphosis into a social venture started with defining the players in the economic cycle of such interventions. First, the 'beneficiaries', who HERA was designed for, and then the payer, or cost bearer in refugee healthcare. These are usually either large international organizations such as UNHCR, WHO, or host country governments themselves. Often, these organizations are also the providers of the health services, or the beneficiaries that HERA was designed to connect the refugees with.

While there are other major players in refugee healthcare, these two are the largest ones. For the team, it was clear that the financial sustainability had to include them. Not only that but working with the payer – keeping in mind that they are usually the service provider too – made the most sense.

At the end of this multi-year process, a clear business model with multiple actors were created. HERA, as an organization, was to provide the service of integration of the HERA App to the providers' services, allowing them to keep real time data while connecting with the beneficiaries directly. This service provision also meant that the team would work in the field, with the payer to modify HERA to the specific needs of the population. One other reason to focus on the payer was also the decision to always keep HERA free of charge to the end-users, refugees. Additional funding could then be used to implement HERA in other countries.

While it is a simple model of financial sustainability, the team also had to consider using this monopsomy model. Ministries of health or large international organizations are usually the sole provider of healthcare in refugee hosting countries.

CONCLUSION

However great an idea or potential it has for creating social value, it will stay as an idea if it is not operationalized. An operational intervention, product, or a service needs continuity beyond proving its impact. This is the core idea behind a social enterprise model.

There are other business models that can be used for scaling up and sustainability of a project. However, the strategies considered by the HERA team are viable and realistic for the context of refugee crisis and the region. While the political and economic context of social issues may change, the case of HERA could provide insight into long and cumbersome way of in front of social enterprises.

Figure 2. Screenshots from HERA App

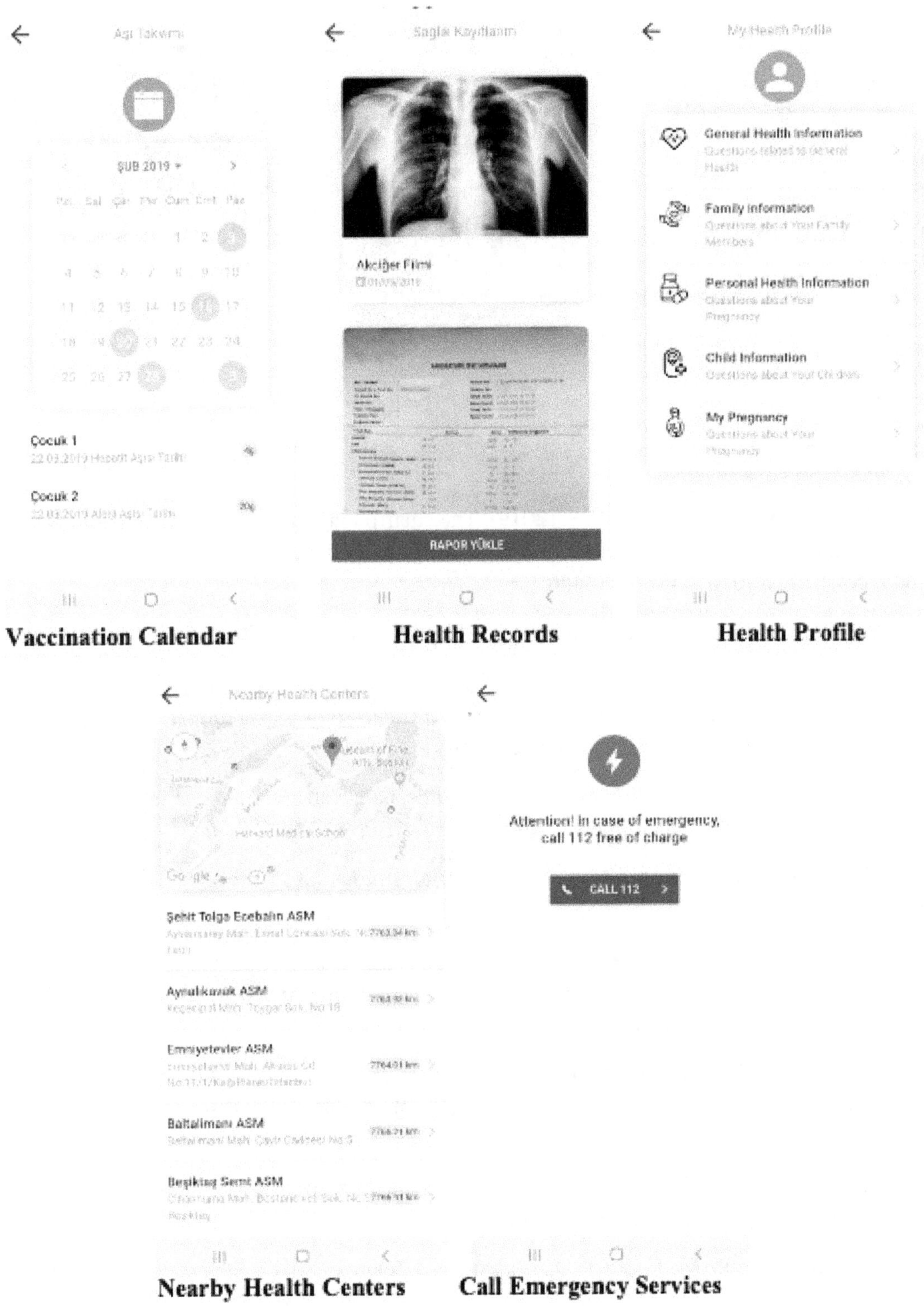

Figure 3. Business Model

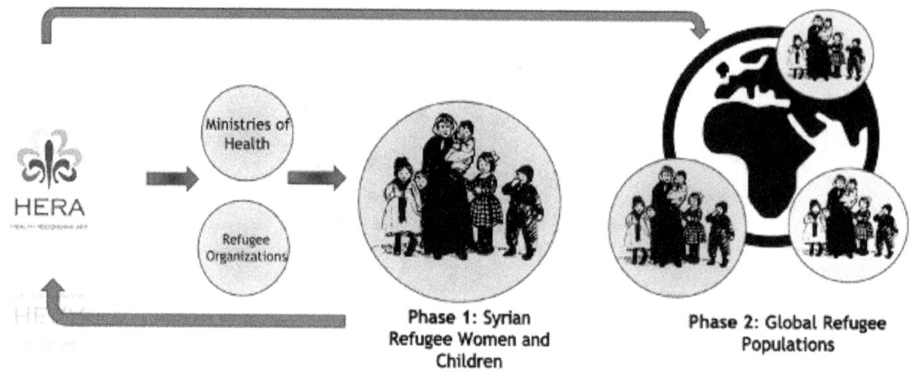

REFERENCES

Alencar, A., Kondova, K., & Ribbens, W. (2019). The smartphone as a lifeline: An exploration of refugees' use of mobile communication technologies during their flight. *Media Culture & Society*, *41*(6), 828–844. doi:10.1177/0163443718813486

Beaglehole, R., & Bonita, R. (2010). What is global health? *Global Health Action, 3*. doi:10.3402/gha.v3i0.5142

Center for Disease Control. (2019, December 19). *Social Determinants of Health*. Retrieved from https://www.cdc.gov/nchhstp/socialdeterminants/index.html

Eisenmann, T. R., Ries, E., & Dillard, S. (2012). Hypothesis-driven entrepreneurship: The lean startup. *Harvard Business School Entrepreneurial Management Case*, (812-095).

Farmer, P. (2013). *Reimagining Global Health: An Introduction*. University of California Press. doi:10.1525/9780520954632

Ferris, E., & Kirişci, K. (2016, July 29). *What Turkey's open-door policy means for Syrian refugees*. Retrieved October 29, 2020, from https://www.brookings.edu/blog/order-from-chaos/2015/07/08/what-turkeys-open-door-policy-means-for-syrian-refugees/

Finnegan, C. (2020, February 12). *Trump budget proposes cuts to global health amid two global health crises*. Retrieved from https://abcnews.go.com/Politics/trump-budget-proposes-cuts-global-health-amid-global/story

Ghorai, K., Akter, S., Khatun, F., & Ray, P. (2014). mHealth for Smoking Cessation Programs: A Systematic Review. *Journal of Personalized Medicine*, *4*(3), 412–423. doi:10.3390/jpm4030412 PMID:25563359

Griggs, D., Stafford-Smith, M., Gaffney, O., Rockström, J., Öhman, M. C., Shyamsundar, P., Steffen, W., Glaser, G., Kanie, N., & Noble, I. (2013). Sustainable development goals for people and planet. *Nature*, *495*(7441), 305–307. doi:10.1038/495305a PMID:23518546

Hall, A. K., Cole-Lewis, H., & Bernhardt, J. M. (2015). Mobile text messaging for health: A systematic review of reviews. *Annual Review of Public Health, 36*(1), 393–415. doi:10.1146/annurev-publhealth-031914-122855 PMID:25785892

ILO | Social Protection Platform |Syria: Social security programmes. (n.d.). Retrieved October 29, 2020, from https://www.social-protection.org/gimi/gess/ShowWiki.action?wiki.wikiId=707

IMHE Syria. (2017, September 19). Retrieved October 29, 2020, from http://www.healthdata.org/syria

Koplan, J. P., Bond, T. C., Merson, M. H., Reddy, K. S., Rodriguez, M. H., Sewankambo, N. K., & Wasserheit, J. N. (2009). Towards a common definition of global health. *Lancet, 373*(9679), 1993–1995. doi:10.1016/S0140-6736(09)60332-9 PMID:19493564

Mair, J., & Lanuza, M. (2006). Social Entrepreneurship Research: A Source of Explanation, Prediction, and Delight. *Journal of World Business, 41*(1), 36–44. doi:10.1016/j.jwb.2005.09.002

Mcneil, D., & Jacobs, A. (2020, May 29). *Blaming China for Pandemic, Trump Says U.S. Will Leave the W.H.O.* Retrieved from https://www.nytimes.com/2020/05/29/health/virus-who.html

Myers, N. (2005). *Environmental refugees: an emergent security issue*. Academic Press.

Nicholls, A. (2010). The legitimacy of social entrepreneurship: Reflexive isomorphism in a pre-paradigmatic field. *Entrepreneurship Theory and Practice, 34*(4), 611–633. doi:10.1111/j.1540-6520.2010.00397.x

Raifman, J. R., Lanthorn, H. E., Rokicki, S., & Fink, G. (2014). The impact of text message reminders on adherence to antimalarial treatment in northern Ghana: A randomized trial. *PLoS One, 9*(10), e109032. doi:10.1371/journal.pone.0109032 PMID:25350546

Rawlings, L. B., & Rubio, G. M. (2005). Evaluating the impact of conditional cash transfer programs. *The World Bank Research Observer, 20*(1), 29–55. doi:10.1093/wbro/lki001

Roberts, M., Hsiao, W., Berman, P., & Reich, M. (2003). *Getting health reform right: a guide to improving performance and equity*. Oxford University Press.

Rodgers, L., Gritten, D., Offer, J., & Asare, P. (2016, March 11). *Syria: The story of the conflict*. Retrieved October 29, 2020, from https://www.bbc.com/news/world-middle-east-26116868

Schmitt, C., & Husson, J. (2017). Entrepreneurial situations, definition and interests for entrepreneurial research. *International Journal of Entrepreneurship and Small Business, 30*(1), 22. doi:10.1504/IJESB.2017.081037

Snyder, L. B., Hamilton, M. A., Mitchell, E. W., Kiwanuka-Tondo, J., Fleming-Milici, F., & Proctor, D. (2004). A meta-analysis of the effect of mediated health communication campaigns on behavior change in the United States. *Journal of Health Communication, 9*(sup1, S1), 71–96. doi:10.1080/10810730490271548 PMID:14960405

Syria Population. (2020). Retrieved October 29, 2020, from https://worldpopulationreview.com/countries/syria-population

Todd, Z. (2019, November 19). *By the Numbers: Syrian Refugees Around the World*. Retrieved October 29, 2020, from https://www.pbs.org/wgbh/frontline/article/numbers-syrian-refugees-around-world/

UNHCR. (2020, October 14). *Operational Portal*. Retrieved October 29, 2020, from https://data2.unhcr.org/en/situations/syria

United Nations. (2020). *Sustainable Development Goals*. Retrieved from https://unfoundation.org/what-we-do/issues/sustainable-development-goals

Vernon, A., Deriche, K., & Eisenhauer, S. (2016). *Connecting refugees: How internet and mobile connectivity can improve refugee well-being and transform humanitarian action (Rep.)*. UNHCR.

Wakadha, H., Chandir, S., Were, E. V., Rubin, A., Obor, D., Levine, O. S., Gibson, D. G., Odhiambo, F., Laserson, K. F., & Feikin, D. R. (2013). The feasibility of using mobile-phone based SMS reminders and conditional cash transfers to improve timely immunization in rural Kenya. *Vaccine, 31*(6), 987–993. doi:10.1016/j.vaccine.2012.11.093 PMID:23246258

World Health Organization. (2020, June 29). *Syrian Arab Republic: WHO and UNICEF estimates of immunization coverage: 2019 revision*. Retrieved October 29, 2020, from https://www.who.int/immunization/monitoring_surveillance/data/syr.pdf

World Health Organization. (2020). *Social Determinants of Health*. Retrieved from https://www.who.int/social_determinants/en

Yates, R., & Humphreys, G. (2013). *Arguing for Universal Health Coverage*. Retrieved from https://www.who.int/health_financing/UHC_ENvs_BD.PDF

ENDNOTE

1 This graph is adapted from Dr. Rıfat Atun's ID552 Innovation and Global Health Systems Course Lecture: Translating ideas to a scalable plan: agile design, November 2018. The scaling up strategy explained here is from the same course.

Chapter 12 Creating Equal Opportunities through Social Entrepreneurship: The Case of Future is Brighter Youth Platform

Tuba Bozaykut-Buk
Istanbul Medipol University, Turkey

Serra Titiz
Mikado Consulting, Turkey

ABSTRACT

Giving priority to creating value for sustainable development rather than accepting the dominance of the profit-centered perspective has been gaining more momentum. Within this changing perspective, social entrepreneurs are the most notable group, whose innovative initiatives create valuable contributions by becoming pioneer forces required for economic and social development. Further, their efforts in showing the significance of social value creation result in a new business model, "social business." Although the social business shares some common features with the traditional business, the social business differentiates itself by acting as a social change actor accompanied by a socially sensitive mission, a hybrid flexible design, innovative ways of finding/using resources for creating new solutions to needs. Thereby, this study aims to understand the features of social business models together with their contribution to social inclusion and creating equal opportunities for all in terms of a developing country context.

INTRODUCTION

As the complexity and the prevalence of social problems increase, their consequences have started to affect more people than ever. The climate crisis, unequal distribution of wealth and natural resources

DOI: 10.4018/978-1-7998-4727-4.ch012

accompanied by increasing poverty undermine the prevalent economic system, and traditional way of doing business. Additionally poverty, resource crises and ecological degradation have transformed the perceptions of development by giving equal importance to social and ecological values besides economic interests (Schaltegger et al., 2016; Stubbs and Cocklin, 2008). Further, the prevailing economic system in terms of equal income generation creates the question of inclusiveness of the disadvantaged groups in the system. Thereby, economic growth not as an impediment but as an accelerator for equity becomes the required view for the welfare of current and forthcoming generations (Ranieri and Ramos, 2013).

The quest for equal opportunities, social integration and social welfare are embraced by inclusive growth paradigm. Inclusive growth, though have defined by various angles, refers to a growth process that embraces all without discriminating the poor, minorities, the disabled etc. (Klasen, 2010). Inclusive growth also questions the value creation through businesses and transforms created value to shared value that offers value to disadvantaged groups through redesigning products/services and transforming value chain (Kramer and Porter, 2011; Porter and Kramer, 2019). Parallel to inclusive growth, the shared value perspective advocates the sustainability of business success and competitiveness only if the given business operations support the economic and social development of societies (Porter and Kramer, 2019). More to that, inclusive growth through creating shared value can be regarded as a solution to distrust directed at corporate mentality that is believed to put all its' efforts and will on profit maximization (Porter and Kramer, 2019).

Inclusive growth through creating shared value also requires innovative products and processes in the value chain regarding disadvantaged groups. Since Schumpeter's arguments (1934), entrepreneurs and their innovative initiatives are regarded as triggers of social and economic transformation (Hall et al. 2010). In line with Schumpeter's entrepreneurship definition, this study follows the 'social innovation' school's approach to social entrepreneurship (Dees and Anderson, 2006a, b). Within this school, social entrepreneurs are evaluated as "change makers as they carry out 'new combinations' in at least one the following areas: new services, new quality of services, new methods of production, new production factors, new forms of organizations or new markets" (Defourny and Nyssens, 2010:44). As an explicit example, the social entrepreneur, Muhammed Yunus and his idea of Microfinance method with his socially innovative product, Grameen Bank can be given. In his case, the created value is enlarged to the poor women of Bangladesh through small loans so that Bangladeshi women can earn their living through minor activities as buying animals for breeding.

Based on not only to the social innovation school but also to other related studies, this chapter aims to discuss the contributions of social enterprises on social inclusiveness through a Turkish initiative; Future is Brighter Youth Platform which offers solutions to the fight against the inequality and social exclusion experienced by Turkish youth related to skill development and employment.

THEORETICAL BACKGROUND

The Social Business Model

The literary background provides a variety of definitions for social businesses. For instance, to the Social Business Initiative (2011:2), social businesses are "operators in the social economy whose main objective is to have a social impact rather than make a profit for their owners or shareholders." Similarly, OECD (1999:105) explains the social enterprise as "any private activity conducted in the public interest, organized with an entrepreneurial strategy, but whose main purpose is not the maximization of profit but the attainment of certain economic and social goals and which has the capacity for bringing innovative solutions to the problems of social exclusion and unemployment". Among others, this study adopts the social enterprise explanation of Boons and Lüdeke-Freund (2013:16) due to its emphasis on sustainable innovation and the business model: "Social business models are enterprises that create the opportunity for "social entrepreneurs to create social value and maximize social profit; of significance is the business model's ability to act as market device that helps in creating and further developing market for innovations with a social purpose."

The business model of a social enterprise refers to a systematically designed value creation process for all stakeholders (Teece, 2010). In line with this, the previous studies indicate that there is an association between the way of organizing the value creation process, namely the business model, and social innovation (Boons and Lüdeke-Freund, 2013). Based on Osterwalder (2004), Doganova and Eyquem-Renault (2009), Boons and Lüdeke-Freund (2013) argue that a generic business model stands on four pillars: a. the value offered to stakeholders, b. supply chain structure, c. customer relations and d. financial structure. Moreover, in case of social businesses, the business model with its four pillars can become a competitive advantage factor due to the differentiated value offered to stakeholders.

In terms of the value offered, the social businesses mainly aim at meeting a social need accompanied by a financial design for generating profit, which is a secondary objective. In other words, social businesses also get beyond the limits of the traditional profit-maximization oriented business model by indicating a different motive, social wealth maximization. As an alternate business model, it is thereby glorified as a model that saves societies from "the egocentric value creation" mindset (Schaltegger et al., 2016; 5).

The Social Entrepreneur

The entrepreneur is a critical element of the social business. In the traditional manner, an entrepreneur refers to someone who seizes opportunities in the market by taking risks and failures on himself/herself. This definition is also applicable to social entrepreneurs but the difference between the two lies in social entrepreneur's dedication to creating social value rather than generating profits (Dees, 1998). The social mission embraced by the social entrepreneur determines value to be generated thereby differentiating the business model from the traditional business models. The social entrepreneur approaches the traditional resources, networks, processes in a novel way (Schumpeter, 1934) in order to create innovative solutions to social/economic or ecological problems. Therefore based on Schumpeter, the social innovation school defines social entrepreneurs as "individuals who reform or revolutionize the patterns of producing social value, shifting resources into areas of higher yield for society" (Dess and Anderson, 2006b:44).

Within the perspective of social innovation school, social entrepreneurs are regarded as social transformation agents (Partzsch and Ziegler, 2011) that struggle for achieving their ideals. Thorough their insistence of realizing their aims, social entrepreneurs go beyond the limits of organizational boundaries. Their dedication to their mission both facilitate the creation of new patterns and formation of new relationships between sectors by deforming the organizational boundaries (Dess and Anderson, 2006b). All attempts to share experiences, ideas together with forming partnerships between business, NGOs and academia are common activities of the social entrepreneurship ecosystem.

The social entrepreneur also has different motives. Not excluding monetary gains, social entrepreneur has motives of reaching self-actualization through achieving personal aim in serving society. Along with the social entrepreneur, the other actors and institutions in the supply chain are noteworthy as they have to be on the same socially responsible side of the social business. This is valid for customers, as well. The customers that seek for the social business' products or services are among those who are more alert to ecological, economic and social problems. Within these premises, it would not be wrong to come to the conclusion that the developed country markets welcome and host most of the social businesses in the world (Bansal et al., 2019); whereas underdeveloped countries' markets have some time to "unfold the sustainability potential" of social businesses (Schaltegger and Wagner, 2008; 2011,cited in Boons and Lüdeke-Freund, 2013:13). Moreover, private sector partnerships are vital for social initiatives both for encouraging social entrepreneurship system and the sustainability of social initiatives. Yet, it is difficult for social initiatives to have the attention of private sector as monetary gains can't function as an outcome (Hall, 2004).

Features of Social Businesses

Besides the entrepreneurial features, another differentiation related with social businesses is their organizational design. Most social businesses are labelled as "hybrid" organizations because of their dependence of networks that cover governmental agencies, private sector, universities and other NGOs (Defourny, and Nyssens, 2013; Tykkyläinen and Ritala, 2020). Participation of these actors and participation of users or customers are welcomed by social businesses; thus, a participative management perspective often is an important characteristic of social enterprises. Parallel to this participatory structure, most social businesses rely on voluntary work as an important factor of production (Defourny and Nyssens, 2013; Mulgan et al., 2007). Additionally, in the contexts that offer no legal, governmental and financial incentives for social businesses and even being subjected to same taxes designed for profit oriented businesses (e.g. Turkey), it becomes more difficult to balance the budget and to reach the financial resources. Thereby, in these cases, social businesses find the solution by establishing associations and foundations. This solution enables them to benefit from the incentives already offered to associations.

Yet the life cycle of the social business also differs as they show a pattern of slow growth. Mulgan (2019:32) puts this as in the following lines: "social organizations tend to have different patterns of growth: as a rule they don't grow as fast as private ones, but they also tend to be more resilient." A recent British Council study on Turkish social enterprises confirms Mulgan for the Turkish case. The study findings show that Turkish social enterprises don't grow fast and operate on a micro scale.

Besides transgressing boundaries, social businesses are inclusive models covering groups that lack power, resources, representation and thereby access to basic social services. As their target is answering social needs, the disadvantaged groups are beneficiaries of the social business in the forms of producers, suppliers or customers. This inclusiveness is one of the reasons why new methods of answering social needs are labelled as "social innovation". From this perspective, social innovation is closely related to working with and for the disadvantaged groups and it arouses interest and action towards "addressing human needs that were previously unmet" (Marques et al.,2018:500).

Social Businesses and Social Innovation

In the similar line, social innovation is defined as 'a novel solution to a social problem that is more effective, efficient, sustainable, or just than existing solutions and for which the value created accrues primarily to society as a whole rather than private individuals' (Phills et al., 2008: 39). To Hall (2004), innovation would not create the effect it desires on societies if it is not diffused. Diffusion refers both to the process and to the degree of adoption of the given novelty. Likewise, Rogers (2003:35) define diffusion as "the process by which an innovation is communicated through certain channels over time among the members of a social system. Diffusion is seen as a special type of communication concerned with the spread of messages that are perceived as new ideas".

Aligned with the target oriented social entrepreneurial tactics and manners, social businesses are closely associated with innovation and more to that they also help instilling innovative behavior into the lives of their stakeholders and value chain. Moreover, the participatory, flexible structure together with cross-sectoral partnerships render social businesses advantageous in diffusing social innovation. Through these mechanisms, social businesses diffuse its' novelties to the society by sharing the mind-set and practices together with offering opportunities for diffusion by creating a mutual social learning atmosphere (Baker and Mehmood, 2015). Also, as Yunus et al. (2010) explain in the case of Grameen Bank, strategic experimentation is critical and the constant experimentation for finding radical solutions to problems is one of the main practices of social businesses.

To the studies, the adaptation and replications of new ideas are very common in the entrepreneurship practices. For instance, British Council's (2019) recent study on Turkish social businesses prove evidence that 86% of the social businesses that participated in the study have developed a new service, product or model in the last 12 months. In the report, this percentage- compared with the innovation activities of traditional Turkish businesses measured between 2014 and 2016, which is 47%, - is evaluated as very high. Another interesting finding of the study (British Council, 2019:47) is that participants describe the basic qualities of their social enterprises as "being social/environmental impact-oriented (88%), innovative (60%) and they also report that they invest a certain percentage of profit back to their mission (49%)".

Concordantly, spread and adoption of new ideas in the social entrepreneurship ecosystem is encouraged and commonly experienced. Institutions such as Ashoka Foundation function as facilitators of social innovation by offering funds, prizes, networks and platforms though which social entrepreneurship can flourish in the society. Besides providing institutional efforts and resources for innovation diffusion, the individual attempts of the social entrepreneur also help in the diffusion. The social entrepreneur playing the roles of liaison and spokesperson of the social business not only spreads his/her innovative ideas but also helps other social entrepreneurs by being a role model. As in the Ashoka case, most Ashoka fellows also act as influencers. They share their ideas by talking about their own social business experience and try to help to-be social entrepreneurs in establishing their social businesses and in diffusing their new ideas in the society.

All these features render social businesses unique in their approach to target achievement, forming networks, designing new organizational structures and social innovation. In the following sections of the chapter, these features are to be examined through a Turkish social enterprise founded by a social entrepreneur. The social entrepreneur in question is one of the first Ashoka fellows in Turkey, Serra Titiz. Titiz is among the entrepreneurs that pioneers the development of social entrepreneurship ecosystem and leads two of the social enterprises in Turkey. Moreover, she is also among the founders of Turkish social entrepreneurship network. Her entrepreneurial spirit, mission-oriented mindset, her efforts in helping other social entrepreneurs result in diffusing her new approach to others.

Accordingly, this chapter analyses Titiz's initiative, Future is Brighter Youth Platform that offers an innovative method for youth recruitment. Her social enterprise is noteworthy and chosen for analysis because of its' deep attachment to sustainability, equality, and social inclusiveness. Social inclusiveness is one of the main pillars for sustainable development and targets at creating equity for all in terms of reaching natural resources and accessing social services. Offering equal opportunities for education and skill development is one of the critical goals of sustainability and have attracted the attention of both policy makers and social entrepreneurs (Vavik and Keitsch, 2010). All in all, the need for equal opportunities for education is essential for developing countries such as Turkey. In these cases, young people generally graduate with no significant qualifications beside the traditional curriculum, while some face exclusion because they don't have a degree from mainstream universities (Ainscow and Sandil, 2010; Okolie et al., 2019). Thereby, as a developing country, Turkish society is in the need for social cohesion and equality in accessing skill development trainings and followingly generating employment opportunities.

In order to understand youth employment in Turkey, some statistics can be given. According to Turkish Statistical Institute's (TSI) 'Youth Statistics, 2019', 16% of the population, equals to12 million 955 thousand people, is aged between 14 and 25 years. Moreover, to June 2020 data, youth unemployment is 26% in Turkey (https://www.tuik.gov.tr/PreHaberBultenleri.do?id=33790). More to that, in Turkey class and academic success is highly correlated and both school and employment achievement rates are lower for disadvantaged groups such as minorities or the low-incomed (Eğitim Reformu Girişimi 2011; Çelik, 2017). Additionally, for the disadvantaged youth, it becomes more difficult to stand on their own choices and control their lives (Erikli, 2016) and most are taught to refrain from asking questions and passively follow the choices adults make for them. Another important issue that causes unemployment is skills mismatch, the disparity between the skills of the labor force and market requirements. According to 2019 labor market report of Turkish employment agency (2019), the main problem of labor supply in the market is the difficulty of finding employees with the required professional skills/qualifications (https://media.iskur.gov.tr/34629/turkiye.pdf).

Thereby on such a background, a social enterprise model offering an online skill development platform with the target of offering equal opportunities for Turkish youth requires a detailed analysis.

AIM AND METHODOLOGY

In a developing country context, social business models are more required and relevant for social welfare development. Within this perspective and based on the literary background discussed, the current study aims to examine the propositions given below by analyzing Future is Brighter Youth Platform through secondary data including website and social impact report analyses. Previous literature has stated that the social entrepreneur (mostly the founder of the social business), his/her *dedication* to finding solutions to *meeting social problems* and *creating social value is critical* and influential on finding new ways in their search for new sources (such as volunteering) and *forming partnerships* that blend actors/organizations from NGOs, private sector, governmental domain (Dees and Anderson, 2006). Beyond their dedication, their organizational design should also be aligned with their strategy, which means that their structure complies with their culture as well as their vision of creating social value.

Based on social entrepreneurship's strategy the *organizational designs* of social business (either planned or emergent after the establishment) are known *flexible, decentralized and hybrid* that stands on *cooperation and constant learning* embracing actors and partnerships from diverse industries and disciplines (Mulgan et al., 2007; Defourny and Nyssens, 2013; Yunus et al. 2010). Within the scope of answering problems, social businesses adopt *inclusiveness perspective* and thereby more sensitive to the problems of disadvantaged groups' needs in terms of providing their services/products for creating substantial benefits (Hall et al., 2012). Equality in all aspects is an important motivator. In some cases, they can even help the formation of a new market by answering societal needs through innovative products and services. Because of their targets of answering social problems by being inclusive without a profit-maximization mindset, social enterprises are sources both for *creating and diffusing social innovation* as they can trigger a dynamic process through which each innovation can lead to the possibility of another innovation (Bornstein, 2004; Mughan et al. 2007; Westley and Antadze, 2010).

In the light of this point of view, by adopting a case study in the Turkish context, our aim is to question what ways a social entrepreneur takes to realize her vision and how she does it. Especially as this is a recently developed research domain, social business studies are more apt to analyze the phenomenon in detail and examine various cases for a better understanding (e.g. Comini et al., 2012; Mumford, 2002; Nielsen and Samia 2008; Yunus et al., 2010). The secondary data is used for case analysis as the official website, together with the analysis of 2016, 2017 and 2018 social impact reports of Future is Brighter Youth Platform. Moreover, especially for the historical background of the study, the founder, Titiz contributes to the study as the co-author.

FUTURE IS BRIGHTER YOUTH PLATFORM

The history of Future is Brighter Youth Platform (FBYP) is also worth examining as it takes its' roots from another social enterprise founded by Titiz, namely Mikado Sustainable Development Consulting (from now on referred as Mikado). Established in 2007, Mikado is a social business registered as a limited company, committed to serve sustainable development and to yield social impact through crafting innovative models and solutions. Mikado's main business strategy is to support the creation of a sustainable corporate and social environment in Turkey through creating partnerships among private sector, civil society, academic, public and international organizations. Moreover, creating an awareness for sustainability in Turkish society and participating in various projects that promote social, ecological and economic sustainability are the distinguishing features of Mikado. Another significant feature is that it earns the privilege to be Turkey's first certified B Corporation. This certification assures that Mikado's business model is designed for the good of the society. Furthermore, it is a key player in shaping the social entrepreneurship ecosystem in Turkey by developing platforms, by designing social innovation centers and by developing researches. Besides providing consultancy, Mikado also develops capacity building programs, provides trainings and issues publications.

By incubating FBYP, Mikado transfers its' social sustainability DNA to FBYP. FBYP was established in 2009. Through creating a social network between these two organizations, Titiz achieves to get beyond the organizational boundaries to collaborate with more organizations, more people for her dream of a sustainable world. More to that, through the resources and networks of Mikado, Titiz is able to realize what has been in her mind for several years—a global initiative providing youth with guidance, inspiration, and empowerment to lead self-determined lives. FBYP, which began as a pillar of Mikado, gradually becomes a more independent national initiative.

Problem Awareness and Innovative Solution

Creating equal employment opportunities cover not only older age workers and disabled people, but also youth and women employment. For example, based on OECD or World Bank statistics, youth who are neither employed nor in education or training together with early school leavers represent an increasing segment of the disadvantaged youth (Acar and Afacan Fındıklı, 2020). Creating job opportunities for those groups and supporting their social development become one of the most critical social problems for societies. Before establishing FBYP, the social entrepreneur- Titiz- worked for and with youth in the civil society and had the opportunity to witness and share their needs. Titiz notices that young people cannot reach sufficient knowledge and guidance when they make decisions about their life. Consequently, they do not know what to expect from themselves truly and are not knowledgeable enough about occupations and career paths. Thereby, they face with difficulties in deciding on a suitable occupation or career path for themselves. While planning her own future, Titiz, herself, had difficulties and she is aware that many youths lose their direction in their career search. The idea of creating an "online, free and equal access to everyone" type of platform came to her while she was establishing Mikado. She prioritized Mikado and then started devising the model and the infrastructure of FBYP. The idea became a project under Mikado, then became a brand itself and was separated from Mikado to act under an NGO.

With this innovative and inclusive idea, Titiz founded FBYP as a first online platform on youth employment. During its first 5 years, FBYP is registered as an NGO and functions as a vocational orientation platform for youth aged 15-29. Volunteering is an important functioning mechanism for FBYP and the platform works with volunteers (+2100 by March 2020) who are matched with youngsters according to their interest areas for better life, education and career decisions. Online mentoring, online trainings, videos and offline workshops are all designed to provide solutions for increasing employability and decrease skills mismatch.

Concordantly, FBYP aims to increase employability of young people in Turkey through online and offline services targeted at empowering young people. Services vary from online mentoring, coaching, trainings, surveys, workshops, youth camps, etc. The founder, Titiz, has taken advantage of the power of internet at the time when people were questioning its outreach and designed FBYP's model on online sharing. She was able to secure in-kind technology providers to set the virtual rooms and online trainings. Her experience in the social sector, her reputation as a sustainable development expert and her network help her introduce FBYP as a solution for the career counseling need of youngsters in Turkey.

Created Social Value: Social Inclusiveness and Empowerment

Targeting at offering solutions to the social problems of youth unemployment and skills mismatch, FBYP provides opportunities for rendering young people as self-determined, proactive, and well-informed citizens by proving free career mentoring and skill development programs. The initiative inspires youth with role models, raises awareness of existing social and personal opportunities, encourages them to make choices, and empowers them through a combination of guidance, mentoring, coaching, and skill development services/opportunities. To exemplify, to FBYP's 2018 social impact report, the young people participating to the platform confirm that the platform contributes their personal and career development, improves their knowledge about professions and required skills, gives the chance to get in contact with the professionals in their areas of interest. Besides these social impacts, the platform offers certified educations such as project management or group management and shares online webinars on career opportunities for free.

Concordantly, FBYP empowers and encourages youth self-determination with the ability to make informed education, career choices and life choices and this can help to minimize lower high school, university and job dropout rates, fulfilled personal lives and a more productive economy and society (FBYP social impact report 2019, 2018, 2017). Moreover, FBYP aims to encourage youth to be proactive members of society, gears them up with 21st century life-skills and empowers them to make more informed life, education and career choices (https://www.gelecekdaha.net/hakkimizda). Moreover, the initiative combines on-and offline mentoring-, coaching- and skill development approaches involving hundreds of professionals as volunteers, a majority of which engages with youth or volunteers for the first time. All these efforts are directed for more fulfilled lives, lower high school, university & job dropout rates, increased employability, more successful careers, a stronger economy and a more proactive and productive society overall. FBYP targets at leveraging the experience, knowledge, skills and networks of hundreds of volunteer role models, professionals, organizations, and companies all over Turkey by providing youth with mentors and training. The rationality behind is to create an knowledge exchange experience which is mutually beneficial. Volunteer mentors and coaches connect to a younger generation and youth receive access to inspiration, experience, knowledge, and guidance from professionals in Turkey's private sector and civil organizations.

Accordingly, the main social value created through FBYP is to increase the employment opportunities for all young Turkish job seekers. Social inclusiveness in terms of skill development for employability is one of the most significant social impacts of FBYP. The opportunities FBYP provide include all young people who have an internet access. FBYP adds value to existing services/opportunities by placing them under one initiative that is easily accessible through a free of charge web platform. The youth may access the platform at anytime and anywhere, regardless of economic or social status. In addition to its web platform and online modules, FBYP facilitates offline forums and workshops countrywide, and introduces mentoring manuals, handbooks, and training modules to allow high schools and universities to replicate and localize the initiatives.

Another social impact of FBYP is to offer employment and skill development opportunities for young people coming from not- privileged universities or wealthy families. A critical social problem related with employment in Turkey is the employers' intention to favor those who are graduated from top universities (Kurnaz Baltacı, 2020). The young job seekers coming from other universities may face with a discrimination based on the university reputation. To minimize discriminations and for a better inclusion of young graduates in the labor market, FBYP aims to function as a bridge between possibly excluded job seekers and employers by developing an online platform. The platform targets at covering all young Turkish people regardless of their universities and offers them opportunities for interacting with mentors.

Furthermore, the innovative idea of offering on-and offline mentoring-, coaching- and skill development of FBYP has reproduced another social program, Embark. Through Embark, FBYP extends its services to Syrian youth in Turkey through its reversing mentoring program. In the Embark program, talented Syrian university students and graduates living in Turkey are matched with business leaders from companies like Unilever and Mastercard. The program components include mentoring sessions, a soft skills bootcamp and a goal setting program called Goals for Good.

Consequently, social innovation, social impact and sustainability are main pillars of FBYP, Mikado and Embark. Additionally, all these social initiatives act as social innovation enablers reproducing social innovation through incubating platforms, projects and products in Turkey. Their business ethics lie in common values such as building partnerships, impact-orientation, good of the society and lifelong learning. Although most of the social business models have problems in continuing their operations (Oeij et al., 2019), both Mikado and FBYP celebrated their 12th and 10th year respectively and FBYP recently achieved to take private sector investment. Through this investment, the platform is at the verge of developing its future version with the investment of its present sponsors and will be reestablished to focus more on the social problem of skills mismatch.

The achievements of Mikado and FBYP are closely associated with the experience, dedication and social network of the social entrepreneur, Serra Titiz. Her experience in the civil society that spans from working in the field with disadvantaged communities to developing capacity building programs, from fundraising to corporate partnerships enabled her to see what's missing and led her to initiate her own social initiatives. Moreover, both her dedication and her experience in the civil society sector qualified Mikado and FBYP as significant social initiatives in Turkey.

DISCUSSION AND CONCLUSION

The business model centered on social innovation offers opportunities for extending the traditional business model assessed primarily by the financial (sales, profit etc.) and customer (satisfaction, loyalty etc.) related outcomes. The motive for creating social transformation puts its' stamp on the values, strategies, interactions, designs, and management of social business models. Realizing social problems or needs, developing creative products, services, designs, dispersing these novelties into other organizations through network of enabling actors/institutions and creating social impact as the prioritized organizational outcome are major features of social business models. Within this perspective, the current chapter examines a Turkish social initiative to have a deeper understanding of the social enterprises' contribution to social inclusion.

In terms of the case analyzed, it can be stated that the social entrepreneur of the case is a highly mission-oriented person and she realizes her missions through establishing a social business on sustainability and a platform on youth empowerment. The past research asserts that the social entrepreneur is highly dedicated to finding solutions for social problems and thereby creates social value by finding new ways and new sources. In the analysed case, Titiz, through her social business, looks for new ways for youth empowerment and achieves to establish a novel online platform for mentoring, trainings, workshops that would help to increase youth employability and decrease the skills mismatch. For organizational design, FBYP cooperates with universities and governmental agencies and starting from its' establishment, FBYD stands on a cooperative structure accompanied by a constant learning atmosphere as diverse actors such as private sector professionals, academics, other NGOs and volunteers working for youth are included.

As discussed previously, social businesses put efforts in creating equality for all regardless of age, gender, ethnicity, religion etc. In case of Turkey, FBYP plays a noteworthy role since Turkey is amongst the countries that have a high rate of youth population together with the related social problem of unemployment. The platform offers a solution to that problem by empowering the youth. Providing opportunities for skill development and including every young person in the labor market has been a concern for Turkey. Besides governmental efforts, civil society and social initiatives focusing on equal opportunities for skill development or career mentoring for all young people are noteworthy for social and economic development.One of the main distinguishing features of FBYP is to offer a free and easily accessible online platform for all young people in order to minimize the disparities based on gender, location or class. Furthermore, FBYP can be regarded as the realization of providing skill development and employment opportunities to all youth in Turkey, leaving no one behind. Trying to minimize the opportunity gaps between young people from diverse social backgrounds, FBYP has the mission of offering equal mentoring and skill development opportunities to all Turkish youth. The understanding of the social problem that Turkish youth is in the need for mentoring both for their personal and professional development is the main reason of being for FBYP. Thereby, trying to offer an inclusive recruitment process result in the establishment of FBYP. Through the platform, the youth can reach skill development educations or can match with a mentor just by an Internet connection regardless of their location and improve their personal skills.

Furthermore, as a social business, FBYP incubated the basis of another social initiative, Embark which also tries to create equal opportunities for Syrian young people in Turkish society. The case of Embark is an explicit example of the relation between social businesses and diffusion of social innovation. Before discussing Embark, the relation between Mikado and FBYP has to be outlined to have a better understanding of how social innovation can be contagious and has the potential of inspiring other social innovations. The values of the former establishment, Mikado, creating social impact and innovation are also shared by FBYP and hence the social structure, network, organizational design are also transferred to FBYP.

Both Mikado and FBYP depend on constant experimentation and learning. As a result, Mikado incubated FBYP, FBYP incubates programs such as Embark. Embark answers the needs of Syrian youth which is increasing in Turkey by a collaborative solution. As meeting the needs of the refugees become a global debate, the Embark program is to be adopted by other initiatives and can turn into a global model. Through Embark, first-hand work experience, personal skill development opportunities are offered to young Syrians in Turkey. Through mentoring process, Turkish businesspeople also find the opportunity to understand how they can integrate young Syrians into the economic system for a shared social welfare. Both FBYP and Embark clearly underlines how an innovative solution can lead other innovative solutions covering sectors and cultures.

To conclude, some indications can be offered to researchers and authorities. The social problem of employment and skill development of Turkish youth are significant issues. To answer these needs, all actors should act together for equal opportunities. Social initiatives that operate for finding solutions covering all have to be encouraged by both economic and social terms. In Turkey, the interest in social entrepreneurship is on the rise but legal infrastructure needed for supporting the interest isn't developed yet. Thereby, social entrepreneurs in Turkey are looking for ways to achieve their social value creation ideals within the limited support. The legal infrastructure and governmental framework have to be designed in a manner to empower social businesses as the power of social businesses will increase the power of societal development. Additionally, funding opportunities that can answer the needs of social innovation businesses have to be developed for a strong social business circle.

The main limitation of the study is its' methodology which makes it difficult to make generalizations for Turkish social businesses. However, the study aims to provide some insight about the phenomenon by offering a detailed data through case analysis. For the forthcoming studies, it can be advised to study more cases especially the cross-cultural cases for understanding the cultural differences of the phenomenon.

ACKNOWLEDGMENT

This research received no specific grant from any funding agency in the public, commercial, or not-for-profit sectors.

REFERENCES

Acar, A. & Afacan Fındıklı, M. (2020) Employment of disadvantaged groups in OECD countries, *International Journal of Research in Business and Social Science*, *9*(4), 330-342.

Ainscow, M., & Sandill, A. (2010). Developing inclusive education systems: The role of organisational cultures and leadership. *International Journal of Inclusive Education*, *14*(4), 401–416. doi:10.1080/13603110802504903

Baker, S., & Mehmood, A. (2015). Social innovation and the governance of sustainable places. *Local Environment*, *20*(3), 321–334. doi:10.1080/13549839.2013.842964

Bansal, S., Garg, I., & Sharma, G. D. (2019). Social entrepreneurship as a path for social change and driver of sustainable development: A systematic review and research agenda. *Sustainability*, *11*(4), 1091. doi:10.3390u11041091

Boons, F., & Lüdeke-Freund, F. (2013). Business models for sustainable innovation: State-of-the-art and steps towards a research agenda. *Journal of Cleaner Production*, *45*, 9–19. doi:10.1016/j.jclepro.2012.07.007

Bornstein, D. (2004). *How to change the world: social entrepreneurs and the power of new ideas*. Oxford University Press.

British Council. Türkiye. (2019). *Türkiye'de Sosyal Girişimlerin Durumu*. Retrieved February 25, 2020, from https://www.britishcouncil.org.tr/programmes/education/social-enterprise-research

Çelik, Ç. (2017). Parental networks, ethnicity, and social and cultural capital: The societal dynamics of educational resilience in Turkey. *British Journal of Sociology of Education*, *38*(7), 1007–1021. doi:10.1080/01425692.2016.1218753

Comini, G., Barki, E., & de Aguiar, L. T. (2012). A three-pronged approach to social business: A Brazilian multi-case analysis. *Revista ADM*, *47*(3), 385–397.

Dees, J. G., & Anderson, B. B. (2006a). Framing a theory of social entrepreneurship: building on two schools of practice and thought. Research on social entrepreneurship, *ARNOVA Occasional Paper Series*, *1*(3), 39–66.

Dees, J. G., & Anderson, B. B. (2006b). Framing a theory of social entrepreneurship:Building on two schools of practice and thought. In J. Gregory (Ed.), Research on social entrepreneurship: Understanding and contributing to an emerging field (pp. 39–66). Academic Press.

Dees, J. G. (1998). The meaning of social entrepreneurship. Retrieved January 29, 2020, from http://www.fuqua.duke.edu/centers/case/documents/dees_SE.pdf.http://www.fuqua.duke.edu/centers/case/documents/dees_SE.pdf

Defourny, J., & Nyssens, M. (2010). Conceptions of social enterprise and social entrepreneurship in Europe and the United States: Convergences and divergences. *Journal of Social Entrepreneurship*, *1*(1), 32–53. doi:10.1080/19420670903442053

Defourny, J., & Nyssens, M. (2013). Social innovation, social economy and social enterprise: what can the European debate tell us? *The International Handbook on Social Innovation*, 40-53.

Doganova, L., & Eyquem-Renault, M. (2009). What do business models do?: Innovation devices in technology entrepreneurship. *Research Policy*, *38*(10), 1559–1570. doi:10.1016/j.respol.2009.08.002

Eğitim Reformu Girişimi. (2011). Eğitim İzleme Raporu 2010. Retrieved February 7, 2020, from http://erg.sabanciuniv.edu/sites/erg.sabanciuniv.edu/files/EIR2010_SON.pdf

Erikli, S. (2016). Genç yoksulluğunun temel belirleyicileri: Eğitim ve düzgün iş. *Gazi Universitesi Iktisadi ve Idari Bilimler Fakultesi Dergisi*, *18*(1), 283.

Hall, B. H. (2004). Innovation and diffusion (No. w10212). National Bureau of Economic Research.

Hall, J., Matos, S., Sheehan, L., & Silvestre, B. (2012). Entrepreneurship and innovation at the base of the pyramid: A recipe for inclusive growth or social exclusion? *Journal of Management Studies*, *49*(4), 785–812. doi:10.1111/j.1467-6486.2012.01044.x

Hall, J. K., Daneke, G. A., & Lenox, M. J. (2010). Sustainable development and entrepreneurship: Past contributions and future directions. *Journal of Business Venturing*, *25*(5), 439–448. doi:10.1016/j.jbusvent.2010.01.002

İşkur. 2019 Turkish Labour Market Research Report. Retrieved January 13, 2020 from https://media.iskur.gov.tr/34629/turkiye.pdf

Klasen, S. (2010). Measuring and monitoring inclusive growth: Multiple definitions, open questions, and some constructive proposals. *ADB Sustainable Development Working Paper Series*, No.12.

Kramer, M. R., & Porter, M. (2011). Creating shared value. *Harvard Business Review*, *89*(1/2), 62–77.

Kurnaz Baltaci, I. (2020). Genç İşsizliği ve Geleceğe Uzanan Zorlu İşgücü Piyasası Koşulları: Diyarbakır, Suriçi Bölgesi Örneği. *Amme Idaresi Dergisi*, *53*(1).

Marques, P., Morgan, K., & Richardson, R. (2018). Social innovation in question: The theoretical and practical implications of a contested concept. *Environment and Planning C. Politics and Space*, *36*(3), 496–512.

Mulgan, G. (2019). *Social Innovation: How societies find the power to change*. Bristol University Press. doi:10.2307/j.ctvs89dd3

Mulgan, G., Tucker, S., Ali, R., & Sanders, B. (2007). Social innovation: what it is, why it matters and how it can be accelerated. The Young Foundation. London: The Hasingstoke Press.

Mumford, M. D. (2002). Social innovation: Ten cases from Benjamin Franklin. *Creativity Research Journal*, *14*(2), 253–266. doi:10.1207/S15326934CRJ1402_11

Nielsen, C., & Samia, P. M. (2008). Understanding key factors in social enterprise development of the BOP: A systems approach applied to case studies in the Philippines. *Journal of Consumer Marketing*, *25*(7), 446–454. doi:10.1108/07363760810915662

OECD (1999). Social Enterprises, OECD Publishing:Paris. Retrieved January 08, 2020 from http://dx.doi.org/ doi:10.1787/9789264182332-en

Oeij, P. R., van der Torre, W., Vaas, F., & Dhondt, S. (2019). Understanding social innovation as an innovation process: Applying the innovation journey model. *Journal of Business Research, 101*, 243–254. doi:10.1016/j.jbusres.2019.04.028

Okolie, U. C., Igwe, P. A., Nwosu, H. E., Eneje, B. C., & Mlanga, S. (2020). Enhancing graduate employability: Why do higher education institutions have problems with teaching generic skills? *Policy Futures in Education, 18*(2), 294–313. doi:10.1177/1478210319864824

Osterwalder, A. (2004). *The business model ontology a proposition in a design science approach* (Unpublished doctoral dissertation). Université de Lausanne, Faculté des hautes études commerciales.

Partzsch, L., & Ziegler, R. (2011). Social entrepreneurs as change agents: A case study on power and authority in thewater sector. *International Environmental Agreement: Politics, Law and Economics, 11*(1), 63–83. doi:10.100710784-011-9150-1

Phills, J. A., Deiglmeier, K., & Miller, D. T. (2008). Rediscovering social innovation. *Stanford Social Innovation Review, 6*(4), 34–43.

Porter, M. E., & Kramer, M. R. (2019). Creating shared value. In Lenssen G.G. & Smith G.N. (Eds.) Managing sustainable business (pp. 323-346). Springer, Dordrecht. doi:10.1007/978-94-024-1144-7_16

Ranieri, R., & Almeida Ramos, R. (2013). *Inclusive growth: building up a concept* (No. 104). Working Paper, International Policy Centre for Inclusive Growth.

Rogers, E. (2003). *Diffusion of Innovations* (5th ed.). Free Press.

Schaltegger, S., Hansen, E. G., & Lüdeke-Freund, F. (2016). Business models for sustainability: Origins, present research, and future avenues. *Organization & Environment, 29*(1), 3–10. doi:10.1177/1086026615599806

Schumpeter, J. A. (1934). *The Theory of Economic Development* (3rd ed.). Oxford University Press.

Social Business Initiative. (2011). *Communication from the Commission: Social Business Initiative: Creating a favourable climate for social enterprises, key stakeholders in the social economy and innovation.* Retrieved January 17, 2020 from https://eurlex.europa.eu/LexUriServ/LexUriServ.do?uri=COM:2011:0682:FIN:EN:PDF

Stubbs, W., & Cocklin, C. (2008). Conceptualizing a "sustainability business model.". *Organization & Environment, 21*(2), 103–127. doi:10.1177/1086026608318042

Teece, D. J. (2010). Business models, business strategy and innovation. *Long Range Planning, 43*(2), 172–194. doi:10.1016/j.lrp.2009.07.003

Turkish Statistical Institute. Youth Statistics. (2019). http://tuik.gov.tr/HbPrint.do?id=33731

The Future is Brighter Platform. The Social Impact Reports. Retrieved from https://www.gelecekdaha.net

Turkish Statistical Institute. (2020). Retrieved February 15, 2020 from https://www.tuik.gov.tr/PreHaber-Bultenleri.do?id=33790

Tykkyläinen, S., & Ritala, P. (2020). Business model innovation in social enterprises: An activity system perspective. *Journal of Business Research.*

Vavik, T., & Keitsch, M. (2010). Exploring relationships between universal design and social sustainable development: Some methodological aspects to the debate on the sciences of sustainability. *Sustainable Development, 18*(5), 295–305. doi:10.1002d.480

Westley, F., & Antadze, N. (2010). Making a difference: Strategies for scaling social innovation for greater impact. *The Innovation Journal, 15*(2).

Yunus, M., Moingeon, B., & Lehmann-Ortega, L. (2010). Building social business models: Lessons from the Grameen experience. *Long Range Planning, 43*(2-3), 308–325. doi:10.1016/j.lrp.2009.12.005

KEY TERMS AND DEFINITIONS

Inclusive Growth: Growth that adopts the principle of equity and that covers the development of conditions of the disadvantaged. Growth without the neglected groups' development would be unhealthy and unsustainable.

Social Business Model: The business model that focuses on creating social welfare by developing solutions to social problems.

Social Entrepreneurship: The social entrepreneur is someone who develops innovative solutions to social problems with a motive for generating social impact.

Social Impact: Social impact is the consequences of activities, projects, programs, or policies that can create a change in the knowledge and behaviors of individuals, groups, or organizations.

Social Innovation: The social innovation is the developing new perspectives, new approaches, new solutions to social problems.

Chapter 13
Smart Specialization Based on the Concept of Creating Shared Value for the Development and Revitalization of an Entrepreneurial Ecosystem

Manuel Mendez Pinzon
Politecnico Grancolombiano, Colombia

Adela Velez Rolon
CESA, Colombia

Marcela Gomez Osorio
https://orcid.org/0000-0003-0464-2548
Independent Researcher, Colombia

ABSTRACT

This research aims to make a methodological and theoretical contribution to smart and sustainable regional development that includes the shared value approach and also aims to create innovative strategies that use a smart specialization strategy methodology to invigorate an entrepreneurial ecosystem. From a conceptual standpoint, the authors established the implementation guidelines for strategies to allow to resolving existing development problems in society and support regional entrepreneurial ecosystems as a way to help their sustainable growth and development. As a result of this research, they propose a smart specialization strategy that allows the development of shared value strategies that contribute to the implementation of procedures and practices that improve the conditions of traditionally excluded populations, while generating a positive economic and environmental impact on entrepreneurial ecosystems.

DOI: 10.4018/978-1-7998-4727-4.ch013

INTRODUCTION

Today's world faces more than ever great challenges and complex problems related to the environment and society, which are greatly pressured by globalization, technological changes, and new consumption patterns. In this sense, the understanding of these problems must be seen from a territorial approach.

Thus, strategies must be formulated in the territory that allows the resolution of these complex problems and at the same time allow the creation of a competitive advantage, based on the potentization of their capacities. The smart specialization strategy arises in response to the need to find a mechanism that allows territorial development based on the capacities and vocations of the same territory (Foray & Van Ark, 2007), according to this strategy, search and prioritization mechanisms for vocations should be described as the entrepreneurial discovery (Foray & Goenaga, 2013)

This discovery involves the creation of a competitive advantage based on research and experimentation processes of the different actors involved in the strategy. In this context, an entrepreneur must have the innovative capacity to design and implement models that generate social and environmental value. The literature describes these models from different perspectives; social business, environmental business, sustainable business, or social entrepreneurship (Elkington & Hartigan, 2008; Hahn, Spieth, & Ince, 2018; Yunus, 2010). This variety of views highlights the difficulty of finding a consensus regarding their understanding and the relationship with economic development, which in the literature has been associated with dependence on the context where these emerge (Sengupta, Sahay & Croce, 2018). Thus, territorial development is directly linked to the modes of entrepreneurship that arise.

Faced with this, Porter and Kramer (2011) propose a strategy that allows generating value, promoting innovation, and increasing competitiveness. Shared value, a concept that glimpses social needs, such as business opportunities for the company. The idea proposes to redefine the relationship already existing between capitalism and society. For the authors, companies that know how to take advantage of these opportunities for the creation of shared value will be successful organizations, insofar as they can establish and focus their efforts towards satisfying social needs, not only in product development but also in developing processes that allow them to be competitive. Therefore, the creation of shared value can influence regional development in the construction of strong local communities and social capital capable of generating value "(Lüth & Stierl, 2015)

Although the concept is linked to business development, it can be extrapolated to the territories understanding them as innovation systems, being the smart specialization strategy one of them. This research aims to contribute to two main bodies of knowledge, first to understand the capabilities of entrepreneurship or social business models in developing countries for the generation of shared value (Sinthupundaja, et, al. 2020) under the strategy of smart specialization and therefore another part, make an approximation. In this sense, this research aims to answer the following questions:

- How to generate an intelligent specialization strategy based on the concept of Shared Value for development that contributes to social entrepreneurship?
- How does the smart specialization strategy contribute to the development of a social entrepreneurship ecosystem?

There is an ever-growing awareness of significant societal challenges, and government and NGOs lack sufficient resources and capabilities to meet these challenges. Therefore, the imperative for entrepreneurship for sustainable development and innovative solutions is profound,

This chapter analyzes how an entrepreneurial ecosystem can be generated under the concept of the smart specialization strategy, starting with a preliminary research phase, a field phase for information gathering and analysis, and a bibliometric analysis of sources queried in the Scopus bibliographic database, then a model was generated ending with an analysis and discussion of the results obtained.

LITERATURE REVIEW

Research and Innovation Strategy for Smart Specialization and the Entrepreneurial Ecosystem

Regional Development is a concept associated with progress that includes a set of geographic, economic, social, and environmental elements that interact with each other, the literature reviewed shows different approaches to Regional Development. On the one hand, regional development is seen as a unit of analysis in methodological individualism, specialization, and economic growth; on the other, cooperation, competitiveness, innovation, and development considers it from an interdisciplinary perspective that includes economic, social, and environmental elements. (CEPAL. 2001; Fernández-Satto, Alfaro-Re & Davies-Vidal, 2009; Manet, 2014; Moncayo, 2003)

Territorial development can be understood from the vocation of the territory, in which two important elements are innovation and alliances. Smart Specialization (SS) grew from this context, in which specialization must be seen as an agenda for territorial development and economic growth (Foray et al. 2012). The following elements are important for its fulfillment: the knowledge of territorial needs, the focus of policy and investment to solve these needs, and the understanding of competitive advantage as a factor of competitiveness, alliances, and innovation.

The scientific research around Smart Specialization, "Guide on Research and Innovation Strategies for Smart Specialization" (RIS3), Stems from the Europe 2020 strategy, which seeks to promote smart, sustainable, and inclusive growth based on research and innovation and through the creation of competitive advantages, for the regions and economies of the EU in the period 2014-2020. (Mccann & Ortega-Argilés, 2013; Glińska & Kononiuk, 2013; Foray et al., 2012. Glińska & Kononiuk, 2013, Paliokaitė, Martinaitis & Reimeris, 2015, Kamrowska & Soltys, 2016).

The difference between traditional industrial policies and SS lies in the notion of entrepreneurial discovery, a process of discovering emerging and promising routes based on existing agents, competencies, and activities in the region (Marinelli and Perianez Forte, 2017).

The entrepreneurial discovery highlights what a country or region does or will do best in R+D and innovation (RDI). In "business" terms, it identifies priorities; entrepreneurs discover new activities through an interactive process in which the private sector produces and discovers information about new activities, and the government considers empowering the actors capable of realizing their potential (Rodrik, 2004 in Foray, 2017). Entrepreneurs are in the best position to discover the areas of R+D and innovation in which a region is likely to excel, considering its capabilities and production assets. In terms of "discovery," the author clearly states the importance of distinguishing between innovation and discovery and stresses that the innovations that matter and should be supported and identified are not those undertaken by individual companies. Policy should focus on activities that seek to explore, experiment, and learn about what needs to be done about R+D and innovation in the future of a sector or between different sectors.

Some of the common challenges to implementing the Entrepreneurial Discovery Process (EDP) within the SS framework are, aligning the activities of universities, maintaining, and stimulating the interest of companies, and integrating civil society in the process. In this context, clusters can play a crucial role as they are areas of specialization in the region and can provide the basis for the new development of routes. While clusters have regional limits, SS transcends regional limits, seeks general competitiveness, and its goal is the regional transformation of the economy. In terms of participation, data indicates that EDP is primarily a triple helix business model.

The discussion about clusters, value chains, and innovation frames shared value as the strategy that business ventures can apply in the territory to promote Smart Specialization.

Shared Value Creation and the Entrepreneurial Ecosystem

The economic transformations of globalization processes and their pressures on the environment and society show the need to find new forms of business development that allow the generation of value companies while also facing these challenges. As a response, the concept of shared value has boomed in recent years.

The concept of creating shared value was developed by Porter, M; Kramer, M, in 2011. Theoretically, generating shared value is explained as the generation of social and environmental value in organizations, and its final goal is the reinvention of capitalism and the inclusion of innovation in business value generation. Shared value is achieved through three strategies: reconceiving products and markets, by redefining productivity in the value chain, and by enabling local cluster development.

Despite being a recent theory, the topic of shared value has been debated by several authors (Rangan, 2015; Pfitzer, Bockstette, and Stamp, 2013; Bertini and Gourville, 2012; Pavlovich and Corner, 2013; Michelini & Fiorentino, 2012; Kramer and Pfitzer, 2016; Pongwiritthon, 2015; Naipinit, Kojchavivong, Kowittayakorn and Sakolnakorn, 2014; Bowe and van der Horst, 2015; Trevena, Kaldor and Downs, 2014; Xing, 2015, Crane et al., 2014, Jones & Wright, 2018). However, there is no single approach to its definition.

A very clear trend is the use of the triple bottom line (TBL). In terms of Sustainability, this proven approach enables awareness of the fundamental dimensions, social, economic, and environmental. However, TBL is not focused on measuring value creation, which represents a challenge in influencing strategic decision-making processes within companies.

Understanding the territory from the standpoint of betting on value generation requires the implementation of innovation systems and the development of an entrepreneurial ecosystem that includes the entire population. In this regard, this section intends to present an analysis of existing literature on how the creation of shared value drives the entrepreneurial ecosystem in a territory.

Dembek, Singh & Bhakoo (2016) describpoe some concepts associated with the concept of shared value as defined by several authors; not only from theoretical and application consensus, but also from corporate social responsibility (CSR), combined value, corporate citizenship, social technology, interest group theory, social innovation, social entrepreneurship, and the base of the pyramid (BoP).

Alternatively, the creation of shared value can also be interpreted from the classification of social business models proposed by Elkington & Hartigan (2008): non-profit companies, hybrid companies, and social companies.

There are several definitions for companies that generate value as part of their business, beyond the three dimensions proposed by Porter & Kramer (2011), which are by reconceiving products and markets, by redefining productivity in the value chain, and by allowing the development of local clusters. Regardless of how they are defined, that definition needs to be approached from the incorporation of social or environmental needs in their value proposition.

In this regard, Pfitzer, Bockstette, and Stamp (2013) determined elements that companies should incorporate if they want to implement shared value in their business core:

1. Embedding a social purpose, which "entails embedding a social mission in the corporate culture and channeling resources to the development of innovations that can help solve social problems."
2. Define the social need, because "If a company doesn't devote time and resources to developing a deep understanding of a social problem, it risks pursuing ineffective solutions."
3. Measuring shared value, through estimating the business and social value, establishing intermediate measures, and tracking progress, and assessing the shared value produced.
4. Creating the optimal innovation structure. The options for structuring initiatives include: the integration with a legacy business, creating a semi-autonomous unit, obtaining philanthropic or government support, and financing external entrepreneurs.
5. Co-creating with external stakeholders, where it can generate practices such as enlisting a wide range of stakeholders and leveraging others' capabilities (p. 4 - 9.)

While these five steps can be used to understand individual entrepreneurship, from the perspective of Smart Specialization, it becomes necessary to understand how the ecosystem can be potentialized toward generating social and environmental value.

One of the Smart Specialization principles is related to entrepreneurship, and it describes how entrepreneurial opportunities are potentiated from the identification of territorial vocations, which is clearly related to a successful innovation system (Foray, David & Hall, 2011, Foray & Goenaga, 2013, McCann and Ortega-Argilés 2011.)

Hausmann & Rodrik (2003) raise the matter that open economies show a general imbalance that consists of having is too little investment and entrepreneurship ex-ante, and too much production diversification ex-post. Facing this requires understanding not only the territorial vocation but also the social and environmental problems that must be solved in the territory.

METHODOLOGY

The methodology used in this research was developed in the following phases: a preliminary research phase, a field phase for information gathering and analysis, and a bibliometric analysis of sources queried in the Scopus bibliographic database, using the following search criteria.

((TITLE-ABS-KEY ("Smart Specialization") OR TITLE-ABS-KEY ("shared value") AND TITLE-ABS-KEY (entrepreneurship) OR TITLE-ABS-KEY ("business model")) AND (LIMIT-TO (PUBYEAR, 2020) OR LIMIT-TO (PUBYEAR, 2019) OR LIMIT-TO (PUBYEAR, 2018) OR LIMIT-TO (PUBYEAR, 2017) OR LIMIT-TO (PUBYEAR, 2016))

In this research, we sought to apply bibliometric analysis as a method to illustrate and identify key elements for the development of the proposal, using the following steps:

- Definition of the central topic under study.
- Database selection.
- Adjustment of research criteria.
- Full export of the material found.
- Processing and analysis of the data obtained.

For the processing and analysis of the data, we used Rstudio, using the Bibliometrix package, developed by M. Aria and C. Cuccurullo (2017). Official information sources were also consulted and then finished with the information analysis phase.

RESULTS

The literature review identifies three major issues that must be considered

- Regional economic development
- A sustainability-based strategy.
- Business models.

Regional Economic Development

Studies focused on regional development concentrate their interest in understanding the relationship between entrepreneurship, knowledge-based systems, innovation, and economic growth. These studies highlight the role of the industry in the development of programs focused on corporate social responsibility and aligned with the business strategy and their economic activity.(Grillitsch et al., 2018; Spieth et al., 2019) the mechanisms to achieve regional development are research and the development of alliances, especially with higher education (Kangas& Aarrevaara, 2020.)

The literature also shows the relevance of the relationship between generating social and environmental value and business strategy and its role in competitiveness. However, there is a vacuum concerning this concept and the construction and implementation of public policies that allow this type of initiative to have an effective impact on regional development (clusters.)

Some sectors appear as global trends: aerospace, lithium, electricity, education, and are shown as major global trends, A European trend stands out. However, its weight is not as great as the associated concepts, which demonstrates that the Smart Specialization strategy transcends borders due to the universality of its associated concepts, rather than being limited to its place of origin.

New Business Models as Drivers of Competitiveness

In the literature, the generation of social and environmental value is defined from the perspective of Sustainability and sustainable business models, and how they enhance competitiveness; this means that the Smart Specialization strategy bets on business models that, in their value proposition, seek to solve social and environmental problems. Issues such as information management and the use of social networks also become relevant in this context (De los Reyes, 2019; Uyarra et al., 2019)

Figure 1. Thematic cluster
Source: Bibliometrix (2020)

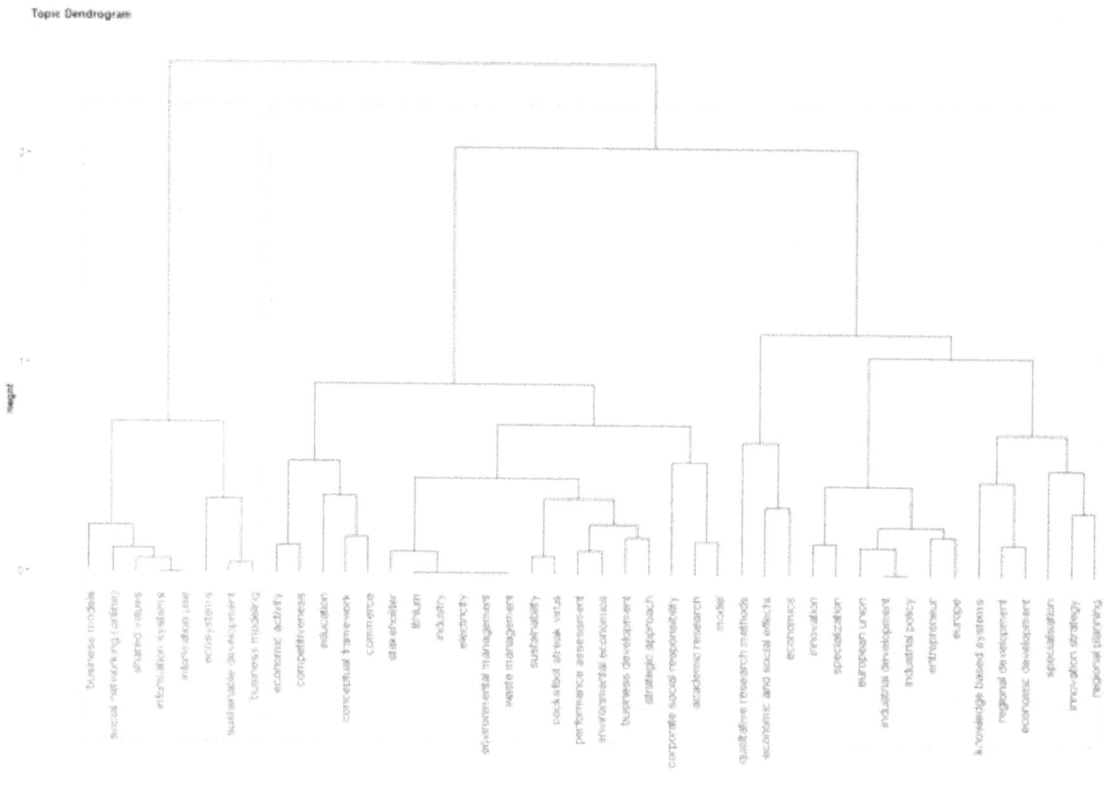

Figure 2. Relevant concepts
Source: Bibliometrix (2020)

However, while "shared value" appears in the search results, "sustainable development" does not, making it evident that the discourse on this topic needs to steer toward concepts more related to entrepreneurship and production instead of only being environmentally focused.

The following chart shows how all the writings stem from or share three key concepts: innovation, Sustainability, and shared value. It is particularly noteworthy that shared value is positioned so strongly as a fundamental concept for the development of Smart Specialization strategies.

The reason for this positioning might be that a Smart Specialization strategy requires a connecting bridge to mediate between productive interests and society to achieve a mutually beneficial relationship effectively, and shared value is this bridge.

Figure 3. Relevance of associated concepts
Source: Bibliometrix (2020

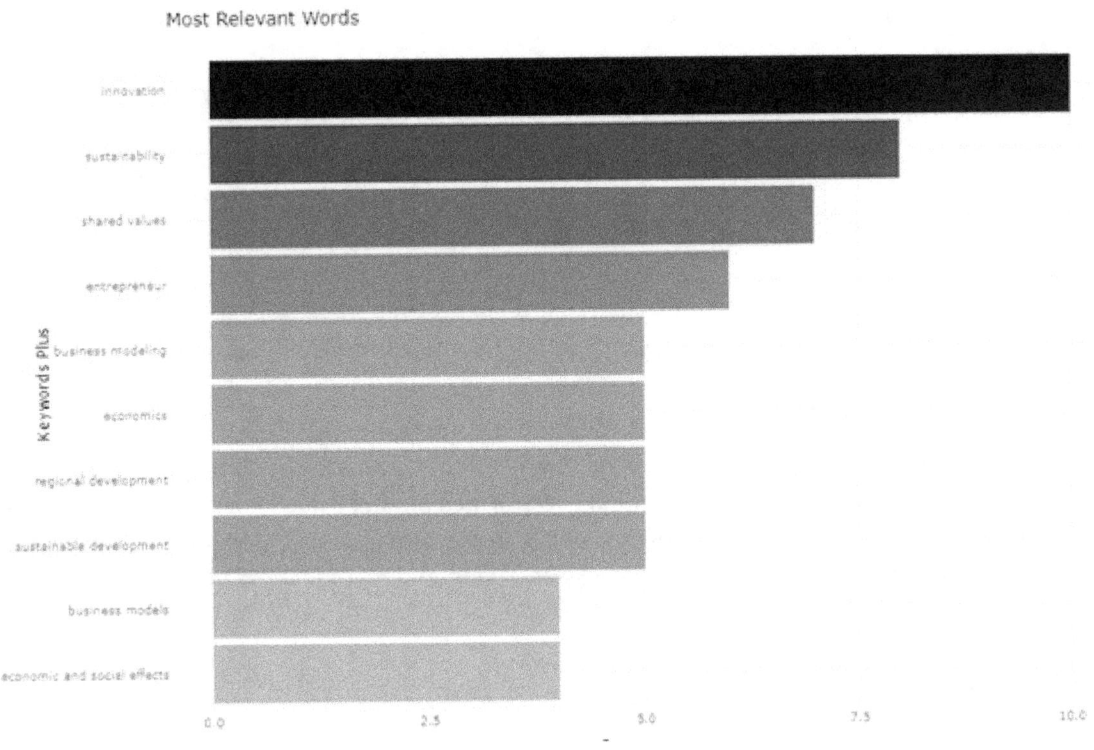

The preceding figure introduces a topic that was not shown in the previous ones, the "economic and social effects" of the implementation of the strategy. Firstly, this shows that the economic and social effects are a concern. Secondly, this might be that, as time has elapsed since the beginning of implementing Smart Specialization in some European regions, results are already showing its evolution.

Figure 4. Growth of concepts
Source: Bibliometrix (2020)

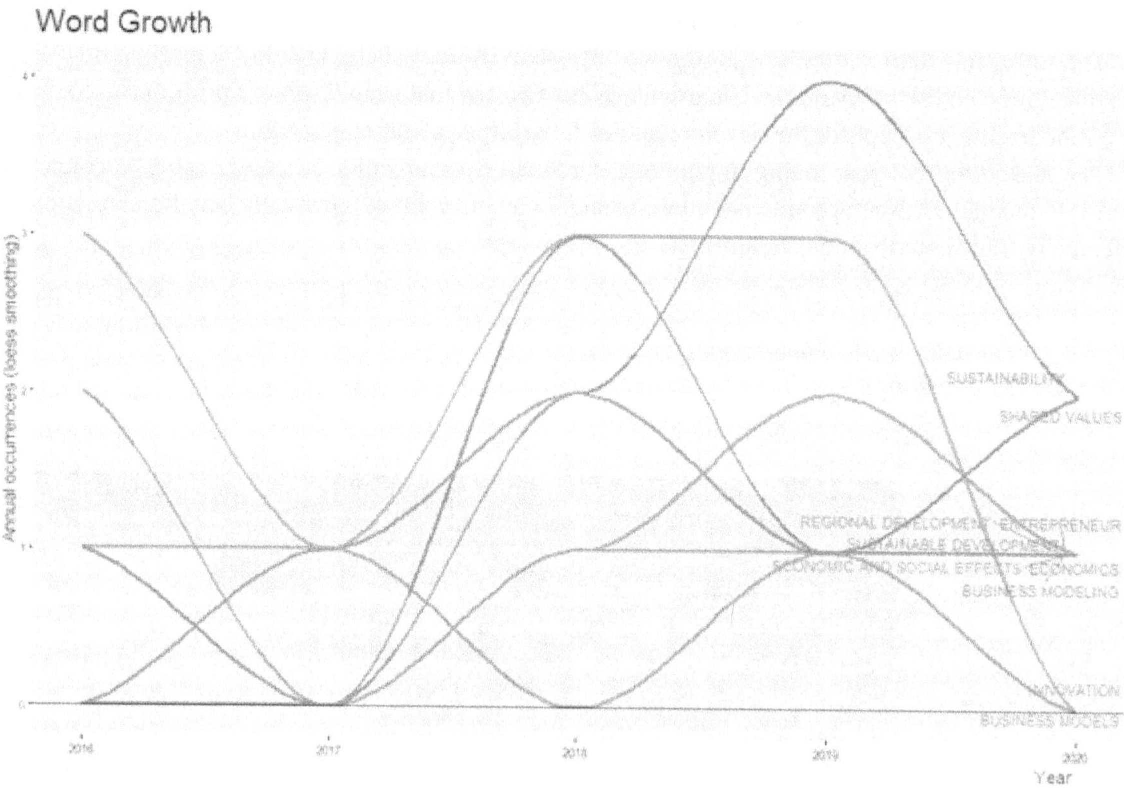

Figure 4 shows clearly that, while shared value was initially not included as a relevant concept, it is becoming increasingly a trend in the conception of SS, which might be due to the equally growing trend of considering the social and economic effects of the implementation of the SS, as the three concepts of shared value are clearly related.

PRACTICAL IMPLICATIONS

From the results obtained, the following scheme is proposed to include in the Smart Specialization Methodology to generate Shared Value and promote the entrepreneurial ecosystem of the city.

1. **Characterization of the productive vocation** and the inclusion of shared value generation from local development and the promotion of Sustainable Development Goals (SDGs), using the Smart Specialization Strategy for the Generation of Shared Value.
2. Implementation of a Smart Specialization Strategy:
    a. **Planning and governance model:** Define the advisory committee, steering committee, map of stakeholders, and interactions. Characterization of the productive vocation, map of stakeholders, and contact with local governments.

   b. **Analysis of the regional context and the entrepreneurial ecosystem:** Diagnosis of existing programs, analysis of documentation, government plans, figures and statistics of the department and municipalities, central challenges of the territory in boosting the economy, generating employment and income, general characterization of the population, description of the stakeholders in the territory, identification of clusters and/or macro sectors.
   c. **Identification of challenges and alignment of vocations:** Analysis of the main economic activities.
   d. **Identification and prioritization of areas of specialization:** Definition of competitive strengths and advantages in the region, potential and innovation, scientific, economic, and technological capabilities, relevant stakeholders.
   e. **Identification of opportunities and niches of specialization:** Identification of segments within the areas of specialization, which are comprised of productive activities and any gaps identified that constitute opportunities to develop shared value strategies.
   f. **Validation of specialization niches and identification of projects:** Identification of alternatives with potential to generate income, employment, and qualification to select the most important ones. Socialization of results, validation of programs, and strategies for food security in the regions, socialization, and validation. Validation of areas of specialization and productive vocation niches.
   g. **Definition of the portfolio of projects and socialization of the strategy:** Consolidation of a portfolio of shared value projects (project idea, identification of needs, resources, and stakeholders for its execution.) Identification of needs within the framework of Shared Value strategies and SDGs.
3. **Design and dissemination of public policy guidelines** under the Shared Value scheme for the development of the territories and government plans.

DISCUSSION AND CONCLUSIONS

This research explored the relationship between the implementation of the Smart Specialization Strategy and the entrepreneurial ecosystem, from the perspective of creating shared value. In this sense, the creation of shared value must be understood as a conditioning factor for regional development.

The literature review carried out as the first step to develop a model that allows integrating the three proposed elements shows that:

1. The literature presents gaps regarding the role of social innovation in this area (Hassink & Gong,2019)
2. To include the generation of shared value from local development, the implementation of the Smart Specialization strategy requires characterizing the productive vocation and target population. According to Veldhuizen (2020) this also requires understanding the social and environmental challenges of the region.
3. Cluster development should be understood as the strategy that allows the territory to be integrated into the generation of social and environmental value, which coincides with the postulates of Porter y Kramer (2011)

Figure 5.
Source: Own elaboration.

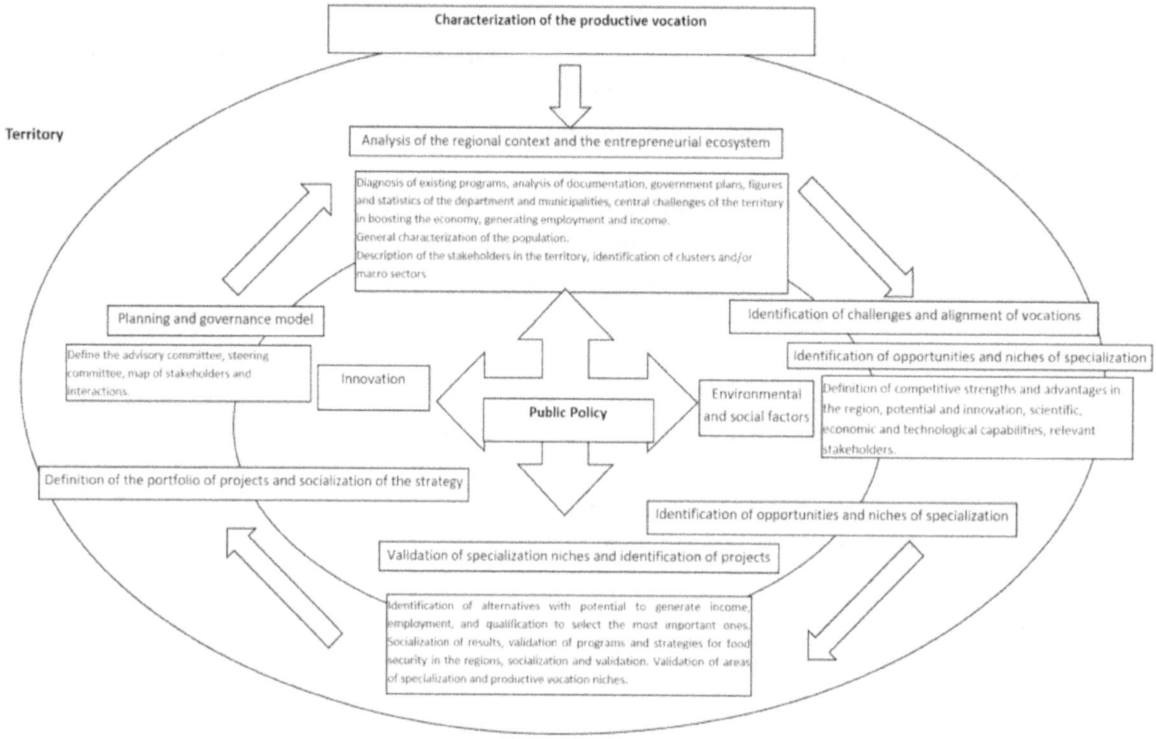

In this way, strategies to generate shared value can contribute to the development of practices and procedures that improve the conditions of traditionally excluded populations, while generating positive economic and environmental impacts in the territories.

This must be understood from a public policy framework under the Shared Value scheme aimed at the development of the territories and government plans.

The Smart Specialization Strategy methodology allows the characterization of the productive vocation of the territories, generating local development and the promotion of SDGs, enabling the invigoration of socio-economic development that creates an entrepreneurial ecosystem.

For the application of this model, it is important to develop activities with all the possible participants or stakeholders, to implement tools that accompany their action.

REFERENCES

Aria, M., & Cuccurullo, C. (2017). Bibliometrix: An R-tool for comprehensive science mapping analysis. *Journal of Informetrics*, *11*(4), 959–975. doi:10.1016/j.joi.2017.08.007

Bertini, M., & Gourville, J. T. (2012). *Pricing to create shared value*. Academic Press.

Bowe, C., & van der Horst, D. (2015). Positive externalities, knowledge exchange and corporate farm extension services; a case study on creating shared value in a water scarce area. *Ecosystem Services, 15*, 1–10. doi:10.1016/j.ecoser.2015.05.009

CEPAL. (2001). *Evolución de los paradigmas y modelos interpretativos del desarrollo territorial. Serie Gestión Pública 13*. Santiago de Chile, Instituto Latinoamericano y del Caribe de Planificación Económica y Social.

Crane, A., Palazzo, G., Spence, L. J., & Matten, D. (2014). Contesting the value of "creating shared value." *California Management Review, 56*(2), 130–153. doi:10.1525/cmr.2014.56.2.130

de los Reyes, G. Jr, & Scholz, M. (2019). The limits of the business case for sustainability: Don't count on 'Creating Shared Value' to extinguish corporate destruction. *Journal of Cleaner Production, 221*, 785–794. doi:10.1016/j.jclepro.2019.02.187

Dembek, K., Singh, P., & Bhakoo, V. (2016). Literature review of shared value: A theoretical concept or a management buzzword? *Journal of Business Ethics, 137*(2), 231–267. doi:10.100710551-015-2554-z

Elkington, J., & Hartigan, P. (2008). *The power of unreasonable people: How social entrepreneurs create markets that change the world*. Harvard Business Press.

Fernández-Satto, V., Alfaro-re, M., & Davies-Vidal, C. (2009). Aglomeraciones productivas y territorio: En busca de una manera más holística de entender sus contribuciones al desarrollo. *Economía, Sociedad y Territorio*, (septiembre-diciembre), 629–680. doi:10.22136/est002009164

Foray, D. (2012). *Guide to Research and Innovation Strategies for Smart Specialisation (RIS 3)*. DG Regional Policy.

Foray, D. (2017). The economic fundamentals of smart specialization strategies. In *Advances in the theory and practice of smart specialization* (pp. 37–50). Academic Press. doi:10.1016/B978-0-12-804137-6.00002-4

Foray, D., David, P. A., & Hall, B. H. (2011). *Smart specialisation from academic idea to political instrument, the surprising career of a concept and the difficulties involved in its implementation (No. REP_WORK)*. EPFL.

Foray, D., & Goenaga, X. (2013). *The goals of smart specialization*. European Commission: JRC Scientific and Policy Report, S3 Policy Brief Series No. 01/2013.

Foray, D., & Van Ark, B. (2007). Smart specialisation in a truly integrated research area is the key to attracting more R&D to Europe. *Knowledge Economists Policy Brief, 1*, 1-4.

Glińska, E & Kononiuk, A. (2013). *The concept of regional strategy of Smart Specialization*. Prace naukowe uniwersytetu ekonomicznego we wrocławiu research papers of wrocław university of economics.

Grillitsch, M., Asheim, B., & Trippl, M. (2018). Unrelated knowledge combinations: The unexplored potential for regional industrial path development. *Cambridge Journal of Regions, Economy and Society, 11*(2), 257–274. doi:10.1093/cjres/rsy012

Grillitsch, M., Asheim, B., & Trippl, M. (2018). Unrelated knowledge combinations: The unexplored potential for regional industrial path development. *Cambridge Journal of Regions, Economy and Society, 11*(2), 257–274. doi:10.1093/cjres/rsy012

Hahn, R., Spieth, P., & Ince, I. (2018). Business model design in sustainable entrepreneurship: Illuminating the commercial logic of hybrid businesses. *Journal of Cleaner Production, 176*, 439–451. doi:10.1016/j.jclepro.2017.12.167

Hassink, R., & Gong, H. (2019). Six critical questions about Smart Specialization. *European Planning Studies, 27*(10), 2049–2065. doi:10.1080/09654313.2019.1650898

Hausmann, R., & Rodrik, D. (2003). Economic development as self-discovery. *Journal of Development Economics, 72*(2), 603–633. doi:10.1016/S0304-3878(03)00124-X

Jones, S., & Wright, C. (2018). Fashion or future: Does creating shared value pay? *Accounting and Finance, 58*(4), 1111–1139. doi:10.1111/acfi.12243

Kamrowska, D., & Soltys, J. (2016). Process of Emergence of Smart Specialisation in Pomeranian Voivodeship in Poland. *World Multidisciplinary Civil Engineering-Architecture-Urban Planning Symposium 2016, WMCAUS 2016*. 10.1016/j.proeng.2016.08.791

Kangas, R., & Aarrevaara, T. (2020). Higher Education Institutions as Knowledge Brokers in Smart Specialisation. *Sustainability, 12*(7), 3044. doi:10.3390u12073044

Kramer, M. R., & Pfitzer, M. W. (2016). The ecosystem of shared value. *Harvard Business Review, 94*(10), 80–89.

Lüth, A., & Stierl, M. (2015). Creating Shared Value by Fostering Regional Development: The 'Partners in Responsibility 'Method for SME. *Global Policy, 6*(4), 507–509. doi:10.1111/1758-5899.12238

Manet, L. (2014). Modelos de desarrollo regional: teorías y factores determinantes. Nóesis. *Revista de Ciencias Sociales y Humanidades*, 18-56.

Marinelli, E., & Perianez Forte, I. (2017). *Smart specialisation at work: The entrepreneurial Discovery as a continuous process*. S3 Working paper Series NO. 12/2017, Sevilla: European Commission Joint Research Centre.

McCann, P., & Ortega-Argilés, R. (2011). *Smart Specialisation, regional growth and applications to EU Cohesion Policy*. Economic Geography Working Paper. University of Groningen. http://i3s.ec.europa.eu/commitment/30/download/5250.html;i3sid=Q116Tz8hQ

Michelini, L., & Fiorentino, D. (2012). *Nuevos modelos de negocio para crear valor compartido*. Revista de Responsabilidad Social.

Moncayo, É. (2003). Nuevas teorías y enfoques conceptuales sobre el desarrollo regional: ¿hacia un nuevo paradigma? *Revista de Economía Institucional*, 32-65.

Naipinit, T., Kojchavivong, S., Kowittayakorn, V., & Sakolnakorn, T. P. N. (2014). McKinsey 7S model for supply chain management of local SMEs construction business in the upper northeast region of Thailand. *Asian Social Science, 10*(8), 35. doi:10.5539/ass.v10n8p35

Paliokaitė, A., Martinaitis, Z., & Reimeris, R. (2015). Foresight methods for smart specialisation strategy development in Lithuania. Disponible en. *Technological Forecasting and Social Change*, *101*, 185–199. doi:10.1016/j.techfore.2015.04.008

Pavlovich, K., & Corner, P. D. (2014). Conscious enterprise emergence: Shared value creation through expanded conscious awareness. *Journal of Business Ethics*, *121*(3), 341–351. doi:10.100710551-013-1726-y

Pfitzer, M., Bockstette, V., & Stamp, M. (2013). Innovating for shared value. *Harvard Business Review*, *91*(9), 100–107.

Pongwiritthon, R. (2015). Creating shared value of Thai SMEs for competitive advantage. *International Journal of Applied Business and Economic Research*, *13*(5), 3109–3120. www.scopus.com

Poponi, S., Arcese, G., Mosconi, E. M., & Arezzo di Trifiletti, M. (2020). Entrepreneurial drivers for the development of the circular business model: The role of academic spin-Off. *Sustainability*, *12*(1), 423. doi:10.3390u12010423

Porter, M. E., & Kramer, M. R. (2011). *La creación de Valor Compartido*. Harvard Bussines Review.

Rangan, K., Chase, L., & Karim, S. (2015). The truth about CSR. *Harvard Business Review*, *93*(1/2), 40–49.

Reinhardt, G. Y., & Ross, A. D. (2019). Expanding Social Science Through Disaster Studies. *Social Science Quarterly*, *100*(7), 2523–2529. doi:10.1111squ.12668

Rodrik, D. (2004). *Industrial policy for the twenty-first century*. Academic Press.

Sengupta, S., Sahay, A., & Croce, F. (2018). Conceptualizing social entrepreneurship in the context of emerging economies: An integrative review of past research from BRIICS. *The International Entrepreneurship and Management Journal*, *14*(4), 771–803. doi:10.100711365-017-0483-2

Sinthupundaja, J., Kohda, Y., & Chiadamrong, N. (2020). Examining capabilities of social entrepreneurship for shared value creation. *Journal of Social Entrepreneurship*, *11*(1), 1–22. doi:10.1080/19420676.2018.1543726

Spieth, P., Schneider, S., Clauß, T., & Eichenberg, D. (2019). Value drivers of social businesses: A business model perspective. *Long Range Planning*, *52*(3), 427–444. doi:10.1016/j.lrp.2018.04.004

Trevena, H., Kaldor, J. C., & Downs, S. M. (2015). 'Sustainability does not quite get the attention it deserves': Synergies and tensions in the sustainability frames of Australian food policy actors. *Public Health Nutrition*, *18*(13), 2323–2332. doi:10.1017/S136898001400295X PMID:25543824

Uyarra, E., Ribeiro, B., & Dale-Clough, L. (2019). Exploring the normative turn in regional innovation policy: Responsibility and the quest for public value. *European Planning Studies*, *27*(12), 2359–2375. doi:10.1080/09654313.2019.1609425

Veldhuizen, C. (2020). Smart Specialisation as a transition management framework: Driving sustainability-focused regional innovation policy? *Research Policy*, *49*(6), 103982. doi:10.1016/j.respol.2020.103982

Xing, M. (2015). *The impact of a strong local supply chain on regional economic impacts of mining*. Academic Press.

Yunus, M., Moingeon, B., & Lehmann-Ortega, L. (2010). Building social business models: Lessons from the Grameen experience. *Long Range Planning*, *43*(2-3), 308–325. doi:10.1016/j.lrp.2009.12.005

Chapter 14
The Role of Social Entrepreneurship in Women's Empowerment:
Case of Cöp(m)adam

Duygu Acar Erdur
Beykent University, Turkey

ABSTRACT

This chapter discusses the role of social entrepreneurship in one of the long-lasting challenges of all cultures, women's empowerment. Empowering women is critical for development, and more importantly, it's a human rights issue. However, especially in developing country contexts, governments, international and non-governmental organizations may fall short to address the issue effectively. In this respect, social entrepreneurship may be an alternative to offer inclusive solutions. This chapter aims to generate a deeper understanding of how social entrepreneurship creates social value about women's empowerment. Following the qualitative methodology, a successful entrepreneurial initiative in Turkey, Çöp(m)adam is examined. Findings demonstrate that Çöp(m)adam contributes to both women's economic and psychological empowerment.

INTRODUCTION

During the last decades, social, economic, and environmental dimensions of sustainable development of countries have come to the top of agendas across the world. In this respect, women's empowerment and gender equality is a sine qua non for sustainable development. Also as a human rights issue, women's empowerment is accepted both as a precondition for and indicator of sustainable development (Warth & Koparanova, 2012). Women both are affected by the implications of development and contribute to sustainable development. Thus, women's empowerment requires an enabling and supportive environment where all obstacles are removed and women are more involved in economic, political, and social spheres of life. In fact, lack of women's empowerment leads to unfair conditions for women, in turn, prevents

DOI: 10.4018/978-1-7998-4727-4.ch014

the whole society to realize its full potential. However, women across the World, still face challenges to access critical resources to gain economic, psychological and political empowerment. Although, governments, non-governmental organizations, women associations, etc. take various attempts, there are still major difficulties in eliminating gender inequality and empowering women in the social, economic, and political spheres.

In such a context, social entrepreneurs are emerging as significant actors generating solutions for such unmet problems. As an increasingly growing area of interest, social entrepreneurship is accepted as catalyze of social transformation through alleviating social problems such as poverty, education, environmental pollution (Alvord et al., 2004). By using innovative business approaches and combining resources creatively, social entrepreneurs address long-lasting problems and may alter existing social structures. In this respect, social entrepreneurship is particularly important for developing countries to fight against various problems considering their limited budgets and structural inadequacies. Yet, comparing to developed country contexts (e.g. United-States, UK) little is known about the social entrepreneurial activities in emerging and developing economies.

From this point of view, the purpose of this chapter is to add to the emerging literature on social entrepreneurship by focusing on a developing country, Turkey, in which social entrepreneurship has started to develop but still remains an understudied context. Chapter aims to reveal how social entrepreneurship generates a solution for a long lasting problem of the country, women empowerment. As a matter of fact, in developing countries, gender inequality is highly widespread and gender-based discrimination is apparent. Turkey has also some significant problems in gender equality and women empowerment (Arat, 2010; Dedeoğlu, 2012). Government's NGOs', and businesses' attempts may fall short to reach every corner and address all women's needs. In this vein, this chapter provides a deeper understanding of how social entrepreneurship can support women's empowerment based on the case of Çöp(m)adam which provides income for local women who are often ignored.

After the introduction, the chapter continues with a brief explanation on women's empowerment concept. Following that, based on the related literature, the role of social entrepreneurship in creating solutions to social problems is discussed. Accordingly, the case of Çöp(m)adam is presented. First, in order to reveal the innovative business approach, its business model is explained. Then, based on the interview data, which is gathered from primary and secondary data sources, the role of Çöp(m)adam in supporting women's economic and psychological empowerment is revealed.

WOMEN'S EMPOWERMENT

Status of women and gender inequality continue to be one of the long-lasting problems in all countries. In this respect, women's empowerment is critical for women as well as men and the whole society, in order to improve the quality of life, create stronger economies, and achieve development and sustainability goals. Economically empowered women are also one of the building blocks of the development of a nation. The empowerment concept is one of the major concerns in addressing the issue of human rights and development (Tripathi, 2011). There are various definitions of empowerment that tackle different aspects of the phenomenon. Although the conceptualizations vary, most of the definitions stress gaining control and power (Batliwala, 1997). In this perspective, power emphasizes the ability to make choices which necessarily implies the possibility of alternatives (Kabeer, 1999:437). Thus, empowerment is defined as "a multi-dimensional social process which helps people gain control over their own lives" (Page & Czuba, 1999). The concept refers to the processes by which those who have been denied the ability to make choices acquire that ability, and therefore it entails change (Kabeer, 2005:13). In other words, it is about changing power relations in favor of those who previously exercised little or no power over their own lives which is identified as disempowerment (Batliwala, 1997:2). Empowerment means acquiring the power to act freely, exercises choice and fulfil one's own potential as a full and equal member of society. Thus, it is very essential for the development of society. Due to the connection between empowerment and development and with the help of the United Nations Millennium Declaration that signed in 2000, the goal of promoting gender equality and women's empowerment has become one of the significant topics of this era.

Women's empowerment can be defined as the process of women taking control and ownership of their lives. It is defined by Kabeer (1999, 2002) as the process by which women who have been denied the ability to make strategic life choices acquire such an ability. Kabeer (1999) define, strategic life choices as the ability to decide where to live, whether and whom to marry, whether to have children, how many children to have etc. In her influential work about the conceptualization of the ability to exercise choice, Kabeer (2005:14) identifies three interrelated dimensions: *agency*, which is central to the concept of empowerment representing the processes by which choices are made and put into effect; *resources*, as the medium through which agency is exercised; *achievements* as the outcomes of agency. While Kabeer (1999, 2001) defines women's empowerment at the individual level and describes it as a process which women gain capacity for exercising strategic forms of agency in relation to their own lives and also to the larger structures of constraint that positioned them as subordinate to men in her early works, the later versions of her definition emphasize more collective forms of agency and points out a sustained structural change. For instance, she points out "the ability of women to participate on equal terms with men in reshaping the societies in which they live in ways that contribute to a more just and democratic distribution of power and possibilities" (Kabeer, 2008: 27).

Accordingly, empowerment is accepted to be possible and sustainable if there are changes at these three levels; changes in the capability and self-esteem of women at the individual level, changes in societal norms at the community level, and political and legal changes in broader levels (Golla et al. 2011). Thus, empowerment is understood as a process of change. Indeed, drawing mainly from the human rights and feminist perspectives, women's empowerment is discussed in terms of gender inequality and of course need of a fundamental transformation in perceptions is emphasized that will challenge the restrictive cultural and social norms which sustain inequity (Cornwall, 2016:345). For instance, Batliwala (1993:31) emphasizes that changing women's self-image which is shaped as weak, inferior and limited beings will enable them to challenge existing power equations in family, in their community and in the society.

Economic independence of women takes an important place in terms of empowerment. Women's economic empowerment refers to the ability of women to control and benefit from the resources, assets, income and their own time, and improve their economic status and well-being (Malhotora et al., 2002). Economic empowerment increases women's agency, mobility, economic independence, and purchasing power (Kabeer, 2011). At the household level, women's economic empowerment ensures control over income, contribution to family support, access to and control of family, resources. At the community level it refers to access to credit, ownership of assets and land, involvement in trade etc. In a broader level, women's economic empowerment refers to the pay structures, job positions, and macro-economic policies (Malhotora, et al., 2002: 13). Employment status can also be related to women's empowerment.

Various scholars emphasize the positive relationship between employment and women's empowerment. For instance, Moghadam (1996) argues that women's participation to the workforce enables them to become independent and to contribute to social development beyond their household duties. Similarly, Cindoğlu and Toktaş (2002, p. 44) also reveal that working women have better bargaining position in their families and so their lives. However, Kabeer(2005:14) asters that providing objective resources such as education or employment support the empowerment but also it may result in a disregard of broader power inequalities and not necessarily mean that a woman would feel herself empowered. Although, economic empowerment is an end in itself, it is a means to other development goals and intertwined with other dimensions of empowerment. For instance, Oladipo (2009:126) asserts that the attainment of economic empowerment depends strongly on the extent to which people are psychologically feel that and highlights the importance of psychological empowerment in the empowerment process.

Empowerment concept was first defined from a psychological perspective by Conger and Kanungo(1988) as enabling or enhancing personal efficacy. From a psychological perspective, one of the primary psychological states fundamental to the experience of empowerment is accepted to be the sense of perceived control over one's environment and others. (Thomas & Velthouse, 1990). This conceptualization reflects the definition of personal empowerment which is something internal that one can develop and strengthen (Rowlands, 1997). From this perspective, psychological empowerment is associated with the happiness of the individual which reflects as pleasant, engaged and a meaningful life (Seligman, 2002) and identified as a facet of psychological well-being (Diener & Biswas-Diener, 2005). Also, Kabeer (2005: 14) reveal that "empowerment often begins from within and rooted in how people see themselves, their sense of self-worth". Therefore, psychological empowerment is gets especially critical for women as it includes women believing that they can act at personal and social levels to improve their condition. Moreover, it challenges the learned helplessness and the supports the development of self-esteem and confidence of women (Stromquist, 1988). As Oladipo (2009) argues, psychologically empowerment creates a change in attitude, cognition and behavior, and psychological well-being which will culminate in a peaceful and developing society. So, disctinct from objective measure, the subjective measures of empowerment such as satisfaction and well-being also make sense.

Women entrepreneurship poses several difficulties. Such that studies reveal that empowerment is context specific. For instance, Charrad (2010:517) argues that women's empowerment can only be understood "within the context of specific social structures in given times and places ranging from states, social institutions, groups, culture, or norms to name only a few". Indeed, for a women, the ability to move out of their culture or context specific gender roles (Rowland, 1997) make sense in terms of economic and psychologic empowerment. Especially in developing countries such as Bangladesh, India, it is demonstrated that women's access to employment increases her household bargaining power (e.g. Anderson & Eswaran, 2009; Rahman & Rao, 2004) and challenges the patriarchal norms and beliefs Banks (2013). Thus, the earned income has an important role in empowering women which contributes to women's autonomy and development (Anderson & Eswaran, 2009).

In this context, Turkey represents an interesting case as a Muslim county which offered political rights to women early on, even ahead of many Western nations. Yet, despite these advancements in political sphere, many Turkish women still struggle with various shortcomings in empowerment. The county ranks 130st among the 144 countries in the World Economic Forum (WEF)'s gender gap index and a woman in Turkey has to wait for 167 years for the world to close the gender gap completely, according to the WEF report. (WEF, 2019). Also, according to Turkish Statistical Institute (TUIK), labor participation rate was 34.5% for women in 2019, which can be considered low.

Moreover, the deeply rooted religious based conservative societal norms that assign women merely roles of wives and mothers which are taken for granted even by women, maintain the secondary status of women in society as well as in the job market (Arat, 2010 Even, the gender equality polices may be insufficient to bring about a permanent change in these traditional gender roles (Dedeoğlu, 2012). Considering the contemporary socioeconomic and political setting, Çınar & Köse (2018:365) define Turkey's situation a 'gender inequality trap' due to the dominance of conservatism and patriarchal norms in the country. Although there are several governmental regulations and non-governmental initiatives toward women that aims to increase the women's empowerment, they are not adequate in terms of reaching all segments and providing widespread impact. Unfortunately, women's secondary position in society has remained. In recent years, other mechanisms seeking solutions to long-lasting problems of the societies that governments, NGOs, international organizations cannot fall short have begun to come into play. Social entrepreneurship is one of these alternative mechanisms, which is tried to be explained in the following section.

THE ROLE OF SOCIAL ENTREPRENEURSHIP IN CREATING SOLUTIONS TO SOCIAL PROBLEMS

The social entrepreneurship concept has become one of the key phenomena during the last decades as a response towards the long-lasting problems (academic arena in the late 1990s (Bornstein 1998; Dees 1998; Drayton 2002). The related literature provides a variety of definitions for the concept. For instance, Seelos & Mair (2005: 41) explain it as "a version of commercial entrepreneurship which has a social mission to change society". Numerous scholars emphasize its innovativeness in treating social problems, which are becoming complex and multi-dimensional such as poverty, lack of health care, education, gender inequality (Dacin, Dacin, & Matear, 2010; Dees, 1998; Lumpkin, Moss, Gras, Kato, & Amezcua, 2011). For instance, Mair & Marti (2006:37) identify social entrepreneurship as a process that involves the innovative use and combination of resources to pursue opportunities to address social needs. Besides, scholars place the concept as a powerful solution mechanism to the significant social problems that are not addressed effectively by governments, businesses, and nonprofit organizations (e.g.Alvord, Brown, & Letts, 2004; Ansari, Munir, & Gregg, 2012; Azmat, Ferdous, & Couchman, 2015; Bloom, 2009; Datta & Gailey, 2012; Ghauri, Tasavori, & Zaefarian, 2014; Nicholls, 2008). Thus, social entrepreneurs are recognized as change agents who find innovative solutions to the long-lasting social problems (Dacin et al. 2010; Dees, 1998; Sharir & Lerner 2006).

The superiority of social entrepreneurship over governments, businesses and non-profit/philanthropic organizations is explained through several factors. First, the dual mission and the attempt to combine the social and economic missions that makes social enterprises unique. Similar to commercial entrepreneurship, social entrepreneurs engage in entrepreneurial activities, such as opportunity identification, exploitation, resource mobilization, and innovation to achieve their social missions (Austin, Stevenson, and Wei-Skillern, 2006; Zahra et al., 2009). They adopt some form of commercial activity to generate revenue and pursuing social goals that differentiates social entrepreneurship from CSR, governments' and NGOs' activities. By performing income-generating activities social enterprises free themselves from being dependent on funds or grants and a gain sustainability to a certain degree (e.g. Austin et al., 2006; Doherty et al., 2014; Mair & Marti, 2006; Pache & Santos, 2013). In addition, the embeddedness of social entrepreneurs in their local communities facilitate the discovery of the localized social needs and problems (Seelos et al., 2011; Shaw & Carter, 2007). Social entrepreneurs, belonging to their territory with a close-knit relationship act as local actors who create the change and the local development

(Marin, 2017). Thus, it gets easier to identify and fulfill the long-lasting social needs. Moreover, comparing to commercial entrepreneurship, social entrepreneurs generally create social value by addressing social problems through the mobilization of their networks and with collaboration to the other actors for diffusing the created social value (Trivedi & Stokols, 2011).

As an increasingly growing area of interest, the initial studies have focused on conceptualization of social entrepreneurship (Dees, 1998, Leadbetter, 1997; Mair & Marti, 2004; Mort, Weerawardena & Carnegie, 2002). For instance in their well-known study, Zahra et al. (2009) suggest that social entrepreneurs vary in the ways of social value creation and identify three types of social entrepreneurship. These are *Social Bricoleur, Social Constructionists and Social Engineer*. According to this typology (Zahra et al. 2009: 523), the *Social Bricoleur* type of social entrepreneurship perceive and focus on the local social problems. Their initiatives are small-scale and local in scope which allows them to generate quick responses. The second type of social entrepreneurship which is named as the *Social Constructionists*, generate alternative structures to provide goods and services addressing social needs that are mostly ignored by governments, agencies or businesses. Their organizations generally require professional volunteers and employees to operate. They primarily differs from *Social Bricoleur*s in the market focus, they can be small to large scale and local to international in scope. The last form of social entrepreneurship, the *Social Engineers,* seek to build long-lasting structures that will change the existing order and so they are very large scale that is national to international in scope. On the other hand, former studies concentrate on revealing how social value is created (e.g. Di Domenico, Haugh, & Tracey, 2010; Smith & Stevens, 2010). In addition, a specific branch of social entrepreneurship focus on the role of social entrepreneurship in women's empowerment. Various studies discuss that social entrepreneurship is playing a significant role in empowerment mechanisms. However, most of the research on social entrepreneurship has been based on developed country contexts such as United-States, UK. Yet, social enterprises that employ women especially from disadvantaged backgrounds is accepted as a vital source of income especially in developing country contexts such as India, Pakistan etc. (British Council, 2017) However, little is known about the social entrepreneurial activities in emerging and developing economies (Al-Dajani & Marlow, 2013; Datta & Gailey, 2012 Haugh & Talwar, 2016). In terms of Turkey, social entrepreneurship is still a relatively new concept. The research in this area have accelerated in late 2000s that focus on the development and distinct characteristics of social enterprises in the Turkish context (e.g. Aslan, et. al., 2012; Gümüşay, 2015; Özdevecioğlu and Cingöz, 2009). In recent years, a gender perspective has become more significant in studies on social enterprises (e.g. Çiçek & Türkmenoglu, 2019; Kapusuz, Çavuş, & Pekkan, 2018). This study focus on a successful social enterprise in Turkish context, Çöp(m)adam, in order to provide a deeper understanding about the role of social entrepreneurship in women's empowerment. Below the business model and the social value created by Çöp(m)adam is explained.

THE CASE OF ÇÖP(M)ADAM

This chapter focus on the role of social entrepreneurship in women's empowerment. For this purpose, Çöp(m)madam (Garbage Lady) is examined which is presented as one of the most successful social enterprises in Turkey (Sanje & Dinç, 2012). Çöp(m)adam is an innovative social initiative that creates women employment in impoverished communities and has been evaluated as one of Turkey's most successful social entrepreneurship projects by the United Nations Development Program (UNDP) in 2011. Çöp(m)adam has founded in 2008, in Ayvalık, in Turkey and its ateliers which are in İstanbul, Van, and

Diyarbakır have been opened with the help of two associations, *KEDV (Kadın Emeğini Değerlendirme Vakfı, [Association for the Support of Women's Labor])*, which aims to increase the economic well-being of women from lower classes, and *KAMER (Kadın Merkezi Eğitim Üretim Danışma ve Dayanışma Vakfı [Foundation for Women's Central Education Production Advisory and Solidarity*]) which aims to identify and challenge the local practices of the sexist system. Çöp(m)adam uses garbage, waste and discarded materials and turns them into fashionable bags and accessories through upcycling, which is a creative reuse process of transforming waste, useless, or unwanted materials into new products that are useful and have value. The founder of çöp(m)adam, Tara Hopkins is an American anthropologist who lives in Turkey and has worked in various universities as an instructor and consultant. She also performed as a coordinator of Civic Involvement Projects of Sabancı University between the years 1998 and 2009.

This study is based on case study method, which is accepted to be a prominent and a promising method in order to understand the dynamics and impacts of social entrepreneurship in the recent years (e.g. Datta & Gailey, 2012; Marshall, 2011). The primary data of the study is obtained from the semi-structured interview conducted with the founder of Çöp(m)adam, Tara Hopkins. The sample questions included; "*How would you describe the primary mission of Çöp(m)adam?, How Çöp(m)adam creates employment for women*?, *What kind of changes have you observed in the women's life working for Çöp(m) adam*?" As a secondary data source, the website of çöp(m)adam, the published media and the internet news were examined meticulously and the identified information which is relevant to the purpose of the study were included. The findings of the study are revealed in two sections below; the business model and the social impact created by Çöp(m)adam.

Business Model of Çöp(m)adam

It has been revealed in many studies that social entrepreneurs have difficulties in initiating and especially maintaining their enterprises (e.g.Smith, Besharov, Wessels, and Chertok(2012); Renko, 2012; Zahra et. al., 2009). Following a social mission in one hand, struggling with production, operation and sales management, recruitment of human resource, legal challenges and gaining legitimacy on the other hand cerate challenges. In this respect, it is not very easy for social enterprises to maintain their existence due to their dual missions. Thus, the business model gets critical as it determines how the operations will generate both financial benefits as well as social benefits, how to create impact. In other words, a social enterprise's business model is the means by which it pursues both profit and social mission.

In these terms, Çöp(m)adam has a quite creative and innovative business model that draws attention in various aspects. Drawing on the work of Osterwalder (2004) on business model canvas, business model of Çöp(m)adam is tried to be revealed in Table 1. The initiative is a community project that hires local women to produce fashionable bags and accessories from packing waste and discarded materials. It aims to provide women a reliable income for women in rural parts of Turkey, who have never worked for salary before and also support recycling by reducing the waste of companies and houses. The scope of the project is revealed on their website as follows (Çöpmadam, 2020):

Questioning what is worth saving or not, çöp(m)adam started as an experimental project in Ayvalık addressing the issues of women's employment in Turkey and the importance of recycling/re-using. Çöp(m) adam aims to utilize waste in a creative, aesthetically and unique way. Çöp(m)adam items are produced from the packaging that would be or has been thrown away, by women who have never previously earned a salary. All the products are one-of-a-kind and signed by its producer.

Table 1. Business model of Çöp(m)adam

Key Partners	Key Activities	Value Proposition	Customer Relationships	Customer Segments
Unilever Sabancı University Coca Cola KAMER KEDV ASHOKA	Providing waste, discarded material Recycling waste to products Training of women	Women's economic empowerment Women's psychological empowerment Upcycling	Website Sabancı University's PR support Unilever's PR support	Women Environmentally conscious people
	Key Resources Packing wastes Discarded materials		**Channels** Stores E-commerce sites Corporate orders	
Cost Structure Wages Rent of ateliers Cost of materials			**Revenue Streams** Direct sales Corporate sales Sponsorships of companies	

Çöp(m)adam brings various parties; multinational companies, non-governmental organizations, and university together through its business model. This multi-stakeholder approach helps it to overcome the difficulties of sustaining the initiative. Indeed, two significant components, *collaboration* and *networking* draw attention in the business model of Çöp(m)adam, which are explained below.

Collaboration

The main activity of Çöp(m)adam is to produce bags, wallets, accessories, aprons, greeting cards, and more from waste, discarded and recycled materials. Therefore, the supply of these materials is extremely critical for the continuance of the initiative. Çöp(m)adam ensure its raw materials through several ways such as collaborations with the organizations such as YünSA, Prima, Sabancı University, the waste donated by local people and collected by women working in the enterprise. However, the primary raw material supplier of Çöp(m)adam is the Unilever company. Through a long-lasting collaboration, the company contributes its waste and renewed materials to the social enterprise and also has provided financial support for Çöp(m)adam in the early stage of the initiative as a solution partner. Tara Hopkins explains the role of Unilever as follows:

Unilever provides material for our products, they give us their waste materials and we use it as a raw material. Also they supported us financially; they paid our rent for several years. It was a very good way for us to start.

Apart from the supply of raw materials, Çöp(m)adam has corporate partnerships with different companies in different areas. A well-known company Coca-Cola is one of them. The company has started a global initiative named "5by20" in 2010 aiming to reach 5 million women worldwide by 2020 and empower them both in the workplace and throughout the world. The initiative supports women entrepreneurs by providing business skills training, access to financial services and assets, and connections with peers and mentors (Coca-Cola Company, Better Shared Future). Çöp(m)adam is one of the social enterprises that has included in this program from Turkey. Tara Hopkins explained how Coca-Cola Company contributed to her social initiative as follows:

People like the idea but sometimes they do not want to pay for that because they do not know the brand. Creating awareness, creating recognition is difficult for me. My marketing skills are limited. Here, the collaboration with the corporations like Coca-Cola, their visibility helped me hugely. They focused on the advertising part... Also, we regularly receive orders from Coca-Cola to be used both at Coca-Cola stores and at their expositions and conferences so they became our customer. Coca-Cola have kept my business alive for long years.

Based on the explanations above, it is possible to say that corporate collaborations plays an important role in the business model of the Çöp(m)adam. Indeed, in recent years, various studies demonstrate the necessity of collaborations between various actors of society in creating solutions to the complex social problems (Austin, 2012a, 2012b, Sakarya, et al., 2012). Following this perspective, Çöp(m)adam, represents a successful example of cross-sector alliances between various organizations and social enterprises that are formed to address social problems.

Networking

The second point that attracts attention in the Çöp(m)adams business model is the benefits of the networks. Tara Hopkins was the first representative of Ashoka in Turkey, in 2000. Ashoka is a network platform that identifies and supports the social entrepreneurs from all around the world, by providing peers, partners and financial support. The platform facilitates the functioning of social enterprises and enables them to achieve their social mission with a broader impact. Tara Hopkins commented on Ashoka as follows:

My social entrepreneurship journey started with Ashoka. I did not know what it meant before. I learned what it is, I identified myself as a social entrepreneur and I had the chance to realize my ideas.

Moreover as Tara Hopkins worked for Sabancı University for years, she benefitted from the network of the university consisting of strong and influential names. The university announced the project via its own channels, engaged the students to be part of the project and tried to make the project visible in the media through its PR capabilities. From the statement below it appears the most critical collaboration of Çöp(m)adam is provided through this social network. She explained:

Sabancı University provided a social capital and also through that network Çöp(m)adam reached Unilever, which have been a key partner.

It is clear that networking is necessary to carry out the projects of the social enterprises as it allows social entrepreneurs to access information, skills and resources that are not available in their enterprise. As a complementary feature for social enterprises, networks are critical in realization of the social mission and generation of the social impact.

The Social Value Created by Çöp(m)adam

When its business model and the related findings are analyzed, it becomes evident that çöp(m)adam creates social value mainly in three different areas. These are women's economic empowerment, women's psychological empowerment, and upcycling. As this study focus on the empowerment of women, the role of çöp(m)adam in women's economic and psychological empowerment is analyzed and discussed in detail below.

Women's Economic Empowerment

As explained above, Stromquist (1995:16) argue that empowerment efforts should target below/non-income adult women which are under the dominance of their husbands in households. In parallel to this, Çöp(m)adam provides employment opportunity to a disadvantaged group, rural women in Turkey. The primary goal of the enterprise is to support women's participation in the workforce especially that have never received a regular income in their life. As it aims to create employment for women, production is made entirely by women workers. In order for a woman to become a Çöp(m)adam worker, she must first go through training and learn how to wash, cut, sew the discarded materials to turn them into product that has a certain labor price. Women receive their payments at the beginning of the following month, regardless of whether their product sold or not. Tara Hopkins explained the scope and recruitment conditions of her initiative as follows.

Nearly 450 women worked in Çöp(m)adam till now and most of them were over 40. I have one condition for recruitment; the ladies should have never worked and have never earned money before. They are charged per piece, the process is fair and transparent.

Çöp(m)adam addresses a commonly overlooked group of people in Turkey; women especially not regularly or never worked for salary or excluded from work life for cultural and socioeconomic reasons. The enterprise gives women the opportunity to have income in an environment where patriarchal values are dominant and women's participation in working and social life is very limited. Çöp(m)adam offers local women the opportunity to realize their potential within their own living spaces without radically changing their lifestyle which facilities the transition process. One of the women who works for Çöp(m)adam explained as follows:

I have never worked before. It's the first time. It is very good to work here, because we spend time here at the atelier working and still we are able to do our housework.

Various studies discuss that the embeddedness of social entrepreneurs in their local communities ensures a deeper understanding of the context and facilitates the discovery of the local social needs (Seelos et al., 2011; Shaw and Carter, 2007). Indeed, this is very critical when challenging the status quo. Because aiming a transformation in the traditional structure that dominates the context requires an awareness of the contextual sensitivities and local customs. Tara Hopkins explain this situation comparing her efforts to the companies' CSR efforts and draws attention to the role of embeddedness. She demonstrated:

Companies have several strengths but they are not always able to see the local needs, the local people. They have no idea what am I doing… I have a perspective of civil society. The mindset and the perspective is so different. They don't have my structure and also they don't understand the women I work with. I mean you have to speak the local language, you have to touch them. I can do that.

Studies discuss that access to work increases their economic independence of women, in turn independence in general. Earning an income empowers women by generating an economic presence and having the opportunity to make a contribution to the family budget (Datta &Gailey, 2012). In this respect, one of the women workers Çöp(m)adam commented:

My husband works as a waitress in a restaurant. We have always been living with a single salary until now. Now it's two. It provides comfort, of course, if we spend one, we save the other.

According to Hashemi and Schuler (1993), decision-making power within the household is accepted as one of the key dimensions of women's empowerment. Thus, a regular income may enable women to "increase their bargaining power in the household, enable sharing of household chores and childcare responsibilities" (Hashemi, Schuler, & Riley, 1996: 648). In this vein, Çöp(m)adam aims to empower women by changing the mindset of women and their families in rural part of Turkey without causing a major disruption in their lives. Still, the social impact of this minor change creates a significant difference in these women's life in terms of economic existence and fighting with poverty. Çöp(m)adam creates a significant economic value directly for women and indirectly for their children. One of the women who works for Çöp(m)adam demonstrates her feelings as follows:

My husband is not someone to let me work at all, but I said I will do this. Because I have an ambition. I never earned money before. As I earn now, I enjoy it. I love to earn, I love to spend my own money and this money is spent for good reasons, it is spent for my children for example.

This statement demonstrates how increased contributions to the family needs strengths women status in the household. Moreover, it illustrates the objection to the sociocultural norms that men's control over women which is taken for granted even by women themselves for long years. Women in developing countries are usually in secondary status due to socio-cultural and economic context. Especially in patriarchal cultures, male dominance mutes women's voice. However, the sense of independence provided by Çöp(m)adam challenges the subordination role of women which is deeply rooted in sociocultural norms. In fact, this is an objection to the patriarchal ideology. Also, it is good example of how a women can gain the capacity for exercising strategic forms of agency toward the constraints that positioned herself as subordinate to men (Kabeer, 1999). Moreover, they have a greater sense of control over their lives and more control over resources (Stromquist 1995:16). The income earned by women helps them to improve their authority in the home and ensure social inclusion. Tara Hopkins explained her observations through a memory, she recalled:

One day I heard the chat of my two ladies about buying cloth for themselves, they were discussing that how it is important for them because they have never ever considered spending money for something like that before. I mean this is very good example of how they own sense of self, own sense of doing something for themselves and that translates to them being happier and stronger.

It is obvious that the economic empowerment ensure women to make strategic life choices or to choices which had been denied to them in the past. As they engage in a productive activity and have a degree of financial autonomy, they gain the ability to exercise greater control over key aspects of their lives and make independent choices in critical arenas of their lives such as marriage, friendship etc.

(Kabeer, 1999:458; Stromquist 1995:16). Thus, women's dependency on their husbands are reduced. Tara Hopkins emphasized that the women working in Çöp(m)adam gain confidence, started to be encouraged to make life decisions and exercise voice. She commented:

They are gaining their economic power, and some of them decide to divorce for example... I mean they gain encourage and confidence to do that. They feel better about themselves, they speak up for themselves. They are happier, that's what I see, what I want.

These findings reveal that working for a salary, earning an income provides an economic existence for women. This existence reduces their dependency on other people -generally their husbands- and provides an area of freedom. With the help of economic power, women become able to support their family, spend money freely for themselves, and make strategic life choices on their own lives. This, in turn, challenges the secondary status of women and provides an existence which helps them to gain self-esteem. Women who made a considerable contribution to household also increase the women's psychological empowerment. Relatedly, Çöp(m)adam's contributions to the psychological empowerment of women are revealed below.

Women's Psychological Empowerment

Kabeer (2008, 2011) discusses that once women economically empowered, they will be able to make changes in other areas of their lives. In fact, the psychological and economic elements of empowerment are related. In this vein, as economic empowerment enables women who are silenced in the economic fields to have economic independence it supports developing a sense of psychological empowerment. Stromquist (1995:14), defines the psychological empowerment as "*the development of feelings that women can act at personal and societal levels to improve their condition as well as the formation of the belief that they can succeed in their change efforts*". Thus, psychological empowerment is related to generating a sense of self identity, self-confidence, and self-esteem. Relatedly, Tara Hopkins emphasizes the importance of women getting psychologically stronger, she demonstrated:

If you ask my ladies why they are here, why they continue to cöp(m)adam, none of them will say firstly money, it is ok, but it is maybe the second or third reason. The first reason is the space for them to feel good about themselves and to grow as an individual.

Generating a sense of self identity, self-confidence, and self-esteem are not teachable but the conditions which these will be developed can be provided. At this point, social entrepreneurs play an intermediary role in creating these conditions. A woman that works for Çöp(m)adam mention this as follows:

I would like to thank Tara very much, she did such a great job. Women support their families thanks to her. I am very happy, we, women produce and create, everyone is doing something here, and this is super.

Oladipo (2009) reveal that when women are psychologically empowered there will be a change in their cognitions, attitudes, and behaviors. Thus, they will have an improved self-esteem, self-efficacy, self-consciousness as well as better psychological well-being which will culminate in a peaceful and developing society. Through Çöp(m)adam, women who experience social exclusion before realize their potential. In this perspective, Tara Hopkins shared her observations about how women working for Çöp(m)adam started to recognize their selves as an individual, recognize their own desires and gain identity. She explained:

Nobody have ask them before what do they want. They were saying this is it, its ok. And I said them, come on it's not ok. What do you really want? Stand up and make your own decisions! Now they are saying I know what to do as Sıdıka, as Ayşe, what Aysun wants, what Hatice wants. They gained identity, they gained self-confidence. This is very important, this is the real social impact.

It is argued that entry to the workforce enables women to become autonomous and to contribute to social development beyond their household duties. It is obvious in the Çöp(m)adam ateliers, women get an environment where they can socialize outside their homes or neighborhoods and they feel useful. This socialization is very important in the rural areas. One of the women explained how their daily routine have changed, she commented:

Previously, I was spending my whole day on housework or walking around simply. We were doing nothing more than that, we were not creative, we were not productive. We were spending time watching TV. I quit it now, now I am focusing on my job...We were never given an opportunity before, if it was given, women would not spend time just sitting at home.

It is revealed that the justification for empowerment often arises when an individual or group of individuals is incapable of or prevented from actualizing their potentials due to barriers created by others within that environment (Francina & Joseph, 2013). The statement above proves how women start to change their "normal" and how they start to believe their efficacy when they free themselves to the preventions. Rather than complying with gender norms and stereotypes of passivity they start to challenge their "learned helplessness". Thus, it is possible to reveal that Çöp(m)adam supports women to generate sense of self-identity, self-esteem, and self-confidence by strengthening them psychologically.

CONCLUSION

This chapter reveals the role of social entrepreneurship in one of the long-lasting problems of all cultures, women's empowerment. Past studies well-articulated the financial and social challenges of the women entrepreneurs face. Especially in patriarchal cultures like Turkey, low education levels, low labor participation and family or house related roles create difficulties for women to adopt an entrepreneur role. Thus, in such contexts, efforts for women entrepreneurship especially addressing long lasting problems such as women empowerment gets critical. In this vein, following a qualitative methodology, the chapter illustrates a successful social entrepreneurship case, Çöp(m)adam, practiced by a woman, with women and for women's empowerment in a developing country, Turkey. Using an innovative business model, Çöp(m)adam transforms waste material into fashionable bags that provide work opportunities to women and also supports recycling. Observing economic and social problems of women in her geographic region, the founder of Çöp(m)adam, Hopkins generated an innovative solution for the rural women which is small in scale but effective for her target group. Via Çöp(m)adam, she played a significant role in women's empowerment that she may be considered as a Social Bricoleur (Zahra et al.,2009).

The qualitative data suggests that Çöp(m)adam is making a direct positive contribution to the women's empowerment in Turkey in two main areas; economic and psychological empowerment. First, concentrating in local geographies, Çöp(m)adam offers work opportunities to local women that have never earned a regular income before. This income enables women to have economic independence and strengthen their position both in their family and in the society. Thus, women gain to ability to make strategic life choices (Kabeer, 1999). Moreover, the ateliers enable women a social atmosphere that supports sense of socialization and solidarity. Also, women are able to gain awareness as an individual and generate self-confidence. Briefly, Çöp(m)adam exemplify that a successful social initiative can support the women's labor force participation and development in Turkey, and make a positive contribution to the role of women in family and society.

Of course, women's empowerment is an ongoing process (Mosedale, 2005) that encompasses the creation of an enabling environment for women free from inequality and strengthening them in economic and psychological aspects. Social entrepreneurship can play a significant role in women's empowerment with its social mission and innovative solutions. Social entrepreneurship is playing a growing role in women's empowerment through its impact on beneficiaries, employees and society. Yet, there is a promising potential for it to achieve. However, as women's empowerment requires a fight against strong patriarchal societal norms and countries' structural deficiencies, in order to create long-term positive changes, this process needs to be addressed with a collaboration of governments, the companies, and civil society. Thus, further studies can concentrate on the collaboration of distinct actors with social entrepreneurs that will enhance the social value.

REFERENCES

Al-Dajani, H., & Marlow, S. (2013). Empowerment and entrepreneurship: A theoretical framework. *International Journal of Entrepreneurial Behaviour & Research, 19*(5), 503–524. doi:10.1108/IJEBR-10-2011-0138

Alvord, S. H., Brown, L. D., & Letts, C. W. (2004). Social entrepreneurship and societal transformation. *The Journal of Applied Behavioral Science, 40*(3), 260–282. doi:10.1177/0021886304266847

Anderson, S., & Eswaran, M. (2009). What determines female autonomy? Evidence from Bangladesh [November.]. *Journal of Development Economics, Elsevier, 90*(2), 179–191. doi:10.1016/j.jdeveco.2008.10.004

Arat, Y. (2010). Religion, Politics and Gender Equality in Turkey: Implications of a democratic paradox? *Third World Quarterly, 31*(6), 869–884. doi:10.1080/01436597.2010.502712 PMID:20857566

Aslan, G., Araza, A., & Bulut, Ç. (2012). Sosyal girişimciliğin kavramsal çerçevesi. *Girişimcilik ve Kalkınma Dergisi, 7*(2), 69–88.

Austin, J., Stevenson, H., & Wei-Skillern, J. (2006). Social and commercial entrepreneurship: Same, different, or both? *Entrepreneurship Theory and Practice, 31*(1), 1–22. doi:10.1111/j.1540-6520.2006.00107.x

Austin, J. E., & Seitanidi, M. M. (2012a). Collaborative value creation: A review of partnering between nonprofits and businesses: Part I: value creation spectrum and collaboration stages. *Nonprofit and Voluntary Sector Quarterly, 41*(5), 726–758. doi:10.1177/0899764012450777

Austin, J. E., & Seitanidi, M. M. (2012b). Collaborative value creation: A review of partnering between nonprofits and businesses: Part II: Partnership Processes and Outcomes. *Nonprofit and Voluntary Sector Quarterly*, *41*(6), 929–968. doi:10.1177/0899764012454685

Bacq, S., & Janssen, F. (2011). The multiple faces of social entrepreneurship: A review of definitional issues based on geographical and thematic criteria. *Entrepreneurship and Regional Development*, *23*(5–6), 373–403. doi:10.1080/08985626.2011.577242

Bayeh, E. (2016). "The role of empowering women and achieving gender equality to the sustainable development of Ethiopia". Pacific Science Review B. *Humanities and Social Sciences.*, *2*(1), 38.

British Council. (2017). Activist to entrepreneur: the role of social enterprise in supporting women's empowerment. https://www.britishcouncil.org/sites/default/files/social_enterprise_and_womens_empowerment_july.pdf

Cicek, B., & Türkmenoğlu, M. A. (2019). Women as Social Entrepreneurs in Turkey. In Social Entrepreneurship: Concepts, Methodologies, Tools, and Applications (pp. 1075-1090). IGI Global.

Çınar, K., & Köse, T. (2018). The Determinants of Women's Empowerment in Turkey: A Multilevel Analysis. *South European Society & Politics*, *23*(3), 365–386. doi:10.1080/13608746.2018.1511077

CocaCola Company. (n.d.). *Better Shared Future*. https://www.coca-colacompany.com/shared-future/women-empowerment

Çöpmadam. (n.d.). *Home*. http://www.copmadam.com/

Cornwall, A. (2016). Women's empowerment: What works? *Journal of International Development*, *28*(3), 342–359. doi:10.1002/jid.3210

Datta, P. B., & Gailey, R. (2012). Empowering Women Through Social Entrepreneurship: Case Study of a Women's Cooperative in India. *Entrepreneurship Theory and Practice*, *36*(3), 569–587. doi:10.1111/j.1540-6520.2012.00505.x

Dedeoglu, S. (2012). Equality, protection or discrimination: Gender equality policies in Turkey. *Social Politics*, *19*(2), 269–290. doi:10.1093p/jxs004

Di Domenico, M., Haugh, H., & Tracey, P. (2010). Social bricolage: Theorizing social value creation in social enterprises. *Entrepreneurship Theory and Practice*, *34*(4), 681–703. doi:10.1111/j.1540-6520.2010.00370.x

Duflo, E. (2012). Women empowerment and economic development. *Journal of Economic Literature*, *50*(4), 1051–1079. doi:10.1257/jel.50.4.1051

Gümüsay, A. A. (2015). Entrepreneurship from an Islamic perspective. *Journal of Business Ethics*, *130*(1), 199–208. doi:10.100710551-014-2223-7

Haugh, H. M., & Talwar, A. (2016). Linking social entrepreneurship and social change: The mediating role of empowerment. *Journal of Business Ethics*, *133*(4), 643–658. doi:10.100710551-014-2449-4

Kabeer, N. (1999). Resources, agency, achievements: Reflections on the measurement of women's empowerment. *Development and Change*, *30*(3), 435–464. doi:10.1111/1467-7660.00125

Kabeer, N. (2005). Gender equality and women's empowerment: A critical analysis of the third millennium development goal 1. *Gender and Development, 13*(1), 13–24. doi:10.1080/13552070512331332273

Kabeer, N. (2011). *Contextualising the Economic Pathways of Women's Empowerment: Findings from a Multi-Country Research Programme.* Pathways Policy Paper, Brighton: Pathways of Women's Empowerment RPC. Retrieved from: http://eprints.lse.ac.uk/89807/1/Kabeer_Contextualising-Economic-Pathways_Published.pdf

Kapusuz, A. G., Çavuş, M. F., & Pekkan, N. Ü. (2018). Perceived social support and social entrepreneurship: Gender perspective from Turkey. In *Knowledge, Learning and Innovation* (pp. 75–90). Springer. doi:10.1007/978-3-319-59282-4_6

Leadbetter, C. (1997). *The rise of social entrepreneurship.* Demos.

Mair, J., & Marti, I. (2004). *Social entrepreneurship: what are we talking about? A framework for future research.* Barcelona: IESE Business School Working Paper No.546.

Malhotra, A., Schuler, S. R., & Boender, C. (2002, June). Measuring women's empowerment as a variable in international development. In *Background paper prepared for the World Bank Workshop on Poverty and Gender: New Perspectives* (Vol. 28). Academic Press.

Marin, A. (2017). Value creation through sense making: Social entrepreneurship for local sustainable development. *Projectics, 18*(3), 89–106. doi:10.3917/proj.018.0089

Mort, G. S., Weerawardena, J., & Carnegie, K. (2002). Social entrepreneurship: Towards conceptualization and measurement. In *American Marketing Association. Conference Proceedings* (Vol. 13, p. 5). American Marketing Association.

Mosedale, S. (2005). Assessing women's empowerment: Towards a conceptual framework. *Journal of International Development, 17*(2), 243–257. doi:10.1002/jid.1212

Oladipo, S. E. (2009). Psychological empowerment and development. *Edo Journal of Counselling, 2*(1), 118–126.

Osterwalder, A. (2004). *The Business Model Ontology: A Proposition In A Design Science Approach* (Ph.D. thesis). Lausanne: University of Lausanne.

Özdevecioğlu, M., & Cingöz, A. (2009). Sosyal girişimcilik ve sosyal girişimciler: Teorik çerçeve. *Erciyes Üniversitesi İktisadi ve İdari Bilimler Fakültesi Dergisi*, (32), 81–95.

Page, N., & Czuba, C. E. (1999). Empowerment: What is it. *Journal of Extension, 37*(5), 1–5.

Renko, M. (2013). Early challenges of nascent social entrepreneurs. *Entrepreneurship Theory and Practice, 37*(5), 1045–1069. doi:10.1111/j.1540-6520.2012.00522.x

Sakarya, S., Bodur, M., Yildirim-Öktem, Ö., & Selekler-Göksen, N. (2012). Social alliances: Business and social enterprise collaboration for social transformation. *Journal of Business Research, 65*(12), 1710–1720. doi:10.1016/j.jbusres.2012.02.012

Sara, K., & Head, S. Z. (2014). *Women's Lives and Challenges: Equality and Empowerment since 2000.* United States Agency for International Development.

Schuler, S. R., Hashemi, S. M., & Riley, A. P. (1996). Rural credit programs and women's empowerment in Bangladesh. *World Development, 24*(4), 635–653. doi:10.1016/0305-750X(95)00159-A

Seligman, M. (2002). *Authentic happiness*. Free Press.

Smith, B. R., & Stevens, C. E. (2010). Different types of social entrepreneurship: The role of geography and embeddedness on the measurement and scaling of social value. *Entrepreneurship and Regional Development, 22*(6), 575–598. doi:10.1080/08985626.2010.488405

Smith, W. K., Besharov, M. L., Wessels, A. K., & Chertok, M. (2012). A paradoxical leadership model for social entrepreneurs: Challenges, leadership skills, and pedagogical tools for managing social and commercial demands. *Academy of Management Learning & Education, 11*(3), 463–478. doi:10.5465/amle.2011.0021

Stromquist, N. (1988). The Theoretical and Practical bases For Empowerment. In *Women, Education and Empowerment: Pathways towards Autonomy*. Report of the International Seminarheldat UIE. https://unesdoc.unesco.org/ark:/48223/pf0000100662

Stromquist, N. (1988). Women's education in development: From welfare to empowerment. *Convergence (Toronto), 21*(4), 5–17.

Thomas, K. W., & Velthouse, B. A. (1990). Cognitive elements of empowerement: An interpretive model of intrinsic task motivation. *Academy of Management Review, 15*(4), 666–681.

Trivedi, C., & Stokols, D. (2011). Social enterprises and corporate enterprises: Fundamental differences and defining features. *The Journal of Entrepreneurship, 20*(1), 1–32. doi:10.1177/097135571002000101

Warth, L., & Koparanova, M. S. (2012). *Empowering women for sustainable development*. United Nations Economic Commission for Europe.

Zahra, S. A., Gedajlovic, E., Neubaum, D. O., & Shulman, J. M. (2009). A typology of social entrepreneurs: Motives, search processes and ethical challenges. *Journal of Business Venturing, 24*(5), 519–532. doi:10.1016/j.jbusvent.2008.04.007

Zimmerman, M. A. (1995). Psychological empowerment: Issues and illustrations. *American Journal of Community Psychology, 23*(5), 581–599. doi:10.1007/BF02506983 PMID:8851341

KEY TERMS AND DEFINITIONS

Business Model: A holistic framework that describes how an organization creates, delivers, and captures value.

Embeddedness: The degree of closeness of interpersonal relationships and social ties.

Local Needs: The specific needs of the local community.

Long-Lasting Problems: Situations that causes difficulties for societies for long years.

Social Enterprise: Social entrepreneurial organization that address a basic unmet need or solve a social or environmental problem through a market-driven approach.

Social Value: The benefits provided to the community that creates positive changes in people's lives.

Women's Empowerment: The process of empowering women.

Section 4
Social Entrepreneurship in the Face of COVID-19

Chapter 15
When Music Changes, so Does the Dance:
The Role of Social Entrepreneurship in Recovery Response to the COVID-19 Pandemic

Gözde Morgül
Beykent University, Turkey

Mine Afacan Fındıklı
Beykent University, Turkey

ABSTRACT

This chapter examines the role of social enterprises/entrepreneurs from the perspective of the COVID-19 outbreak and discussed the importance of social entrepreneurship. In this context, answers to the following questions are sought: Did social enterprises/entrepreneurs stand out during the COVID-19 era, particularly the social value they created? Do social enterprises/entrepreneurs perform studies especially for groups experiencing social exclusion during the COVID-19 era? The study based on qualitative research reveals that by producing innovative, fast, and effective solutions social initiatives have won the approval of society. The headlines of leading media outlets published between December 2019 and June 2020 and discourses from social actors confirm the rising critical value of social entrepreneurs.

INTRODUCTION

"When Music Changes, So Does The Dance" This world-famous African proverb expresses the importance of adapting to the dynamic nature of change for governments, for-profit and non-profit organizations, and humanity as a whole. With the Covid-19 outbreak, music changed for all the countries of the world simultaneously.

DOI: 10.4018/978-1-7998-4727-4.ch015

Emerged in Wuhan, China in December 2019 with a high spreading rate and contagiousness, the Coronavirus disease 2019 (Covid-19) affected the world in a short time (Gao, Tian, & Yang, 2020). On January 30, 2020, the World Health Organization (WHO, 2020) announced that the Covid-19 outbreak was declared an "international public health emergency". Despite the emergence of Covid-19 as a health crisis, its socio-economic effects and possible post-corona scenarios began to be discussed in a short time (Bavel, 2020; Fernandes 2020; Nicola et. al., 2020). This crisis also brought up some of the hidden problems in societies. For example, in April, which coincided with the Corona-19 outbreak in England, government officials had a hard time due to the 50 percent increase in mortality in elderly care homes (Financial Times, 2020). The Covid-19 era also exposed other issues such as unemployed people with no permanent jobs, working mostly uninsured and in part-time or daily jobs (e.g. babysitters, cleaners, etc.) (CBS News, 2020) as well as the exclusion and otherization of migrant workers in Singapore (Financial Times, 2020). Thus, the gap between different segments of the society in terms of access to resources and living conditions became clearer. This outbreak demonstrated governments and policymakers the need to quickly implement measures and new practices to improve the well-being of society's vulnerable and perhaps neglected segments (WEF, 2020). For example, in India, Omidyar officials called for a rapid response fund to overcome the challenges of the negative socio-economic impact brought by Covid-19, with the statement "We know that slowdown will affect the vulnerable segments of our population and small businesses the most". (Economic times, 2020).

Providing aid packages to those who are liable to suffer more in society is a temporary solution for them to improve their lives. Creating new job opportunities and introducing sustainable new initiatives are the steps to be taken for the development of society. From this perspective, social entrepreneurs and social enterprises seem to have the capacity to offer new and diverse solutions through the networks they establish. The main motivation in writing this section was that social entrepreneurs, with their awareness of the specific needs of the society as they are embedded in it, can focus on the problems that are not in the spotlight. With their innovative problem-solving skills, their collaboration with different actors (governments, NGOs, universities, etc.), they can play a triggering role in increasing public welfare. In particular, they can offer constructive and permanent solutions in remedying the negative effects of the crisis caused worldwide in the Covid-19 era.

In this section, answers to the following questions are sought: Do social enterprises/entrepreneurs stand out during the Covid-19 era, particularly the social value they created? Do social enterprises/entrepreneurs perform studies especially for groups experiencing social exclusion during the Covid-19 era?

Written statements of social enterprises and secondary data related to Covid-19 were used to find answers to the research questions. For this purpose, reports from academic publications, news from important publications, and reports prepared by organizations such as WHO, IMF, UNESCO, UNDP, ILO, WIEGO were examined. The content of the section was planned to asses the socio-economic effects of the Covid-19 outbreak, the role and importance of social entrepreneurship in creating social value, how the groups experiencing "social exclusion" were affected by the Covid-19 process, and the studies conducted by the social entrepreneurs during this period

Evaluation Of The Socioeconomic Effects Of Covid-19

It is stated that the socioeconomic and political effects of the Covid-19 pandemic are different from previous pandemics, such as Global influenza (1918), Sars (2002), and Ebola (2013-2016) (Fernandes, 2020). Uncertainties about the spread and evolution of the Covid-19 virus and the greater integration of the countries worldwide due to globalization are among the differences with previous outbreaks (Fernandes, 2020; Guerrieri, et al., 2020).

As the consequence of physical distancing, which is one of the most important measures taken to reduce the speed of the disease, countries closed their international borders and sanctioned travel restrictions, quarantines, and social distance regulations within the country (Fox News, 2020). These *"new normal"* conditions led to the breaking of global supply chains, cessation of commercial activities, and the deterioration of supply-demand balances for imported and domestic goods and services (Allen, 2020; Yap, 2020). While the direct and indirect effects of the Covid-19 outbreak at the global, country, and society level cannot be precisely estimated, all related institutions and organizations are working on the necessary measures.

One of the economic impacts of the Covid-19 pandemic is that the slowing global growth rate (IMF, 2019-2020) has dragged the world economy into recession, which last occurred during the 2008-2009 financial crisis (UNSDG, 2020). National gross domestic product (GDP) is expected to fall by 5% in the USA, by 7% in European countries (Greece, Italy, Portugal, Germany, Spain) and 5% in Turkey (Fernandes, 2020). The United Nations forecasted the immediate, medium- and long-term socio-economic impacts of the Covid-19 on countries, societies, and vulnerable groups and put forward the strategies to be taken in their Development Program Report (UNDP, 2020). The International Labor Organization (ILO, 2020) announced that, by the end of 2020, between 5.3 million and 24.7 million jobs will be lost due to the economic crisis caused by the Covid-19. Moreover, since informal workers (the most vulnerable group in the labor market) represent 1.6% of the global workforce of 2 billion to 3.3 billion, it is estimated that there will be a 60% decrease in their income levels.

Apart from economic projections, UNESCO (2020) has announced that approximately 1.2 billion students globally are negatively affected by the interruption of formal education. Although efforts are made to provide education through distance education modules during the pandemic, there are serious difficulties for disadvantaged communities to benefit from distance education opportunities due to geographical and socio-economic conditions (UNICEF, 2020). However, even though the economic implications of the long-term closure of educational institutions around the world are not fully known, the research by Chen et al. in Taiwan in 2011 on the effects of the 2009 H1N1 pandemic helps to predict the impact. The authors reported that 27% of families who could not go to work to be able to look after their children due to the closure of schools during the 2009 H1N1 pandemic experienced 18% loss of income (Nicola, et al., 2020). Similarly, interrupting face-to-face education in schools poses a serious problem for families who have to meet their children's daily nutritional needs normally catered by schools. Thus, the economic burdens caused by the Covid-19 outbreak are likely to be heavier for families.

It is known that the Covid-19 pandemic causes important problems in healthcare services at the global level (including developing countries) because of how the virus spreads, the rate of spread, and the supply of drugs and equipment used in the treatment phase. At certain times, healthcare workers had great difficulty in supplying the necessary equipment (masks, gloves, protective overalls) (Euro News 2020; BBC 2020; New York Times 2020). This further unearthed the existing injustices and inequalities in accessing and benefiting from health services for the vulnerable and disadvantaged groups (Whitehead 1992, Whitehead et al., 2001) (WHO, 2020). As the examples illustrate, the effects of the outbreak vary between countries (developed and developing countries), sectors, and socioeconomic classes (rich and poor) (Fernandes 2020; Hoque et al., 2020; Gössling, Scott, & Hall 2020). The policies developed by the countries within the scope of the measures taken include extending the coverage of existing social support programs for citizens and support packages consisting of unemployment, food and child aids, provision of mandatory health equipment, state guarantees for small- and medium-sized enterprises, commercial grants, low interest loans and tax deferral and deduction (IMF, 2020).

Besides all these constructive efforts, another important issue that should be considered by states and international organizations is what can be done for the groups who cannot benefit from emergency support interventions (elderly people, colored people, unregistered workers). These groups are even more fragile than before in terms of poverty, inequality, and access to vital needs. The Covid-19 pandemic increased the restrictions on vulnerable and neglected groups' access to livelihoods, health and education services, and deepened the gap between other segments of society. Thus, there is an increasing need for actors who play a key role and can support the process by creating social value, provide continuity in livelihoods, education, and health. It is understood that social entrepreneurship, with its innovative and collaborative approaches to creating permanent social value and leading social change, is one of the complements of this puzzle (Mair & Marti, 2006; Jackson & Jackson, 2014; Hellström et al., 2015).

The Role and Importance of Social Entrepreneurship in Creating Social Value

Actors such as governments, international organizations, non-governmental organizations work for permanent solutions in solving social problems and achieving development goals. However, the multi-dimensional and complex nature of social problems makes it difficult for actors to produce permanent solutions with initiatives on their own (Acar Erdur, Afacan Fındıklı, 2020). In today's world, where the Covid-19 crisis has made the existing problems more prominent, governments fail to reach every part of the society due to their bureaucratic and formal structures. Aid projects of global organizations cannot offer specific solutions for developed and developing countries (Easterly, 2009). Non-governmental organizations (NGOs) can often provide limited benefits in creating social benefits due to their structure. While they do contribute to community needs, NGOs cannot act in an entrepreneurial manner as long as they continue to adhere to contributions from individuals and subsidies from the state, in other words, unless they have income from their own through a sustainable project. (Kummitha, 2017: 16). Businesses, on the other hand, provide support through projects for the needs of a part of the society within the scope of their corporate social responsibility (CSR) projects, but after a while, the majority of these projects discontinue. These efforts cannot achieve a satisfactory outcome because the establishment objectives of the enterprises are to create and achieve corporate value (Visser, 2012; Kummitha, 2017).

Looking at the areas where these actors are fall short in improving social development and welfare, social entrepreneurship, which involves innovative use of resources to create lasting social value and catalyze social change, emerges as a complement (Mair & Marti, 2006: 37). Social entrepreneurs are generally ahead of the actors mentioned above with a "bottom-up" approach to discovering social needs and providing innovative solutions (Dacin et al., 2010). At the same time, focusing on value creation instead of value capture are prominent focal points in responding to social needs.

When looking at the global current situation of social entrepreneurs, the special report published by the Global Entrepreneurship Monitor 2015 (GEM), which is considered as the most comprehensive entrepreneurship project in the world, stands out. In the research conducted on 31 economies, the result obtained about creating social value, which is regarded as one of the criteria defining social entrepreneurs can be summarized by the following statement: *"Many economies report that between 50 and 70% of operational social entrepreneurs (according to the broad definition) are 'value creators'"* (GEM, 2015: 15). On the other hand, from the perspective of the figure, for example, there are around 9,000 social enterprises in Turkey amounting to 20 million in size according to the Status Report of the Social

Enterprises in Turkey prepared by the British Council (2019), and the Social Enterprise: Market Trend: 2017 report estimates that there are 99,000 social enterprises in the UK. It is therefore possible to say that there is an ecosystem with much room for development in Turkey.

In the relevant literature, value creation is measured at the social level, while value capture is measured at the organizational level. In other words, while entrepreneurs achieve value and accomplish their corporate goals, social entrepreneurs create value and aim to create value at the social level. In this sense, social entrepreneurs and the social enterprises they establish distribute the income they earn in line with their activities proportionally among stakeholders to improve the welfare of the society (Kummitha, 2017). While social entrepreneurship is emerging in response to a social need with its social mission and goals, it increases economic and social development and welfare through the creation and employment of new jobs (Wennekers et al. 2005). For this reason, social entrepreneurs and social enterprises are considered as important actors of social development with their value-creating activities, networks, and collaborations (Littlewood & Khan, 2018; Maclean et al. 2013).

In summary, there are two main elements that have helped social entrepreneurship stand out in the academic literature and society over the past 20 years. First of all, as mentioned above, governments and other institutional structures are inadequate in achieving social goals. In the capitalist system, which captures the value for themselves and is based on maximizing profit, social development, and sustainability goals are not achieved even though improvements are made with corporate social responsibility projects or funds. Another factor is that social entrepreneurs have an understanding, behavior, and vision that sees opportunities for improvement instead of problems, unlike other actors in the third sector, including NGOs (Mair & Marti, 2006; Jackson & Jackson, 2014). It is their capacity to create value through networks, realizing where the opportunity is to meet unmet needs and gathering the necessary resources (Thompson, 2002). In their field of activity, they are embedded within the society and encourage the participation of stakeholders to respond effectively to community needs.

Previous studies have also confirmed that community involvement and embeddedness are two necessary mechanisms to both make a successful social contribution and sustain their initiative (Kummitha, 2017: 22). Thus, they are superior to other actors in accurately identifying social needs and generating timely responses in offering innovative solutions, via their reverse-flowing bottom-up mechanisms developed by social entrepreneurs instead of top-down approaches. (Hellström et al., 2015; Korsgaard, 2011). From this perspective, we believe that the role of social entrepreneurship for the vulnerable and neglected groups in the Covid-19 pandemic crisis becomes much more important.

FROM EXCLUSION TO INCLUSION: THE VALUE OF SOCIAL ENTREPRENEURSHIP FOR DIFFERENT SECTIONS OF SOCIETY

Social exclusion is generally related to social status and implies the lack of access to resources, benefits, and opportunities for contribution and self-realization (Wacquant, 2008). Individuals are defined as socially excluded when they live in a society where they cannot participate in normal social activities for reasons beyond their control to improve their welfare (Saith, 2001). Thus, inability to take part in economic employment and benefit from optimum living conditions, economic and financial resources, and benefits are considered the foundations of social exclusion (Seyfang, 2003). Burchardt et al. (2002) argued that the individual or group would be socially excluded if they could not participate in four core activities. These are: 1) Consumption: capacity to purchase goods and services, 2) Production:

participation in socially valuable activities, 3) Political Participation: participation in local or national decision-making processes, 4) Social Interaction: integration with family, friends, and society (p: 30). If a person or group suffers from one of these, the possibility of social exclusion arises (Levitas, 2005).

Social entrepreneurs have become one of the best practices of the third sector with their long-term initiatives to cover those excluded from the society in these four areas (Kummitha, 2016). The negative effects of the Covid-19 pandemic crisis on a global level have caused these groups to suffer severe injuries in particular, to the best of our knowledge. As the first measures and processes implemented with the onset of the pandemic, the governments first attempted to take precautions in healthcare and economic areas, as a natural course of action. The governments' priorities have therefore been the small, medium, and large enterprises within the system. Meanwhile, governments have been slow to take action against the groups we discussed below. With this point of view, examples are searched on how vulnerable groups are affected by the pandemic and how social initiatives/entrepreneurs can contribute to these generally neglected groups.

Groups Over 60 Years Old Who Need Health and Care Support

While some uncertainties about the effects of the Covid-19 virus persist, scientists agree that age and chronic conditions increase the risk of death (Lloyd-Sherlock, et al., 2020; Jordan, Adab, & Cheng, 2020; Brooke & Jackson, 2020). Thus, the elderly are announced as the most vulnerable group that can suffer the most from the pandemic (WHO, 2020). However, the elderly also experienced great difficulties in accessing medical treatment and other healthcare services (obtaining information, prescribing, etc.) during the pandemic. For example, the British Medical Association (BMA, 2020) has published a guideline that includes the use of limited resources in hospitals and decisions to be taken if hospitals exceed their capacity. In the guideline, BMA recommended that resources be used primarily for patients with higher survival rates. Moreover, in the elderly care centers of countries such as America, Germany, Spain, France, and England, the elderly were left to die, in a manner of speaking, because of lack of masks, care abuses, and because they were not admitted to hospitals (The Guardian, 2020; Euro News, 2020).

While the process continues, the World Economic Forum (WEF, 2020) shares the efforts of social entrepreneurs for disadvantaged and vulnerable groups through its website. Sharing announcements about social initiatives on WEF's page can be considered as an indication of how important they are to the community. In the Covid-19 era, there were important disruptions especially in healthcare services and the existence of social initiatives in resolving such disruptions proved very valuable. Altibbi and Senior Citizen Home Safety Association (SCHSA) are examples. Altibbi is a social enterprise that offers reliable and simplified health information on a digital platform in the Middle East and North Africa region. With the emergence of the pandemic, it quickly established a free Corona Hotline to address the difficulties experienced by individuals over 65 years of age. Senior Citizen Home Safety Association (SCHSA), another social enterprise, provides free masks and disinfectants for the elderly as well as personal care and emergency services. As can be understood from these two examples, social entrepreneurs are trying to create social value through new business models that they have developed to solve the difficulties of obtaining reliable information and access to healthcare in the pandemic process.

Groups Combating Poverty

While there are different views on the definition and criteria of poverty, the World Bank describes the absolute global poverty line in more measurable and simplified numerical numbers. Accordingly, the absolute poverty threshold is $ 1.90, which corresponds to the number of calories to be consumed per person per day (2400k / cal) (TWB, 2015). On the other hand, the United Nations Development Program (UNDP), the United Nations Children's Fund (UNICEF), the Organization for Economic Cooperation and Development (OECD) go beyond the numerical data and define the relative poverty line as people who are unable to meet their basic social needs and fall below the average welfare level, even if they have reached the minimum subsistence level (OECD, 2008).

The poor who meet the definition of socially excluded groups (Seyfang, 2003) and are among the disadvantaged groups (UNDP) are significantly affected by the pandemic. For example, the figures published by Office for National Statistic (2020), the UK's largest independent official statistics producer, revealed the impact of the Covid 19 outbreak on different socioeconomic groups in society. According to the analysis, Covid-19-associated mortality was 55.1 per 100 thousand in the poorest regions of the country and 25.3 per 100 thousand in the highest income regions. Also, the World Bank's April (2020) report claims that 40-60 million people may face extreme poverty due to the pandemic, while the international non-governmental organization OXFAM (2020) predicts that the number of people who earn below $ 1.90 a day and are defined as extremely poor can reach 1 billion following the pandemic. In the report of United Nations Population Fund (UNPD) (2020) Covid-19 Situation Report 4 for UNFPA Latin America and the Caribbean, the inequality between groups became more evident with the decrease in the growth rate of America and the Caribbean, and poverty/extreme poverty rates are on the rise. However, in June, the World Bank has updated its predictions of April about poverty, estimating that 100 million people may face extreme poverty.

Although the fight against poverty is at the top of the agenda of governments, institutions, and organizations at the global level, it is very difficult to realize the needs of all groups and to access and create sustainable solutions at the regional level. Especially at the regional level, fast and effective opportunities in line with the needs can be provided through social entrepreneurs who are familiar with these needs. For example, in Paraguay, Fundación Paraguaya (FP), which struggles with the multidimensional poverty of families and allows people to live in dignity, continues to work in the pandemic era. It facilitates the conditions of obtaining microloans for the poor and vulnerable people living in Paraguay and supports them to go through the process with minimal damage by developing alternative options for those who cannot afford a microloan. (Fundacionparaguaya, 2020)

Youth Fighting Unemployment

Youth employability is one of the increasing problems for both developed and developing countries. Individuals between the ages of 15-24 who are looking for a job, want to work but cannot find a job are considered as the young unemployed by the United Nations. Low education levels (WEF, 2013), lack of basic academic skills (reading, writing) (OECD, 2013) make young people the cheapest and unskilled labor force in the market (Alcaraz et al., 2011; Arias & Khamis, 2008). On the other hand, young people who do not have the financial support necessary for their education and who are obliged to work are in the first layoff group due to the nature of their work (part-time, seasonal) (Morsy, 2012).

Therefore, young people (15-24) are more likely to be affected by the crises (health, financial) that countries may experience (Helgesson, et al. 2013). As a matter of fact, while the global youth unemployment rate was around 13% in 2007, after the 2008 economic crisis, the global youth unemployment rate reached almost 19-21% (4 to 5.5 million) at the EU level (Scarpetta, Sonnet, & Manfredi, 2010; Nita & Fleser, 2011). In fact, employment problems of disadvantaged and/or poorly educated male youth started before the 2008 financial crisis and continued after the crisis (Edelman & Holzer, 2013). The Covid-19 outbreak, which started as a health crisis and spread to the economic field in a short time, will have similar negative effects on youth unemployment. ILO's report titled "Covid-19 and the World of Work" (2020) reveals that young unemployed people are disproportionately affected by the labor markets. According to a survey, one of every six young people has stopped working since the outbreak of Covid-19, while the working hours have decreased by 23%.

Similarly, Turkey has been struggling with the problem of youth unemployment as one of the countries with a high proportion of the young population. Social initiatives have rolled up their sleeves to go beyond existing solutions for the youth unemployment problem and offer benefits at a social level. For example, Future is Bright Youth Platform (FBYP), which was in established in Turkey by Titiz, emerges as one of the most effective examples of social initiatives. In order to contribute to the professional and personal development of young people, FBYP provides online trainings that will improve their skills and promote career opportunities, regardless of their geographical location, social and economic conditions. Moreover, volunteer professionals offer youth (online) mentoring and coaching practices. Volunteer mentors and coaches come together on this platform to convey their knowledge and experience, to give information about the sector and organization they work in, and to guide them. Another example is the Konexio project based in Paris. This social enterprise, founded by Jean Guo, was launched to integrate vulnerable communities to the workforce. During the Covid-19 pandemic, it continues to provide personal development and education support with online workshops to motivate young people who stay at home and prepare them for business life. (Globalshaper, 2020)

Unregistered Employment Groups

Another group that is threatened globally is those with unregistered employment (workers, domestic workers, daily/hourly workers, refugees, and migrants, etc.). This group of employees is deprived of securities such as insurance, job security, health services, unemployment/child benefit, and retirement. Informal workers are among the vulnerable groups due to their lack of social security and exclusion from income support programs.

The International Labor Organization (ILO) is working to investigate the effects of the Covid-19 outbreak on labor markets. These studies suggest that approximately 1.6 billion people with unregistered employment worldwide will face increased vulnerability to both the virus and the pandemic measures implemented. They show that most of the unregistered workers earn their livelihood with low-skilled jobs that require physical strength in small enterprises of sectors such as manufacturing, textile, construction, tourism, retail, agriculture, which are the sectors that were most negatively affected by the pandemic. Consequently, many of them do not have the opportunity to work at home and they thus have irregular income (WEF, 2020; ILO, 2020). On the other hand, the circumstances are not much different for home workers. In the status evaluation made by WIEGO (2020), it is announced that more than 50 million workers, mostly women, in South Asia, have come to the point of losing their income sources due to small-scale entrepreneurs interrupting production, disruptions in the supply chain, not getting new orders or general pandemic measures. Similarly, in countries such as Africa, Brazil, India where unregistered employment is intense, labor losses are expected to increase the poverty rate (ILO, 2020).

In this context, "Merida Hub", founded by Sergio Alanis in Mexico, is developing a project to help vulnerable and mostly unregistered groups (e.g. home workers, textile workers) who have lost their income sources during the Covid-19 pandemic. Within the scope of the project, they help people have jobs again by contacting various businesses so that they can work in jobs where they can both maintain their health and earn income. (Globalshaper, 2020)

Immigrants and refugees are also involved in unregistered employment. (Connel, 2009; Manning & Trimmer, 2020). Social distance measures and curfews taken during the outbreak generally affect the refugees and immigrants who have to travel to find daily or part-time jobs. Besides, the joint press release by Universal Declaration of Human Rights (OHCHR), International Organization for Migration (IOM), UN Refugee Agency (UNHCR), and WHO (2020), emphasizes that refugees, migrants, and stateless people living in inadequate health conditions are at high risk during the pandemic.

In summary, the existing disadvantages of globally excluded and vulnerable groups seem to have increased further due to the outbreak. In the course of the pandemic, social entrepreneurs are developing new business models in areas such as obtaining reliable information, generating income sources, food aid, psychological support, maintenance service, and procuring protective equipment. With the projects they initiated, they offer measures to reduce the negative effects of Covid-19 in a short time. Each solution they develop for existing problems increases the likelihood of developing another innovation (Bornstein, 2007; Antadze & Westley, 2010).

The ecosystem created by social entrepreneurs to sustain their contribution to the society and to transform the dynamic and innovative approaches of social entrepreneurs to create value is supported by 40 leading global organizations in the fight against the Covid-19. This initiative, called the "Covid Response Alliance", makes an important contribution to overcoming the problems of social entrepreneurs in finding resources (Schwabfound, 2020).

In the light of the literature and the information obtained from various secondary sources, it became even more evident with in this era that social entrepreneurs have an important place among other actors of the society. It seems that the increasing entrepreneurship tendencies of young generations and the innovation and dynamism they bring to the society will be appreciated even further in time. In today's world, where public resource use is decreasing in many social fields and social issues are gradually taken over by market functions, social entrepreneurship stands out as a promising and increasingly important value (Koorsgaad, 2011).

RESEARCH DESIGN

This study was shaped based on the social value created by social entrepreneurs and focused on socially excluded groups of the society in the context of social inclusion especially during the Covid-19 pandemic. The study questioned whether the inclusion of the social entrepreneurship has become more distinct during the Covid-19 outbreak.

Based on the theoretical background above, this study seeks to address the following research question: Do social entrepreneurs become more important in solving social and economic problems caused by the COVID-19 period? What are the responses (project examples) given by social entrepreneurs in solving the social and economic problems caused by the COVID-19 period?

Discourse analysis (Silverman, 2002), a qualitative research method, was used to find answers to the research questions. As is known, data can be obtained from interviews, individual meetings, statements, organizational reports and descriptions, corporate brochures, TV programs, cartoons, and videos in discourse analysis (Adolphus, 2020; Phillips, Lawrence, & Hardy, 2004).

In this study, firstly, in the context of Covid-19, search was made with the keywords "social entrepreneurs", "Covid-19", "disadvantage group", "vulnerable populations", from the Google Scholar database and Google search engine. In the second stage, the search continued by adding the keywords "social entrepreneurs response", "social value" and "critical". In this context, the data required for discourse analysis were obtained from academic publications related to social enterprise (Haider & Bawden, 2007) and important written media discourses published between December 2019 and June 2020 (Ferguson, 2007). In addition, reports prepared by international organizations such as WF, WEF, WHO, IMF, UNESCO, UNDP, ILO, WIEGO were examined and included in the literature. Furthermore, the written text discourses of communities, organizations (e.g. WEF, Schwab Foundation, Skoll Foundation, Global Shaper) (Pollach, 2005) and their advisors that connect the social entrepreneurship ecosystem and offer international support programs are quoted and qualitatively interpreted. The examples given to the studies carried out by social entrepreneurs during the Covid-19 pandemic process were selected by randomization method. In order to ensure the validity and reliability of the research, data from different sources were collected and examined by two researchers. The findings are meaningful and consistent in themselves and at the same time, the value of the social entrepreneur in the Covid-19 era was confirmed by different sources from the research results' perspective (Yin, 1994).

RESULTS

The Increasing Importance of Social Entrepreneurs in Creating Social Value in the Covid-19 Era

Social entrepreneurs, thanks to their innovative and dynamic structures, take rapid action by creating necessary social networks and resources in line with new needs in sudden changes in environmental conditions (Thompson, 2002; Weerawardena & Mort, 2006). Moreover, social entrepreneurs are seen as creators of regional change (Drayton, 2002). Statements about social enterprises during the Covid-19 pandemic reveal that social enterprises can comprehend problems at regional level faster and produce innovative solutions for these problems, which in turn may be more effective than government practices at the regional level. It is possible to support these thoughts from the explanations and statements below.

A session titled "China social innovators response: actions and response during Covid-19" was organized in the 2020 Virtual Skoll World Forum with the motto "Collective Strength" of China Alliance of Social Value Investment (CASVI). The aim was to demonstrate the positive role of Chinese social initiatives in the Covid-19 pandemic process, to bring the solutions they developed to a global level, to promote their impact, and to inspire new social initiatives that will start to fight the pandemic. Tedxchengdu Curator Changkun Shen also said the following about the high impact of China's social initiatives in the pandemic process:

The rapid actions of these Chinese social entrepreneurs in mobilizing resources, integrating information, and connecting communities are the sort of innovations that ought not be ignored in China's response to the pandemic. Hopefully, these efforts made here from Chinese social entrepreneurs will be seen by the wider international community, and help those still fighting in the center of the COVID-19 crisis. (Changkun Shen, 2020).

In his article titled "Why social entrepreneurs are critical to our response to and recovery from the COVID-19 crisis" published in The World Economic Forum COVID Action Platform, François Bonnici made the following statement to highlight the outstanding value of social entrepreneurs in the Covid-19 pandemic process in terms of vulnerable groups.

Social entrepreneurs solve market and government failures by serving excluded and vulnerable populations, which are most at risk to impacts of COVID-19. From providing reliable information, services and care for the most vulnerable, to developing community tracing initiatives or mental health support through mobile phones, the work of social entrepreneurs is even more critical during the COVID-19 pandemic, as they reach those who the market and governments are unable to account for. (Bonnici, 2020)

Supporting social initiatives, the Schwab Foundation made a similar statement regarding the failure of governments to address the problems of different groups, their inability to meet their needs, and the value of social initiatives to fill these gaps.

From providing access to food & water to developing mobile community tracing initiatives, the work of social entrepreneurs is even more critical during the COVID-19 pandemic, as they reach those who the market and governments are unable to account for. (Schwabfound, 2020).

The most important issue in the Covid-19 pandemic was the fact that even developed countries could not reach the groups that could be more easily harmed, both in healthcare and other measures they took. In particular, the admissions made by government representatives, lawmakers and healthcare professionals for the elderly as a subgroup in the vulnerable population also support this argument. For example, the words of Swedish Prime Minister Stefan Löfven are relevant:

We did not manage to protect the most vulnerable people, the most elderly, despite our best intentions. (BBC news, 2020)

In addition, the statement of French Lawmaker Eric Ciotti and Dr. Mike Osborn also confirms the bitter picture.

Most of the Covid-19 patients in elderly nursing homes were not admitted to hospitals, these people who needed treatment were left to die. (The Guardian, 2020).

People have lain undiscovered during the pandemic for seven to 14 days. (The Guardian, 2020).

It is likely that a new crisis will occur if the vaccine required for Covid-19 virus cannot be developed, as discussed in some printed media (CNN health, 2020). In this context, the idea that social entrepreneurs will be an important tool in dealing with all possible negative scenarios can be deduced from the following statements of Managing Director, World Economic Forum Adrian Monck:

If a vaccine doesn't work, social entrepreneurs fight COVID and top stories of the week. (Monck, 2020)

The article titled "COVID-19 and social entrepreneurship" written by Jasna Pocek, acting as Postdoctoral Researcher at Sten K Johnson Center for Entrepreneurship, Lund University School of Economics and Management published on the Raoul Wallenberg Institute (RWI) website includes another statement supporting the idea that social enterprises/entrepreneurs may be more effective than governments or companies in the private sector in meeting the needs of vulnerable groups, as mentioned above.

Since in both **developed** *and developing economies some vulnerable communities seem to be comparably more affected by Covid 19 than the rest of the population, also because of a lack of communication between the government and the individuals inside those communities, social entrepreneurship could offer indeed possible solutions in these cases. (Pocek, 2020)*

Another statement that the colored people, defined among vulnerable and disadvantaged groups, are disproportionately affected from the socioeconomical perspective and that the already existing inequalities between other groups are growing can be found in the article of the guest researcher Michael McEachrane, titled "Covid-19: Disproportionally Hits Segregated Communities" on the RWI website:

Across the world, the infection, lockdown, and economic ramifications of COVID-19 are disproportionally affecting Black and Brown people. This is true both domestically and internationally. The preexisting racial inequities that COVID-19 is exposing are antithetical to principles of equal human dignity, rights, and non-discrimination. (McEachrane, 2020)

On the other hand, social entrepreneurs seem ready to meet new needs that will arise within the framework of scenarios that are foreseen or unforeseen in health, social or economic fields. For example, Executive Director, SCA Group of Companies Bhairavi Jani's article titled "From me to we: COVID-19 heralds a new model of entrepreneurship" supports this idea:

Entrepreneurship has taken a leading role in fighting COVID-19. In the fight against COVID-19, entrepreneurship has taken a lead role in developing contact tracing apps, repurposing factories to manufacture ventilators and PPE, creating makeshift hospitals, and accelerating the search for a vaccine, to name a few examples. (WEF, 2020)

At the academic level, the following article, *"The COVID-19 Virtual Idea Blitz: Marshaling social entrepreneurship to rapidly respond to urgent grand challenges"* was published by Bacq et al. (2020) to demonstrate and prove the value of social entrepreneurs' ability to respond quickly to imminent and sudden challenges (health, education, economy, etc.). The article describes the "Virtual idea blitz" project, a rapid intervention attempt of a group of academicians from Indiana University's Kelley School of Business. In this article, it is pointed out that the "virtual idea blitz" project is organized in a very short time and it is a community-based project in which volunteer students, academicians, professionals, and financial groups participate. This social responsibility project generated approximately 95 ideas that produced a high impact in solving the difficulties occurring during the Covid-19 era (Bacq et al., 2020).

Projects Started by Social Entrepreneurs in the Covid-19 Era

Covid-19 health crisis and socio-economic changes that it brings together in many countries of the world cause the existing social problems to grow or new social problems to arise. In this context, social entrepreneurs have taken action to meet new needs arising from socio-economic changes. Below are some examples of social values that social entrepreneurs attempt to capture with the innovative solutions they produce within the framework of the problem-solving nature (Shapiro, 2012) of Covid-19 pandemics.

Our first example is about a social initiative from Turkey where Ebru Baybara Demir, a social entrepreneur, chef, and farmer from Mardin, runs a tourism business and manufactures Allepo soups and Sorgül wheat with women, some from the local people and some from Syrian refugees. She explains what she is doing for the beneficiaries in the projects to alleviate their anxiety about the pandemic:

It is a source of income for women who left their home for the first time or who work for the first time in Mardin's provincial touristic business. The closure of the restaurant due to the outbreak has disrupted the income of working women. But I rolled up the sleeves and increased soap production for a new road map suitable for the period. (Ergu, 2020).

Our second example, also from Turkey, is a social enterprise which aims to create environmental awareness to individuals and works to find solutions to climate change problems. According has stopped some of their ongoing work during the Covid-19 pandemic and launched the "#evdekal" forest project that will create synergies between the Covid-19 pandemic and environmental solutions. The project aims to directly contribute to climate change by throwing a seed with unmanned aerial vehicles they develop for each day people stay at home. According to founder Mert Karslıoğlu talks about the indirect impact of the project as follows:

The production of seed balls is carried out by women experiencing income inequality arising due to climate change, thereby both supporting women's employment and combating climate change collectively. (Sosyalup.net, 2020)

Our third example is Crisis Text Line SMS line organization, which identifies themselves as social entrepreneurs. It is a global non-profit organization that provides free support via SMS in the USA, UK, Ireland, and Canada for issues such as bullying, anxiety, suicide, depression, loneliness, emotional abuse. Individuals can get support by contacting the counselors via sms at the time of the crisis. It also involves consultants who want to work voluntarily by providing training and the organization keeps personal information confidential in all crisis interviews. During the pandemic, they started to provide support for parents, students, healthcare professionals affected by the Covid-19 crisis, and those experiencing financial stress (Crisistextline, 2020).

One of Hong Kong's most established social initiatives and the self-financing Senior Citizen Home Safety Association (SCHSA) has decided to provide 24-hour care and emergency assistance, especially masks and cleaning supplies. It also provides services for elderly people living alone to maintain their mental and emotional health. (Pocek, 2020)

Founded in USA by Jonathan Jackson, the social enterprise and technology company Dimagi creates digital solutions for the least serviced regions of the world to improve healthcare delivery. The initiative, whose domain is Greater China, North America, Africa, the Middle East and North Africa, South Asia,

Latin America, provides support by giving "pro bono" subscriptions during the Covid-19 pandemic for "ComeCare" which is a mobile data platform providing information on the number of cases, patient monitoring and follow-up, topics which healthcare professionals have the most difficulty with. (WEF, 2020).

Link Accessibility, established in Shenzhen, China, is a social enterprise that offers everyone accessibility in mobile applications. In particular, it cooperates with Alibaba, Tencent, Baidu, Oppo and Huawei to provide accessibility in mobile applications for the visually and hearing impaired and the elderly. In the course of the pandemic, they launched the "Wechat" project. The WeChat project is a software that individuals with disabilities can easily use and access Covid-19 information, taking into account their needs. It is reported that it has reached approximately 13,000 people after its introduction in February, preventing their current obstacles from causing further difficulties in outbreak conditions. In their interviews titled "*During Covid-19, this social enterprise reached out to 17 million people*", Xiao Longdan and Liquan Wu expressed their thoughts about the process as follows:

In our call for action, we called upon the society to not forget those persons with disabilities, especially in times of crisis. (Linkedin interview, 2020).

As can be understood from the two examples we have given above, the social value that social entrepreneurs try to create in the period of Covid-19 contributes to wide masses. In this context, a social entrepreneurship program against the Covid-19 pandemic was launched by Çukurova Development Agency (ÇKA) within the emerging ecosystem in Turkey. Within the scope of the development of social entrepreneurship, it is aimed to develop new business and project ideas in successfully fighting the pandemic.

Another example of social entrepreneurship is Simprints, another social enterprise founded by Jonathan Jackson. In 12 countries, they established a biometric patient identification system so that healthcare workers can effectively follow the pandemic process, and they made it easier for patients to be followed. Thanks to biometric patient identities, community-based health data will be created and health problems that may develop later can be predicted (Simprints, 2020).

First Respond is China's first social initiative (90,000) certified at the B level that provides the highest level of first aid training at the global level. The sudden onset and rapid spread of the outbreak caused great pressures in the health system, and First Respond, by fighting information pollution during this pandemic, gave people the right information about the pandemic and started online courses on how to protect themselves (mask, disinfectant) (Scoll, 2020).

Within the increasing importance of social entrepreneurship worldwide, and especially with the Covid-19 outbreak, UNESCO, IBM and SAP2 Covid 19 launched the project "Code The Curve Hackathon" to develop digital solutions for the effects of the pandemic and to support young innovators, data scientists and designers globally. By presenting their innovative solutions, participants will benefit from the trainings and events to be provided by IBM, SAP, FOSSASIA and iHackOnline organizations. It also takes into account the efforts initiated by UNESCO for young female software developers to develop their digital and professional competencies (UNESCO, 2020).

The "Hack for Sweden" and "Hack the crisis" project initiated during the Covid-19 era by the Swedish government for the future of Sweden were developed to support innovative social initiatives that can find a cure for the Covid 19 outbreak. (Hackforsweden, 2020)

As can be seen from the examples above, governments and organizations have also announced their support for the solution of the problems experienced during the Covid-19 period.

FUTURE RESEARCH DIRECTIONS

This research aims to reveal the increasing importance of social enterprises in the Covid-19 period and the social value they create. In this context, four different groups that are considered to be vulnerable during the pandemic process are focused around the world and the projects carried out by social enterprises for these groups are mentioned. Future studies, the effects of Covid 19 could be conducted in a cultural context and through more regional studies through different groups.

CONCLUSION

Covid-19, which actually started as a health crisis, caused unexpected global socio-economic effects in a short time due to its ease of transmission. Furthermore, the effects of COVID-19 continue, and there is still uncertainty about how this will affect humanity. In this context ıt is very important to use an entrepreneurial perspective to generate new ideas, solutions and methods in dealing with unexpected crisis situations.

İt is considered important to evaluate the importance and role of the social entrepreneurs in creating social value under the uncertain conditions of the health, social or economic crisis. For this reason, the Covid-19 outbreak and the importance of social entrepreneurship, which are very up-to-date topics, were discussed in this part of the book. The socioeconomic effects of the Covid-19 pandemic, the state of the disadvantaged and vulnerable groups experiencing social exclusion during the pandemic, and information and explanations on the social value created by social enterprises and the projects they realized are provided.

Overall, social initiatives respond to social challenges recognized by the United Nations with a global perspective and regional innovations they bring. The efforts of social entrepreneurs to create social value by providing solutions to specific problems and needs are also supported by many governments and organizations. At the same time during the Covid-19 process, more than 50 global organizations come together with "The COVID Response Alliance for Social Entrepreneurs" to support social entrepreneurs, and continue to support more than 15000 social entrepreneurs (Schwab, 2020)

Social enterprises have entered into a rapid transformation to meet the new needs that emerged with the Covid -19 pandemic process. According to the findings obtained, it can be said that by producing innovative, fast and effective solutions during the Covid-19 pandemic process, social initiatives have won the approval of the society. The headlines of leading media outlets published between December 2019 and June 2020, and discourses from social actors confirm the rising critical value of social entrepreneurs.

The following statements in Social Enterprise UK's "Social Enterprise and Covid-19" report again confirm this view: *"Social entrepreneurs are using the COVID-19 crisis to showcase the best of what they do and to further differentiate themselves from mainstream business. As the UK looks towards recovery, social entrepreneurs that demonstrate strong community and social engagement may to do better and many are already innovating in how they combine agile business approaches with an ongoing commitment to social value."* (Social Enterprise UK, 2020:7). It seems that in the fight against an unprecedented challenge called Covid-19, Social Entrepreneurship will become even more valuable in the near future in their responses to local needs, including vulnerable groups.

REFERENCES

Acar Erdur, D., & Afacan Fındıklı, M. (2020). A Conceptual Model Proposal for Co-Creation of Social Value: Insights from Social Entrepreneurs. *Istanbul Gelisim University Journal of Social Sciences*, *7*(1), 1–20.

Adolphus, M. (2020). *How to use discourse analysis*. Available at: https://www.emeraldgrouppublishing.com/archived/research/guides/methods/discourse_analysis.htm

Alsafi, Z., Abbas, A. R., Hassan, A., & Ali, M. A. (2020). *The Coronavirus Pandemic: Adaptations in Medical Education*. International Journal of Surgery.

Antadze, N., & Westley, F. (2010). funding social innovation: How do we know what to grow? *Philanthropist*, *23*(3).

Bacq, S., Geoghegan, W., Josefy, M., Stevenson, R., & Williams, T. A. (2020). The COVID-19 Virtual Idea Blitz: Marshaling social entrepreneurship to rapidly respond to urgent grand challenges. *Business Horizons*.

Bbcnews. (2020a). *Coronavirus deaths: How big is the epidemic in care homes?* Available at: https://www.bbc.com/news/health-52284281

Bbcnews. (2020b). *Coronavirus: What's going wrong in Sweden's care homes?* Available at: https://www.bbc.com/news/world-europe-52704836

Bonnici, F. (2020). *Why social entrepreneurs are critical to our response to and recovery from the COVID-19 crisis*. Available at: https://www.weforum.org/agenda/2020/05/schwab-foundation-covid-response-alliance-social-entrepreneurs-coronavirus-recovery response/?utm_source=sfmc&utm_medium=email&utm_campaign=2718479_Agenda_weekly-8May2020&utm_term=&emailType=Newsletter [Accessed: 06 JUNE 2020]

Bornstein, D. (2007). *How to change the world: Social entrepreneurs and the power of new ideas*. Oxford University Press.

Brooke, J., & Jackson, D. (2020). Older people and COVID-19: Isolation, risk and ageism. *Journal of Clinical Nursing*.

Burchardt, T., Le Grand, J., & Piachaud, D. (2002b). Degrees of exclusion: Developing a dynamic, multidimensional measure. In J. Hills, J. Le Grand, & D. Piachaud (Eds.), *Understanding social exclusion*. Oxford University Press.

CBSNEWS. (2020). Available at: https://www.cbsnews.com/news/coronavirus-quarantine-workers-without-pay-help/

Chen, W. C., Huang, A. S., Chuang, J. H., Chiu, C. C., & Kuo, H. S. (2011). Social and economic impact of school closure resulting from pandemic influenza A/H1N1. *The Journal of Infection*, *62*(3), 200–203. doi:10.1016/j.jinf.2011.01.007 PMID:21256153

CNNhealth. (2020). *What happens if a coronavirus vaccine is never developed? It has happened before.* Available at: https://edition.cnn.com/2020/05/03/health/coronavirus-vaccine-never-developed-intl/index.html

Connell, J., Burgess, J., Theodore, N., Valenzuela, A., & Meléndez, E. (2009). Worker centers: Defending labor standards for migrant workers in the informal economy. *International Journal of Manpower.*

Crisistextline. (2020). *How to Handle Coronavirus.* Available at: https://www.crisistextline.org/topics/get-help-coronavirus/#for-healthcare-workers-6

Yap. (2020, Feb. 8). China's factories struggle to resume operations after virus shutdown. *Wall St. J.* Available at: https://www.wsj.com/articles/chinas-factories-struggle-to-resume-operations-after-virus-shutdown-11581157800

Dacın, P. A., Dacın, M. T., & Matear, M. (2010). Social entrepreneurship: Why we don't need a new theory and how we move forward. *The Academy of Management Perspectives, 24*(3), 37–57.

Dacin, P. A., Dacin, M. T., & Tracey, P. (2011). Social entrepreneurship: A critique and future directions. *Organization Science, 22*(5), 1203–1213. doi:10.1287/orsc.1100.0620

Drayton, W. (2006). Everyone a changemaker: Social entrepreneurship's ultimate goal. *Innovations: Technology, Governance, Globalization, 1*(1), 80–96. doi:10.1162/itgg.2006.1.1.80

Easterly, W. (2009). How the millennium development goals are unfair to Africa. *World Development, Vol, 37*(1), 26–35. doi:10.1016/j.worlddev.2008.02.009

Economictimes. (2020). *Omidyar Network India announces Rapid Response Funding for Covid-19.* Available at: https://economictimes.indiatimes.com/small-biz/sme-sector/omidyar-network-india-announces-rapid-response-funding-for-covid19/articleshow/74789991.cms?from=mdr

Ergu, E. (2020). *İlham Veren Kadınlar.* Available at: https://www.hurriyet.com.tr/ekonomi/ebru-baybara-demir-avrupaya-sorgul-bugdayi-ve-mardin-sabununu-online-anlatacak-avrupaya-ilham-olacak-41502929

Euronews. (2020). Available at: https://www.euronews.com/2020/05/21/are-care-homes-the-dark-side-of-sweden-s-coronavirus-strategy

FernandesN. (2020). Economic effects of coronavirus outbreak (COVID-19) on the world economy. Available at SSRN 3557504. doi:10.2139srn.3557504

Financial Tımes. (2020). Available at: https://www.ft.com/content/9d6b46e2-55f4-4de1-ba21-f1ab9f-14bcbf

Financial Tımes. (2020). *Covid-19.* Available at: https://www.ft.com/content/0fdb770a-a57a-11ea-92e2-cbd9b7e28ee6

Fundacionparaguaya. (2020). *Covıd-19.* Available at: http://www.fundacionparaguaya.org.py/v2/?noticias=nos-cuidamos-y-te-cuidamos

FOXNEWS. (2020). Available at: https://www.foxnews.com/category/health/infectious-disease/coronavirus

Gao, J., Tian, Z., & Yang, X. (2020). Breakthrough: Chloroquine phosphate has shown apparent efficacy in treatment of COVID-19 associated pneumonia in clinical studies. *Bioscience Trends*, *14*(1), 72–73. doi:10.5582/bst.2020.01047 PMID:32074550

Globalshapers. (2020). *Konexio's Online Mentoring and Training During COVID-19*. Available at: https://www.globalshapers.org/impact/konexios-online-mentoring-and-training-during-covid-19

Gössling, S., Scott, D., & Hall, C. M. (2020). Pandemics, tourism and global change: A rapid assessment of COVID-19. *Journal of Sustainable Tourism*, 1–20.

Groot, A., & Dankbaar, B. (2014). Does social innovation require social entrepreneurship? *Technology Innovation Management Review*, *4*(12), 17–26. doi:10.22215/timreview/854

Guerrieri, V., Lorenzoni, G., Straub, L., & Werning, I. (2020). *Macroeconomic Implications of COVID-19: Can Negative Supply Shocks Cause Demand Shortages?* (No. w26918). National Bureau of Economic Research.

Hackforsweden. (2020). Available at: https://www.hackthecrisis.se/challenges

Helgesson, M., Johansson, B., Nordqvist, T., Lundberg, I., & Vingård, E. (2013). Unemployment at a young age and later sickness absence, disability pension and death in native Swedes and immigrants. *European Journal of Public Health*, *23*(4), 606–610. doi:10.1093/eurpub/cks099 PMID:22930745

Hellström, E., Hämäläinen, T., Lahti, V. M., Cook, J. W., & Jousilahti, J. (2015). *Towards a Sustainable Well-Being Society*. Academic Press.

Hoque, A., Shikha, F. A., Hasanat, M. W., Arif, I., & Hamid, A. B. A. (2020). The effect of Coronavirus (COVID-19) in the tourism industry in China. *Asian Journal of Multidisciplinary Studies*, *3*(1), 52–58.

ILO. (2020). *Available at: As job losses escalate, nearly half of global workforce at risk of losing livelihoods*. https://www.ilo.org/global/about-the-ilo/newsroom/news/WCMS_743036/lang--en/index.htm

ILO Monitor. (2020). *COVID-19 and the world of work. Fourth edition Updated estimates and analysis*. Available at: https://www.ilo.org/wcmsp5/groups/public/@dgreports/@dcomm/documents/briefingnote/wcms_745963.pdf

IMF. (2020). *Policy Responses To Covid-19*. Available at: https://www.imf.org/en/Topics/imf-and-covid19/Policy-Responses-to-COVID-19#U

Jackson, W. T., & Jackson, M. J. (2014). Social Enterprises And Social Entrepreneurs: One Size Does Not Fit All. *Academy of Entrepreneurship Journal*, *20*(2), 152–162.

Jani, B. (2020). *From me to we: COVID-19 heralds a new model of entrepreneurship*. Available at: https://www.weforum.org/agenda/2020/05/covid-19-is-showing-us-a-new-model-of-entrepreneurship/

Jordan, R. E., Adab, P., & Cheng, K. K. (2020). *Covid-19: risk factors for severe disease and death*. Academic Press.

Kummitha, R. K. R. (2016). Social Entrepreneurship As A Tool To Remedy Social Exclusion: A Win–Win Scenario? *South Asia Research*, *36*(1), 1–19. doi:10.1177/0262728015615485

Kummitha, R. K. R. (2017). *Social Entrepreneurship and Social Inclusion*. Palgrave., doi:10.1007/978-981-10-1615-8

Korsgaard, S. (2011). Opportunity formation in social entrepreneurship. *Journal of Enterprising Communities: People and Places in the Global Economy*, *5*(4), 265–285. doi:10.1108/17506201111177316

Levitas, R. (2005). *The inclusive society? Social exclusion and new labour*. Palgrave Macmillan.

Linkedininterwiev. (2020). *Interview I During COVID-19, this social enterprise reached out to 17 million people*. Available at: https://www.linkedin.com/pulse/interview-during-covid-19-social-enterprise-reached-out-shenzhen/

Lloyd-Sherlock, P., Ebrahim, S., Geffen, L., & McKee, M. (2020). *Bearing the brunt of covid-19: older people in low and middle income countries*. Academic Press.

Littlewood, D., & Kahn, Z. (2018). Insights from a systematic review of literature on social enterprise and networks Where, how and what next? *Social Enterprise Journal*, *14*(4), 390–409. doi:10.1108/SEJ-11-2018-068

Maclean, M., Harvey, C., & Gordon, J. (2013). Social innovation, social entrepreneurship and the practice of contemporary entrepreneurial philanthropy. *International Small Business Journal*, *31*(7), 747–763. doi:10.1177/0266242612443376

Maır, J., & Martı, I. (2006). Social Entrepreneurship Research: A Source of Explanation, Prediction, and Delight. *Journal of World Business*, *41*(1), 36–44. doi:10.1016/j.jwb.2005.09.002

Manning, P., & Trimmer, T. (2020). *Migration in world history*. Routledge. doi:10.4324/9781351256681

McEachrane, M. (2020). *COVID-19: Disproportionally Hits Segregated Communities*. Available at: https://rwi.lu.se/2020/05/covid-19-disproportionally-hits-segregated-communities/

Monck, A. (2020). *If a vaccine doesn't work, social entrepreneurs fight COVID and top stories of the week*. Available at https://www.weforum.org/agenda/2020/05/if-a-vaccine-doesnt-work-social-entrepreneurs-fight-covid-and-top-stories-of-the-week/

MorsyH. (2012). Scarred generation. Available at SSRN 3093019

Nicola, M., Alsafi, Z., Sohrabi, C., Kerwan, A., Al-Jabir, A., Iosifidis, C., Agha, M., & Agha, R. (2020). The socio-economic implications of the coronavirus and COVID-19 pandemic: A review. *International Journal of Surgery*, *78*, 185–193. doi:10.1016/j.ijsu.2020.04.018 PMID:32305533

OECD. (2008). *Growing unequal? Income distribution and poverty in OECD countries*. Paris, France: Organisation for Economic Co-operation and Development. Available at: https://www.oecd.org/els/soc/growingunequalincomedistributionandpovertyinoecdcountries.htm

Office for National Statistic. (2020). *Deaths involving COVID-19 by local area and socioeconomic deprivation: deaths occurring between 1 March and 17 April 2020*. Available at: https://www.ons.gov.uk/peoplepopulationandcommunity/birthsdeathsandmarriages/deaths/bulletins/deathsinvolvingcovid-19bylocalareasanddeprivation/deathsoccurringbetween1marchand17april

Phillips, N., Lawrence, T. B., & Hardy, C. (2004). Discourse and institutions. *Academy of Management Review, 29*(4), 635–652. doi:10.5465/amr.2004.14497617

Pocek, J. (2020). *COVID-19: Social Entrepreneurship*. Available at: https://rwi.lu.se/2020/04/covid-19-social-entreprenurship/

Saith, R. (2001). *Social Exclusion: The Concept and Application to Developed Countries* (Working Paper No. 72). QEH Working Paper Series.

Seyfang, G. (2003). Growing cohesive communities one favour at a time: Social exclusion, active citizenship, and time banks. *International Journal of Urban and Regional Research, 27*(3), 699–706. doi:10.1111/1468-2427.00475

Schwabfound. (2020). *COVID Response Alliance for Social Entrepreneurs*. Available at: https://www.schwabfound.org/covid-response-alliance-for-social-entrepreneurs

Scarpetta, S., Sonnet, A., & Manfredi, T. (2010). *Rising youth unemployment during the crisis*. Academic Press.

Scoll. (2020). *How Chinese Social Entrepreneurs Stepped up to Respond to COVID-19*. Available at: https://skoll.org/2020/05/04/how-chinese-social-entrepreneurs-stepped-up-to-respond-to-covid-19/

Shen, C. (2020). *How Chinese Social Entrepreneurs Stepped up to Respond to COVID-19*. Available at: https://skoll.org/2020/05/04/how-chinese-social-entrepreneurs-stepped-up-to-respond-to-covid-19/

Silverman, D. (2002). Analyzing talk and text. In N. K. Denzin & Y. S. Lincoln (Eds.), *Handbook of Qualitative Research* (2nd ed., pp. 821–834). Sage Publications.

Simprints. (2020). Available at: https://www.simprints.com/impact

Social EnterprıseU. K. (2020). Available at: https://www.socialenterprise.org.uk/wp-content/uploads/2020/05/Social-Enterprise-COVID-19-research-report-2020.pdf

Sohrabi, C., Alsafi, Z., O'Neill, N., Khan, M., Kerwan, A., Al-Jabir, A., ... Agha, R. (2020). World Health Organization declares global emergency: A review of the 2019 novel coronavirus (COVID-19). *International Journal of Surgery*.

Sosyalup.net. (2020). *Türkiye'nin ilk EvdeKal Ormanı teknolojiyle kuruluyor*. Available at: http://sosyalup.net/turkiyenin-ilk-evdekal-ormani-teknolojiyle-kuruluyor/

Time. (2020). *If We Don't Work, We Don't Get Paid.' How the Coronavirus Is Exposing Inequality Among America's Workers*. Available at: https://time.com/5795651/coronavirus-workers-economy-inequality/

The Guardian. (2020). *Virus patients more likely to die may have ventilators taken away*. Available at: https://www.theguardian.com/society/2020/apr/01/ventilators-may-be-taken-from-stable-coronavirus-patients-for-healthier-ones-bma-says

The Guardian. (2020). *UK coronavirus victims have lain undetected at home for two weeks*. Available at: https://www.theguardian.com/world/2020/jun/07/uk-coronavirus-victims-have-lain-undetected-at-home-for-two-weeks

Thompson, J. L. (2002). The World Of The Social Entrepreneur. *International Journal of Public Sector Management, 15*(5), 412–431. doi:10.1108/09513550210435746

UNDP. (2020). *Socio-economic impact of COVID-19*. Available at https://www.undp.org/content/undp/en/home/coronavirus/socio-economic-impact-of-covid-19.html

UNESCO. (2020). *UNESCO launches CodeTheCurve Hackathon to develop digital solutions in response to COVID-19*. Available at: https://en.unesco.org/news/unesco-launches-codethecurve-hackathon-develop-digital-solutions-response-covid-19 [Accessed: 02 JUNE 2020]

UNESCO. (2020). *Education: From disruption to recovery*. Available at: https://en.unesco.org/covid19/educationresponse

UNSDG. (2020). *Shared Responsıbılıty, Global Solıdarıty: Responding To The Socio-Economic İmpacts Of Covıd-19 March 2020*. Author.

Van Bavel, J. J., Baicker, K., Boggio, P. S., Capraro, V., Cichocka, A., Cikara, M., ... Drury, J. (2020). Using social and behavioural science to support the COVID-19 pandemic response. *Nature Human Behaviour*, 1–12. PMID:32355299

Wacquant, L. (2008). *Urban outcasts: A comparative sociology of advanced marginality*. Polity.

WEF. (2020a). *The pandemic will leave the poor further disadvantaged – IMF*. Available at: https://www.weforum.org/agenda/2020/05/pandemics-poor-rich-economics-coronavirus-covid19/

WEF. (2020b). *6 ways social innovators are responding to the COVID-19 pandemic*. Available at https://www.weforum.org/agenda/2020/03/how-social-innovators-are-responding-to-the-covid19-pandemic/

WEF. (2013). *The Challenge of Youth Unemployment*. Available at http://www3.weforum.org/tools/gac/youth-unemployment-visualization-2013/

Wennekers, S., van Stel, A., Thurik, R., & Reynolds, P. (2005). Nascent entrepreneurship and the level of economic development. *Small Business Economics, 24*(3), 293–309. doi:10.100711187-005-1994-8

WHO. (2020). *OHCHR, IOM, UNHCR and WHO joint press release: the rights and health of refugees, migrants and stateless must be protected in COVID-19 response*. Available at: https://www.who.int/news-room/detail/31-03-2020-ohchr-iom-unhcr-and-who-joint-press-release-the-rights-and-health-of-refugees-migrants-and-stateless-must-be-protected-in-covid-19-response

WİEGO. (2020). *Covid-19: Impact on Home-Based Workers in South Asia Charter of Demands by HomeNet South Asia*. https://www.wiego.org/resources/homenet-south-asias-demands-covid-19-crisis

World Bank. (2002-2009). Globalization, Growth, and Poverty. In Poverty Measures. World Bank Policy Research Report.

World Bank. (2020). *The impact of COVID-19 (Coronavirus) on global poverty: Why Sub-Saharan Africa might be the region hardest hit*. Available at https://blogs.worldbank.org/opendata/impact-covid-19-coronavirus-global-poverty-why-sub-saharan-africa-might-be-region-hardest

World Bank. (2020). *Updated estimates of the impact of COVID-19 on global poverty*. Available at https://blogs.worldbank.org/opendata/updated-estimates-impact-covid-19-global-poverty

Yin, R. K. (1994). Case study research: Design and methods (2nd ed.). Thousand Oaks, CA: Sage.

KEY TERMS AND DEFINITIONS

COVID-19 Response of Social Entrepreneurs: The solutions developed by social enterprises for socioeconomic problems arising with the Covid-19 pandemic.

Disadvantaged Group: Groups that have difficulty accessing social protection systems for different reasons (women, older persons, color people, refugees, and migrants)

Inequality in Social Life: The differentiation preference of access of social goods in the society brought about by power, religion, race, ethnicity, gender, age, sexual orientation, and class.

Social Entrepreneurs Project: Projects initiated by the social enterprises in the era of covid-19 to create social value.

Social Exclusion: Being excluded from communities for various reasons, not being able to utilize general rights and benefits.

Social Value Creation: All kinds of projects or models that will provide access to resources that can create social impact.

Socioeconomic Impacts: Financial and social impact on people, communities resulting from an action or inaction, event, project, or policy.

Chapter 16
Massive Open Online Course (MOOC) Platforms as Rising Social Entrepreneurs:
Creating Social Value Through Reskilling and Upskilling the Unemployed for After COVID-19 Conditions

Çağla Arıker
Istanbul Gelisim University, Turkey

ABSTRACT

Educational social entrepreneurs which offer massive open online courses (MOOCs) create social value through removing inequality in terms of reaching educational resources to develop new skills required by the business world through offering free or low cost, high quality online courses to anyone anywhere and removing the barriers of traditional education cost, location, and access. The negative effects of COVID-19 pandemic on unemployment levels and new graduates' expectations about finding a job are apparent. As known, there has also been a long-standing debate over the insufficiency of traditional education models in terms of satisfying human resources qualifications needed by contemporary business world. After the pandemic, new jobs and new business models requiring new employee skills are also expected to occur. As a result, the understanding behind the MOOCs and the importance of social entrepreneurs which offer MOOCs increased. For these reasons, the purpose of this chapter is to examine MOOCs platforms and their actions to create social value during the COVID-19 pandemic.

INTRODUCTION

Continuous digitalization has been affecting all industries and resulting in a rise of new business models with a new understanding. There has also been a long-standing debate over the insufficiency of traditional education models in terms of satisfying human resources qualifications needed by thecontemporary busi-

DOI: 10.4018/978-1-7998-4727-4.ch016

ness world. Another dimension of these ongoing discussions includes the criticisms toward inequality of education opportunities. Creating social value through giving equal chance to access quality education and democratization of education have been positioned as an ideal vision for all societies. Digitalization creates an opportunity to make this dream true since it eliminates all constraints such as location, time, prerequisites, financial power that hinder people to reach educational resources and institutes. As a result, transformation of traditional education understanding toward a more open, equitable and affordable one has also been a discussion under the shadow of digitalization for a long time especially from the perspective of higher education and with the leadership of universities with high reputation.

Use of open online courses for educational purposes has appeared as an inevitable result of digitalization. Educational social entrepreneurs which offer Massive Open Online Courses (MOOCs) create social value through to removing inequality in terms of reaching educational resources to develop new skills required by the business world through offering free or low cost, high quality online courses to anyone anywhere and removing the barriers of traditional education cost, location and access. The trend to reskill and upskill oneself through participating in courses provided by MOOCs social entrepreneurs has been a rising one since 2012. Three major MOOCs social entrepreneurs represented by Coursera, Udacity, and edX have been cooperated with top universities around the world since 2012 and many others have been also founded to provide online education services (Zhao et al., 2020, pp. 3). Millions of people from all around the world have already taken hundreds of different courses provided by several MOOCs social entrepreneurs until 2019. As known, a pandemic, called as COVID-19, appeared at the end of 2019, caused many unpredictable, sharp and compulsory changes creating almost a dystopian world. Most governments are forced to take measurements such as lockdowns, home working and distance education in order to decrease the speed of disease which creates enormous amount of burden on hospitals, health professionals and finally the economies of countries. All of these measurements created a new revolutionary environment that accelerated people's adoption to online learning.

The negative effects of COVID-19 pandemic on unemployment levels and new graduates' expectations about finding a job are apparent. After the pandemic, new jobs and new business models requiring new employee skills are also expected to occur. As a result, the understanding behind the MOOCs and the importance of social entrepreneurs which offer MOOCs increased. For these reasons, the purpose of this chapter is to examine MOOCs platforms and their actions to create social value during the COVID-19 pandemic.

The chapter is organized as follows. First of all, definitions of MOOCs and historical development of MOOCs social entrepreneurs are explained. Secondly, the negative effects of COVID-19 pandemic are examined. Thirdly, some examples of MOOCs social entrepreneurs are introduced, their social impacts are discussed and their responses to COVID-19 pandemic in terms of creating a social value during hard times are examined. Finally, a conclusion about the future revolutionary impact of MOOCs social entrepreneurs is provided.

BACKGROUND

MOOC stands for four words, namely "Massive" meaning broad participation of global users with various background and demography, "Open" meaning freedom of participation, "Online" meaning connecting through the Internet and finally "Course" meaning lectures designed for online learning (Lubis et al., 2020, pp. 2716).

In "Institutional MOOC Strategies in Europe" report of EADTU (European Association of Distance Teaching Universities), MOOCs are defined as "online courses designed for large numbers of participants, that can be accessed by anyone anywhere as long as they have an internet connection, are open to everyone without entry qualifications, and offer a full/complete course experience online for free" (Jansen & Schuwer, 2015, pp. 4) McAuley et al. (2010, pp. 10) defined Massive Open Online Courses (MOOCs) as "an online course with the option of free and open registration, a publicly shared curriculum, and open-ended outcomes". Fini (2009, pp. 4) defined MOOCs as "live courses, which include direct participation of teachers and rich and valuable interaction among participants".

The main advantages of MOOCs include flexibility without being limited by distance, space and time; reduction of costs both for MOOCs providers and participants; no entrance requirements for the participants other than Internet Access, and no limits to set a maximum number of participants (Verawardina et al., 2020, pp. 386; Castaño-Muñoz et al., 2018, pp. 608).

MOOCs support "many-to-many relationship" since they allow large number of participators from around the world instead of traditional "ono-to-many model of interactions" that are just between a teacher and students (Fini, 2009, pp. 3). Another words, MOOC participators may also contribute to the content and quality of courses at a large scale which in turn creates a richer learning environment while teachers have the role of moderators as well as their traditional roles of teaching a structural content. Srivastava et al. (2020, pp. 5) states that students in online learning have more learning engagement, learn in less time and their retention of information is better relative to traditional learning.

The first large scale MOOC, "The Connectivism & Connective Knowledge / CCK08" was introduced at the University of Manitoba through the Learning Technologies Centre and Extended Education by George Siemens and Stephen Downes in 2008 as a part of the program leading to the Certificate in Adult and Continuing Education (CACE) (Downes, 2008, pp. 1). Before CCK08, there were many universities offering online courses to a small, limited audience (Ng & Widom, 2014, pp. 1). What makes CCK08 different from its precedents is a total of 2,200 people from around the World participating in the course (Downes, 2009). The course was offered formal, informal and hybrid ways. The name formal states for course participants from University of Manitoba students earning credits as a result of completing the course and its assignments while informal means participants from outside the University who took the course with their own choice and without any obligation, academic certification and grading (Fini, 2009, pp. 2). The third type of participants were allowed to choose a mixed way of taking the course as enrolling to the online course and being evaluated by their own institution (Fini, 2009, pp. 2). As seen, the first occurrence of MOOC type of courses is to support lifelong learning.

In 2011, Stanford University offered three courses free to the public, each garnering signups of about 100,000 learners or more and giving the opportunity to watch online lectures, do machine-graded homework, and earn a "Statement of Accomplishment" after passing the class (Ng & Widow, 2014, pp. 1). The platform developed for two of these courses called as "Databases" taught by Jeniffer Widom and "Machine Learning" taught by Andrew Ng, became the genesis of today's Coursera while the third one called as "Artificial Intelligence" taught by Sebastian Thrun and Peter Norvig, became the genesis of today's Udacity (Ng & Widow, 2014, pp. 1).

The main difference between the open course of University of Manitoba and the courses of Stanford University is the allowed level of live interaction between the participators. The type of MOOCs similar to the Stanford University's is called as xMOOCs (eXtended MOOCs) while the type of MOOCs similar to the University of Manitoba's is called as cMOOCs (connectivist MOOCs). Both types include some pros and cons. xMOOCs are structural and traditional university courses allowing high number of people to take university level courses but eliminating interaction between the instructor and student as well as between students (Lu & Dzikria, 2020, pp. 2). On the contrary, cMOOCs allow a high-level communication and collaboration between participants although traditional teacher-student interaction is limited (Lu & Dzikria, 2020, pp. 2). Use of cMOOCs require the capability of self-regulated learning for participators (Littlejohn et al., 2016, pp. 41) since it emphasizes on learner centered, learner directed and collaborative style of learning process in which the lecturer becomes a motivator, a guide and a resource person (Masaviru, 2020, pp. 59).

The hybrid uses of xMOOCs and cMOOCs can be called blended learning. Blended learning (flipped classroom), once the primary motivation of universities to partner with MOOC platforms like Coursera and edX, includes uploading the primary course content as online videos by the instructor to be learnt at home by the students which in turn brings the advantage of using face-to-face class time for discussions or laboratory experiments more efficiently (Ng & Widow, 2014: 7).

SOCIAL IMPACT OF SOCIAL ENTREPRENEURS OFFERING MASSIVE OPEN ONLINE COURSES

Concepts of Social Entrepreneurship, Social Value and Social Impact

The concept of social entrepreneur is defined in a variety of ways. Abu Saifan (2012, pp. 25) defines the concept as "The social entrepreneur is a mission-driven individual who uses a set of entrepreneurial behaviors to deliver a social value to the less privileged, all through an entrepreneurially oriented entity that is financially independent, self-sufficient, or sustainable." The author states that social entrepreneurs may operate within the boundaries of two business strategies as "non-profit with earned income strategies" that includes a social entrepreneur operating for both social and commercial purposes but revenues and profits generated are used only to further improve the delivery of social values and "for-profit with mission-driven strategies" that includes a social entrepreneur operating again for both social and commercial purposes but the founders and investors can also benefit from personal monetary gain (Abu Saifan, 2012, pp. 26-27).

Tan et al. (2005, pp. 358) defines a social entrepreneur as "a legal person is a social entrepreneur from t1 to t2 just in case that person attempts from t1 to t2, to make profits for society or a segment of it by innovation in the face of risk, in a way that involves that society or segment of it". The author states that a social entrepreneur's objective may be either to profit only society or to profit both society and himself (Tan et al., 2005, pp. 359). They claim that in the latter case there is a continuum of social entrepreneurs in six descending degrees of altruism as the social entrepreneur may attempt to profit society alone at risk of personal loss or foregoing personal profit, to profit society by profiting himself at risk of incurring personal loss or forgoing personal profit, to profit himself by profiting society at risk of personal loss or foregoing personal profit (2005, pp. 359).

In their famous article, Bacq & Janssen define (2011, pp. 388) social entrepreneurship as "the process of identifying, evaluating and exploiting opportunities aiming at social value creation by means of commercial, market-based activities and of the use of a wide range of resources". The authors also state that different forms of social entrepreneurship can be found in the private for-profit sector and in the public sector (Bacq & Janssen, 2011, pp. 388).

Darko and Koranteg (2015, pp. 8) avoid from fixing a tight definition for the concept instead they prefer to classify five different types of social entrepreneurs along a non-profit to for-profit spectrum. Accordingly, social entrepreneurs are classified into five groups as Non-Governmental Organizations (NGOs) that try to build in revenue generating activities to become more sustainable but also rely on grant funding or in-kind support; Non-Profit Organizations that are set up to be self-sustaining or revenue generating; Self-Defined Social Enterprises that are for-profit or nonprofit, have social / environmental purposes, seek sustainability and reinvest profits in business or social / environmental projects; For-Profit Businesses with equal emphasis given to commercial and social / environmental mission; and finally a second group of For-Profit Businesses with strong social / environmental mission but sharing some or all profits with owner.

Eggers and Macmillan (2013, pp. 35) states that social entrepreneurs may mix profit making and social mission at varying degrees. Societal mission is in front for some of social entrepreneurs while both making profit and offering socially responsible goods and services that disrupt the status quo is in balance for others (Eggers and Macmillan, 2013, pp. 35).

Yunus (2010, pp.4) defines social entrepreneurs as non-economic, charity or business initiatives of social consequences created by an entrepreneur with a social vision and with or without profit objectives. De Ruysscher et al. (2016, pp. 2532) define the concept of social entrepreneurship as ''a systematic process that aims to create social value at three levels: improving people's lives, community-building, and improving society".

De Ruysscher et al. (2016, pp. 2536 -2537) define the concept of social value at two levels as "improving people's lives in reference to valued personal outcomes such as individual and /family quality of life" at the individual level and "improving society as reflected in indices reflecting socioeconomic position like education, occupation and income; positive health like longevity, wellness and, access to health care; environmental quality like air, water, and green space; and subjective well-being like life satisfaction, positive affect and absence of negative affect" at the societal level.

Singh (2016, pp. 60) defines social value as the total impact that a social entrepreneur has on the beneficiaries (individuals and societies). When a social entrepreneur contributes to social value creation, a measurable impact is expected to occur at individual and societal level. Cramer et al. (1980, pp. 56) define the concept of social impact as "a significant improvement or deterioration in people's well-being or a significant change in an aspect of community concern." Antadze & Westley (2012, pp. 148) define the concept of social impact as "measurable outcomes that can be causally linked to a specific set of deliberative actions, interventions or programs focused on addressing a social issue or problem.

Social Value Created by MOOCs Social Entrepreneurs

As definitions of social entrepreneurship make explicit, MOOCs entrepreneurs are also in the class of social entrepreneurs that pursue both social and profit missions to varying degrees. MOOC entrepreneurs create social value through offering equal education opportunities for everyone which in turn improve personal life quality and society's well-being as a whole. The basic logic behind Massive Open Online Courses (MOOCs) is to open up educational material to a global audience without time and place constraints. The philosophy behind MOOCs is to provide equal opportunities of education for all people independent from citizenship, ethnicity, prior majors and purchasing power. MOOCs generally carry no fees or affordable level of fees and require no prerequisites except from the Internet connection and necessary hardware to follow the online courses (McAuley et al., 2010, pp. 5). Open courses also offer flexible conditions for participators to choose a time, rhythm and place compatible with their work and family responsibilities (OECD, 2020, pp. 4). As a result, MOOC providers are accepted as social entrepreneurs because of the great potential of MOOCs to contribute in lifelong personal development of individuals which in turn create a real social value through supporting the continuous improvement of the society. When an individual participates in an online course provided by a MOOCs social entrepreneur, he improves himself which in turn opens the doors of better jobs that enhance individual quality of life. Additionally, MOOCs contribute to society's well-being since it depends on individual human beings.

Technology-based teaching has been revolutionizing traditional higher-education since CCK08 and the initiatives of Stanford University (Chen, 2013, pp. 1). On the other hand, the role of MOOCs has been not restricted within the borders of higher-education. Over the years, MOOCs social entrepreneurs have gained acceptance as online course providers for lifelong learning as well as traditional university education (Bylieva et al., 2020, pp. 1084).

Today, having a university degree is not sufficient and a continuous update of post-degree knowledge and competencies, namely lifelong learning, is needed due to the speed of technological innovation (Castaño-Muñoz et al, 2018, pp. 607). The need for lifelong learning has been being discussed for years by many global institutions. For instance, the report of UNESCO, published in 2009, highlighted the significance of adult learning and education as a lifelong learning process to create a knowledge-based society (UNESCO, 2009). Lifelong learning is offered to all members of society as a value and culture by the developed countries (Yamamoto & Altun, 2020, pp. 26).

When MOOCs have begun to enhance, they also targeted people from developing countries struggling with low income that hinder their enrollment to top universities abroad (Hone & Said, 2016, pp. 157). In years, MOOCs social entrepreneurs have created their own value and reputation as providers of an alternative and more equitable way of education for anyone who has necessary hardware. Today, their position is not limited to being a blended education tool for higher education students and institutions, but also being a personal development tool for individuals who just want to take new courses to support their career or satisfy their self-actualization needs. As a result, MOOCs gained a new value as the symbols of new education understanding which is totally digitized.

Examples of Social Entrepreneurs Offering MOOC to Create Social Value and Social Impact

As Ayub et al. (2017, pp. 34) underline, the free accessibility of MOOCs is expected to replace the traditional teaching and learning methods which in turn create a great social value through making education affordable and attainable for anyone. All of these companies offer a mix of some fee-based and free courses. As a result, MOOCs create a social value through eliminating constraints of education such as availability of education institutions in a country, affordability of education fees, accessibility to the location of education institutions and, acceptability of the quality of education (Lane, 2012, pp. 136; Lane et al., 2014, pp. 117). MOOCs social entrepreneurs create social value through bringing an understanding of more socially conscious education as a result of their high flexibility that allows people around the world to shape their learning according to the constraints of their life (Drăgușin & Welsh, 2015, pp.81).

Coursera, Udemy, Udacity and edX, are the examples of the first social entrepreneurs providing xMOOCs. On the other hand, there are also other social entrepreneurs such as FutureLearn, NovoEd, Canvas, Open2Study, Khan Academy which contribute to the social value through cMOOCs. The first examples of MOOCs social entrepreneurs are examined below.

Coursera: Coursera was founded by Daphne Koller and Andrew Ng from Stanford University in 2012 with a vision of providing life-transforming learning experiences to anyone, anywhere (Coursera, 2020). Today, Coursera is one of the leading MOOCs social entrepreneurs that partners with more than 200 top universities and industry educators to offer courses, certificates, specializations and some degree programs. Its main target markets to offer courses divided into three as Coursera for Business, Coursera for Government, and Coursera for Campus (Coursera, 2020).

The main mission of Coursera for Business is to help transform the human resources of companies through taking training and development programs developed by top universities and businesses for Coursera (Coursera for Business, 2020). Coursera provide collection of courses under some packages such as Data Science for Business Analysts containing six different courses; Digital Marketing containing ten different courses; Mini MBA with seven different courses; Digital Transformations containing nine different courses; Web Development with eight different courses; Machine Learning and Artificial Intelligence with five different courses (Coursera for Business, 2020). Enterprises can also select or order tailored course programs for their teams. Enterprises should pay for the courses.

Coursera for Campus is a service for universities to offer job-relevant, credit-ready, online education to their students, faculty, and staff through more than 4200 available courses provided by top universities (Coursera for Campus, 2020).

Coursera for Government includes courses for government institutions to improve their citizens and employees with essential skills needed for the future of work (Coursera for Government, 2020). The main courses are grouped under business, technology, data science and human resources clusters. Coursera have already cooperated with the governments of countries such as Australia, Colombia, Egypt, India, Kazakhstan, Philippines, Singapore, United Arab Emirates and United States as well as United Nations. For instance, The Egyptian Government's Next Technology Leaders (NTL) Programme, designed to prepare young Egyptians for jobs in tech and entrepreneurship, cooperated with Coursera in 2017 under the arm of Coursera for Government (The Technology Learning, 2020). Similarly, Coursera is also working with The Digital Learning & Skills Enrichment Initiative (DLSEI), an initiative under Prime Minister's Laptop Scheme executed through the Higher Education Commission (HEC) of Pakistan, to combat the rising unemployment through enhancing online learning and skills development among students of Pakistan (An Initiative, 2020).

The vision of Coursera is expressed in this sentence: "We envision a world where anyone, anywhere can transform their life by accessing the world's best learning experience". Coursera is a MOOC social entrepreneur that is positioned to create a social value through closing the gap for access to education and career-skills training (Swersky et al, 2017: 129). The company creates social value through many alternatives of free courses for individuals to contribute to the improvement of individuals' skills and society's welfare. There is no restriction of time, place and financial power as well as any prerequisite to take available courses.

When Coursera cooperated with the U.S. Department of State, and nonprofit organizations around the world to start an initiative, known as Coursera for Refugees, this action was accepted as a testament to the broad social impact potential of MOOCs (Swersky et al, 2017: 128). According to the results of Coursera's Learner Outcomes Survey (2020) which is sent learners six months after completing a course, 73% of course completers report a career outcome such as pay increases, promotions, finding a new job, becoming better at a current job, starting a business, picking a new career path, and improving candidacy for new positions (Hickey et al, 2020, pp. 24). This is an example of social impact measurement for MOOCs social entrepreneurs.

Udemy: Udemy is another MOOCs provider founded by Eren Bali, Oktay Caglar and Gagan Biyani with the objective of making quality education more accessible and improving lives through learning. The company offers 130,000 course alternatives in more than 65 languages and 35 million students have completed courses (Udemy). Business, finance & accounting, IT & software, office productivity, personal development, design, marketing, lifestyle, photography, health & fitness, music, teaching & academics are some examples of main course categories provided by Udemy. The company also divided its customers into three as individuals, businesses and government institutions. In 2020, Udemy found a place at the rank of 34 in Fortune's Change the World list that selects and ranks companies having a positive social impact through activities that are part of their core business strategy (Methodology for Change, 2020).

Udacity: Udacity born as a result of an experiment in online learning at Stanford University when instructors Sebastian Thrun and Peter Norvig offered "Introduction to Artificial Intelligence" course online to 160,000 students in more than 190 countries for free (Udacity, 2020). The company's mission is summarized as to democratize education through making learning accessible and convenient for everyone and to train the world's workforce in the jobs of the future (Udacity, 2020). Udacity partners with leading technology companies and teaches the critical tech skills that companies are looking for in their workforce (Udacity, 2020). Udacity also defines two main customer segments as consumers and enterprises.

The company also develops programs with governments such as Next Generation Abu Dhabi that included nanodegree programs of Business Analytics, Digital Marketing, Front End Developer and AI programming with Python and was launched in partnership with Abu Dhabi School of Government and the Abu Dhabi Youth Council (Next Generation, 2020). One Million Arab Coders is another program to which Udacity contributes through its partnership with the Dubai government to teach Arab youth being interested in developing their digital skills (1 Million, 2020). Udacity partnered with MiSK (Mohammed bin Salman) Foundation in Saudi Arabia, to teach courses such as Android Development, Web Development, and Data Science through providing 2,650 scholarships at the first phase and 6,000 more at the second phase within the framework of this collaboration (Udacity, 2020). Another government partnership was announced with the Ministry of ICT of Egypt to introduce Intro to Programming Nanodegree to 6,000 Egyptian high school students (Shen, 2017).

Udacity announced scholarship programs such as Pledge to Equality Scholarship Program to award 1,000 Nanodegree program scholarships to African Americans in order to create a more diverse talent pool with skills like machine learning, artificial intelligence, cybersecurity and data analysis (New York Amsterdam News, 2020).

Udemy and Udacity are given as examples of social entrepreneurs that balance profit and social value through providing low fee-based education services for the poorest of the poor (Eggers and Macmillan, 2013, pp. 93-98).

edx: edX was founded by Harvard and MIT in 2012. The company is still managed by universities and colleges (edX, 2020). edX, one of the leading MOOCs provider, expressed its position as "The leading MOOC provider that is both nonprofit and open source" or "A global nonprofit that is transforming traditional education, removing the barriers of cost, location and access through providing high-quality education for everyone, everywhere" (edX, 2020). A wide variety of courses from different subjects and degrees are offered by the non-profit company to individuals, university students and enterprises. Some examples of the most popular subjects are Business & Management, Computer Science, Data Analysis & Statistics, Humanities and Language. Other subjects include Architecture, Art & Culture, Chemistry, Communication, Design, Ethics, Energy & Earth Sciences, Medicine, Music, Philanthropy, Science and many others (edX, 2020). edX is accepted as one of the leading educational social entrepreneurs creating social value through contributing education of individual and society. The company has reached 24 million unique users, 80 million unique enrollments, 5,743 instructors, 196 countries, 1.6 million certificates, over 3,000 courses and more than 145 partners (2020 Impact Report). Additionally, 87% of industry professionals who completed edX's MicroMasters Program as well as 81% industry professionals who completed edX's Professional Certificate Program reported positive career outcomes as stated in the company's 2020 Impact Report.

Social Value Created by MOOCs Social Entrepreneurs During Hard Times: The Case of COVID-19 Pandemic

As known, the outbreak of Coronavirus disease 2019 (COVID-19) affected all countries. It engendered an epidemic emergency that endangers the public health and calls for some urgent measures (Feng et al., 2020, pp. 167). Beside from the health considerations, the pandemic has also many negative effects on the economy. It is a pandemic directing many governments to take lockdown measures against the infection. In many countries, schools were closed, flights were canceled, many service companies such as restaurants, hotels and theaters were prohibited from accepting visitors and many companies shifted to home offices.

The pandemic has changed all traditional approaches and created new rules for many industries. Unfortunately, it also resulted in a significant increase at unemployment levels due to the negative effects of lockdowns on the economic growth rates (Bilawar, 2020, pp. 8). The most affected companies which laid off employees or reduced working hours are from the industries such as retail, transportation, commodity supply chains, sales, leisure, and tourism.

According to the OECD Employment Outlook 2020 Report, the impact of the COVID-19 pandemic in the first three months has been ten times bigger than in the first months of the 2008 global financial crisis in terms of collapse in the number of hours people work at OECD markets, 12.2% to 1.2%, respectively.

In the US, the number of unemployed persons was 12.6 million (7.9%) in September 2020 which is almost double of 6.8 million (4.4%) in February, 2020 (U.S. Department of Labor, 2020: 2). The figures were sharper as 14.7% in April up from 4.4% in March (Aratani, 2020). The number of unemployed people living in the OECD countries increased by 18.4 million to 55 million in April 2020 (Unemployment Rates, OECD, June 2020). Even the shares of countries fluctuate, the United States accounted for the main part of this increase, these figures prove an urgent need for measurements since they are worse than many crisis times such as the Great Depression or 2008 financial crisis.

In its optimistic scenario, the unemployment rate peaks at 9.4% on average across the OECD by the end of 2020 which is 5.3% more relative to the end of 2019. OECD also adjusted its projection of unemployment rate as 12.6% in case of the emergence of a second wave in late 2020. The projections by the end of 2021 are also not very hopeful as 7.7% without a second wave and 8.9% with a second wave.

In the UK, the number of people claiming benefits for being out of work or on very low incomes rose 120% to 2.7 million between March and August 2020 as an indicator showing that the real situation can be worse, (King, 2020).

Figures were more drastic for developing or underdeveloped countries. In India, 22 million people lost their jobs in April (Inamdar, 2020). The unemployment rate was up to 24 percent in May, 2020 and the economy is still fragile even though the rate decreased to 6.67% in September 2020 (Keelery, 2020). In South Africa, the unemployment rate reached at 30% which resulted in 350.000 new jobless people taking the total up to 7 million in June 2020 which may hit 50% in the worst-case scenario (The Unemployment Rate, 2020).

Similarly, while higher-earning white-collar workers who can easily adapt to digital technologies often worked from home, lower-earning blue-collar workers often had to stop working which underlines the need for training to adapt to the new world after the pandemic (The OECD Employment Outlook 2020).

Governments allocated a high amount of funds to support businesses to continue hiring workforce and/or to support unemployed ones that create a great burden on the budget. On the other hand, these are short-term measures. More importantly, since COVID-19 pandemic accelerates the transformation of traditional business models, people may not find their works after the recovery. As a result, people may not return to working when economies reboot and many adults may need to upskill, reskill, or seek new occupations (Boeren et al., 2020, pp. 2). This requires also a fast transformation of skills and competencies of human resources to remain competitive in the new world.

One of the most important sectors that was affected by the pandemic is education. After COVID-19 pandemic, a quick, drastic, and unprecedented transformation from face-to-face education to online education has appeared as a must (Al-Matari & Al-Maqbali, 2020, pp. 6).

As lockdowns are being ordered to cope with the global pandemic, face-to-face education opportunities disappear both for students from all school levels and adults who aim lifelong learning (HundrED Research Report, 2020, pp. 10). Although MOOCs social entrepreneurs have existed as new channels of education since 2012 and they have earned a wide acceptance, they have been accepted as supplementary of traditional face-to face education not as mainstreams until COVID-19 pandemic. As Fenwick et al. states (2020, pp. 13), changing the status quo of face-to-face learning has always been difficult, but COVID-19 pandemic caused the birth of a new status quo in which online learning became a standard. The lockdowns and social distancing appeared as the results of a force majeure situation which forced decision makers to implement an online learning strategy and convince students, teachers, academics and lifelong learners to try them. A quick and total return to the old normal is not expected after adapting new normal such as online learning and working from home and experiencing their advantages (Fenwick et.al., 2020: 3). For this reason, the MOOCs social entrepreneurs' role in supporting lifelong learning appears more strongly. They have been invested in online learning technology for years while traditional education institutes were sleeping (HundrED Research Report, 2020, pp. 4).

The MOOCs social entrepreneurs provide many opportunities of self-improvement and adding new skills to individual capabilities through participating in available MOOCs especially for people who lost their jobs during the pandemic.

MOOCs can help the workforce to adapt to the new business conditions after COVID-19 pandemic. Some experts evaluate the period of pandemic as a revolutionary process which changes all traditional molds and people will not return to the status quo when things return to normal (HundrED Research Report, 2020, pp. 5). As a result, some old school jobs may not exist anymore as well as numerous new jobs and ways of conducting a business may appear after the pandemic. This reality requires rapid acquirement of new skills for human resources of all countries.

At this point, MOOCs providers can create a great social value through availing high-quality learning opportunities to mass workforce (Srivastava, et al., 2020, pp. 4). The need for lifelong learning had been discussed for a long time before COVID-19 crisis appeared for sustainability of a technology-based world. In a UN Report called as "Transforming our world: the 2030 Agenda for Sustainable Development", one of the seventeen sustainable development goals was determined as "Ensure inclusive and equitable quality education and promote lifelong learning opportunities for all" (2015, pp. 14).

Since COVID-19 pandemic created a compulsory change that accelerates the transformation of traditional business models, experienced professionals also need to adapt themselves to new environmental conditions. This requires a renewed and more comprehensive lifelong learning view. As a result, the need for lifelong learning to support taking new skills to match with technological changes is now more stunning (Mathes, 2019, pp. 18). MOOCs social entrepreneurs create a social value through providing an opportunity of transformative learning which has the potential to transform a global and individual crisis into a learning experience for people who lost their jobs or want to gain new skills during the COVID-19 crisis (Eschenbacher & Fleming, 2020, pp. 14). MOOCs social entrepreneurs may also contribute in creating social value through offering some open courses targeting the older members of society who are more vulnerable against the social isolation in terms of both physical and mental health at times of COVID-19 crisis (Talmage et al., 2020, pp. 2).

Examples of Initiatives Taken by Social Entrepreneurs Offering MOOC during COVID-19 Pandemic

When searched at Google Trends, a significant increase is observed for the search of words such as MOOCs, online learning, online courses, Coursera, edX, Udacity, FutureLearn, "Khan Academy", "Harvard Online Courses" after the second half of March, 2020. This is a clue that proves the increased interest of people in online learning during the COVID-19 pandemic.

As Bran & Grosseck states (2020, pp. 40), the virtual realm opened up while governments were implementing lockdowns during COVID-19 pandemic. Many institutions such as universities, libraries, museums, and publishers opened their digital sources to the public. Several MOOCs social entrepreneurs also offered numerous courses available for different fields freely as a contribution to diminish the financial effects of lockdowns (Raju, 2020, pp. 27).

Governments in many countries allocated new funds to support online training programs organized by public employment services, municipalities or other government institutions to invest on their workforce against all the odds of COVID-19 pandemic. Public institutions mostly cooperated with course providers like MOOCs social entrepreneurs, universities or volunteers. Many MOOCs social entrepreneurs also partnered with government institutions to support lifelong education of the adults with the purpose of bringing the new skills to adapt after pandemic world conditions.

In the UK, a new online learning platform called as The Skills Toolkit has been launched in April 2020 by the government to help citizens who lost their jobs during the outbreak, are on furlough, want to boost the new skills while working from home for shorter time, graduate recently or own a business and want to upskill their employees through offering free online courses ("New Free", 2020). The Skills Toolkit courses are provided by The Open University, Google, Amazon and FutureLearn with which the government cooperated (The Skills Toolkit, 2020). There are many alternative courses regarding Computer Essentials, Digital Design and Marketing, Computer Science and Coding, Business and Finance, Practical Maths, Personal Growth and Wellbeing and Professional Development. Under Computer Essentials courses, the participants can learn about very basic knowledge such as how to use a computer or device, find a job online, use online public service, use office programs like Microsoft Word or Excel, send emails, create a CV, edit photos, book a meeting, manage personal calendar, organize a to-do list and stay safe online through registering short-time courses. Under Digital Design and Marketing courses, the participants can enhance their digital skills through courses with intermediate level of content such as content planning, use of social media channels, search engine optimization (SEO), display advertising, pay per click, email marketing, targeting customers, data insights, how to design mobile applications, guidance and regulations covering user interfaces, CSS stylesheet language, JavaScript programming language and Photoshop. As seen, each of these concepts have been rising for years and their emergence was accelerated by the pandemic of COVID-19 that created a greater need for online business models. Under the Computer Science section, more advanced level of courses such as cybersecurity, computer networks, artificial intelligence and cloud computing can be found. Similarly, under the Coding section, programming courses such as HTML, CSS and Python exist. These higher-level courses are targeting professionals who want to improve themselves and generally planned for longer hours to complete. Under the Business and Finance section, people can find courses regarding introductory level bookkeeping and financial management as well as sales management, customer service and entrepreneurship. Subjects such as effective communication, skills for career development, working in teams, presentation techniques are offered under the Professional Development section. Resilience at work, dealing with stressful situations, growth mindset and neuroscience for personal development are some examples of courses under the Personal Growth and Wellbeing group. As seen, a wide range of courses are available for beginners, intermediates and advanced ones within the Skills Toolkit.

In September, 29 2020, Prime Minister, Boris Johnson, has also announced a new program called as 'Lifetime Skills Guarantee' in which adults without an A level or equivalent qualification will be offered free college courses so that they can find work in a post-COVID world (Northern Council for Further Education, 2020). Johnson said the government cannot "save every job" amid the Covid-19 pandemic but it's possible to give people new skills to find and create new jobs through offering free and online college courses and encourage their participation across their lifetimes (BBC News, 2020). UK Education Secretary, Gavin Williamson said that current jobs have all changed overnight as a result of the profound effect created by COVID-19 disease which calls for an urgent action (Williamson, 2020). Free college courses, paid for through the National Skills Fund, will be available from April 2020 in England and participators will be given the opportunity to study at a time and location that suits them (BBC News, 2020).

In Canada, Ontario, the government established a partnership with Apple both to provide videos, apps, books and free one-to-one virtual coaching by Apple Professional Learning Specialists to the teachers with the aim of enhancing their digital learning abilities and to deliver I-pad devices to the students and teachers (Ontario Newsroom, 2020).

A high level of demand appeared for online training programs during the COVID-19 pandemic. In the Flemish Region of Belgium, 19,000 online courses, provided by the Public Employment Service (VDAB) offering online training for the workforce, have been applied in the second half of March 2020 that was four times as high as in the same period last year. Some of these courses were accounting, language courses, learning to work with excel and artificial intelligence.

In Nigeria, Kaduna, the Click-On Kaduna program has been launched by the government cooperating with WACOM and Natview Technology that support the program as a CSR project as well as IBM-DNA and the World Bank (Click-On Kaduna, 2020). Free courses such as Content Marketing for a Digital Era, Creative Designs and Animation Illustrations and Entrepreneurship were offered to upscale the digital preparedness of the workforce for the post COVID-19 period (Click-On Kaduna, 2020).

Coursera has also taken some actions during the period of COVID-19 pandemic through starting its Coursera Work Recovery Initiative. The company provided government agencies the opportunity to access its online courses on a free basis to serve citizens who became unemployed due to the pandemic (Leighton, 2020a). As a result, any government institution that applied can be able to open more than

3800 available courses under 400 specializations of Coursera to its unemployed workforce and provide reskilling and upskilling of them for after the pandemic new era. Coursera provided up to 50,000 licenses per government between October 31, 2020 and December 31, 2020.

Hawaii Technology Development Corporation, Government of Barbados Ministry of Labour, The Directorate of Science, Technology and Innovation (DSTI) of Sierra Leone, State of Illinois, American Job Centers at the USA are the examples of local government institutes that cooperated with Coursera's Work Recovery Initiative to create a social value through offering free online courses to reskill and upskill masses who became unemployed due to the pandemic (Governor Pritzker, 2020). COL (Commonwealth of Learning, Canada) and Coursera also partnered through the Workforce Recovery Initiative to help governments in the Commonwealth Nations (COL) and 2,300 learners from 17 African nations participated in these courses (Thousands of African, 2020)

In Turkey, The Municipality of Beylikdüzü, a district in Istanbul, signed a collaboration contract with one of the most known MOOCs social entrepreneurs, Coursera, to offer online courses covering all geographical regions of Turkey. The education movement started in September, 23 2020 and 5983 people participated in 14872 online training courses from 2428 program alternatives until October, 2 2020 (Municipality of Beylikdüzü, 2020). The cooperation was planned to continue until the end of 2020 and the total capacity of learners was 50000 people which were offered a total of 3800 different program alternatives (Coursera Beylikdüzü, 2020). The primary purpose was determined as to support young people who lost the chance of education, employees who lost their jobs or want to adapt to emerging jobs and working requirements of "new normal" due to the COVID-19 pandemic (Coursera Beylikdüzü, 2020). The participants can take several courses from different fields such as Data Science, Business, Computer Science, Information Technology, Personal Development, Language Learning, Math and Logic, Social Sciences, Health, Physical Science and Engineering and Arts and Humanities. These courses were prepared with the collaboration of world class universities such as Stanford University, Yale University, Duke University, Princeton University and Imperial College of London. Coursera also collaborates with Koc University, one of the leading universities of Turkey. The Municipality also shared the certificates acquired after completing the courses and CV's of participants with 2400 international companies. As seen, the cooperation between government institutions and MOOCs social entrepreneurs can contribute to the creation of social value at a larger scale especially during crisis times like Covid-19 pandemic.

Coursera also started Coursera for Campus Response Initiative to minimize the impact of the COVID-19 pandemic on students through offering free access to more than 450 Guided Projects as well as 3,800 courses for students whose universities signed up to the initiative for free (Leighton, 2020b).

Udemy offered a collection from the 614 free courses to support hard times of people during COVID-19 pandemic through investing in self-improvement for after the pandemic period.

In March and April 2020, Udacity provided free access to one of 40 premium Nanodegree programs such as School of Data Science, School of Artificial Intelligence, School of Programming, School of Autonomous Systems, School of Cloud Computing and School of Business covering U.S., Canada and Europe for one month as an opportunity to learn new skills during COVID-19 crisis times (Lager, 2020). This offer attracted 30000 new enrollments to Udacity's nanodegree programs (Johnson, 2020). The company also offered worldwide special discounts for people who had impacted from COVID-19 pandemic, such as laid-off workers, students, and workers managing remote teams (Pradhan, 2020).

Udacity provided 7,000 challenge scholarships and 1,175 Nanodegree scholarships until August, 2020 and target to offer a total of 20,000 scholarships until the end of 2020 for employees who have been laid off due to the COVID-19 pandemic (New York Amsterdam News, 2020).

Another MOOCs social entrepreneur, edX, started a program, Workforce Recovery Acceleration, with the purpose of providing re-entrance of individuals who lost their jobs to the workforce as soon as possible. In the Workforce Recovery Acceleration Program, edX offered a 30% discount for employees negatively impacted from the environmental conditions that occurred as a result of COVID-19 pandemic (A Message from, 2020). This was an offer for courses under MicroMasters Programs, Professional Certificate Programs or MicroBachelors Programs. These programs were based on a segmentation of employees with different needs.

MicroMasters programs target graduate learners who seek an advance for their career through more deep learning in their specialization and cover some advanced courses such as Artificial Intelligence, Entrepreneurship, International Law, International Hospitality Management, Cloud Computing, Big Data, Cybersecurity, Bioformatics, Digital Product Management, Marketing Analytics, Quantum Technology: Computing and so on (MicroMasters Programs, 2020).

Professional Certificate programs target people who need to build and enhance critical professional skills needed in today's most in-demand fields and include large variety of courses such as Risk Management, Retail and Omnichannel Management, Virtual Reality App Management, Java and Android Foundation, Public Library Management, Food, Nutrition and Health, Solar Energy in Hot Desert Climates, Python Data Science and so on (Professional Certificate Programs, 2020).

MicroBachelors programs target adult learners independent from a prerequisite of college degree and include introductory level courses such as Introduction to Information Technology, Computer Science Fundamentals, Professional Writing, Marketing Essentials, Elements of Data Science, Introduction to Databases, Programming & Data Structures and Cybersecurity Fundamentals (MicroBachelors® Programs, 2020). This program is a proper example to prove one of the main features of MOOCs which is learning opportunity for everyone without any prerequisite.

EdX also presented some free courses for medical professionals who influenced from COVID-19 pandemic deeply, and for academic institutions. Examples of free courses offered for medical professionals include Mechanical Ventilation for COVID-19 developed by Harvard University, Safe Surgical Care: Strategies During a Pandemic launched by University of British Columbia, Crisis Resource Management launched by Columbia University and three courses in Spanish as COVID - 19: Ventilación Mecánica Para No Intensivistas (Mechanical Ventilation for Non-Intensivists), COVID-19: Abordaje İnicial Del Paciente Con Infección Por COVID-19 (Revention, Management And General Measures Of COVID-19 İnfection) And, COVID-19: Comunicarnos Sin Daño Durante La Pandemia (Communication Without Harm During The Pandemic) (A Message from, 2020). edX also made some free courses and programs available for qualified accredited higher education institutions (A Message from, 2020).

FUTURE RESEARCH DIRECTIONS

Covid-19 pandemic showed that MOOCs are rising as the new valuable sources of training and education. They will realize their potential as one of the available channels of education as a result of the pandemic's influence on changing traditional habits of people. On the other hand, extensive use of MOOCs also call for many researches to investigate issues such as the most effective content and ways of online teaching, the fields that fit best for online learning, the measurement of conversion rates like return of investment of employees participation in MOOCs and percentage of finding a job after completing different varieties of course programs. The course content should result in a significant reskilling and upskilling of the workforce which in turn creates a higher level of demand from the employers to hire course participators (OECD, 2020: 2). The course content, design and availability of alternative courses may also influence the motivation of participators to complete the course which seems to be a problem currently due to as low as 10% completion rate of online courses (OECD, 2020: 3).

Although MOOCs social entrepreneurs have a great potential to create social value through supporting lifelong learning of the workforce, some problems such as inadequate infrastructure, lack of time, lack of digital competencies and skills have to be solved to provide wider use of MOOCs (Malita et.al., 2018: 235). Lu & Dzikria (2020, pp. 10) found that capacity of intellectual and social capital affect the intention to use MOOCs. For this reason, research to investigate the effectiveness of participation in MOOCs in terms of the ability of students to internalize the course content as a function of intellectual and social capital as well as the ability to use information in business life is needed.

There are also a number of legal issues accompanying online learning like copyright, licensing, and online learning contractual agreements (Milakovich & Wise, 2019, pp. 187). As a result, one major problem regarding MOOCs is the issue of copyright which arises when materials such as text, images, displays, illustrations, audio and video clips and other contents produced by third parties are used in online courses (Wahid et.al, 2015, pp.25). Content of a MOOC must be free from copyright constraints (Kaushik, 2015, pp.114). For this reason, use of third-party materials calls for a need of permission from the copyright owner in order to avoid any possible jurisdiction (Wahid et.al, 2015, pp.26). On the other hand, this process may require another expertise, take time and be expensive or copyright owners may refuse to license for a use of their material in an online course (Butler, 2012, pp.2). In any case, a creator of an online course should be aware of his/her responsibilities to obtain copyright permission when third party materials are used because infringement of copyright may result in varied degrees of fine or even imprisonment although regulations regarding copyright sanctions may be different from one country to another. (Wahid et.al, 2015, pp.25). For instance, Udemy highlights that it takes no responsibility for the material that an online course creator places on their platform and suggests either not including a material infringing somebody else's content or contacting them to ask their permission.

It is a fact that the copyright issue is multi-dimensional. On one hand, the content providers have obligations not to infringe copyright of third-parties. Another dimension of the copyright issue is to protect the rights of online content providers who upload their original online course videos to MOOCs providers' web sites. Many MOOCs providers use some services and/or technologies to protect the uploaded content. For instance, Udacity established Udacity's Copyright Agent for third-parties who think that their work is misrepresented or used in a way that constitutes copyright infringement (Udacity). A similar agent also exists in edX. Udemy employs an anti-piracy technology although the company states that this is a huge problem for the industry and even the giants such as Amazon and Netflix struggle with it (Udemy). Another dimension that should be taken into consideration regarding copyright issues of MOOCs content is the fact that copyright laws between countries have not been unified which in turn results in many conflicts between legal systems of various countries such as lack of legislation or problems of legal application for digital copyright infringement (Zhuo, 2019: pp. 257). For this reason, studies about the conflicting legal systems in various countries, lack of legislation and legal application regarding digital copyright infringement within the scope of MOOCs are also needed to develop solutions.

CONCLUSION

Main contribution of this chapter is to clarify the position of MOOCs companies as both profit and social value oriented social entrepreneurs fitting the theoretical definitions of social entrepreneurs through linking the social value and tangible social impact created by MOOCs social entrepreneurs to the definitions of these concepts. The chapter also summarized how MOOCs can be valuable sources of social value creation and significant social impact through examples, especially during and after crisis times which in turn highlight the possible future contributions of MOOCs social entrepreneurs both for individuals and policy makers.

MOOCs social entrepreneurs first appeared in 2012, globally. Since then, they earned wide acceptance from individuals who want to improve themselves, companies that aim to train their human resources to adapt the latest technologies and government institutes that try to realize transformation of their societies to have a competitive power in a globalized and digitalized world. MOOCs social entrepreneurs have been creating social value through making online contemporary courses available for all people around the world and minimizing the financial constraints as well as time and location limits. They are classified as social entrepreneurs that mix profit making and social mission. Even though they also set prices for their courses to reach profit objectives, they have been always offering a large number of free course alternatives to create a social value through realizing their primary reason for existence: democratization and equality of education. Under most circumstances, the resources of government are not sufficient to support the improvement of individuals and society as a whole. As a result, private social entrepreneurs can be accepted as important centers of social value creation. The figures regarding people who find a job, start a new business, feel upskilled or reskilled after completing MOOCs are promising to benefit from the transforming power of MOOCs social entrepreneurs.

The period of COVID-19 pandemic resulted in many people to lose their jobs and many others work in diminished hours. The futurists anticipate that after this period, some old-school jobs will not exist anymore which means unemployed people may not find their work again. As a result, reskilling and upskilling the society occurs as a must for all governments. On the other hand, the limited monetary and intellectual resources of most governments direct them to cooperate with MOOCs social entrepreneurs. The period of COVID-19 shows that MOOCs social entrepreneurs can carry some of the burden appeared at crisis times. This situation increases the importance of MOOCs social entrepreneurs whose philosophy is to create social value through supporting the lifelong learning of any individual independent from their nationality. COVID-19 pandemic also resulted in an inevitable revolution in traditional education models that have been argued for years and gave way to the rise of MOOCs social entrepreneurs that have been already increasing their value as new and more equitable education systems that create social value through democratizing lifelong education and have measurable impact at the society in terms of making people find new jobs, start new businesses, feel upskilled and reskilled. It was only a matter of time to enlarge the acceptance of MOOCs social entrepreneurs as alternative and credible education institutions and COVID-19 pandemic accelerated this process. As Ray (2020, pp. 875) underlines, MOOCs are the best solution to the problems such as unemployment and sustainability of face-to-face education occurred due to the COVID-19 pandemic at present, whether it will replace traditional learning or not - is a question only time can tell, but it can definitely add a social value to the learning system as a whole.

REFERENCES

A Message from Anant Agarwal, edX Founder and CEO. (2020). https://www.edx.org/covid-19

Abu-Saifan, S. (2012). Social entrepreneurship: Definition and boundaries. *Technology Innovation Management Review*, *2*(2), 23–27.

Al-Matari, A. S., & Al-Maqbali, H. A. (2020). Using Massive Open Online Courses (MOOCs) on Microsoft's educational community platform for professional development for teachers in Oman under Covid-19. *IOSR Journal of Mobile Computing & Application (IOSR-JMCA)*, *7*(2), 6-15.

An Initiative under Prime Minister's Laptop Scheme executed through the Higher Education Commission of Pakistan. (n.d.). https://dlsei.pk/

Antadze, N., & Westley, F. R. (2012). Impact metrics for social innovation: Barriers or bridges to radical change? *Journal of Social Entrepreneurship*, *3*(2), 133–150.

Aratani, L. (2020, May 28). Jobless America: the coronavirus unemployment crisis in figures. *The Guardian*. https://www.theguardian.com/business/2020/may/28/jobless-america-unemployment-coronavirus-in-figures

Ayub, E., Wei, G. W., & Yue, W. S. (2017). Exploring factors affecting learners' acceptance of MOOCs based on Kirkpatrick's model. *Proceedings of the 8th International Conference on E-Education, E-Business, E-Management and E-Learning*, 34-39.

Bacq, S., & Janssen, F. (2011). The multiple faces of social entrepreneurship: A review of definitional issues based on geographical and thematic criteria. *Entrepreneurship and Regional Development*, *23*(5-6), 373–403.

BBC News. (2020, September 29). *Covid: PM promises 'radical' shake-up of adult education*. https://www.bbc.com/news/uk-politics-54330880

Bilawar, P. B. (2020). Lockdown period and information sources. *International Journal of Engineering Research and Management*, *7*(6).

Boeren, E., Roumell, E. A., & Roessger, K. M. (2020). COVID-19 and the future of adult education: An Editorial. *Adult Education Quarterly*, *1*(4).

Bran, R. A., & Grosseck, G. (2020). Press RESET: Digitalising education in disruptive times. *Revista Romaneasca pentru Educatie Multidimensionala*, *12*(1Sup2), 39-48.

Butler, B. (2012). Massive open online courses: Legal and policy issues for research libraries. Association of Research Libraries, 1-15.

Bylieva, D., Bekirogullari, Z., Lobatyuk, V., & Nam, T. (2020). Analysis of the consequences of the transition to online learning on the example of MOOC philosophy during the COVID-19 pandemic. *Humanities & Social Sciences Reviews*, *8*(4), 1083–1093.

Castaño-Muñoz, J., Kalz, M., Kreijns, K., & Punie, Y. (2018). Who is taking MOOCs for teachers' professional development on the use of ICT? A cross-sectional study from Spain. *Technology, Pedagogy and Education*, *27*(5), 607–624.

Change the World. (n.d.). https://www.udemy.com/courses/free/

Chen, J. C. C. (2013). *Opportunities and challenges of MOOCS: Perspectives from Asia*. IFLA WPIC 2013 Singapore. http://library.ifla.org/157/1/098-chen-en.pdf

Click-On Kaduna. (2020). https://skills.click-onkaduna.ng/

Coursera Workforce Recovery Initiative. (2020). https://www.dsti.gov.sl/coursera/

Coursera Workforce Recovery Programme. (2020a). https://labour.gov.bb/coursera-workforce-recovery-programme/

Coursera Workforce Recovery Programme. (2020b). https://covid19.bergenworkforce.org/coursera/

Cramer, J. C., Dietz, T., & Johnston, R. A. (1980). Social impact assessment of regional plans: A review of methods and issues and a recommended process. *Policy Sciences*, *12*(1), 61–82.

Darko, E., & Koranteng, K. (2015). *Social enterprise landscape in Ghana*. British Council. https://www.britishcouncil.org/sites/default/files/social_enterprise_landscape_in_ghana_report_final.pdf

De Ruysscher, C., Claes, C., Lee, T., Cui, F., Van Loon, J., De Maeyer, J., & Schalock, R. (2017). A systems approach to social entrepreneurship. *Voluntas*, *28*(6), 2530–2545.

Downes, S. (2008). Places to go: Connectivism & connective knowledge. *Innovate: Journal of Online Education*, *5*(1), 6.

Downes, S. (2009). *New technology supporting informal learning* [Web log post]. https://halfanhour.blogspot.com/2009/04/new-technology-supportinginformal.html

Drăgușin, M., & Welsh, D. H. (2015). Innovative and sustainable business models in digital higher education: A comparative analysis of global reach MOOCs platforms. *New Trends in Sustainable Business and Consumption*, 75-83.

Eggers, W. D., & Macmillan, P. (2013). *The solution revolution: How business, government, and social enterprises are teaming up to solve society's toughest problems*. Harvard Business Press.

Eschenbacher, S., & Fleming, T. (2020). Transformative dimensions of lifelong learning: Mezirow, Rorty and COVID-19. *International Review of Education*, 1–16.

Feng, X. L., Hu, X. C., Fan, K. Y., & Yu, T. (2020, April). A brief discussion about the impact of coronavirus disease 2019 on teaching in colleges and universities of China. In *Proceedings of 2020 International Conference on E-Commerce and Internet Technology (ECIT)*, (pp. 167-170). IEEE.

Fenwick, M., McCahery, J. A., & Vermeulen, E. P. (2020). Will the world ever be the same after COVID-19? Two lessons from the first global crisis of a digital age. *European Business Organization Law Review*, 1–21.

Fini, A. (2009). The technological dimension of a massive open online course: The case of the CCK08 course tools. *International Review of Research in Open and Distributed Learning*, *10*(5).

Governor Pritzker launches "get hired" website to connect workers impacted by covid-19 with employment and career resources. (2020). https://www2.illinois.gov/Pages/news-item.aspx?ReleaseID=21545

Hickey, A., Urban, A., & Karsten, E. (2020). *Drivers of Quality in Online Learning*. https://about.coursera.org/press/wp-content/uploads/2020/10/Coursera_DriversOfQuality_Book_MCR-1126-V4-lr.pdf

Hone, K. S., & El Said, G. R. (2016). Exploring the factors affecting MOOC retention: A survey study. *Computers & Education*, *98*, 157–168.

https://theskillstoolkit.campaign.gov.uk/

Inamdar, N. (2020, May 6). Coronavirus lockdown: India jobless numbers cross 120 million in April. *BBC News*. https://www.bbc.com/news/world-asia-india-52559324

Jansen, D., & Schuwer, R. (2015). *Institutional MOOC strategies in Europe.* Status Report Based on a Mapping Survey Conducted in October-December 2014.

Johnson, K. (2020). Back by Popular Demand! Udacity is Offering 1 Month of Free Access to Nanodegree Programs. *Udacity Blog*. https://blog.udacity.com/2020/04/one-month-free-on-nanodegrees-2.html

Kaushik, A. (2015). Massive Open Online Course (MOOC). *Library Waves-A Biannual Peer Reviewed Journal*, *1*(2), 110–118.

Keelery, S. (2020). *COVID-19 impact on unemployment rate in India 2020*. https://www.statista.com/statistics/1111487/coronavirus-impact-on-unemployment-rate/

King, B. (2020, October 13). Unemployment rate: How many people are out of work? *BBC News*. https://www.bbc.com/news/business-52660591

Lager, S. (2020). Udacity's Contribution to the COVID-19 Crisis: One Free Month Access to Nanodegree Programs. *Udacity Blog*. https://blog.udacity.com/2020/03/one-month-free-on-nanodegrees.html

Lane, A. (2012). A review of the role of national policy and institutional mission in European distance teaching universities with respect to widening participation in higher education study through open educational resources. *Distance Education*, *33*(2), 135–150.

Lane, A., Caird, S., & Weller, M. (2014). The potential social, economic and environmental benefits of MOOCs: Operational and historical comparisons with a massive 'closed online' course. *Open Praxis*, *6*(2), 115–123.

Leighton, M. (2020a). Coursera is offering 90% of its online classes to college students for free until September 30, 2020 — here's how to enroll. *Business Insider*. https://www.businessinsider.com/coursera-free-classes-college-students

Leighton, M. (2020b). Coursera's Workforce Recovery Initiative gives unemployed workers free access to 90% of its online course catalog — here's how it works. *Business Insider*. https://www.businessinsider.com/coursera-workforce-recovery-initiative

Littlejohn, A., Hood, N., Milligan, C., & Mustain, P. (2016). Learning in MOOCs: Motivations and self-regulated learning in MOOCs. *Internet and Higher Education*, *29*, 40–48.

Lu, H. P., & Dzikria, I. (2020). The role of intellectual capital and social capital on the intention to use MOOC. *Knowledge Management Research and Practice*, 1–12.

Lubis, A. H., Idrus, S. Z. S., & Abd Rashid, S. (2020). The exposure of MOOC usage In Indonesia. *International Journal of Scientific & Technology Research*, *9*(2).

Malita, L., Tiru, L. G., & Grosseck, G. (2018). MOOCs for teachers professional development—A university challenge. *International Journal of Information and Education Technology (IJIET)*, *8*(3), 235–239.

Masaviru, M. (2020). From physical classrooms to e-learning and online teaching: A case study of Light International School, Mombasa. *Journal of Education and Practice*, *11*(13), 2020.

Mathes, J. (2019). *Global quality in online, open, flexible and technology enhanced education: An analysis of strengths, weaknesses, opportunities and threats*. International Council for Open and Distance Education.

McAuley, A., Stewart, B., Siemens, G., & Cormier, D. (2010). *The MOOC model for digital practice*. Academic Press.

Methodology for Change the World. (n.d.). https://fortune.com/franchise-list-page/methodology-change-the-world-2020

MicroBachelors Programs for Undergraduate Education. (2020). https://www.edx.org/microbachelors

MicroMasters Programs. (2020). https://www.edx.org/micromasters#program-list

Milakovich, M. E., & Wise, J. M. (2019). *Copyright, legal issues, and intellectual property in Digital Learning*. Edward Elgar Publishing.

Million Arab Coders Initiative. (2020). Error! Hyperlink reference not valid.*2020 Impact Report*. https://www.edx.org/assets/2020-impact-report-en.pdf

Municipality of Beylikdüzü. (2020). https://www.courserabeylikduzu.org/

New free online learning platform to boost workplace skills. (2020). https://www.gov.uk/government/news/new-free-online-learning-platform-to-boost-workplace-skills

New York Amsterdam News. (2020, October 17). *Udacity to provide 1,000 scholarships to African Americans*. http://amsterdamnews.com/news/2020/aug/25/udacity-provide-1000-scholarships-african-american/

Next Generation Abu Dhabi Partners. (n.d.). https://www.udacity.com/l/Next-Gen-AbuDhabi

Ng, A., & Widom, J. (2014). Origins of the modern MOOC (xMOOC). MOOCs: Expectations and Reality: Full Report, 34-47.

Northern Council for Further Education. (2020). *PM announces new Lifetime Skills Guarantee*. https://www.ncfe.org.uk/blog/pm-announces-new-lifetime-skills-guarantee#:~:text=Prime%20Minister%2C%20Boris%20Johnson%2C%20has,%2C%20fully%2Dfunded%20FE%20course

OECD. (2020). *The OECD Employment Outlook 2020*. OECD. https://www.oecd-ilibrary.org/sites/1686c758-en/index.html?itemId=/content/publication/1686c758-en

OECD. (2020). *The potential of online learning for adults: early lessons from the COVID-19 crisis*. OECD.

Ontario Newsroom. (2020, April 17). *Ontario Establishes Key Partnerships to Make Home Learning More Accessible*. https://news.ontario.ca/en/release/56697/ontario-establishes-key-partnerships-to-make-home-learning-more-accessible

Petrie, C., Aladin, K., Ranjan, P., Javangwe, R., Gilliland, D., Tuominen, S., & Lasse, L. (2020). *Spotlight: Quality education for all during Covid-19 crisis*. https://hundred.org/en/research

Pradhan, R. (2020). Turn Downtime into an Online Learning Opportunity With Our New Global Offer. *Udacity Blog*. https://blog.udacity.com/2020/04/covid19-onlinelearning-offer.html

Professional Certificate Programs. (2020). https://www.edx.org/professional-certificate

Raju, H. (2020). Covid-19 Lockdown-challenges to higher education. *Cape Comorin An International Multidisciplinary Research Journal*, *2*(4), 26–28.

Ray, A. E-learning: the new normal in the post-covid world. *International Research Journal of Modernization in Engineering Technology and Science*, *2*(9), 866-876.

Shen, C. (2017). Udacity Launches in MENA. *Udacity Blog*. https://blog.udacity.com/2017/12/udacity-launches-in-mena.html

Singh, A. (2016). *The process of social value creation: A multiple-case study on social entrepreneurship in India*. Springer.

Srivastava, S., Singh, P., & Singh, V. P. (2020). Impact of COVID-19 on education system in India: A review. *Iconic Research and Engineering Journals*, *4*(1), 1–7.

Swersky, L., Behnke, K. A., & Mays, J. (2017). Coursera for Refugees: Universal Access to World-Class Education. EMOOCs-WIP, 128-132.

Talmage, C. A., Baker, A. L., Guest, M. A., & Knopf, R. C. (2020). Responding to social isolation among older adults through lifelong learning: Lessons and questions during COVID-19. *Local Development & Society*, 1-8.

Tan, W. L., Williams, J., & Tan, T. M. (2005). Defining the 'social' in 'social entrepreneurship': Altruism and entrepreneurship. *The International Entrepreneurship and Management Journal*, *1*(3), 353–365.

Telli Yamamoto, S. G., & Altun, D. (2020). Coronavirüs ve çevrimiçi (online) eğitimin önlenemeyen yükselişi. *Journal of University Research*, *3*(1), 25–34.

The technology learning initiative "Next Technology Leaders (NTL)". (n.d.). https://www.itida.gov.eg/English/Pages/Next-Technology-Leaders.aspx

The unemployment rate in South Africa soars to 30% as a result of the Covid-19 pandemic. (2020, June 23). *Asian News*. https://en.as.com/en/2020/06/23/latest_news/1592936714_614525.html

Thousands of African graduates recognized at virtual convocation through COL-Coursera Workforce Recovery Initiative. (2020). https://web.aflia.net/thousands-of-african-graduates-recognized-at-virtual-convocation-through-col-coursera-workforce-recovery-initiative/

Unemployment Rates. (2020). *OECD*. http://www.oecd.org/newsroom/unemployment-rates-oecd-update-june-2020.htm

UNESCO. (2009). *Belém framework for action: Harnessing the power and potential of adult learning and education for a viable future*. UNESCO. http://www.unesco.org/en/confinteavi

United Nations General Assembly. (2015). Resolution adopted by the General Assembly on 25 September 2015. Washington, DC: United Nations.

U.S. Department of Labor. (2020). *The Employment Situation — September 2020, News Release Bureau Labor Statistics*. https://www.bls.gov/news.release/pdf/empsit.pdf

Verawardina, U., Asnur, L., Lubis, A. L., Hendriyani, Y., Ramadhani, D., Dewi, I. P., Darni, R., Betri, T. J., Susanti, W., & Sriwahyuni, T. (2020). Reviewing online learning facing the COVID-19 outbreak. *Talent Development & Excellence*, *12*, 385–392.

Wahid, R., Mohd Sani, A., Mat, B., Subhan, M., & Saidin, K. (2015). Sharing works and copyright issues in massive open online courseware (MOOC). *International Journal for Research in Emerging Science and Technology*, *2*(10), 24–29.

Williamson, G. (2020, September 29). Lifetime Skills Guarantee: Education Secretary outlines new measures to help more people get the skills they need to get ahead. *FE News*. https://www.fenews.co.uk/fevoices/55849-lifetime-skills-guarantee-education-secretary-outlines-new-measures-to-help-more-people-get-the-skills-they-need-to-get-ahead

Workforce Recovery Initiative. (2020). https://www.htdc.org/workforce-recovery-initiative-by-coursera/

Yunus, M. (1998). Alleviating Poverty Through Technology. *Science, New Series*, *282*(5388), 409–410.

Zhao, J., Xiao, H., Li, Y., Wen, D., Xu, P., Fu, Y., Piao, J., Liu, J., Cao, D., Zhong, Z., & Zhao, G. (2020). *Experience of massive distance online education for medical colleges and universities in China to counter the COVID-19 pandemic*. Research Square.

Zhuo, W. (2019). Research on Copyright Law Conflict under the Network Environment. *5th International Conference on Finance, Investment, and Law (ICFIL 2019)*, 256-259.

KEY TERMS AND DEFINITIONS

COVID-19: An infectious disease caused by a newly discovered coronavirus and spread throughout the world.

Digitalization: Use of digital technologies as businesses, governments, educational institutes, and individuals.

Lifelong Learning: Improving oneself through taking courses for new interests, reskilling and upskilling.

MOOCs: Massive open online courses provided by online education platforms offering free or low cost, high quality online courses to anyone anywhere and removing the barriers of traditional education cost, location, and access.

Reskilling: Training employees to teach a completely new job.

Social Entrepreneurs: Entrepreneurs whose core business create a social value as well as profit.

Social Impact: Effect of companies' actions on larger society and members of society.

Social Value: Creating benefits to solve some social problems and to satisfy some social needs.

Upskilling: Training employees to teach additional skills.

Conclusion

Since its emerging, the social entrepreneurship concept has attracted attention and has become a global phenomenon. Over the years, a valuable knowledge has been formed about the concept. This book tries to further the social entrepreneurship understanding focusing on social value creation. We sought to bring together a comprehensive collection of chapters that focus different aspects. The sixteen chapters aimed to show both theoretical and empirical evidence about the various challenges, tools, and ways of social value creation through social entrepreneurship regarding the question of how it can be created and sustained.

The first conceptual chapter, Chapter 1, extends the theoretical framework of sustainability towards social entrepreneurship. As known, at the United Nation's Sustainable Development Summit (2015), 193 countries were accepted to take action for 17 Sustainable Development Goals (SDGs) of 'The 2030 Agenda for Sustainable Development'. However, the sustainability issues such as increased inequality in economic participation and opportunity, educational attainment, health issues, and the deterioration of a natural livelihood are aggravating, and the gap between developed and developing countries still stays by far. In this vein, describing social entrepreneurship as an important contributor to the sustainability goas, Toker draws a path from sustainability to social entrepreneurship.

To ponder the question of how social entrepreneurship has been progressed, in Chapter 2, Şengüllendi helps us to monitor the scientific evolution of social entrepreneurship, via bibliometric analysis within the scope of social impact theory and the social value creation approach. This book also presents successful examples of social value creation. For instance, Chapter 14 draws attention to the role of social entrepreneurship on women empowerment, which is a long lasting problem in the Turkish context. Through a single case study method, Acar Erdur reveals how çöp(m)adam, a social enterprise founded by a woman also, have contributed to economic and psychological empowerment of women that have never able to get a regular income before. Chapter 12 focuses on the role of social entrepreneurship on equal opportunity for young population. Through the case of Future is Brighter, Bozaykut and Titiz who is the founder of the enterprise, chapter explains the social impact that have been created for the youth in terms of social inclusion. Chapter 16 puts forward an alternative way of creating social value by giving an equal chance to access high quality education and democratization of education. In this perspective, it explicit MOOCs (Massive open online courses) entrepreneurs who pursue both social and profit missions at varying degrees, and explains how they share educational material to a global audience without any time and any place restrictions via technology-based tools. Similarly, in Chapter 11, Sürmeli, Narla and Hoeflin present the case of HERA, a digital platform which is designed to increase access to healthcare for refugee and migrant populations. It also explains how the HERA project evolved into a social enterprise from a grant-based field project. In fact, these two cases prove how digitalization transforms the social entrepreneurship concept as explained in Chapter 6 by Cide Demir as a new way of social entrepreneurship.

As these examples confirm, pursing social missions, social enterprises have been identified as powerful mechanisms to deliver innovative solutions to the deep-rooted societal problems. However, although social entrepreneurs prioritize social value creation they still need to pursue business logic for commercial activity and maintain the organization, as they are acting with a dual mission (Costanzo et al., 2014; Doherty et al., 2014). In Chapter 4, Saraç points out the tensions between value creation and value capture strategies of social enterprises, and suggests that rather than suffered from this tension, there is another way of creating value as hybrid organizations. In a similar vein, in Chapter 3, using netnography methodology, Güneştepe, Arıoglu and Tunçalp, questions how social enterprises manage symbolic meanings while pursuing their dual missions in the Turkish context.

Besides trying to manage these tensions, social enterprises face also various challenges such as scarcity of financial resources, leadership challenges, regulative environment, impact assessment, ethical issues or gaining legitimacy (e.g. André & Pache, 2016; Costanzo et al., 2014; Pret & Carter, 2017, Shaw & Carter, 2007; Sulphey & Alkahtani, 2017). Among these, financial challenges are in the forefront. In this respect, Chapter 7, 8 and 9 provides a financial lens for social value creation. For instance, in Chapter 7, Erkut describes crowdfunding as an alternative tool for social entrepreneurship and explains the potential benefits. In a similar vein, in Chapter 8, Yılmaz and Yaşar focus on the funding performance of social and environmental projects in crowdfunding and provide guidelines for social entrepreneurs seeking to fund their projects on crowdfunding. Presenting a different perspective, in Chapter 9, Kara introduces the social impact bond as a tool for social impact investment.

Despite the financial challenges, an unfavorable institutional context, especially in developing country contexts, makes the ecosystem difficult to grow. In this respect, in chapter 13, Pinzon, Rolon and Osorio establish the implementation guidelines for strategies to allow to resolving existing development problems in society and support regional entrepreneurial ecosystems. From a conceptual standpoint, they propose a Smart Specialization strategy that allows the development of shared value. In Chapter 5, Karaçay draws our attention to the influence of societal culture on social innovation, specifically by shaping the perceptions of social entrepreneurs for social value creation, as their social initiatives are influenced by cultural values where they belong. To illustrate the relationship between social innovation and culture, Chapter 10 presents cases of success from in Colombia, Peru, and Chile. Through the cases, Kuchel and Mendez enables us to see the dynamics of social innovation in the South American context.

Of course, in today's world, social problems arise from and persist due to the complex combination of situations and hard to predict. The pace and the depth of these ongoing changes necessitate a rapid adaptation. For instance, Covid-19 pandemic is a current process that triggers this adaptation and change the accustomed processes in the world. In this context, Chapter 15 focuses on the prominent role of social entrepreneurship by underlining their initiatives, especially for groups experiencing social exclusion. Morgül and Afacan Fındıklı first discuss the impacts of the Covid-19 pandemic on economic indicators, healthcare services, access to education, and disadvantaged groups such as elderly people and unregistered workers. Then, they bring these rapid and inclusive responses to light in solving social and economic problems caused by the COVID-19 period by discourse analysis obtained from academic and media discourses published between December 2019 and June 2020. In chapter 16, Arıker argues that social entrepreneurs create new opportunities to ensure equality in access to educational resources by online courses to anyone anywhere and removing the barriers of traditional education. Arıker examines MOOC platforms regarding their strategies to enhance their online learning initiatives and how they collaborate with stakeholders including government institutions during the COVID-19 pandemic. She gives examples of social entrepreneurs offering MOOC such as Coursera, Khan Academy, edX, Udacity, and Examples of universities offering MOOC such as Harvard Online Courses, Koc Akademy.

Is it Possible to co-create Social Value?

Although social entrepreneurs can be regarded as agents of positive social change with their social missions and valuable efforts, tackling various challenges, social entrepreneurship ceases to be an endeavor that can be carried out by a single person, an individual entrepreneur. Despite the dominant conceptualization that has centered on the understanding of the ''heroic'' view of the lone social entrepreneur as a change agent, an alternative view is that social entrepreneurship may be better understood as a collective action involving groups, networks, governments, or organizations (Austin, 2000, Austin & Seitanidi,2012a, 2012b; Nicholls & Huybrechts 2016). Social value can be created from a single hand, yet collaboration is a beneficial vehicle to scale and maintain the created impact. Indeed, most of today's social problems are too complex for one individual or organization to tackle alone and require multi-dimensional, multi-sectoral, and multi-organizational approaches to resolve (Kania & Kramer 2011). Thus, the growing commitment to social responsible behavior aiming collective impact (Kania &Kramer 2011, 2013), recognition of the shared value model (Porter & Kramer 2011), the social and solidarity economy perspective (Utting 2015), and the new co-operativism' (Ridley-Duff, 2016) contributes to the collaboration idea (de Bruin et al, 2017).

From this point of view, it is well demonstrated that much of the social entrepreneurship activities occurs to be collective, drawing on support, cooperation, networks or/and alliances to improve access to resources and funding, build awareness, provide sustainability, gain legitimacy, scale the social impact and eventually stimulating positive social change (Chalmers & Balan-Vnuk 2013; Huybrechts & Nicholls 2013; Shaw & de Bruin 2013). In this sense, Montgomery, Dacin & Dacin (2012:376) define collective social entrepreneurship (CSE) concept as a "collaboration amongst similar as well as diverse actors for the purpose of applying business principles to solving social problems".

Of course, collaboration is not a new concept. Different approaches have generated a valuable analytic framework for collaborative arrangements (e.g. Austin & Seitanidi, 2012a, 2012b). Yet, it is not free from challenges. While a large number of theoretical and applied research demonstrates the benefits of collaboration, it is also highlighted that there are risks and challenges (e.g. Keast & Mandell 2014). Collective social value creation, from intention to impact, is a rocky road, and there are several critical factors regarding collaborative arrangements for co-creations to be successful.

First of all, resource complementation is considered critical in collaborations (Austin, 2000). In this regard, agreeing on a common agenda, identifying the motives of the parties, clarifying the partners' intentions and expected benefits, and understanding the potential of the resources that each partner will contribute may enable to generate linked interests, strengthen the fit between partners, and increase the potential for value creation (Austin & Seitanidi, 2012a; Seitanidi, 2010). However, when in collaboration, the resource dependence of the social enterprise to its partner may lead to an asymmetric power relation (Pffefer & Salancik, 2003), which can be hard to manage for the social enterprise. Thus, successful collaborations may require a specific form governance, management and leadership to support power, decision, and risk sharing (e.g. Ansell & Gash 2012; Caldwell, et al., 2017; Crosby & Bryson, 2010; Kania & Kramer, 2011) that will function a process catalyst (Mandell & Keast, 2009). As Austin (2000) notes, this may require the partners' missions, people, and activities to act in a collective way, even a change in organizational culture (Seitanidi 2010), in order to show commitment to the collaboration.

In these terms, developing a long-term and high trust relationship between partners identified as one of the key element of a collaboration (Keast & Mandell, 2014). Such a relationship is described by a recognized need to collaborate, interdependency, shared risk and power, and a transparent communication (Barraket & Loosemore, 2017). This kind of relationship may facilitate the internalization and the institutionalization of the partnership, and contribute to the generation common understanding (Seitanidi & Crane, 2008).Naturally, this requires a smooth coordination between partners. In this regard, understanding how coordination is addressed in different collaborative arrangements, its role on the initiation and the evolution of the collaborations is determinative on the co-creation process (Bruin & Stangl, 2014).

Knowledge sharing and collaborative learning between partners is also accepted essential in order to realize a change. Trustworthy, consistent, and well-coordinated partnerships may also lead to knowledge sharing and organizational learning which is identified as one of the most significant benefits of collaboration (Austin & Seitanidi 2014; Chalmers & Balan-Vnuk 2013; Weerawardena & Sullivan Mort, 2012). Thus, understanding the triggers, facilitators, and barriers for knowledge transfer, learning capability, and co-learning between partners is critical for the creation of collaborative know-how and so the sustainability of co-creation. Moreover, considering the potential of open innovation may contribute to co-creation and influence the nature of social impact. (West et al., 2014).

Recent studies also draw attention to the role of legitimacy as a key driver of emergence and development of collaborations, especially in different stages of the process (e.g. Huybrechts & Nicholls 2013; Sarpong & Davies, 2014). Gaining and maintaining the legitimacy is critical for social enterprises that perform a contested logic. Thus, there is a growing interest on legitimacy issues in collaborations. For instance, the role of legitimacy in the justification of collaboration and partner selection, may become challenging. Also, the type of legitimacy that partners seek, and how the legitimacy evolves during the collaborative process are important topics to consider (Huybrechts & Nicholls 2013).

Collaborations are seen as an effective way to tackle societal problems that one individual or single organization cannot overcome. As de Briun (2016:18)'s expresses, "a spark that is ignited locally can spread flames beyond the local level … to a sustainable future". However, to increase its benefits for society we need to further our understanding of the dynamics of the co-creation, collaborative patterns, organizational and institutional factors that drive collaboration, and the success factors. In this way, collaborations may create a social change at the system level (de Bruin, et al., 2017). We hope that generating social value through a collaborative approach can find more place in the agendas of profit/nonprofit distinct actors who can make a real positive change together.

REFERENCES

André, K., & Pache, A. C. (2016). From caring entrepreneur to caring enterprise: Addressing the ethical challenges of scaling up social enterprises. *Journal of Business Ethics*, *133*(4), 659–675. doi:10.100710551-014-2445-8Ansell, C., & Gash, A. (2012). Stewards, mediators, and catalysts: Toward a model of collaborative leadership1. *The Innovation Journal*, *17*(1), 2.

Austin, J., Stevenson, H., & Wei-Skillern, J. (2006). Social and commercial entrepreneurship: Same, different, or both? *Entrepreneurship Theory and Practice*, *30*(1), 1–22. doi:10.1111/j.1540-6520.2006.00107.x

Austin, J. E. (2000). Strategic collaboration between nonprofits and businesses. *Nonprofit and Voluntary Sector Quarterly*, *29*(1, suppl), 69–97. doi:10.1177/089976400773746346

Austin, J. E., & Seitanidi, M. M. (2012a). Collaborative Value Creation: A Review of Partnering between Nonprofits and Businesses: Part I. Value Creation Spectrum and Collaboration Stages. *Nonprofit and Voluntary Sector Quarterly*, *41*(5), 726–758. doi:10.1177/0899764012450777

Austin, J. E., & Seitanidi, M. M. (2012b). Collaborative Value Creation: A Review of Partnering between Nonprofits and Businesses. Part 2: Partnership Processes and Outcomes. *Nonprofit and Voluntary Sector Quarterly*, *41*(6), 929–968. doi:10.1177/0899764012454685

Austin, J. E., & Seitanidi, M. M. (2014). *Creating value in nonprofit-business collaborations: New thinking and practice*. John Wiley & Sons.

Chalmers, D. M., & Balan-Vnuk, E. (2013). Innovating not-for-profit social ventures: Exploring the microfoundations of internal and external absorptive capacity routines. *International Small Business Journal*, *31*(7), 785–810. doi:10.1177/0266242612465630

Costanzo, L. A., Vurro, C., Foster, D., Servato, F., & Perrini, F. (2014). Dual-Mission Management in Social Entrepreneurship: Qualitative Evidence from Social Firms in the United Kingdom. *Journal of Small Business Management*, *52*(4), 655–677. doi:10.1111/jsbm.12128

Crosby, B. C., & Bryson, J. M. (2010). Integrative leadership and the creation and maintenance of cross-sector collaborations. *The Leadership Quarterly*, *21*(2), 211–230. doi:10.1016/j.leaqua.2010.01.003

Dart, R. (2004). The legitimacy of social enterprise. *Nonprofit Management & Leadership*, *14*(4), 411–424. doi:10.1002/nml.43

de Bruin, A., Lewis, K. V., & Shaw, E. (2016). *The collaborative dynamic in social entrepreneurship*. Academic Press.

de Bruin, A., Shaw, E., & Lewis, K. V. (2017). The collaborative dynamic in social entrepreneurship. *Entrepreneurship and Regional Development*, *29*(7-8), 575–585. doi:10.1080/08985626.2017.1328902

de Bruin, A., & Stangl, L. (2014). Insights on scaling social enterprise. *Social entrepreneurship and enterprise: Concepts in context*, 153-172.

Doherty, B., Haugh, H., & Lyon, F. (2014). Social enterprises as hybrid organizations: A review and research agenda. *International Journal of Management Reviews*, *16*(4), 417–436. doi:10.1111/ijmr.12028

Huybrechts, B., & Nicholls, A. (2013). The role of legitimacy in social enterprise-corporate collaboration. *Social Enterprise Journal*, *9*(2), 130–146. doi:10.1108/SEJ-01-2013-0002

Kania, J., & Kramer, M. (2011, Winter). Collective impact. *Stanford Innovation Review*, 36–41.

Keast, R., & Mandell, M. (2014, February). The collaborative push: Moving beyond rhetoric and gaining evidence. *The Journal of Management and Governance*, *18*(1), 9–28. doi:10.100710997-012-9234-5

Keast, R., & Mandell, M. P. (2013). Network performance: A complex interplay of form and action. *International Review of Public Administration*, *18*(2), 27–45. doi:10.1080/12294659.2013.10805251

Kramer, M. R., & Porter, M. (2011). *Creating shared value* (Vol. 17). FSG.

Loosemore, M., & Barraket, J. (2017). The co-creation of social value between social enterprises and private firms in the construction industry. *Thirty-Third Annual Conference*.

Low, T., Chaves, A., Caldwell, J. D., Kumar, A., Fang, N. X., Avouris, P., Heinz, T. F., Guinea, F., Martin-Moreno, L., & Koppens, F. (2017). Polaritons in layered two-dimensional materials. *Nature Materials, 16*(2), 182–194. doi:10.1038/nmat4792 PMID:27893724

Mandell, M. P., & Keast, R. (2009). A new look at leadership in collaborative networks: Process catalysts. *Public sector leadership: International challenges and perspectives*, 163-178.

Montgomery, A. W., Dacin, P. A., & Dacin, M. T. (2012). Collective social entrepreneurship: Collaboratively shaping social good. *Journal of Business Ethics, 111*(3), 375–388. doi:10.100710551-012-1501-5

Mulgan, G. (2006). The process of social innovation. *Innovations: Technology, Governance, Globalization, 1*(2), 145–162. doi:10.1162/itgg.2006.1.2.145

Pfeffer, J., & Salancik, G. R. (2003). *The external control of organizations: A resource dependence perspective*. Stanford University Press.

Pret, T., & Carter, S. (2017). The importance of 'fitting in': Collaboration and social value creation in response to community norms and expectations. *Entrepreneurship and Regional Development, 29*(7-8), 639–667. doi:10.1080/08985626.2017.1328903

Ridley-Duff, R. (2016). *Rendering the social solidarity economy: exploring the case for a paradigm shift in the visibility of co-operative and mutual enterprises in business education, research and policy-making*. Academic Press.

Sarpong, D., & Davies, C. (2014). Managerial organizing practices and legitimacy seeking in social enterprises. *Social Enterprise Journal, 10*(1), 21–37. doi:10.1108/SEJ-05-2013-0019

Seitanidi, M. M. (2010). *The politics of partnerships: A critical examination of nonprofit-business partnerships*. Springer Science & Business Media. doi:10.1007/978-90-481-8547-4

Seitanidi, M. M., & Crane, A. (2008). Corporate social responsibility in action. Partnership management: Selection-design-institutionalisation. *Journal of Business Ethics*.

Shaw, E., & Carter, S. (2007). Social entrepreneurship. *Journal of Small Business and Enterprise Development, 14*(3), 418–434. doi:10.1108/14626000710773529

Shaw, E., & de Bruin, A. (2013). Reconsidering capitalism: The promise of social innovation and social entrepreneurship? *International Small Business Journal, 31*(7), 737–746. doi:10.1177/0266242613497494

Sulphey, M. M., & Alkahtani, N. (2017). Economic security and sustainability through social entrepreneurship: the current Saudi scenario. *Journal of Security and Sustainability Issues, 6*(3).

Utting, P. (2015). Corporate accountability, fair trade and multi-stakeholder regulation. In *Handbook of research on fair trade*. Edward Elgar Publishing. doi:10.4337/9781783474622.00013

Weerawardena, J., & Mort, G. S. (2012). Competitive strategy in socially entrepreneurial nonprofit organizations: Innovation and differentiation. *Journal of Public Policy & Marketing*, *31*(1), 91–101. doi:10.1509/jppm.11.034

West, J., Salter, A., Vanhaverbeke, W., & Chesbrough, H. (2014). *Open innovation: The next decade*. Academic Press.

Compilation of References

Million Arab Coders Initiative. (2020). Error! Hyperlink reference not valid.*2020 Impact Report*. https://www.edx.org/assets/2020-impact-report-en.pdf

A Message from Anant Agarwal, edX Founder and CEO. (2020). https://www.edx.org/covid-19

AB. (2020). *Microfinance and social entrepreneurship*. Retrieved from https://www.ab.gov.tr/files/SBYPB/birlik%20 programlari/easi_brosur.pdf

Abu-Saifan, S. (2012). Social entrepreneurship: Definition and boundaries. *Technology Innovation Management Review*, *2*(2), 23–27.

Acar Erdur, D., & Afacan Fındıklı, M. (2020). A Conceptual Model Proposal for Co-Creation of Social Value: Insights from Social Entrepreneurs. *Istanbul Gelisim University Journal of Social Sciences*, *7*(1), 1–20.

Acar, A. & Afacan Fındıklı, M. (2020) Employment of disadvantaged groups in OECD countries, *International Journal of Research in Business and Social Science*, *9*(4), 330-342.

Adolphus, M. (2020). *How to use discourse analysis*. Available at: https://www.emeraldgrouppublishing.com/archived/research/guides/methods/discourse_analysis.htm

Afonasova, M., Panfilova, E., Galichkina, M., & Slusarczyk. (n.d.). Digitalization in Economy and Innovation: The Effect on Social and Economic Processes. *Polish Journal of Management Studies, 19*(2), 22-32.

Agafonow, A. (2014). Toward a positive theory of social entrepreneurship. On maximizing versus satisficing value capture. *Journal of Business Ethics*, *125*(4), 709–713. doi:10.100710551-013-1948-z

Agrawal, A., Catalini, C., & Goldfarb, A. (2011). The Geography of Crowdfunding. SSRN Electronic Journal. doi:10.3386/w16820

Agrawal, A., Catalini, C., & Goldfarb, A. (2016). Are Syndicates the Killer App of Equity Crowdfunding? *California Management Review*, *58*(2), 111–124. doi:10.1525/cmr.2016.58.2.111

Ahmadi, H. B., Kusi-Sarpong, S., & Rezaei, J. (2017). Assessing the social sustainability of supply chains using Best Worst Method. *Resources, Conservation and Recycling*, *126*, 99–106. doi:10.1016/j.resconrec.2017.07.020

Ainscow, M., & Sandill, A. (2010). Developing inclusive education systems: The role of organisational cultures and leadership. *International Journal of Inclusive Education*, *14*(4), 401–416. doi:10.1080/13603110802504903

Akar, H., & Üstüner, M. (2017). Mediation role of self-efficacy perceptions in the relationship between emotional intelligence levels and social entrepreneurship traits of pre-service teachers. *Journal of Education and Future*, (12), 95–115.

Akbaş, S. (2019). *Girişimciler ve Yatırımcıları Buluşturan Alternatif Finansman Yöntemi: Kitlesel Fonlama (Yüksek Lisans Tezi)*. Pamukkale Üniversitesi Sosyal Bilimler Enstitüsü.

Aksoy, B., Koçanci, M., & Namal, M. K. (2019). *Girişimcilik motivasyonu: Uygulamalı girişimcilik eğitimi katılımcıları örneği*. Yönetim Ve Ekonomi. *Celal Bayar Üniversitesi İktisadi Ve İdari Bilimler Fakültesi Dergisi, 26*(1), 109–129. doi:10.18657/yonveek.526604

Alberti, F. G., & Varon, M. A. (2017). Can profit and sustainability goals co-exist? New business models for hybrid firms. *The Journal of Business Strategy, 38*(1), 3–13. doi:10.1108/JBS-12-2015-0124

Al-Dajani, H., & Marlow, S. (2013). Empowerment and entrepreneurship: A theoretical framework. *International Journal of Entrepreneurial Behaviour & Research, 19*(5), 503–524. doi:10.1108/IJEBR-10-2011-0138

Alencar, A., Kondova, K., & Ribbens, W. (2019). The smartphone as a lifeline: An exploration of refugees' use of mobile communication technologies during their flight. *Media Culture & Society, 41*(6), 828–844. doi:10.1177/0163443718813486

Alexiou, K., Wiggins, J., & Preece, S. B. (2020). Crowdfunding Acts as a Funding Substitute and a Legitimating Signal for Nonprofit Performing Arts Organizations. *Nonprofit and Voluntary Sector Quarterly, 49*(4), 1–22. doi:10.1177/0899764020908338

Alhaddi, H. (2015). Triple bottom line and sustainability: A literature review. *Business and Management Studies, 1*(2), 6–10. doi:10.11114/bms.v1i2.752

Alkire, S., Foster, J. E., Seth, S., Santos, M. E., Roche, J. M., & Ballon, P. (2015). *Multidimensional poverty measurement and analysis*. Oxford University Press. doi:10.1093/acprof:oso/9780199689491.001.0001

Allison, T. H., Davis, B. C., Short, J. C., & Webb, J. W. (2015). Crowdfunding in a prosocial microlending environment: Examining the role of intrinsic versus extrinsic cues. *Entrepreneurship Theory and Practice, 39*(1), 53–73. doi:10.1111/etap.12108

Allon, G., & Babich, V. (2020). Crowdsourcing and Crowdfunding in the Manufacturing and Services Sectors. *Manufacturing & Service Operations Management, 22*(1), 102–112. doi:10.1287/msom.2019.0825

Al-Matari, A. S., & Al-Maqbali, H. A. (2020). Using Massive Open Online Courses (MOOCs) on Microsoft's educational community platform for professional development for teachers in Oman under Covid-19. *IOSR Journal of Mobile Computing & Application (IOSR-JMCA), 7*(2), 6-15.

Alsafi, Z., Abbas, A. R., Hassan, A., & Ali, M. A. (2020). *The Coronavirus Pandemic: Adaptations in Medical Education*. International Journal of Surgery.

Alvord, S. H., Brown, L. D., & Letts, C. W. (2004). Social entrepreneurship and societal transformation: An exploratory study. *The Journal of Applied Behavioral Science, 40*(3), 260–282. doi:10.1177/0021886304266847

An Initiative under Prime Minister's Laptop Scheme executed through the Higher Education Commission of Pakistan. (n.d.). https://dlsei.pk/

Anderson, S., & Eswaran, M. (2009). What determines female autonomy? Evidence from Bangladesh [November.]. *Journal of Development Economics, Elsevier, 90*(2), 179–191. doi:10.1016/j.jdeveco.2008.10.004

Andreoni, J. (1990). Impure altruism and donations to public goods: A theory of warm-glow giving. *Economic Journal (London), 100*(401), 464–477. doi:10.2307/2234133

Angelica, M. H. (2019). Social entrepreneurship: Evolutions, characteristics, values and motivations. *The Annals of The University of Oradea. Economic Sciences, 28*(1), 63–71.

Antadze, N., & Westley, F. (2010). funding social innovation: How do we know what to grow? *Philanthropist*, *23*(3).

Antadze, N., & Westley, F. R. (2012). Impact metrics for social innovation: Barriers or bridges to radical change? *Journal of Social Entrepreneurship*, *3*(2), 133–150.

Apostolos, G., & Ioannis, M. (2012). Crowd-funding: Developing a Strategy for Crowd Participation. In *12th International Conference*. Economic Society of Therssaloniki.

Aratani, L. (2020, May 28). Jobless America: the coronavirus unemployment crisis in figures. *The Guardian*. https://www.theguardian.com/business/2020/may/28/jobless-america-unemployment-coronavirus-in-figures

Arat, Y. (2010). Religion, Politics and Gender Equality in Turkey: Implications of a democratic paradox? *Third World Quarterly*, *31*(6), 869–884. doi:10.1080/01436597.2010.502712 PMID:20857566

Aria, M., & Cuccurullo, C. (2017). Bibliometrix: An R-tool for comprehensive science mapping analysis. *Journal of Informetrics*, *11*(4), 959–975. doi:10.1016/j.joi.2017.08.007

Arias, J. A., Franco, L. C., Sánchez, M., & Rojas, M. J. (2019). Prácticas innovadoras en el contexto de la de educación superior: Una experiencia de la Institución Universitaria Politécnico Grancolombiano y la Corporación Universitaria Rafael Núñez. In *Investigación e innovación en la enseñanza superior. Nuevos contextos, nuevas ideas, primera edición* (pp. 470-480). Recuperado de https://octaedro.com/wp-content/uploads/2019/11/16152-Investigacion-e-innovacion-en-la-ES.pdf

Arnold, L., Brennecke, M., Camus, P., Fridgen, G., Guggenberger, T., Radszuwill, S., & Urbach, N. (2019). *Blockchain and Initial Coin Offerings: Blockchain's Implications for Crowdfunding*. Business Transformation through Blockchain.

Aslan, G., Araza, A., & Bulut, Ç. (2012). Sosyal girişimciliğin kavramsal çerçevesi. *Girişimcilik ve Kalkınma Dergisi*, *7*(2), 69–88.

Aspelund, A., Fjell, L., & Rødland, S. E. (2017). Doing good and doing well? international entrepreneurship and social responsibility. *International Journal of Entrepreneurship*, *21*(2).

Austin, J. E., & Seitanidi, M. M. (2012a). Collaborative value creation: A review of partnering between nonprofits and businesses: Part I: value creation spectrum and collaboration stages. *Nonprofit and Voluntary Sector Quarterly*, *41*(5), 726–758. doi:10.1177/0899764012450777

Austin, J. E., & Seitanidi, M. M. (2012b). Collaborative value creation: A review of partnering between nonprofits and businesses: Part II: Partnership Processes and Outcomes. *Nonprofit and Voluntary Sector Quarterly*, *41*(6), 929–968. doi:10.1177/0899764012454685

Austin, J., Stevenson, H., & Wei-Skillern, J. (2006). Social and commercial entrepreneurship: Same, different, or both? *Entrepreneurship Theory and Practice*, *30*(1), 1–22. doi:10.1111/j.1540-6520.2006.00107.x

Austin, J., Stevenson, H., & Wei-Skillern, J. (2012). Social and commercial entrepreneurship: Same, different, or both? *Revista ADM*, *47*(3), 370–384.

Ayub, E., Wei, G. W., & Yue, W. S. (2017). Exploring factors affecting learners' acceptance of MOOCs based on Kirkpatrick's model. *Proceedings of the 8th International Conference on E-Education, E-Business, E-Management and E-Learning*, 34-39.

Bacq, S., Geoghegan, W., Josefy, M., Stevenson, R., & Williams, T. A. (2020). The COVID-19 Virtual Idea Blitz: Marshaling social entrepreneurship to rapidly respond to urgent grand challenges. *Business Horizons*.

Bacq, S., & Eddleston, K. A. (2016). A Resource-Based View of Social Entrepreneurship: How Stewardship Culture Benefits Scale of Social Impact. *Journal of Business Ethics*, 1–23.

Bacq, S., & Janssen, F. (2011). The multiple faces of social entrepreneurship: A review of definitional issues based on geographical and thematic criteria. *Entrepreneurship and Regional Development*, *23*(5-6), 373–403. doi:10.1080/08985626.2011.577242

Bağdaş, Ç. K. (2019). Sosyal İş Modelleri ve Sosyal Girişimcilik: Boğaziçi Üniversitesi Tüketim Kooperatifi Örneği. *İşletme Araştırmaları Dergisi*, *11*(3), 1433-1449.

Baierl. (2019). *Digital Entrepreneurship – Interfaces between Digital Technologies and Entrepreneurship Reihe: FGF Studies in Small Business and Entrepreneurship*. Springer. doi:10.1007/978-3-030-20138-8

Baker, S., & Mehmood, A. (2015). Social innovation and the governance of sustainable places. *Local Environment*, *20*(3), 321–334. doi:10.1080/13549839.2013.842964

Baker, T., Miner, A. S., & Eesley, D. T. (2003). Improvising firms: Bricolage, account giving and improvisational competencies in the founding process. *Research Policy*, *32*(2), 255–276. doi:10.1016/S0048-7333(02)00099-9

Baker, T., & Nelson, R. E. (2005). Creating something from Nothing: Resource Construction through Entrepreneurial Bricolage. *Administrative Science Quarterly*, *50*(3), 329–366. doi:10.2189/asqu.2005.50.3.329

Baliga, S. (2013). Shaping the Success of Social Impact Bonds in The United States: Lessons Learned from the Privatization of U.S. Prisons. *Duke Law Journal*, *63*, 437–479.

Bansal, S., Garg, I., & Sharma, G. D. (2019). Social entrepreneurship as a path for social change and driver of sustainable development: A systematic review and research agenda. *Sustainability*, *11*(4), 1091. doi:10.3390u11041091

Barbosa, A. M. (2020). What's in a Hybrid? Framing, Meaning, and Symbols in Hybrid Organizing. *The Academy of Management Annals*, *2020*(1), 20690. Advance online publication. doi:10.5465/AMBPP.2020.20690abstract

Barbosa, L. (2020). Social Entrepreneurship and Digital Technology – Case Study of the Blockchain for Zero Hunger Initiative. *52nd International Scientific Conference on Economic and Social Development*.

Barcevicius. (2019). *Exploring Digital Government Transformation in the EU*. European Commission JRC Science for Policy Report, 12.

Battilana, J., & Dorado, S. (2010). Building Sustainable Hybrid Organizations: The Case of Commercial Microfinance Organizations. *Academy of Management Journal*, *53*(6), 1419–1440. doi:10.5465/amj.2010.57318391

Baumgartner, R. J., & Ebner, D. (2010). Corporate sustainability strategies: Sustainability profiles and maturity levels. *Sustainable Development*, *18*(2), 76–89. doi:10.1002d.447

Bayeh, E. (2016). "The role of empowering women and achieving gender equality to the sustainable development of Ethiopia". Pacific Science Review B. *Humanities and Social Sciences.*, *2*(1), 38.

BBC News. (2020, September 29). *Covid: PM promises 'radical' shake-up of adult education*. https://www.bbc.com/news/uk-politics-54330880

Bbcnews. (2020a). *Coronavirus deaths: How big is the epidemic in care homes?* Available at: https://www.bbc.com/news/health-52284281

Bbcnews. (2020b). *Coronavirus: What's going wrong in Sweden's care homes?* Available at: https://www.bbc.com/news/world-europe-52704836

Beaglehole, R., & Bonita, R. (2010). What is global health? *Global Health Action, 3*. doi:10.3402/gha.v3i0.5142

Because International. (2020). *A shoe that expands 5 sizes and lasts for years, created for kids living in poverty*. Retrieved June 9, 2020, from https://becauseinternational.org/the-shoe-that-grows

Béchervaise, N. E., & Benjamin, C. G. (2013). Visionary or criminal: From profit through morality to socially sustainable entrepreneurship. *Procedia: Social and Behavioral Sciences, 99*, 339–350. doi:10.1016/j.sbspro.2013.10.502

Becker, S., Kunze, C., & Vancea, M. (2017). Community energy and social entrepreneurship: Addressing purpose, organisation and embeddedness of renewable energy projects. *Journal of Cleaner Production, 147*, 25–36. doi:10.1016/j.jclepro.2017.01.048

Beije, P. (2000). *Technological Change in the Modern Economy*. Edward Elgar.

Belleflamme, P., Lambert, T., & Schwienbacher, A. (2014). Crowdfunding: Tapping the right crowd. *Journal of Business Venturing, 29*(5), 585–609. doi:10.1016/j.jbusvent.2013.07.003

Benford, R. D., & Snow, D. A. (2000). Framing Processes and Social Movements: An Overview and Assessment. *Annual Review of Sociology, 26*(1), 611–639. doi:10.1146/annurev.soc.26.1.611

Berndt, C., & Wirth, M. (2018). Market, Metrics, Morals: The Social Impact Bond as an Emerging Social Policy Instrument. *Geoforum, 90*, 27–35. doi:10.1016/j.geoforum.2018.01.019

Bertini, M., & Gourville, J. T. (2012). *Pricing to create shared value*. Academic Press.

Better World Books. (2020). *Better World Books: History*. Retrieved June 19, 2020, https://about.betterworldbooks.com/history/

Betts, S. C., Laud, R., & Kretinin, A. (2018). Social entrepreneurship: A contemporary approach to solving social problems. *Global Journal of Entrepreneurship, 2*(1), 31–40.

Beugré, C. (2016). *Social entrepreneurship: Managing the creation of social value*. Taylor & Francis. doi:10.4324/9780203442609

Biancone, P. P., Secinaro, S., & Kamal, M. (2019). Crowdfunding and Fintech: Business Model Sharia Compliant. *European Journal of Islamic Finance*, (12), 1–10.

Biggiero, L. (2007). Industrial and Knowledge Relocation Strategies Under the Challenges of Globalization and Digitalization: The Move of Small and Medium Enterprises Among Territorial Systems. *Entrepreneurship and Regional Development, 18*(6), 443–471. doi:10.1080/08985620600884701

Bilawar, P. B. (2020). Lockdown period and information sources. *International Journal of Engineering Research and Management, 7*(6).

Bi, S., Liu, Z., & Usman, K. (2017a). The influence of online information on investing decisions of reward-based crowdfunding. *Journal of Business Research, 71*, 10–18. doi:10.1016/j.jbusres.2016.10.001

Blanchard, K., & Gray, D. (2019). Can shared value and entrepreneurship contribute to SME development within rural locations? *Strategic Change, 28*(2), 147–155. doi:10.1002/jsc.2256

Bocken, N. M., Short, S. W., Rana, P., & Evans, S. (2014). A literature and practice review to develop sustainable business model archetypes. *Journal of Cleaner Production, 65*, 42–56. doi:10.1016/j.jclepro.2013.11.039

Bodenhausen, G. V., & Hugenberg, K. (2009). Attention, perception, and social cognition. In F. Strack & J. Förster (Eds.), *Social cognition: the basis of human interaction* (pp. 1–22). Psychology Press.

Boelman V., Kwan A., Lauritzen J.R.K., Millard J., & Schon, R. (2014). *Growing social innovation: A guide for policy makers, A deliverable of the TEPSIE project*. EU 7th Framework Programme, Brussels: EU, DG Research.

Boeren, E., Roumell, E. A., & Roessger, K. M. (2020). COVID-19 and the future of adult education: An Editorial. *Adult Education Quarterly, 1*(4).

Bolton, E. (2010). Social Impact Bonds Unlocking investment in rehabilitation. *Social Finance*. https://www.socialfinance.org.uk/resources/publications/social-impact-bonds-unlocking-new-investment-rehabilitation

Bonini, S., & Capizzi, V. (2019). The role of venture capital in the emerging entrepreneurial finance ecosystem: Future threats and opportunities. *Venture Capital, 21*(2–3), 137–175. doi:10.1080/13691066.2019.1608697

Bonnici, F. (2020). *Why social entrepreneurs are critical to our response to and recovery from the COVID-19 crisis*. Available at: https://www.weforum.org/agenda/2020/05/schwab-foundation-covid-response-alliance-social-entrepreneurs-coronavirus-recovery response/?utm_source=sfmc&utm_medium=email&utm_campaign=2718479_Agenda_weekly-8May2020&utm_term=&emailType=Newsletter [Accessed: 06 JUNE 2020]

Bonzanini, D., Giudici, G., & Patrucco, A. (2016). The Crowdfunding of Renewable Energy Projects. In *Handbook of Environmental and Sustainable Finance* (pp. 429–444). doi:10.1016/B978-0-12-803615-0.00021-2

Boons, F., & Lüdeke-Freund, F. (2013). Business Models For Sustainable Innovation: State of the Art and Steps Towards a Research Agenda. *Journal of Cleaner Production, 45*, 9–19. doi:10.1016/j.jclepro.2012.07.007

Bornstein, D. (2004). *How to change the world: social entrepreneurs and the power of new ideas*. Oxford University Press.

Bornstein, D. (2007). *How to change the world: Social entrepreneurs and the power of new ideas*. Oxford University Press.

Borst, I., Moser, C., & Ferguson, J. (2018). From Friendfunding to Crowdfunding: Relevance of Relationships, Social Media, and Platform Activities to Crowdfunding Performance. *New Media & Society, 20*(4), 1396–1414. doi:10.1177/1461444817694599 PMID:30581357

Boschee, J. (1995). Social entrepreneurship. *Across the Board, 32*(3), 20–25.

Bottiglia, R., & Pichler, F. (Eds.). (2016). *Crowdfunding for SMEs: A European Perspective*. Springer. doi:10.1057/978-1-137-56021-6

Bourdieu, P. (1986). The Forms of Capital. In J. G. Richardson (Ed.), *Handbook of Theory and Research for the Sociology of Education* (pp. 241–258). Greenwood Press.

Bourdieu, P. (1993). *The Field of Cultural Production*. Polity Press.

Bourdieu, P., & Wacquant, L. J. D. (Eds.). (1992). *An Invitation to Reflexive Sociology*. University of Chicago Press.

Bowe, C., & van der Horst, D. (2015). Positive externalities, knowledge exchange and corporate farm extension services; a case study on creating shared value in a water scarce area. *Ecosystem Services, 15*, 1–10. doi:10.1016/j.ecoser.2015.05.009

Bowman, C., & Ambrosini, V. (2000). Value creation versus value capture: Towards a coherent definition of value in strategy. *British Journal of Management, 11*(1), 1–15. doi:10.1111/1467-8551.00147

Boyack, K., Klavans, R., & Börner, K. (2005). Mapping the backbone of science. *Scientometrics, 64*(3), 351–374. doi:10.100711192-005-0255-6

Bran, R. A., & Grosseck, G. (2020). Press RESET: Digitalising education in disruptive times. *Revista Romaneasca pentru Educatie Multidimensionala, 12*(1Sup2), 39-48.

Brennan, M., & Micklas, K. (2020). 5 things to know about climate change and coronavirus with WHO Climate Lead Dr . Campbell- Lendrum. *CBS News*, 1–4.

Bretschneider, U., Knaub, K., & Wieck, E. (2014). *Motivations for crowdfunding: What drives the crowd to invest in start ups?* Paper presented at the 22nd European Conference on Information Systems (ECIS 2014), Tel Aviv, Israel.

Brickson, S. L. (2007). Organizational identity orientation: The genesis of the role of the firm and distinct forms of social value. *Academy of Management Review*, *32*(3), 864–888. doi:10.5465/amr.2007.25275679

British Council. (2017). Activist to entrepreneur: the role of social enterprise in supporting women's empowerment. https://www.britishcouncil.org/sites/default/files/social_enterprise_and_womens_empowerment_july.pdf

British Council. (2019). *The State of Social Enterprise in Turkey Report.* Retrieved September 3, 2020 from https://www.britishcouncil.org.tr/en/programmes/education/social-enterprise-research

British Council. Türkiye. (2019). *Türkiye'de Sosyal Girişimlerin Durumu.* Retrieved February 25, 2020, from https://www.britishcouncil.org.tr/programmes/education/social-enterprise-research

Brooke, J., & Jackson, D. (2020). Older people and COVID-19: Isolation, risk and ageism. *Journal of Clinical Nursing.*

Brüntje, D., & Gajda, O. (2016). *Crowdfunding in Europe State of the Art in Theorey and Practice.* Springer.

Burchardt, T., Le Grand, J., & Piachaud, D. (2002b). Degrees of exclusion: Developing a dynamic, multidimensional measure. In J. Hills, J. Le Grand, & D. Piachaud (Eds.), *Understanding social exclusion.* Oxford University Press.

Bureau of European Policy Advisors. (2011). *Empowering people, driving change, social innovation in European Union.* Retrieved from https://ec.europa.eu/archives/bepa/pdf/publications_pdf

Busenitz, L. W., & Barney, J. B. (1997). Biases and heuristics in strategic decision-making: Differences between entrepreneurs and managers in large organizations. *Journal of Business Venturing*, *12*(1), 9–30. doi:10.1016/S0883-9026(96)00003-1

Butler, B. (2012). Massive open online courses: Legal and policy issues for research libraries. Association of Research Libraries, 1-15.

Bylieva, D., Bekirogullari, Z., Lobatyuk, V., & Nam, T. (2020). Analysis of the consequences of the transition to online learning on the example of MOOC philosophy during the COVID-19 pandemic. *Humanities & Social Sciences Reviews*, *8*(4), 1083–1093.

Byungku, L., & Louise, K. (2019). Cultural leadership ideals and social entrepreneurship: An international study. *Journal of Social Entrepreneurship*, *10*(1), 108–128. doi:10.1080/19420676.2018.1541005

Cahill, G. (2010). Primer on social innovation: A compendium of definitions developed by organizations around the world. *The Philantropist*, *23*, 259–271.

Cajaiba-Santana, G. (2014). Social innovation: Moving the field forward: a conceptual framework. *Technological Forecasting and Social Change*, *82*, 42–51. doi:10.1016/j.techfore.2013.05.008

Calabretta, G., Durisin, B., & Ogliengo, M. (2011). Uncovering the intellectual structure of research in business ethics: A journey through the history, the classics, and the pillars of Journal of Business Ethics. *Journal of Business Ethics*, *104*(4), 499–524. doi:10.100710551-011-0924-8

Calderini, M., Chiodo, V., & Michelucci, F. V. (2018). The Social Impact Investment Race: Toward an Interpretative Framework. *European Business Review*, *30*(1), 66–81. doi:10.1108/EBR-10-2016-0134

Calic, G., & Mosakowski, E. (2016). Kicking off social entrepreneurship: How a sustainability orientation influences crowdfunding success. *Journal of Management Studies*, *53*(5), 738–767. doi:10.1111/joms.12201

Canestrino, R., Ćwiklicki, M., Di Nauta, P., & Magliocca, P. (2019). Creating social value through entrepreneurship: The social business model of La Paranza. *Kybernetes*, *48*(10), 2190–2216. doi:10.1108/K-03-2018-0135

Canestrino, R., Ćwiklicki, M., Magliocca, P., & Pawełek, B. (2020). Understanding social entrepreneurship: A cultural perspective in business research. *Journal of Business Research*, *110*, 132–143. doi:10.1016/j.jbusres.2020.01.006

Cantele, S., Moggi, S., & Campedelli, B. (2020). Spreading Sustainability Innovation through the Co-Evolution of Sustainable Business Models and Partnerships. *Sustainability*, *12*(3), 1–19. doi:10.3390u12031190

Carè, R., & De Lisa, R. (2019). Social Impact Bonds for a SustainableWelfare State: The Role of Enabling Factors. *Sustainability*, *11*(2884), 2–23.

Castaño-Muñoz, J., Kalz, M., Kreijns, K., & Punie, Y. (2018). Who is taking MOOCs for teachers' professional development on the use of ICT? A cross-sectional study from Spain. *Technology, Pedagogy and Education*, *27*(5), 607–624.

Castellas, E. I., Ormiston, J., & Findlay, S. (2018). Financing social entrepreneurship The role of impact investment in shaping social enterprise in Australia. *Social Enterprise Journal*, *14*(2), 130–155. doi:10.1108/SEJ-02-2017-0006

Caulier-Grice, J., Davies, A., Patrick, R., & Norman, W. (2012). Defining social innovation: A deliverable of TEPSIE project. EU 7th Framework Programme, EU, DG Research, Brussels.

Çavuş, M. F., & Pekkan, N. Ü. (2017). Algılanan sosyal desteğin sosyal girişimciliğe etkisi: Üniversite öğrencileri üzerinde bir araştırma 1. *Business and Economics Research Journal*, *8*(3), 519–532. doi:10.20409/berj.2017.64

CBSNEWS. (2020). Available at: https://www.cbsnews.com/news/coronavirus-quarantine-workers-without-pay-help/

CCAF. (2020). *The Global Alternative Finance Market Benchmarking Report*. https://www.jbs.cam.ac.uk/faculty-research/centres/alternative-finance/publications/the-global-alternative-finance-market-benchmarking-report/

Çelik, Ç. (2017). Parental networks, ethnicity, and social and cultural capital: The societal dynamics of educational resilience in Turkey. *British Journal of Sociology of Education*, *38*(7), 1007–1021. doi:10.1080/01425692.2016.1218753

Center for Disease Control. (2019, December 19). *Social Determinants of Health*. Retrieved from https://www.cdc.gov/nchhstp/socialdeterminants/index.html

CEPAL. (2001). *Evolución de los paradigmas y modelos interpretativos del desarrollo territorial. Serie Gestión Pública 13*. Santiago de Chile, Instituto Latinoamericano y del Caribe de Planificación Económica y Social.

Certo, S. T., & Miller, T. (2008). Social entrepreneurship: Key issues and concepts. *Business Horizons*, *51*(4), 267–271. doi:10.1016/j.bushor.2008.02.009

Chakraborty, S., & Swinney, R. (2020). Signaling to the Crowd: Private Quality Information and Rewards-Based Crowdfunding. *Manufacturing & Service Operations Management*, •••, 1–15. doi:10.1287/msom.2019.0833

Chalmers, D., Matthews, R., & Hyslop, A. (2019). Blockchain as an External Enabler of New Venture Ideas: Digital Entrepreneurs and the Disintermediation of the Global Music Industry. *Journal of Business Research*. Advance online publication. doi:10.1016/j.jbusres.2019.09.002

Change the World. (n.d.). https://www.udemy.com/courses/free/

Chang, S. H., Chang, C. W., & Chiu, H. J. (2020). A social impact theory perspective on consumers' intention to adopt recycling in China. *International Journal of Organizational Innovation (Online)*, *12*(4), 220–232.

Charvet, F., Cooper, M. C., & Gardner, J. T. (2008). The intellectual structure of supply chain management: A bibliometric approach. *Journal of Business Logistics*, *29*(1), 47–73. doi:10.1002/j.2158-1592.2008.tb00068.x

Chen, J. C. C. (2013). *Opportunities and challenges of MOOCS: Perspectives from Asia*. IFLA WPIC 2013 Singapore. http://library.ifla.org/157/1/098-chen-en.pdf

Chen, W. C., Huang, A. S., Chuang, J. H., Chiu, C. C., & Kuo, H. S. (2011). Social and economic impact of school closure resulting from pandemic influenza A/H1N1. *The Journal of Infection*, *62*(3), 200–203. doi:10.1016/j.jinf.2011.01.007 PMID:21256153

Cherrier, H., Goswami, P., & Ray, S. (2018). Social entrepreneurship: Creating value in the context of institutional complexity. *Journal of Business Research*, *86*, 245–258. doi:10.1016/j.jbusres.2017.10.056

Chertok, M., Hamaoui, J., & Jamison, E. (2008). The Funding Gap. *Stanford Social Innovation Review*, *6*(2), 44–52.

Choi, D. Y., & Gray, E. R. (2008). The venture development processes of "sustainable" entrepreneurs. *Management Research News*, *31*(8), 558–569. doi:10.1108/01409170810892127

Ciborra, C. U. (1996). The platform organization: Recombining strategies, structures and surprises. *Organization Science*, *7*(2), 103–118. doi:10.1287/orsc.7.2.103

Cicek, B., & Türkmenoğlu, M. A. (2019). Women as Social Entrepreneurs in Turkey. In Social Entrepreneurship: Concepts, Methodologies, Tools, and Applications (pp. 1075-1090). IGI Global.

Çınar, K., & Köse, T. (2018). The Determinants of Women's Empowerment in Turkey: A Multilevel Analysis. *South European Society & Politics*, *23*(3), 365–386. doi:10.1080/13608746.2018.1511077

Clarke, A., & Fuller, M. (2010). Collaborative Strategic Management: Strategy Formulation and Implementation by Multi-Organizational Cross-Sector Social Partnerships. *Journal of Business Ethics*, *94*(S1), 85–101. doi:10.100710551-011-0781-5

Click-On Kaduna. (2020). https://skills.click-onkaduna.ng/

CNNhealth. (2020). *What happens if a coronavirus vaccine is never developed? It has happened before*. Available at: https://edition.cnn.com/2020/05/03/health/coronavirus-vaccine-never-developed-intl/index.html

Cobo, M. J., López-Herrera, A. G., Herrera-Viedma, E., & Herrera, F. (2011). Science mapping software tools: Review, analysis, and cooperative study among tools. *Journal of the American Society for Information Science and Technology*, *62*(7), 1382–1402. doi:10.1002/asi.21525

CocaCola Company. (n.d.). *Better Shared Future*. https://www.coca-colacompany.com/shared-future/women-empowerment

Colombo, M. G., Franzoni, C., & Rossi-Lamastra, C. (2015). Internal Social Capital and the Attraction of Early Contributions in Crowdfunding. *Entrepreneurship Theory and Practice*, *39*(1), 75–100. doi:10.1111/etap.12118

Comini, G., Barki, E., & de Aguiar, L. T. (2012). A three-pronged approach to social business: A Brazilian multi-case analysis. *Revista ADM*, *47*(3), 385–397.

Congress of the United States Congressional Budget Office. (2019). *The 2019 Long-Term Budget Outlook*. https://www.cbo.gov/system/files/2019-06/55331-LTBO-2.pdf

Connell, J., Burgess, J., Theodore, N., Valenzuela, A., & Meléndez, E. (2009). Worker centers: Defending labor standards for migrant workers in the informal economy. *International Journal of Manpower*.

Çöpmadam. (n.d.). *Home*. http://www.copmadam.com/

Corley, K. G., & Gioia, D. A. (2011). Building theory about theory building: What constitutes a theoretical contribution? *Academy of Management Review*, *36*(1), 12–32. doi:10.5465/amr.2009.0486

Cornforth, C. (2014). Understanding and combating mission drift in social enterprises. *Social Enterprise Journal*, *10*(1), 3–20. doi:10.1108/SEJ-09-2013-0036

Cornwall, A. (2016). Women's empowerment: What works? *Journal of International Development*, *28*(3), 342–359. doi:10.1002/jid.3210

Costanza, R., & Daly, H. E. (1992). Natural capital and sustainable development. *Conservation Biology*, *6*(1), 37–46. doi:10.1046/j.1523-1739.1992.610037.x

Costanzo, L. A., Vurro, C., Foster, D., Servato, F., & Perrini, F. (2014). Dual-Mission Management in Social Entrepreneurship: Qualitative Evidence from Social Firms in the United Kingdom. *Journal of Small Business Management*, *52*(4), 655–677. doi:10.1111/jsbm.12128

Coulter, N., Monarch, I., & Konda, S. (1998). Software engineering as seen through its research literature: A study in co-word analysis. *Journal of the American Society for Information Science*, *49*(13), 1206–1223. doi:10.1002/(SICI)1097-4571(1998)49:13<1206::AID-ASI7>3.0.CO;2-F

Coursera Workforce Recovery Initiative. (2020). https://www.dsti.gov.sl/coursera/

Coursera Workforce Recovery Programme. (2020a). https://labour.gov.bb/coursera-workforce-recovery-programme/

Coursera Workforce Recovery Programme. (2020b). https://covid19.bergenworkforce.org/coursera/

Cramer, J. C., Dietz, T., & Johnston, R. A. (1980). Social impact assessment of regional plans: A review of methods and issues and a recommended process. *Policy Sciences*, *12*(1), 61–82.

Crane, A., Palazzo, G., Spence, L. J., & Matten, D. (2014). Contesting the value of "creating shared value." *California Management Review*, *56*(2), 130–153. doi:10.1525/cmr.2014.56.2.130

Cresswell, K., Worth, A., & Sheikh, A. (2010). Actor-Network Theory and Its Role in Understanding the Implementation of Information Technology Developments in Healthcare. *BMC Medical Informatics and Decision Making*, *10*(1), 67. doi:10.1186/1472-6947-10-67 PMID:21040575

Crisistextline. (2020). *How to Handle Coronavirus.* Available at: https://www.crisistextline.org/topics/get-help-coronavirus/#for-healthcare-workers-6

Crowdfunding - Statistics & Facts. (2020). *Statistica*. https://www.statista.com/topics/1283/crowdfunding/

Çubukçu, C. (2017). Kitlesel fonlama: Türkiye'deki Kitlesel Fonlama Platformları Üzerinden Bir Değerlendirme. *Girişimcilik ve İnovasyon Yönetimi Dergisi*, *6*(2), 155–172.

Cumming, D. J., & Johan, S. A. (2019). *Crowdfunding: Fundamental Cases, Facts, and Insights*. Academic Press.

Dacin, M. T., Dacin, P. A., & Tracey, P. (2011). Social entrepreneurship: A critique and future directions. *Organization Science*, *22*(5), 1203–1213. doi:10.1287/orsc.1100.0620

Dacin, P. A., Dacin, M. T., & Matear, M. (2010). Social entrepreneurship: Why we don't need a new theory and how we move forward from here. *The Academy of Management Perspectives*, *24*(2), 36–56.

Dacın, P. A., Dacın, M. T., & Matear, M. (2010). Social entrepreneurship: Why we don't need a new theory and how we move forward. *The Academy of Management Perspectives*, *24*(3), 37–57.

Darko, E., & Koranteng, K. (2015). *Social enterprise landscape in Ghana*. British Council. https://www.britishcouncil.org/sites/default/files/social_enterprise_landscape_in_ghana_report_final.pdf

Dart, R. (2004). The legitimacy of social enterprise. *Nonprofit Management & Leadership*, *14*(4), 411–424. doi:10.1002/nml.43

Datta, A. , Sahaym, A., & Brooks, S. (2018). Unpacking the Antecedents of Crowdfunding Campaign's Success: The Effects of Social Media and Innovation Orientation. *Journal of Small Business Management*. Advance online publication. doi:10.1111/jsbm.12498

Datta, P. B., & Gailey, R. (2012). Empowering Women Through Social Entrepreneurship: Case Study of a Women's Cooperative in India. *Entrepreneurship Theory and Practice*, *36*(3), 569–587. doi:10.1111/j.1540-6520.2012.00505.x

De Clercq, D., & Voronov, M. (2009). Role of cultural and symbolic capital in entrepreneurs' ability to meet expectations about conformity and innovation. *Journal of Small Business Management*, *47*(3), 398–420. doi:10.1111/j.1540-627X.2009.00276.x

de los Reyes, G. Jr, & Scholz, M. (2019). The limits of the business case for sustainability: Don't count on 'Creating Shared Value' to extinguish corporate destruction. *Journal of Cleaner Production*, *221*, 785–794. doi:10.1016/j.jclepro.2019.02.187

De Mooij, M. (2017). Comparing dimensions of national culture for secondary analysis of consumer behavior data of different countries. *International Marketing Review*, *34*(3), 444–456. doi:10.1108/IMR-02-2016-0047

De Ruysscher, C., Claes, C., Lee, T., Cui, F., Van Loon, J., De Maeyer, J., & Schalock, R. (2017). A systems approach to social entrepreneurship. *Voluntas*, *28*(6), 2530–2545.

Dean, T. J., & McMullen, J. S. (2007). Toward a theory of sustainable entrepreneurship: Reducing environmental degradation through entrepreneurial action. *Journal of Business Venturing*, *22*(1), 50–76. doi:10.1016/j.jbusvent.2005.09.003

Dedeoglu, S. (2012). Equality, protection or discrimination: Gender equality policies in Turkey. *Social Politics*, *19*(2), 269–290. doi:10.1093p/jxs004

Dees, J. G. (1998). The meaning of social entrepreneurship. Retrieved January 29, 2020, from http://www.fuqua.duke.edu/centers/case/documents/dees_SE.pdf.http://www.fuqua.duke.edu/centers/case/documents/dees_SE.pdf

Dees, J. G. (1998). *The meaning of social entrepreneurship*. Retrieved June 16, 2020, from https://centers.fuqua.duke.edu/case/wp-content/uploads/sites/7/2015/03/Article_Dees_MeaningofSocialEntrepreneurship_2001.pdf

Dees, J. G. (1998). *The meaning of social entrepreneurship*. Revised May 2001, original draft, available at http://www.fuqua.duke.edu/centers/case/documents/ Dees_SEdef. pdf

Dees, J. G., & Anderson, B. B. (2006a). Framing a theory of social entrepreneurship: building on two schools of practice and thought. Research on social entrepreneurship, *ARNOVA Occasional Paper Series*, *1*(3), 39–66.

Dees, J. G., & Anderson, B. B. (2006b). Framing a theory of social entrepreneurship:Building on two schools of practice and thought. In J. Gregory (Ed.), Research on social entrepreneurship: Understanding and contributing to an emerging field (pp. 39–66). Academic Press.

Dees, J. G. (1998). Enterprising nonprofits: What do you do when traditional sources of funding fall short. *Harvard Business Review*, *76*(1), 55–67. PMID:10176919

Dees, J. G., & Anderson, B. B. (2003). For-profit social ventures. In M. L. Kourilsky & W. B. Walstad (Eds.), *Social Entrepreneurship* (pp. 1–26). Senate Hall.

Dees, J. G., Emerson, J., & Economy, P. (2001). *Enterprising Nonprofits: A Toolkit for Social Entrepreneurs*. Wiley.

Defazio, D., Franzoni, C., & Rossi-Lamastra, C. (2020). How Pro-social Framing Affects the Success of Crowdfunding Projects: The Role of Emphasis and Information Crowdedness. *Journal of Business Ethics*. Advance online publication. doi:10.100710551-020-04428-1

Defourny, J., & Nyssens, M. (2013). Social innovation, social economy and social enterprise: what can the European debate tell us? *The International Handbook on Social Innovation*, 40-53.

Defourny, J., & Nyssens, M. (2010). Conceptions of social enterprise and social entrepreneurship in Europe and the United States: Convergences and divergences. *Journal of Social Entrepreneurship*, *1*(1), 32–53. doi:10.1080/19420670903442053

Del Giudice, A., & Migliavacca, M. (2019). Social Impact Bonds and Institutional Investors: An Empirical Analysis of a Complicated Relationship. *Nonprofit and Voluntary Sector Quarterly*, *48*(1), 50–70. doi:10.1177/0899764018797480

Dembek, K., Singh, P., & Bhakoo, V. (2016). Literature review of shared value: A theoretical concept or a management buzzword? *Journal of Business Ethics*, *137*(2), 231–267. doi:10.100710551-015-2554-z

Dentchev, N., Baumgartner, R., Dieleman, H., Jóhannsdóttir, L., Jonker, J., Nyberg, T., Rauter, R., Rosano, M., Snihur, Y., Tang, X., & van Hoof, B. (2016). Embracing the variety of sustainable business models: Social entrepreneurship, corporate intrapreneurship, creativity, innovation, and other approaches to sustainability challenges. *Journal of Cleaner Production*, *113*, 1–4. doi:10.1016/j.jclepro.2015.10.130

Denzin, N., & Lincoln, Y. S. (2018). Introduction: the discipline and practice of qualitative research. In N. Denzin & Y. S. Lincoln (Eds.), *The Sage Handbook of Qualitative Research*. Sage.

Desa, G. (2007). *Social entrepreneurship: snapshots of a research field in emergence*. Paper presented at the 3rd International Social Entrepreneurship Research Conference, Centre for Corporate Values and Responsibility (CVR), Frederiksberg.

Dey, P., & Steyaert, C. (2016). Rethinking the space of ethics in social entrepreneurship: Power, subjectivity, and practices of freedom. *Journal of Business Ethics*, *133*(4), 627–641. doi:10.100710551-014-2450-y

Di Domenico, M., Haugh, H., & Tracey, P. (2010). Social bricolage: Theorizing social value creation in social enterprises. *Entrepreneurship Theory and Practice*, *34*(4), 681–703. doi:10.1111/j.1540-6520.2010.00370.x

Díaz-Correa, J. E., & López-Navarro, M. A. (2018). Managing sustainable hybrid organisations: A case study in the agricultural sector. *Sustainability*, *10*(9), 3010. doi:10.3390u10093010

Diaz, J. T., Bolivar, H., Gomez, J., & Prada, J. (2018). Business diagnostic technology for sharing value and social innovation in one-person companies. *2017 Congreso Internacional De Innovacion y Tendencias En Ingenieria, CONIITI 2017 - Conference Proceedings*, 1-6. doi:10.1109/CONIITI.2017.8273342

Dickel, P., & Eckardt, G. (2020). Who wants to be a social entrepreneur? The role of gender and sustainability orientation. *Journal of Small Business Management*, 1–23. doi:10.1080/00472778.2019.1704489

Diener, E., Oishi, S., & Lucas, R. E. (2003). Personality, culture, and subjective well-being: Emotional and cognitive evaluations of life. *Annual Review of Psychology*, *54*(1), 403–425. doi:10.1146/annurev.psych.54.101601.145056 PMID:12172000

Dionisio, M. (2019). The evolution of social entrepreneurship research: A bibliometric analysis. *Social Enterprise Journal*, *15*(1), 22–45. doi:10.1108/SEJ-05-2018-0042

Disley, E., Rubin, J., Scraggs, E., Burrowes, N., & May Culley, D. (2011). *Lessons Learned from the Planning and Early Implementation of the Social Impact Bond at HMP Peterborough*. Rand Europe.

Doganova, L., & Eyquem-Renault, M. (2009). What do business models do?: Innovation devices in technology entrepreneurship. *Research Policy, 38*(10), 1559–1570. doi:10.1016/j.respol.2009.08.002

Doherty, B., Haugh, H., & Lyon, F. (2014). Social enterprises as hybrid organizations: A review and research agenda. *International Journal of Management Reviews, 16*(4), 417–436. doi:10.1111/ijmr.12028

Domanski, D., Howaldt, J., & Schröder, A. (2017). Social Innovation in Latin America. *Journal of Human Development and Capabilities, 18*(2), 307–312. doi:10.1080/19452829.2017.1299698

Dorfleitner, G., Hornuf, L., & Weber, M. (2018). Dynamics of investor communication in equity crowdfunding. *Electronic Markets, 28*(4), 523–540. doi:10.100712525-018-0294-5

Douglas, E., & Prentice, C. (2019). Innovation and profit motivations for social entrepreneurship: A fuzzy-set analysis. *Journal of Business Research, 99*, 69–79. doi:10.1016/j.jbusres.2019.02.031

Douglas, H. (2008). Creating knowledge: A review of research methods in three societal change approaches. *Journal of Nonprofit & Public Sector Marketing, 20*(2), 141–163. doi:10.1080/10495140802224787

Downes, S. (2009). *New technology supporting informal learning* [Web log post]. https://halfanhour.blogspot.com/2009/04/new-technology-supportinginformal.html

Downes, S. (2008). Places to go: Connectivism & connective knowledge. *Innovate: Journal of Online Education, 5*(1), 6.

Drăguşin, M., & Welsh, D. H. (2015). Innovative and sustainable business models in digital higher education: A comparative analysis of global reach MOOCs platforms. *New Trends in Sustainable Business and Consumption*, 75-83.

Drayton, W. (2006). Everyone a changemaker: Social entrepreneurship's ultimate goal. *Innovations: Technology, Governance, Globalization, 1*(1), 80–96. doi:10.1162/itgg.2006.1.1.80

Drencheva, A. (2019). Social Entrepreneurship: Blending Prosocial Motivation and Self-Interests in Business. In D. Ochnik (Ed.), *Selflessness in Business* (pp. 15–32). Vernon Press.

Duflo, E. (2012). Women empowerment and economic development. *Journal of Economic Literature, 50*(4), 1051–1079. doi:10.1257/jel.50.4.1051

Duque Oliva, E. J., Cervera Taulet, A., & Rodríguez Romero, C. (2006). A bibliometric analysis of models measuring the concept of perceived quality inproviding internet service. *Innovar (Universidad Nacional de Colombia), 16*(28), 223–243.

Durak, İ. (2016). Sosyal Gırısımcılık Ve Ahılık Teskılatı: Teorık Çerçeve/Socıal Entrepreneurshıp And Akhı Organızatıon: Theoretical Framework. *Erciyes Üniversitesi Iktisadi ve Idari Bilimler Fakültesi Dergisi*, (47), 101.

Dworkin, G. (2010). Paternalism. The Stanford Encyclopedia of Philosophy.

Dy, A. M. (2016). A Web of Opportunity or the Same Old Story? Women Digital Entrepreneurs and Intersectionality Theory. *Human Relations*, 286–311.

Dyer, W. G. Jr, & Wilkins, A. L. (1991). Better stories, not better constructs to generate better theory: A rejoinder to Eisenhardt. *Academy of Management Review, 16*(3), 613–619. doi:10.5465/amr.1991.4279492

Easterly, W. (2009). How the millennium development goals are unfair to Africa. *World Development, Vol, 37*(1), 26–35. doi:10.1016/j.worlddev.2008.02.009

Economictimes. (2020). *Omidyar Network India announces Rapid Response Funding for Covid-19.* Available at: https://economictimes.indiatimes.com/small-biz/sme-sector/omidyar-network-india-announces-rapid-response-funding-for-covid19/articleshow/74789991.cms?from=mdr

Eggers, W. D., & Macmillan, P. (2013). *The solution revolution: How business, government, and social enterprises are teaming up to solve society's toughest problems*. Harvard Business Press.

Eğitim Reformu Girişimi. (2011). Eğitim İzleme Raporu 2010. Retrieved February 7, 2020, from http://erg.sabanciuniv.edu/sites/erg.sabanciuniv.edu/files/EIR2010_SON.pdf

Eichler, G., & Schwarz, E. (2019). What sustainable development goals do social innovations address? A systematic review and content analysis of social innovation literature. *Sustainability*, *11*(522), 1–18. doi:10.3390u11020522

Eisenhardt, K. M., & Graebner, M. E. (2007). Theory building from cases: Opportunities and challenges. *Academy of Management Journal*, *50*(1), 25–32. doi:10.5465/amj.2007.24160888

Eisenmann, T. R., Ries, E., & Dillard, S. (2012). Hypothesis-driven entrepreneurship: The lean startup. *Harvard Business School Entrepreneurial Management Case*, (812-095).

El Ebrashi, R. (2013). Social Entrepreneurship Theory and Sustainable Social Impact. *Social Responsibility Journal*, *9*(2), 188-209.

Elamrani, J., & Lemtaoui, M. (2016). Creating shared value in Moroccan companies: A case study of OCP SA. *Transnational Corporations Review*, *8*(4), 280–288. doi:10.1080/19186444.2016.1266131

Elia, G., Margherita, A., & Passiante, G. (2020). Digital Entrepreneurship Ecosystem: How Digital Technologies and Collective Intelligence are Reshaping the Entrepreneurial Process. *Technological Forecasting and Social Change*, *150*, 1–12. doi:10.1016/j.techfore.2019.119791

Elkington, J. (1998). Partnerships from cannibals with forks: The triple bottom line of 21st-century business. *Environmental Quality Management*, *8*(1), 37–51. doi:10.1002/tqem.3310080106

Elkington, J., & Hartigan, P. (2008). *The power of unreasonable people: How social entrepreneurs create markets that change the world*. Harvard Business Press.

Emerson, J., Freundlich, T., Fructerman, J., Berlin, L., & Stevenson, K. (2007). Nothing ventured, nothing gained. In Nothing ventured, nothing gained: Addressing the critical gaps in risk-taking capital for social enterprise. doi:10.1108/09657960110696708

Eneza Education. (2017). Retrieved October 1, 2020 from http:// enezaeducation.com/

Erdur, D., & Fındıklı, M. (2020). A conceptual model proposal for co-creation of social value: Insights from social entrepreneurs. *Istanbul Gelisim University Journal of Social Sciences*, *7*(1), 1–20.

Ergu, E. (2020). *İlham Veren Kadınlar*. Available at: https://www.hurriyet.com.tr/ekonomi/ebru-baybara-demir-avrupaya-sorgul-bugdayi-ve-mardin-sabununu-online-anlatacak-avrupaya-ilham-olacak-41502929

Erikli, S. (2016). Genç yoksulluğunun temel belirleyicileri: Eğitim ve düzgün iş. *Gazi Universitesi Iktisadi ve Idari Bilimler Fakultesi Dergisi*, *18*(1), 283.

Eschenbacher, S., & Fleming, T. (2020). Transformative dimensions of lifelong learning: Mezirow, Rorty and COVID-19. *International Review of Education*, 1–16.

Eurodiaconia Briefing for Members, Measuring Social Value, What Do We Mean by Measuring Social Value? (n.d.). Retrieved September, 10 from www.eurodiaconia.org

Euronews. (2020). Available at: https://www.euronews.com/2020/05/21/are-care-homes-the-dark-side-of-sweden-s-coronavirus-strategy

European Commission. (2016). *Social Enterprises and Their Eco-systems: Developments in Europe, Directorate-General for Employment Social Affairs and Inclusion, 8. European Union Digital Transformation.* Retrieved August 21, 2020 from https://www.i-scoop.eu/digital-transformation/digitization-digitalization-digital-transformation-disruption/

Eurostat. (2019). *At risk of poverty or social exclusion in the EU-28, 2018.* Retrieved July 17, 2020, from https://ec.europa.eu/eurostat/news/themes-in-the-spotlight/poverty-day-2019

Everett, J. (2002). Organizational Research and the Praxeology of Pierre Bourdieu. *Organizational Research Methods*, *5*(1), 56–80. doi:10.1177/1094428102051005

Fanea-Ivanovici, M. (2018). Crowdfunding – A Viable Alternative Source of Finance for the Film Industry? *Revista Economica*, *70*(3), 79–88.

Farmer, P. (2013). *Reimagining Global Health: An Introduction*. University of California Press. doi:10.1525/9780520954632

Feilhauer, S., & Hahn, R. (2019). Firm-Nonprofit Collaboration: Explaining the Rationale Behind Firms' Cross-Sector Partner Choices. *Long Range Planning*, *3*, 1–19. doi:10.1016/j.lrp.2019.101952

Feng, X. L., Hu, X. C., Fan, K. Y., & Yu, T. (2020, April). A brief discussion about the impact of coronavirus disease 2019 on teaching in colleges and universities of China. In *Proceedings of 2020 International Conference on E-Commerce and Internet Technology (ECIT)*, (pp. 167-170). IEEE.

Fenwick, M., McCahery, J. A. and Vermeulen, E. P. M. (2018). Fintech and the Financing of Smes and Entrepreneurs: From Crowdfunding to Marketplace Lending. *The Economics of Crowdfunding*, 103–129.

Fenwick, M., McCahery, J. A., & Vermeulen, E. P. (2020). Will the world ever be the same after COVID-19? Two lessons from the first global crisis of a digital age. *European Business Organization Law Review*, 1–21.

FernandesN. (2020). Economic effects of coronavirus outbreak (COVID-19) on the world economy. Available at SSRN 3557504. doi:10.2139srn.3557504

Fernández-Satto, V., Alfaro-re, M., & Davies-Vidal, C. (2009). Aglomeraciones productivas y territorio: En busca de una manera más holística de entender sus contribuciones al desarrollo. *Economía, Sociedad y Territorio*, (septiembre-diciembre), 629–680. doi:10.22136/est002009164

Ferreira, J. J., Fernandes, C. I., Peres-Ortiz, M., & Alves, H. (2017). Conceptualizing social entrepreneurship: Perspectives from the literature. *International Review on Public and Nonprofit Marketing*, *14*(1), 73–93. doi:10.100712208-016-0165-8

Ferris, E., & Kirişci, K. (2016, July 29). *What Turkey's open-door policy means for Syrian refugees.* Retrieved October 29, 2020, from https://www.brookings.edu/blog/order-from-chaos/2015/07/08/what-turkeys-open-door-policy-means-for-syrian-refugees/

Fettahoğlu, S., & Khusayan, S. (2017). Yeni finansman olanağı: Kitle fonlama. *Uşak Üniversitesi Sosyal Bilimler Dergisi*, *10*(4), 497–521.

Financial Tımes. (2020). Available at: https://www.ft.com/content/9d6b46e2-55f4-4de1-ba21-f1ab9f14bcbf

Financial Tımes. (2020). *Covid-19.* Available at: https://www.ft.com/content/0fdb770a-a57a-11ea-92e2-cbd9b7e28ee6

Fini, A. (2009). The technological dimension of a massive open online course: The case of the CCK08 course tools. *International Review of Research in Open and Distributed Learning*, *10*(5).

Finnegan, C. (2020, February 12). *Trump budget proposes cuts to global health amid two global health crises.* Retrieved from https://abcnews.go.com/Politics/trump-budget-proposes-cuts-global-health-amid-global/story

Fisscher, O., Frenkel, D., Lurie, Y., & Nijhof, A. (2005). Stretching the frontiers: Exploring the relationships between entrepreneurship and ethics. *Journal of Business Ethics*, *60*(3), 207–209. doi:10.100710551-005-0128-1

FitzGerald, C., Carter, E., Dixon, R., & Airoldi, M. (2019). Walking the Contractual Tightrope: A Transaction Cost Economics Perspective on Social Impact Bonds. *Public Money & Management*, *39*(7), 458–467. doi:10.1080/09540962.2019.1583889

Folke, C., Carpenter, S., Elmqvist, T., Gunderson, L., Holling, C. S., & Walker, B. (2002). Resilience and sustainable development: Building adaptive capacity in a world of transformations. *Ambio*, *31*(5), 437–440. doi:10.1579/0044-7447-31.5.437 PMID:12374053

Foray, D., & Goenaga, X. (2013). *The goals of smart specialization.* European Commission: JRC Scientific and Policy Report, S3 Policy Brief Series No. 01/2013.

Foray, D., & Van Ark, B. (2007). Smart specialisation in a truly integrated research area is the key to attracting more R&D to Europe. *Knowledge Economists Policy Brief*, *1*, 1-4.

Foray, D. (2012). *Guide to Research and Innovation Strategies for Smart Specialisation (RIS 3).* DG Regional Policy.

Foray, D. (2017). The economic fundamentals of smart specialization strategies. In *Advances in the theory and practice of smart specialization* (pp. 37–50). Academic Press. doi:10.1016/B978-0-12-804137-6.00002-4

Foray, D., David, P. A., & Hall, B. H. (2011). *Smart specialisation from academic idea to political instrument, the surprising career of a concept and the difficulties involved in its implementation (No. REP_WORK).* EPFL.

Fossen, F. M., & Sorgner, A. (2019). Digitalization of Work and Entry into Entrepreneurship. *Journal of Business Research*, *148*(2963), 1–16. doi:10.1016/j.jbusres.2019.09.019

FOXNEWS. (2020). Available at: https://www.foxnews.com/category/health/infectious-disease/coronavirus

Freudenreich, B., Ludeke-Freund, F., & Schaltegger, S. (2019). A Stakeholder Theory Perspective on Business Models: Value Creation for Sustainability. *Journal of Business Ethics*, *166*(1), 3–18. doi:10.100710551-019-04112-z

Fundacionparaguaya. (2020). *Covid-19.* Available at: http://www.fundacionparaguaya.org.py/v2/?noticias=nos-cuidamos-y-te-cuidamos

Gafni, H., Marom, D., & Sade, O. (2019a). Are the life and death of an early-stage venture indeed in the power of the tongue? Lessons from online crowdfunding pitches. *Strategic Entrepreneurship Journal*, *13*(1), 3–23. Advance online publication. doi:10.1002ej.1293

Galindo-Martin, M. A., Castano-Martinez, M. S., & Mendez-Picaso, M. T. (2019). Digital Transformation, Digital Dividends, and Entrepreneurship: A Quantitative Analysis. *Journal of Business Research*, *101*, 522–527. doi:10.1016/j.jbusres.2018.12.014

Gao, J., Tian, Z., & Yang, X. (2020). Breakthrough: Chloroquine phosphate has shown apparent efficacy in treatment of COVID-19 associated pneumonia in clinical studies. *Bioscience Trends*, *14*(1), 72–73. doi:10.5582/bst.2020.01047 PMID:32074550

Gardner. (2018). *Gardner Glossary.* Digital Library Federation.

Garmendia, J., Barrientos, E., & Castro, J. (2019). Management context of entrepreneurship in engineers and architects in Tachira, Venezuela. *Journal of Physics: Conference Series*, *1418*, 012015. doi:10.1088/1742-6596/1418/1/012015

Gasca, L. (2017). *Why Do Social Enterprises Fail? New Research Reveals Three Reasons (And Some Surprises).* https://nextbillion.net/why-do-social-enterprises-fail-new-research-reveals-three-reasons-and-some-surprises/

Gehman, J., Glaser, V. L., Eisenhardt, K. M., Gioia, D., Langley, A., & Corley, K. G. (2018). Finding Theory–Method Fit: A Comparison of Three Qualitative Approaches to Theory Building. *Journal of Management Inquiry*, *27*(3), 1–18. doi:10.1177/1056492617706029

Geissdoerfer, M., Vladimirova, D., & Evans, S. (2018). Sustainable business model innovation: A review. *Journal of Cleaner Production*, *198*, 401–416. doi:10.1016/j.jclepro.2018.06.240

Gerber, E. M., & Hui, J. (2013). Crowdfunding: Motivations and deterrents for participation. *ACM Transactions on Computer-Human Interaction*, *20*(6), 1–32. Advance online publication. doi:10.1145/2530540

Ghorai, K., Akter, S., Khatun, F., & Ray, P. (2014). mHealth for Smoking Cessation Programs: A Systematic Review. *Journal of Personalized Medicine*, *4*(3), 412–423. doi:10.3390/jpm4030412 PMID:25563359

Giddens, A. (1984). *The Constitution of Society*. Polity Press.

Gierczak, M. M., Bretschneider, U., Haas, P., Blohm, I., & Leimeister, J. M. (2016). Crowdfunding: Outlining the New Era of Fundraising. In *Crowdfunding in Europe*. Springer. doi:10.1007/978-3-319-18017-5_2

Gill, J. C., Mankelow, J., & Mills, K. (2019). The role of Earth and environmental science in addressing sustainable development priorities in Eastern Africa. *Environmental Development*, *30*, 3–20. doi:10.1016/j.envdev.2019.03.003

Gimenez, C., Sierra, V., & Rodon, J. (2012). Sustainable operations: Their impact on the triple bottom line. *International Journal of Production Economics*, *140*(1), 149–159. doi:10.1016/j.ijpe.2012.01.035

Gioia, D. A., Corley, K. G., & Hamilton, A. L. (2012). Seeking Qualitative Rigor in Inductive Research: Notes on the Gioia Methodology. *Organizational Research Methods*, *16*(1), 15–31. doi:10.1177/1094428112452151

Giorgi, S., & Weber, K. (2015). Marks of Distinction: Framing and Audience Appreciation in the Context of Investment Advice. *Administrative Science Quarterly*, *60*(2), 333–367. doi:10.1177/0001839215571125

Giudici, G., Guerini, M., & Rossi-Lamastra, C. (2018). Reward-based crowdfunding of entrepreneurial projects: The effect of local altruism and localized social capital on proponents' success. *Small Business Economics*, *50*(2), 307–324. doi:10.100711187-016-9830-x

Glińska, E & Kononiuk, A. (2013). *The concept of regional strategy of Smart Specialization*. Prace naukowe uniwersytetu ekonomicznego we wrocławiu research papers of wrocław university of economics.

Globalshapers. (2020). *Konexio's Online Mentoring and Training During COVID-19*. Available at: https://www.globalshapers.org/impact/konexios-online-mentoring-and-training-during-covid-19

Gobble, M. (2018). Digitalization, Digitization, and Innovation. *Research Technology Management*, *61*(4), 56–59. doi:10.1080/08956308.2018.1471280

Goffman, E. (1974). *Frame analysis: An essay on the organization of experience*. Harvard University Press.

Goodland, R. (1995). The concept of environmental sustainability. *Annual Review of Ecology and Systematics*, *26*(1), 1–24. doi:10.1146/annurev.es.26.110195.000245

Görün, M., & Kara, M. (2010). Kentsel dönüşüm ve sosyal girişimcilik bağlamında Türkiye'de kentsel yaşam kalitesinin artırılması. *Yönetim Bilimleri Dergisi*, *8*(2), 137–164.

Gössling, S., Scott, D., & Hall, C. M. (2020). Pandemics, tourism and global change: A rapid assessment of COVID-19. *Journal of Sustainable Tourism*, 1–20.

Governor Pritzker launches "get hired" website to connect workers impacted by covid-19 with employment and career resources. (2020). https://www2.illinois.gov/Pages/news-item.aspx?ReleaseID=21545

Granados, M. L., Hlupic, V., Coakes, E., & Mohamed, S. (2011). Social enterprise and social entrepreneurship research and theory. *Social Enterprise Journal*, *7*(3), 198–218. doi:10.1108/17508611111182368

Gras, D., & Lumpkin, G. T. (2012). Strategic Foci in Social and Commercial Entrepreneurship: A Comparative Analysis. *Journal of Social Entrepreneurship*, *3*(1), 6–23. doi:10.1080/19420676.2012.660888

Greenfield, S. M., & Strickon, A. (1981). A new paradigm for the study of entrepreneurship and social change. *Economic Development and Cultural Change*, *29*(3), 467–499. doi:10.1086/451267

Griffiths, A. & Meinicke, C. (2014). *Introduction To Social Impact Bonds And Early Intervention*. Early Intervention Foundation: Initial Report.

Griggs, D., Stafford-Smith, M., Gaffney, O., Rockström, J., Öhman, M. C., Shyamsundar, P., Steffen, W., Glaser, G., Kanie, N., & Noble, I. (2013). Policy: Sustainable development goals for people and planet. *Nature*, *495*(7441), 305–307. doi:10.1038/495305a PMID:23518546

Grillitsch, M., Asheim, B., & Trippl, M. (2018). Unrelated knowledge combinations: The unexplored potential for regional industrial path development. *Cambridge Journal of Regions, Economy and Society*, *11*(2), 257–274. doi:10.1093/cjres/rsy012

Groot, A., & Dankbaar, B. (2014). Does social innovation require social entrepreneurship? *Technology Innovation Management Review*, *4*(12), 17–26. doi:10.22215/timreview/854

Guerrieri, V., Lorenzoni, G., Straub, L., & Werning, I. (2020). *Macroeconomic Implications of COVID-19: Can Negative Supply Shocks Cause Demand Shortages?* (No. w26918). National Bureau of Economic Research.

Gümüsay, A. A. (2015). Entrepreneurship from an Islamic perspective. *Journal of Business Ethics*, *130*(1), 199–208. doi:10.100710551-014-2223-7

Gümüsay, A. A., Smets, M., & Morris, T. (2020). "God at Work": Engaging Central and Incompatible Institutional Logics through Elastic Hybridity. *Academy of Management Journal*, *63*(1), 124–154. doi:10.5465/amj.2016.0481

Gundolf, K., & Filser, M. (2013). Management research and religion: A citation analysis. *Journal of Business Ethics*, *112*(1), 177–185. doi:10.100710551-012-1240-7

Gundry, L., Kickul, J., Griffiths, M., & Bacq, S. (2011). Creating Social Change Out of Nothing: The Role of Entrepreneurial Bricolage in Social Entrepreneurs' Catalytic Innovations. In Social and Sustainable Entrepreneurship (Advances in Entrepreneurship, Firm Emergence and Growth, Vol. 13). Emerald Group Publishing Limited. doi:10.1108/S1074-7540(2011)0000013005

Günes, M. (2017). *Sosyal Sorunların Yönetim ve Çözümünde Geleceği Şekillendirmek: Sosyal Girişimci Kooperatifçilik Ve Avrupa Girişimcilik Ağı Örneği*. Third Sector Social Economic Review.

Güngör, E. (2008). *Ahlak Psikolojisi ve Sosyal Ahlak*. Ötüken Yayınları.

Hackforsweden. (2020). Available at: https://www.hackthecrisis.se/challenges

Hagedorn, A., & Pinkwart, A. (2016). The financing process of equity-based crowdfunding: An empirical analysis. In *Crowdfunding in Europe* (pp. 71–85). Springer. doi:10.1007/978-3-319-18017-5_5

Hahn, R., Spieth, P., & Ince, I. (2018). Business model design in sustainable entrepreneurship: Illuminating the commercial logic of hybrid businesses. *Journal of Cleaner Production*, *176*, 439–451. doi:10.1016/j.jclepro.2017.12.167

Haigh, N., & Hoffman, A. J. (2014). The new heretics: Hybrid organizations and the challenges they present to corporate sustainability. *Organization & Environment*, *27*(3), 223–241. doi:10.1177/1086026614545345

Haigh, N., Walker, J., Bacq, S., & Kickul, J. (2015). Hybrid Organisations: Origins, Strategies, Impacts and Implications. *California Management Review*, *57*(3), 5–12. doi:10.1525/cmr.2015.57.3.5

Hall, B. H. (2004). Innovation and diffusion (No. w10212). National Bureau of Economic Research.

Hall, A. K., Cole-Lewis, H., & Bernhardt, J. M. (2015). Mobile text messaging for health: A systematic review of reviews. *Annual Review of Public Health*, *36*(1), 393–415. doi:10.1146/annurev-publhealth-031914-122855 PMID:25785892

Hall, J. K., Daneke, G. A., & Lenox, M. J. (2010). Sustainable development and entrepreneurship: Past contributions and future directions. *Journal of Business Venturing*, *25*(5), 439–448. doi:10.1016/j.jbusvent.2010.01.002

Hall, J., Matos, S., Sheehan, L., & Silvestre, B. (2012). Entrepreneurship and innovation at the base of the pyramid: A recipe for inclusive growth or social exclusion? *Journal of Management Studies*, *49*(4), 785–812. doi:10.1111/j.1467-6486.2012.01044.x

Hamamura, T., Heine, S. J., & Paulhus, D. L. (2008). Cultural differences in response styles: The role of dialectical thinking. *Personality and Individual Differences*, *44*(4), 932–942. doi:10.1016/j.paid.2007.10.034

Hanninen, M., Smedlund, A., & Mitronen, L. (2018). Digitalization in Retailing: Multi-Sided Platforms as Drivers of Industry Transformation. *Baltic Journal of Management*, *13*(2), 152–168. doi:10.1108/BJM-04-2017-0109

Harding, R. (2006). *Social entrepreneurship monitor*. London Business School.

Harrison, R. (2013). Venture Capital An International Journal of Entrepreneurial Finance Crowdfunding and the revitalisation of the early stage risk capital market: Catalyst or chimera? *Venture Capital*, *15*(4), 283–287. Advance online publication. doi:10.1080/13691066.2013.852331

Hassink, R., & Gong, H. (2019). Six critical questions about Smart Specialization. *European Planning Studies*, *27*(10), 2049–2065. doi:10.1080/09654313.2019.1650898

Haugh, H. M., & Talwar, A. (2016). Linking social entrepreneurship and social change: The mediating role of empowerment. *Journal of Business Ethics*, *133*(4), 643–658. doi:10.100710551-014-2449-4

Hausmann, R., & Rodrik, D. (2003). Economic development as self-discovery. *Journal of Development Economics*, *72*(2), 603–633. doi:10.1016/S0304-3878(03)00124-X

Havrylchyk, O. (2018). Regulatory framework for the loan-based crowdfunding platforms. Organisation for Economic Co-operation and Development Unclassified Document.

Hayton, J. C., George, G., & Zahra, S. A. (2002). National culture and entrepreneurship: A review of behavioral research. *Entrepreneurship Theory and Practice*, *26*(4), 33–52. doi:10.1177/104225870202600403

Helgesson, M., Johansson, B., Nordqvist, T., Lundberg, I., & Vingård, E. (2013). Unemployment at a young age and later sickness absence, disability pension and death in native Swedes and immigrants. *European Journal of Public Health*, *23*(4), 606–610. doi:10.1093/eurpub/cks099 PMID:22930745

Hellström, E., Hämäläinen, T., Lahti, V. M., Cook, J. W., & Jousilahti, J. (2015). *Towards a Sustainable Well-Being Society*. Academic Press.

Helmsing, A. B. (2015). Conditions for social entrepreneurship. *The International Journal of Social Quality*, *5*(1), 51–66. doi:10.3167/IJSQ.2015.050104

Helvacıoğlu, E. (2013). Sosyal Girişimcilik Boyutunda Kütüphaneler. *Bilgi Dünyası*, *14*(1), 199–203.

Hemer, J. (2011). A snapshot on crowdfunding. In *Arbeitspapiere Unternehmen und Region, No. R2/2011*. Fraunhofer ISI. doi:10.1227/01.NEU.0000349921.14519.2A

Hesse, A., Kreutzer, K., & Diehl, M.-R. (2019). Dynamics of Institutional Logics in a Cross-Sector Social Partnership: The Case of Refugee Integration in Germany. *Journal of Business Ethics*, *159*(3), 679–704. doi:10.100710551-017-3775-0

Hickey, A., Urban, A., & Karsten, E. (2020). *Drivers of Quality in Online Learning*. https://about.coursera.org/press/wp-content/uploads/2020/10/Coursera_DriversOfQuality_Book_MCR-1126-V4-lr.pdf

Hille, I. G. A., de Bakker, H. E., Ferguson, J., & Groenewegen, P. (2018). Navigating Tensions in a Cross-Sector Social Partnership: How a Convener Drives Change for Sustainability. *Corporate Social Responsibility and Environmental Management*, *26*(2), 317–329. doi:10.1002/csr.1684

Hille, I. G. A., de Bakker, H. E., Ferguson, J., & Groenewegen, P. (2020). Cross-Sector Partnerships for Sustainability: How Mission-Driven Conveners Drive Change in National Coffee Platforms. *Sustainability*, *2020*(12), 1–23.

Hill, T. L., Kothari, T. H., & Shea, M. (2010). Patterns of meaning in the social entrepreneurship literature: A research platform. *Journal of Social Entrepreneurship*, *1*(1), 5–31. doi:10.1080/19420670903442079

Hitt, M. A., Ireland, R. D., Sirmon, D. G., & Trahms, C. A. (2011). Strategic entrepreneurship: Creating value for individuals, organizations, and society. *The Academy of Management Perspectives*, *25*(2), 57–75.

Hlady-Rispal, M., & Servantie, V. (2018). Deconstructing the way in which value is created in the context of social entrepreneurship. *International Journal of Management Reviews*, *20*(1), 62–80. doi:10.1111/ijmr.12113

Hofstede, G. (1980). *Culture's consequences: International differences in work-related values*. Sage.

Holon, I. Q. (2020). *LATAM EdTech 100*. Available from: https://www.holoniq.com/notes/latam-edtech-100/

Hone, K. S., & El Said, G. R. (2016). Exploring the factors affecting MOOC retention: A survey study. *Computers & Education*, *98*, 157–168.

Hong, Y., Y. H., & Burtch, G. (2015). How does Social Media Affect Contribution to Public versus Private Goods in Crowdfunding Campaigns? *Thirty Sixth International Conference on Information Systems*, 1–15.

Hoogendoorn, B., Pennings, E., & Thurik, A. (2010). What do we know about social entrepreneurship: An analysis of empirical research. *International Review of Entrepreneurship*, *8*(2), 1–42.

Hoque, A. S. M. M., Awang, Z., Muda, H., & Salleh, F. (2018). Ramification of Crowdfunding on Bangladeshi Entrepreneur's Self-efficacy. *Accounting*, *4*(4), 129–138. doi:10.5267/j.ac.2018.4.001

Hoque, A., Shikha, F. A., Hasanat, M. W., Arif, I., & Hamid, A. B. A. (2020). The effect of Coronavirus (COVID-19) in the tourism industry in China. *Asian Journal of Multidisciplinary Studies*, *3*(1), 52–58.

Hoque, N., Hasmat Ali, M., Arefeen, S., Masrurul Mowla, M., & Mamun, A. (2018). Use of Crowdfunding for Developing Social Enterprises: An Islamic Approach. *International Journal of Business and Management*, *13*(6), 156–164. doi:10.5539/ijbm.v13n6p156

Hörisch, J. (2015a). Crowdfunding for environmental ventures: An empirical analysis of the influence of environmental orientation on the success of crowdfunding initiatives. *Journal of Cleaner Production*, *107*, 636–645. doi:10.1016/j.jclepro.2015.05.046

Hornuf, L., & Cumming, D. (2018). *The Economics of Crowdfunding: Startups, Portals and Investor Behavior. Taylor &amp*. Francis Limited.

Horton, P., & Horton, B. P. (2019). Re-defining sustainability: Living in harmony with life on Earth. *One Earth*, *1*(1), 86–94. doi:10.1016/j.oneear.2019.08.019

House, R. J., Hanges, P. J., Javidan, M., Dorfman, P. W., Gupta, V., & Globe Associates. (2004). *Leadership, culture and organizations: The Globe study of 62 societies*. Thousand Oaks, CA: Sage.

Houston, R. (2019). *Social value and its relation to the SDGs*. Retrieved July 26, 2020, from https://www.ice.org.uk/ICEDevelopmentWebPortal/media/Documents/News/Blog/Social-Value-and-its-relation-to-SDGs-Simetrica-April-25-2019.pdf

Hsu, C. (2015). The Informational Role of Volume. University of British Columbia.

https://theskillstoolkit.campaign.gov.uk/

Huang, S., & Cox, J. L. (2014). Establishing a Social Entrepreneurial System to Bridge the Digital Divide for the Poor: A Case Study for Taiwan. *Universal Access in the Information Society*, 219–236.

Hubbard, G. (2009). Measuring organizational performance: Beyond the triple bottom line. *Business Strategy and the Environment*, *18*(3), 177–191. doi:10.1002/bse.564

Hui, J. S., Greenberg, M. D., & Gerber, E. M. (2014). Understanding the role of community in crowdfunding work. *Proceedings of the ACM Conference on Computer Supported Cooperative Work, CSCW*, 62–74. 10.1145/2531602.2531715

Human Development Report. (2015). *Work for Human Development*. New York: United Nations Development Program.

Hure, E., Picot-Koupey, K., & Ackermann, C. (2017). Understanding Omni-Channel Shopping Value: A Mixed Method Study. *Journal of Retailing and Consumer Services*, *39*, 314–330. doi:10.1016/j.jretconser.2017.08.011

İedaNest Blog. (n.d.). *Türkiye'de Kitlesel Fonlamanın Faydaları ve Destekçi Motivasyonu*. https://blog.ideanest.org

ILO | Social Protection Platform |Syria: Social security programmes. (n.d.). Retrieved October 29, 2020, from https://www.social-protection.org/gimi/gess/ShowWiki.action?wiki.wikiId=707

ILO Monitor. (2020). *COVID-19 and the world of work. Fourth edition Updated estimates and analysis*. Available at: https://www.ilo.org/wcmsp5/groups/public/@dgreports/@dcomm/documents/briefingnote/wcms_745963.pdf

ILO. (2020). *Available at: As job losses escalate, nearly half of global workforce at risk of losing livelihoods*. https://www.ilo.org/global/about-the-ilo/newsroom/news/WCMS_743036/lang--en/index.htm

IMF. (2020). *Polıcy Responses To Covıd-19*. Available at: https://www.imf.org/en/Topics/imf-and-covid19/Policy-Responses-to-COVID-19#U

IMHE Syria. (2017, September 19). Retrieved October 29, 2020, from http://www.healthdata.org/syria

Inamdar, N. (2020, May 6). Coronavirus lockdown: India jobless numbers cross 120 million in April. *BBC News*. https://www.bbc.com/news/world-asia-india-52559324

Inglehart, R., & Baker, W. (2000). Modernization, cultural change and the persistence of traditional values. *American Sociological Review*, *65*(1), 19–51. doi:10.2307/2657288

Inkpen, A. C., & Tsang, E. W. (2005). Social capital, networks, and knowledge transfer. *Academy of Management Review*, *30*(1), 146–165. doi:10.5465/amr.2005.15281445

Investment, I. (n.d.). *The Invisible Heart of Markets.* http://gsgii.org/wp-content/uploads/2017/05/Impact-Investment-Report.pdf

Isenberg, D. J. (2011). *The entrepreneurship ecosystem strategy as a new paradigm for economic policy: principles for cultivating entrepreneurship.* Babson Entrepreneurship Ecosystem Project, Babson College. Available at: http://www.innovationamerica.us/images/stories/2011/The-entrepreneurship-ecosystem-strategy-for-economic-growth-policy-20110620183915.pdf

Isenberg, D. J. (2010). How to start an entrepreneurial revolution. *Harvard Business Review, 88*(6), 40–50.

Isenberg, D. J. (2014). What an entrepreneurship ecosystem actually is. *Harvard Business Review, 5*, 1–7.

Işık, C., & Aydın, E. (2017). Kişisel değerlerin sosyal girişimcilik eğilimine etkisi: Turizm öğrencileri üzerine bir araştırma. *Girişimcilik ve İnovasyon Yönetimi Dergisi, 6*(2), 131–154.

İşkur. 2019 Turkish Labour Market Research Report. Retrieved January 13, 2020 from https://media.iskur.gov.tr/34629/turkiye.pdf

Istanbul International Center for Private Sector in Development. (2019). The Impact Investing Ecosystem in Turkey. United Nations Development Programme.

Jackson, T. (2013). Evaluating Social Impact Bonds: Questions, Challenges, Innovations, and Possibilities in Measuring Outcomes in Impact Investing. *Community Development (Columbus, Ohio), 44*(5), 608–616. doi:10.1080/15575330.2013.854258

Jackson, W. T., & Jackson, M. J. (2014). Social Enterprises And Social Entrepreneurs: One Size Does Not Fit All. *Academy of Entrepreneurship Journal, 20*(2), 152–162.

Jamali, D. (2006). Insights into triple bottom line integration from a learning organization perspective. *Business Process Management Journal, 12*(6), 809–821. doi:10.1108/14637150610710945

Jani, B. (2020). *From me to we: COVID-19 heralds a new model of entrepreneurship.* Available at: https://www.weforum.org/agenda/2020/05/covid-19-is-showing-us-a-new-model-of-entrepreneurship/

Jansen, D., & Schuwer, R. (2015). *Institutional MOOC strategies in Europe.* Status Report Based on a Mapping Survey Conducted in October-December 2014.

Jennifer Ho, L. C., & Taylor, M. E. (2007). An empirical analysis of triple bottom-line reporting and its determinants: Evidence from the United States and Japan. *Journal of International Financial Management & Accounting, 18*(2), 123–150. doi:10.1111/j.1467-646X.2007.01010.x

Johnson, K. (2020). Back by Popular Demand! Udacity is Offering 1 Month of Free Access to Nanodegree Programs. *Udacity Blog.* https://blog.udacity.com/2020/04/one-month-free-on-nanodegrees-2.html

Jones, S., & Wright, C. (2018). Fashion or future: Does creating shared value pay? *Accounting and Finance, 58*(4), 1111–1139. doi:10.1111/acfi.12243

Jordan, R. E., Adab, P., & Cheng, K. K. (2020). *Covid-19: risk factors for severe disease and death.* Academic Press.

Jovanovic, M., Okanovic, M., & Dlacic, J. (2018). Digitalization and Society's Sustainable Development – Measures and Implications. *Proceedings of Rijeka School of Economics, 36*(2), 905–928.

Joy, M., & Shields, J. (2013). Social Impact Bonds. *The Next Phase of Third Sector Marketization Canadian Journal of Nonprofit and Social Economy Research, 4*(2), 39–55.

Joy, M., & Shields, J. (2018). Austerity in the Making: Reconfiguring Social Policy through Social Impact Bonds. *Policy and Politics*, *46*(4), 681–695. doi:10.1332/030557318X15200933925397

Kabeer, N. (2011). *Contextualising the Economic Pathways of Women's Empowerment: Findings from a Multi-Country Research Programme*. Pathways Policy Paper, Brighton: Pathways of Women's Empowerment RPC. Retrieved from: http://eprints.lse.ac.uk/89807/1/Kabeer_Contextualising-Economic-Pathways_Published.pdf

Kabeer, N. (1999). Resources, agency, achievements: Reflections on the measurement of women's empowerment. *Development and Change*, *30*(3), 435–464. doi:10.1111/1467-7660.00125

Kabeer, N. (2005). Gender equality and women's empowerment: A critical analysis of the third millennium development goal 1. *Gender and Development*, *13*(1), 13–24. doi:10.1080/13552070512331332273

Kamrowska, D., & Soltys, J. (2016). Process of Emergence of Smart Specialisation in Pomeranian Voivodeship in Poland. *World Multidisciplinary Civil Engineering-Architecture-Urban Planning Symposium 2016, WMCAUS 2016*. 10.1016/j.proeng.2016.08.791

Kangas, R., & Aarrevaara, T. (2020). Higher Education Institutions as Knowledge Brokers in Smart Specialisation. *Sustainability*, *12*(7), 3044. doi:10.3390u12073044

Kantur, D. (2017). Sosyal Girişimcilikte Yerleşiklik: Coğrafi Yayılım ve Kültürel Değerlerin Rolü. *Journal of Entrepreneurship and Innovation Management*, *6*(1), 173–196.

Kapusuz, A. G., Çavuş, M. F., & Pekkan, N. Ü. (2018). Perceived social support and social entrepreneurship: Gender perspective from Turkey. In *Knowledge, Learning and Innovation* (pp. 75–90). Springer. doi:10.1007/978-3-319-59282-4_6

Karaçay, G., & Alpkan, L. (2019). The effects of digital transformation on labor markets: Social policy recommendations for labor market of Turkey [Dijital dönüşümün işgücü piyasalarına etkileri: Türkiye işgücü piyasası için sosyal politika önerileri]. *Türk İdare Dergisi*, *91*(488), 345–373.

Karğin, M., Aktaş, H., & Gökbunar, R. (2018). Üniversitelerde Sosyal Girişimcilik: Fırsatlar ve Öneriler. *Yonetim ve Ekonomi*, *25*(1), 155–170.

Kaushik, A. (2015). Massive Open Online Course (MOOC). *Library Waves-A Biannual Peer Reviewed Journal*, *1*(2), 110–118.

Kedmenec, I., & Strašek, S. (2017). *Are some cultures more favourable for social entrepreneurship than others?* Economic research-. *Ekonomska Istrazivanja*, *30*(1), 1461–1476. doi:10.1080/1331677X.2017.1355251

Keelery, S. (2020). *COVID-19 impact on unemployment rate in India 2020*. https://www.statista.com/statistics/1111487/coronavirus-impact-on-unemployment-rate/

Kibler, E., Salmivaara, V., Stenholm, P., & Terjesen, S. (2018). The evaluative legitimacy of social entrepreneurship in capitalist welfare systems. *Journal of World Business*, *53*(6), 944–957. doi:10.1016/j.jwb.2018.08.002

Kickul, J., Gundry, L., Mitra, P., & Berçot, L. (2018). Designing with purpose: Advocating innovation, impact, sustainability, and scale in social entrepreneurship education. *Entrepreneurship Education and Pedagogy*, *1*(2), 205–221. doi:10.1177/2515127418772177

King, B. (2020, October 13). Unemployment rate: How many people are out of work? *BBC News*. https://www.bbc.com/news/business-52660591

Klasen, S. (2010). Measuring and monitoring inclusive growth: Multiple definitions, open questions, and some constructive proposals. *ADB Sustainable Development Working Paper Series*, No.12.

Klymenko, O., Halse, L., Jeger, B., Nerger, A.J., (2019). Digitalization and Environmental Sustainability: Where are the Opportunities? *7th EurOMA Book of Proceedings,* 3880-3889.

Koçak, S., & Özdemir, M. (2015). Öğretmen Adaylarının Okul Yöneticiliğine Yönelik Tutumları Üzerinde Sosyal Girişimciliğin Rolü. *Mersin University Journal of the Faculty of Education, 11*(3).

Konaklı, T., & Göğüş, N. (2013). Aday Öğretmenlerin Sosyal Girişimcilik Özellikleri Ölçeği: Geçerlik ve Güvenirlik Çalışması. *Gazi University Journal of Gazi Educational Faculty (GUJGEF), 33*(2).

Koplan, J. P., Bond, T. C., Merson, M. H., Reddy, K. S., Rodriguez, M. H., Sewankambo, N. K., & Wasserheit, J. N. (2009). Towards a common definition of global health. *Lancet, 373*(9679), 1993–1995. doi:10.1016/S0140-6736(09)60332-9 PMID:19493564

Korosec, R. L., & Berman, E. M. (2006). Municipal support for social entrepreneurship. *Public Administration Review, 66*(3), 448–462. doi:10.1111/j.1540-6210.2006.00601.x

Korsgaard, S. (2011). Opportunity formation in social entrepreneurship. *Journal of Enterprising Communities: People and Places in the Global Economy, 5*(4), 265–285. doi:10.1108/17506201111177316

Koseoglu, M. A., Rahimi, R., Okumus, F., & Liu, J. (2016). Bibliometric studies in tourism. *Annals of Tourism Research, 61*, 180–198. doi:10.1016/j.annals.2016.10.006

Kozinets, R. V. (2018). Netnography for Management and Business Research. In C. Cassell, A. L. Cunliffe, & G. Grandy (Eds.), *The SAGE Handbook of Qualitative Business and Management Research Methods* (pp. 384–397). Sage.

Kozinets, R. V. (2019). *Netnography: The essential guide to qualitative social media research* (3rd ed.). Sage.

Kramer, M. R., & Pfitzer, M. W. (2016). The ecosystem of shared value. *Harvard Business Review, 94*(10), 80–89.

Kramer, M. R., & Porter, M. (2011). *Creating shared value.* FSG.

Kraus, S., Filser, M., O'Dwyer, M., & Shaw, E. (2014). Social entrepreneurship: An exploratory citation analysis. *Review of Managerial Science, 8*(2), 275–292. doi:10.100711846-013-0104-6

Kraus, S., Palmer, C., Kailer, N., Kallinger, F. L., & Spitzer, J. (2018). Digital Entrepreneurship: A Research Agenda on New Business Models for the Twenty-First Century. *International Journal of Entrepreneurial Behaviour & Research, 25*(2), 353–375. doi:10.1108/IJEBR-06-2018-0425

Krlev, G., Bund, E., & Mildenberger, G. (2014). Measuring what matters? Indicators of social innovativeness on the national level. *Information Systems Management, 31*(3), 200–224. doi:10.1080/10580530.2014.923265

Kromidha, E., & Robson, P. (2016). Social identity and signalling success factors in online crowdfunding. *Entrepreneurship and Regional Development, 28*(9–10), 605–629. doi:10.1080/08985626.2016.1198425

Kümbül Güler, B. (2011). Yoksullukla mücadelede sosyal girişimcilik: Ashoka üyelerinden sosyal yenilikçi örnek uygulamalar. *Dokuz Eylül Üniversitesi Sosyal Bilimler Enstitüsü Dergisi, 13*(3), 79–111.

Kummitha, R. K. R. (2016). Socıal Entrepreneurshıp As A Tool To Remedy Socıal Exclusıon: A Wın–Wın Scenarıo? *South Asia Research, 36*(1), 1–19. doi:10.1177/0262728015615485

Kummitha, R. K. R. (2017). *Social Entrepreneurship and Social Inclusion.* Palgrave., doi:10.1007/978-981-10-1615-8

Kurnaz Baltaci, I. (2020). Genç İşsizliği ve Geleceğe Uzanan Zorlu İşgücü Piyasası Koşulları: Diyarbakır, Suriçi Bölgesi Örneği. *Amme Idaresi Dergisi, 53*(1).

Kuti, M., Bedő, Z., & Geiszl, D. (2017). Equity-based Crowdfunding. *Financial and Economic Review, 16*(4), 187–200.

La Torre, M., Trotta, A., Chiappini, H. & Rizzello, A. (2019). Business Models for Sustainable Finance: The Case Study of Social Impact Bonds. *Sustainability, 11*(1887), 2-23.

Lagazio, C., & Querci, F. (2018). Exploring the multi-sided nature of crowdfunding campaign success. *Journal of Business Research, 90*(May), 318–324. doi:10.1016/j.jbusres.2018.05.031

Lager, S. (2020). Udacity's Contribution to the COVID-19 Crisis: One Free Month Access to Nanodegree Programs. *Udacity Blog*. https://blog.udacity.com/2020/03/one-month-free-on-nanodegrees.html

Lall, S. A. (2019). From Legitimacy to learning: How impact measurement perceptions and practices evolve in social enterprise–social finance organization relationships. *Voluntas, 30*(3), 562–577. doi:10.100711266-018-00081-5

Lam, P. T. I., & Law, A. O. K. (2016). Crowdfunding for renewable and sustainable energy projects: An exploratory case study approach. *Renewable & Sustainable Energy Reviews, 60*, 1–18. doi:10.1016/j.rser.2016.01.046

Landström, H., Parhankangas, A., & Mason, C. (Eds.). (2019). *Handbook of Research on Crowdfunding*. Edward Elgar Publishing. doi:10.4337/9781788117210

Lane, A. (2012). A review of the role of national policy and institutional mission in European distance teaching universities with respect to widening participation in higher education study through open educational resources. *Distance Education, 33*(2), 135–150.

Lane, A., Caird, S., & Weller, M. (2014). The potential social, economic and environmental benefits of MOOCs: Operational and historical comparisons with a massive 'closed online'course. *Open Praxis, 6*(2), 115–123.

Lan, H., Zhu, Y., Ness, D., Xing, K., & Schneider, K. (2014). The role and characteristics of social entrepreneurs in contemporary rural cooperative development in China: Case studies of rural social entrepreneurship. *Asia Pacific Business Review, 20*(3), 379–400. doi:10.1080/13602381.2014.929300

Latane´, B. (1981). The Psychology of Social İmpact. *The American Psychologist, 36*(4), 343–356. doi:10.1037/0003-066X.36.4.343

Latane´, B., & Wolf, S. (1981). The Social İmpact of Majorities and Minorities. *Psychological Review, 88*(5), 438–453. doi:10.1037/0033-295X.88.5.438

Laville, J.-L., & Nyssens, M. (2001). The social enterprise: towards a theoretical socio-economic approach. In C. Borzaga & J. Defourny (Eds.), *The Emergence of Social Enterprise* (pp. 312–332). Routledge.

Le Blanc, D. (2015). Towards integration at last? The sustainable development goals as a network of targets. *Sustainable Development, 23*(3), 176–187. doi:10.1002d.1582

Leadbetter, C. (1997). *The rise of social entrepreneurship*. Demos.

Leadbetter, C. (1997). *The Rise of the Social Entrepreneur*. Demos.

Lee, R., & Shaw, E. (2016). Bourdieu's non-material forms of capital: Implications for startup policy. *Environment and Planning C. Politics and Space, 34*(8), 1734–1758.

Legner, C. (2017). Digitalization: Opportunity and Challenge for the Business and Information Systems Engineering Community, *Business. Information Systems, 59*(4), 301–308.

Lehner, O. M., & Nicholls, A. (2014). Social finance and crowdfunding for social enterprises: a public-private case study providing legitimacy and leverage. In Venture Capital (Vol. 16, Issue 3, pp. 271–286). Taylor & Francis. doi:10.1080/13691066.2014.925305

Lehner, O. M. (2013). Crowdfunding social ventures: A model and research agenda. *Venture Capital, 15*(4), 289–311. doi:10.1080/13691066.2013.782624

Lehner, O. M. (2014). The formation and interplay of social capital in crowdfunded social ventures. *Entrepreneurship and Regional Development, 26*(5–6), 478–499. doi:10.1080/08985626.2014.922623

Leighton, M. (2020a). Coursera is offering 90% of its online classes to college students for free until September 30, 2020 — here's how to enroll. *Business Insider*. https://www.businessinsider.com/coursera-free-classes-college-students

Leighton, M. (2020b). Coursera's Workforce Recovery Initiative gives unemployed workers free access to 90% of its online course catalog — here's how it works. *Business Insider*. https://www.businessinsider.com/coursera-workforce-recovery-initiative

Lepak, D. P., Smith, K. G., & Taylor, M. S. (2007). Value creation and value capture: A multilevel perspective. *Academy of Management Review, 32*(1), 180–194. doi:10.5465/amr.2007.23464011

Lepeley, M. T. (forthcoming). Soft Skills: The lingua franca of Human Centered Management. In *Soft Skills in Human Centered Management. Global Dimensions*. Routledge.

Levitas, R. (2005). *The inclusive society? Social exclusion and new labour*. Palgrave Macmillan.

Light, P. C. (2006). Reshaping social entrepreneurship. *Stanford Social Innovation Review, 4*(3), 47–51.

Lindenberg, S., & Steg, L. (2007). Normative, gain and hedonic goal frames guiding environmental behavior. *The Journal of Social Issues, 63*(1), 117–137. doi:10.1111/j.1540-4560.2007.00499.x

Linkedininterwiev. (2020). *Interview | During COVID-19, this social enterprise reached out to 17 million people*. Available at: https://www.linkedin.com/pulse/interview-during-covid-19-social-enterprise-reached-out-shenzhen/

Lin, Y., Yin, P., & Lee, W. C. (2018). Modeling Dynamic Competition on Crowdfunding Markets. *World Wide Web Conference*, 1815–1824.

Lipusch, N., Dellermann, D., Oeste-Reiß, S., & Ebel, P. (2018). Innovating Beyond the Fuzzy Front End: How to Use Reward-Based Crowdfunding to Co-create with Customers. *Proceedings of the 51st Hawaii International Conference on System Sciences*, 4202–4211. 10.24251/HICSS.2018.528

Littlejohn, A., Hood, N., Milligan, C., & Mustain, P. (2016). Learning in MOOCs: Motivations and self-regulated learning in MOOCs. *Internet and Higher Education, 29*, 40–48.

Littlewood, D., & Holt, D. (2018). Social entrepreneurship in South Africa: Exploring the influence of environment. *Business & Society, 57*(3), 525–561. doi:10.1177/0007650315613293

Littlewood, D., & Kahn, Z. (2018). Insights from a systematic review of literature on social enterprise and networks Where, how and what next? *Social Enterprise Journal, 14*(4), 390–409. doi:10.1108/SEJ-11-2018-068

Lloyd-Sherlock, P., Ebrahim, S., Geffen, L., & McKee, M. (2020). *Bearing the brunt of covid-19: older people in low and middle income countries*. Academic Press.

Lobe, B., Morgan, D., & Hoffman, K. A. (2020). Qualitative Data Collection in an Era of Social Distancing. *International Journal of Qualitative Methods, 19*, 1–8. doi:10.1177/1609406920937875

Lounsbury, M., & Glynn, M. A. (2001). Cultural Entrepreneurship: Stories, Legitimacy and the Acquisition of Resources. *Strategic Management Journal, 22*(6-7), 545–564. doi:10.1002mj.188

Lubis, A. H., Idrus, S. Z. S., & Abd Rashid, S. (2020). The exposure of MOOC usage In Indonesia. *International Journal of Scientific & Technology Research, 9*(2).

Lu, H. P., & Dzikria, I. (2020). The role of intellectual capital and social capital on the intention to use MOOC. *Knowledge Management Research and Practice*, 1–12.

Lumpkin, G. T., Moss, T. W., Gras, D. M., Kato, S., & Amezcua, A. S. (2013). Entrepreneurial processes in social contexts: How are they different, if at all? *Small Business Economics, 40*(3), 761–783. doi:10.100711187-011-9399-3

Lundvall, B. (1988). Innovation as an Interactive: From User-Producer Interaction to the National System of Innovation. In *Technical Change and Economic Theory* (pp. 349–369). Pinter.

Lundvall, B. (2007). National Innovation Systems-Analytical Concept and Development Tool. *Industry and Innovation, 14*(1), 95–119. doi:10.1080/13662710601130863

Lustig, N. (2019). *An Overview of Edtech in Latin America*. Available from: https://www.nathanlustig.com/an-overview-of-edtech-in-latin-america/

Lüth, A., & Stierl, M. (2015). Creating Shared Value by Fostering Regional Development: The 'Partners in Responsibility 'Method for SME. *Global Policy, 6*(4), 507–509. doi:10.1111/1758-5899.12238

Macht, S., & Chapman, G. (2019). Getting more than money through online crowdfunding. *Asia-Pacific Journal of Business Administration, 11*(2), 171–186. doi:10.1108/APJBA-05-2019-0101

Macke, J., Sarate, J. A. R., Domeneghini, J., & da Silva, K. A. (2018). Where do we go from now? Research framework for social entrepreneurship. *Journal of Cleaner Production, 183*, 677–685. doi:10.1016/j.jclepro.2018.02.017

Macke, J., Vallejos, R. V., Faccin, K., & Genari, D. (2012). Social Capital in Collaborative Networks Competitiveness: The case of the Brazilian Wine İndustry Cluster. *İnt. J. Comput. İntegr. Manuf., 25*, 1–8.

Maclean, M., Harvey, C., & Gordon, J. (2013). Social innovation, social entrepreneurship and the practice of contemporary entrepreneurial philanthropy. *International Small Business Journal, 31*(7), 747–763. doi:10.1177/0266242612443376

Maiolini, Marra, A., Baldassarri, C., & Carlei, V. (2016). Digital Technologies for Social Innovation: An Empirical Recognition on the New Enablers. *Journal of Technology Management & Innovation, 11*(4), 22–28. doi:10.4067/S0718-27242016000400004

Mair, J., & Marti, I. (2004). Social entrepreneurship: What are we talking about? A framework for future research (No. D/546). IESE Business School.

Mair, J., & Marti, I. (2004). *Social entrepreneurship: what are we talking about? A framework for future research.* Barcelona: IESE Business School Working Paper No.546.

Mair, J., & Martı´, I. (2006). Social entrepreneurship research: A source of explanation, prediction, and delight. *Journal of World Business, 41*(1), 36–44. doi:10.1016/j.jwb.2005.09.002

Mair, J., & Martí, İ. (2009). Entrepreneurship in and around İnstitutional voids: A case study from Bangladesh. *Journal of Business Venturing, 24*(5), 419–435. doi:10.1016/j.jbusvent.2008.04.006

Malhotra, A., Schuler, S. R., & Boender, C. (2002, June). Measuring women's empowerment as a variable in international development. In *Background paper prepared for the World Bank Workshop on Poverty and Gender: New Perspectives* (Vol. 28). Academic Press.

Malita, L., Tiru, L. G., & Grosseck, G. (2018). MOOCs for teachers professional development—A university challenge. *International Journal of Information and Education Technology (IJIET), 8*(3), 235–239.

Mamabolo, A., & Myres, K. (2020). Performance Measurement in Emerging Market Social Enterprises using a Balanced Scorecard. *Journal of Social Entrepreneurship, 11*(1), 65–87. doi:10.1080/19420676.2018.1561499

Manet, L. (2014). Modelos de desarrollo regional: teorías y factores determinantes. Nóesis. *Revista de Ciencias Sociales y Humanidades*, 18-56.

Manning, P., & Trimmer, T. (2020). *Migration in world history*. Routledge. doi:10.4324/9781351256681

Manning, S., & Bejarano, T. A. (2017). Convincing the crowd: Entrepreneurial storytelling in crowdfunding campaigns. *Strategic Organization, 15*(2), 194–219. doi:10.1177/1476127016648500

Marchegiani, L. (2017). From Mecenatism to Crowdfunding: Engagement and Identification in Cultural-Creative Projects. *Journal of Heritage Tourism, 13*(2), 1–9.

Marin, A. (2017). Value creation through sense making: Social entrepreneurship for local sustainable development. *Projectics, 18*(3), 89–106. doi:10.3917/proj.018.0089

Marinelli, E., & Perianez Forte, I. (2017). *Smart specialisation at work: The entrepreneurial Discovery as a continuous process*. S3 Working paper Series NO. 12/2017, Sevilla: European Commission Joint Research Centre.

Marques, P., Morgan, K., & Richardson, R. (2018). Social innovation in question: The theoretical and practical implications of a contested concept. *Environment and Planning C. Politics and Space, 36*(3), 496–512.

Martez, N., & Dieste, E. (2019). Measurement system for the analysis of social innovation in projects. *Proceedings - 2019 7th International Engineering, Sciences and Technology Conference, IESTEC 2019*, 311-316. 10.1109/IESTEC46403.2019.00064

Martin, R. L., & Osberg, S. (2007). *Social entrepreneurship: The case for definition*. Academic Press.

Martin-Pena, M.L. (2018). *The Digitalization and Servitization of Manufacturing: A Review on Digital Business Models*. Wiley.

Martin, R. L., & Osberg, S. (2007). Social Entrepreneurship: The Case for Definition. *Stanford Social Innovation Review*.

Martin, R. L., & Osberg, S. (2007, Spring). Social entrepreneurship: The case for definition. *Stanford Social Innovation Review*, 29–39.

Masaviru, M. (2020). From physical classrooms to e-learning and online teaching: A case study of Light International School, Mombasa. *Journal of Education and Practice, 11*(13), 2020.

Mathes, J. (2019). *Global quality in online, open, flexible and technology enhanced education: An analysis of strengths, weaknesses, opportunities and threats*. International Council for Open and Distance Education.

Matinheikki, J., Rajala, R., & Peltokorpi, A. (2017). From the profit of one toward benefitting many–Crafting a vision of shared value creation. *Journal of Cleaner Production, 162*, S83–S93. doi:10.1016/j.jclepro.2016.09.081

Matten, D., & Moon, J. (2008). Implicit and explicit CSR: A conceptual framework for a comparative understanding of corporate social responsibility. *Academy of Management Review, 33*(2), 404–424. doi:10.5465/amr.2008.31193458

McAuley, A., Stewart, B., Siemens, G., & Cormier, D. (2010). *The MOOC model for digital practice*. Academic Press.

McCann, P., & Ortega-Argilés, R. (2011). *Smart Specialisation, regional growth and applications to EU Cohesion Policy*. Economic Geography Working Paper. University of Groningen. http://i3s.ec.europa.eu/commitment/30/download/5250.html;i3sid=Q116Tz8hQ

McEachrane, M. (2020). *COVID-19: Disproportionally Hits Segregated Communities*. Available at: https://rwi.lu.se/2020/05/covid-19-disproportionally-hits-segregated-communities/

McHugh, N., Sinclair, S., Roy, M., Huckfield, L., & Donaldson, C. (2013). Social Impact Bonds: A Wolf in Sheep's Clothing? *The Journal of Poverty and Social Justice: Research, Policy, Practice*, *21*(3), 247–257. doi:10.1332/204674313X13812372137921

McKenzie, S. (2004). *Social sustainability: towards some definitions*. Hawke Research Institute Working Paper Series, 27. Hawke Research Institute, University of South Australia.

Mcneil, D., & Jacobs, A. (2020, May 29). *Blaming China for Pandemic, Trump Says U.S. Will Leave the W.H.O.* Retrieved from https://www.nytimes.com/2020/05/29/health/virus-who.html

Mebratu, D. (1998). Sustainability and sustainable development: Historical and conceptual review. *Environmental Impact Assessment Review*, *18*(6), 493–520. doi:10.1016/S0195-9255(98)00019-5

Méndez, M., Henao, A., & Vélez, A. (2017). Factores críticos de éxito para el desarrollo de una empresa en sus primeras fases de desarrollo. Espacios, 38(18).

Méndez, M., & Gómez, M. (2017). Factores incidentes para crear valor compartido en las mipymes de Bogotá. *Suma de Negocios*, *8*(18), 96–105. doi:10.1016/j.sumneg.2017.10.003

Merton, R. (1988). The Matthew Effect in science, II: Cumulative advantage and the symbolism of intellectual property. *Isis*, *79*(4), 606–623. doi:10.1086/354848

Methodology for Change the World. (n.d.). https://fortune.com/franchise-list-page/methodology-change-the-world-2020

Michelini, L., & Fiorentino, D. (2012). *Nuevos modelos de negocio para crear valor compartido*. Revista de Responsabilidad Social.

MicroBachelors Programs for Undergraduate Education. (2020). https://www.edx.org/microbachelors

MicroMasters Programs. (2020). https://www.edx.org/micromasters#program-list

Miglo, A. (2020). Crowdfunding in a Competitive Environment. *Journal of Risk and Financial Management*, *13*(3), 1–38. doi:10.3390/jrfm13030039

Milakovich, M. E., & Wise, J. M. (2019). *Copyright, legal issues, and intellectual property in Digital Learning*. Edward Elgar Publishing.

Mitchell, R. K., Smith, J. B., Morse, E. A., Seawright, K. W., Peredo, A. M., & McKenzie, B. (2002). Are entrepreneurial cognitions universal? Assessing entrepreneurial cognitions across cultures. *Entrepreneurship Theory and Practice*, *27*(2), 9–29. doi:10.1177/104225870202600402

Mitra, P., Kickul, J., Gundry, L., & Orr, J. (2019). The Rise of Hybrids: A Note for Social Entrepreneurship Educators. *International Review of Entrepreneurship*, *17*(2).

Moed, H. F. (2005). *Citation analysis in research evaluation* (Vol. 9). Springer Science & Business Media.

Molecke, G., & Pinkse, J. (2020). justifying social impact as a form of impression management: Legitimacy judgements of social enterprises' impact accounts. *British Journal of Management*, *31*(2), 387–402. doi:10.1111/1467-8551.12397

Mollick, E. (2014). The dynamics of crowdfunding: An exploratory study. *Journal of Business Venturing*, *29*(1), 1–16. doi:10.1016/j.jbusvent.2013.06.005

Moncayo, É. (2003). Nuevas teorías y enfoques conceptuales sobre el desarrollo regional: ¿hacia un nuevo paradigma? *Revista de Economía Institucional*, 32-65.

Monck, A. (2020). *If a vaccine doesn't work, social entrepreneurs fight COVID and top stories of the week.* Available at https://www.weforum.org/agenda/2020/05/if-a-vaccine-doesnt-work-social-entrepreneurs-fight-covid-and-top-stories-of-the-week/

Monteiro, P., & Nicolini, D. (2015). Recovering Materiality in Institutional Work: Prizes as an Assemblage of Human and Material Entities. *Journal of Management Inquiry*, *24*(1), 61–81. doi:10.1177/1056492614546221

MorsyH. (2012). Scarred generation. Available at SSRN 3093019

Mort, G. S., Weerawardena, J., & Carnegie, K. (2002). Social entrepreneurship: Towards conceptualization and measurement. In *American Marketing Association. Conference Proceedings* (Vol. 13, p. 5). American Marketing Association.

Mosedale, S. (2005). Assessing women's empowerment: Towards a conceptual framework. *Journal of International Development*, *17*(2), 243–257. doi:10.1002/jid.1212

Moss, T. W., Neubaum, D. O., & Meyskens, M. (2015). The Effect of Virtuous and Entrepreneurial Orientations on Microfinance Lending and Repayment: A Signaling Theory Perspective. *Entrepreneurship Theory and Practice*, *39*(1), 27–52. doi:10.1111/etap.12110

Moss, T. W., Short, J. C., Payne, G. T., & Lumpkin, G. T. (2011). Dual identities in social ventures: An exploratory study. *Entrepreneurship Theory and Practice*, *35*(4), 805–830. doi:10.1111/j.1540-6520.2010.00372.x

Moulaert, F., Martinelli, F., Swyngedouw, E., & Gonzalez, S. (2005). Towards alternative model(s) of local innovation. *Urban Studies (Edinburgh, Scotland)*, *42*(11), 1969–1990. doi:10.1080/00420980500279893

Moysidou, K., & Hausberg, J. P. (2020). In crowdfunding we trust: A trust-building model in lending crowdfunding. *Journal of Small Business Management*, *58*(3), 511–543. doi:10.1080/00472778.2019.1661682

Mukkamala, Vatrapu, R., Ray, P. K., Sengupta, G., & Halder, S. (2018). Blockchain for Social Business: Principles and Applications. *IEEE Engineering Management Review*, *46*(4), 94–99. doi:10.1109/EMR.2018.2881149

Mulgan, G., Tucker, S., Ali, R., & Sanders, B. (2007). Social innovation: what it is, why it matters and how it can be accelerated. The Young Foundation. London: The Hasingstoke Press.

Mulgan, G., Tucker, S., Ali, R., & Sanders, B. (2007). *Social innovation: what it is, why it matters and how it can be accelerated.* Working Paper, Skoll Centre for Social Innovation.

Mulgan, G. (2006). The process of social innovation. *Innovations: Technology, Governance, Globalization*, *1*(2), 145–162. doi:10.1162/itgg.2006.1.2.145

Mulgan, G. (2019). *Social Innovation: How societies find the power to change*. Bristol University Press. doi:10.2307/j.ctvs89dd3

Mulgan, G., Reeder, N., Aylott, M., & Bo'sher, L. (2011). *Social Impact Investment: The Challenge and Opportunity of Social Impact Bonds*. The Young Foundation.

Mumford, M. D. (2002). Social innovation: Ten cases from Benjamin Franklin. *Creativity Research Journal*, *14*(2), 253–266. doi:10.1207/S15326934CRJ1402_11

Municipality of Beylikdüzü. (2020). https://www.courserabeylikduzu.org/

Muñoz, P., & Kibler, E. (2016). Institutional complexity and social entrepreneurship: A fuzzy-set approach. *Journal of Business Research, 69*(4), 1314–1318. doi:10.1016/j.jbusres.2015.10.098

Munoz, P., & Kimmitt, J. (2019). A Diagnostic Framework for Social Impact Bonds in Emerging Economies. *Journal of Business Venturing Insights, 12*, 1–9. doi:10.1016/j.jbvi.2019.e00141

Muñoz, P., & Kimmitt, J. (2019). Social mission as competitive advantage: A configurational analysis of the strategic conditions of social entrepreneurship. *Journal of Business Research, 101*, 854–861. doi:10.1016/j.jbusres.2018.11.044

Muro, M. (2017). *Digitalization and the American Workforce*. Metropolitan Policy Program.

Murray, R., Caulier-Grice, J., & Mulgan, G. (2010). *The open book of social innovation*. NESTA.

Murschetz, P. (2019). Editorial to Special Issue on "Digital Entrepreneurship". In P. Faustino & T. Flew (Eds.), *Journal of Creative Industries and Cultural Studies* (pp. 9–13). Routledge.

Myers, N. (2005). *Environmental refugees: an emergent security issue*. Academic Press.

Naipinit, T., Kojchavivong, S., Kowittayakorn, V., & Sakolnakorn, T. P. N. (2014). McKinsey 7S model for supply chain management of local SMEs construction business in the upper northeast region of Thailand. *Asian Social Science, 10*(8), 35. doi:10.5539/ass.v10n8p35

Nandan, M., London, M., & Bent-Goodley, T. (2015). Social workers as social change agents: Social innovation, social intrapreneurship, and social entrepreneurship. *Human Service Organizations, Management, Leadership & Governance, 39*(1), 38–56. doi:10.1080/23303131.2014.955236

Nelson, R. R. (1993). *National innovation systems: A comparative analysis*. Oxford University Press.

Neumeier, S. (2012). Why do social innovations in rural development matter and should they be considered more seriously in rural development research? Proposal for a stronger focus on social innovations in rural development research. *Sociologia Ruralis, 52*(1), 48–69. doi:10.1111/j.1467-9523.2011.00553.x

Nevin, S., Gleasure, R., O'Reilly, P., Feller, J., Li, S., & Cristoforo, J. (2017). Social identity and social media activities in equity crowdfunding. *Proceedings of the 13th International Symposium on Open Collaboration*, 1–8. 10.1145/3125433.3125461

New free online learning platform to boost workplace skills. (2020). https://www.gov.uk/government/news/new-free-online-learning-platform-to-boost-workplace-skills

New York Amsterdam News. (2020, October 17). *Udacity to provide 1,000 scholarships to African Americans*. http://amsterdamnews.com/news/2020/aug/25/udacity-provide-1000-scholarships-african-american/

Next Generation Abu Dhabi Partners. (n.d.). https://www.udacity.com/l/Next-Gen-AbuDhabi

Ng, A., & Widom, J. (2014). Origins of the modern MOOC (xMOOC). MOOCs: Expectations and Reality: Full Report, 34-47.

Nicholls, A. (2009). 'We do good things, don't we?':'Blended Value Accounting'in social entrepreneurship. *Accounting, Organizations and Society, 34*(6-7), 755–769. doi:10.1016/j.aos.2009.04.008

Nicholls, A. (2010). The institutionalization of social investment: The interplay of investment logics and investor rationalities. *Journal of Social Entrepreneurship, 1*(1), 70–100. doi:10.1080/19420671003701257

Nicholls, A. (2010). The legitimacy of social entrepreneurship: Reflexive isomorphism in a pre-paradigmatic field. *Entrepreneurship Theory and Practice, 34*(4), 611–633. doi:10.1111/j.1540-6520.2010.00397.x

Nicholls, A. (Ed.). (2008). *Social entrepreneurship: New models of sustainable social change.* OUP Oxford.

Nicola, M., Alsafi, Z., Sohrabi, C., Kerwan, A., Al-Jabir, A., Iosifidis, C., Agha, M., & Agha, R. (2020). The socio-economic implications of the coronavirus and COVID-19 pandemic: A review. *International Journal of Surgery, 78*, 185–193. doi:10.1016/j.ijsu.2020.04.018 PMID:32305533

Nielsen, C., & Samia, P. M. (2008). Understanding key factors in social enterprise development of the BOP: A systems approach applied to case studies in the Philippines. *Journal of Consumer Marketing, 25*(7), 446–454. doi:10.1108/07363760810915662

Nielsen, K. R. (2018). Crowdfunding through a partial organization lens – The co-dependent organization. *European Management Journal, 36*(6), 695–707. doi:10.1016/j.emj.2018.01.006

Nikolaou, I. E., Tasopoulou, K., & Tsagarakis, K. (2018). A typology of green entrepreneurs based on institutional and resource-based views. *The Journal of Entrepreneurship, 27*(1), 111–132. doi:10.1177/0971355717738601

Nogueira, A. (2018). *Digital Entrepreneurship: What is it and How to Get Started.* Retrieved October, 7, 2020 from https://blog.hotmart.com/en/digital-entrepreneurship/

Nominet Trust Reveals 100 Leading Ventures Using Tech to Solve World's Biggest Social Problems. (n.d.). Retrieved September 27, 2020 from http://www.nominettrust. org.uk/news-events/news/nominet-trust-reveals-100-leading-ventures-using-tech-to-solve-world%E2%80%99s-biggest-soci

Norman, W., & MacDonald, C. (2004). Getting to the bottom of the "triple bottom line". *Business Ethics Quarterly, 14*(2), 243–262. doi:10.5840/beq200414211

North, D., Baldock, R., & Ullah, F. (2013). Funding the growth of UK technology-based small firms since the financial crash : Are there breakages in the finance escalator? *Venture Capital, 15*(3), 237–260. doi:10.1080/13691066.2013.804755

Northern Council for Further Education. (2020). *PM announces new Lifetime Skills Guarantee.* https://www.ncfe.org.uk/blog/pm-announces-new-lifetime-skills-guarantee#:~:text=Prime%20Minister%2C%20Boris%20Johnson%2C%20has,%2C%20fully%2Dfunded%20FE%20course

O'Connor, A., Stam, E., Sussan, F., & Audretsch, D. B. (Eds.). (2018). *Entrepreneurial Ecosystems. Place-Based Transformations and Transitions.* Springer.

OECD (1999). Social Enterprises, OECD Publishing:Paris. Retrieved January 08, 2020 from http://dx.doi.org/doi:10.1787/9789264182332-en

OECD. (2008). *Growing unequal? Income distribution and poverty in OECD countries.* Paris, France: Organisation for Economic Co-operation and Development. Available at: https://www.oecd.org/els/soc/growingunequalincomedistributionandpovertyinoecdcountries.htm

OECD. (2014). *Cultivating successful entrepreneurs.* Available at: http://www.oecd.org/cfe/leed/entrepreneurship.htm

OECD. (2015). *Policy brief on social ımpact measurement for social enterprises.* Retrieved August 08, 2020, from https://www.oecd.org/social/PB-SIM-Web_FINAL.pdf

OECD. (2016). *Understanding Social Impact Bonds.* http://www.oecd.org/cfe/leed/UnderstandingSIBsLux-WorkingPaper.pdf

OECD. (2020). *The OECD Employment Outlook 2020.* OECD. https://www.oecd-ilibrary.org/sites/1686c758-en/index.html?itemId=/content/publication/1686c758-en

OECD. (2020). *The potential of online learning for adults: early lessons from the COVID-19 crisis.* OECD.

Oeij, P. R., van der Torre, W., Vaas, F., & Dhondt, S. (2019). Understanding social innovation as an innovation process: Applying the innovation journey model. *Journal of Business Research*, *101*, 243–254. doi:10.1016/j.jbusres.2019.04.028

Office for National Statistic. (2020). *Deaths involving COVID-19 by local area and socioeconomic deprivation: deaths occurring between 1 March and 17 April 2020*. Available at: https://www.ons.gov.uk/peoplepopulationandcommunity/birthsdeathsandmarriages/deaths/bulletins/deathsinvolvingcovid19bylocalareasanddeprivation/deathsoccurringbetween-1marchand17april

Okolie, U. C., Igwe, P. A., Nwosu, H. E., Eneje, B. C., & Mlanga, S. (2020). Enhancing graduate employability: Why do higher education institutions have problems with teaching generic skills? *Policy Futures in Education*, *18*(2), 294–313. doi:10.1177/1478210319864824

Oladipo, S. E. (2009). Psychological empowerment and development. *Edo Journal of Counselling*, *2*(1), 118–126.

Ontario Newsroom. (2020, April 17). *Ontario Establishes Key Partnerships to Make Home Learning More Accessible*. https://news.ontario.ca/en/release/56697/ontario-establishes-key-partnerships-to-make-home-learning-more-accessible

Ordanini, A., Miceli, L., Pizzetti, M., & Parasuraman, A. (2011). Crowd-funding: Transforming customers into investors through innovative service platforms. *Journal of Service Management*, *22*(4), 443–470. doi:10.1108/09564231111155079

Osterwalder, A. (2004). *The business model ontology a proposition in a design science approach* (Unpublished doctoral dissertation). Université de Lausanne, Faculté des hautes études commerciales.

Osterwalder, A. (2004). *The Business Model Ontology: A Proposition In A Design Science Approach* (Ph.D. thesis). Lausanne: University of Lausanne.

Oxfam. (2020). *World's billionaires have more wealth than 4.6 billion people*. Retrieved July 22, 2020, from https://www.oxfam.org/en/press-releases/worlds-billionaires-have-more-wealth-46-billion-people

Özdemir, F., & Ar, İ. M. (2015). Sosyal yenilik üzerine bir alan araştırması. *Girişimcilik ve İnovasyon Yönetimi Dergisi*, *4*(1), 17–43.

Özdevecioğlu, M., & Cingöz, A. (2009). Sosyal girişimcilik ve sosyal girişimciler: Teorik çerçeve. *Erciyes Üniversitesi İktisadi ve İdari Bilimler Fakültesi Dergisi*, (32), 81–95.

Pache, A. C., & Santos, F. (2013). Inside the Hybrid Organization: Selective Coupling as a Response to Competing Institutional Logics. *Academy of Management Journal*, *56*(4), 972–1001. doi:10.5465/amj.2011.0405

Page, N., & Czuba, C. E. (1999). Empowerment: What is it. *Journal of Extension*, *37*(5), 1–5.

Paliokaitė, A., Martinaitis, Z., & Reimeris, R. (2015). Foresight methods for smart specialisation strategy development in Lithuania. Disponible en. *Technological Forecasting and Social Change*, *101*, 185–199. doi:10.1016/j.techfore.2015.04.008

Paredo, A. M., & McLean, M. (2006). Social Entrepreneurship: A Critical Review of the Concept. *Journal of World Business*, *41*(1), 56–65. doi:10.1016/j.jwb.2005.10.007

Parida, Sjödin, D., & Reim, W. (2019). Reviewing Literature on Digitalization, Business Model Innovation, and Sustainable Industry: Past Achievements and Future Promises. *Sustainability*, *11*(2), 391. doi:10.3390u11020391

Parkinson, C., & Howorth, C. (2008). The language of social entrepreneurs. *Entrepreneurship and Regional Development*, *20*(3), 285–309. doi:10.1080/08985620701800507

Partzsch, L., & Ziegler, R. (2011). Social entrepreneurs as change agents: A case study on power and authority in thewater sector. *International Environmental Agreement: Politics, Law and Economics*, *11*(1), 63–83. doi:10.100710784-011-9150-1

Pathak, S., & Muralidharan, E. (2016). Informal institutions and their comparative influences on social and commercial entrepreneurship: The role of in-group collectivism and interpersonal trust. *Journal of Small Business Management, 54*(S1), 168–188. doi:10.1111/jsbm.12289

Pavlovich, K., & Corner, P. D. (2014). Conscious enterprise emergence: Shared value creation through expanded conscious awareness. *Journal of Business Ethics, 121*(3), 341–351. doi:10.100710551-013-1726-y

Pearce, J. (2003). *Social Enterprise in Anytown*. Calouste Gulbenkian Foundation.

Petrie, C., Aladin, K., Ranjan, P., Javangwe, R., Gilliland, D., Tuominen, S., & Lasse, L. (2020). *Spotlight: Quality education for all during Covid-19 crisis*. https://hundred.org/en/research

Petteni, O. (2020). *Capitalisme, progrès et entropie: Notes sur les chiffonniers du temps présent*. Retrieved May 19, 2020, from https://terrabayt.com/yasam/gunumuz-pacavracilarina-dair-notlar-brukselde-kolektif-mutfak-deneyimi/

Pfitzer, M., Bockstette, V., & Stamp, M. (2013). Innovating for shared value. *Harvard Business Review, 91*(9), 100–107.

Phillips, M. (2006). Growing pains: The sustainability of social enterprises. *International Journal of Entrepreneurship and Innovation, 7*(4), 221–230. doi:10.5367/000000006779111648

Phillips, N., Lawrence, T. B., & Hardy, C. (2004). Discourse and institutions. *Academy of Management Review, 29*(4), 635–652. doi:10.5465/amr.2004.14497617

Phillips, W., Lee, H., Ghobadian, A., O'Regan, N., & James, P. (2015). Social innovation and social entrepreneurship: A systematic review. *Group & Organization Management, 40*(3), 428–461. doi:10.1177/1059601114560063

Phills, J. A., Deiglmeier, K., & Miller, D. T. (2008). Rediscovering social innovation. *Stanford Social Innovation Review, 6*(4), 34–43.

Phills, J. A., Deiglmeier, K., & Miller, D. T. (2008). Rediscovering Social Innovation. *Stanford Social Innovation Review, 6*(4), 34–43.

Pico Bonilla, C. M., Pico Bonilla, A., Méndez Pinzón, M., Ramírez Triana, C. A., Chicas Sierra, S. M., Mateus Tovar, R. F., & Tunjano Pinzón, I. F. (2018). *Experiencias de aprendizaje significativo para la apropiación de conocimientos en ciencias económicas, administrativas y contables*. Institución Universitaria Politécnico Grancolombiano.

Pitelis, C. N. (2009). The co-evolution of organizational value capture, value creation and sustainable advantage. *Organization Studies, 30*(10), 1115–1139. doi:10.1177/0170840609346977

Pitschner, S., & Pitschner-Finn, S. (2014). Non-profit differentials in crowd-based financing: Evidence from 50,000 campaigns. *Economics Letters, 123*(3), 391–394. doi:10.1016/j.econlet.2014.03.022

Pocek, J. (2020). *COVID-19: Social Entrepreneurship*. Available at: https://rwi.lu.se/2020/04/covid-19-social-entreprenurship/

Polanyi, K. (1977). *The Livelihood of Man*. Academic Press.

Pongwiritthon, R. (2015). Creating shared value of Thai SMEs for competitive advantage. *International Journal of Applied Business and Economic Research, 13*(5), 3109–3120.

Poponi, S., Arcese, G., Mosconi, E. M., & Arezzo di Trifiletti, M. (2020). Entrepreneurial drivers for the development of the circular business model: The role of academic spin-Off. *Sustainability, 12*(1), 423. doi:10.3390u12010423

Popov, E.V., Veretennikova, A.Y., & Kozinskaya, K.M. (2020). *The Impact of Digitalization on the Social Entrepreneurship Development, Institute of Economics*. The Ural Branch of the Russian Academy of Sciences.

Porter, M. E., & Kramer, M. R. (2019). Creating shared value. In Lenssen G.G. & Smith G.N. (Eds.) Managing sustainable business (pp. 323-346). Springer, Dordrecht. doi:10.1007/978-94-024-1144-7_16

Porter, M. E., Hills, G., Pfitzer, M., Patscheke, S., & Hawkins, E. (2011). *Measuring shared value: How to unlock value by linking social and business results*. Available at: https://www.hbs.edu/faculty/publication%20files/measuring_shared_value_57032487-9e5c-46a1-9bd8-90bd7f1f9cef.pdf

Porter, M. (2012). *New Opportunities for Company Performance and Purpose: Creating Shared Value*. Hitachi Innovation Forum 2012, *Video Conference*, Boston, MA.

Porter, M. E., & Kramer, M. R. (2006). Strategy & Society. *Harvard Business Review*, 84. PMID:17183795

Porter, M. E., & Kramer, M. R. (2011). *La creación de Valor Compartido*. Harvard Bussines Review.

Porter, M., & Kramer, M. R. (2011). Creating shared value. *Harvard Business Review*, *89*(1/2), 62–77.

Pörtner, H. O., Roberts, D., Masson-Delmotte, V., Zhai, P., Tignor, M., Poloczanska, E., Mintenbeck, K., Nicolai, M., Okem, A., & Petzold, J. (2019). *IPCC Special Report on the Ocean and Cryosphere in a Changing Climate*. IPCC Intergovernmental Panel on Climate Change.

Poverty, U. S. A. (2020). *The Population of Poverty USA*. Retrieved June 21, 2020, from https://www.povertyusa.org/facts

Pradhan, R. (2020). Turn Downtime into an Online Learning Opportunity With Our New Global Offer. *Udacity Blog*. https://blog.udacity.com/2020/04/covid19-onlinelearning-offer.html

Preece, J. (2004). Online Communities: Researching sociability and usability in hard to reach populations. *AJIS. Australasian Journal of Information Systems*, *11*(2), 146–152. doi:10.3127/ajis.v11i2.132

Premier Line. (n.d.). *Crowdfunding Definition Page*. https://www.premierline.co.uk/

Pret, T., & Carter, S. (2017). The importance of 'fitting in': Collaboration and social value creation in response to community norms and expectations. *Entrepreneurship and Regional Development*, *29*(7), 639–667. doi:10.1080/08985626.2017.1328903

Pret, T., Shaw, E., & Drakopoulou-Dodd, S. (2016). Painting the Full Picture: The Conversions of Economic, Cultural, Social and Symbolic Capital. *International Small Business Journal*, *34*(8), 1004–1027. doi:10.1177/0266242615595450

Price Water House Coopers (PWC). (n.d.). *Crowdfunding Page*. www.pwc.com.tr

Professional Certificate Programs. (2020). https://www.edx.org/professional-certificate

Public Policy and International Affairs Fellowship Domestic Policy Workshop. (2014). *Social Impact Bonds A New Tool for Social Financing*. Academic Press.

Puumalainen, K., Sjögrén, H., Syrjä, P., & Barraket, J. (2015). Comparing social entrepreneurship across nations: An exploratory study of institutional effects. *Canadian Journal of Administrative Sciences*, *32*(4), 276–287. doi:10.1002/cjas.1356

Rachinger, Rauter, R., Müller, C., Vorraber, W., & Schirgi, E. (2018). Digitalization and Its Influence on Business Model Innovation. *Journal of Manufacturing Technology Management*, *30*(8), 1143–1160. doi:10.1108/JMTM-01-2018-0020

Rahdari, A., Sepasi, S., & Moradi, M. (2016). Achieving sustainability through Schumpeterian social entrepreneurship: The role of social enterprises. *Journal of Cleaner Production*, *137*, 347–360. doi:10.1016/j.jclepro.2016.06.159

Raifman, J. R., Lanthorn, H. E., Rokicki, S., & Fink, G. (2014). The impact of text message reminders on adherence to antimalarial treatment in northern Ghana: A randomized trial. *PLoS One*, *9*(10), e109032. doi:10.1371/journal.pone.0109032 PMID:25350546

Raju, H. (2020). Covid-19 Lockdown-challenges to higher education. *Cape Comorin An International Multidisciplinary Research Journal*, *2*(4), 26–28.

Ramirez, R. (1999). Value co-production: Intellectual origins and implications for practice and research. *Strategic Management Journal*, *20*(1), 49–65. doi:10.1002/(SICI)1097-0266(199901)20:1<49::AID-SMJ20>3.0.CO;2-2

Ramus, T., & Vaccaro, A. (2017). Stakeholders matter: How social enterprises address mission drift. *Journal of Business Ethics*, *143*(2), 307–322. doi:10.100710551-014-2353-y

Ramus, T., Vaccaro, A., & Berrone, P. (2020). Time Matters! How hybrid organizations use time to respond to divergent stakeholder demands. *Organization Studies*. Advance online publication. doi:10.1177/0170840619900341

Randhawa, A., & Kumar, A. (2017). Exploring sustainability of smart development initiatives in India. *International Journal of Sustainable Built Environment*, *6*(2), 701–710. doi:10.1016/j.ijsbe.2017.08.002

Rangan, K., Chase, L., & Karim, S. (2015). The truth about CSR. *Harvard Business Review*, *93*(1/2), 40–49.

Rangan, V. K., & Gregg, T. (2019). How social entrepreneurs zig-zag their way to impact at scale. *California Management Review*, *62*(1), 53–76. doi:10.1177/0008125619876903

Ranieri, R., & Almeida Ramos, R. (2013). *Inclusive growth: building up a concept* (No. 104). Working Paper, International Policy Centre for Inclusive Growth.

Rao, P. K. (1999). *Sustainable Development* (Vol. 1). Blackwell Publishers.

Rasouli, A. H., & Kumarasuriyar, A. (2016). The social dimensions of sustainability: Towards some definitions and analysis. *Journal of Social Science for Policy Implications*, *4*(2), 23–34. doi:10.15640/jsspi.v4n2a3

Rauthmann, J. F. (2012). You say the party is dull, I say it is lively: A componential approach to how situations are perceived to disentangle perceiver, situation, and perceiver situation variance. *Social Psychological & Personality Science*, *3*(5), 519–528. doi:10.1177/1948550611427609

Rawhouser, H., Cummings, M., & Newbert, S. L. (2019). Social impact measurement: Current approaches and future directions for social entrepreneurship research. *Entrepreneurship Theory and Practice*, *43*(1), 82–115. doi:10.1177/1042258717727718

Rawhouser, H., Villanueva, J., & Newbert, S. (2017). Strategies and Tools for Entrepreneurial Resource Access: A Cross-Disciplinary Review and Typology. *International Journal of Management Reviews*, *19*(4), 473–491. doi:10.1111/ijmr.12105

Rawlings, L. B., & Rubio, G. M. (2005). Evaluating the impact of conditional cash transfer programs. *The World Bank Research Observer*, *20*(1), 29–55. doi:10.1093/wbro/lki001

Ray, A. E-learning: the new normal in the post-covid world. *International Research Journal of Modernization in Engineering Technology and Science*, *2*(9), 866-876.

Reinhardt, G. Y., & Ross, A. D. (2019). Expanding Social Science Through Disaster Studies. *Social Science Quarterly*, *100*(7), 2523–2529. doi:10.1111squ.12668

Renko, M. (2013). Early challenges of nascent social entrepreneurs. *Entrepreneurship Theory and Practice*, *37*(5), 1045–1069. doi:10.1111/j.1540-6520.2012.00522.x

Resnick, P., & Kraut, R. (2012). *Building successful online communities: Evidence-based social design*. MIT Press.

Rey-Martí, A., Mohedano-Suanes, A., & Simón-Moya, V. (2019). Crowdfunding and social entrepreneurship: Spotlight on intermediaries. *Sustainability, 11*(4), 1–23. doi:10.3390u11041175

Rey-Martí, A., Ribeiro-Soriano, D., & Palacios-Marqués, D. (2016). A bibliometric analysis of social entrepreneurship. *Journal of Business Research, 69*(5), 1651–1655. doi:10.1016/j.jbusres.2015.10.033

Rivera-Santos, M., Holt, D., Littlewood, D., & Kolk, A. (2015). Social entrepreneurship in sub-Saharan Africa. *The Academy of Management Perspectives, 29*(1), 72–91. doi:10.5465/amp.2013.0128

Rizzello, A., & Carè, R. (2016). Insight into the Social Impact Bond Market: An Analysis of Investors. *ACRN Oxford Journal of Finance and Risk Perspectives, 5*(3), 145–171.

Roberts, M., Hsiao, W., Berman, P., & Reich, M. (2003). *Getting health reform right: a guide to improving performance and equity*. Oxford University Press.

Rodgers, L., Gritten, D., Offer, J., & Asare, P. (2016, March 11). *Syria: The story of the conflict*. Retrieved October 29, 2020, from https://www.bbc.com/news/world-middle-east-26116868

Rodrik, D. (2004). *Industrial policy for the twenty-first century*. Academic Press.

Rogers, E. (2003). *Diffusion of Innovations* (5th ed.). Free Press.

Roy, A., Brumagim, A., & Goll, I. (2014). Predictors of social entrepreneurship success: A cross-national analysis of antecedent factors. *Journal of Social Entrepreneurship, 5*(1), 42–59. doi:10.1080/19420676.2013.820783

Ryan, S., & Young, M. (2018). Social Impact Bonds: The Next Horizon of Privatization. *Studies in Political Economy, 99*(1), 42–58. doi:10.1080/07078552.2018.1440985

Sachs, J. D. (2012). From millennium development goals to sustainable development goals. *Lancet, 379*(9832), 2206–2211. doi:10.1016/S0140-6736(12)60685-0 PMID:22682467

Sahut, J. M., Iandoli, L., & Teulon, F. (2019, September). The Age of Digital Entrepreneurship. *Small Business Economics*, 1–19.

Saith, R. (2001). *Social Exclusion: The Concept and Application to Developed Countries* (Working Paper No. 72). QEH Working Paper Series.

Sakarya, Ş., & Bezirgan, E. (2018). Kitlesel Fonlama Platformları: Türkiye Ve Yurtdışı Karşılaştırması. *Düzce Üniversitesi Sosyal Bilimler Enstitüsü Dergisi, 8*(2), 18–33.

Sakarya, S., Bodur, M., Yildirim-Öktem, Ö., & Selekler-Göksen, N. (2012). Social alliances: Business and social enterprise collaboration for social transformation. *Journal of Business Research, 65*(12), 1710–1720. doi:10.1016/j.jbusres.2012.02.012

Santana, M. (2017). Digital Entrepreneurship: Expanding the Economic Frontier in the Mediterranean. European Institute of the Mediterranean, 1-51.

Santos, F. M. (2012). A positive theory of social entrepreneurship. *Journal of Business Ethics, 111*(3), 335–351. doi:10.100710551-012-1413-4

Sara, K., & Head, S. Z. (2014). *Women's Lives and Challenges: Equality and Empowerment since 2000*. United States Agency for International Development.

Sarason, Y., Dean, T., & Dillard, J. F. (2006). Entrepreneurship as the nexus of individual and opportunity: A structuration view. *Journal of Business Venturing, 21*(3), 286–305. doi:10.1016/j.jbusvent.2005.02.007

Sarasvathy, S. (2008). *Effectuation: Elements of entrepreneurial expertise*. Edward Elgar., doi:10.4337/9781848440197

Sarıkaya, M. (2010). Üçüncü Sektörde Yönetsel ve Kavramsal Dönüşüm: Sosyal Kâr Amaçlı Örgütler. *CÜ İktisadi ve İdari Bilimler Dergisi, 11*(1), 87–100.

Sarma & Sunny. (2017). Civic Entrepreneurial Ecosystems: Smart City Emergence in Kansas City. *Business Horizons*, 843–853.

Sassmannshausen, S. P., & Volkmann, C. (2013). *A bibliometric based review on social entrepreneurship and its establishment as a field of research (No. 2013-003)*. Schumpeter Discussion Papers.

Sastre-Castillo, M. A., Peris-Ortiz, M., & Danvila-Del Valle, I. (2015). What is different about the profile of the social entrepreneur? *Nonprofit Management & Leadership, 25*(4), 349–369. doi:10.1002/nml.21138

Saunila, M., Ukko, J., & Rantala, T. (2018). Sustainability as a driver of green innovation investment and exploitation. *Journal of Cleaner Production, 179*, 631–641. doi:10.1016/j.jclepro.2017.11.211

Saxena, G. (2019). Multidimensional competency construct for social entrepreneurs: A logistic regression approach. *Kasetsart Journal of Social Sciences, 40*(3), 684–688.

Scarpetta, S., Sonnet, A., & Manfredi, T. (2010). *Rising youth unemployment during the crisis*. Academic Press.

Schäfer, M. S., Metag, J., Feustle, J., & Herzog, L. (2018). Selling science 2.0: What Scientific Projects Receive Crowdfunding Online? *Public Understanding of Science (Bristol, England), 27*(5), 496–514. doi:10.1177/0963662516668771 PMID:27647666

Schaltegger, S., Hansen, E. G., & Lüdeke-Freund, F. (2016). Business models for sustainability: Origins, present research, and future avenues. *Organization & Environment, 29*(1), 3–10. doi:10.1177/1086026615599806

Schimmack, U., Radhakrishnan, P., Oishi, S., Dzokoto, V., & Ahadi, S. (2002). Culture, personality, and subjective well-being: Integrating process models of life satisfaction. *Journal of Personality and Social Psychology, 82*(4), 582–593. doi:10.1037/0022-3514.82.4.582 PMID:11999925

Schinckus, C. (2017). Financial Innovation as a Potential Force for a Positive Socialchange: The Challenging Future of Social Impact Bonds. *Research in International Business and Finance, 39*, 727–736. doi:10.1016/j.ribaf.2015.11.004

Schmitt, C., & Husson, J. (2017). Entrepreneurial situations, definition and interests for entrepreneurial research. *International Journal of Entrepreneurship and Small Business, 30*(1), 22. doi:10.1504/IJESB.2017.081037

Schmutzler, J., Andonova, V., & Diaz-Serrano, L. (2019). How context shapes entrepreneurial self-efficacy as a driver of entrepreneurial intentions: A multilevel approach. *Entrepreneurship Theory and Practice, 43*(5), 880–920. doi:10.1177/1042258717753142

Schneider, S., & Clauß, T. (2019). Business Models for Sustainability: Choices and Consequences. *Organization & Environment, 00*(0), 1–24.

Schrötgens, J., & Boenigk, S. (2017). Social Impact Investment Behavior in the Nonprofit Sector: First Insights from an Online Survey Experiment. *Voluntas, 28*(6), 2658–2682. doi:10.100711266-017-9886-5

Schuler, S. R., Hashemi, S. M., & Riley, A. P. (1996). Rural credit programs and women's empowerment in Bangladesh. *World Development, 24*(4), 635–653. doi:10.1016/0305-750X(95)00159-A

Schumpeter, J. A. (1934). *The Theory of Economic Development* (3rd ed.). Oxford University Press.

Schwab Foundation for Social Entrepreneurship. (2017). Retrieved October 7, 2020 from http://www. schwabfound.org/

Schwabfound. (2020). *COVID Response Alliance for Social Entrepreneurs*. Available at: https://www.schwabfound.org/covid-response-alliance-for-social-entrepreneurs

Schwartz, S. H. (1994). Beyond individualism/collectivism: New cultural dimensions of values. In U. Kim, H. C. Triandis, C. Kagitcibasi, S.-C. Choi, & G. Yoon (Eds.), *Individualism and collectivism: theory, method, and applications*. Sage.

Schwienbacher, A., & Larralde, B. (2010). Crowdfunding of small entrepreneurial ventures. In *Handbook of Entrepreneurial Finance* (Vol. 11, p. 3,10). Oxford University Press. http://ssrn.com/abstract=1699183

Scoll. (2020). *How Chinese Social Entrepreneurs Stepped up to Respond to COVID-19*. Available at: https://skoll.org/2020/05/04/how-chinese-social-entrepreneurs-stepped-up-to-respond-to-covid-19/

Sekliuckiene, J., & Kisielius, E. (2015). Development of social entrepreneurship initiatives: A theoretical framework. *Procedia: Social and Behavioral Sciences*, *213*, 1015–1019. doi:10.1016/j.sbspro.2015.11.519

Seligman, M. (2002). *Authentic happiness*. Free Press.

Semeen, H., & Islam, M. (2020). Social impact disclosure and symbolic power: Evidence from UK Fair Trade Organizations. *Critical Perspectives on Accounting*, (102182), 102182. Advance online publication. doi:10.1016/j.cpa.2020.102182

Sengupta, S., Sahay, A., & Croce, F. (2018). Conceptualizing social entrepreneurship in the context of emerging economies: An integrative review of past research from BRIICS. *The International Entrepreneurship and Management Journal*, *14*(4), 771–803. doi:10.100711365-017-0483-2

Seyfang, G. (2003). Growing cohesive communities one favour at a time: Social exclusion, active citizenship, and time banks. *International Journal of Urban and Regional Research*, *27*(3), 699–706. doi:10.1111/1468-2427.00475

Sharma, S. ve Lertnuwat, N. (2016). The Financial Crowdfunding with Diverse Business Models. *Journal of Asian and African Social Science and Humanities*, *2*(2), 74–89.

Shaw, E., & Carter, S. (2007). Social entrepreneurship. *Journal of Small Business and Enterprise Development*, *14*(3), 418–434. doi:10.1108/14626000710773529

Shen, C. (2017). Udacity Launches in MENA. *Udacity Blog*. https://blog.udacity.com/2017/12/udacity-launches-in-mena.html

Shen, C. (2020). *How Chinese Social Entrepreneurs Stepped up to Respond to COVID-19*. Available at: https://skoll.org/2020/05/04/how-chinese-social-entrepreneurs-stepped-up-to-respond-to-covid-19/

Shen, W., Crandall, J. W., Yan, K., & Lopes, C. V. (2018). Information design in crowdfunding under thresholding policies. In *Proceedings of the 17th International Conference on Autonomous Agents and MultiAgent Systems* (pp. 632-640). International Foundation for Autonomous Agents and Multiagent Systems.

Shepherd, D. A., & Patzelt, H. (2011). The new field of sustainable entrepreneurship: Studying entrepreneurial action linking "what is to be sustained" with "what is to be developed". *Entrepreneurship Theory and Practice*, *35*(1), 137–163. doi:10.1111/j.1540-6520.2010.00426.x

Short, J. C., Moss, T. W., & Lumpkin, G. T. (2009). Research in social entrepreneurship: Past contributions and future opportunities. *Strategic Entrepreneurship Journal*, *3*(2), 161–194. doi:10.1002ej.69

Siebold, N., Günzel-Jensen, F., & Müller, S. (2018). Balancing dual missions for social venture growth: A comparative case study. *Entrepreneurship and Regional Development, 31*(9-10), 710–734. doi:10.1080/08985626.2018.1554710

Sikdar, S. K. (2003). Sustainable development and sustainability metrics. *AIChE Journal. American Institute of Chemical Engineers, 49*(8), 1928–1932. doi:10.1002/aic.690490802

Silverman, D. (2002). Analyzing talk and text. In N. K. Denzin & Y. S. Lincoln (Eds.), *Handbook of Qualitative Research* (2nd ed., pp. 821–834). Sage Publications.

Simprints. (2020). Available at: https://www.simprints.com/impact

Singelis, T. M., & Brown, W. J. (1995). Culture, self, and collectivist communication: Linking culture to individual behavior. *Human Communication Research, 21*(3), 354–389. doi:10.1111/j.1468-2958.1995.tb00351.x PMID:12349710

Singh, A. (2016). *The process of social value creation: A multiple-case study on social entrepreneurship in India*. Springer.

Sinthupundaja, J., Kohda, Y., & Chiadamrong, N. (2020). Examining capabilities of social entrepreneurship for shared value creation. *Journal of Social Entrepreneurship, 11*(1), 1–22. doi:10.1080/19420676.2018.1543726

Situmorang, D. B. M., & Mirzanti, I. R. (2012). Social entrepreneurship to develop ecotourism. *Procedia Economics and Finance, 4*, 398–405. doi:10.1016/S2212-5671(12)00354-1

Slaper, T. F., & Hall, T. J. (2011). The triple bottom line: What is it and how does it work. *Indiana Business Review, 86*(1), 4–8.

Small, A. (2014, Feb. 5). The New Social Entrepreneurs: Young, Tech-Savvy – and Improving the World. *The Guardian.*

Smallbone, D., Welter, F., & Ateljevic, J. (2014). Entrepreneurship in Emerging Market Economies: Contemporary Issues and Perspectives. *International Small Business Journal, 32*(2), 113–116. doi:10.1177/0266242613511479

Smith, B. R., & Stevens, C. E. (2010). Different types of social entrepreneurship: The role of geography and embeddedness on the measurement and scaling of social value. *Entrepreneurship and Regional Development, 22*(6), 575–598. doi:10.1080/08985626.2010.488405

Smith, P. B. (2015). To lend helping hands: In-group favoritism, uncertainty avoidance, and the national frequency of pro-social behaviors. *Journal of Cross-Cultural Psychology, 46*(6), 759–771. doi:10.1177/0022022115585141

Smith, W. K., Besharov, M. L., Wessels, A. K., & Chertok, M. (2012). A paradoxical leadership model for social entrepreneurs: Challenges, leadership skills, and pedagogical tools for managing social and commercial demands. *Academy of Management Learning & Education, 11*(3), 463–478. doi:10.5465/amle.2011.0021

Snyder, L. B., Hamilton, M. A., Mitchell, E. W., Kiwanuka-Tondo, J., Fleming-Milici, F., & Proctor, D. (2004). A meta-analysis of the effect of mediated health communication campaigns on behavior change in the United States. *Journal of Health Communication, 9*(sup1, S1), 71–96. doi:10.1080/10810730490271548 PMID:14960405

Social Business Initiative. (2011). *Communication from the Commission: Social Business Initiative: Creating a favourable climate for social enterprises, key stakeholders in the social economy and innovation.* Retrieved January 17, 2020 from https://eurlex.europa.eu/LexUriServ/LexUriServ.do?uri=COM:2011:0682:FIN:EN:PDF

Social Enterprise Coalition. (2020). *How do social enterprises work?* Retrieved April 5, 2020, from https://www.socialenterprise.org.uk/faq/

Social Enterprises and Their Ecosystems in Europe. (2020). Comparative Synthesis Report, European Commission.

Social EnterpriseU. K. (2020). Available at: https://www.socialenterprise.org.uk/wp-content/uploads/2020/05/Social-Enterprise-COVID-19-research-report-2020.pdf

Social innovation mapping: Social entrepreneurs changing lives through ICT. (2014). *Ashoka.* Retrieved September 15, 2020 from https://sipa.columbia.edu/ system/files/ICT-Based-Social-Impact_09- 2014-report.pdf

Sohrabi, C., Alsafi, Z., O'Neill, N., Khan, M., Kerwan, A., Al-Jabir, A., ... Agha, R. (2020). World Health Organization declares global emergency: A review of the 2019 novel coronavirus (COVID-19). *International Journal of Surgery.*

Sorenson, O., Assenova, V., Li, G. C., Boada, J., & Fleming, L. (2016). Expand innovation finance via crowdfunding. *Science, 354*(6319), 1526–1528. doi:10.1126cience.aaf6989 PMID:28008025

Sosyalup.net. (2020). *Türkiye'nin ilk EvdeKal Ormanı teknolojiyle kuruluyor.* Available at: http://sosyalup.net/turkiyenin-ilk-evdekal-ormani-teknolojiyle-kuruluyor/

Spanos, L. (2016). Complementarity and Interconnection Between CSR and Crowdfunding: A Case Study in Greece. *5th International Conference on Social Responsibility, Ethics and Sustainable Business*, 1–15. 10.2139srn.2883191

Sparviero, S. (2019). The case for a socially oriented business model canvas: The social enterprise model canvas. *Journal of Social Entrepreneurship, 10*(2), 232–251. doi:10.1080/19420676.2018.1541011

Spieth, P., Schneider, S., Clauß, T., & Eichenberg, D. (2019). Value drivers of social businesses: A business model perspective. *Long Range Planning, 52*(3), 427–444. doi:10.1016/j.lrp.2018.04.004

Srivastava, S., Singh, P., & Singh, V. P. (2020). Impact of COVID-19 on education system in India: A review. *Iconic Research and Engineering Journals, 4*(1), 1–7.

Stadtler, L. (2011). Aligning a Company's Economic and Social Interests in Cross-Sector Partnerships. *Journal of Corporate Citizenship, 44*(44), 85–106. doi:10.9774/GLEAF.4700.2011.wi.00007

Steffen, W., Richardson, K., Rockström, J., Cornell, S. E., Fetzer, I., Bennett, E. M., Biggs, R., Carpenter, S. R., De Vries, W., De Wit, C. A., Folke, C., Gerten, D., Heinke, J., Mace, G. M., Persson, L. M., Ramanathan, V., Reyers, B., & Sörlin, S. (2015). Planetary boundaries: Guiding human development on a changing planet. *Science, 347*(6223), 1259855. Advance online publication. doi:10.1126cience.1259855 PMID:25592418

Steiner, S. D., Brock, D. D., Pittz, T. G., & Liguori, E. (2018). Multi-disciplinary involvement in social entrepreneurship education: A uniquely threaded ecosystem. *Journal of Ethics & Entrepreneurship, 8*(1), 73–91.

Stephan, U., Uhlaner, L. M., & Stride, C. (2015). Institutions and social entrepreneurship: The role of institutional voids, institutional support, and institutional configurations. *Journal of International Business Studies, 46*(3), 308–331. doi:10.1057/jibs.2014.38

Stiglitz, J. E. (2002). Information and the Change in the Paradigm in Economics. *The American Economic Review, 92*(3), 460–501. doi:10.1257/00028280260136363

Stromquist, N. (1988). The Theoretical and Practical bases For Empowerment. In *Women, Education and Empowerment: Pathways towards Autonomy.* Report of the International Seminarheldat UIE. https://unesdoc.unesco.org/ark:/48223/pf0000100662

Stromquist, N. (1988). Women's education in development: From welfare to empowerment. *Convergence (Toronto), 21*(4), 5–17.

Strulak-Wójcikiewicz, R., & Lemke, J. (2019). Concept of a simulation model for assessing the sustainable development of urban transport. *Transportation Research Procedia, 39*, 502–513. doi:10.1016/j.trpro.2019.06.052

Stubbs, W. (2019). Strategies, Practices, and Tensions in Managing Business Model Innovation for Sustainability: The Case of an Australian BCorp. *Corporate Social Responsibility and Environmental Management*, 1063–1072. doi:10.1002/csr.1786

Stubbs, W., & Cocklin, C. (2008). Conceptualizing a "Sustainability Business Model. *Organization & Environment, 21*(2), 103–127. doi:10.1177/1086026608318042

Surie, G. (2017). Creating the innovation ecosystem for renewable energy via social entrepreneurship: Insights from India. *Technological Forecasting and Social Change, 121*, 184–195. doi:10.1016/j.techfore.2017.03.006

Swersky, L., Behnke, K. A., & Mays, J. (2017). Coursera for Refugees: Universal Access to World-Class Education. EMOOCs-WIP, 128-132.

Syed Azman, S. M. & Engku Ali, E. R. (2016). Potential Role of Social Impact Bond and Socially Responsible Investment Sukuk as Financial Tools that Can Help Address Issues of Poverty and Socio-Economic Insecurity. *Intellectual Discourse*, 343-364.

Syria Population. (2020). Retrieved October 29, 2020, from https://worldpopulationreview.com/countries/syria-population

Talmage, C. A., Baker, A. L., Guest, M. A., & Knopf, R. C. (2020). Responding to social isolation among older adults through lifelong learning: Lessons and questions during COVID-19. *Local Development & Society*, 1-8.

Talonen, A., Pasanen, J., & Ruuskanen, O. P. (2020). Exploring the Co-operative Form ' s Potential in Crowdfunding : A Non-monetary Perspective. *FIIB Business Review*, 1–13.

Tan, W. L., Williams, J., & Tan, T. M. (2005). Defining the 'social'in 'social entrepreneurship': Altruism and entrepreneurship. *The International Entrepreneurship and Management Journal, 1*(3), 353–365.

Tarhan, M. (2019). MEB 2023 Eğitim Vizyonu Çerçevesince Türkiye'de Girişimcilik Eğitiminin Geleceğine Yönelik Bir Değerlendirme. *Abant İzzet Baysal Üniversitesi Eğitim Fakültesi Dergisi, 19*(2), 667–682. doi:10.17240/aibuefd.2019.19.46660-528071

Tatli, A., Vassilopoulou, J., Özbilgin, M., Forson, C., & Slutskaya, N. (2014). A Bourdieuan Relational Perspective for Entrepreneurship Research. *Journal of Small Business Management, 52*(4), 615–632. doi:10.1111/jsbm.12122

Teece, D. J. (2010). Business models, business strategy and innovation. *Long Range Planning, 43*(2), 172–194. doi:10.1016/j.lrp.2009.07.003

Telli Yamamoto, S. G., & Altun, D. (2020). Coronavirüs ve çevrimiçi (online) eğitimin önlenemeyen yükselişi. *Journal of University Research, 3*(1), 25–34.

Testa, S., Nielsen, K. R., Bogers, M., & Cincotti, S. (2019). The role of crowdfunding in moving towards a sustainable society. *Technological Forecasting and Social Change, 141*(December), 66–73. doi:10.1016/j.techfore.2018.12.011

The Future is Brighter Platform. The Social Impact Reports. Retrieved from https://www.gelecekdaha.net

The Guardian. (2020). *UK coronavirus victims have lain undetected at home for two weeks*. Available at: https://www.theguardian.com/world/2020/jun/07/uk-coronavirus-victims-have-lain-undetected-at-home-for-two-weeks

The Guardian. (2020). *Virus patients more likely to die may have ventilators taken away*. Available at: https://www.theguardian.com/society/2020/apr/01/ventilators-may-be-taken-from-stable-coronavirus-patients-for-healthier-ones-bma-says

The technology learning initiative "Next Technology Leaders (NTL)". (n.d.). https://www.itida.gov.eg/English/Pages/Next-Technology-Leaders.aspx

The unemployment rate in South Africa soars to 30% as a result of the Covid-19 pandemic. (2020, June 23). *Asian News*. https://en.as.com/en/2020/06/23/latest_news/1592936714_614525.html

Thomas, K. W., & Velthouse, B. A. (1990). Cognitive elements of empowerement: An interpretive model of intrinsic task motivation. *Academy of Management Review*, *15*(4), 666–681.

Thompson, J. L. (2002). The World Of The Social Entrepreneur. *International Journal of Public Sector Management*, *15*(5), 412–431. doi:10.1108/09513550210435746

Thompson, J., & Doherty, B. (2006). The diverse world of social enterprise: A collection of social enterprise stories. *International Journal of Social Economics*, *33*(5-6), 361–375. doi:10.1108/03068290610660643

Thomson Reuters Foundation & Deutsche Bank. (2019). *The best countries to be a social entrepreneur*. Retrieved from https://poll2019.trust.org/

Thousands of African graduates recognized at virtual convocation through COL-Coursera Workforce Recovery Initiative. (2020). https://web.aflia.net/thousands-of-african-graduates-recognized-at-virtual-convocation-through-col-coursera-workforce-recovery-initiative/

Time. (2020). *If We Don't Work, We Don't Get Paid.' How the Coronavirus Is Exposing Inequality Among America's Workers*. Available at: https://time.com/5795651/coronavirus-workers-economy-inequality/

Todd, Z. (2019, November 19). *By the Numbers: Syrian Refugees Around the World*. Retrieved October 29, 2020, from https://www.pbs.org/wgbh/frontline/article/numbers-syrian-refugees-around-world/

Toker, K. (2017). Supply networks, value and sustainability. In I. M. Pekdemir (Ed.), *Sustainability Dynamics in Business* (pp. 271–323). Beta Publishing.

Toker, K. (2018). Industry 4.0 Declaration and its effects on sustainability. *Istanbul Management Journal*, *29*(84), 51–64.

Toker, K., Çinar, F., & Görener, A. (2020). Circular Economy Measurement and a Case of the Developing Country Context. In U. Akkucuk (Ed.), *Handbook of Research on Creating Sustainable Value in the Global Economy* (pp. 241–257). IGI Global. doi:10.4018/978-1-7998-1196-1.ch014

Tortia, E., Degavre, F., & Poledrini, S. (2020). Why are social enterprises good candidates for social innovation? Looking for personal and institutional drivers of innovation. *Annals of Public and Cooperative Economics*, *91*(3), 1–19. doi:10.1111/apce.12265

Tracey, P., Phillips, N., & Jarvis, O. (2011). Bridging institutional entrepreneurship and the creation of new organizational forms: A multilevel model. *Organization Science*, *22*(1), 60–80.

Tracey, P., & Stott, N. (2017). Social innovation: A window on alternative ways of organizing and innovating. *Innovation*, *19*(1), 51–60. doi:10.1080/14479338.2016.1268924

Trevena, H., Kaldor, J. C., & Downs, S. M. (2015). 'Sustainability does not quite get the attention it deserves': Synergies and tensions in the sustainability frames of Australian food policy actors. *Public Health Nutrition*, *18*(13), 2323–2332. doi:10.1017/S136898001400295X PMID:25543824

Triandis, H. C. (1990). Cross-cultural studies of individualism and collectivism. In J. Berman (Ed.), *Nebraska Symposium on Motivation* (pp. 41-133). Lincoln: University of Nebraska Press.

Trivedi, C. (2010). Towards a social ecological framework for social entrepreneurship. *The Journal of Entrepreneurship*, *19*(1), 63–80. doi:10.1177/097135570901900104

Trivedi, C., & Stokols, D. (2011). Social enterprises and corporate enterprises: Fundamental differences and defining features. *The Journal of Entrepreneurship*, *20*(1), 1–32. doi:10.1177/097135571002000101

TÜİK. (n.d.). https://www.tuik.gov.tr/

Tunçalp, D., & Le, P. L. (2014). (Re)Locating boundaries: A systematic review of online ethnography. *Journal of Organizational Ethnography*, *3*(1), 59–79.

Turkish Statistical Institute. (2020). Retrieved February 15, 2020 from https://www.tuik.gov.tr/PreHaberBultenleri.do?id=33790

Turkish Statistical Institute. Youth Statistics. (2019). http://tuik.gov.tr/HbPrint.do?id=33731

Tykkyläinen, S., & Ritala, P. (2020). Business model innovation in social enterprises: An activity system perspective. *Journal of Business Research*.

U.S. Department of Labor. (2020). *The Employment Situation — September 2020, News Release Bureau Labor Statistics*. https://www.bls.gov/news.release/pdf/empsit.pdf

Überbacher, F. (2014). Legitimation of New Ventures: A Review and Research Programme. *Journal of Management Studies*, *51*(4), 667–698. doi:10.1111/joms.12077

UN. (2020a). *World economic situation and prospects: October 2019 Briefing, No. 131*. Retrieved July 21, 2020, from https://www.un.org/development/desa/dpad/publication/world-economic-situation-and-prospects-october-2019-briefing-no-131/

UN. (2020b). *No poverty: why it matters*. Retrieved September 21, 2020, from https://www.un.org/sustainabledevelopment/wp-content/uploads/2016/08/1_Why-It-Matters-2020.pdf

UNDP. (2020). *Socio-economic impact of COVID-19*. Available at https://www.undp.org/content/undp/en/home/coronavirus/socio-economic-impact-of-covid-19.html

UNDP. (2020). *Sustainable development goals*. Retrieved September 11, 2020, from https://www.un.org/sustainabledevelopment/sustainable-development-goals/

UNDP. (2020). *What are the Sustainable Development Goals?* Available at: https://www.undp.org/content/undp/en/home/sustainable-development-goals.html

UNDP's Istanbul International Center for Private Sector in Development. (2019). *The Impact Investing Ecosystem in Turkey*. Retrieved from https://www.iicpsd.undp.org/content/dam/istanbul/docs/The%20Impact%20Investing%20Ecosystem%20in%20Turkey_final.pdf

Unemployment Rates. (2020). *OECD*. http://www.oecd.org/newsroom/unemployment-rates-oecd-update-june-2020.htm

UNESCO. (2009). *Belém framework for action: Harnessing the power and potential of adult learning and education for a viable future*. UNESCO. http://www.unesco.org/en/confinteavi

UNESCO. (2020). *Education: From disruption to recovery*. Available at: https://en.unesco.org/covid19/educationresponse

UNESCO. (2020). *UNESCO launches CodeTheCurve Hackathon to develop digital solutions in response to COVID-19*. Available at: https://en.unesco.org/news/unesco-launches-codethecurve-hackathon-develop-digital-solutions-response-covid-19 [Accessed: 02 JUNE 2020]

UNHCR. (2020, October 14). *Operational Portal*. Retrieved October 29, 2020, from https://data2.unhcr.org/en/situations/syria

United Nations (2015). *Transforming our world: The 2030 agenda for sustainable development.* General Assembly a/ res/70/1.

United Nations General Assembly. (2015). Resolution adopted by the General Assembly on 25 September 2015. Washington, DC: United Nations.

United Nations. (2015). *Transforming our world: The 2030 agenda for sustainable development.* General Assembley 70 Session.

United Nations. (2020). *Sustainable Development Goals.* Retrieved from https://unfoundation.org/what-we-do/issues/sustainable-development-goals

UNSDG. (2020). *Shared Responsıbılıty, Global Solıdarıty: Responding To The Socio-Economic İmpacts Of Covıd-19 March 2020.* Author.

US Census Bureau. (2020). *United States | 2018 Poverty Statistics, All People Below Poverty Level Percent.* Retrieved July 21, 2020, from https://www.census.gov/search-results.html?searchType=web&cssp=SERP&q=Poverty

Uyarra, E., Ribeiro, B., & Dale-Clough, L. (2019). Exploring the normative turn in regional innovation policy: Responsibility and the quest for public value. *European Planning Studies, 27*(12), 2359–2375. doi:10.1080/09654313.2019.1609425

Van Bavel, J. J., Baicker, K., Boggio, P. S., Capraro, V., Cichocka, A., Cikara, M., ... Drury, J. (2020). Using social and behavioural science to support the COVID-19 pandemic response. *Nature Human Behaviour*, 1–12. PMID:32355299

Van de Ven, A. H., Sapienza, H. J., & Villanueva, J. (2007). Entrepreneurial pursuits of self-and collective interests. *Strategic Entrepreneurship Journal, 1*(3–4), 353–370. doi:10.1002ej.34

VanSandt, C. V., Sud, M., & Marmé, C. (2009). Enabling the original intent: Catalysts for social entrepreneurship. *Journal of Business Ethics, 90*(3), 419–428. doi:10.100710551-010-0419-z

Vasileiadou, E., Huijben, J. C. C. M., & Raven, R. P. J. M. (2016). Three is a crowd? Exploring the potential of crowdfunding for renewable energy in the Netherlands. *Journal of Cleaner Production, 128*, 142–155. doi:10.1016/j.jclepro.2015.06.028

Vavik, T., & Keitsch, M. (2010). Exploring relationships between universal design and social sustainable development: Some methodological aspects to the debate on the sciences of sustainability. *Sustainable Development, 18*(5), 295–305. doi:10.1002d.480

Veldhuizen, C. (2020). Smart Specialisation as a transition management framework: Driving sustainability-focused regional innovation policy? *Research Policy, 49*(6), 103982. doi:10.1016/j.respol.2020.103982

Venkataraman, S. (1997). The distinctive domain of entrepreneurship research: An editor's perspective. In J. Katz & R. Brockhaus (Eds.), Advances in entrepreneurship, firm emergence, and growth vol. 3: Firm emergence and growth (pp. 119—138). Greenwich, CT: JAI Press.

Véras, E. Z. (2015). Female entrepreneurship: from women's empowerment to shared value creation. Journal on Innovation and Sustainability. *RISUS, 6*(2), 109-123.

Verawardina, U., Asnur, L., Lubis, A. L., Hendriyani, Y., Ramadhani, D., Dewi, I. P., Darni, R., Betri, T. J., Susanti, W., & Sriwahyuni, T. (2020). Reviewing online learning facing the COVID-19 outbreak. *Talent Development & Excellence, 12*, 385–392.

Vernon, A., Deriche, K., & Eisenhauer, S. (2016). *Connecting refugees: How internet and mobile connectivity can improve refugee well-being and transform humanitarian action (Rep.).* UNHCR.

Villalobos Araya, R. (2020). School "brillo DE luna": Sustainable business model. *Emerald Emerging Markets Case Studies, 10*(1), 1–22. Advance online publication. doi:10.1108/EEMCS-11-2019-0314

Vira, K. S. (2020). Promoting Entrepreneurship Through Crowd Funding In India. *Studies in Indian Place Names, 40*(35), 418–424.

Vismara, S. (2016). Equity retention and social network theory in equity crowdfunding. *Small Business Economics, 46*(4), 579–590. doi:10.100711187-016-9710-4

Vitell, S. J., Nwachukwu, S., & Barnes, J. (1993). The effects of culture on ethical decision-making: An application of Hofstede's typology. *Journal of Business Ethics, 12*(10), 753–760. doi:10.1007/BF00881307

Vural, A. (2019). Girişimciler İçin Yeni Nesil Bir Finansman Modeli "Kitle Fonlaması - Crowdfunding": Dünya Ve Türkiye Uygulamaları Üzerine Bir İnceleme Ve Model Önerisi (Doktora Tezi). Başkent Üniversitesi: Sosyal Bilimler Enstitüsü, Ankara.

Wacquant, L. (2008). *Urban outcasts: A comparative sociology of advanced marginality*. Polity.

Waddock, S. A., & Post, J. E. (1991). Social entrepreneurs and catalytic change. *Public Administration Review, 51*(5), 393–401. doi:10.2307/976408

Wahid, R., Mohd Sani, A., Mat, B., Subhan, M., & Saidin, K. (2015). Sharing works and copyright issues in massive open online courseware (MOOC). *International Journal for Research in Emerging Science and Technology, 2*(10), 24–29.

Wakadha, H., Chandir, S., Were, E. V., Rubin, A., Obor, D., Levine, O. S., Gibson, D. G., Odhiambo, F., Laserson, K. F., & Feikin, D. R. (2013). The feasibility of using mobile-phone based SMS reminders and conditional cash transfers to improve timely immunization in rural Kenya. *Vaccine, 31*(6), 987–993. doi:10.1016/j.vaccine.2012.11.093 PMID:23246258

Wallmeroth, J. (2019). Investor Behavior in Equity Crowdfunding. *Venture Capital, 21*(2–3), 273–300. doi:10.1080/13691066.2018.1457475

Warth, L., & Koparanova, M. S. (2012). *Empowering women for sustainable development*. United Nations Economic Commission for Europe.

WCED. (1987). *Out Common Future*. Oxford University Press.

WEF. (2013). *The Challenge of Youth Unemployment*. Available at http://www3.weforum.org/tools/gac/youth-unemployment-visualization-2013/

WEF. (2020a). *The pandemic will leave the poor further disadvantaged – IMF*. Available at: https://www.weforum.org/agenda/2020/05/pandemics-poor-rich-economics-coronavirus-covid19/

WEF. (2020b). *6 ways social innovators are responding to the COVID-19 pandemic*. Available at https://www.weforum.org/agenda/2020/03/how-social-innovators-are-responding-to-the-covid19-pandemic/

Wei-Skillern, J., Austin, J. E., Leonard, H., & Stevenson, H. (2007). *Entrepreneurship in the social sector* (Vol. 13). Sage.

Welter, F. (2011). Contextualizing entrepreneurship—Conceptual challenges and ways forward. *Entrepreneurship Theory and Practice, 35*(1), 165–184. doi:10.1111/j.1540-6520.2010.00427.x

Wennekers, S., van Stel, A., Thurik, R., & Reynolds, P. (2005). Nascent entrepreneurship and the level of economic development. *Small Business Economics, 24*(3), 293–309. doi:10.100711187-005-1994-8

Wessel, M., Thies, F., & Benlian, A. (2017). Opening the floodgates: The implications of Increasing Platform Openness in Crowdfunding. *Journal of Information Technology, 32*(4), 344–360. doi:10.105741265-017-0040-z

Westley, F., & Antadze, N. (2010). Making a difference: Strategies for scaling social innovation for greater impact. *The Innovation Journal*, *15*(2), 1–20.

Westley, F., & Antadze, N. (2010). Making a difference: Strategies for scaling social innovation for greater impact. *The Innovation Journal*, *15*(2).

WHO. (2020). *OHCHR, IOM, UNHCR and WHO joint press release: the rights and health of refugees, migrants and stateless must be protected in COVID-19 response*. Available at: https://www.who.int/news-room/detail/31-03-2020-ohchr-iom-unhcr-and-who-joint-press-release-the-rights-and-health-of-refugees-migrants-and-stateless-must-be-protected-in-covid-19-response

Wieczorek, A. J., & Hekkert, M. P. (2012). Systemic instruments for systemic innovation problems: A framework for policy makers and innovation scholars. *Science & Public Policy*, *39*(6), 74–87. doi:10.1093cipolcr008

WİEGO. (2020). *Covid-19: Impact on Home-Based Workers in South Asia Charter of Demands by HomeNet South Asia*. https://www.wiego.org/resources/homenet-south-asias-demands-covid-19-crisis

Williamson, G. (2020, September 29). Lifetime Skills Guarantee: Education Secretary outlines new measures to help more people get the skills they need to get ahead. *FE News*. https://www.fenews.co.uk/fevoices/55849-lifetime-skills-guarantee-education-secretary-outlines-new-measures-to-help-more-people-get-the-skills-they-need-to-get-ahead

Wilson, F., & Post, J. E. (2013). Business models for people, planet (& profits): Exploring the phenomena of social business, a market-based approach to social value creation. *Small Business Economics*, *40*(3), 715–737. doi:10.100711187-011-9401-0

Wongphuka, K., Chai-Aroon, T., Phainoi, S., & Boon-Long, P. (2017). Social entrepreneur competencies of social activists involved with children and youths: A case study of Nan province, Thailand. *Kasetsart Journal of Social Sciences*, *38*(2), 143–149. doi:10.1016/j.kjss.2016.02.002

Wood, A. (2010). New Legal Structures to Address the Social Capital Famine. *Vermont Law Review*, *35*(045), 45–52.

Workforce Recovery Initiative. (2020). https://www.htdc.org/workforce-recovery-initiative-by-coursera/

World Bank. (2002-2009). Globalization, Growth, and Poverty. In Poverty Measures. World Bank Policy Research Report.

World Bank. (2013). Crowdfunding's Potential for the Developing World. In infoDev, Finance and Private Sector Development Department. Author.

World Bank. (2020). *The impact of COVID-19 (Coronavirus) on global poverty: Why Sub-Saharan Africa might be the region hardest hit*. Available at https://blogs.worldbank.org/opendata/impact-covid-19-coronavirus-global-poverty-why-sub-saharan-africa-might-be-region-hardest

World Bank. (2020). *Updated estimates of the impact of COVID-19 on global poverty*. Available at https://blogs.worldbank.org/opendata/updated-estimates-impact-covid-19-global-poverty

World Economic Forum. (2020). *6 ways social innovators are responding to the COVID-19 pandemic*. Author.

World Health Organization. (2020). *Social Determinants of Health*. Retrieved from https://www.who.int/social_determinants/en

World Health Organization. (2020, June 29). *Syrian Arab Republic: WHO and UNICEF estimates of immunization coverage: 2019 revision*. Retrieved October 29, 2020, from https://www.who.int/immunization/monitoring_surveillance/data/syr.pdf

Worldreader. (2017). Retrieved September 2, 2020 from https://www. worldreader.org/

Xing, M. (2015). *The impact of a strong local supply chain on regional economic impacts of mining*. Academic Press.

Xu, L. Z. (2018). Will a Digital Camera Cure Your Sick Puppy? Modality and Category Effects in Donation-Based Crowdfunding. *Telematics and Informatics, 35*(7), 1914–1924. doi:10.1016/j.tele.2018.06.004

Yang, Y., Wu, M., & Cui, L. (2011). Integration of three visualization methods based on co-word analysis. *Scientometrics, 90*(2), 659–673. doi:10.100711192-011-0541-4

Yan, X., Lin, H., & Clarke, A. (2018). Cross-Sector Social Partnerships for Social Change: The Roles of Non-Governmental Organizations. *Sustainability, 10*(558), 1–17. doi:10.3390u10020558

Yap. (2020, Feb. 8). China's factories struggle to resume operations after virus shutdown. *Wall St. J.* Available at: https://www.wsj.com/articles/chinas-factories-struggle-to-resume-operations-after-virus-shutdown-11581157800

Yasar, B., Kiesssling, T., & Martin, T. (2020). An Empirical Test of Signaling Theory. *Management Research Review*. doi:10.1108/MRR-08-2019-0338

Yates, R., & Humphreys, G. (2013). *Arguing for Universal Health Coverage*. Retrieved from https://www.who.int/health_financing/UHC_ENvs_BD.PDF

Yavuz, M. S. (2019). Digital Transformation in Economy: A Review of Blockchain Technology and Application Areas. *Research of Financial, Economic, and Social Studies, 4*(1), 15–29.

Yıldırım, B., & Tuncay, T. (2019). Sosyal İnovasyonun Ve Sosyal Girişimciliğin Sosyal Hizmet Mesleğinin Geleceğindeki Rolü. *Hacettepe Üniversitesi İktisadi ve İdari Bilimler Fakültesi Dergisi, 37*(1), 169–188. doi:10.17065/huniibf.350375

Yin, R. K. (1994). Case study research: Design and methods (2nd ed.). Thousand Oaks, CA: Sage.

Yin, R. K. (1994). *Case Study Research: Design and Methods*. Sage Publications.

Yitshaki, R., & Kropp, F. (2016). Entrepreneurial passions and identities in different contexts: A comparison between high-tech and social entrepreneurs. *Entrepreneurship and Regional Development, 28*(3), 206–233.

Yunus, M. (1998). Alleviating Poverty Through Technology. *Science, New Series, 282*(5388), 409–410.

Yunus, M. (2007). *Creating a world without poverty: Social business and the future of capitalism* (1st ed.). PublicAffairs.

Yunus, M., Moingeon, B., & Lehmann-Ortega, L. (2010). Building social business models: Lessons from the Grameen experience. *Long Range Planning, 43*(2-3), 308–325. doi:10.1016/j.lrp.2009.12.005

Zahra, S. A., Gedajlovic, E., Neubaum, D. O., & Shulman, J. M. (2009). A typology of social entrepreneurs: Motives, search processes and ethical challenges. *Journal of Business Venturing, 24*(5), 519–532. doi:10.1016/j.jbusvent.2008.04.007

Zahra, S. A., Rawhouser, H. N., Bhawe, N., Neubaum, D. O., & Hayton, J. C. (2008). Globalization of social entrepreneurship opportunities. *Strategic Entrepreneurship Journal, 2*(2), 117–131. doi:10.1002ej.43

Zahra, S. A., Wright, M., & Abdelgawad, S. G. (2014). Contextualization and the advancement of entrepreneurship research. *International Small Business Journal, 32*(5), 479–500. doi:10.1177/0266242613519807

Zan, B. U. (2012). *Türkiye'de Bilim Dallarında Karşılaştırmalı Bibliyometrik Analiz Çalışması*. Yayımlanmamış Doktora Tezi, Ankara Üniversitesi, Sosyal Bilimler Enstitüsü.

Zhang, D. D., & Swanson, L. A. (2014). Linking social entrepreneurship and sustainability. *Journal of Social Entrepreneurship, 5*(2), 175–191. doi:10.1080/19420676.2014.880503

Zhao, J., Xiao, H., Li, Y., Wen, D., Xu, P., Fu, Y., Piao, J., Liu, J., Cao, D., Zhong, Z., & Zhao, G. (2020). *Experience of massive distance online education for medical colleges and universities in China to counter the COVID-19 pandemic.* Research Square.

Zhao, Y., Harris, P., & Lam, W. (2019). Crowdfunding Industry-History, Development,Policies, and Potential Issues. *Journal of Public Affairs*, *19*(1), 1–9. doi:10.1002/pa.1921

Zheng, H., Li, D., Wu, J., & Xu, Y. (2014). The role of multidimensional social capital in crowdfunding: A comparative study in China and US. *Information & Management*, *51*(4), 488–496. doi:10.1016/j.im.2014.03.003

Zhuo, W. (2019). Research on Copyright Law Conflict under the Network Environment. *5th International Conference on Finance, Investment, and Law (ICFIL 2019)*, 256-259.

Zhu, Y., Rooney, D., & Phillips, N. (2016). Practice-based wisdom theory for integrating institutional logics: A new model for social entrepreneurship learning and education. *Academy of Management Learning & Education*, *15*(3), 607–625. doi:10.5465/amle.2013.0263

Zimmerman, M. A. (1995). Psychological empowerment: Issues and illustrations. *American Journal of Community Psychology*, *23*(5), 581–599. doi:10.1007/BF02506983 PMID:8851341

Zott, C., & Huy, N. (2007). How Entrepreneurs Use Symbolic Management to Acquire Resources. *Administrative Science Quarterly*, *52*(70), 70–105.

Zupic, I., & Čater, T. (2015). Bibliometric methods in management and organization. *Organizational Research Methods*, *18*(3), 429–472. doi:10.1177/1094428114562629

Zvilichovsky & Inbar. (2015). *Playing both sides of the market: Success and reciprocity on crowdfunding platforms.* Available at SSRN 2304101

About the Contributors

Duygu Acar Erdur is an Assistant Professor at the Faculty of Business Administration Department at Beykent University. She received her Ph.D. in Business Administration from Uludag University .Her research interests and expertise include institutional theory, diversity, equality, and gender studies.

Mine Afacan Fındıklı received her Ph.D. degree from Institute of Social Sciences at Istanbul University - Department of Management and Organization in December 2012.After completing her Ph.D., she worked as vice-dean of the FEAS and the head of Department of International Logistics and Transportation for three years. She was the Assistant Editor of the Journal of Social Sciences at Gelisim University. In 2016, she has received her associate professorship degree in strategy and management. She worked as vice-dean in the FEAS at Beykent University between 2017 February-2020 February. Currently, she has been funded by the Scientific and Technological Research Council of Turkey (TUBITAK) and she has been a visiting fellow at the University of Bath, School of Management, Future of Work Research Centre for six months. She continues her academic studies within the framework of human resources management, organizational behavior and social entrepreneurship.

***

Erkut Altındağ is an Associated Professor of Economic and Administrative Sciences at Beykent University, Turkey. His papers have appeared in Social Behavior and Personality, International journal and The European Journal of Health Economics, Sage Open and Kybernetes. His research interests include family firms, strategic management, technology management, modern management theories and strategic human resources management.

Merve Güngördü Arıoğlu is a Ph.D. Candidate in Istanbul Technical University, with a specialization in Management and Organization Studies. Arıoğlu's current research focuses on hybrid organizations, the process of hybridization and social entrepreneurship.

Çağla Arıker received her MBA in Production Management and Marketing from Marmara University in 2005 and PhD in Marketing from Istanbul University in 2011. She is currently teaching Marketing at Istanbul Gelisim University, Faculty of Economics, Administrative and Social Sciences, Business Administration Department. She writes and presents widely on issues of consumer behavior, digital marketing, retailing, entrepreneurship, social entrepreneurship, and CSR.

Tuba Bozaykut-Buk earned her PhD in Management and Organisation from Istanbul University. Since 2014, she has been working at various foundation universities and teaching undergraduate/graduate courses. Her current research interests are corporate sustainability management, sustainability reporting and bottom-of-the -pyramid.

Hale Cide Demir received her Ph.D. degree from Marmara University Faculty of Business Administration and Organization in 2016. Her dissertation subject was "Digitalization and Organizational Impression Management". Her most recent work is on digital social entrepreneurship, remote working, digital leadership, and digital-organization issues. She has over 20 years of experience in sales, marketing, and channel management. She currently works as a Vice President in Retail Banking. She teaches Digital Strategic Management and Organizational Dynamics at Kadir Has University.

Marcela Gomez Osorio is an advisor and consultant in subjects of sustainable development, shared value, knowledge management, science, innovation, and technology. Gomez Osorio has extensive experience in higher education entities, private companies, and public entities of national, departmental, and municipal order. She is a marine biologist with a master in environmental management for sustainable development from the Javeriana University.

Kutay Güneştepe has a Ph.D. degree in Management Engineering from Istanbul Technical University, with a specialization in Organization Theory. Dr. Güneştepe's Research focuses on the participation of space and materiality in practices and particularly the role of these constructs in organizational resistance and maintenance. Moreover, Dr. Güneştepe also studies resource acquisition and conversion models of new ventures during their entrepreneurial journey. His research has appeared in Research in the Sociology of Organizations.

Caitlyn Hoeflin is the international program manager of HERA Inc. She has a BA in Psychology from Reed College, Oregon. Her research experience is focused on refugees and emerging technologies.

Esen Kara is an Assistant Professor at the Faculty of Economics and Administrative Sciences at Bursa Uludag University. She received her Ph.D. in management. Her research focuses on financial markets, financial crises and financial volatility. She is currently teaching finance at Bursa Uludag University.

Gaye Karacay is an Assistant Professor at the Management Faculty of Istanbul Technical University. Her Ph.D. in Management and Organization is from Bogazici University. Before her Ph.D. studies, Dr. Karacay worked in the strategic management of public and private sector institutions. She has a joint-MBA degree from London Business School (LBS) and UCLA Anderson School of Management. Her research interests include leadership, cross-cultural management, talent management, and social entrepreneurship. Her research published in the journals including Journal of International Management, Human Resource Management Journal, Journal of World Business, and Personnel Review.

Katherina Kuschel explores women in technology ventures at CENTRUM Graduate Business School (Peru). She studied women's innovation and entrepreneurship from an ecosystem perspective at Universidad Tecnológica Metropolitana (Chile, 2018-2019). In 2017, she participated in a comprehensive international study on the role of women entrepreneurs in the development of regional innovation ecosystems at Lazaridis School of Business and Economics (Canada). She was a Visiting Researcher at University of Siegen (Germany) where she led an international collaborative research project on entrepreneurial failure. She was Assistant Professor of Management at the School of Economics and Business - Universidad del Desarrollo in Chile. She holds a Ph.D. in Social Psychology from Universitat Autònoma, Barcelona (Spain). Her main area of research is the identity of female founders in technology ventures. Besides leading a research group on work-life issues among entrepreneurs, she participated as guest editor at the International Entrepreneurship and Management Journal on Women Entrepreneurship within STEM fields and a Routledge edited book entitled The Wellbeing of Women in Entrepreneurship.

Manuel Méndez Pinzón Professor and researcher in the areas of creating shared value (CSV), competitiveness, and corporate social responsibility at the Politécnico Grancolombiano. Prof. Méndez has extensive teaching and research experience in higher education. He is a founding member and part of the technical committee of the academic network of shared value (Colombia). He is a Research Associate by the Ministry of Science, Technology and Innovation (Colombia), as well as a consultant in both the public and private sectors. Director and organizer of international academic events, B.B.A, and MBA (ESAN Graduate School of Business, Peru).

Gözde Morgül worked as a Guidance-Psychological Counselor, Head of Guidance and Psychological Counseling Department, General Coordinator in the K12 education sector for 10 years. She started her Ph.D education in business administration in 2017 and works as a research assistant in the Department of Business Administration (English) at Beykent University. Her research focuses on organizational behavior and human resources management.

Neeru Narla is a U.S.-based pediatrician and public health specialist. She has collaborated with international partners in Africa, Asia, and Europe on the delivery of context-specific interventions to improve maternal and child health with locally driven solutions, and supplemented her medical training with a clinical fellowship in global health delivery. Her work focuses on promoting health equity, capacity building, and innovative preventive services primarily for children and families in resource-denied settings.

Mehlika Saraç is an Assistant Professor at the Faculty of Economics and Administrative Sciences at Bursa Uludag University. She received her Ph.D. in management. Her research focuses on organizational behavior, human resources management, and strategic management.

Muhammet Fatih Şengüllendi is a faculty member at Beykent University Business Administration Department. He graduated from Yıldız Technical University, Department of Business Administration. He completed his master's degree in Yıldız Technical University's "Innovation, Entrepreneurship and Management" department with his thesis titled "The Relationship Between Transformational Leadership and Positive Psychological Capital". In 2017, he started his PhD education in the Department of Business Management at Yıldız Technical University. He has academic publications on leadership, positive psychological capital, perceived organizational support, and organizational innovation.

Aral Sürmeli is the CEO of HERA Inc., a nonprofit focused on digital health interventions for refugee populations around the world, and the co-founder and current president of Medical Rescue Association of Turkey (MEDAK), the first and only nonprofit focused on medical rescue in Turkey. He is an MD, MPH, and his work has been focused on healthcare access in disasters and humanitarian crises.

Serra Titiz has been working on sustainable development since 2003. She worked with youth, with women and vocational groups at large NGOs at managerial levels, has participated to international programs on NGOs and Civic Activism. Her work has always been a reflection of social innovation.

Kerem Toker is an assistant professor of business management and organization at Bezmiâlem Vakif University, Faculty of Health Sciences, Istanbul-Turkey. Dr. Toker received a BSc degree in Business Management from Trakya University, Turkey, in 2005, and he received an MSc degree in Business Management from Trakya University (2006). In July 2015, he completed his Ph.D. studies in Business Management and Organization at Istanbul University. He has been working as an assistant professor in the Health Management Department of Bezmiâlem Vakif University since 2018. His research interests are logistics management, sustainability, business management, and strategy.

Deniz Tunçalp is working as an Associate Professor in the Department of Management Engineering at Istanbul Technical University. He received a Ph.D. in Management (Organization Studies) from the School of Management at Sabanci University in Istanbul in 2006. He holds his BSc in Industrial Engineering (1992), M.Sc. in Information Systems (1999), M.Sc. in Industrial Engineering (2000) from Middle East Technical University, M.A. in Law (2009) from Istanbul Bilgi University. He also worked as a Visiting Associate Professor in Politecnico di Milano in 2017-2018. Previously, he was a visiting scholar at Carnegie Mellon University in 2009-2010. Dr. Tuncalp's research interests are organizational change/stability, technological change, high-technology entrepreneurship, and qualitative research methodologies. His research has appeared in various journals, including Organizational Research Methods, Management Decision, Research in the Sociology of Organizations, Journal of Organizational Ethnography, Computers in Human Behavior, and Operations Research. He aims to contribute to the intersection between organization theory and entrepreneurship research.

Adela Velez Rolon is an Associate Professor and researcher Colegio de Estudios Superiores de Administración (CESA). She studied a B.Sc. in Biology from Universidad de los Andes. She received a postgraduate certificate of Management and Environmental Education, and a master's degree in Research in Scientific Education. Prof. Vélez held her Ph.D. in Education from Universitat Autònoma, Barcelona (Spain). She is a Research Associate by the Ministry of Science and Technology and Innovation (Colombia), Researcher in the areas: sustainability, shared value, corporate social responsibility, knowledge management, and innovation. She is a founding member and part of the technical committee of the academic network of shared value (Colombia).

Burze Yasar is an assistant professor at the Department of Business Administration at TED University in Ankara, Turkey. Her research interests are crowdfunding, social entrepreneurship, social finance, and sustainability.

Işıl Sevilay Yılmaz is an assistant professor at the Department of Business Administration at TED University in Ankara, Turkey. Her research interests include corporate finance, mergers & acquisitions, crowdfunding, social finance and sustainability.

Index

G

H

I

K

L

M

P

Q

R

S

T

U

V

W

www.ingramcontent.com/pod-product-compliance
Lightning Source LLC
LaVergne TN
LVHW060409300926
849162LV00006B/1379